UNDERSTANDING POLITICS:
IDEAS, INSTITUTIONS,
and
ISSUES

Sixth Edition

Thomas M. Magstadt, Ph.D.

Adjunct Professor, Rockhurst University

THOMSON
* ™
WADSWORTH

Australia · Canada · Mexico · Singapore · Spain
United Kingdom · United States

THOMSON

WADSWORTH

Publisher: Clark Baxter
Senior Editor: David Tatom
Development Editor: Stacey Sims
Assistant Editor: Heather Hogan
Editorial Assistant: Dianne Long
Technology Project Manager: Melinda Newfarmer
Marketing Manager: Janise Fry
Marketing Assistant: Mary Ho
Advertising Project Manager: Stacey Purviance
Project Manager, Editorial Production: Ray Crawford
Print/Media Buyer: Karen Hunt
Permissions Editor: Stephanie Keough-Hedges

Production Service: Stratford Publishing Services
Photo Researcher: Stratford Publishing Services
Copy Editor: Leslie Connor
Cover Designer: Jeanette Barber
Cover Image: © Mitch Hrdlicka /Getty Images
Cover Printer: Vail-Ballou Press
Compositor: Stratford Publishing Services
Printer: Vail-Ballou Press

For more information about our products, contact us at:
Thomson Learning Academic Resource Center
1-800-423-0563
For permission to use material from this text,
contact us by: **Phone:** 1-800-730-2214
Fax: 1-800-730-2215
Web: http://www.thomsonrights.com

Library of Congress Control Number: 2002107912

ISBN 0-534-60381-5

Wadworth/Thomson Learning
10 Davis Drive
Belmont, CA 94002-3098
USA

Asia
Thomson Learning
5 Shenton Way #01-01
UIC Building
Singapore 068808

Australia
Nelson Thomson Learning
102 Dodds Street
South Melbourne, Victoria 3205
Australia

Canada
Nelson Thomson Learning
1120 Birchmount Road
Toronto, Ontario M1K 5G4
Canada

Europe/Middle East/Africa
Thomson Learning
High Holborn House
50/51 Bedford Row
London WC1R 4LR
United Kingdom

Latin America
Thomson Learning
Seneca, 53
Colonia Polanco
11560 Mexico D.F.
Mexico

Spain
Paraninfo Thomson Learning
Calle/Magallanes, 25
28015 Madrid, Spain

CONTENTS IN BRIEF

CONTENTS

iv

Dystopia: From Dream to Nightmare
    Orwell's World   •   Utopia and Terrorism

Final Thoughts

PART IV   POLITICS BY VIOLENT MEANS

PREFACE

Today, political and economic instability anywhere in the world can affect people everywhere. Terrorist acts, military clashes, civil wars, ethnic conflicts, economic downturns, banking crises, and volatile stock markets are everyday occurrences. Seismic events such as the terrorist attacks on the United States in the fall of 2001 can affect our lives in countless ways, as can less dramatic acts such as the passage by Congress of a major new campaign finance law in the spring of 2002 or yet another transnational merger of corporate giants.

Things change with blinding speed, but the basic nature of politics remains unchanged. The struggle for power continues; so, too, does the search for order and justice all over the world. The limits of power even in its most concentrated forms are glaringly apparent—from ancient places such as Palestine in the Middle East and Afghanistan in Central Asia to the United States of America, with its relatively short history and even shorter memory.

The costs of failed politics and corrupt, cynical, or simply incompetent leadership are clearly apparent in the contemporary world. Nor is the quality of citizenship cause for celebration. This double deficiency—both at the top and bottom of political society—is a kind of stealth crisis, one that gives ample evidence of its existence but continues to go largely unnoticed. Meanwhile, there is no absence of injustice, intolerance, misguided idealism, zealotry, and human suffering—proof enough that the ever-more polluted and crowded planet we inhabit has not changed for the better, even though the West's fortunate few are far more secure and comfortable than the vast majority who live in the so-called developing regions of the globe.

Since *Understanding Politics* made its debut in 1984, nothing has shaken my conviction that politics matters. I continue to believe that students need to acquire at least a rudimentary knowledge of the political and economic forces that shape our world in order to reap the benefits of liberty and assume the responsibilities of citizenship in a democratic republic. Ironically, as knowledge, news, and information have become more and more accessible—thanks in no small part to the proliferation of desktop computers and the World Wide Web—many Americans have become less and less engaged in the political process. This fact is all the more discouraging because a heightened political awareness is only the first step in the educational preparation—and empowerment—of the next generation of citizens who will be called upon to vote, pay taxes, and, yes, to lead the nation in the difficult decades that lie ahead.

The study of politics is a gateway to a broader and better understanding of human nature, of society, and of the world. This belief, more than any other, is what originally motivated two struggling young professors to write the first edition of this book. It is also what has continued to inspire its multiple revisions—that, plus a sense that the book was, is, and always will be essentially a work in progress.

A successful introduction to politics must balance two key objectives: (1) dispelling anxieties associated with the attempt to understand political science, especially for the uninitiated, and (2) providing the intellectual stimulation necessary to challenge today's college student. This book is testimony to the fact that the science and philosophy of politics fall squarely within the liberal arts tradition. The phrase "science and philosophy of politics" points to one of the deepest cleavages within the discipline: Analysts who approach politics from the standpoint of science often stress the importance of power, whereas those who view it through the wide-angle lens of philosophy often emphasize the importance of justice. But the distinction between power and justice—like that between science and philosophy—is too often exaggerated.

Moral and political questions are ultimately inseparable in the real world. That is, the exercise of power in itself is not what makes an action political; rather, what makes power *political* is the debate about its proper or improper uses and who benefits or suffers as a result. Thus, whenever questions of fairness are raised in the realm of public policy (for example, questions concerning abortion, capital punishment, or the use of force by police or the military), the essential ingredients of politics are present. Excessive attention to either the concept of power or to morality is likely to confound our efforts to make sense of politics or, for that matter, to find lasting solutions for the problems that afflict and divide us. Thus, it is always necessary to balance the equation, tempering political realism with a penchant for justice.

Similarly, the dichotomy so often drawn between facts and values is misleading. Rational judgments, in the sense of reasoned opinions about what is good and just, are sometimes more definitive (or less elusive) than facts. (The statement "Adolf Hitler and the Nazis abused human rights" is such a judgment.) Other value-laden propositions can be stated with a high degree of probability but not absolute certainty. (For example, "If you want to reduce violent crime, first reduce poverty.") Still other questions of this kind may be too difficult or too close to call—in the abortion controversy, for example, does the right of a woman to biological self-determination outweigh the right to life of the unborn? It makes no sense to ignore the most important questions in life simply because the answers are not easy. Even when the right answers are unclear, it is often possible to recognize wrong answers—a moderating force in itself.

The book gives due attention to contemporary political issues without ignoring the more enduring questions that often underlie them. For example, a voter's dilemma as to who would make the best mayor, governor, or president raises deeper questions. For example, what qualifications are necessary for public office? What is wrong with a system that fails to produce more distinguished—or distinctive—choices? Similarly, conflicts between nation-states or social groups raise general questions about what causes people to fight and kill each other on a mass scale?

Although I have tried to minimize the use of names and dates, political ideas cannot be discussed fruitfully in an historical vacuum. The choice of historical examples throughout the text is dictated by a particular understanding of politics. Some episodes in twentieth-century history (among them the October Revolution in Russia, the rule of National Socialism in Hitler's Germany, the breakup of colonial empires after World War II, the Cold War, the U.S. Civil Rights movement, and the collapse of communism in Europe) are so important and raise such fundamental questions that anyone who claims to be liberally educated must come to grips with what they mean.

Inevitably, some themes and events are discussed in more than one chapter: The world of politics is more like a seamless web than a chest of drawers. In politics as in nature, a given event or phenomenon often has many meanings and is connected to other events and phenomena in ways that are not immediately apparent. Emphasizing the common threads among major political ideas, institutions, and issues helps beginning students make sense of seemingly unrelated bits and pieces of the political puzzle. Seeing how the various parts fit together is a necessary step toward understanding politics.

Understanding Politics presents a bottom-up approach to the study of politics and government. It begins by identifying political phenomena (such as war and terrorism) that students find interesting, and then seeks to describe and explain them. In an effort to build on students' natural curiosity, I try to avoid much of the jargon and many of the technical or arcane disputes that characterize so much of the more advanced literature.

Rather than turning inward toward the deep recesses of a single discipline, the book turns outward to disciplines such as history and philosophy. It is intended to be a true liberal arts approach to the study of government and politics. The goal is ambitious: to challenge students to begin a lifelong learning process that alone can lead to a generation of citizens who are well-informed, actively engaged, self-confident, and thoughtful, and who have a capacity for indignation in the face of public hypocrisy, dishonesty, stupidity, or gross ineptitude.

Chapter 1, "Introduction: The Study of Politics," defines the basic concepts of politics and centers on how and why it is studied. This chapter lays the groundwork for the remainder of the text and thus stands alone as its introduction.

Part I ("Comparative Political Systems") analyzes utopian, democratic, and authoritarian forms of government, as well as political systems caught in the difficult transition from authoritarian to democratic institutions. This foundation-building section (encompassing Chapters 2 through 5), looks at different kinds of political regimes in a theoretical light.

Part II ("Established and Emerging Democracies") consists of three chapters (6 through 8) and examines established democracies (Chapter 6), transitional states (Chapter 7), and developing countries (Chapter 8). Virtually all governments in today's world either aspire to some form of democracy or claim to be "democratic." That fact is itself arresting evidence of the power of an idea. Although it is often abused, the idea of democracy has fired the imagination of people everywhere for more than two centuries. In an age when bad news is written in blood and body counts are more likely to refer to innocent civilians than armed combatants it is well to remember that democratic ideals have never before been so warmly embraced or widely (if imperfectly) institutionalized.

In Part III, "Politics by Civil Means," Chapters 9 through 13 focus on the political process. The United States is featured in this section, which examines citizenship and political socialization, political participation (including opinion polling and voting behavior), political organization (parties and interest groups), political leadership, political ideologies (or divergent "approaches to the public good"), and contemporary public policy issues.

Part IV, "Politics by Violent Means," examines conflict as a special and universal problem in politics. It divides the problem into three categories: revolution, terrorism, and war (corresponding to Chapter 14, 15, and 16, respectively). This section invariably stimulates the curiosity of students and provokes spirited class discussions.

Finally, Part V, "Politics Without Government," introduces students to key concepts in the study of world affairs, describes key patterns, and discusses perennial problems. Thus, Chapter 17 combines the material covered in two chapters in the previous edition. It examines the basic principles and concepts in international relations and the evolving structure and context of world politics, as well as drawing attention to a number of global issues. Chapter 18 looks at international law and organizations and the search for world order—a fitting note on which to end the course.

In this new edition—the sixth!—I have retained the pedagogical features that characterized the previous five editions of the book. Thus, each chapter begins with an outline and ends with a summary, highlights key terminology, presents review questions for measuring comprehension, and provides an annotated list of recommended readings. In addition, the text contains a wide variety of photos, figures, maps, tables, and boxed features, many of which have been revised or replaced with updated materials.

What's New

This new edition keeps the fundamental organization of *Understanding Politics* intact, but the structure has been streamlined to better fit into the time frame of many college and university calendars. The sixth edition retains noteworthy features and materials that were added in the last edition.

- A consideration of the importance of technology and computers in the emerging world order explores the potential of such technology to weaken governments worldwide.

- The addition of World Wide Web boxes in most chapters enables students to explore chapter topics in greater detail while providing them with an important resource for research assignments.

- A complete revision of the section on China emphasizes the vast economic and political changes that today characterize this emerging world power.

- A discussion of terrorism in Algeria illustrates how a country can be torn apart by fanatical groups that recognize no moral limits in the fight to oust the government.

- A discussion of alliances addresses the distinctive and important role played by international organizations, with a particular emphasis on the emergence of NATO as an unusual or perhaps unique alliance.

- A case study of Hafez al-Assad of Syria presents a prototype of a contemporary authoritarian ruler.

- An expanded discussion of Japan as an example of modern democracy features new materials on the judicial branch.

In the sixth edition, I have added several more new features.

- Chapter 6 combines two chapters from the previous edition; it examines Great Britain as the "model" of parliamentary government and then looks at four adaptations of the British model (France, Germany, Japan, and India).

- Chapter 7 has been recast to focus on states in transition rather than concentrating exclusively on postcommunist states; it includes many of the same case-study countries but also looks at South Korea and Taiwan, as well as Latin America's fledgling democracies.

- Chapter 8 contains much of the original material on developing countries, but now includes a discussion of dysfunctional states (Somalia, Yugoslavia, Sierra Leone, and Afghanistan) and introduces the notion of "overdeveloped states" (prosperous countries facing problems such as pollution and drug dependency often associated with a very advanced state of economic development).

- Chapter 10 is the result of a merger of two chapters (on political participation and political organization) from the previous edition. The new subtitle of this chapter "The Price of Influence" reflects a stronger emphasis on the role of campaign contributions in amplifying the voice of the privileged few at the expense of the many.

- Chapter 15 ("Terrorism: The Weapon of the Weak") is expanded and updated to reflect the tragic events of September 11, 2001, and the surge of both information and interest those events precipitated. Also, I have added a considerable amount of material to the discussion of the bloody guerrilla–terrorist campaign in Algeria.

- Chapter 17 on world politics, like Chapters 6 and 10, combines two chapters from the previous edition. The "new" chapter examines the balance of power before and after the two world wars, looks at American foreign policy during and after the Cold War, considers the opposing views of idealists and realists, discusses seven contemporary global issues, and concludes with a brief look at two controversial visions of the future world order. The chapter is a kind of sampler—if it does not totally satisfy the strongest appetites for knowledge of the subject perhaps it will at least stimulate weaker ones.

Note to Instructors   An *Instructor's Manual and Test Bank* is available in both print form and on the Wadsworth Publishers' Web site <www.wadsworth. com>. It consists of a brief chapter summary, true/false, multiple choice, and essay questions for each chapter. A test item file is available in a format for IBM-compatible and Macintosh computers. A book-specific Web site provides access to the links presented in the textbook.

Also, an *InfoTrac® College Edition* workbook is available for this textbook for the first time. InfoTrac is a searchable online library that gives students access to full-text articles from more than 700 popular and scholarly periodicals. Among the journals available are *American Political Science Review, Foreign Policy, Political Science Quarterly, Policy Studies Journal,* and many more. Instructors may obtain passwords for the InfoTrac database from Wadsworth/Thomson Learning representatives; students receive passwords on purchase of the text. The workbook provides instructors for using the database and a set of key words that can be used to locate articles on topics specifically related to the course.

A Personal Note

Understanding Politics was originally the product of a close professional and personal relationship. With this edition, it is now my privilege to continue the project on my own. My longtime collaborator, Dr. Peter Schotten, is in no way responsible for any of the changes—or errors of logic or fact—found in this edition, but the imprint of his diligence and intelligence will of course remain for as long as this book continues to reappear in new editions—that is, for a very long time if fate is so kind.

Acknowledgments

Through six editions and almost two decades, many individuals associated with several different publishing houses and universities have helped make this book a success. Among the scholars and teachers who reviewed the work for this edition in manuscript, offering criticisms and suggestions that in many cases proved to be invaluable, were Peter Longo, University of Nebraska at Kearney; Donald G. Baker, Southampton College, Long Island University; Henry Steck, the State University of New York, Cortland; Ruth Ann Strickland, Appalachian State University; and Iraj Paydar, Bellevue Community College. In addition, I would like to thank David Atkinson and Dale Neuman, friends and colleagues who graciously reviewed parts of the manuscript and gave me useful comments.

I am indebted to several editors at Wadsworth, especially Stacey Sims. Caroline Croley, Margaret Parks, and Brian Chaffee helped with marketing and marketing communications. I also want to thank editors of previous editions, especially Michael Weber and Doug Bell, both formerly at St. Martin's Press, and James Headley, during the brief time the book was the property of St. Martin's/Worth Publishers. The book continues to benefit from the contribution they and others have made. Amy McConathy and Marilea Polk Fried played a crucial role in initiating the review stage of this edition at Bedford/St. Martin's.

Nadya Nedelsky again prepared the instructor's manual in a most conscientious and able fashion. I look forward to a close and continuing relationship with the editors at Wadsworth, who acquired this book as part of the political science list from Bedford/St. Martin's in 2001.

Finally, as always, I owe a big debt of gratitude to my family—Mary Jo (who died in 1990), David, Amy, Michael, Barbara, and Rebecca.

About the Author

Thomas M. Magstadt earned his doctorate at the Johns Hopkins School of Advanced International Studies (SAIS). He has taught at several colleges and universities—including Augustana College, the University of Nebraska at Kearney, and the Air War College—and has twice chaired political science departments. He has also worked as a foreign affairs specialist in the executive branch of the federal government. Magstadt is currently an adjunct professor at Rockhurst University in Kansas City, and is the author of *Nations and Governments: Comparative Politics in Regional Perspective,* fourth edition (Bedford/St. Martin's/Wadsworth, 2002).

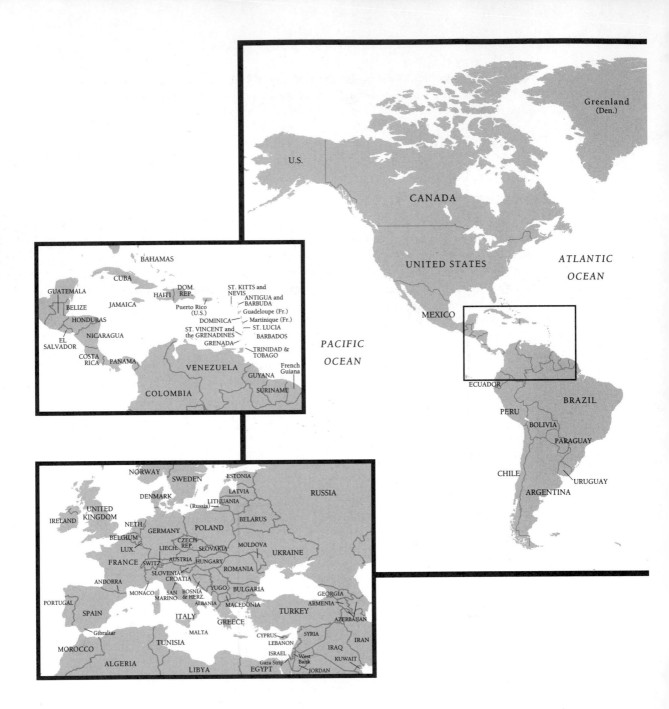

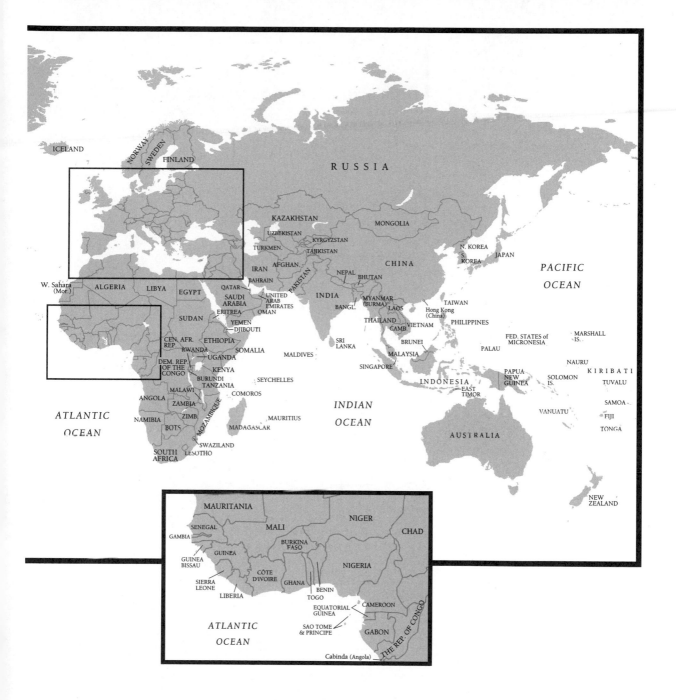

V. C. L. / Getty Images

Chapter 1

INTRODUCTION
THE STUDY OF POLITICS

Politics and Everyday Life

Basic Concepts of Politics
Order • Power and Its Correlates • Justice

How Politics Is Studied
For What Purposes? • By What Methods?
• From What Perspective?

Why Study Politics?
Self-Interest • The Public Interest

Most Americans lead ordinary lives. We are rightly concerned with routine yet vital details of our daily existence, such as paying bills (and tuition!), advancing or securing the well-being of family and loved ones, deciding what car to buy (or simply determining if our car will even start), and so forth. At some level, we all understand that these ordinary but not insignificant concerns about individual safety, economic security, and personal happiness depend not merely on our own efforts, but also on the character and results of our public deliberations—that is, on politics. If nothing else, we are reminded of the omnipresence of politics from watching or listening to the nightly news which brings into our homes deadly ethnic conflicts in remote African states, scenes of violent clashes in the Middle East, and acts of political terrorism.

Politics matters. For this reason, responsible membership in civil society requires a basic understanding of the ideas, institutions, and issues that constitute the stuff of politics.

POLITICS AND EVERYDAY LIFE

Politics is about the way human beings govern and are governed. Politics affects our lives in countless ways on a daily basis, as the following two hypothetical examples serve to illustrate:

Hypothetical #1
A man named John Doe, who has confessed to two rapes, a variety of lesser sex offenses too numerous to mention, and several armed robberies and assaults is released from prison by a district court judge on a legal technicality. Doe, who has been undergoing psychiatric examination at a state mental facility, announces to the press that he is a changed man, that he has found religion, and that he hopes to return to his hometown of Pleasantville and resume a normal life. The same week he comes back to town several brutal rapes occur in Pleasantville. Although there is no reason to believe that Doe is responsible for these crimes, local residents are up in arms. The latest rapes serve to reinforce their opinions that (1) dangerous criminals lurk in their midst; (2) it is very difficult to apprehend such criminals, no matter how boldly and frequently they strike; and (3) even when apprehended, self-confessed robbers, murderers, and rapists sometimes go free because of loopholes in our system of justice. The people of Pleasantville vow to hold the judges and politicians responsible for the terror that envelops their town each night. "There is something wrong with a legal system that allows things like this to happen," they tell each other.

Hypothetical #2
An elderly woman named Mary Smith, who just turned ninety, lives alone in the house she and her husband built in a little northern Minnesota community nearly sixty-five years ago. Smith is still capable of caring for herself and refuses to move to a retirement home. Because her wants and needs are simple, she managed to get along quite nicely on her modest pension until the price of home heating fuel skyrocketed. Since then, her savings, like those of many senior citizens trying to care for themselves, have dwindled with each passing year. The past two winters, which were severe even for northern Minnesota, have nearly wrecked Smith's personal finances. Recently, Smith gained new hope from a newspaper article that stated the federal government had

enacted a law providing fuel oil subsidies to the elderly. When she called the toll-free number, however, she was informed that if she had any savings left in the bank, she was not eligible for a subsidy. Now Smith is desperate. "What will become of me?" she asks. "The government will not be satisfied until I am penniless and homeless. Where is the justice in this world?"

The cases of John Doe and Mary Smith illustrate how the practical problems of everyday politics, which at first glance may appear to affect only one individual, become inextricably bound up with the perpetual quest for what is fair or just in light of the public interest. In other words, issues are more or less political to the extent that the use of public power affects the lives and well-being of private citizens.

BASIC CONCEPTS OF POLITICS

Politics has been variously defined as "the art of the possible," as the study of "who gets what, when, and how," as the "authoritative allocation of values," and in countless other ways. Whether or not we can agree on a definition, most of us know it when we see it. Like any other branch of human knowledge, political science—the systematic study of politics—has a lexicon and language all its own. We start our language lesson with "three little words" that carry a lot of political freight: *order, power,* and *justice*.

Order

Order exists on several levels. Politically, order denotes structures, rules, rituals, procedures, and practices that comprise a political system. The latter is built upon the foundations of the social order (or simply "society"). What exactly *is* society? Society used in the present context is closely related to the word, ***community,*** which is an association of individuals who share a common identity. Usually that identity is at least partially defined by geography because people who live in close proximity often know each other, enjoy shared experiences, speak the same language, and have similar values and interests. Sometimes a new community can be created by instilling a sense of common purpose or a single political allegiance among diverse groups, but, as the breakup of the Soviet Union and Yugoslavia in the early 1990s illustrates, it is not easy to build a new social order even in the presence of a tightly structured political system.

Government is the artifice by which societies are ruled and binding rules are made. Given the rich variety of governments in the world, how might they all be categorized? A common distinction traditionally has been made between ***republics*** (where sovereignty ultimately resides in the people) and governments such as monarchies or tyrannies where sovereignty rests with the rulers. Today, almost all republics are democratic (or representative) republics, meaning that sovereign power is exercised by elected representatives responsible to the people.[1]

Some political scientists are content to draw a simple distinction between democracies, which hold free elections, and dictatorships, which do not. Others emphasize political economy, distinguishing between governments enmeshed in capitalist or market-based systems and governments based on socialist or state-regulated systems. Lastly, governments in developing countries face different kinds of challenges, problems, and predicaments than governments in developed countries—not surprisingly, the kinds of government found in low-income regions of the world are often quite different from the kinds found in high-income regions.

In the modern world, the *state* is the sole repository of *sovereignty*. A sovereign state is a community with well-defined territorial boundaries administered by a single government. In the language of politics, a state is usually synonymous with *country*. France, for instance, may be called either a state or a country. (In certain federal systems of government, a state is an administrative subdivision, such as New York, Florida, Texas, or California in the United States, but states of this sort are not sovereign.)

A *nation* is made up of a distinct group of people who share a common background, including any or all of the following: geographic location, history, racial or ethnic characteristics, religion, language, culture, and belief in common political ideas. Geography heads this list because members of a nation typically exhibit a strong collective sense of belonging that is associated with a particular territory for which they are willing to fight and die if necessary.

Nations vary in terms of history and homogeneity (similarity among members). Countries with relatively homogeneous populations are most commonly found in Europe. Poland, for example, is a very homogeneous nation, as are the Scandinavian countries (Denmark, Sweden, and Norway), Finland, France, Austria, Portugal, and Greece. The United Kingdom, Germany, the Netherlands, Spain, and Italy are somewhat more diverse, but they also speak with one national tongue (although there are different dialects spoken in different parts of these countries). Belgium is one of the few countries on the Continent that is clearly divided culturally and linguistically (French-speaking Walloons versus the Dutch-speaking Flemish). By contrast, the United States as a nation of immigrants is exceptionally diverse. But the "melting pot" eventually assimilates newcomers into the mainstream of American society, thus reinforcing a singular nationhood.[2]

It is obvious that the *nation-state*, both as idea and ideal, is rooted in a specific time and place—that is, in modern European history, particularly in Western Europe. It fits less comfortably into other regions of the world, where the political boundaries of sovereign states—many of which were European colonies before World War II—often do not coincide with ethnic or cultural geography. In some instances, ethnic, religious, or tribal groups that were bitter traditional enemies were thrown together in new "states," resulting in societies prone to great instability or even to civil war.

Decolonization after World War II gave rise to many instant *multinational states* in which the various national (ethnic or tribal) groups were not assimilated into the new social order—many decades later, the task of nation-building in these new states is still far from finished. A few examples will underscore this point. In 1967, Nigeria was plunged into a vicious civil war when one large ethnic group (the Ibo) tried (unsuccessfully) to secede and form an independent state

(Biafra). In 1994, Rwanda witnessed one of the bloodiest massacres in modern times when the numerically superior Hutus slaughtered hundreds of thousands of Tutsis, not sparing women and children in the process. In India, where there are frequent communal clashes between Hindus and Muslims and sporadic outbreaks of violence involving militant Sikhs in Punjab, and where hundreds of languages and dialects are spoken, characterizing the country as a *nation-state* simply misses the point altogether. In Sri Lanka (formerly Ceylon), Hindu Tamils have long waged a terrorist guerrilla war against the majority Sinhalese, who are Buddhist.

Even in the Slavic-speaking parts of Europe, age-old ethnic rivalries have caused the breakup of preexisting states. The Soviet Union, Yugoslavia, and Czechoslovakia are all examples of multinational states that self-destructed in the 1990s.

Finally, there are *stateless nations*, such as the Palestinians and Kurds, who share a sense of common identity (or community) but have no homeland. The existence of these nations without states has created highly volatile situations, most notably in the Middle East.

Power and Its Correlates

The ability of governments, and of governmental leaders, to make and enforce rules and to influence the behavior of individuals or groups by rewarding or punishing certain behaviors constitutes *power*. Governments cannot maintain peace, guarantee security, promote economic growth, or pursue effective policies without power. The effective exercise of political authority involves much more, however, than the ability to use physical force. Indeed, the sources of power are many and varied. An overwhelming election mandate, a gift for eloquent oratory, vast wealth, or a repressive secret police all represent quite different sources of power. Of course, the more abundant the power sources (or resources), the greater the capabilities of government. Weak governments often cannot do much harm (at least not directly), but they seldom can do much good either.

Power can never be equally distributed in any society or state. Yet the need to concentrate power in the hands of a few inevitably raises questions, doubts, and sometimes suspicions among the many. Who wields power and whether power is exercised effectively are important to the common welfare. Thus, the question "Who rules?" may give rise to a highly controversial political issue. Sometimes the answer is simple; one only has to look at a nation's constitution and observe the workings of its government. But it may be difficult to determine who *really* rules when the government is cloaked in secrecy or when, as is often the case, informal patterns of power deviate sharply from the formal structures of authority outlined in the nation's basic law. In any nation-state, the number of people holding political office and exercising power is minuscule compared to the population at large. No less important than the question "Who rules?" and how effectively is whether political power is wielded justly.

Power and *authority* are often confused because they are so closely associated and, in fact, even used interchangeably. In reality, they are two distinct concepts denoting two distinct dimensions of politics. Mao Zedong, the late Chinese Communist leader, once said that power flows from the barrel of a gun, which is true but grossly oversimplified. Political power *does* come in part from possession of coercive instruments (the police, the secret police, the militia, the military), but not exclusively from such sources. Power can also flow from wealth, personal charisma, ideology, religion, and many other sources, including the moral standing of a particular individual or group in society.

Authority, by definition, does not only (or even mainly) flow from the barrel of a gun, but also from *norms* that are recognized and embraced by the vast majority of a society's members. These norms are variously rooted in moral, spiritual, and legal codes of behavior or good conduct. Authority as it is used in this text, therefore, implies *legitimacy*—a condition in which power is exercised through established institutions and according to rules that are freely accepted by the people as right and proper. Note that this definition does not mean (nor is it meant to imply) that democracy is the only legitimate form of government possible. On the contrary, a monarchy or other form of dictatorship could qualify as legitimate. The acid test of *legitimate authority* is not whether people have the right to vote or to strike or to dissent openly, but how much *value* people attach to any or all of these rights. If people are content with the existing political order just as it is (with or without voting rights), the legitimacy of the ruler(s) is simply not in question. Power in this case is married to authority, and the stability of the state follows as a natural consequence. As history amply demonstrates, it is possible to *seize* power and to rule without a popular mandate or public approval, without moral, spiritual, or legal justification—in other words, without true (that is, legitimate) authority. Examples of power seizures in recent decades can be found in the Middle East and North Africa, Asia, and elsewhere; prior to the 1980s, such power seizures were common in Latin America, as well.

Authority, on the other hand, *cannot* be seized: It can only be asserted or claimed. Claiming authority, however, is useless without the means to enforce it. Whether the right to rule is seriously challenged (and enforcement becomes necessary) hinges in large part on the question of legitimacy. If people refuse to accept a government's authority, illegitimate rulers are faced with a choice: relinquish power or repress opposition. Whether repression works or not depends, in turn, on the answer to two questions. First, how widespread and determined is the opposition? Second, does the government have enough financial resources and coercive capabilities to defeat its opponents and deter future challenges?

In general, it is better for rulers to have public approval than not to have it. This principle is true of dictatorships as well as democracies if for no other reason than the relatively high cost of repression over a long period of time. Obviously, if people respect their ruler(s) and play by the rules without being forced to do so (or threatened with the consequences of not doing so) the task of maintaining order and stability in society is going to be much easier. Moreover, people who are sullen, discontent, and oppressed are unlikely to be highly motivated and productive workers—this peril has been the Achilles' heel of many dictatorships in the last century. Indeed, it accounts in no small measure for the collapse of communism in Eastern Europe and the former Soviet Union.

Justice

The fact that the governors are always vastly outnumbered by the governed gives rise to competing—and sometimes conflicting—claims regarding the fairness of a government's policies and programs. It is often asserted that the rule of some citizens over others can be accepted only if the public interest is significantly advanced in the process. Thus the exercise of power must be tempered by the question of *justice:* Is power exercised fairly, in the interest of the ruled, or merely for the sake of the rulers? For more than 2,000 years, political observers have maintained the distinction between the public-spirited exercise of political power on the one hand and self-interested rule on the other; this attests to the importance of justice in political life.

Not all states allow questions of justice to be raised; in fact, throughout history most have not. Even today, some governments brutally and systematically repress political discussion and debate because they fear that if public attention focuses on basic issues of justice and the common good, the legitimacy of the existing political order might come under attack. All too often, criticism of the *way* a government rules may call into question its moral or legal *right* to rule. This is one reason political liberty is so important. In contemporary times, justice is often defined by the extent to which individual rights (that is, natural, human, or civil rights) are

Kevin McKiernan/Sipa Press

Citizens can publicize their claims of political injustice in any number of ways, including demonstrations and marches. One of the goals of Louis Farrakhan's October 1995 Million Man March was to question whether African American citizens in the United States were being fairly treated.

respected by government. Among the most important of these rights is that which permits citizens to question whether their government is acting justly.

Although questions of public morality may be suppressed, they can never be extinguished. Questions about which ruler is legitimate or what policy is desirable naturally crop up in everyday conversation. This fact seems to stem from human nature itself. The Greek philosopher Aristotle (384–322 B.C.E) observed that, in contrast to animals, who can only make sounds signifying pleasure and pain, human beings use reason and language "to declare what is advantageous and what is just and unjust." Therefore, "it is the peculiarity of man, in comparison with the rest of the animal world, that he alone possesses a perception of good and evil, of the just and unjust. . . ."[3] Thus the same human faculties that make moral judgment possible also make political discussion necessary.

HOW POLITICS IS STUDIED

The Greek philosopher Aristotle is the father of political science.[4] Not only did he write about politics and ethics, he also described different political orders and suggested a scheme for classifying and evaluating them. For Aristotle, political science simply meant political investigation; thus a political scientist was one who sought, through systematic inquiry, to understand the truth about politics. In this sense, Aristotle's approach to studying politics more than 2,000 years ago has much in common with what political scientists do today. Yet the discipline has changed a great deal since Aristotle's time.

Today, there is no consensus on how politics can best be studied. The result is a multifaceted discipline with different political scientists choosing different approaches, asking different kinds of questions, and addressing different audiences. The resulting ferment is not necessarily bad. Rather, it reflects the diversity and vitality of the discipline, as well as the vast universe of human activity with which political science must deal. The following pages explore why and how contemporary political scientists study politics.

For What Purposes?

In one sense, the study of politics is no different from the study of biology, history, or psychology. Just as students in other disciplines seek the truth about their respective subjects, political scientists attempt to understand the truth about politics and government.

Besides gaining knowledge for its own sake, practical advantages accompany the disciplined study of politics. Studying interest groups in the United States not only reveals a great deal of information about the number, composition, and influence of interest groups but also can shed light on ways for interest groups to become more effective. By the same token, public opinion surveys tell voters how elections are likely to turn out, but also can (and are) used by candidates to tailor campaign strategy and fine-tune tactics in different regions and states (see Chapter 10). Similarly, an expert in foreign policy or international relations is not only aware of various treaties the United States has signed and ratified over the past twenty-five years but also can offer advice regarding the implications and long-term consequences of entering into new alliances or making new commitments around the world (see Chapter 18).

Yet experts and specialists frequently disagree. In political science, this disagreement goes beyond specific issues and involves such basic questions as whether it is possible to have a "true" science of politics. Should political science strive to predict or forecast events to the degree that chemists and physicists can? Should we hold political scientists to the same standards as, say, meteorologists? To appreciate the diversity among political scientists, we will look first at what is commonly called "methodology."

By What Methods?

There are many ways of classifying political scientists. However, we will focus on two divisions in contemporary political science, *traditionalists* versus *behaviorists* and *political economists* versus *Marxists*. Bear in mind that these categories are not mutually exclusive and that political scientists often integrate different approaches.

The Traditional Approach   Although mastery of the nuts and bolts of politics is important, traditionalists give equal emphasis to evaluation. They want to assess not merely *how* a particular policy, process, or institution works, but *how well* it works according to certain moral or legal standards. In considering Congress's committee system, nuclear deterrence, or the efficacy of the United Nations, for example, they would ask, "Are there better alternatives?"

The possible criteria for making such judgments are diverse—philosophy and formal logic, constitutions, treaties, the texts of official documents, court cases, expert opinions, and the like, can all come into play. In addition, the choice of research topics and methods are often rooted in what the individual investigator considers most important. For example, the study of the separation of powers (into executive, legislative, and judicial branches of government) might begin with a review of the Constitution that would no doubt include James Madison's famous commentary in *The Federalist* (1787–88). Or, alternatively, it might focus on the economic interests the Founders supposedly represented or the social class they were virtually all rooted in—but such an approach would take the investigator beyond the pale of traditional political science into the realm of behaviorism, political economy, or, quite possibly, Marxist analysis. We turn next to behaviorism.

The Behavioral Approach   In contrast to traditionalists' emphasis on normative political questions, behaviorists emphasize the scientific method. This school of thought, which became prominent after World War II, focuses on the more concrete task of describing and predicting political behavior and the dynamics and outcomes of political processes. Unlike traditional political scientists, behaviorists generally avoid moral and philosophical judgments about politics because they believe that such judgments are little more than speculations and cannot be proved scientifically.

Behavioral scientists shy away from "values," preferring instead to concentrate on "facts." (Whether there is a clear distinction between values and facts in political life deserves careful attention, which it rarely gets.) Behaviorists employ the scientific method so familiar to investigators in such fields as biology, physics, and chemistry, asking the sort of questions that can only be answered by carefully putting together a research design, gathering empirical data, using the tools of statistical analysis, and constructing experiments to test hypotheses. Some behaviorists use deductive rather than inductive methods, developing elaborate mathematical models to explain the behavior of voters, political parties, decisionmakers, coalition members, and the like. In this vein, for more than half a century now, elaborate statistical and mathematical studies have been undertaken in an attempt to identify the correlates and causes of war.

An example of the behavioral approach helps illustrate its methods. In December 1996, a study titled "Partisan Effects of Voter Turnout in Senatorial and Gubernatorial Elections" was published in a well-known scholarly journal.[5] The study asked the following precise question that could theoretically be answered using quantitative methods: Is it really true, as is widely believed, that high voter turnout favors Democrats? The prevailing belief that Democrats benefited from high voter turnout assumed that: (1) people with lower socioeconomic status (SES) voted less often than people with higher SES; (2) as voter turnout rose, more lower SES citizens voted; and (3) these lower SES voters were likely to vote for the party they thought would most effectively advance working-class interests—namely, the Democratic party. Many political observers had accepted this theory, contending that low voter turnout helped explain recent Republican election successes. Politicians also believed that high voter turnout aided Democrats, which was one reason that Democrats generally favored (and Republicans opposed) the 1995 National Voter Registration Act (popularly known as the motor voter bill, this law eased voter registration procedures).

The researchers used statistics that started in 1928, examining 1,842 state elections: 983 for senator, 859 for governor. The study omitted two kinds of elections: (1) elections in the Deep South between 1928 and 1965 in which there was effectively only one party with any chance of winning (the Democratic party); and (2) elections in which third-party candidates received more than 5 percent of the vote. Applying a mathematical test, the researchers concluded that from 1928 to 1964 high voter turnout aided the Democratic party, just as was generally believed, but after 1964 the results were markedly different. In senatorial races, there was no relationship between turnout and votes for Democrats; in gubernatorial elections, Republicans, rather than Democrats, fared slightly better, but the difference was not statistically significant.

Why was the conventional theory of voter turnout invalidated after 1964? Although this question was beyond the scope of the study, its findings were consistent with another complex theory of American voting behavior. The rise in the number of independents since 1964 (decline in party identification and partisan voting) has made it increasingly difficult to calculate which party will benefit from increased voter turnout.

This sophisticated research project epitomizes the kind of methodology employed by behavioral political scientists. Behaviorists, like other research scientists, are content to take small steps on the road to knowledge. Each step along the way points to future studies.

Studying human behavior is markedly different from studying the behavior of gases or laboratory rats. There are almost always multiple explanations for human behavior. It is extremely difficult to sort out and isolate a single cause of behavior, to distinguish a true cause from a mere statistical correlation. For instance, several studies indicate that criminals tend to be less intelligent than law-abiding citizens. If so, is low intelligence a *cause* of crime (perhaps because many criminals cannot understand the consequences of violating the law or the value of deferred gratification in civil society)? How does low intelligence relate to other correlates (and perhaps causes) of crime, including age, gender, personality type, a history of being abused or neglected as a child, and drug or alcohol addiction? What about free will? Are we to believe that society—rather than the individual who commits a crime—is responsible?

Behavioral and traditional political scientists often disagree not only about how to study politics but also about what questions to ask. Behaviorists prefer to examine specific and narrowly defined questions, answering them by applying quantitative techniques. Many broader questions of politics, especially those raising questions of justice, lie beyond the scope of this sort of investigation. Questions such as "What is justice?" or "What is the best political system?" are dismissed because answers are said to involve subjective policy preferences or value judgments. Traditionalists counter by arguing that even if such questions cannot be resolved scientifically, not all value judgments are arbitrary or based on mere prejudice. Confining the study of politics only to questions with quantifiable answers, they argue, runs the risk of turning political science into an academic game of Trivial Pursuit.

Given the complexity of understanding human behavior, it is not surprising that experts argue over methodology. Today, the dispute between these two schools of thought—traditional and behavioral—is less intense than it used to be. Each has made notable contributions to the study of politics and government. Political economy and Marxian schools of thought have also made important contributions to the study of politics. We turn to these two contending approaches next.

Political Economy Many political scientists look at politics through the prism of political economy, which views politics and macroeconomics as two sides of the same coin rather than as two separate disciplines. From this perspective, political analysis that ignores economics ignores reality. By the same token, economic analysis divorced from politics ends up as an empty theoretical exercise. In the real world, politics and economics are so mutually dependent that separating them is like trying to separate sunshine and daylight.

The questions that interest political economists are dictated by this expanded definition of politics. Economics emphasizes a different set of concepts than politics—competition instead of conflict, wealth instead of power, consumer choice instead of voter preference, and so on. In addition, economists are more attuned than political scientists to fiscal and monetary policies—including taxes and public spending, interest rates and the money supply, tariffs and trade—as powerful *political* instruments in the hands of decisionmakers. Political scientists, on the other hand, are more prone to focus on the impact of interest groups on public policy, and on the political implications of economic decisions such as interest-rate changes, deficit spending, tax cuts, or trade liberalization.

Political economists seek to combine the best of both worlds—politics and economics—to produce a higher level of analysis, one with greater explanatory and even predictive value. The tools of political economy provide a fruitful way to study comparative and international politics, as well as politics and policy in one country. Here is a brief profile of the world as it looks from the perspective of political economy:

1. The world's material wealth is maldistributed. More than four-fifths of the poor live in two regions: sub-Saharan Africa and South Asia. Per capita gross national product (GNP) in 1998 was fifty times higher in North America and Western Europe than in sub-Saharan Africa and about thirty-five times higher than in Asia and the Pacific (which includes rich countries such as Japan, South Korea, and Taiwan).

2. Economic growth rates have declined in many countries in the past three decades, but this decline has hit the poorest regions of the world the hardest. The full impact of declining growth rates on developing countries can best be appreciated by comparing them with population growth rates, which yields the *annual per capita growth rate* for the economy as a whole. By this measure, the economies of many developing countries—especially in sub-Saharan Africa, as well as parts of the Arab world and South Asia—are losing ground every year.

3. The distribution of wealth is more unequal in developing (poor) nations and regions than within developed (rich) nations and regions. For example, the top 10 percent of the population owns 50 percent of the wealth in Brazil and 40 percent of the wealth in Kenya, Zambia, Peru, and Mexico. In the United States and Japan, by contrast, the top 10 percent owns less than 25 percent of the wealth.

Perhaps the foregoing profile is enough to demonstrate how important the approach or perspective we use can be in determining what we see or what we consider important. Both the topics chosen and the tools of analysis used by the investigator are to a large extent determined by the approach we adopt. Among the approaches that have made a major impact on political science (and world politics), Marxian analysis stands out as one that demands our attention—whether we like it or not.

The Marxian Approach   Marxism as an ideology is discussed in Chapters 5 and 12 of this book. As an ideology, Marxism is forever connected with left-wing totalitarianism and with the excesses of the Stalinist era in the former Soviet Union and communist regimes elsewhere in the world (China, North Korea, and Cuba are among the few communist-ruled states still in existence). But there is another way to apply Marx's ideas. Scholars in communist countries are forced to embrace the official version of Marxism publicly whether they agree with it privately or not, but many scholars in non-communist countries (including the United States) find Marxian categories of analysis to be fruitful in explaining political-economic processes. Some of these scholars may have personal political agendas—that is, ideological motives—but it would be unscientific in the extreme to ignore Marxian critiques of democratic capitalism out of blind prejudice against anything that smacks of socialism.

In the United States, Marxism has had limited academic (or political) appeal due in part to the Cold War and the obvious connection between Marxism and Soviet-style communism. In many other countries, however, Marxism has greatly influenced the study of politics, economics, and society—on both the domestic and international levels.

For example, a whole school of thought among scholars interested in developing countries has taken up a form of Marxian analysis called *dependency theory*. Starting with the proposition that the planet Earth has a finite amount of natural resources, dependency theorists posit that the world (or global society) is divided into three basic classes: the industrial core (the United States, Western Europe, and Japan); the semiperiphery (new industrial countries such as South Korea, Taiwan, Singapore, Chile, and Brazil); and the periphery (the vast majority of countries in the former colonial areas of Asia, Africa, and Latin America). The states of both the periphery and the semiperiphery are dependent on the industrial core for markets, capital, and technology. The industrial nations purportedly have a vested interest in perpetuating this state of dependency.

The dependency system perpetuates global inequality in various ways. First, the core states produce costly manufactures, and the peripheral states supply cheap raw materials (foodstuffs and minerals). Prices are manipulated by the dominant economic powers—consequently, the *terms of trade* (the price of industrial goods and services versus the price of commodities) favor the core states. Commodity prices fluctuate widely from one year to the next; many developing countries are dependent on the export of one or two commodities (such as sugar, coffee, bananas, or jute). Export revenues for commodities are extremely sensitive to price fluctuations beyond the control of the exporting countries. But the developing countries must continue to import and must pay for imports with convertible currency (such as dollars). Often they must borrow from abroad, with no option but to pay whatever interest rates international financiers in the core states demand. Further, any foreign aid they receive comes with strings attached. Finally, in a crisis, they are left with little choice but to accept the conditions imposed by the US–led International Monetary Fund for short-term loans.

An especially unfair aspect of this whole system, according to dependency theorists, is the collusion between capitalists in the core states and economic elites in the peripheral states. These elites profit hugely from the arrangement, but it is mutually beneficial: The core states back the governments in power (often dictatorships), which in turn maintain order and stability while keeping domestic markets open for (and to) international business. Grants of military and economic aid, seen in this light, are bribes that reap larger dividends for the donor nations than for the recipients in part because corrupt rulers often siphon off most of the funds.

Most political economists in the West reject dependency theory. They stress that many developing nations have been plagued by weak institutions, corrupt or incompetent leaders, and chronic sociopolitical instability. The path to economic development is political. Adoption of rational laws and policies aimed at promoting economic growth is the key to unlocking the door to development—a door that will otherwise remain closed. Nonetheless, Marxian analysis continues to be a potent force in academic circles abroad and even within a small but prolific minority of political scientists in the United States.

From What Perspective?

Political economy is but one of several sub-fields into which political science can be divided. Other prominent sub-fields include *political theory, American government, comparative politics, international relations,* and *public administration* as well. Several other more specialized areas of political science deserve mention. Generally, depending on how they are studied, these specialties fit within one or more of the subfields just listed. *Constitutional law,* for example, is a traditional specialty that focuses on a specific aspect of American government. *Public policy,* which stresses modern management techniques such as zero-based budgeting, cost accounting, and systems analysis, involves both American government and public administration. *Political parties* and *interest groups* (as a special research and teaching area) fall within either American government or comparative politics. Now let's look more closely at the six subfields into which political science programs are often divided.

Political Theory   Normative political theory, or political philosophy, dates back to Plato (circa 400 B.C.E). Plato's method in searching for the truth was to ask important questions: What is the good life? What is good government? To what extent will good government produce the good life? Can good government actually be achieved? What is the basic nature of human beings? Are people basically good or bad? Is human nature easily changed? What kind of state best takes account of that nature without sacrificing the common good? Beyond order and security, is the primary end of the state to improve human beings morally, to make them equal, to guarantee individual liberties, or to do something else? Pursuant to these ends, should government be strong and vigilant or weak and permissive? When is revolution justified? How can political stability be safeguarded?

Political theory tries to answer these questions through reason and logic supported by the writings of political thinkers, such as Aristotle, Jean-Jacques Rousseau, John Locke, and John Stuart Mill, among others. The aim of this type of inquiry is to make judgments as to right and wrong or good and bad. Because people who advocate change and those who oppose it both do so in the belief that they are morally right, understanding politics requires familiarity with the criteria by which policies and programs are judged good and bad.[6] Normative theorists contend that without knowledge of the moral costs and consequences of politics, citizens and leaders alike will lack direction and a clear sense of purpose.

American Government   Understanding our own political institutions is important but not always easy. The only way to do it is by careful and continuous study. American government (like all of politics) is far more complex than is often imagined. Political scientists who teach courses on American government and politics are, in effect, engaging in civic education. For obvious reasons, it is crucial that citizens in a democracy understand how the government works, what rights they are guaranteed by the Constitution, and so on. Also, politics in America merits study because the United States is home to both the oldest constitutional democracy of the modern era and the largest economy in the world.

Comparative Politics   Comparative politics seeks to contrast and evaluate governments and political systems. Comparative analysis of forms of government, stages of economic development, domestic and foreign policies, and political traditions leads political scientists to formulate meaningful generalizations. Some comparative political scientists specialize in a particular region of the world or a particular nation intensively. Others focus on a particular political phenomenon such as instability or voting behavior.

All political systems share certain characteristics. Figure 1-1 depicts one famous model, first formulated by political scientist David Easton in 1965. It postulates that all political systems function within the context of political cultures, which consist of traditions, values, and common knowledge. Furthermore, it holds that citizens invariably have expectations and place demands on the political system. But they also support the system in various ways: They may participate in government, vote, or simply obey the laws of the state. Citizens' demands and support, influenced by popular beliefs about what is and should be happen-

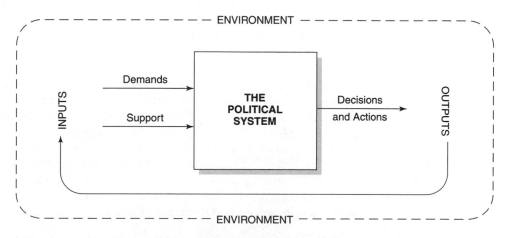

FIGURE 1-1   A Simplified Model of the Political System
SOURCE: Copyright 1965, 1979 by David Easton. All rights reserved.

ing in society, in turn influence the decision-making capacity of the political system. From this ongoing process, governmental decisions and actions emerge, usually in such forms as edicts, laws, and orders.

Countries, of course, differ in countless ways. Some political scientists see the differences among countries as being more significant than the similarities, and they differentiate among political systems in various ways. This text, for example, emphasizes how democratic, authoritarian, and totalitarian states differ. Some political scientists are uncomfortable with the totalitarian category, and so they merely contrast democratic and non-democratic states. Others stress the economic context of politics in different places: in the post-industrial world (North America, Western Europe, Australia, and Japan) and in the rapidly growing states of East Asia (China, South Korea, Taiwan, and Singapore); in the impoverished remnants of the communist world (Vietnam, North Korea, and Cuba); and in the "less developed countries" (LDCs). More recently, the distinction between established liberal democracies and "transitional states" has gained currency (see Chapter 7). Still other political scientists, as we noted earlier, point to the maldistribution of the world's wealth and posit a politically significant division (commonly called the "North-South conflict") between richer nations north of the equator and poorer nations to the south. Finally some observers distinguish between viable states and so-called failed states (see Chapter 8).

International Relations   Specialists in international relations analyze how nations interact. Why do nations sometimes live in peace and harmony but go to war at other times? What is the relative impact of diplomacy, economic interdependence, the United Nations, and nuclear deterrence on efforts to maintain peace? The advent of the nuclear age, of course, brought new urgency to the study of international relations.

War and peace are the most pressing concerns of international relations, but they are by no means the only ones. Other issues run the gamut from trade and tourism to terrorism, from foreign policy to farm policy, from economic integration to emigration. Issues in these and many other areas are valid pursuits for experts in international relations, but no individual can hope to master the intricacies of them all. Hence, international relations, like the other subfields of political science, is multifaceted.

The role of morality in foreign policy continues to be a matter of lively debate. Some political scientists (generally called realists) argue that considerations of national interest have always been paramount in international politics and always will be.[7] Other political scientists (sometimes called idealists) contend that a heightened concern for morality will lead to world peace and an end to the "war system," which the realists accept fatalistically. Still others suggest that the distinction between national interest and international morality is false; democracies, for example, can actively promote the health of other democracies and by so doing serve both their own self-interest and the cause of world peace and prosperity.[8]

Public Administration   In recent years the study of public administration has emerged in some schools not simply as a subfield of political science but as a separate discipline designed to train people seeking a career in public service. Essentially, public administration focuses on how the bureaucracy implements governmental policies. Usually the emphasis is on national government, but public administration is also concerned with state and local government and with intergovernmental relations. Students of public administration seek to understand what helps as well as what hinders the bureaucracy in carrying out its assigned functions. Bureaucratic structures, procedures, and processes are examined in an attempt to improve efficiency and reduce waste and duplication. Of particular concern are how and why bureaucracies develop their own policy interests, quite apart from the governmental policies they are established to implement.

Political scientists who study public administration frequently concentrate on case studies, paying attention not only to the ways in which governmental power is exercised but also to whether power is exercised in a manner consistent with the public interest. In this sense, public administration shares the concerns of political science as a whole.

WHY STUDY POLITICS?

How professional political scientists study politics reveals a great deal about the discipline in general but little about the importance of political science for beginning students. A basic understanding of politics is a vital part of any undergraduate's education, for reasons spelled out in the following pages. To realize the benefits that can flow from the study of politics, however, students must make a sincere effort to learn and, above all, must keep an open mind.

Self-Interest

Because personal happiness depends in no small degree on what government does or does not do, we all have a considerable stake in understanding how government works (or why it is not working). To college students, for example, federal work-study programs, state subsidies to public education, low-interest loans, federal grants, and court decisions designed to protect (or not protect) students' rights are political matters of great significance. Through the study of politics, we become more aware of our dependence on the political system and better equipped to determine when to favor and when to oppose change. At the same time, such study helps to reveal the limits of politics and of our ability to bring about positive change. It is sobering to consider that each of us is only one person in a nation of millions (and a world of billions), most of whom have opinions and prejudices no less firmly held than are our own.

The Public Interest

What could be more vital to the public interest than the moral character and conduct of the citizenry? Civil society is defined by and reflected in the kinds of everyday decisions and choices made by ordinary people leading ordinary lives. At the same time, people are greatly influenced by civil society and the prevailing culture and climate of politics. People with very similar capabilities and desires can develop quite different moral dispositions, depending on the circumstances. Politics plays a vital role in the shaping of these circumstances, and the public interest in the broadest possible sense hangs in the balance.

A Negative Example   The rise and fall of Nazi Germany (1933–45) illustrates the tremendous impact a political regime can have on the moral character of citizens. Headed by Adolf Hitler, the most significant and striking aspects of Nazism were its tenets. Its political doctrine was explicitly grounded in a doctrine of virulent racial supremacy. Hitler ranted about the superiority of the so-called Aryan race. The purity of the German nation was supposedly threatened with adulteration by inferior races or *untermenschen*. Policies based on this *weltanschauung* (worldview) resulted in the systematic murder of millions of innocent men, women, and children. Approximately 6 million Jews and millions of others, including Poles, Gypsies, homosexuals, and people with disabilities, were killed in cold blood. So intent were the Nazis on carrying out the "final solution" to the alleged problem of racial contamination that the operation of extermination camps in the closing months of World War II continued even at the expense of military campaigns.

The Holocaust—a gruesome spectacle of gas chambers and mass murder—forces us to ask how horrors on this scale could take place in a supposedly civilized country. How could a nation with an impressive humanistic tradition, which nurtured so many of the world's greatest composers, writers, and thinkers, have permitted such a thing to happen?

In the Nazi era, the German nation appears, at first glance, to have become little more than an extension of Hitler's will; in other words, the awesome moral responsibility for the Holocaust somehow rested on the shoulders of one man—Adolph Hitler. But some observers dispute this interpretation, pointing out that Hitler could not have carried out his program of mass murder without a community of accomplices. What about those who helped to plan, coordinate, and administer his policies? According to one observer, Irving Kristol:

> When one studies the case of The Nazi there comes a sickening emptiness of the stomach and a sense of bafflement. Can this be all? The disparity between the crime and the criminal is too monstrous.
>
> We expect to find evil men, paragons of wickedness, slobbering, maniacal brutes; we are prepared to trace the lineaments of The Nazi on the face of every individual Nazi in order to define triumphantly the essential features of his character. But the Nazi leaders were not diabolists, they did not worship evil. For—greatest of ironies—the Nazis, like Adam and Eve before the fall, knew not of good and evil, and it is this cast of moral indifference that makes them appear so petty and colorless and superficial.[9]

Kristol is not alone in thinking that many Nazis were not so much morally evil as morally ignorant. Some observers have characterized Albert Speer, Hitler's minister of armaments and munitions, as just such a person.[10] Another, according to political theorist Hannah Arendt, was Adolf Eichmann, a Nazi functionary who administered much of the extermination program. In Arendt's view, Eichmann was not a particularly unusual man.[11] He had a strong desire to get ahead, to be a success in life. He took special pride in his ability to do a job efficiently. Although not particularly thoughtful or reflective, he was intelligent. Arendt also describes him as somewhat insecure, but not noticeably more so than many "normal" people. Eichmann claimed to have no obsessive hatred toward Jews (although, obviously, he was not sufficiently skeptical or mentally independent to resist the widespread anti-Semitism that existed in Germany at that time). In short, Eichmann was morally indifferent; in Kristol's words, he "knew not of good and evil."

These writers tell a story of ordinary people who participated in acts of extraordinary evil, people who remind us of people we all know—perhaps even of ourselves. It would not be difficult, for example, to picture an Eichmann in surroundings more familiar to us, perhaps as an ambitious up-and-coming executive in a large American corporation or as a young foreign service officer determined to get ahead. Such a person would most likely be a workaholic, devoted to company or country, concerned with advancement, and eager to please superiors. Not lacking decent human qualities, he or she might, for instance, be a faithful spouse and loving parent. (It was not unusual for the Nazis to display great affection for their families.) The key point is that this make-believe person is so caught up in the "real world," as defined in terms of narrow career objectives, that he or she has no time for, or interest in, "abstract" moral questions.

If it is true that Adolf Eichmann was an ordinary man, why are there so few Eichmanns? In large measure, the answer can be found in the fortunate fact that the political regimes under which most people live are nothing like Nazi Germany. The Nazi experience was a crucial factor in shaping the personality and character of all the Eichmanns in Germany between the two world wars. Just as every conscientious grocery store manager knows that the goal is profit, so Eichmann and his ilk understood that goal was killing masses of people in gas chambers. In addition, he knew his success, like that of the grocery store manager, would be measured largely in terms of a single criterion: efficiency. What mattered to Eichmann was not what he was doing but how well he did it. Very likely he would have discharged his responsibilities with equal zeal had he been in charge of park planning or flower planting rather than mass extermination. The banality of this evildoer and the magnitude of his evil are both appalling and instructive, for they accurately reflected Germany's prevailing policies.[12]

The German leadership equated mass extermination with patriotism and the public interest. It would have required a rare combination of intellectual independence and moral courage not to go along with this prevailing view. Tragically, those were precisely the qualities countless people like Eichmann so sorely lacked. Knowing that the public interest can never be served by blind obedience to authority illustrates the importance of understanding politics.

GATEWAYS TO THE WORLD: EXPLORING CYBERSPACE

On a recent afternoon, a search of a popular subject catalog on the World Wide Web revealed nearly 500 category and 2,000 site matches for the search term *politics*. These were grouped into general headings that included Current Politics Headlines, Citizenship, Elections, Humor, Interest Groups, Organizations, Parties, Political Issues, Political Opinion, and Political Science. There were also links to a directory of various Usenet groups for those interested in any and every facet of politics. Clearly, you are not alone in your interest in this subject, as this list indicates. Throughout the rest of this book, you will find more of these Gateways to the World boxes.

Here you will discover practical advice on how to find out more about concepts covered in the chapter by utilizing the resources of the Internet. This advice will range from suggested search terms to uniform resource locators [URLs] of specific Web sites. This section should prove useful as you seek to learn about a concept in more depth or in researching and writing papers. The URLs in this section will provide you with hints for getting involved in organizations that deal with issues relevant to the chapter. You should keep in mind that the Web is constantly changing, so some of the sites to which this text refers may no longer be available.

Summary

The study of politics is based on three fundamental concepts: order, power, and justice. Understanding that human life is ordered constitutes the first recognition of political life. Specifically, political order is reflected in communities where human beings live and share a common identity. Communities are ordered, maintained, and perpetuated by government. The addition of government, imposing a structure on the most consequential and self-sufficient communities, has produced the modern nation-state.

Power, which has many sources, refers to government's ability to perform its required tasks. Questions of justice arise if the public interest is not advanced by the exercise of governmental power. Thus politics plays a vital and pervasive role in everyday life, for the irrepressible human pursuit of justice is intimately bound up with the exercise of public power, even though moral questions may at times be obscured from public view.

Political scientists study their discipline to discover the truth about political institutions, forces, movements, and processes. Traditional political scientists are interested in assessing the workings of government, whereas behaviorists use scientific methods to describe and predict political outcomes. Almost all political scientists specialize, with the broadest subfields of the discipline being political theory (or philosophy), American government, comparative politics, international relations, and public administration.

Among the many valid reasons for studying politics, two are worthy of special emphasis: (1) Understanding politics is a matter of self-interest, and (2) by exploring politics, an individual gains a better appreciation of what is, and what is not, in the public interest. The critical importance of this awareness among ordinary citizens was tragically illustrated by the rise of Nazism in Germany.

Key Terms

politics	power
order	authority
community	legitimacy
government	legitimate authority
republics	justice
state	traditionalists
sovereignty	behaviorists
country	political economists
nation	Marxists
nation-state	dependency theory
multinational states	terms of trade
stateless nations	

Review Questions

1. On what three fundamental concepts is the study of politics based?

2. How does one identify a political problem? Are some conflicts more political than others? Explain.

3. How do political scientists differ from one another?

4. In what ways can individuals benefit from the study of politics and government?

Recommended Reading

ARISTOTLE. *The Politics.* Edited and translated by Ernest Barker. New York: Oxford University Press, 1962. An account of the necessity and value of politics.

BETTELHEIM, BRUNO. "Remarks on the Psychological Appeal of Totalitarianism." *Surviving and Other Essays.* New York: Random House, 1980. Bettelheim provides an excellent account of the less obvious ways the Nazi regime imposed conformity and obedience on its citizens.

CRICK, BERNARD. *In Defense of Politics.* Magnolia, Mass.: Peter Smith Publisher, 1994. An argument that politics is an important and worthy human endeavor.

DRUCKER, PETER. "The Monster and the Lamb." *Atlantic* (December 1978): 82–87. A short but moving account of the effects of the Nazi government on several individuals.

EASTON, DAVID. *The Political System: An Inquiry into the State of Political Science.* 2nd ed. Chicago: University of Chicago Press, 1981. A pioneering book that laid the foundation for a systems theory approach to political analysis.

Lewis, C. S. *The Abolition of Man*. New York: Simon & Schuster, 1996. An elegant discussion of the necessity of moral judgments.

Milgram, Stanley. *Obedience to Authority*. New York: HarperCollins, 1983. A report on a series of social science experiments that demonstrated the degree to which many individuals obey authority.

Schlesinger, Arthur M., Jr. *The Disuniting of America: Reflections on a Multicultural Society*. New York: W. W. Norton, 1993. A sober consideration of the extent to which the people of the United States comprise a nation.

Strauss, Leo. "What Is Political Philosophy?" *What Is Political Philosophy? and Other Studies*. Chicago: University of Chicago Press, 1988. A cogent introduction to the value and necessity of political philosophy.

Tinder, Glenn. *Political Thinking: The Perennial Questions*. 6th ed. Reading, Mass.: Addison-Wesley, 1995. A topical consideration of politics' enduring controversies.

Notes

1. Baron de Montesquieu's (1689–1755) classification of political governments in Book II of his *Spirit of the Laws* has proved most influential. Montesquieu distinguished among republics, monarchies, and despotic governments, further subdividing democratic republics, ruled by the whole people, from aristocratic republics, ruled by part of the people (specifically by the wealthy class). Republics also have been historically distinguished from direct democracies. Thus, James Madison (perhaps the leading U.S. Founder) called governments where the people directly participated in their own governing (and did not rely on representation) *direct democracies*. Because the government of the United States provided for representation, it was called a *republic*.

2. For a discussion of some worrisome tendencies, see Arthur Schlesinger, Jr., *The Disuniting of America: Reflections on a Multicultural Society* (New York: Norton, 1993).

3. Aristotle, *The Politics*, trans. and ed. Ernest Barker (New York: Oxford University Press, 1962), 4.

4. As opposed to Plato, who is sometimes classified as the first political "philosopher."

5. Jack H. Nagel and John E. McNulty, "Partisan Effects of Voter Turnout in Senatorial and Gubernatorial Elections," *American Political Science Review* 90 (December 1996): 780–793.

6. See Leo Strauss, *What Is Political Philosophy? and Other Studies* (New York: Free Press, 1959), 10–12.

7. There are variations of this approach; for instance, traditional realist theory has been updated (but not without controversy) by political scientists referred to as *neorealists* or *structural realists*. A leading work here is Kenneth Waltz, *Theory of International Politics* (Reading, Mass.: Addison-Wesley, 1979). Also see his "Realist Thought and Neo-Realist Theory," *Journal of International Affairs* XLIV (Spring/Summer 1990): 21–37.

8. For a scholarly attempt to reconcile the two approaches, see Robert O. Keohane, *International Institutions and State Power* (Boulder, Colo.: Westview Press, 1989). Keohane's theory is sometimes referred to as *neoliberal institutionalism*.

9. Irving Kristol, "The Nature of Nazism," in *The Commentary Reader*, ed. Norman Podhoretz (New York: Atheneum, 1965), 16.

10. See Albert Speer, *Inside the Third Reich*, trans. R. Winston and C. Winston (New York: Avon, 1971). Compare Stanley Haverwas and David Burrell, "Self-deception and Autobiography: Reflections on Speer's *Inside the Third Reich*," in *Truthfulness and*

Tragedy: Further Investigations in Christian Ethics, ed. Stanley Haverwas et al. (South Bend, Ind.: University of Notre Dame Press, 1977), 82–97.

11.   Hannah Arendt, *Eichmann in Jerusalem: A Report on the Banality of Evil* (New York: Penguin Books, 1964). Compare Gideon Hausner, *Justice in Jerusalem* (New York: Schocken Books, 1968), 465.

12.   Not all Germans, or Europeans, were as indifferent or self-serving in the face of evil as was Eichmann. A notable if atypical exception was Oskar Schindler (whose renown has increased enormously due to the movie *Schindler's List*). Schindler was a German businessman who belonged to the Nazi party and at first exploited labor, but then used his business and political connections to save the lives of his Jewish workers. An attempt to examine Schindler and the courageous acts of other righteous Christians is set forth in Eva Fogelman, *Conscience and Courage: Rescuers of Jews during the Holocaust* (New York: Doubleday, 1994). Also see Samuel P. Oliner and Pearl M. Oliner, *The Altruistic Personality: Rescuers of Jews in Nazi Europe* (New York: Free Press, 1988). No doubt most of us would identify more with the Christian rescuers or with Schindler than with Eichmann, but the disturbing fact remains that far more Germans (including tens of thousands of Hitler Youth), mesmerized by Hitler's message of hate, behaved more like Eichmann than like Schindler.

Susan LeVan / Getty Images

© Ted Spiegel / CORBIS

© Bettmann / CORBIS

PART I

COMPARATIVE POLITICAL SYSTEMS

UTOPIAS

MODEL STATES

As CITIZENS, WE often favor (or oppose) policies and leaders because we believe they will help us make ours a better or more just society. Behind many of our political preferences is some idea of what constitutes the public good and the good society. Usually, this notion is unexamined—that is, though we believe in a certain kind of political order, we are often unable to spell out the specific reasons why.[1] Yet it is important to articulate and analyze the underlying assumptions behind our political ideas and ideals. If we are to make meaningful comparisons between or among political systems (the goal of Part I of this text), we need to clarify what the public good is and is not. Ideas about utopia found in the writings of philosophers, theologians, and others can help us better understand both the possibilities and limits of politics. What would the best political order look like? Why is it often said that the best is the enemy of the good? Is it more dangerous in politics to settle for too little or to strive for too much?

The word *utopia* comes from the title of a book written by Sir Thomas More (1478–1535), the lord chancellor of England under King Henry VIII and an influential humanist. More coined the term from the Greek words *ou topos*, meaning "no place," and *eutopos*, "a place where all is well." In common usage *utopia* tends to incorporate both of these meanings. Hence we might say that a **utopia** is a nonexistent place where people dwell in perfect health, harmony, and happiness.

The literature of Western political philosophy contains a number of elaborate utopian blueprints, each of which represents its author's best attempt to formulate the complete and good (or completely good) political order. Utopian models differ in specific features, but they all serve similar purposes. Without exception, all utopia inventors have sought to pursue the logic of political life to its final conclusions. And in doing so, they have often engaged in implicit and explicit criticism of existing political, social, and economic conditions. Because of this critical function, utopian constructs can be and have been used as standards of political measurement or as criteria for judging the performance of political systems. Then, too, abstract models of the perfect society have occasionally served as practical guides to political action. Thus, despite its appearance of impracticality, utopian thought serves significant purposes and affects political activities, directly or indirectly.

Our exploration of famous utopias begins with Plato's *Republic*, which we contrast with three later versions of utopia—those found in Sir Francis Bacon's *New Atlantis*, in Karl Marx's writings extolling the virtues of the "classless society," and in B. F. Skinner's *Walden Two*. The choice of utopian works featured in this chapter is based on the fact that each finds answers in a different place. For Plato, the answer lies in the realm of philosophy; for Bacon, in science; for Marx, in economics; and for Skinner, in psychology.

There are many other worthy examples of utopian literature. Thus Thomas More's *Utopia* (1516) remains essential reading, as do Tommaso Campanella's *City of the Sun*, James Harrington's *The Commonwealth of Oceana* (1656), the writings of such French utopian socialists as Charles Fourier and the Comte de Saint-Simon, and American writer Edward Bellamy (1850–1898), who incorporated a number of similar proposals in *Looking Backward, 2000–1887* (1888). These visionaries and many others have all helped to keep the idea and the ideals of utopia alive.

Hardly less important is the literature on dystopia—political experiments aimed at achieving perfect justice in society which went terribly wrong. The purpose of these works is to demonstrate the dangers inherent in trying to build a perfect order in an imperfect world.

PLATO'S *REPUBLIC:* PHILOSOPHY IS THE ANSWER

Plato's *Republic* is a long dialogue between Socrates and interlocutors. Socrates (469–399 B.C.E.), considered the first Western political philosopher, held that "the unexamined life is not life worth living"—an idea that has become a cornerstone of Western civilization. As preserved and elaborated on by Plato, Socrates' most brilliant student, Socratic philosophy represents a fundamental alternative to the earlier works of Homer, who praised the virtues of courage and honor, and the later teachings of Jesus, who proclaimed belief in God and moral behavior in accordance with God's Word to be the basis of the most exalted life.

Because of his penchant for relentlessly seeking answers to penetrating philosophical questions, Socrates was mistrusted by the rulers of Athens. Eventually he was accused, in court, of undermining belief in the established gods and corrupting Athenian youth. He was convicted and sentenced to death. The execution of Socrates (by a self-administered drink of hemlock) stands as a poignant reminder of the tension between intellectual freedom and the political order.

In *The Republic,* Plato has Socrates begin with an inquiry into the meaning of justice. He then proceeds to describe the best political order: a society devoid of all tension between philosophers and rulers.[2] (In such a society, the charges leveled against Socrates would have been groundless. There would be no fear of teachers making youth disloyal, for it would be possible to be *both* philosophic and patriotic.) The founding and construction of such a city would reflect nothing less than the perfection of political thought.

The Just City

Initially, Socrates is prompted to elaborate on his conception of the ultimate political good by a skeptical listener, who challenges him to explain why it is better to be just than unjust. Is it not true, he is asked, that the successful man who gains power and possessions from unjust actions is much happier than the just man who, like Socrates, has neither power nor possessions? Because justice will be easier to identify in a city than in a person, the search for the just city begins.[3]

Socrates first proposes that political life arises from the fact that no individual can be self-sufficient. He then describes a very simple society with no government and no scarcity, whose farmers, shoemakers, and other artisans produce just enough for the perpetuation of a plain and placid way of life. In this society, which seeks to satisfy the basic needs of the body (food, drink, shelter, and so on), each person performs one specialized function.

To avoid monotony, however, adornments are required. But the creation of luxury liberates desire and gives rise to restless spirits. The city then becomes "feverish" and needs to expand. Specifically, it must acquire more land, and for

Culver Pictures

One of the great philosophers of ancient Greece, Plato (c. 428–348 B.C.E.) believed that ideal state authority should rest in the hands of the philosopher-king: "Until philosophers are kings, . . . cities will never have rest from their evils."

that task soldiers are necessary. The soldiers, who form the second class in the republic, are initially called guardians. Their task becomes clearer as the dialogue progresses: They are to protect the polis as sheepdogs protect a flock of lambs.

As described in *The Republic,* the education of the guardians encompasses the entire range of human activities, including the aesthetic, intellectual, moral, and physical aspects of life. Socrates suggests that the purpose of education is to teach the truth. Therefore, censorship of untrue or dangerous ideas is required. Throughout the course of this training, strict discipline is maintained. Everything is held in common, including personal property and spouses. Love of the community replaces ordinary human love.

At age twenty, the students are divided into two groups. Some are designated auxiliaries and are assigned the role of defending the city; they will be the republic's soldiers. The others, who retain the name of guardian, continue their education. Other, later screenings determine the jobs eventually held by those in the guardian class. All choices are based on merit. At the end of a prolonged period of study, a guardian, by understanding the truth of things, may become a philosopher. Supreme in wisdom, philosophers alone are fit to hold the highest offices. In this manner, the republic is governed by *philosopher-kings.*

Thus Plato's republic is made up of a class of farmers and artisans, a class of warrior-auxiliaries, and a class of philosopher-guardians. This tripartite division reflects Plato's idea that the human soul is divided into three parts: an appetitive part, which derives from physical desires; a spirited part, which produces anger and indignation when something dear is threatened; and a reasoning part, which seeks to know the truth. Each class embodies one essential virtue. The workers and artisans, who provide for the city's physical necessities, possess moderation: Their lives are governed in an orderly and proper fashion. Although the warrior-auxiliaries also possess moderation, their particular virtue is courage, which is the perfection of the spirited part of the soul. The perfection of the reasoning part, wisdom, is reserved for the philosophers (who, of course, also possess the other two virtues). Only philosophers possess a completely excellent soul; every part of their being is perfect, as is the relationship among the parts of their soul. Because of their all-encompassing excellence, the philosophers alone understand justice, the most comprehensive virtue of all. Furthermore, because each component of the republic does its job well (growing food and making things, defending the city, or ruling), and in so doing prominently displays a particular cardinal virtue (moderation, courage, or wisdom), this imaginary city is also considered just.

And what a city it is! One commentator has suggested that "all of Western man's aspirations to justice and the good life are given expression and fulfillment in Socrates' proposals."[4] This is a city where

> men's faculties are not denied their exercise by poverty, birth, or sex, where the accidental attachments of family and city do not limit a man's understanding and pursuit of the good; it is a regime, finally, where wise, public-spirited men rule for the common good.[5]

All citizens perform the tasks for which they are best equipped, and they receive recognition, honors, and respect in proportion to the value of their contributions to society. This city suggests an answer to the question Socrates was asked originally. It is the philosophers who are just and who seem to be the happiest of all persons (certainly happier than the unjust), but their happiness does not depend on possession of power unjustly obtained. Of course, in the republic, philosophers are not persecuted; they are placed in charge, not put on trial.

Because philosophers rule and because they are just and wise, otherwise objectionable practices can be instituted. For example, to ensure that public servants place the public interest above private interests, family relationships are banned among the soldier and guardian classes. The continued existence of exceptional individuals is ensured by a eugenics program that provides for state control of human sexual relations. The guardian class is to propagate only through a system of carefully orchestrated "marriage festivals" planned for the sole purpose of collective (and selective) breeding. Nothing is to be left to chance.

The Noble Lie

To placate the members of the lower class (considering that they would probably neither understand nor accept their humble status), the philosopher-kings are in charge of perpetuating the noble lie—an official myth—on which the just city depends. Thus all citizens (except the philosophers) are told that their memories of past experiences are only dreams, and that they had once lived beneath the earth, where they had been fashioned and trained. When they were ready, their mother, the earth, sent them up to the surface. Furthermore, during the formative process they were given souls fashioned out of gold (in the case of philosophers), silver (auxiliaries), or iron and bronze (farmers and artisans). This myth is designed to persuade residents of the republic that they are all brothers and sisters, and to ensure popular acceptance of the class system essential to the republic's existence.

In describing the best political state, Socrates also reveals the difficulties involved in its creation and maintenance. Not only is the republic concept impractical, but it also seems impossible to realize. Socrates clearly shows the price that would have to be paid for the creation of such a political order. As we have seen, that price includes the abolition of families, the establishment of censorship, the presence of a widespread falsehood regarding the moral basis of the regime, and the rule of people who do not desire to rule.

Although *The Republic* may not be a blueprint for some future political regime, it is valuable in several other respects. Above all, it insightfully explores important political ideas, such as justice, tyranny, and education. It also demonstrates a thoughtful model of the best political order while simultaneously exposing the practical impediments to its implementation. In sum, *The Republic* should be taken less as a political prescription than as a philosophical exercise. Socrates' excursion into utopia represents an attempt to perfect human thought, not a formula for the perfection of human deeds.

FRANCIS BACON'S *NEW ATLANTIS*: SCIENCE IS THE ANSWER

The idea that utopias can be actually achieved in the here and now became increasingly prevalent after the fifteenth century. Francis Bacon (1561–1626) was the first and most influential utopian advocate of the idea that science could secure for human beings their most desired human good—comfortable self-preservation. Those who today believe in or proclaim the glories of human progress, scientific advancement, technological innovation, or worldwide political modernization and development (see Chapter 9) generally assume the rightness of a political regime at least somewhat similar in orientation to that outlined by Bacon.

In *The New Atlantis* (1627), Bacon describes the imaginary voyage of travelers who discover an island called Bensalem. They suffered greatly during their long sojourn in the Pacific, and they need food and rest. At first the islanders warn them not to land, but after some negotiations, the travelers are allowed to disembark. The visitors' negative first impressions fade as they come to see the island as it really is: a blissfully happy place.

Stability and Science

Most of the practical details of day-to-day life in Bensalem are merely sketched in by Bacon. Although its envoys have made secret expeditions to Europe to learn about advances in science, the island is otherwise completely cut off from other

Culver Pictures

Francis Bacon (1561–1626)—English philosopher, scientist, essayist, and states-man—promulgated the idea that science is the key to humanity's comfortable self-preservation: "Nature, to be commanded, must be obeyed."

societies. This geographic isolation precludes the need for self-defense. The island is also economically self-sufficient. Bacon creates the unmistakable impression of a land endowed with an abundance of natural resources.

Bensalem is a Christian society, but one that emphasizes religious freedom. Members of various religious faiths hold important positions, and toleration is the norm. The religious disputes that had torn apart many European nations are absent from this utopian island.

The social basis of Bensalem is the family; marriage is described as the foundation of society. During a holiday known as the Feast of the Family, instituted and paid for by the state, the heads of particularly large families are honored, and family unit and moral behavior are celebrated as the cornerstones of a close-knit and stable community life. The stability of the community is underlined by the fact that it was founded some 2,000 years earlier by a benevolent ruler, Solamona, who promulgated laws so perfect that they have never required revision.

Bensalem is a very progressive society. The best minds of Bensalem are assembled at a great college, appropriately called Solomon's House, where the rules of science are applied, through experimentation and observation, to the discovery of "knowledge of the causes and secret motions of things; and the enlarging of the bounds of human empire, to the effecting of all things possible." In contrast to Plato's *Republic,* knowledge is pursued not simply for its own sake in Bensalem but also for the conquest of nature. Greater material comfort, better health, and a more secure and prosperous way of life make up the great legacy of the academy's laboratories, experimental lakes, medicine shops, and observatories. In Bensalem, science can and should be used for "the relief of man's estate."

Bacon's seventeenth-century vision seems prophetic in many respects. Through science, for example, life expectancy on the island increases dramatically as whole strains of illness are eradicated. New types of fruits and flowers are produced, some with curative powers. Medical treatment undergoes a technological revolution. The Bensalemites can even predict impending natural disasters, for their science can uncover nature's darkest secrets.

Blueprint for the Future

Although scholars disagree about Bacon's true intentions in *The New Atlantis*, a seriousness of purpose marks his work. One noted authority sees Bacon as the "first really modern utopian" because Bacon expected his ideal society to come into existence.[6] *The New Atlantis* was not meant to be a *precise* outline of the future; however, Bacon did suggest one possible form for a society in which scientific progress would be allowed to proceed unimpeded. Bacon's vision of a technological utopia was not intended as a protest against existing society, but it comprised an outline for the radical improvement of the human condition.

KARL MARX'S CLASSLESS SOCIETY: ECONOMICS IS THE ANSWER

Karl Marx (1818–1883) was also a utopian thinker, but in a different way from Plato or Bacon. Marx's predecessors began with elaborate descriptions of their paradises, and when they engaged in social criticism, it was usually implicit rather than explicit. Marx, by contrast, began with an explicit criticism of existing society and sketched only the broadest outlines of his utopia. He thought of himself as a hardheaded realist rather than a starry-eyed idealist. Because he considered his worldview to be the product of a correct empirical understanding of

Granger Collection

Karl Marx (1818–1883)—German philosopher, economist, and revolutionary—believed that a just world could only be achieved through the evolution of humanity from a capitalist to a socialist economy and society: "The history of all hitherto existing society is the history of class struggle."

historical and socioeconomic reality, Marx would have adamantly objected to any suggestion that his ideas were rooted in visionary thinking.

Nevertheless, the utopian element in Marxism is evident. Unlike earlier utopians, Marx believed that his ideal society was not only possible but inevitable. The bitter class struggle he envisaged (see Chapter 14) can be properly understood only as the necessary prelude to a utopian life in a promised land of peace and plenty. This prophecy represented to Marx the end product of supposedly irresistible forces that were propelling human history toward its inevitable destiny—the classless society.

The Centrality of Economics

Marx's attack on economic inequality was influenced by the harsh working conditions and widespread suffering associated with capitalism in the mid-nineteenth century. The wealthy commercial and industrial elites (the bourgeois capitalist class) opposed reforms aimed at improving the living conditions of the impoverished working class (the proletariat). Marx's *Das Kapital* is punctuated with vivid descriptions of employment practices that aroused his anger, such as the following:

> Mary Anne Walkley had worked without intermission for 26 1/2 hours, with 60 other girls, 30 in one room, that only afforded 1/3 of the cubic feet of air required for them. . . . Mary Anne Walkley fell ill on the Friday [and] died on Sunday. . . . The doctor, Mr. Keys, called in too late to the death-bed, duly bore witness before the coroner's jury that "Mary Anne Walkley had died from long hours of work in an overcrowded workroom."[7]

To Marx, the deaths of Mary Anne Walkley and others like her were not mere accidents. He believed that economics—the production and distribution of material necessities—was the ultimate determinant of human life and that, historically, human societies rose and fell according to the inexorable dynamic of economic forces. He believed that Mary Anne Walkley, having been born into the age of capitalism, was preordained to spend a brief and meager life working for subsistence wages so that the owners of the means of production—the capitalist class—could further enrich themselves. Her harsh life and premature death had been dictated by the profit-driven economics of the mid-nineteenth century. But the internal progressive logic of capitalism made it equally inevitable, according to Marx, that the superstructures of power built on these foundations of greed and exploitation would collapse in a great social upheaval led by the impoverished and alienated working class—Marx's beloved proletariat.

The Dictatorship of the Proletariat

Marx referred to the first stage of the revolutionary process immediately following the overthrow of capitalism as the *dictatorship of the proletariat.* This historical epoch, Marx asserted, would comprise the *first stage of communism* and represent the advent of the socialist millennium in human history. As a temporary phenomenon, the dictatorship of the proletariat would survive only as long as there remained a need to guard against counterrevolution. During this time, revolutionary new programs would be launched, based on the principle "From each according to his abilities, to each according to his needs." These policies would include the abolition of all private ownership of property, a heavily progressive income tax, the abolition of the right of inheritance, the centralization of all credit in the state and of all means of communications and transportation, the introduction of free education for all children, the abolition of child labor, the extension "of factories and instruments of production owned by the State," and "the bringing into cultivation of waste-lands, and the improvement of the soil generally in accordance with a common plan."[8]

Following these steps, the government would simply wither away. As (according to Marx's collaborator, Friedrich Engels) class differences and antagonisms naturally fade away, the injection of state power in social relations becomes unnecessary, and "the government of persons is replaced by the administration of things and the direction of the process of production." In the end, "The State is not 'abolished.' It dies out."[9]

In essence, then, Marx viewed the dictatorship of the proletariat (the socialist stage of communism) as a necessary way station on the road to a classless utopia. Marx believed that human beings come into the world with a clean slate and that what is subsequently written on that slate is determined by the nature of human society rather than by individual genetic inheritance. Further, Marx saw no inherent tension between the true interests of the individual and the interests of society. During the socialist era, therefore, people would naturally acquire socialist values. Unlike capitalist states, which allegedly produce competitive citizens who degrade and exploit one another, the socialist state would produce cooperative citizens who respect and support one another. Class conflict would inevitably disappear, displaced by a natural harmony of interests.

The Marxist belief in the withering away of the state was thus based on a kind of harmony-of-interest logic: Eliminate private property and the division of labor, and you eliminate social inequality. Eliminate social inequality, and you eliminate the cause of armed conflict. Obviously, no class struggle is possible when classes no longer exist. Finally, eliminate armed conflict, and you eliminate the need for the state. After all, past societies were nothing more than human contrivances for the perpetuation of class dominance. With the disappearance of social classes, according to Marx, government as we have known it will simply atrophy as a result of its own obsolescence.

The Classless Society

The natural demise of government, Marx prophesied, would usher in the *second stage of communism,* the classless society. In this communist utopia, true human fulfillment would be possible. Under capitalism, Marx wrote, "everyone has a definite, circumscribed sphere of activity, which is put upon him and from which he cannot escape. He is a hunter, a fisherman, a shepherd or a 'critical critic,' and he must remain so if he does not want to lose his means of subsistence."[10] Under communism, in contrast,

> when each one does not have a circumscribed sphere of activity but can train himself in any branch he chooses, society by regulating the common production makes it possible for me to do this today and that tomorrow, to hunt in the morning, to fish in the

afternoon, to carry on cattle-breeding in the evening, also to criticize the food—just as I please—without becoming a hunter, fisherman, shepherd or critic.[11]

Along with individual self-fulfillment, social bliss would blossom in the new order, which would be populated by "loyal, wise and incorruptible friends, devoted to one another with an absolutely unselfish benevolence."[12] Marx's classless society resembles virtually every other utopia in this respect. One student of Marxist utopianism observes that Marx's description of communist society shares with most other utopian works a "single ethical core," characterized by "cooperative rather than competitive labor, purposeful achievement for societal ends rather than self-indulgence or private hedonism, and an ethic of social responsibility for each member rather than of struggle for survival of the fittest."[13]

The picture of the future that Marx and Engels presented to the world was indeed exciting—and utopian:

> Crime would disappear, the span of life would increase, brotherhood and cooperation would inculcate a new morality, scientific progress would grow by leaps and bounds. Above all, with socialism spreading throughout the world, the greatest blight of humankind, war, and its twin brother, nationalism, would have no place. International brotherhood would follow. . . . With the socialist revolution humanity will complete its "prehistoric" stage and enter for the first time into what might be called its own history.
> . . . After the revolution a united classless society will be able for the first time to decide which way to go and what to do with its resources and capabilities. For the first time we shall make our own history! It is a "leap from slavery into freedom; from darkness into light."[14]

B. F. SKINNER'S *WALDEN TWO:*
BEHAVIORAL PSYCHOLOGY IS THE ANSWER

Psychologist B. F. Skinner (1904–1990) has been perhaps the most influential contemporary writer on *behavioral psychology*. Skinner believed that all human behavior is environmentally determined, a mere response to external stimuli. His experiments, designed to control animal behavior (including the training of pigeons to play Ping-Pong), and his theories about the relationship of human freedom to behavior modification have been the object of both acclaim and alarm. In the fictional work *Walden Two* (1948), Skinner outlined his notion of a modern utopian society. It is noteworthy that Skinner actually believed it possible to create the society described in *Walden Two* with the tools made available by the new science of human behavior.

The Good Life

As described in *Walden Two*, Skinner's utopia is a world within a world. Its founder, psychologist T. E. Frazier, has managed to obtain "for taxes" a tract of land that previously contained seven or eight run-down farms. Bounded on one side by a river and rolling hills and on the other three sides by densely wooded terrain, the land is conveniently self-enclosed, symbolizing that it is also largely self-sufficient.

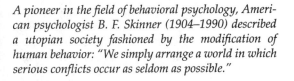

A pioneer in the field of behavioral psychology, American psychologist B. F. Skinner (1904–1990) described a utopian society fashioned by the modification of human behavior: "We simply arrange a world in which serious conflicts occur as seldom as possible."

Although concerned about the problem of creating a good society, Frazier is not a philosopher. In fact, he disdains philosophy. Difficult questions such as "What constitutes the good life?" are dismissed as irrelevant. "We all know what's good, until we stop to think about it," he declares.[15] For Frazier, the basic ingredients of the good life are obvious: good health, an absolute minimum of unpleasant labor, a chance to exercise one's talents and abilities, and true leisure (that is, freedom from the economic and social pressures that, in Frazier's view, render the so-called leisure class the least relaxed of people). These goals are realized at Walden Two in its pleasant atmosphere of noncompetitive social harmony.

The Science of Behavioral Engineering

Frazier sums up his view about how to produce individual happiness and group harmony in this way:

> I can't give you a rational justification for any of it. I can't reduce it to any principle of "the greatest good." This *is* the Good Life. We know it. It's a fact, not a theory. . . . We don't puzzle our little minds over the outcome of Love versus Duty. We simply *arrange* a world in which serious conflicts occur as seldom as possible or, with a little luck, not at all.[16]

The key word here is *arrange*. The kind of world to be arranged is of only passing interest to Frazier; what commands his attention is the question of how to do the arranging. He is concerned not with ends but with means, not with philosophy but with scientific experimentation. He is the quintessential methodologist.

Frazier has no time for politics or politicians. Because political action has not helped build a better world, "other measures" are required. What other measures? A revolution in the science of behavior modification:

Considering how long society has been at it, you'd expect a better job. But the campaigns have been badly planned and the victory has never been secure. The behavior of the individual has been shaped according to revelations of "good conduct," never as the result of experimental study. But why not experiment? The questions are simple enough. What's the best behavior for the individual so far as the group is concerned? And how can the individual be induced to behave in that way? Why not explore these questions in a scientific spirit?[17]

The Walden Two experiment represents this kind of scientific exploration. Initially, an experimental code of good behavior is developed. Everyone at Walden Two is expected to adhere to the code, under the supervision of certain behavioral scientists, such as Frazier, called managers. In the outside world, Frazier notes, behavioral technology has been misused by psychologists, educators, religious leaders, politicians, ideologues, advertisers, and salespeople, among others. At Walden Two, positive reinforcement, rather than punishment, is employed to instill desired behavioral patterns, and a system of finely tuned frustrations and annoyances is used to eliminate the destructive emotions of anger, fear, and lust. For example, to engender self-restraint Frazier has the schoolteachers hang lollipops around the children's necks. If a child, having been instructed not to lick the candy, fails to resist the temptation, further self-control training is administered. Such *behavioral engineering* will prove successful, Frazier asserts, not because it physically controls outward behavior but because the conscious manipulation of stimuli effectively influences "the *inclination* to behave-the motives, the desires, the wishes."[18]

To ensure proper socialization, children are placed in a scientifically controlled environment from infancy. They are raised in nurseries, and at no time during childhood or adolescence do they live with their parents. (Nor do their parents live with each other.) The overriding importance of community is emphasized in other ways: Private property is abolished, meals are taken together in common dining halls, and boys and girls customarily marry and have children at age fifteen or sixteen, according to the dictates of Walden Two's genetic plan.

The Behavioral Scientist as God

Much that is familiar in the outside world is notably absent at Walden Two. Although its residents feel free, there is no freedom in this community. The idea of freedom is illusory, Frazier argues, because all behavior is conditioned. History is viewed "only as entertainment"; schoolchildren do not even study this "spurious science." Religion is not forbidden, but, like government in Marx's utopia, it has simply withered away through social obsolescence ("psychologists are our priests," Frazier asserts). Moral codes of right and wrong have given way to "experimental ethics." Politics has no value: "You can't make progress toward the Good Life by political action! Not under *any* current form of government! You must operate upon another level entirely."[19]

It soon becomes apparent that life at Walden Two has been organized to create the most propitious circumstances for the managers' experiments in behavior modification. Although Frazier justifies this manipulation on the basis of increased human happiness, we are left with the gnawing sense that something significant is missing here—some sort of check on the power of the behavioral engineers who run the community.

We are told that the managers will not become corrupted by their power because the planners "are part of a noncompetitive culture in which a thirst for power is a curiosity."[20] Then, too, we are assured, the managers do not use force (nobody does at Walden Two), and the offices they hold are not permanent—in time, they will once again become ordinary citizens. These reassurances have a hollow ring, however. Clearly, the love of power is not absent from Frazier's own soul. As the founder of Walden Two, he appears to view himself as a kind of messiah who has discovered the secret to a whole new way of life: "I look upon my work and, behold, it is good."[21] Another brave new world, it would seem, has arrived.

UTOPIAS REVISITED

In every utopia we have examined, there are no conflicts, jealousies, rivalries, rancorous disputes, or individual frustrations. No deep-seated tensions divide individuals, and no great antagonisms exist between society and the state. Each of these ideal states, however, is inspired by a different vision and ordered according to a different plan.

The Inspiration for Utopia

As we have observed, political thinkers construct utopias for a variety of reasons. In *The Republic,* Plato explored the limits of human perfection; that is, he sought not only to depict his conception of the best political order but also to make clear the problems that would accompany any attempt to bring about such a political order. In contrast, Bacon wrote *The New Atlantis* not to show the limits of human achievement but to indicate what a society wholly predicated on modern science might achieve. Bacon was concerned with the possibilities, not the limitations, of humanity. His is a hopeful work that promises a tangible improvement in human welfare.

Marx's utopian vision also is hopeful; even more, however, it constitutes a logical and necessary part of his worldview. Without the promise of a classless society at the end of the road, the violence and suffering that Marx believed would inevitably accompany the end of capitalism would seem senseless. Marx's utopia, then, provides a beacon of hope in an otherwise dark vision of revolution and struggle. Skinner's *Walden Two,* by contrast, was written as an indictment of what its author saw as the ineffective and incorrect use of behavioral engineering. Skinner sought to demonstrate how a rational and scientific approach to behavior modification could produce dramatic social improvements.

The Road to Utopia

To create a completely happy and harmonious world, a writer must postulate a breakthrough in the way society is constituted. Plato saw philosophy as the key. His republic could not exist until or unless the wisest philosophers ruled (an unlikely prospect at best). Not so with Bacon, for whom it was not the abstract quest for human knowledge that would blaze the trail but the technical mastery of the scientific method. His Solomons were not philosophers concerned about the intangible realm of ideas; they were scientists who analyzed, observed, classified, recorded, and verified natural phenomena in an attempt to improve the human condition. For Marx, philosophy and science were overshadowed by economics; nonexploitative economic relationships, he believed, would guarantee a peaceful and plentiful world. Finally, Skinner viewed the scientific manipulation of human behavior as the key to social and personal fulfillment.

The Practicality of Utopia

With the advent of modern science and technology, some political thinkers began to take more seriously the practical possibility of achieving utopia. Armed with increasingly sophisticated tools—a new science, a new economics, a new behavioral psychology—utopians increasingly tended to view the possibility of heaven on earth as something more than a pipe dream.

This trend is clearly reflected in the utopian works we have examined. Plato, for example, demonstrated that it would be difficult, if not impossible, to bring his utopia into being and to keep it going. Bacon, in contrast, described the kind of society that might herald a radical improvement in human welfare if only the potential of modern science were realized to the fullest possible extent. To be sure, Bacon viewed utopia only as a future possibility, but one well within our power to achieve. Marx's classless society, however, was not so much a possibility as an inevitability—a ratification of and reward for the final victory of the proletariat. In the sense that Marx's utopia supposedly lies within our grasp, it resembles Skinner's Walden Two. The latter, however, was to be brought into being immediately and without violence or revolution. The techniques of behavioral engineering were well enough known, Skinner believed; all that was required to achieve Walden Two was the will to put them to use.

In sum, utopias have increasingly assumed the form of blueprints for the future. Underlying these blueprints have been certain shared assumptions about human beings and what is best for them.

Utopia and Human Nature

Almost immediately after the ideal city is described in *The Republic,* its demise is outlined. According to one interpretation of the work, Plato understood that even if a perfectly ordered human community could be brought into existence, its degeneration could not be prevented. Plato thus raised a question that has plagued all subsequent utopians: How can change be avoided? A utopia, by definition, represents the best political system; therefore, all important change within it must be change for the worse. Hence, paradoxically, change necessarily becomes the deadly enemy of these innovative societies.

To guard against change, most utopian writers have left nothing to chance in the ideal society, especially when it comes to *human nature.* Fundamental human characteristics such as vice and maliciousness and human unpredictability must be eradicated, or at least rigidly controlled, if people are to live together in peace and harmony.

In the pursuit of this blissful state, utopias typically feature *eugenics* programs, compulsory education, and the abolition of private property. Both eugenics programs, which seek to control hereditary traits of people by selective breeding, and compulsory education have been viewed as necessary methods of ensuring the perpetuation of the best human qualities while eliminating undesirable characteristics. In the same vein, utopian thinkers have advocated eliminating private property in order to banish egoism, greed, and avarice from human nature. Most utopians have taken the position that human selfishness is caused by socioeconomic institutions that protect, sanction, and perpetuate inequalities and that these institutions can be eliminated only by a fundamental reordering of society. In many utopias, therefore, communal activities, common residences, and public meals replace the private ownership of property, in the hope that cooperation will triumph over competition.

A specific view of human nature underlies most proposals for the radical restructuring of society. Conflicts among human beings, in this view, grow out of badly organized or corrupt societies, what is often called simply "the system." If the negative effects of fundamentally flawed institutions are eliminated, human behavior will take a positive turn. At the heart of the utopian impulse, then, is the belief that human nature, if not good, is at least malleable (and therefore potentially good).

Utopia and the Neglect of Politics

The utopian belief that human nature can and should be easily molded raises some serious concerns. If it is true that environment can influence individuals so profoundly, they become potential candidates not only for moral perfection but also for moral corruption. Any flaw in the construction of a utopia can therefore turn a dream into a nightmare.

In almost every utopia (including Marx's dictatorship of the proletariat stage), political power is centralized. Accordingly, utopian governments have at their disposal powerful tools with which to control human behavior. By themselves, these tools are neutral; everything depends on how they are used—wisely or foolishly, efficiently or wastefully, morally or immorally. Utopian thinkers tend to assume that these tools will always be used benignly. But given the power of the modern technocratic state and the malleability of human nature, this assumption seems tenuous at best. What has troubled many critics of utopian schemes is not simply the concentration of power they tend to countenance but also the total absence of checks and balances in the exercise of that power.

Utopian thinkers generally display little interest in politics and government. They see no real need to reconcile the conflicting claims of power and justice. Given material abundance, public-spirited citizens, and little or no conflict between human desires and human well-being (or between socioeconomic equality and individual excellence), the achievement of social justice becomes a technical, rather than a political, problem. Hence the nuts-and-bolts workings of actual governments—mechanisms for separation of powers, checks and balances, judicial review, and so forth—hold no interest for most utopians.

DYSTOPIA: FROM DREAM TO NIGHTMARE

The dangers of unchecked political power, and the more general theme of utopia-turned-nightmare, are vividly developed in such well-known works as George Orwell's *Nineteen Eighty-Four* (1961) and Aldous Huxley's *Brave New World* (1932). Both books provide graphic descriptions of a *dystopia*—a society whose creators set out to build a perfect political order only to discover that having promised the impossible, they could remain in power only by maintaining a ruthless monopoly through coercion and communication.

Orwell's World

In *Nineteen Eighty-Four,* the totalitarian rulers (personified by a shadowy figure called Big Brother) retain power by manipulating not only the people's actions and forms of behavior but also their sources and methods of thought. Thus, the Ministry of Truth is established for the sole purpose of systematically lying to the citizenry; a new language ("Newspeak") is invented to purge all words, ideas, and expressions considered dangerous by the government; and a contradictory kind of logic ("double-think") is introduced to make the minds of the citizenry receptive to the opportunistic zigzags of official propaganda.

According to the official ideology, the purpose behind state terror, strict censorship, and constant surveillance is to prevent enemies of the revolution from stopping the march toward full communism—a workers' paradise in which everyone will be happy, secure, prosperous, and equal. In theory, the masses are finally put in control of their own destiny; in practice, they become a new class of slaves whose fate is in the hands of the most ruthless tyrant(s) imaginable—or perhaps unimaginable (without Orwell's help).

Utopia and Terrorism

In Chapter 15, we will explore the nature and impact of terrorism on domestic and international politics in the contemporary world. Acts of terror are often associated with religious or ideological zeal, especially where those acts involve the ultimate sacrifice as in the case of suicide bombers. Normal people wonder what could possibly motivate another human being to carry out a mission that is at once barbaric and self-destructive. The case of the September 11, 2001, coordinated attacks on the World Trade Center in New York City and the Pentagon in Washington, D.C., which involved numerous individuals using hijacked commercial airliners as weapons, are particularly shocking and difficult to understand. What is the source of the kind of seething hatred that would motivate not one individual but a group of individuals to plan, engage in lengthy preparations, and finally execute a mass murder based on a joint suicide pact?

---

http://www.levity.com/alchemy/atlantis.html

This site provides the text of Francis Bacon's *New Atlantis*.

http://www.worldmedia.com/manucon/cards/marx.html

A brief, lighthearted look at Karl Marx with an overview of his works and a collection of quotes.

http://swift.eng.ox.ac.uk/jdr/marx.html

An excellent starting point for further study of Marx and/or Marxism. This page includes an overview of Marx and his life's work, but the most useful part of the site is its extensive list of links to other Marx sites. Further research into utopias and dystopias on the Web can be accomplished by entering combinations of the words *utopia* or *dystopia* with other search terms.

There is no simple answer to this question. Perhaps it is a blessing that most of us cannot understand how anyone could ever find "good" reasons to do such bad things to innocent people. But it is quite possible—even likely—that some terrorists are motivated by a perverted idea of what is possible, by a horribly misguided sense of what the world *could* be like if only the source of evil, as they define it, were annihilated.[22] Whether that "evil" is capitalism, materialism, Israel, the United States of America, or whatever is almost incidental. The point is that extremists who imagine a time when, for example, Islamic societies were pure and unadulterated, a time before Western ideas, values, music, money, and military intervention corrupted the faithful, will all too easily find a cause—and an enemy—defined all too clearly by a blinding vision of the past, present, or future. It is a disturbing fact that in modern history a longing for utopia, a place on earth where happiness knows no limits, is often associated with violence that knows no limits.

FINAL THOUGHTS

Perhaps some more modest institutions for ensuring decent government deserve greater consideration than utopians have been willing to grant. As we have seen, utopian plans are fraught with hidden dangers. Although often motivated by the best of intentions and supported by the highest of ideals, utopian schemes, as Plato recognized, are as prone to failure as most other human endeavors. And in the real world, when utopian dreams collapse, they sometimes bring whole societies crashing down with them—as has been demonstrated by twentieth-century totalitarianism, much of which originated in utopian ideals.

Summary

Sir Thomas More coined the term *utopia,* signifying an imaginary society of perfect harmony and happiness. In the sixteenth century, More's *Utopia* was a subtle attack on the ills of English society under Henry VIII. The first important attempt to define the "perfect" political order, however, was made by Plato in *The Republic.*

Four works stand out as representative of utopian thought in the history of Western political philosophy. In *The Republic,* Plato sought the just society through philosophical inquiry. In the seventeenth century, Francis Bacon's *New Atlantis* demonstrated how the human condition could be elevated through modern science. Karl Marx later propounded the view that only through the radical reorganization of economic relationships within society could true justice and an end to human misery be achieved. The ultimate aim of Marx's theory of social transformation is the creation of a classless society. Finally, in B. F. Skinner's *Walden Two,* a prime example of a contemporary utopian scheme, behavioral psychology holds the key to utopia. The form and content of the just society were of less concern to Skinner than the methods for bringing such a society into existence.

In general, utopian thought has been inspired by idealism and impatience with social injustices. However, the presumed desirability of utopia frequently conflicts with its practical possibility. The principal obstacle to utopian society is the decided unpredictability and selfishness of human nature, which utopian thinkers commonly have sought to control through eugenics programs, compulsory education, and the abolition of private property.

Utopian visionaries often blame politics for the failure to improve society. As a result, in many utopian blueprints the role of politics in bringing about desired change is either greatly reduced or eliminated entirely. This neglect of politics leaves most utopian schemes open to criticism, for they could easily become blueprints for totalitarianism. Such blueprints are reflected in writings that describe dystopias as utopias turned into nightmares.

Key Terms

utopia	behavioral psychology
philosopher-kings	behavioral engineering
dictatorship of the proletariat	human nature
first stage of communism	eugenics
second stage of communism	dystopia

Review Questions

1. What is the origin of the term *utopia*? What does the word mean?

2. How have utopian writers differed regarding the practicality of utopia?

3. Utopian writers often make certain basic assumptions about human nature and society. Comment.

4. What can the study of utopian thought teach us about politics in the contemporary world?

5. In the twentieth century, totalitarianism greatly influenced certain novelists who produced chilling stories that turn utopia upside down. Comment.

Recommended Reading

BACON, FRANCIS. *The New Atlantis and the Great Instauration.* 2nd ed. Wheeling, W. Va.: Harlan Davidson, 1989. Bacon's seventeenth-century account of a society blessed by scientific breakthroughs is surprisingly modern.

GILISON, JEROME. *The Soviet Image of Utopia.* Baltimore: Johns Hopkins University Press, 1975. An insightful discussion of the idealist elements in Marxist-Leninist ideology.

HERTZLER, JOYCE. *The History of Utopian Thought.* New York: Cooper Square, 1965. A thoroughgoing discussion of utopian thinkers and their ideas throughout history.

KATEB, GEORGE. *Utopia and Its Enemies.* Rev. ed. New York: Schocken Books, 1972. A sympathetic defense of the value and contributions of utopian thought.

MORE, THOMAS. *Utopia.* Translated by Paul Turner. Baltimore: Penguin, 1965. More's imaginary society inspired many later utopian writers; the work remains a charming account of one man's paradise.

ORWELL, GEORGE. *Nineteen Eighty-Four.* New York: New American Library, 1961. A classic novel that brilliantly describes a dystopia modeled after Stalin's Soviet Union.

PLATO. *The Republic.* Translated by Allan Bloom. New York: Basic Books, 1991. Bloom's literal interpretation and interpretive essay helps make this edition of Plato's classic work especially valuable.

POPPER, KARL. *The Open Society and Its Enemies.* Princeton, N.J.: Princeton University Press, 1966. This work argues that Plato and Marx (among others) were advocates of totalitarian government and opponents of free, democratic societies.

SKINNER, B. F. *Walden Two.* New York: Macmillan, 1976. A fictionalized account of a small community founded and organized according to the principles of behavioral psychology.

Notes

1. See Leo Strauss, *What Is Political Philosophy? and Other Studies* (New York: Free Press, 1959), 10.

2. Allan Bloom, "Interpretive Essay," in *The Republic of Plato,* trans. Allan Bloom (New York: Basic Books, 1968), 308–310.

3. Plato's ideal political order is most accurately translated as "city." The Greek word *polis* implies a small self-sufficient community that provides for all human relationships. Modern distinctions between, for example, society and government or church and state are quite foreign to this concept.

4. Bloom, *The Republic of Plato,* 410.

5. Ibid.

6. Howard White, *Peace among the Willows: The Political Philosophy of Francis Bacon* (The Hague: Martinus Nijhoff, 1968), 97, 102.

7. Karl Marx, "Capital: Selections," in *The Marx-Engels Reader,* ed. Robert C. Tucker (New York: Norton, 1972), 259.

8. Karl Marx and Friedrich Engels, "Manifesto of the Communist Party," in *The Marx-Engels Reader,* ed. Robert C. Tucker (New York: Norton, 1972), 352.

9. Friedrich Engels, "Socialism: Utopian and Scientific," in *The Marx-Engels Reader,* ed. Robert C. Tucker (New York: Norton, 1972), 635.

10. Karl Marx, "Outlines of a Future Society, from 'The Germany Ideology,'" in *Capital, Communist Manifesto, and Other Writings,* ed. Max Eastman (New York: Modern Library, 1932), 1.

11. Ibid.

12. Joseph Cropsey, "Karl Marx," in *History of Political Philosophy,* ed. Leo Strauss and Joseph Cropsey (Skokie, Ill.: Rand McNally, 1969), 717.

13. Jerome Gilison, *The Soviet Image of Utopia* (Baltimore: Johns Hopkins University Press, 1975), 110.

14. Roy Macrides, *Contemporary Political Ideologies* (Cambridge, Mass.: Winthrop, 1980), 180.

15. B. F. Skinner, *Walden Two* (New York: Macmillan, 1962), 159.

16. Ibid., 161.

17. Ibid., 104–105.

18. Ibid., 262.

19. Ibid., 193.

20. Ibid., 272.

21. Ibid., 295.

22. See, for example, the writings of Daniel Pipes, especially *The Hidden Hand: Middle East Theories of Conspiracy* (New York: Free Press, 1997) and *Conspiracy: How the Paranoid Style Flourishes and Where It Comes From* (New York: Free Press, 1998); see also Fouad Ajami, *The Dream Palace of the Arabs: A Generation's Odyssey* (New York: Pantheon, 1998).

Chapter 3

CONSTITUTIONAL DEMOCRACY

THE REVOLUTION OF REPRESENTATION

CONSTITUTIONAL DEMOCRACIES FEATURE governments that are freely elected—governments that in the words of the American Founders involve a "scheme of representation." In *republics* (based on *indirect* democratic rule), the people participate in the political process both directly and through elected representatives. Countries as diverse as France, Poland, India, South Africa, Brazil, and Mexico are all examples of *constitutional democracy* in action. Official names such as the Federal Democratic Republic of Germany or the Republic of South Korea reflect the fact that the essence of modern democracy is representation. For this reason, nothing is more vital to the political life of republics than regular elections based on universal suffrage (the right to vote) and the secret ballot. It is easy to forget that many people in many places have fought and died for this right in the last two centuries. Today, far more people enjoy the right to vote in far more places than at any other time in the history of the world. In retrospect, the history of the two centuries since the American and French Revolutions is all about the struggle for *human dignity* and *popular self-government*—two terms that are, in the minds of many, virtually synonymous.

But even where the people are the ultimate source of political power, they cannot simply do anything they wish. Every existing democracy imposes limitations on majority rule. These limitations often take form of minority rights—that is, rights that are guaranteed even to citizens who are totally out of step with the majority. By the same token, standard rules and regulations dictate the procedures according to which government operates.

DEMOCRATIC CONSTITUTIONS

A nation's *constitution* delineates the basic organization and operation of government, setting forth both its powers and limitations. Most contemporary democracies have written constitutions, but they differ markedly. Constitutions vary greatly in age and in length. Some, like those of the United States and France, are models of brevity. Others, including those of India and Kenya, are lengthy and detailed. India's constitution devotes no fewer than ninety-seven items to federal control, sixty-six to state jurisdiction, and another forty-seven to joint federal-state control (or *concurrent powers*). Kenya's constitution is so explicit in allocating authority between the central and regional governments that it covers such subjects as animal disease control, the regulation of barbers and hairdressers, and houses occupied by disorderly residents.

The United Kingdom and Israel are two democracies that do not even have a formal (written) constitution. The British constitution is inscribed in the minds and hearts of the British people. It is a deeply ingrained and highly consensual social contract consisting of custom and convention as well as certain constitutional principles found in historic documents, royal decrees, acts of Parliament, and judicial precedent that have animated British political life for centuries.

Nonetheless, democratic constitutions are designed with certain core values in mind, including liberty, some type of equality, and impartial justice under law. In recent years, the threat of international terrorism has loomed far larger in Western democracies than any plausible threat of military invasion or missile attack. This threat poses a serious dilemma for democracies: how to preserve the civil liberties consistent with limited government while giving the executive branch, and the law-enforcement agencies it controls, broader powers required for effective government in the face of a malignancy that infiltrates society, spreads quietly, and strikes without warning.

Constitutional democracies must satisfy three competing, and sometimes conflicting, requirements. First, because such governments are democratic, they must be *responsive* to the people. Second, because they are governed in accordance with established rules and procedures, they are *limited* in the goals they can pursue and the means by which they can pursue them. Finally, like all governments, constitutional democracies cannot succeed or long survive unless they are *effective* in maintaining law and order, managing complex economies, and protecting the civilian population against external threats such as incursions and invasions by foreign armies (as well as violent crime, natural disasters, and terrorism).

Inherent in the concept of constitutional democracy, then, is the ideal of a government that is at once responsive, limited, and effective. Maintaining a proper balance among these basic requirements is one way of gauging the success of any democracy. Doing so in times of crisis is one of democracy's greatest—and recurring—challenges.

DEMOCRACY AS RESPONSIVE GOVERNMENT

Constitutional democracies exercise popular control according to the principle of majority rule. Through free elections (and occasionally by means of direct participation), citizens play an important role in government—namely, choosing who will hold high office and, therefore, make the laws, formulate the policies, and administer the programs on which well-ordered civil societies depend. This principle of government seems so self-evident in the United States, Canada, and other Western democracies that we (and they) seldom question its validity.

Majority Rule

The validity of democracy itself, however, can indeed be questioned. As Socrates pointed out some twenty-five centuries ago, in matters of vital importance people naturally seek out experts. If we are ill, for example, we go to a doctor—a medical expert. Why, then, if we want good government, would we turn to the people, many of whom are politically apathetic and ignorant? A contemporary commentator has pointed out that "if you visited a physician and sought advice as to whether to undergo an operation, you would be appalled if he explained that his policy in such cases was to poll a random sampling of passersby and act in accordance with the will of the majority."[1] Yet that is what democracies do all the time.

Perhaps the most straightforward defense of majority rule was provided by Alexis de Tocqueville in *Democracy in America* (1835): "The moral authority of the majority is partly based upon the notion, that there is more intelligence and more wisdom in a great number of men collected together than in a single individual."

Tocqueville believed that the approximate equality of human intellect was a basic assumption of democratic government. In addition, he argued, "The moral power of the majority is founded upon yet another principle, which is, that the interests of the many are to be preferred to those of the few"—a democratic precept that, in the final analysis, also rests on a belief in human equality.[2]

Whereas Socrates emphasized the great human differences in wisdom, intellect, and virtue, Tocqueville stressed the moral equality of human beings as the basis for his defense of majority rule. Furthermore, because the majority is always changing, and today's minority can become tomorrow's majority, the principle of majority rule is appealing to all. In the United States, according to Tocqueville, "all parties are willing to recognize the rights of the majority, because they all hope to turn those rights to their own advantage at some future time."[3]

The political principle of *majority rule* therefore finds support both in the ideal of equality and in self-interest. However, achieving majority rule is not as easy, nor is it always prized as highly, as we might think. In the United States, where the two-party system is well entrenched, elections typically produce a clear majority in both state and national legislatures. They also produce the *appearance* of a clear majority in most presidential elections. But as we discovered in the 2000 presidential election, the candidate who wins a majority of the popular votes is not automatically assured of getting elected. (The winner-takes-all system in which the candidate who gets a plurality of the popular votes in a given state gets all that state's electoral votes is discussed in Chapters 6 and 10.)

In parliamentary systems, the problem of majority rule is rather different. Most parliamentary systems have multiple political parties represented in the national legislature. (You will discover why this is so later.) Multiparty systems typically do not produce a clear majority of parliamentary seats for any single party. Two or more parties are then forced into a coalition in order to form a government with enough votes to get its programs and policies approved. As a result, the very *possibility* of majority rule is called into question. When the voters divide into, say, five or six sides rather than just two, there is obviously no clear signal as to where the "majority" stands on anything. Nor can any single party in a coalition government hew to its own platform and ignore the wishes of its partners in the coalition. The upshot is a watering down of positions—a government based more on rule by the lowest common denominator than on majority rule. Consequently, voters often become frustrated and cynical at what they perceive to be ineffective government.

Even in the United Kingdom, world's foremost two-party parliamentary system, majority rule is problematical. British elections nearly always produce a clear majority in Parliament (see Chapter 6), but the winning party seldom garners more than 45 percent of the popular votes (and often significantly less). In other words, British democracy is more accurately characterized as *plurality vote* system. To a lesser extent, the same could be said of American democracy because members of the U.S. Congress are elected in single-member districts and whoever gets the most votes, no matter how far short of a majority, in each district wins the seat.

The distinction between majority and plurality voting raises a theoretical problem. If a candidate or government is chosen on the basis of a plurality rather than a majority it means that more voters did *not* vote for that candidate or government than did—possibly many more. The logic of this analysis, however, can easily take a wrong turn. The reason the majority does not rule is not because the minority has usurped power but because *there is no majority*. Thus, to talk about the myth of the majority is not to denigrate majority rule but rather to recognize the difficulty of putting it into practice.

Governing by majority rule is easier said than done for another reason, as well. The fact that the majority is often elusive raises a problem for democratic theory; the fact that it is often tyrannical raises a problem for democratic practice. We turn next to this problem and how democracies try to solve it.

The Tyranny of the Majority

The desirability of responsible government appears obvious, but the presence of such a government is no guarantee that grave injustices will not occur. To illustrate this point, consider the Wild West scenario in which an innocent drifter, falsely accused of the cold-blooded murder of one of the town's most upstanding citizens, is jailed pending trial by a judge and jury. Almost everyone in town is indignant or drunk (or both), and an angry mob clamors for instant justice. Against this throng stand two solitary figures, a crotchety old deputy and the brave sheriff. The inevitable showdown takes place in the street in front of the sheriff's office. Led by the mayor and town council members (as well as by the man who actually committed the murder), a lynch mob demands that the "killer" be handed over immediately. In the end, only heroic action by the sheriff saves the innocent man from being dragged off and hanged from the nearest tree.

The hackneyed plot actually represents an object lesson in political science—a vivid example of responsive government in action. The majority of townspeople have made their wishes clearly known to the sheriff, who symbolizes authority and the rule of law. The easy way out for the sheriff would be to hand over the (innocent) prisoner to the angry crowd. Could any action be more in accordance with the principle of majority rule, or less in accordance with the requirements of elementary justice? Democratic government—when defined as the unlimited rule of the majority—*can* become synonymous with mob rule. Commonly viewed as a defense against tyranny, majority rule, ironically, can produce a new kind of tyranny, which Tocqueville called the ***tyranny of the majority***.[4] For this reason, political thinkers through the ages have often rejected democracy, fearing that a majority based on one dominant class, religion, or political persuasion would trample on the rights of minorities.

Americans witnessed the danger of mob rule in the fall of 2001 during the crisis following terrorist attacks in which thousands of New Yorkers died and thousands more were injured. When the perpetrators were identified as Muslim extremists, many Americans, horrified by the enormity of the crime, turned against Arab and Muslim minorities living in the United States. Only after President George W. Bush made an impassioned plea for tolerance and reason did the public furor against anyone appearing to be from the Middle East calm down.

In Western Europe, the specter of a majority steamrolling the rights of minorities has been raised in recent years over the issue of immigration. In France, for example, a party called the National Front momentarily captured headlines by gaining a strong following in local and even national elections. This party's meteoric rise alarmed some observers in part because opinion polls showed that many French voters who did not vote for the National Front nonetheless sympathized with its aims. National Front candidate Jean-Marie Le Pen's second place finish in the 2002 presidential election shocked France and Europe. Le Pen lost in a landslide to incumbent Jacques Chirac in the runoff, but the fact that he had earlier beaten the Socialist candidate, Prime Minister Lionel Jospin, was a wake-up call for those who had underestimated the strength of the anti-immigration movement in Europe.

There are many democracies around the world where the majority can be seen to tyrannize over minorities. In Germany, for example, there is a sizeable Turkish minority that has never been granted equal rights. In the Czech Republic (and elsewhere in Eastern Europe), the Czech majority systematically discriminates against the Roma. In Israel, the Arab minority (that is, Arab-Palestinians who are Israeli citizens rather than residents of the West Bank and Gaza) do not enjoy full political and social equality with the Jewish majority. In Turkey, the rights of the Kurdish minority have often fallen victim to the fears and prejudices of the Turkish majority.

The foregoing is only a sampling of majority tyranny in the world today. It is appallingly easy to find examples *in democratic societies* of minorities whose rights are routinely trampled on by the majority. Calling attention to this fact can be misconstrued as an attack on democracy, but just the opposite is true. Indeed, a willingness to tolerate self-criticism and a capacity to benefit from it are among the strongest arguments for the superiority of democracy as a political system.

Ask yourself the following questions: When nobody is talking about the tyranny of the majority in a democracy, what does it mean? Does it mean there is no tyranny? Does it mean there is no majority? Or does it mean, perhaps, that the silent majority has allowed a highly vocal fraction within its ranks to ride roughshod over the rights of minorities? We turn now to the ways democracies seek to protect the rights of citizens both from government and from fellow citizens.

DEMOCRACY AS LIMITED GOVERNMENT

Limited government means that there are clear restrictions on majority rule. The need for limited government should be clear from our Wild West lynch mob example. Hanging a person who has not been tried and convicted is murder, and even the majority must not be allowed to get away with murder. Obviously, the notion of a morally infallible majority is nonsense—every majority consists of a collection of individuals, many of whom may be misled, misguided, or misinformed on any given issue. Therefore, to prevent miscarriages of justice (such as lynchings), limitations must be placed on popular rule. These take many forms. In the United States, government is restricted as to how it can make laws or punish

Although almost 800 years old, the Magna Carta endures as one of the first and most important documents helping establish the idea that governments were bound to obey the rule of law and to respect citizens' rights.

citizens accused of breaking laws. Under the Constitution (Article I, Sections 9 and 10), it cannot, for example, pass an *ex post facto law,* which retroactively penalizes acts, or a *bill of attainder,* a legislative act that declares a person guilty.

The Constitution limits governmental powers in another important respect. The Bill of Rights (consisting of the first ten Amendments) forbids the government to deny citizens freedom of speech, press, assembly, and privacy, and guarantees the accused a fair trial (see Chapter 13).

Minority Rights

Constitutional restrictions on government clearly limit the principle of majority rule in the United States. No matter how many people want to deprive an individual of his or her right to free speech, and no matter how keen they are to do so, no voice can be silenced in this manner.

For limited government to be anything other than a hollow concept, the government must at least be able to protect minorities against intimidation by aroused majorities. In practice, however, the line between majority rule and minority rights is often unclear and open to debate. Then, too, constitutional rights are not self-defining; citizens are entitled to express themselves, but this right is not absolute. For example, freedom of speech does not give one the right to make obscene phone calls or to send death threats through the mail, though it is not always as clear where to draw the line between "speaking one's mind" and jeopardizing the rights or safety of others.

By comparison, the United States goes to greater lengths to protect civil rights and personal freedoms than do most other democracies. For example, many Europeans are bemused by the use of quotas in the United States as part of a broader "affirmative action" program to promote equal opportunities in education and the workplace. Similarly, the feminist movement (or women's liberation) does not resonate in many other countries around the world, including those with democratic traditions, open societies, and secularized cultures. The rights of the accused in the United States go well beyond the practices found in many other democracies. In most democracies, where trial by jury does not exist, the use of courtroom maneuvers to exclude evidence is rare. In addition, most democracies allow far less latitude for citizens to file civil suits than in the United States (the world's most litigious society).

The Rule of Law

The idea that nations ought to be governed by impartial, binding laws is not new. Aristotle argued that the *rule of law* is almost always superior to the rule of unrestrained individuals. He based this argument on the concept of fairness, contending that while individuals are subject to appetites and passions for physical, material, and psychic satisfaction, the law represents "reason free from all passion."[5] Therefore, a government of laws is superior to one of individuals, even though the laws must be interpreted and enforced by individuals (magistrates and ministers of justice).

More than 2,000 years later, English philosopher John Locke (1632–1704) defended the rule of law on the basis of its close relationship to individual freedom. Locke believed freedom could not exist without written law and that good government must follow certain precepts (for instance, that taxes should not be levied without the consent of the people).

To Locke, these rules constituted "laws" of the highest order because they embody what civil society is all about. They are "laws above the law" that necessarily and justly place limitations on lawmakers, no matter how large a majority such lawmakers command. From Locke's concept of a "higher law," the idea of constitutionalism evolved. As Locke noted (and as the inscription above the entrance to the Department of Justice building in Washington, D.C., reads), "Wherever Law ends, Tyranny begins."[6]

Locke was part of a proud English tradition that had sought since 1215 to establish limits on government. In that year, rebellious barons forced King John to sign the famous *Magna Carta.* Originally, this document made concessions only to the feudal nobility, but its broad clauses were subsequently interpreted more flexibly and expanded to cover increased numbers of people. Ultimately, the Magna Carta became the foundation of British liberties. Containing some sixty-three clauses, it was the beginning outline of a checks-and-balances system that limited the absolute authority of the monarchy. It declared, for instance, royal vassals must be summoned to councils to give their advice on and consent to important affairs of the realm, and that extraordinary taxes had to be approved by the royal vassals. Perhaps most important was Clause 39, which expressed an essential pledge of due process of law, one that guaranteed the accused an impartial trial as well as a protection against arbitrary imprisonment and punishment. To that end it stated, "no free man shall be taken or imprisoned, or disposed, or outlawed, or banished, or in any way destroyed . . . except by the legal judgment of his peers or by the law of the land."

During the seventeenth century, in Locke's time, great advances were made in the limitation of government by law. For example, the *Petition of Right* (1628) advanced the idea of due process of law while limiting the monarch's power of taxation. In addition, abolishing the dreaded *Star Chamber* (in 1641) ended the authority of a court that used torture to gain confessions and that imposed punishment on subjects at the request of the Crown. Finally, the ***Habeas Corpus Act*** (1679) limited government's power to imprison people arbitrarily. It imposed substantial penalties on judges who failed in a timely manner to issue writs of habeas corpus, thereby demonstrating that the accused had been legally detained and properly charged with the commission of a crime.

Also originating in the seventeenth century was a judicial precedent that came to have enormous influence in the United States. Renowned English jurist Sir Edward Coke's opinion in ***Dr. Bonham's case*** (1610) asserted that English common law (including the Magna Carta) should be the standard to which ordinary acts of Parliament, as well as the monarchy, had to conform. In Coke's words:

> It appears in our books, that in many cases the common law will controul Acts of Parliament, and sometimes adjudge them to be utterly void: for when an Act of Parliament is against common right or reasons, or repugnant, or impossible to be performed, the common law will controul it and adjudge it to be void.[7]

Although a "higher law" theory was not adopted in England, where parliamentary supremacy became the rule, it eventually found a home in the United States. The U.S. Constitution and Bill of Rights (largely derived from English common law) became the standards against which popularly enacted laws would be judged.

Constitutionalism as Correct Procedure

Constitutionalism is synonymous with correct procedure or the rule of law. For instance, the Constitution as interpreted by the U.S. Supreme Court prohibits the president of the United States, even during wartime, from seizing or nationalizing industries (such as steel mills) without Congressional approval.[8] Similarly, the rule of law and *due process* (another name for correct procedure) dictate that a citizen accused of a crime shall be provided with an attorney, allowed to confront witnesses, informed of the charges brought against him or her, and so on. For the same reason, administrative agencies are compelled by law to provide public notice to those who might be adversely affected by a pending decision.

In each instance, the rationale behind procedural due process is the same: No decision can be accepted as either fair or final unless it can be shown that the "rules of the game" have been strictly followed. Hence, in constitutional democracies if it turns out that the winner of an election cheated—that is, did not play by the rules—the effect is delegitimize the results. In fact, that is exactly what happened when the so-called Watergate scandal forced President Nixon to resign (or face certain impeachment) in 1974.

In the United States, however, due process of law tends to be taken to extremes in the eyes of many outside observers. For example, the police must *immediately* tell a suspect apprehended in connection with a crime that he or she has the right to remain silent (the Fifth Amendment protection against self-incrimination). If the suspect confesses to the crime without being informed of this right (and several others), the confession is inadmissible in court. In virtually every other liberal democracy in the world, including United Kingdom, France, Canada and Australia to cite but a few examples, a confession is a confession so long as it is not extracted by torture or trickery.

It is not enough for a democracy to proclaim the rule of law—words and deeds must coincide. Thus African Americans and other minorities continued to be victims of discrimination for many years after the Civil War was fought and the Fourteenth Amendment, which explicitly guaranteed "equal protection of the laws," was passed. Similarly, women did not gain the right to vote until 1920 and enjoyed few opportunities outside the confines of home and family until recently. Finally, America's prison population is disproportionately made up of young black males, despite the strict adherence of the courts to the rules of evidence and other requisites of due process. In addition, most prisoners awaiting execution on death row are African Americans, prompting critics to question the fairness of the American system of justice.

Correct procedure is essential to equal justice which, in turn, is essential to democracy. At the same time, due process is not an ironclad guarantee against grave injustice. Expecting such a guarantee is perhaps too much to ask of any political-legal order. As we noted in the previous chapter, utopia is not an option.

Federalism

Another way to limit constitutional government is through a division of powers called *federalism.* Modern examples of federal republics are the United States, Germany, Canada, India, Brazil, Mexico, and Nigeria.

In theory, federalism represents a division of power between the national government and regional subdivisions. These subdivisions are often called *states*, but the term is not to be confused with sovereign states or nation-states. In the United States, there is a constitutional division of power between national and state governments. Article 1, Section 8, of the Constitution, for instance, delineates many areas in which Congress is empowered to legislate. At the same time, the Tenth Amendment provides that all powers not granted to the national government are reserved for the states. Traditionally, the states have been empowered to maintain internal peace and order, provide for education, and safeguard the people's health, safety, and welfare (the states' so-called *police powers*). These powers were once exercised almost exclusively by the states, but the role of national (or federal) government has grown enormously since the 1930s, when President Franklin Delano Roosevelt launched a massive set of federal programs called the New Deal in order to create jobs and stimulate the economy in the midst of the Great Depression.

President Richard Nixon (1968–73) tried to reverse this process with a policy called the *new federalism* aimed at making government "more effective as well as more efficient." The two main elements of this policy were the use of so-called block grants to the states and general revenue sharing. Thereafter, other presidents—notably Ronald Reagan (1980–88), a conservative Republican, and Bill Clinton (1992–2000), a Democrat—also favored the transfer of power back to the states. In the United States, this phenomenon is called *devolution.*

What is the rationale for such a division of power? In U.S. history, those who believed the best guarantee of liberty was to keep government as close to the people as possible advocated federalism. Fearing that tyranny might arise from a single central government far removed from popular sentiments and local interests, some delegates at the Constitutional Convention (1787) argued successfully that the existence of states would limit the potentially tyrannical power of the new central government. In the Constitution, therefore, the separate states were given equal representation in the newly created Senate, and the federal method of electing the president (through the electoral college) was adopted. In addition, the states were to play an important role in amending the Constitution. As noted earlier, the First Congress deferred to the states in proposing the adoption of the Tenth Amendment.

The way federalism in the United States functions today differs significantly from the way it functioned during the nation's early history. Originally, great controversies flared over the question of whether a state (Virginia and Kentucky in 1798–99, South Carolina in the 1830s) or a region (the South in 1860) could resort to states' rights federalism to justify dissent from specific policies undertaken by the national government. When questions of interest or principle (the Alien and Sedition Acts of 1798, the tariff in the 1830s, slavery in the 1860s) divided the nation, political wrangling centered on the constitutionality of particular governmental actions or on the issue of whether state governments or the national government could legitimately exercise final authority.

Issues that the supremacy clause of the Constitution (Article 6) could not settle, the Civil War did. Although there have been some notable clashes, especially in the South over school desegregation in the late 1950s and early 1960s, the contemporary relationship between the national government and the states is characterized by cooperation rather than conflict across a wide range of public policies, from building highways to fighting crime.[9]

In recent years, there has been greater competition between these two levels of government, however. In the 1990s, for example, state governments experimented with educational reforms (charter schools, school vouchers, new ways to bring religion into the classroom) and a variety of anticrime measures (mandatory sentencing, three-strikes laws, victims' compensation). Some states also sought to roll back affirmative action.

This trend illustrates the sense in which federalism in the United States is *competitive* as well as cooperative. Even so, the Constitution is seldom seen as a barrier to the routine intergovernmental cooperation that exists throughout the U.S. political system.

Federalism and Liberty   By guarding against the dangers of overcentralization, federalism protects liberty, ensuring that the powers of the national government remain limited. In this way, federalism helps to protect individuals against a potentially overbearing central government.[10] Like systems of *administrative decentralization*, which rely on local bureaucracies to carry out important governmental tasks, American-style federalism protects individual liberty by limiting the scope of the national government. Thus, the aim of modern federalism is the same as that of political decentralization, which, by devolving functions to local governments, helps to limit the size of the central administrative structure and hence to make it less formidable to liberty. At the same time, decentralization draws masses of citizens into political life by multiplying and simplifying the governments accessible to them, thus activating the citizenry and habituating them to self-government. Further, these local governments become organized structures capable, in case of necessity, of resisting centralized authority or mitigating its excesses. Finally, decentralization permits government to be adapted to local needs and circumstances, and makes possible experimentation in the way problems are met. Decentralization is thus a vital safeguard to liberty and a way to educate an energetic and competent citizenry.[11]

The link between federalism and liberty is particularly striking in the case of Germany. Democracy in Germany was reborn after World War II when the nation was exhausted by war, defeated, and occupied by foreign armies. The Allied powers led by the United States were determined to prevent a new German state from once again launching a campaign of military aggression in Europe. The best way to do that, they reasoned, was to inoculate Germany against the virus of dictatorship. The "vaccine" they decided to use was democratic federalism.

How could federalism possibly prevent rise of a new Hitler? The key is to be found in the decentralized structure of Germany's government. The German states (called *Länder*) play an important role in governance *on both the state and national levels*. Delegates appointed by the sixteen state (*Land*) governments comprise the upper house of the German parliament, the Bundesrat. The upper house has veto power over legislation directly affecting the states, including new taxes. In addition, most of the governmental bureaucracy in Germany falls under the control of the *Länder*.

The Alternative: Unitary Systems   Most governments in the world today are not federal systems. A far more common form of government is the **unitary system**, such as that found in the United Kingdom. It is called "unitary" because there is only one primary unit of government, the central government, which often turns over many affairs to local governments but is not required to do so. Notably absent from these systems is an intermediate layer—the equivalent of states in federal systems—between the center and local political-administrative units.

Some unitary systems, for example those found in France and Italy, have guarded the powers and prerogatives of the national government against encroachment by local magistrates, mayors, and politicians more jealously than the British. In France, **prefects** (officials appointed by the central government) mediate between the central government in Paris and the local departments. Until the Socialist government of François Mitterrand instituted reforms in the early 1980s, the prefects were charged with the close supervision of local governments within their departments and had the power to veto local decisions. Admirers have long regarded this system, known as **tutelage**, as a model of rational political administration. Tutelage was so centralized and systematized that one could supposedly tell what subject schoolchildren all over France were studying at any given time simply by glancing at a clock. To many Americans accustomed to a multiplicity of schools, curricula, accreditation requirements, and academic standards, such government-imposed uniformity would no doubt seem curious.

DEMOCRACY AS EFFECTIVE GOVERNMENT

So far we have argued that democratic government cannot ignore the opinions and beliefs of its citizens—who vote, pay taxes, and serve in the armed forces—but that it cannot simply mirror the momentary inclinations of the many, lest it harm the interests and rights of the few. Democratic government that is responsive and limited, however, is not necessarily viable. To succeed or even survive, democracy, like other forms of government, has to be effective. In other words, it must have the capacity to accomplish the purposes for which it was created. If democracy cannot protect its citizens, promote prosperity, and provide essential services (such as education, law enforcement, water treatment, and fire fighting), then what good is it? Simply raising this question points to the possibility that democratic government might be *too* responsive or *too* limited for the good of the people.

A limited, responsive government capable of acting expeditiously must be based on structures that incorporate checks and balances on governmental power but that do not impair the government's ability to act energetically when circumstances dictate. On this point, James Madison's incisive comment on the Constitutional Convention is apropos: "Among the difficulties encountered by the convention, a very important one must have lain, in combining the requisite stability and energy in government, with the inviolable attention due to liberty, and to the Republican form."[12] Madison argued that stability in government is essential to domestic tranquility, national security, and public confidence, while energy is required to meet internal and external challenges. Together, he contended, stability and energy comprise the very essence of effective government.

The Need for Stability

Stability is an essential attribute of effective government. Political and governmental stability can be a particularly acute problem for newly emerging democracies and developing countries, but the problem is not confined to any one type of state or region of the world. Italy, for example, is a developed democracy notorious for having short-lived governments.

Stability can be encouraged in a variety of ways. Elected representatives must be given a sufficient time in office (term) to accomplish something worthwhile. There must be an institutionalized way of peacefully settling the kinds of political disputes and social conflict that might otherwise tear a country apart. (In the United States, the Supreme Court often performs this function, but political parties and legislatures also play a vital role.) Established procedures for changing leaders by regularized methods, such as elections and appointments, are enormously important and represent one of the principal advantages of democracy over modern dictatorships. (Monarchies typically solve this problem by resorting to the principle of inheritance—upon the death of the king power passes automatically to the eldest son.)

History and tradition, along with symbolism and ritual, reinforce the sense of continuity in governments. (Consider the pomp and circumstance surrounding

GATEWAYS TO THE WORLD: EXPLORING CYBERSPACE

http://www.uni-wuerzburg.de/law/home.html

An excellent site containing the texts of over seventy-five countries' constitutional documents. For many countries, there are also accompanying documents, essays, and historical background. From this site, you will be able to compare and contrast the various constitutions around the world.

You may also want to read de Tocqueville's *Democracy in America* to get a sense of an outsider's perspective on the political culture of a constitutional democracy in its early years.

the inauguration of a U.S. president or the marriage of a member of the British royal family.) Citing the need for continuity, James Madison opposed Thomas Jefferson's proposal for recurring constitutional conventions on the grounds that because "every appeal to the people would carry an implication of some defect in the government, frequent appeals would, in great measure, deprive the government of that veneration which time bestows on every thing, and without which perhaps the wisest and freest governments would not possess the requisite stability" and that even "the most rational government will not find it a superfluous advantage, to have the prejudices of the community on its side."[13]

The Need for Energy

To be effective, a government must also be energetic. In the United States, the Founders' commitment to energetic government was clearly reflected in the Constitution they bequeathed. It not only granted government as a whole ample powers but also created a strong executive capable of competing with the legislative branch. Constitutional provisions enabling Congress "to make all Laws which shall be necessary and proper for carrying into Execution the . . . Powers" delineated in Articles I and II is clear evidence of the Founders' intent to ensure that the national government would be able to act decisively when necessary. To this end, Alexander Hamilton noted in *The Federalist* that "a government ought to contain in itself every power requisite to the full accomplishment of the objects committed to its care . . . free from every other control but a regard to the public good and to the sense of the people."[14]

As noted earlier, the powers of the national government have expanded with the passage of time while those of the states have contract in relative terms. In general, however, the powers of government on all levels have grown enormously since 1789. This expansion in the role of government in the United States is a response to changes in society, the economy, and, indeed, the world beyond America's shores. The upshot of this trend, for better or worse, is that the U.S. government is undoubtedly more energetic today than it was a century ago and far more so than two centuries ago. If one considers that the United States is the preeminent military and economic power in the world—the only true superpower at the start of the twenty-first century—it is plain to see that democracy in America has worked rather well. It is one thing to criticize the "system" for not being responsive enough or to argue that government is too invasive (not limited enough), but who can doubt that it has been effective?

As we will see in Chapter 6, France under the Fourth Republic (1945–58) lacked effective government (energy). France finally solved this problem only by scrapping the old constitution and writing a new one, which tipped the balance away from the parliament toward the president (a new office under the Fifth Republic). France also has a prime minister, who is the head of government, but the president, as head of state who is directly elected to a renewable five-year term in office, has the power to make and break governments. By creating a strong presidency, the constitution of the Fifth Republic set the stage for a new era in French democracy—one which has ushered in greater stability and prosperity than France has known in more than two centuries.

In contrast to France, Italy has not solved the riddle of effective democratic rule. More than any other parliamentary democracy in the Western world, Italy has been a showcase of governmental instability. Because it is a parliamentary system, the government is headed by the prime minister, and because Italy has a chaotic party system, the prime minister rarely has the support of a durable or dependable coalition in parliament (much less a parliamentary majority). The upshot is that Italy changed governments on average about every six months for over two decades after World War II. Efforts to reform Italy's electoral system in recent years have so far failed to fix the problem. Fortunately, postwar Italy is an economic success story despite its unenviable political record. One can only guess what economic heights Italy might have scaled if it had been more effectively governed for the last half-century.

These three examples illustrate that democratic government can be effective but there is no guarantee. Of the three requisites for successful democracy discussed in this chapter, effectiveness is the only one that is not unique to democratic rule. Dictatorships do not typically strive to be responsive or limited, but instead seek to be effective with a singularity of purpose impossible in constitutional democracies. No democracy can fulfill its promise unless it is responsive nor can it be punished for failure to keep that promise unless it is limited. Until quite recently, there was a real question whether democracies could compete with dictatorships as effective forms of government. Thanks to a historic reversal of fortunes, however, the question now is whether dictatorships can compete with democracies.

REINVENTING GOVERNMENT: THE ENLIGHTENMENT AND THE IDEA OF AMERICA

The United States is the birthplace of the first modern theory of representative democracy ever put into practice. From its inception, it was not perfect, but it was a daring departure from the past and a bold attempt to reshape the future, which it did. The triumph of the idea that republics are a plausible and preferable alternative to monarchies and other forms of authoritarian rule was a defining moment in the history of the modern world. It so happens that this triumph occurred in a place called America. Today, the idea of America is synonymous with liberty and democracy in minds of people all over the world. (It is the idea far more than the reality that has proven to be a powerful force in modern times.)

The idea of America—that people are capable of self-government within the framework of a written constitution—is, in a very real sense, a product of the eighteenth century Enlightenment, which in turn was a product of the intellectual ferment in Europe that has its origins in the Italian Renaissance of the late fifteenth century. It is important to understand that the American Revolution did not simply spring full-blown from the head of George Washington or Thomas Jefferson or any other revolutionary leader. On the contrary, the political theory that informed the American Founders draws heavily on the contributions of famous thinkers who lived and wrote during this time, including Niccolò Machiavelli, Thomas Hobbes, John Locke, and Baron de Montesquieu. All agreed that the purpose of government was not, as Aristotle had claimed, to inculcate virtue, but rather to combat vice. This unflattering view of human nature led these thinkers to stress the pursuit of realistic goals—liberty or security, for example, which may be politically attainable, rather than virtue, which is not.

THE ARCHITECTURE OF LIBERTY

Here is the universal problem of politics: If people are not by nature virtuous, and rulers are people, how is it possible to insure that any system of rule will not degenerate into tyranny? The American Founders tried to solve this puzzle by developing what they called the *new science of politics*. This "new science" revolved around an ingenious and novel arrangement of political institutions designed to permit a large measure of liberty while guarding against the arbitrary exercise of power (tyranny) by compartmentalizing the functions of government, thus preventing the concentration of power. Just as Sir Isaac Newton revolutionized the modern understanding of natural science, so the Founders believed they were introducing a revolutionary understanding of politics—a new foundation for the quintessential social science.

Alexander Hamilton in *The Federalist* makes the theme of discovery explicit. Arguing that the new American Constitution would prevent "the extremes of tyranny and anarchy" that had plagued previous republics, Hamilton admonished his readers not to dwell on past examples: "The science of politics like most other sciences has received great improvement. . . . The efficacy of various principles is now well understood, which were either not known at all, or imperfectly known to the ancients." Hamilton catalogued the structural improvements built into the Constitution by the pioneers of this new science:

> The regular distribution of power into distinct departments; the introduction of legislative balances and checks; the institution of courts composed of judges holding their offices during good behaviour; the representation of the people in the legislature by deputies of their own election: these are either wholly new discoveries, or have made

their principal progress towards perfection in modern times. They are means, and powerful means, by which the excellences of republican government may be retained and its imperfections lessened or avoided.[15]

The Founders understood that, in James Madison's words, "enlightened statesmen will not always be at the helm."[16] In the absence of exceptional leadership, only the state itself, properly constructed, could check the ambitions of those who claimed to rule in its name. Elections provide one such check, noted Madison, but "experience has taught mankind the necessity of auxiliary precautions."[17] The chief precaution was to set up a permanent rivalry among the main components of government: "The great security against a gradual concentration of the several powers in the same department, consists in giving to those who administer each department the necessary constitutional means, and personal motives to resist encroachments of the others." In short, "Ambition must be made to counteract ambition."[18]

Checks and Balances

In pursuit of this goal, the Founders attempted to make each branch of government largely independent of the other branches—thus the powers of each respective branch derive from specific provisions of the Constitution (Article 1 for the legislature, Article 2 for the executive, Article 3 for the judiciary). Each branch was given constitutional authority to perform certain prescribed tasks, and each was equipped with the tools to resist any illegitimate expansion of power by the other branches. These tools, generally called *checks and balances*, ranged from the mundane (the president's veto power) to the extraordinary (impeachment proceedings brought by Congress against a president).

Together they comprise the "necessary constitutional means" available to members of one branch of government for use against the encroachments of another. "The interest of the [individual] must be connected with the constitutional rights of the place."[19] Institutionalized self-interest, the Founders felt, would infuse officeholders with a sense of the power, importance, and majesty of their particular institution and heighten their desire to maintain its prestige (and thereby advance their own careers). Thus, one reason Congress moved to bring impeachment charges against President Richard Nixon in 1974 was his blatant disregard for its authority in his conducting of both foreign and domestic policy. (Nixon's abuse of power—including his alleged involvement in the Watergate affair—was the general theme of the case against him.) In 1998, President Clinton was impeached, in part, because he resisted efforts by the (Republican) Congress to investigate his conduct in office. His opponents also charged that he flouted the judicial branch of government—for example, by allegedly lying to a grand jury.

In predicating democratic institutions on self-interest, the Founders demonstrated a limited faith in the human goodness and the likelihood of moral improvement. According to Hamilton, "Men are ambitious, vindictive, and rapacious."[20] Madison concurred, although less bluntly:

> It may be a reflection on human nature, that such devices [as checks and balances] should be necessary to control the abuses of government. But what is government itself, but the greatest of all reflections on human nature? If men were angels, no gov-

ernment would be necessary. If angels were to govern men, neither external nor internal controls on government would be necessary.[21]

In a well-ordered republic, enlightened self-interest would work for the good of all: Ideally, politicians would discover that personal interests (getting reelected) could best be achieved by promoting the public interest. If not, however, Madison's system, like Adam Smith's "invisible hand," would automatically adjust itself to ensure that the balance of institutional power would not be upset. Thus it was not on the lofty plane of morality or religious sentiment that the new science of politics in the United States found its justification; rather, it was justified on the firmer (albeit lower) ground of institutionalized self-interest.

The focus on the political thought of the Founders runs the risk of appearing to be a celebration of all things "American," and, as such, of being ethnocentric and narrow-minded. In this case, however, there is a justification grounded in logic and history. It just so happens that the first successful democratic experiment in modern history was launched in North America in the twilight of the eighteenth century. And it also happens that the revolutionaries who launched it were also political philosophers (there were no "political scientists" in those days). By self-consciously constructing a "science of politics," they provided a practical theory of democracy that has far-ranging implications and applications. As noted at the outset, these applications go well beyond any single nation or state or region of the world.

A Presidential System

The government of the United States is often called a *presidential system* because the chief executive is elected in balloting that is separate from the vote for members of Congress. This system is characterized by a *separation of powers* in which the legislative, executive, and judicial branches of the national government are each responsible to different constituencies for the exercise of their respective powers and responsibilities. The government was formally organized along functional lines. Because all governments need to formulate, execute, and interpret laws, it is logical to create a legislature to perform the first of these functions (rule making), an executive to carry out the second (rule implementation), and a judiciary to oversee the third (rule interpretation).

The logic of this arrangement knows no political or geographic boundaries—today it is reflected in the composition of many democracies in all regions of the world. Presidential democracies are especially common in Latin America today, but they are also scattered in various forms in such far-flung places as Russia, France, Yugoslavia, Nigeria, South Africa, Indonesia, and the Philippines.

The Separation of Powers

The U.S. Constitution assigns specific tasks to each branch of government. Congress, for example, is given the so-called power of the purse. The president proposes a budget and attempts to influence congressional appropriations, but Congress always has the final word on governmental spending. This potent constraint on the executive has not been widely emulated by other presidential democracies, which typically give the executive branch the upper hand in setting the budget (expenditures) while giving the legislature the primary role on the revenue side (taxation).

In a few areas, power and authority are shared in the American model. Overlapping responsibilities, for instance, characterize the government's "war powers." Congress is empowered to raise and support armies (although the Constitution limits appropriations to two years), to provide and maintain a navy, to make the rules regulating the armed forces, and to declare war. However, the Constitution makes the president the commander in chief of the armed forces. Therefore, any significant military undertaking, declared or undeclared, requires the cooperation of both branches. In general, this pattern is replicated in other countries with similar institutions, although the principal of civilian control over the military is nowhere more firmly established either in principle or in practice than in the United States. Indeed, in many presidential systems, the possibility of a military takeover (a so-called coup d'état) in times of crisis remains the principal danger to democracy.

Besides the different tasks they perform and the different ways they discharge these tasks, members of the three branches in the United States serve different terms of office and different constituencies. Under the Constitution, as amended, the president must stand for election every four years and is limited to two terms of office. The president and the vice president are the only two governmental officials in the United States who can receive a mandate from the entire national electorate. By contrast, congressional representatives serve particular districts (subdivisions of states) and are elected for two-year terms. Senators represent states as a whole and serve six-year terms in office. Supreme Court justices (and all other federal judges) are not elected; they are appointed by the president with the "advice and consent" of the Senate. The Founders stipulated this mode of appointment because they believed that to render impartial opinions, the judiciary must be free of the political pressures involved in winning and holding elective office.

The precise term of office varies somewhat from country to country, but four years is a fairly standard term. Both Russia and Brazil, for example, are identical in this respect to the United States: presidents are elected to four-year terms and are allowed to run for immediate reelection. By contrast, the presidents of Mexico and Nigeria are elected to six-year terms but cannot run for reelection. Until recently, France's president was elected to a renewable seven-year term. (The term was reduced to five years in 2000; see Chapter 6.) In most presidential systems, the chief executive actually has more power vis-à-vis the legislative branch than in the United States.

As noted earlier, under the U.S. Constitution no one branch of government possesses the power to dominate the others. Power is diffused and, to some extent, up for grabs. Given this political setup, it is not surprising that U.S. politics is often characterized by policy disputes and struggles for ascendancy, particularly between the president and Congress. Similar tension often exists between presidents and parliaments in other countries, as well, although presidents elsewhere often have certain "weapons" in battles with parties and parliaments that the U.S. president pointedly lacks.

The U.S. Congress is divided into two chambers, the Senate and the House of Representatives (pictured here). The founders intended that the legislative branch would both reflect and refine public opinion.

Constraints on Majority Rule

The Founders of the American political system were equally troubled by the potential danger of the tyranny of the majority (the tendency of the majority in a democracy to trample the rights of the minority). To some extent, *bicameralism* (the division of the legislative branch into two houses) was designed to provide a barrier against the majority steamroller. So too was the separation of powers. The presidential veto, the independence of the courts, and federalism were also intended as safeguards against the potential excesses inherent in majority rule.

Again, this political-institutional pattern is discernible in other countries, as well. The bicameral arrangement of the legislature is the rule nearly everywhere. In most cases, presidents have a veto power over legislation but the veto can be overridden by a determined and united legislature. Courts are typically set up to be independent, although whether judges are politically neutral or jurisprudentially impartial is often problematical. Many of the world's federal systems are also presidential—examples include Russia, Mexico, Brazil, and Nigeria. (By contrast Canada, Germany, and India are examples of parliamentary federalism.)

The American Agenda: A Sampler

Curtailing Entitlements

Entitlements include Social Security and Medicare programs. These programs are important to the lives of individual Americans, providing income for retired and disabled citizens and medical care for elderly citizens. But they are expensive, comprising approximately 36 percent of the total outlay of the federal budget. Having been taxed for these programs, Americans feel they are "entitled" to their extension and perhaps their expansion. Yet, as Americans live longer, as the cost of medical care increases, and as the large baby boom generation ages, the cost of these programs increases faster than tax revenues. This has created short-term, intermediate, and long-term funding challenges for continuing these entitlement programs. Still, any threatened cutback of costs gives rise to intense and widespread political pressure exerted by unhappy Americans, prompting the question: How will American political leaders find the resolve to act in a way that likely will be unpopular but will nonetheless meet and solve these problems?

Education

A focus of growing controversy, the American education system has been criticized for not effectively educating students. A particular concern is that the United States has not created workers with skills sufficient to meet the economic and technological challenges of the global marketplace. One controversial reform: encouraging competition with the public schools by allowing parents tax deductions for sending their children to private, secular, and church-affiliated schools.

Crime

In public opinion polls, Americans persistently list crime as their foremost concern. In recent years, the overall violent crime rate has decreased modestly, after showing extraordinary increases over the past half century. One worrisome countertrend has been an increase in violent crimes committed by extremely young offenders.

Debate rages over which government strategies actually reduce crime. One approach has focused on a widespread educational campaign to reduce drug abuse—linking it to incidents of violent crimes, including armed robbery, mugging, murder, and rape. Another strategy, instituted by former Mayor Rudolf Giuliani of New York City, cracked down on "nuisance crimes" such as loud radio playing, loitering, and public intoxication, and the crime rate in the city did decrease markedly. One possible explanation: Crime withers in an environment where citizen security is enhanced and the bonds of community are reinforced.

The Well-Being of Children

As the United States approached the year 2000, both liberals and conservatives worried about the predicament of children. Liberals were concerned that newly enacted welfare reform would unfairly harm poor children whose parents were unemployed. Meanwhile, conservatives worried that the fabric of the traditional family was unraveling, and this would lead to increased problems at school, with the law, and in other aspects of their lives. Conservatives emphasized that one of three children was now born to a single, unmarried mother, while the divorce rate had increased dramatically over the previous three decades. However, conservatives and liberals agreed, albeit for somewhat different reasons, that too many children in the United States were socially, economically, and emotionally at risk.

For a broad discussion of American public policy, see Chapter 13.

How Strong Is Too Strong?

The American system was designed not only to thwart tyranny but also to provide for a strong, energetic government. To this end, the Founders sought to create a powerful and unified executive branch capable of resisting both the encroachments of Congress and the centrifugal pull of the states. They believed (correctly) that the absence of a hereditary monarch, regular elections, and the possibility of impeachment effectively checked the executive power.[22]

Nonetheless, the American president actually has fewer constitutional weapons in the battle with Congress than presidents in other similar democratic republics possess. For better or worse, Congress can easily resist an unpopular president in the United States. Even popular presidents can be impeded, harassed, embarrassed, and frustrated by the opposition party, as former President Clinton would no doubt attest. When President Richard Nixon tried to use the IRS and FBI to intimidate his opponents, it backfired—fortunately. Russia's president, for example, is far more likely to get away with such heavy-handed tactics (see Chapter 7). Where the line is—or ought to be—drawn between capabilities and constraints depends on such key variables as political culture and circumstances.

Summary

In constitutional democracies, governments are both popular and restrained. They exist by virtue of constitutions that may differ widely in format and detail but invariably delineate the powers and boundaries of the governments they create.

Inherent in the idea of constitutional democracy is the belief that a government should be popular, limited, and effective. The concept of popular control through majority rule is central to the creation of a responsive government. The rationale for majority rule holds that the wisdom and interests of the majority are preferable to the wisdom and intelligence of the minority. However, because the majority is not always correct and can sometimes be tyrannical, constitutional democracies also place limits on the powers of the government. Protection of individual rights, the rule of law (constitutionalism), and federalism are the principal strategies used to prevent tyranny of the majority. Finally, democratic governments must act effectively. One requirement of effective government is stability; another is energy, or the ability to act, initiate, and lead.

The idea of America is synonymous with representative democracy in the minds of people all over the world. For inspiration, the Founders drew upon the writings of political thinkers who lived and wrote from the time of the Renaissance to Enlightenment and who were themselves inspired by classical political philosophy, particularly the writings of Plato and Aristotle from the time of ancient Greece. What the author calls "the architecture of liberty" grew out of the new science of politics developed by the American Founders. That new science was designed to prevent tyranny by compartmentalizing the functions of government (separation of powers) and ensuring that each of the compartments (branches) would have the means to defend itself against encroachment by the others (checks and balances).

Key Terms

republics	constitutionalism
constitutional democracy	due process
constitution	federalism
concurrent powers	police powers
majority rule	new federalism
tyranny of the majority	devolution
limited government	administrative decentralization
ex post facto law	unitary system
bill of attainder	prefects
rule of law	tutelage
Magna Carta	new science of politics
Petition of Right	checks and balances
Star Chamber	presidential system
Habeas Corpus Act	separation of powers
Dr. Bonham's case	bicameralism

Review Questions

1. What is a republic?

2. What general characteristics must constitutional democracies possess to serve the public good?

3. What is federalism? What advantages does this form of government offer?

4. Why is effective government a combination of energy and stability? How is each achieved?

5. What is constitutionalism? Why is it important?

6. What is the philosophy behind the "new science of politics"?

7. What is the meaning of the phrase *architecture of liberty* in the context of the American Founding?

Recommended Reading

CORWIN, EDWARD. *The "Higher Law": Background of American Constitutional Law.* Ithaca, N.Y.: Cornell University Press, 1955. A brief account of the rise of constitutionalism in Britain and the United States.

DIAMOND, MARTIN. *The Founding of the Democratic Republic.* Itasca, Ill.: Peacock, 1981. An excellent and readable discussion of the ideas employed by the Founders to create a responsive, limited, and effective political order.

FRIEDRICH, CARL. *Limited Government: A Comparison.* Englewood Cliffs, N.J.: Prentice-Hall, 1974. A brief explanation of the relationship between constitutionalism and the idea of democracy.

GREENE, JACK, ed. *The Reinterpretation of the American Revolution, 1763 to 1789.* Westport, Conn.: Greenwood, 1979. An outstanding collection of essays exploring American political ideas at a critical era; the essays by Bailyn, Diamond, and Kenyon are especially noteworthy.

HAMILTON, ALEXANDER, JOHN JAY, and JAMES MADISON. *The Federalist.* New York: Modern Library, 1964. The foremost exposition of the ideas underlying the American democracy by those responsible for its creation.

MAYO, H. B. *An Introduction to Democratic Theory.* New York: Oxford University Press, 1960. A thorough discussion of the advantages, limitations, and distinctive aspects of democracy.

Notes

1. Stephen Cahn, *Education and the Democratic Ideal* (Chicago: Nelson-Hall, 1979), 3.
2. Alexis de Tocqueville, *Democracy in America,* vol. 1 (New York: Schocken Books, 1961), 299–300.
3. Ibid., 301.
4. Ibid., 304–308.
5. Aristotle, *The Politics,* trans. and ed. Ernest Barker (New York: Oxford University Press, 1962), 1287a, 146.
6. John Locke, *Second Treatise on Civil Government* (New York: New American Library, 1965), sec. 202, 448.
7. 8 Co. Rep. 114a (1610).
8. See *Youngstown Sheet and Tube Company v. Sawyer,* 343 U.S. 579 (1952), especially the concurring opinion of Justice Jackson.
9. See Morton Grodzins, "The Federal System," in *Goals for Americans: The Report of the Presidential Commission on National Goals* (New York: American Assembly, Columbia University, 1960).
10. However, federalism does not protect individuals from abuse by state or local government, which the African American experience in various Southern states well illustrates.
11. Martin Diamond, Winston Fisk, and Herbert Garfinkel, *The Democratic Republic: An Introduction to American National Government* (Skokie, Ill.: Rand McNally, 1970), 136.
12. Hamilton, Jay, and Madison, *The Federalist* (New York: Modern Library, 1964), no. 31, 226–227.
13. Ibid., no. 49, p. 329.
14. Ibid., no. 31, p. 190.
15. Ibid., no. 9, 48-49.
16. Ibid., no. 10, p. 57.
17. Ibid., no. 51, 337.
18. Ibid.
19. Ibid.
20. Ibid., no. 6, 27.
21. Ibid., no. 51, 337.
22. Martin Diamond, Winston Fisk, and Herbert Garfinkel, *The Democratic Republic: An Introduction to American National Government* (Skokie, Ill.: Rand McNally, 1970), 136.

© AFP / CORBIS

Chapter 4

AUTHORITARIAN STATES

TRADITIONAL RULE

The Virtues of Authoritarianism

The Vices of Authoritarian Rulers

The Characteristics of Authoritarian States

The Politics of Authoritarianism

**Authoritarianism in Practice:
The Nigerian Example**

**Authoritarianism in Theory:
Myth versus Reality**
- Authoritarianism Is a Modern Invention
- Authoritarian Regimes Are Tyrannical
- Authoritarian Regimes Are Illegitimate
- Authoritarian Regimes Are Unpopular
- Authoritarian Regimes Neglect the Public
Interest • Authoritarian Rule Is the Worst
Kind Possible

The Twilight of Authoritarianism?

BY FAR THE most common form of rule throughout history is *authoritarianism.* Indeed, until the advance of democracy in Latin America at the beginning of the 1980s and the collapse of communism in Eastern Europe at the end of that decade, democracy was still the exception and authoritarianism was the rule. Authoritarian states come in a variety of sizes and shapes. They can be based on ancient ways (monarchies and theocracies) or modern means (secular dictatorships or military juntas). One modern form of authoritarianism is so extreme that it has been given a new name—totalitarianism (see Chapter 5). At the other end of the authoritarian spectrum, a number of traditional monarchies can still be found, mainly in the Arab Middle East. Examples include Morocco, Saudi Arabia, Jordan, Kuwait, Oman, Bahrain, Qatar, and the United Arab Emirates.

Whatever precise shape and form they assume, authoritarian states share certain telltale traits. They are typically headed by self-appointed rulers, and all political power—in practice and often in principle—resides in one or several persons. Most authoritarian governments posit no utopian goals, although at the extremes totalitarian rulers do, in fact, use a millenarian, or utopian, ideology to justify all state action no matter how harsh or brutal.

Typically, authoritarian rulers do not try to control every aspect of the society and the economy. Rather, they focus on keeping themselves in power and turning back all challenges to the status quo (the existing structures of state power). Authoritarian regimes continue to be the main alternative to constitutional democracy (and vice versa); as such, they warrant closer examination.

THE VIRTUES OF AUTHORITARIANISM

Outside of a few relatively brief historical periods—classical Greece and Rome, medieval and Renaissance Italy, and the contemporary age—monarchy as a political system had few serious challengers (monarchs themselves, however, were often less fortunate). Even during these more "enlightened" eras, monarchy was the most prevalent form of government. In the golden age of the Greek city-state system, for example, the principal alternative to monarchy was another form of authoritarianism—oligarchy—not republican government.

Why is authoritarian rule so common throughout history? First, it is relatively simple: there is no need to develop complex structures, procedures, and laws. Second, it is streamlined and thus (in theory) efficient: there is no need to bargain or compromise or cajole. The bureaucracy is typically staffed by individuals loyal to the regime: recruitment is based on patronage and nepotism rather than merit. Third, the will of the government cannot easily be thwarted by society: that is, neither special interest groups nor public opinion can block or blunt state action. Even to attempt to do so often provokes a violent response. Opposition and repression are two sides of the same coin. Fourth, where security is closely tied to defense against external threats, the ability of a strong leader to collect taxes, build roads necessary for commerce and communication, raise armies, and rally the nation is vital to self-preservation. Fifth, democracies tend to flourish in conditions of economic prosperity where there is a robust middle class. Countries that can afford the luxury of schools and the other social infrastructure essential to an informed citizenry are generally better candidates for democracy than poor, less-developed countries where people are caught up in a daily struggle for survival. Finally, as an astute observer of politics once said, "power corrupts, absolute power corrupts absolutely." There is something at once intoxicating and addictive about power—a first taste gives rise to an appetite that cannot be easily satisfied (as the saying goes, "the appetite grows with the eating").

THE VICES OF AUTHORITARIAN RULERS

Every authoritarian state is governed by a single ruler or an elite ruling group. The single-head form of government is called an *autocracy*, and the elite-group form is known as an *oligarchy* (sometimes referred to as a *junta*, or ruling clique). Authoritarian rulers are the sole repositories of power and authority within the political system. Tenure in office depends not on elections (the active consent of the people) but on a combination of myth and might. On the one hand, the people are often told that obedience to authority is their moral (or sacred) duty; on the other hand, the rulers stand ready to use brute force whenever rebellion threatens their position, which they are determined to maintain at all costs.

Traditionally, authoritarian governments have been headed by a dictator. Several of the most notorious dictators who came to power after World War II have now died or been deposed, including Idi Amin (Uganda), Emperor Bokassa I (the Central African Republic), Rafael Trujillo (the Dominican Republic), François "Papa Doc" Duvalier and his son "Baby Doc" Duvalier (Haiti), Ferdinand Marcos (the Philippines), Anastasio Somoza (Nicaragua), Manuel Noriega (Panama), Shah Reza Pahlavi (Iran), and General Suharto (Indonesia) to name but a few.

Among the most notorious dictators still in power are Muammar Qaddafi (Libya) and Saddam Hussein (Iraq). Three others, Hafez al-Assad (Syria) and Mobutu Sese Seko (the Congo, formerly Zaire), and General Sani Abacha (Nigeria) all died in the late 1990s. Today, Syria is ruled by Assad's son, the Congo is in a state of near-anarchy, and Nigeria's fragile new experiment with democratic rule remains in grave jeopardy due to a recurring cycle of internal ethnic and religious conflicts.

Until the turn toward democracy in the 1980s, Latin America had a long tradition of military rule, but it is not unique in this respect. Indeed, after World War II, such rule was common in most regions of the world, including Asia, the Middle East and North Africa (the so-called Arab world), and sub-Saharan Africa. Although many dictatorships have disappeared, they can still be found in these regions. Even in Latin America, where democracy is now the norm, the possibility of a return to military control cannot be ruled out.

Where the military dominates the political system, it often rules as an *institution* rather than through a single individual. A ruling committee (or junta) consisting of generals headed by a "president," who is also a general, is the usual pattern. The military frequently claims legitimacy on the grounds that civilian leaders are corrupt and venal or that only the military can maintain order and stability.

Hafez al-Assad: Dictator

Sipa Press

From 1971 to 2000, Hafez al-Assad governed Syria with an iron hand. Assad's rise to power and his rule illustrate Machiavelli's teaching that it is better for a ruler to be feared than loved.

Assad was born in poverty to a Shi'ite Alawite family (Shi'ite Muslims remain a minority in Syria, their beliefs considered heretical by the nation's 65 percent plus Sunni Muslims). At the age of sixteen he joined the Ba'ath party, an organization he would one day lead. Strongly championing the causes of nationalism and Arab unity, the Ba'ath party also advocated the creation of a secular, non-Islamic state (Syria had been governed by the French, who relinquished their rule over the region in 1946). Later, Assad would graduate from a military academy as a pilot. But his main interest remained politics, and his motive was always an unquenchable desire for political power. On the road to becoming president of Syria, Assad turned on virtually every political ally who had once helped or befriended him.

Assad's goals for Syria were straightforward—he intended to be the absolute ruler of Syria and to turn Syria into a regional political and military power. He was successful in achieving these goals, but there were disappointments, too. Most notable was the loss of the strategic Golan Heights to Israel in the 1967 Six-Day War, waged while Assad was defense minister. Syria's inability to reclaim the land in 1973 when Syria and Egypt waged war against and were defeated by Israel stands as a perpetual reminder of Assad's failed political ambitions.

Although Assad spent state funds to battle his nation's pervasive poverty, and improved Syria's housing, educational institutions, and medical facilities, these efforts were overshadowed by his unrelenting behind-the-scenes efforts to maintain political power. Symbolic of those efforts were the periodic elections held in Syria under his rule. Assad always garnered over 99 percent of the vote in rigged elections. Little wonder the elections were uncontested and decisive: Assad employed assassins and supported terrorists to murder political opponents throughout the Middle East. He directed the dreaded Moukhabarat (the state security force known for its effective use of electronic surveillance, cruel terror, and the widespread use of torture) against suspected internal enemies. The most notorious exercise of blatant power against perceived political enemies was directed by Assad in 1982. Assad suspected that members of the Muslim Brotherhood (a radical Sunni Muslim organization) were plotting to overthrow his regime. He closed the city of Hamma, a center of strength for the Muslim Brotherhood, and proceeded to massacre thousands of its residents (between 5,000 and 30,000 Syrians, according to various estimates).

Today, Syria is ruled by Assad's son Bashar Assad, an opthalmologist by training who returned to Syria (from the United Kingdom where he was living) after his elder brother died in a car crash in 1994. Bashar was immediately elevated from the rank of colonel to lieutenant general and named commander in chief of the armed forces. Following his father's death in 2000, he assumed the presidency without any opposition. Not surprisingly, Syria's military-based dictatorship remains largely unchanged and unchallenged.

Senior military officers continue to play an important governing role in many of Latin America's emerging democracies which are now headed by popularly elected civilian presidents. In Africa, military rulers still hold sway in various countries and the threat of a military coup against elected civilian governments is always present. Authoritarian rulers generally do not respect individual rights when such rights interfere with the power or policy goals of the state. Authoritarian regimes usually place the interests of the rulers above the welfare of the rank-and-file citizenry. Given the nature of the system, there is nothing to prevent them from doing so.

One way to get a glimpse of the true nature of authoritarianism is to think of it as a place where arbitrary rules are strictly enforced. Now to try to imagine what it would be like to live there.

Yet there are important differences among authoritarian rulers. They vary in the extent to which they impose conformity and suppress intellectual and artistic freedom. Furthermore, the amount of force, repression, and violence employed by authoritarian rulers varies greatly. Some rulers use coercion sparingly, while others, appropriately labelled tyrants, display an enthusiasm for cracking down on dissenters. Finally, whereas most authoritarian rulers are self-aggrandizing in the extreme, a few have made genuine and sustained efforts to exercise political power in ways that also advance the national interest (the late Josef Broz Tito of Yugoslavia and Anwar Sadat of Egypt are two examples). Ambitious national programs undertaken to industrialize, reform, or modernize the economy point to the possibility of a benevolent dictatorship. Of course, even benevolent dictators generally do not tolerate organized political opposition.

These practical distinctions, even if they are sometimes difficult to perceive, have important political implications. Authoritarian states are, by definition, home to regimes that recognize few—if any—constraints on the power they wield. Most of these governments are, at best, only incidentally concerned with the well-being of the citizenry; yet even in the case of authoritarian states headed by self-interested dictators, important variations do exist. In short, all tyrants are dictators, but not all dictators are tyrants (see Figure 4-1).

THE CHARACTERISTICS OF AUTHORITARIAN STATES

Authoritarian rulers frequently come to power by force or violence, first surprising and then overthrowing the government in a *coup d'état.* Until quite recently, power seizures of this kind were quite common in Asia, Latin America, the Middle East, and sub-Saharan Africa, where dictators would come and go with little or no effect on the people in whose name (and for whose sake) they pretended to act.

Maintaining a monopoly of power is the main aim of authoritarian states. Authoritarian leaders thus seek to control the means by which political opponents can be intimidated, harassed, exiled, imprisoned, or even executed. The army and the police are the principal instruments of coercion, hence the high incidence of military rule. For obvious reasons, civilian dictators also typically cultivate close ties to the military. In fact, many civilian rulers of authoritarian states start out as military strongmen and later convert to "civilian" status, largely for the sake of

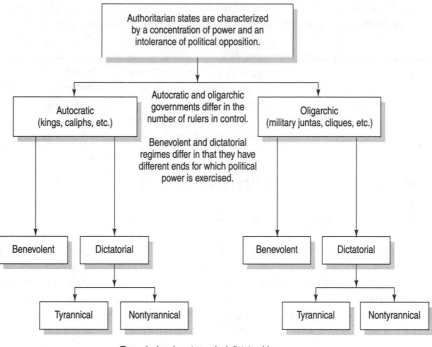

FIGURE 4-1 Types of Authoritarian Governments

appearances. In Egypt, for example, Gamal Abdel Nasser, Anwar Sadat, and now Hosni Mubarak were all military commanders before becoming president.

To frustrate actual or potential political opposition, authoritarian rulers often impose strict press censorship, outlaw opposition parties, and exert firm control over the legal system, which is manipulated to prosecute (and persecute) political opponents. A monopoly over the mass media and the courts gives absolute rulers a highly effective means of perpetuating their rule while also supplying the machinery by which excesses of power can be disguised or legitimized. Repressive institutions and policies are typically justified in the name of order and stability, a plausible ploy given the list of problems faced by many developing nations (foreign enemies, internal ethnic and religious divisions, economic scarcity, and profound class differences).

Although some authoritarian states have actively promoted social and economic modernization (for example, Turkey, South Korea, and Taiwan in the recent past), most are characterized by underdeveloped agrarian economies and sharp gradations between rich and poor. Authoritarian rulers tend to seek control over the economy only to a limited extent and chiefly for the purpose of collecting taxes to underwrite military and economic programs and often lavish personal expenditures.

Paying taxes and showing respect for authority are the principal (if not the only) demands made on ordinary citizens by autocratic regimes. Thus, although the government may exploit its citizens economically, it is ordinarily indifferent to the way they live or what they do, so long as they stay away from politics. Indeed, whether the state tries to invade the private lives of its citizens is, arguably, a kind of litmus test indicating when the rulers have crossed the line between authoritarianism and totalitarianism.

To be sure, authoritarian rulers rarely make the lives of the people better—often doing exactly the opposite—but their governments do tend to leave ordinary citizens alone most of the time. In general, authoritarianism "does not attempt to get rid of or to transform all other groups or classes in the state, it simply reduces them to subservience."[1]

THE POLITICS OF AUTHORITARIANISM

Perhaps subservience is the natural result of the fact that authoritarian rulers are seldom motivated to govern for the people's benefit. Aristotle argued that all authoritarian forms of rule, despite the important differences among them, are a perversion of good government. Asserting that "those constitutions which consider the common interest are *right* constitutions, judged by the standard of absolute justice," he argued that "those constitutions which consider only the personal interests of the rulers are all wrong constitutions, or *perversions* of the right forms. Such perverted forms are despotic."[2] Aristotle also argued that the end of good government should not be the good of one individual or of a privileged few but, insofar as possible, the good of all citizens. Yet by definition dictators and tyrants alike place their own personal interests above the interests of society. Like medical quacks who become wealthy by touting fraudulent medicines as miracle cures, such rulers become powerful by promising great benefits to the people whom they most exploit.

This perversion of ends usually entails a like perversion of means. Often authoritarian rulers justify self-serving policies on the specious grounds that whatever they do is necessary to preserve order and defend the nation from its enemies. The great danger in ritually overstating the case for security is that the rulers will (and often do) resort to excessive force in dealing with domestic unrest which may well be a natural result of their own failed policies.

Throughout history, authoritarian governments have been criticized for their characteristically cruel persecution of political opponents. As a rule, such states hold a negative view of politics: Either the ruler is above politics, or the sphere of politics is greatly restricted. This means that in authoritarian states, questions regarding who should rule or how cannot be raised in public because any criticism of a ruler is considered an act of disloyalty or treason.

AUTHORITARIANISM IN PRACTICE:
THE NIGERIAN EXAMPLE

Nigeria illustrates why authoritarian governments are both so easily instituted and so widely despised. As one of sub-Saharan Africa's potentially great powers, Nigeria under military rule provides an instructive example of the workings of, and the harms caused by, authoritarian governments. Even though Nigeria accounts for only 3 percent of the African landmass, its 120 million people comprise some 20 percent of sub-Saharan Africa's population. With a gross national product second only to South Africa's, and substantial amounts of oil available for export, Nigeria's economy nonetheless remains woefully underdeveloped; its annual per capita gross national product is under $300 per person.

Nigeria's economic development has been undermined by tribal and ethnic diversity, as well as by a series of inept and corrupt military rulers. Nigeria originally existed as a British colony, becoming independent in 1960. As with so many other African nations, its borders were constructed primarily for the administrative convenience of its colonial rulers (see Chapter 8). Within these borders are peoples divided by region, religion, ethnicity, language, and culture. The fact that some 250 languages and dialects are spoken provides a glimpse of Nigeria's astonishing diversity.

Nigeria is a breeding ground for social conflict. First, the country is divided along religious lines: Moslems dominate in the north and Christians dominate in the south. Second, several large ethnic groups (or tribes) dominate different regions of the country: the Hausa-Fulani in the north; the Yorubas in the west; and the Ibos in the east. Third, the different parts of Nigeria have different competitive advantages and sources of political power. For instance, the north is the most populous region, the south contains most of Nigeria's oil deposits, and the east produces a disproportionate percentage of the country's diplomats and administrators.

Given these deep divisions, it is not surprising that Nigeria has been beset with profound social instability since its independence. For instance, in eastern Nigeria the Ibos attempted to secede in 1967 as the independent state of Biafra. The civil war that resulted lasted almost three years and killed over a million people. In the end, the move for secession failed. Frequent religious riots, with thousands of Christian and Moslem citizens perishing, constitute yet another example of endemic social instability.

Thus, Nigeria is a multiethnic state, made up of numerous and diverse groups of people, with little sense of a single national identity. These schisms partially explain why Nigeria's two experiments with democracy and elected government (1960–66 and 1979–83) failed. Against such a chaotic background, political order carries a premium, and a strong national government able to suppress domestic violence has a broad appeal. But from 1983 to 1999, military rule in Nigeria brought virtually nothing but decline, distrust, and dissension.

Although corruption has never been absent from Nigerian politics, it reached new heights during this period. A succession of military dictators and ruling cliques enriched themselves shamelessly while utterly neglecting the country's economic and social well-being. According to one measure, Nigeria prior to 1999 was ruled by the most corrupt government in the world (see Table 4-1). Bribery and extortion were a way of life, and the system of patronage, in which the military rulers bestowed government jobs and other favors on supporters of the regime, produced a bloated, inefficient, irresponsible, and unresponsive bureaucracy.

TABLE 4-1

Corrupt as They Come*

1 Nigeria	19 Bolivia	37 Hong Kong
2 Pakistan	20 Argentina	38 Japan
3 Kenya	21 Italy	39 Austria
4 Bangladesh	22 Turkey	40 United States
5 China	23 Spain	41 Israel
6 Cameroon	24 Hungary	42 Germany
7 Venezuela	25 Jordan	43 Britain
8 Russia	26 Taiwan	44 Ireland
9 India	27 Greece	45 Australia
10 Indonesia	28 South Korea	46 Netherlands
11 Philippines	29 Malaysia	47 Switzerland
12 Uganda	30 Czech Rep.	48 Singapore
13 Colombia	31 Poland	49 Norway
14 Egypt	32 South Africa	50 Canada
15 Brazil	33 Portugal	51 Finland
16 Ecuador	34 Chile	52 Sweden
17 Mexico	35 Belgium	53 Denmark
18 Thailand	36 France	54 New Zealand

*Corruption rankings in 1996, based on the level of corruption in a country perceived by employees of multinational firms and institutions (1 = most corrupt in survey, 54 = least corrupt).
SOURCE: *Transparency International, Berlin.* Reprinted from the *Wall Street Journal,* January 2, 1997, Sec. 1, 5.

Nigeria's military rulers repeatedly promised free elections in the future, but these promises were not kept. When elections were held in 1993, the results displeased the ruler(s). In response, Nigeria's military boss, General Ibrahim Babangida, nullified the election, imprisoned the winner, and charged him with treason. Thereafter, many other critics of the military regime were also imprisoned and persecuted—some were even executed.

Finally, in 1999, following many years of failed military rule and the sudden death of Nigeria's paramount ruler of the day, General Sani Abacha, the country was again given a chance to vote in a meaningful (somewhat free) election. Former military leader Olusegun Obasanjo became Nigeria's first democratically elected president since 1983. Obasanjo represents a rarity in Nigeria: a public figure with a military background and a reputation for personal integrity.

Whether Obasanjo will be able to put Nigeria firmly on the path to democracy and prosperity remains to be seen. One way or the other, the rule of the generals in Nigeria stands as a reminder of two major political truths. First, the overriding aim of authoritarian rulers is to remain in power at all costs. Second, even the most brutal dictatorship ultimately cannot escape the consequences of its own misrule.

AUTHORITARIANISM IN THEORY: MYTH VERSUS REALITY

Ignoring the genuine diversity among authoritarian states often leads people to generalize from extreme cases and end up with a distorted view. The understandable (and usually justified) stigma attached to authoritarianism has promoted certain popular misconceptions. We will now examine six assumptions that are based on a blend of fact and myth.

Authoritarianism Is a Modern Invention

This assertion is plausible on its face but it cannot withstand scrutiny. The fundamental methods of consolidating and maintaining power, in fact, have been well known for at least two millennia.

In *The Politics*, Aristotle provided an impressive catalog of the political tactics used by the earliest known autocrats, whose methods of maintaining power would be familiar to most modern-day dictators. Aristotle astutely observed that these tactics were designed to render individuals incapable of concerted political action by breaking their spirit and making them distrustful of one another. Persons who were thought for whatever reason to represent a political threat were eliminated. By banning common meals, cultural societies, and other communal activities, individuals were isolated from one another. Such actions fostered insecurity and distrust and thus made it difficult for dissidents to create an underground political movement. Secret police increased popular anxiety while obtaining information; spies were used for the same purposes.

Poverty, heavy taxes, and hard work monopolized the subjects' time and attention. (Aristotle cited the construction of the Egyptian pyramids in this regard.) Finally, warmongering was viewed by autocratic rulers as a useful way of providing a diversion "with the object of keeping their subjects constantly occupied and continually in need of a leader."[3]

Aristotle's list of autocratic political tactics was expanded and updated by the Italian political thinker Niccolò Machiavelli (1469–1527), who literally wrote the book on gaining and keeping political power. His book, *The Prince* (1513), can be viewed on one level as a kind of instructor's manual for the successful authoritarian ruler. Those who would rule, Machiavelli contended, must understand the importance of *seeming* to act morally even when committing immoral acts. Successful rulers must be masters of deception. Often they will *have* to act immorally in order to survive; for this reason, they must constantly appear honest and upright, even while practicing "how not to be good."

Machiavelli also advised would-be rulers not to keep promises that are no longer in their best interest; to disguise their intentions; to inspire fear, rather than love, in their subjects; and, if possible, to cultivate the appearance of generosity while always practicing self-interest. Generosity, in his view, meant keeping one's

Niccolò Machiavelli (1469–1527) contended in The Prince *that rulers could maintain their power only by resorting to immoral tactics and strategies.*

own property and giving away that of others. When property must be confiscated or political opponents imprisoned or "traitors" executed—in other words, whenever punishment has to be inflicted—the acts should be done swiftly and simultaneously. The sooner the bloodletting was ended, Machiavelli argued, the sooner it would be forgotten. In contrast, benefits should be doled out little by little, so they can be savored and their recipients reminded of whence all good things come. Finally, Machiavelli counseled, punishment should always be severe as well as swift: Mild retribution, he argued, may arouse a spirit of rebellion; it may also make the ruler look weak and indecisive.

It is not surprising that the word *Machiavellian* has come to be associated with ruthless, immoral acts. Yet Machiavelli did not invent the methods he prescribed. He simply systematized a set of practices that were prevalent in the governmental dealings of the city-states of sixteenth-century Italy. Like Aristotle before him, he merely elaborated on the actual methods and techniques used by the autocratic rulers to maintain political power—techniques that are still used today.

Authoritarian Regimes Are Tyrannical

Many observers have pointed out significant differences in the way authoritarian states wield power. Aristotle, in particular, distinguished between two different forms of authoritarianism. The more common variety, Aristotle noted, relies on such traditional methods of political control as acts of outright cruelty and repression. The purpose of such policies is clear enough: to take away the power to revolt. A second kind of authoritarian ruler seeks to deceive the people. Such dictators give the appearance of being concerned about the common good. They avoid displaying wealth, give no sign of any impropriety, honor worthy citizens, erect public monuments, and so on. In short, these rulers "should appear to [their] subjects not as a despot, but as a steward or a King of [their] people."[4] Of course, the rulers' self-interest is still supreme. They merely attempt to make a good impression in order to take away the motivation (or desire) to revolt. This kind of ruler may do the right thing, but for the wrong reasons. The ruler is, in Aristotle's phrase, "half-good." Nevertheless, life under a "half-good" autocrat would clearly be preferable to life under a "traditional" dictator.

Thus it is not only the *extent* to which authoritarian governments affect individual lives but also the *manner* in which they do so that matters. As we have seen, some rulers imprison and murder all real or imagined political enemies, while others govern with a minimum of force. In another vein, some authoritarian governments show a marked indifference to economic development, preferring to concentrate their energies on the preservation of political power, while others actively seek to improve economic conditions. Shah Muhammad Reza Pahlavi (1920–80) for example, was both an unrelenting persecutor of his political enemies and a progressive modernizer in the realm of cultural, economic, and social policy of Iran, where some measure of personal freedom existed. Similarly, the present-day governments of Taiwan and Singapore represent a curious mixture of democracy and dictatorship, yet both countries for years enjoyed relatively high rates of economic growth and standards of living that were the envy of many Third World states.

Authoritarian Regimes Are Illegitimate

Most Americans would subscribe to John Locke's view that the only legitimate governments are those based on the consent of the governed. But consent is not the only measure of legitimacy—in fact, there have been long periods in history when popular will was not even recognized as a criterion of legitimacy.

From the late Middle Ages through the eighteenth century, the prevalent form of government in Europe was monarchy, based on religion (divine right) and heredity (royal birth). Similarly, in Imperial China the dynastic principle was one source of the emperor's legitimacy, but religion also played a major role—the Chinese emperor ruled under the "mandate of Heaven." Historically, tradition and religion served as two of the principal sources of governmental legitimacy.

Many contemporary dictatorships have relied on a somewhat more informal and personal source of legitimacy, the popular appeal of a ***charismatic leader.*** Often charismatic rule is grounded in the personal magnetism, oratorical skills, or legendary feats of a national hero who has led the country to victory in war or revolution. Post–World War II examples include Nasser of Egypt, Sukarno of Indonesia, and Qaddafi of Libya. Many postcolonial Third World dictatorships were based almost exclusively on hero worship of a "liberator"—a person who rallied the indigenous population in a successful struggle to win independence from European colonial rule.

Culver Pictures

While enjoying the support of the French people, Napoléon Bonaparte (1769–1821) crowned himself emperor of France in 1804: "I am the state—I alone am here the representative of the people."

Divine sanction, tradition, and charisma, then, are the historical pillars of autocratic rule. More often than not, these wellsprings of legitimacy have served effectively to sell the idea that the rulers have a *right* to rule without consulting the people. Having the right to rule does not mean the same thing as ruling rightly, of course. And unfortunately, dictators and tyrants have too often used their "rights" to commit serious wrongs.

Authoritarian Regimes Are Unpopular

People living in a democracy tend naturally to assume that if given the choice, everyone would choose to live in a democracy rather than a dictatorship. Yet the evidence suggests that this assumption is mistaken. Undeniably, some dictators inspire in their people not only fear—stemming from their use of force and terror to suppress political opposition—but also respect, trust, voluntary obedience, and even love. Because authoritarian leaders sometimes provide political stability and economic growth, dictators are occasionally adored.

Personal charisma is another source of popularity. The prototype of the charismatic "man on horseback" was Napoléon Bonaparte. Napoléon seized power in a country convulsed by revolution and led France in a series of spectacularly successful military campaigns, nearly conquering the entire Continent. At the height of his military success, Napoléon enjoyed almost universal popularity in France. Hitler, too, enjoyed broad support among the German rank and file. (Of course, Hitler's totalitarian state exercised powers that far surpassed those of Napoleon's regime.) As one writer has pointed out:

> It is sometimes assumed that one who rules with the support of the majority cannot be a tyrant; yet both Napoleon and Hitler, two of the greatest tyrants of all time, may well have had majority support through a great part of their reigns. Napoleon, in many of his aggressive campaigns, probably had majority support among the French, but his actions . . . were nonetheless tyrannical for that. Hitler, for all we know, might have had at least tacit support of the majority of the German people in his campaign against the Jews; his action was nonetheless tyrannical for that. Let us assume—*per impossible,* one would hope—that [if] a democratically elected Prime Minister were to start on a similar campaign, he would be acting tyrannically; the probable result would be that he would be opposed by a minority so vehemently that he would have to take tyrannical measures to suppress it and thereby cease to depend on the popular vote and thus become an absolute tyrant. A tyrant, then, may in many of his measures have popular support, but in general his power will not depend upon it.[5]

Bad rulers, no matter how reckless or ruthless, will not necessarily be impeded by good people. In this respect, modern tyrannies illustrate a truth expressed most notably by the nineteenth-century Russian author Fyodor Dostoyevsky: In an age of equality, the masses, desiring security above all else, will gladly accept despotism in order to escape the burden of responsibility that accompanies freedom.[6] The truth is that despotic government is often more popular than we care to believe.

Authoritarian Regimes Neglect the Public Interest

This generalization cannot survive close scrutiny. Even the worst tyrants can bring order out of political chaos and material progress out of economic stagnation. Adolf Hitler, it has been argued, should be credited with curing Germany's economic woes. And apologists for Benito Mussolini, Hitler's contemporary and the fascist dictator of Italy, have noted that at least he made the trains run on time. Such public policy successes by no means justified the excesses of these tyrants, but they do help to explain the domestic popularity of Hitler and Mussolini.

Perhaps the most impressive example of an autocratic regime that succeeded in creating sustained social and economic progress comes not from Europe but from China. Baron de Montesquieu, Adam Smith, and Karl Marx were all moved to comment on the classical Chinese system of government.[7] And in our own time, this system continues to be the object of much scholarly attention.[8] Particularly noteworthy was the vast network of dikes, irrigation ditches, and waterways that crisscrossed the immense Chinese realm. This hydraulic system represented a signal achievement, exceeding in scale and scope any public works ever undertaken in the West in premodern times. What kind of a civilization could build public works on such a stupendous scale?

One modern scholar, Karl Wittfogel, theorized that the Chinese system, which he labeled "oriental despotism," owed its distinctive features to the challenges of sustaining a huge population in a harsh and demanding environment.[9] The staple food of China has always been rice, and rice cultivation requires large amounts of water under controlled conditions. Thus, to solve the perennial food problem, Chinese civilization first had to solve the perennial water problem. This meant building sophisticated flood control, irrigation, and drainage works. The end result was a system of *permanent agriculture,* which enabled the Chinese to cultivate the same land for centuries without stripping the soil of its nutrients.

Constructing such a system presupposes a strong central government. A project as ambitious as the transformation of the natural environment in the ancient world could not have been attempted without political continuity and stability, social cohesion, scientific planning, resource mobilization, labor conscription, and bureaucratic coordination on a truly extraordinary scale. Thus, the technology and logistics of China's system of permanent agriculture gave rise to a vast bureaucracy and justified a thoroughgoing, imperial dictatorship with several unusual (by European standards) characteristics. As early European travelers and traders noted, the Chinese government was the largest landowner (private ownership of property was severely restricted). Furthermore, governmental policies and programs were designed and implemented largely by a centralized bureaucracy whose officials were dedicated to efficient administration. Admission to this class was based not on heredity, property ownership, or wealth (as would have been the case in Europe) but on a series of examinations that revealed candidates' knowledge of the Confucian classics—and, through those works, the principles of right conduct—as well as mastery of the immensely complex written language. At the apex of the power pyramid sat the emperor, who ruled under the mandate of Heaven and whose power was absolute.

What about the average Chinese citizen under this highly centralized form of government? The average person traded food for labor and was regarded by the ruling powers primarily as a factor of production. Outside of imposing severe labor discipline on the common people, the bureaucracy left individuals alone. The government did not live in constant fear of popular revolution; Imperial China was a remarkably stable society. The fusion of religion and government, the fact that the masses were kept busy in rice cultivation and large-scale public works projects, the unavailability of modern weapons and communications technology, and the practice of rewarding the scholar-gentry class with great privileges and perquisites all combined to limit potential political opposition. This unique form of "hydraulic despotism" lasted longer than any other system of government the world has ever known.

Asian despotism presents us with a paradox of sorts. On the one hand, it stands as an example of a political regime more despotic than most traditional forms of Western authoritarianism:

> Oriental despotism was stronger and more pervasive than either modern European autocracy of the sixteenth-to-nineteenth-century kind or Roman power at most periods. Vast numbers of people were controlled and exploited by a few and on a scale far greater and with bureaucratic institutions far more elaborate than under the personal tyrannies of the city-states.[10]

On the other hand, Imperial China's economic and technical achievements, along with its art, language, and literature, were extremely impressive by any standard. Also, significant material advances accompanied China's early economic development. Although the emperors and scholar-officials were neither liberal nor politically enlightened, the Chinese system of hydraulic despotism resulted in a sufficient supply of food to support a large and growing population for centuries (albeit not without occasional famines). In view of the difficulties many Third World countries have experienced in trying to provide their people with food and shelter, the agricultural achievements of Imperial China seem even more remarkable.

A less breathtaking but somewhat similar modern-day phenomenon has been Asia's "little dragons," especially Singapore, Taiwan, and South Korea. Today, these countries are in the process of democratizing, a development encouraged by the West. Nonetheless, as essentially authoritarian states until very recently, it is only fair to note that they experienced impressive gains in gross domestic product and standard of living. Cooperation between government and private business was the key—an Asian form of corporatism. These programs implemented large-scale industrialization and encouraged manufacturing and technological developments for the purpose of dramatically increasing exports. The government safeguarded native industry by adopting a variety of protectionist strategies, such as trade barriers and currency manipulation. The current economic prowess of these nations is one of the legacies of authoritarian rule; it suggests that state action can serve the public interest even in the absence of freedom and democracy.

Authoritarian Rule Is the Worst Kind Possible

First, totalitarian states (see Chapter 5) go well beyond traditional autocracies in restricting individual freedom. Second, as noted earlier, different kinds of authoritarian governments exploit individual citizens to greater or lesser degrees. Some aim at economic growth and social reform, others do not. Some provide the essentials of life for their citizens, others are indifferent to the well-being of the masses. A few may even be efficient, reform-minded, and socially progressive. Third, for some developing countries, authoritarianism may be the only effective government possible (see Chapter 8). Finally, if the turbulence in many former Soviet satellite states in Eastern Europe is any indication, left-wing totalitarian government converts less readily to constitutional democracy than does authoritarian government.

When a nation must choose between anarchy, economic collapse, or social chaos on the one hand, and some kind of authoritarian government on the other, a dilemma arises. Under such conditions, some sort of dictatorship is perhaps necessary—at least temporarily. In the modern world, dictatorship increasingly appears to be essentially a temporary solution.

THE TWILIGHT OF AUTHORITARIANISM?

Although authoritarian governments represent the most straightforward and simple solution to establishing political order, some political scientists contend that authoritarianism is currently under siege. Between 1974 and 1990, more than thirty countries in Latin America, Asia, and Eastern Europe shifted from a nondemocratic to a democratic form of government.[11] Sometimes the collapse of communism is cited as an explanation for this phenomenon. Yet even before the collapse of communism in Eastern Europe, nondemocratic governments, especially in Latin America, were falling by the wayside. During the 1980s, Ecuador, Bolivia, Peru, Brazil, Uruguay, Argentina, Chile, and Paraguay replaced military rulers, opting for more democratic alternatives. Central American nations followed suit. Democracy has also made some inroads in sub-Saharan Africa in recent years. In 1990 alone, at least nine African countries held multiparty elections and another dozen or so adopted reforms designed to lead to such elections.[12] A few years later, South Africa's repressive apartheid system, based on a racist ideology of white supremacy, was abolished and replaced by majority rule.

How enduring (or ephemeral) the trend away from authoritarian governments will prove to be remains open to question. Can we look forward to a future when, for the first time in human history, nondemocratic regimes will be the exception and democracy will be the norm?

Certainly, the contemporary world features many examples of successful democracies and failed dictatorships. Furthermore, the prosperity commonly associated with democratic states encourages imitators and admirers (for an extended discussion of this point, see Chapter 8). In recent times, the democratic model appears to shine brightly.

And yet it is premature to proclaim an irreversible worldwide trend toward democracy. In the past, democracy has often suffered reversals.[13] Nor is it certain that this time things will be any different. Despite showing promise at the beginning of the decade, democracy does not appear to be working very well in Africa. For example, in the early 1990s, Zambia was a model of better things to come. In 1991, elections were held and Kenneth Kaunda, who had ruled Zambia for more than twenty-five years, lost to Frederick Chiluba. However, in 1996, when it was time for a new election, Chiluba banned Kaunda from running against him. As a respected British weekly observed, "this has become par for the African course."

> African elections are now seldom genuine tests of popular opinion. Except in one of two places, notably South Africa, democratic travesty is the pattern. All power tends to be concentrated in one person, the president. The government fixes the election; the opposition boycotts it or rejects the result; the government ignores the opposition. The problem is that tyrants have learnt how to control the voting. Boundaries, the media, the economy and the voters' roll are all manipulated. Opponents are squashed. Soldiers have also learnt how to play the game. Half the countries of west and central Africa are ruled by "elected" ex-soldiers, among them the bosses of the Gambia and Niger, both voted into office after recently overthrowing democratically elected governments.[14]

Africa is not the only region with an authoritarian history where fledgling democracies are now under attack. In Latin America, democracy is widespread yet remains fragile. Several countries, including Colombia, Peru, and Mexico, face major internal threats from guerrilla and terrorist groups. Further unrest is reflected in recent polls, with more than 70 percent of respondents stating they

GATEWAYS TO THE WORLD: EXPLORING CYBERSPACE

http://www.pbs.org/newshour/bb/middle_east

This site provides a further examination of the rise to power and the rule of Syrian leader Hafez al-Assad.

http://www.amnesty.org/ailib/intcam/nigeria/hrdint.html

Amnesty International's Web site is an excellent source of information for further exploration of the impact of Nigerian authoritarianism on human rights.

Many countries discussed in this chapter have individual Web sites devoted to aspects of their political, historical, and social culture. To find a list of these sites, use the name of the specific country of interest as your search term. You should pay particular attention to the group or individual who sponsors or maintains each Web site.

For instance, Shell Oil's Nigeria Web site is likely to take a very different stance on the impact of multinational corporations on the Nigerian economy than would the Web site of a patriotic Nigerian business leader.

were "not very satisfied" or "not at all satisfied" with the functioning of democracy in Latin America.[15]

What explains the continuing specter of authoritarianism in the postmodern world? In part, the answer lies in the great disparities in development and living standards found in different parts of today's world. There are countries in Eastern Europe, Asia, Latin America, the Middle East, as well as sub-Saharan Africa, where modern economies have yet to be created. Gross economic and educational disparities persist and worsen with the passage of time. Huge debt payments and a lack of resources burden local economies. Tribal or ethnic divisions destabilize many developing societies. And even in nations where the military has relinquished power or has been removed from office, prominent generals remain, often exerting a behind-the-scenes influence over civilian governments, sometimes biding their time in case the new governments are unable to overcome the severe social, economic, and political challenges they face. Thus, while democracy appears to be advancing around the world, many emerging democracies remain frail. In these circumstances, it is way too soon to write the obituary for authoritarian rule.

Summary

When one or more self-appointed rulers exercise unchecked political power the result is a dictatorship. Benevolent autocrats (who are somewhat concerned with advancing the public good), ordinary dictators (who are concerned solely with advancing their own interests), or tyrants (who exhibit great enthusiasm for violence and bloodletting) all qualify as dictators, but even slight differences can make a significant difference in the lives of the people who by definition have no voice in how they are governed.

Historically, authoritarian rulers have provided the most common form of government. Yet despite their prevalence, authoritarian regimes have been regarded as perversions of good government because they almost always place the ruler's interests ahead of the public good. Nigeria provides a good example of a contemporary authoritarian state.

Misconceptions about authoritarian regimes abound. It is not true that dictatorial rule is a modern phenomenon or that all authoritarian states are identical, illegitimate, or unpopular with their citizens. Further, such governments can be differentiated on moral grounds: Some seek to promote the public interest; others do not. Moreover, authoritarian regimes do not represent the worst possible form of government in all cases.

Finally, although there is some evidence that authoritarian government is giving way to democracy, it is too early to draw any definitive conclusions.

Key Terms

authoritarianism	junta
autocracy	coup d'état
oligarchy	charismatic leader

Review Questions

1. What are the two basic types of nondemocratic government? Are authoritarian governments becoming less prevalent? Where are such governments found today?

2. What are the chief characteristics of authoritarian governments?

3. Are all autocrats tyrannical? Explain.

4. What kind of "advice" did Machiavelli give to rulers bent on maintaining their power?

5. Summarize the six myths that surround authoritarian governments. What are the fallacies associated with these myths?

Recommended Reading

BOESCHE, ROGER. *Theories of Tyranny, from Plato to Arendt.* University Park: Pennsylvania State Press, 1996. Many authoritarian rulers have been tyrants, and tyranny has been a subject of study for the greatest political thinkers. This book examines both.

CRICK, BERNARD. *Basic Forms of Government: A Sketch and a Model.* Magnolia, Mass.: Peter Smith, 1994. A short yet comprehensive outline of types of governments that contrasts authoritarian with totalitarian and democratic states.

LATEY, MAURICE. *Patterns of Tyranny.* New York: Atheneum, 1969. A study that attempts to classify and analyze various tyrannies throughout history.

MACHIAVELLI, NICCOLÒ. *The Prince.* (Trans. Harvey C. Mansfield, Jr.) Chicago: University of Chicago Press, 1985. This classic study describes the methods tyrants must use to maintain power.

MOORE, BARRINGTON. *Social Origins of Dictatorship and Democracy.* Boston: Beacon Press, 1993. A general discussion of the relationship between social conditions and political systems.

RUBIN, BARRY. *Modern Dictators: Third World Coup Makers, Strongmen, and Political Tyrants.* New York: New American Library/Dutton, 1989. A good general discussion of various nondemocratic regimes that have held power in the post–World War II era.

Notes

1. Bernard Crick, *Basic Forms of Government: A Sketch and a Model* (London: Macmillan, 1980), 53.
2. Aristotle, *The Politics,* trans. and ed. Ernest Barker (New York: Oxford University Press, 1962), 1279a, 112. [Emphasis ours.]
3. Ibid., 1313b, 245.
4. Ibid., 1312b, 240.
5. Maurice Latey, *Patterns of Tyranny* (New York: Atheneum, 1969), 115.
6. Fyodor Dostoyevsky, *The Brothers Karamazov,* ed. Ernest Rhys (London: Dent, 1927), 259.
7. Crick, *Basic Forms of Government,* 35.
8. See Karl Wittfogel, *Oriental Despotism: A Comparative Study of Total Power* (New York: Random House, 1981).
9. Ibid.
10. Crick, *Basic Forms of Government,* 36.
11. Samuel P. Huntington, "How Countries Democratize," *Political Science Quarterly* 106, no. 4 (1991–92): 579.
12. Robert M. Press, "Africa's Struggle for Democracy," *Christian Science Monitor,* March 21, 1991, 4.
13. Huntington, "How Countries Democratize," 579.
14. "Polls to Nowhere," *Economist,* November 23, 1996, 20–21.
15. "The Backlash in Latin America," *Economist,* November 30, 1996, 19.

© Bettmann / CORBIS

TOTALITARIAN STATES

FAILED UTOPIAS

ALMOST ALL NONDEMOCRATIC (authoritarian) states have been headed by a dictator or an autocrat intent on maintaining political power, often at any cost (see Chapter 4). In the twentieth century, a new and extreme form of tyranny appeared—*totalitarianism*. The term itself denotes complete domination of a society and its members by tyrannical rulers and imposed beliefs.

This obsession with control extends beyond the public realm into the private lives of citizens. So extensive is governmental power that the regime seeks not simply to control the human beings within its reach, but also to transform human nature. For the totalitarian tyrant, *absolutely everything is political*, including work, education, religion, sports, social organizations, and even the family (as neighbors spy on neighbors and children are encouraged to report "disloyal" parents). Inevitably, as these regimes attempt to transform society according to an ideological blueprint, they exterminate all "enemies of the people." Enemies are defined in terms of whole categories or groups within society and therefore typically encompass hundreds of thousands and even millions of innocent people who in most cases are not "political" by any objective standards. In these two crucial respects, totalitarian regimes differ from more traditional, nondemocratic authoritarian states. Authoritarian governments typically seek to maintain political power (rather than transform society) while more narrowly defining political enemies as individuals (not groups) who are actively involved in opposing the existing state.

Totalitarianism profoundly influenced the course of the twentieth century but, with the collapse of the Soviet-style communism in Eastern Europe in 1989 and the Soviet Union itself a few years later, this extreme form of tyranny appears to have fallen into a steep decline. Why then study totalitarian states at all? At least four reasons come to mind. First, communism is not the only form of totalitarian state possible. The examples of Nazi Germany and Fascist Italy are reminders that totalitarianism is not a product of one ideology, regime, or ruler. Second, totalitarianism is an integral part of contemporary history and stands in sharp contrast to the pronouncements of politicians, professors, theologians, and a host of others who optimistically proclaimed a belief in human progress. Many people who suffered directly at the hands of totalitarian dictators or lost loved ones in Hitler's Holocaust, Stalin's Reign of Terror, Mao's horrific purges, or other, more recent instances of totalitarian brutality are still living. The physical and emotional scars of the victims remain even after the tyrants who inflicted the injuries and perpetrated the injustices are long gone. Third, totalitarian states demonstrate the risks of idealism gone awry. Based on a millenarian vision of social progress and perfection that cannot be pursued without resort to barbaric measures (and cannot be achieved even then), they have all failed miserably as experiments in utopian nationbuilding. Fourth, totalitarianism remains a possibility wherever there is great poverty, justice, and therefore the potential for violence and turmoil—in other words, in vast parts of today's world.

It is dangerous to assume that the world has seen the last of the totalitarian tyrants. Indeed, the terrorist attack on the United States in the fall of 2001 raises a poignant question: Is it possible that future totalitarian threats to peace and freedom will not necessarily be posed by a figure who heads a government or rules a state? Is Osama bin Laden and his al Qaeda network such a threat? After all, the

Taliban regime in Afghanistan, which harbored bin Laden and his organization, itself displayed many of the characteristics of a totalitarian state. We will return to this question several times in the pages that follow. One of the lessons of September 11, 2001, is this: Civilized people everywhere need to study extremism in all its political manifestations in order to guard against the resurgence of powerful *mass movements* with opportunistic leaders for whom civilization has no meaning.

THE ESSENCE OF TOTALITARIANISM

Violence is at the core of every totalitarian state—controlled, systematic, state-inflicted violence. This violence often assumes the form of indiscriminate mass terror and genocide aimed at whole groups, categories, or classes of people who are labeled enemies, counterrevolutionaries, spies, or saboteurs. Even ordinary citizens are expected to demonstrate unconditional loyalty to the regime in a variety of ways and are subject to tight surveillance. Mass mobilization for political and economic purposes is carried out through a highly regimented and centralized one-party system dedicated to an all-encompassing ideology. To disseminate this ideology, the state employs a propaganda and censorship apparatus far more sophisticated and effective than that typically found in authoritarian states.

> Totalitarian governments aim at achieving total political, social, and economic control: Totalitarian dictatorship involves total domination, limited neither by received laws or codes (as in traditional authoritarianism) nor even the boundaries of governmental functions (as in classical tyranny), since they obliterate the distinction between state and society. . . . Totalitarianism is limited only by the need to keep large numbers of people in a state of constant activity controlled by the elite.[1]

Complete domination of society is necessary because totalitarian ideologies promise the advent of a new social order, whether it be the society of racially pure Aryan super race envisioned by Adolf Hitler's Nazi regime in Germany, or the proletarian brotherhood of oppressed and downtrodden workers promised by the Soviet leaders V. I. Lenin and Joseph Stalin, or the new mass society of selfless peasants fashioned in the poetic imagery of China's Mao Zedong. Whatever the specifics, the general vision of community conjured up in totalitarian ideologies—including that of Afghanistan's brutal Taliban rulers in recent times—has been remarkably similar. All such totalitarian prophets "have exhibited a basic likeness . . . in their determination to engender a higher and unprecedented kind of human existence."[2]

The totalitarian leader's claim of political legitimacy can be traced directly to this self-proclaimed aim of creating a new society. According to one expert, "The characteristic feature of totalitarian rule is the subjugation of both state and society together under a utopian, nonpolitical claim to rule."[3] In other words, totalitarian leaders assert that because the perfect social order can only be achieved by the bold action of self-ordained leaders who form a sort of quasi-religious priesthood, the forcible imposition of a set of beliefs on society is justified. A totalitarian ideology, then, can be defined as a "reasonably coherent body of ideas concerning practical means of how totally to change and reform a society by force, or violence, based on an all-inclusive or total criticism of what is wrong with the existing or antecedent society."[4]

The ideal societies prophesied by totalitarian movements commonly exalt such values as equality and community over liberty and individuality. As another authority put it:

> The total revolutionary's true community is perfectly comprehensive and thoroughly egalitarian: no social differences will remain; even authority and expertise, from the scientific to the artistic, cannot be tolerated. Such a radical egalitarianism must necessarily reject all individualism. The rights of the individual against the collectivity disappear, and normal constitutional rights are reinterpreted as rights to conform to the group. Claims against the group—to material goods, to restricted human relationships such as love, and to privacy—are condemned as divisive. In the name of equality, there is postulated a community of such solidarity that it can be said to have a consciousness of its own, and individual consciousness becomes at best an antisocial deviation.[5]

At the heart of this harmonious community lies the concept of a reformulated human nature. In totalitarian states, the wholesale reconstruction of the human personality becomes the nonnegotiable price of admission into the utopian society promised by the official ideology. This impulse to human perfection was reflected in Lenin's repeated references to the creation of a "new Soviet man" and in the Nazi assertion that party workers and leaders represented a new type of human being or a new breed of "racially pure" rulers. Mao Zedong displayed a near obsession with something he called *rectification*—the radical purging of all capitalist tendencies (such as materialism and individualism) at all levels of Chinese society. It is striking that all twentieth-century totalitarian movements have sought to transform not only the public life and outward appearance of society but also the private lives and innermost moral sense of society's members.

Not even the most repressive totalitarian regime, however, has managed to accomplish these transformations completely. In all totalitarian states, there have remained *"islands of separateness"*[6]—the family, the church, and other social institutions through which internal resistance to the prevailing government can survive. Not even the extraordinarily totalitarian government of the fictional state of Oceania, described by the famous British writer George Orwell in his chilling novel, *Nineteen Eighty-Four,* managed to master its citizens totally (although it came close enough to make for extraordinarily grim reading).

But if totalitarian states have not succeeded in reinventing human nature or building utopia, they have often had stunning success in silencing all opponents while carrying out radical (and ultimately disastrous) programs of social transformation. Totalitarian rulers have understood that no new community of fellow believers can survive in the midst of dissenters, deviants, skeptics, and enemies. That the ends and means they have adopted are at odds with reason and common sense matters not. Nor do they recognize moral limits to the exercise of political power. Today's rising star can become tomorrow's enemy of the people depending only on whatever is deemed expedient at a particular moment. When the professed goal is not merely to get and keep control of a government but to change the world, extraordinary political measures can easily be justified—way too easily.

No sacrifice can be too great, no price too high, to follow the leader to the promised land.

The clearest examples of such utopian political orders have been Nazi Germany, the Soviet Union (especially during Stalin's Reign of Terror), and Maoist China. Totalitarianism, however, has not been confined to these countries. Nor has it disappeared entirely from the political map of the world. Finally, even where it has disappeared, the scars of totalitarian tyranny are deep and continue to have a disfiguring effect on the political, social, and economic institutions of countries that are now living through a post-totalitarian era.

THE REVOLUTIONARY STAGE OF TOTALITARIANISM

How do totalitarian movements start? Typically, they are conceived in violence and emerge from the wreckage of a collapsed or collapsing state. Out of the revolutionary ferment of such turbulent times, a charismatic leader often emerges. Leadership is crucial to the success of any revolution. In the case of *total* revolution, leadership is one of five elements that deserve close examination; ideology, organization, propaganda, and violence are the other four.

Leadership

Perhaps the most conspicuous trait of total revolution has been reliance on what may be termed the *cult of leadership.* Virtually every such revolution has been identified with—indeed, personified in—the image of a larger-than-life figure. The Russian Revolution had its Lenin, the Third Reich its Hitler, the Chinese Revolution its Mao, Cuba its Castro, and so forth. Each of these leaders became the object of hero worship. Social thinker Eric Hoffer sums up the importance of leadership in modern mass movements as follows:

> Once the stage is set, the presence of an outstanding leader is indispensable. Without him there will be no movement. The ripeness of the times does not automatically produce a mass movement, nor can elections, laws and administrative bureaus hatch one.
>
> It was Lenin who forced the flow of events into the channels of the Bolshevik revolution. Had he died in Switzerland, or on his way to Russia in 1917, it is almost certain that the other prominent Bolsheviks would have joined a coalition government. The result might have been a more or less liberal republic run chiefly by the bourgeoisie. In the case of Mussolini or Hitler the evidence is even more decisive: without them there would have been neither a Fascist nor a Nazi movement.[7]

Although revolutions have invariably been launched in the name of the masses, the initiative has always come from above. Revolutionary leaders instinctively understand that the masses alone possess the raw power to change the world but lack the will and direction. (For the Bolsheviks, the missing ingredient was "class consciousness"; for the Nazis, it was *Volksgeist* or "spirit of the German nation.") The inspiration and fanatical commitment to fuse a large number of self-interested individuals into a revolutionary mass movement cannot come from a bloodless abstraction such as "the party." But it can come from the personal dynamism of a charismatic leader, who can read the minds, capture the imagination, and win the hearts of the masses. (It is ironic that all modern mass movements have emphasized the personality of the leader while de-emphasizing the individuality of the followers.) A leader such as Lenin or Mao, then, is to a mass movement what a detonator is to a bomb—no matter how powerful (or lethal) the explosive in a bomb might be, it remains dormant and harmless until provided with an efficient trigger.

Ideology

Whatever the quality of leadership, total revolutions depend in the final analysis on the willingness of large numbers of converts to engage in extraordinary acts of self-sacrifice in the name of the cause. Such reckless devotion cannot be inspired by appeals to the rational faculty in human beings. It must arise, rather, from a believer's blind faith in the absolute truth provided by a comprehensive political doctrine.

The Need for a Scapegoat: Reinterpreting the Past   As a critique of the past, ideology generally focuses on some form of absolute evil to which all national (or worldwide) wrongs and social injustices can be attributed. To the revolutionary ideologue, the true causes of economic recession, inflation, military defeat, official corruption, national humiliation, moral decadence, and other perceived problems are rooted in the mysteries and plots of a rejected past.

Rarely is the absolute evil a disembodied force; almost always it assumes the form of a clearly identifiable enemy. If such an enemy does not exist, one must be invented. Usually it has been an individual or a group that was already widely feared, hated, or envied. Lenin blamed the plight of the workers on money-grubbing capitalists. Hitler blamed the German loss in World War I and the economic crises that preceded his assumption of power on Jews and communists. Mao found his enemy first in wealthy landlords and later in "capitalist-roaders." Clearly, the purpose of these ploys was to focus mass attention on a readily identifiable scapegoat, on whose shoulders all of the nation's ills could be placed.

In the words of one authority, "Mass movements can rise and spread without a belief in God, but never without a belief in a devil."[8] Hate and prejudice, rather than love and high principle, are seemingly the most effective forces in bringing people together in a common cause. The deliberate cultivation of a hate object not only serves to focus blame for the injustices of the past but also helps to mobilize the masses against the alleged cause of the miseries of the present.

Revolutionary Struggle: Explaining the Present   As a guide to the present, ideology provides the *true believer* with keys to a "correct" analysis of the underlying forces at work in contemporary society. Concepts such as class struggle for Marxist-Leninists, *Herrenvolk* (the "master race") for the Nazis, and "contradictions" for Mao's followers were used as tools to explain and predict social reality. Yesterday the enemy was preeminent; today the enemy will be defeated.

Advocates of total revolution believe that struggle is the very essence of politics. For Marxist-Leninists, class struggle was the engine of progress in history. For

Maoists, struggle was a desirable end in itself; only through the direct experience of revolutionary struggle, they believed, could the masses (especially the young) learn the true meaning of self-sacrifice. Hitler glorified the struggle for power by proclaiming war to be the supreme test of national greatness. (Revealingly, Hitler outlined his own path to political power in a book titled *Mein Kampf,* "my struggle.") Whether the aim is to overthrow monopoly capitalists or to purify a race, revolutionary struggle is always described in terms of good versus evil. It was common for leading Nazis to depict Jews not simply as enemies of the state but as *untermenschen* ("subhumans") and, frequently, as insects or lice.[9] Of course, the repeated use of such degrading characterizations eventually serves to dehumanize the scapegoat group in the mass mind; it is easier to justify the extermination of insects than of human beings.

Utopia: Foretelling the Future   As a promise of the future, ideology tends to paint a radiant picture of perfect justice and perpetual peace. Marxist-Leninists envisioned this utopia as a classless society, one from which all social and economic inequality would be abolished. The Nazi utopia was a society from which all racial "impurities" would be removed through the extermination or enslavement of racial "inferiors." Whatever its precise character, this motivating vision invariably included the promise of material plenty stemming from the redistribution of property from the haves to the have-nots. Marxism-Leninism promised to take from the rich (the bourgeoisie) and give to the poor (the proletariat). Interestingly, Hitler made a similar promise when he proclaimed his intention to provide *lebensraum* ("living space") in the east; he would take land away from the land-rich but slothful Slavs and give it to the land-poor but industrious Germans.

   Inherent in these visions of utopia is almost always an ironclad guarantee of success in the struggle to achieve them. Thus, Marxism is based on a deterministic worldview (in the sense that the success of the proletarian revolution is dictated by inflexible "laws" of history). Hitler, too, was an unabashed determinist. In *Mein Kampf,* he wrote, "Man must realize that a fundamental law of necessity reigns throughout the whole realm of Nature."[10] And throughout this public career, he spoke frequently of "the iron law of our historical development," the "march of history," and the "inner logic of events." Hitler, no less than Lenin, Stalin, or Mao, claimed that he (and the German *volk*) had a world-shattering mission to accomplish and that success was inevitable. He expressed this notion in what is perhaps his most famous (or infamous) pronouncement: "I go the way that Providence dictates with the assurance of a sleepwalker."

Ideology and Truth   The past, present, and future as described by a given revolutionary ideology may seem far-fetched or even ludicrous to a disinterested observer. For example, the racial theory promulgated by the Nazis utterly lacked historical, sociological, genetic, and moral foundations. By the same token, the economic facet of Hitler's ideology—the "socialism" in National Socialism—was devoid of meaningful content. So watered down was Hitler's conception of socialism that in the words of one authority, "anyone genuinely concerned about the people was in Hitler's eyes a socialist."[11]

Why would anyone take such an ideology seriously? First, it appealed to popular prejudices and made them respectable. Second, it was not the message that counted so much as the messenger—the leader's personal magnetism attracted a following whether or not the words made sense. Third, certitude was far more important than rectitude.

Consider all that an ideology must do for the individual follower if it is to be successful:

> It must claim scientific authority which gives the believer a conviction of having the exclusive key to all knowledge; it must promise a millennium to be brought about for the chosen race or class by the elect who holds this key; it must identify a host of ogres and demons to be overcome before this happy state is brought about; it must enlist the dynamic of hatred, envy, and fear (whether of class or race) and justify these low passions by the loftiness of its aims; every means and every crime is laudable in overcoming the adversary, and the virtues of the enemy can be turned into vices by attaching some simple label, such as "bourgeois," to them; in particular, truth is what is to the advantage of the chosen class or race, falsehood what is contrary to that interest; since this truth is scientifically demonstrable and since no two people are likely to agree about it, there must be a single interpreter, whose will is law, if the ideology is to be fully effective; as the bearer of all truth, the leader is entitled to expect from his followers religious devotion and every sacrifice and every crime that will promote his interest.[12]

In the final analysis, ideologues can often get away with the most absurd allegations and falsehoods if they also address real problems faced by ordinary people. Thus, many Germans recognized the extremist nature of the Nazis' racial theories but probably believed that such absurdities would be discarded by Hitler once the work of unifying the country, reviving the economy, and restoring the nation's lost honor had been accomplished. By the same token, it is doubtful that any but the most committed Bolsheviks believed that the workers' paradise was just around the corner, but the Russian people likely did believe in land reform, an end to Russia's disastrous involvement in World War I, and improvements in nutrition, medical care, and education as promised by Lenin.

Organization

Ideology in total revolutions cannot be implemented without sustained organization. Cohesive structure was one of the missing ingredients in pre-twentieth century rebellions. Most such outbreaks were spontaneous affairs; they burst into flame, occasionally spread, but almost always burned themselves out.

Different revolutionary leaders have stressed different methods of formal organization in their quest for political power. Although the Bolshevik party did not actually seize power in Russia until October 1917, Lenin had founded the party more than fourteen years earlier. Admitting only hard-core revolutionaries into the party, Lenin reasoned that the czar could be defeated only by a long, clandestine struggle. Thus, a small, tightly knit group of professional revolutionaries would be far more effective in the long run than a large, amorphous mass of unruly malcontents.

To ensure secrecy, discipline, and centralized control, Lenin organized the Bolshevik party into tiny *cells,* later called *primary party organizations.* Each cell had a leader, dubbed a secretary, who acted on orders or instructions from above. Ultimately, all important decisions on strategy, tactics, and the "party line" were made by Lenin himself (though he claimed to speak in the name of the party's **Central Committee**). As the Bolsheviks grew in number and established cells in cities outside their St. Petersburg headquarters, intermediate layers of authority became necessary, but the principles of strict party discipline and total subordination of lower levels to higher ones were not relaxed.

Having formed his own faction, Lenin eventually placed a formal ban on factionalism. Any Bolshevik who thereafter opposed the party line stood in danger of being labeled a factionalist. Before the actual seizure of power in October 1917, the penalty for dissent was frequently expulsion from the party; after 1917, revolutionary justice was often less lenient. Factionalism was not tolerated; party members were expected to place party interests above personal interests at all times. This spirit of self-sacrifice and total commitment to the party was given a special name—*partiinost,* a term commonly used in the former Soviet Union to denote the distinctive combination of intangible qualities (such as loyalty, self-discipline, and revolutionary élan) that every party member was expected to exhibit.

In comparison with Lenin's revolution, Mao's took more than twenty years to achieve success and involved many more people. Unlike its Russian counterpart, the Chinese Revolution was primarily a rural phenomenon involving a mass of discontented peasants. Under these circumstances, Mao's most pressing organizational problem was to mold the peasants into an effective military force capable of carrying out a protracted guerrilla war. His success in turning an amorphous peasant mass into an effective fighting force seemed to offer convincing proof that once organized, the poor and downtrodden could overcome seemingly insurmountable obstacles. For this reason, Mao's theory and practice of peasant-based revolution have been regarded by many radicals (especially in developing nations) as the guiding example of revolutionary organization in a rural society.

In contrast to Mao's long, concerted struggle to achieve political power, Hitler's attempts to gain power in Germany followed an erratic course, swinging from a violent, abortive coup in the early 1920s to a successful manipulation of the country's constitutional system in the 1930s. A compliant organization in the form of the Nazi party was crucial to Hitler's ultimate success.

During his rise to power, Hitler made extensive use of brute force to intimidate his opposition, but he also created numerous party-controlled clubs and associations. The Hitler Youth, a Nazi women's league, a Nazi workers' organization, a Nazi student league, and various other academic and social organizations gave the Nazis considerable political power even before Hitler took over the reins of government (see Figure 9-3 on page 270). Later, through a policy called *Gleichschaltung* ("coordination"), he destroyed virtually all preexisting social organizations and substituted Nazi associations in their place. Partly for this reason, Hitler's promises and threats carried great weight throughout German society. Like all modern revolutionaries, Hitler understood the value of a carefully constructed revolutionary organization.

Propaganda

As modern political life has extended its reach to more and more people, *propaganda*—the broad dissemination of ideas and information deliberately tailored to further a political cause—has become a potent political weapon. To be successful, as Hitler noted, propaganda must address the masses exclusively; hence "its effect for the most part must be aimed at the emotions and only to a very limited degree at the so-called intellect."[13]

An avid student of the science of propaganda, Hitler formulated several theorems about the subject that still hold true today. To begin with, he postulated that "all propaganda must be popular and its intellectual level must be adjusted to the most limited intelligence among those it is addressed to." Hence, "the greater the mass it is intended to reach, the lower its purely intellectual level will have to be. . . . Effective propaganda must be limited to a very few points and must harp on these in slogans until the last member of the public understands what you want him to understand." Given these premises, it follows that the "very first axiom of all propagandist activity [is] the basically subjective and onesided

Through the implementation of an immense propaganda campaign in combination with the inculcation of the Nazi ideology, Adolf Hitler (1889–1945) was able to persuade the German people of the need to persecute Jews, the necessity of an eventual war, and the radical transformation of German society.

attitude it must take toward every question it deals with."[14] Furthermore, the bigger the lie, the better.

Hitler argued that the success of any propaganda campaign depends on the propagandists' understanding of the "primitive sentiments" of the popular masses. Propaganda cannot have multiple shadings: Concepts and "facts" must be presented to the public as true or false, right or wrong, black or white. In *Mein Kampf*, Hitler heaped high praise on British propaganda efforts in World War I and expressed contempt for German propaganda, which he faulted for not painting the world in stark black-and-white terms.

Long before Hitler's rise to power, Lenin developed and refined his own techniques of mass propaganda. Lenin began by making a distinction between propaganda and agitation. His explanation of the difference between the two should be considered in light of Hitler's theorems:

> A propagandist, when he discusses unemployment, must explain the capitalist nature of the crisis; he must show the reason for its inevitability in modern society; he must describe the necessity of rebuilding society on a Socialist basis, etc. In a word, he must give many ideas concentrated all together, so many that all of them will not be understood by the average person, and in their totality they will be understood by relatively few.
>
> The agitator, on the other hand, will pick out one more or less familiar and concrete aspect of the entire problem. Let us say the death of an unemployed worker as a result of starvation. His efforts will be concentrated on this fact, to impart to the masses a single idea—the idea of the senseless contradiction between the growth of wealth and the growth of poverty. He will strive to evoke among the masses discontent and revolt against this great injustice and will leave the full explanation for this contradiction to the propagandists.[15]

Unlike Hitler, who was a highly effective orator, Lenin was a master pamphleteer and polemicist who relied most heavily on the written word. In the infancy of his movement, Lenin's chief weapon was the underground newspaper. Endowed with such names as *Iskra* ("The Spark"), *Vperyod* ("Forward"), and *Proletari* ("Proletariat"), these contraband tabloids often had to be produced in some remote corner of the country, or even in a foreign country, and smuggled into Saint Petersburg in false-bottom briefcases or by other methods.

Violence

The fifth and final characteristic of totalitarian revolution is the use of violence and terror as accepted instruments of political policy. For revolutionaries, violence is particularly useful in reinforcing the political effect of propaganda. One student of modern totalitarian tyranny has observed that "terror without propaganda would lose most of its psychological effect, whereas propaganda without terror does not contain its full punch."[16] And according to the Nazi theorist Eugene Hadamovsky, "Propaganda and violence are never contradictions. Use of violence can be part of the propaganda."[17]

The kind of violence commonly associated with terrorism ranges from highly selective acts such as assassinations and kidnappings to indiscriminate bombings and sabotage that result in death and injury to innocent bystanders. Sabotage is designed to disrupt production, transportation, and communications systems and thereby the political stability of the state; terror is aimed at attacking the psychological sense of personal security, a precondition for social stability.

Terror in support of propaganda has played a prominent role in mass movements of both the Right and the Left. One of the most striking examples is that provided by the *fasci di combattimento* ("combat groups") formed by the Italian Fascist party leader Benito Mussolini shortly after World War I. After attempts to gain power by wooing the working class away from the Socialist party had failed, Mussolini began to cultivate the middle classes and to seek financing from the wealthy industrialists and big landowners. Convinced of the impossibility of capturing control of the Italian government by legal means, in the early 1920s he turned increasingly toward terror as a means of dealing with political opponents. His followers thus substituted arson and assassination for the normal, nonviolent means of political competition. One of the more novel forms of terror devised by the Fascists was the *punitive expedition*, in which armed bands conducted raids against unsuspecting and defenseless communities. The local police often would cooperate by doing nothing.

The punitive expeditions mounted by the Italian Fascists epitomized the strategy and tactics of terror as part of totalitarian revolution. Cleverly employed, terrorism can create a sense of utter defenselessness in the face of an imminent but often indistinct danger. The aim of the terrorists is threefold: (1) to create an artificial atmosphere of crisis; (2) to demonstrate that the state is no longer capable of providing law-abiding, taxpaying citizens with protection from unprovoked attacks on their persons and property; and (3) to prod an increasingly fearful, desperate, and fragmented citizenry to turn for refuge and order to the very same political movement that, unbeknown to most, has caused the deepening state of social degeneration.

Hannah Arendt provides an especially lucid explanation of the similar use of terror by the Nazis:

> The Nazis did not strike at prominent figures as had been done in the earlier wave of political crimes in Germany (the murder of Rathenau and Erzberger); instead, by killing small socialist functionaries or influential members of opposing parties, they attempted to prove to the population the danger involved in mere membership. This kind of mass terror, which still operated on a comparatively small scale, increased steadily because neither the police nor the courts seriously prosecuted political offenders on the so-called Right. It was valuable as what a Nazi publicist has aptly called "power propaganda": it made clear to the population at large that the power of the Nazis was greater than that of the authorities and that it was safer to be a member of a Nazi paramilitary organization than a loyal Republican. This impression was greatly strengthened by the specific use the Nazis made of their political crimes. They always admitted them publicly, never apologized for "excesses of the lower ranks"—such apologies were used only by Nazi sympathizers—and impressed the population as being very different from the "idle talkers" of other parties.
>
> The similarities between this kind of terror and plain gangsterism are too obvious to be pointed out. This does not mean that Nazism was gangsterish, as has sometimes been concluded, but only that the Nazis, without admitting it, learned as much from

American gangster organizations as their propaganda admittedly learned from American business publicity.[18]

THE CONSOLIDATION OF POWER

Once the old order has been overthrown or fatally discredited, the totalitarian leadership can operate from a solid power base within the government. The next task it faces is the elimination of any competing political parties and factions. Party officials must then be placed in charge of all governmental functions throughout the country—especially in any provinces that were not particularly supportive of the revolutionary movement during its early stages. The final step in the consolidation process is the elimination of all those within the party who pose a real or potential danger to the totalitarian leader.

Throughout this stage, the totalitarian leader, like the traditional authoritarian ruler, is primarily concerned with the acquisition and maintenance of power. At the ruler's disposal are the same tools and methods used in the revolutionary stage of the movement. Ideology and propaganda serve to justify and popularize the leader's actions. Violence may be used to intimidate and silence opponents. The party organization provides the leader with tangible proof of popularity (the group of loyal followers) and power (the party faithful become the eyes and ears of the omnipotent state).

Perhaps the chief tool available to would-be totalitarian rulers at this stage is their own skill. A number of correct decisions must be made if they are to succeed. They must know exactly what to do and must not shrink from doing it. Careful calculation, not conscience, must be the guide. In these matters, Machiavelli's advice is especially valuable: "One ought not to say to someone whom one wants to kill, 'Give me your gun, I want to kill you with it,' but merely, 'Give me your gun,' for once you have the gun in your hand, you can satisfy your desire."[19] The relevance of such advice becomes obvious as we examine the methods used by aspiring totalitarian rulers to consolidate their power.

Eliminating Opposition Parties

The first step toward political consolidation is the elimination of all competing parties and independent factions. The ruling party must be the only legitimate political organization in the state for two reasons. First, there is the traditional concern of all absolute rulers: Any opposition group, no matter how small or ineffectual it seems, poses a potential danger to the ruler. Second, the mere existence of political opponents inhibits the wholesale changes in domestic and foreign policy mandated by the movement's ideology. Thus, political opposition must be eradicated by any means possible.

Lenin solved the problem of rival parties, one of which (the Socialist Revolutionaries) was substantially more popular than his own (the Bolsheviks), through the brilliant use of the age-old tactic of divide and conquer. (One observer refers to Lenin's strategy as *salami tactics*[20] because of his extraordinary ability to eliminate opponents by slicing up small but potentially dangerous groups, piece by piece.) Thus, after the new revolutionary legislature, called the Constituent Assembly, was elected, Lenin exploited an already existing division in the dominant Socialist Revolutionary party by forming an alliance with its left wing. This alliance enabled Lenin to move against the party's more moderate wing, as well as against other rightist parties, and gave him sufficient legislative support to close down the Constituent Assembly altogether. As expected, the alliance with the left-wing Socialist Revolutionaries was cast aside as soon as it no longer suited Lenin's purposes.

Lenin's strategy was not confined to the dismemberment of opposing political parties. Another target was the Soviet Union's huge peasant population, among whom the Bolshevik leader initially had little support. The lack of peasant support became a particularly acute problem during the civil war (1918–20), when food-stuffs and other basic necessities were extremely scarce. In response, Lenin "instituted in the villages a 'civil war within a civil war' by setting poor peasants against those who were less poor,"[21] thereby helping to undermine the political opposition.

Lenin's salami tactics represent only one method by which opponents and rival parties have been eliminated by totalitarian movements. Mao Zedong, in contrast, was compelled by circumstances to fight his main adversary—the *Kuomintang,* or Nationalist government, led by Chiang Kai-shek—in a protracted guerrilla war. Hitler chose still another strategy. Bolstered by his Nazi party's steadily growing popularity in the polls, a formidable following of true believers, superb oratorical skills, and a special group of shock troops known as storm troopers, he played a waiting game. By 1933, Hitler had maneuvered himself into the chancellorship of Germany by shrewdly preying on the fears and political limitations of the people in power. Once in office, he gradually expanded his authority, first by gaining passage of new emergency powers, then by suspending civil liberties, and, finally, by ending meaningful democracy in Germany.

Only then, operating from a position of strength, did he move to shut down all opposition parties. Unlike Mao, who struggled against opposing forces militarily, Hitler employed native cunning and the charade of legality to destroy his opponents politically before using the power of the state to begin destroying them physically.

Purging Real or Imagined Rivals within the Party

Purges constitute the last step on the road to total power. In conducting purges, totalitarian governments almost invariably charge perceived rivals with subversive activities detrimental to the movement and the nation. Whether the charges are accurate is immaterial: They merely provide the totalitarian ruler with a public rationale for purging individuals perceived as threats or, at the very least, political liabilities. The downfall and, in many cases, sudden death of such "oppositionists" demonstrates to would-be dissidents the high price of crossing the supreme leader.

One author's observation that Mao Zedong "never hesitated to destroy his enemies [including] rival communists, Kuomintang activists, and 'landlords'"[22] can be applied to all successful totalitarian rulers. The scope and severity of such purges, however, can differ significantly from one ruler to the next. Hitler, for example, rid himself of party rivals in a single, almost surgically precise operation. By 1934, Hitler had become worried about the attitudes and actions of some of his oldest supporters, especially Ernst Röhm. As head of the SA (*Sturmabteilung*, or "storm troopers"), a group of roughnecks whose primary function had been to intimidate political opponents during Hitler's rise to power, Röhm had continued to advocate and instigate violent activities at the point when the Führer's "legal" control over the government was about to be consolidated fully. Moreover, Hitler wanted to replace the SA with the more disciplined and reliable legions of the SS (*Schutzstaffel*, or "security echelon"). All attempts to persuade Röhm and his compatriots to go along with these plans failed. So Hitler turned on Röhm and other party members who had been instrumental in the Nazis' rise to power; on the Führer's orders, the Röhm faction was murdered in June 1934. Blaming the whole incident on his political enemies, Hitler used the Röhm purge to his advantage, solidifying his support within Germany and focusing on the (allegedly) grave danger facing the nation.

Lenin's purges were more widespread. In 1921, following the elimination of all competing parties, he turned his attention to the people who challenged his leadership within the movement itself. Thousands of trade unionists and sailors, formerly the backbone of the Bolsheviks' popular support, were murdered by the secret police when they demanded free trade unions and elections. Next Lenin dealt with the so-called Workers' Opposition faction of the Bolshevik party, which was demanding that the party reverse its previous policy and grant the workers control of their own industries. Lenin pronounced the group guilty of "factionalism" and accused it of endangering both the party and the revolution. The members of the Workers' Opposition group were expelled from the party—but, significantly, they were not murdered.

Such relatively mild actions were not characteristic of Lenin's successor, Joseph Stalin, who as the head of the Soviet Communist party (1924–53) did not hesitate to murder those whom he perceived as political enemies. Stalin's ultimate success in subduing his political enemies hinged on two key factors. First, he masterfully adapted Lenin's salami tactics—used by Lenin to subdue rival parties, but by Stalin against rivals within his own party. Second, Stalin showed an extraordinary talent for political infighting. He turned out to be the most active, single-minded, and iron-willed member of Lenin's inner circle, a factor that proved decisive in the succession struggle that followed Lenin's death in 1924.

Creating a Monolithic Society

Totalitarian rule requires enormous organizational control over the larger society, for it seeks a complete societal transformation. Therefore, it must gain control over the economy, the arts, the military, the schools, the government—in short, over every aspect of society. Nothing can be allowed to escape its grasp, and no method of maintaining control can be ruled out. As Nazi propaganda chief Joseph Goebbels remarked, "The revolution we have made is a total revolution . . . it is completely irrelevant what means it uses."[23] No facet of society—not political parties, not religion, not artistic expression, not education or academic freedom—can be allowed to block the creation of the new society. In such matters, the totalitarian leader's will is supreme. In the words of another Nazi official, "If the brains of all university professors were put at one end of the scale and the brains of the Führer at the other, which end, do you think, would tip?"[24]

For this program of total control to succeed, loyal followers must be put in charge of all elements of government and society in every town and region. This process was particularly well documented in Hitler's Germany.[25] Even in small towns, officeholders who had not publicly supported the Nazis were stripped of their power. Simultaneously, numerous "enemies of the people" were "discovered" and swiftly and harshly punished by the brutal *Gestapo* (secret police). The severity of these punishments, the alleged omnipresence of the Gestapo, and the purported manifestations of mass support for the Nazis were well publicized and deliberately exaggerated in the media as well as by word of mouth. Citizens had no doubt about the fate that awaited those who opposed the Nazis. Intimidation and coercion thus contributed immensely to the Nazis' success.

The effectiveness of these terror tactics helps to explain why there was so little overt resistance to the Nazi takeover, but it does not tell the whole story. The Nazis may have been able to gain power primarily through the use of intimidation, but moral apathy and self-interest played important roles as well. This point is perhaps best illustrated by a true story told by a German refugee who had been on the faculty of the prestigious University of Frankfurt. At the time of the Nazi takeover, this university had the reputation of being an exemplary (and unusually liberal) academic institution, with a faculty that epitomized professional commitment to scholarship, freedom of conscience, and democracy.[26] It was believed that if the Nazis could gain control of the University of Frankfurt without major incident, they would be able to use strong-arm methods to control all of German academia. Opponents of the Nazis hoped, in particular, that the party would find it difficult to overcome the opposition of a famous biochemist-physiologist on the Frankfurt faculty whose worldwide academic reputation was matched by his humane and compassionate attitude toward life. Following the appointment of a Nazi commissar at the university, every professor and graduate assistant was summoned for an important faculty meeting:

> The new Nazi commissar wasted no time on the amenities. He immediately announced that Jews would be forbidden to enter university premises and would be dismissed without salary on March 15; this was something no one had thought possible despite the Nazis' loud anti-Semitism. Then he launched into a tirade of abuse, filth, and four-letter words such as had been heard rarely even in the barracks and never before in academia. He pointed his finger at one department chairman after another and said, "You either do what I tell you or we'll put you into a concentration camp." There was silence when he finished; everybody waited for the distinguished biochemist-physiologist.
>
> The great liberal got up, cleared his throat, and said, "Very interesting, Mr. Commissar, and in some respects very illuminating; but one point I didn't get too clearly. Will there be more money for research in Physiology?" The meeting broke up shortly

thereafter with the commissar assuring the scholars that indeed there would be plenty of money for "racially pure science." A few of the professors had the courage to walk out with their Jewish colleagues, but most kept a safe distance from these men who only a few hours earlier had been their close friends.[27]

Such human frailties—weakness of will, moral blindness, and surpassing self-interest—together with ruthless strong-arm tactics, made it comparatively easy for the Nazis to place party members in positions of political authority.

THE TRANSFORMATION OF SOCIETY

Consolidating political power represents only a prelude to the most distinctive stage in the life cycle of the totalitarian state, the attempted transformation of society according to the dominant political doctrines of the state. This stage generally coincides with the regime's assumption of control over the economy and requires active government planning and intervention.[28] In justifying the drive for a new social order, the regime usually cites the widespread social disorder that lingers in the wake of every revolution, charging that all instability is caused by counter-revolutionaries, spies, and saboteurs.

At this point, totalitarian regimes clearly manifest their salient characteristics, which inevitably reflect the revolutionary movements that gave birth to them. Carl Friedrich and Zbigniew Brzezinski, two respected students of this subject, have identified six characteristics shared by all totalitarian governments.[29] Each state posits an official *ideology*, a set of political ideas that explains reality and justifies the actions of the government in the name of some future state of happiness. Each possesses a single, hierarchical *party* that is intertwined with or superior to the government. Each relies on a *secret police* willing and able to carry out campaigns of terror against enemies of the state, and each maintains a tight grip on the *armed forces* and all other instruments of organized violence. Each also seeks to exercise a *monopoly on the means of mass communication*, which are used to spread official propaganda. Finally, each totalitarian state exercises *central control over the economy*, through which it attempts to bring about drastic social change. In essence, these characteristics of totalitarian government derive from the components of the revolutionary movement (leadership, ideology, organization, propaganda, and violence), now redirected to the state's day-to-day administration and transformation.

Generally speaking, the attempted transformation of the state follows predetermined ideological prescriptions, occasionally influenced by more pragmatic concerns. Nonetheless, totalitarian regimes put much greater stock in adhering to their ideology than in responding to practical concerns at this stage. Examples taken from the political careers of Stalin, Hitler, and Mao illustrate this point.

The Soviet Union under Stalin

In 1928, having defeated his political rivals, Stalin stood poised to launch his drive to collectivize and industrialize the Soviet economy. His first Five-Year Plan for the economy (1928–32) marked the beginning of a cataclysmic phase in the history of the Soviet Union. Over the next ten years, millions of innocent people were killed or sent to labor camps, and a whole class of relatively well-to-do landholders, the *kulaks,* ceased to exist. In addition, the whole pattern of Soviet agricultural production was radically reshaped.

To understand why Stalin would visit such a cataclysm on the Soviet countryside, we must first understand the preeminent role of ideology in totalitarian government. Stalin's first Five-Year Plan, which instituted a highly centralized economic system designed to foster rapid development of the Soviet economy, was motivated to a considerable degree by power politics. But the evidence suggests that Stalin was also truly committed to the ideological goal of creating an advanced industrial society based on Marxist-Leninist principles. Realizing this goal would not only provide a Marxist showcase for the rest of the world but would also protect the fledgling revolution from hostile "capitalist encirclement," Stalin decided that the only way to accomplish this remarkable feat would be to invest massively in heavy industry while squeezing every last drop of profit out of agriculture, the traditional foundation of the Russian economy. Here, Marxist-Leninist dogma reigned supreme. Private ownership of farmland, animals, and implements would have to be eliminated and farming "collectivized." Under Stalin's *collectivization* plan, most agricultural production was lodged in large cooperative units known as *kolkhozi* (collective farms), whose members shared whatever income was left after compulsory deliveries were made to the state, or in *sovkhozi* (state farms), whose laborers received wages.

Through this strategy, Stalin believed, industrial production could be doubled or even tripled during the period of the first Five-Year Plan. In effect, Soviet agriculture was collectivized to underwrite Soviet industrialization. By sweeping away all pockets of rural resistance and herding peasants into collective farms, the state could maximize political control and minimize obstacles to its draconian system of tax collections. "Taxes" in this case meant compulsory deliveries to the state of scarce food supplies, which were used to feed the growing army of industrial workers and to pay for imported capital goods.

Seen in this light, Stalin's collectivization drive, however costly in human terms, takes on the even more disturbing dimension of a cold, calculated plan in which moral constraints did not exist. As the plan progressed, Stalin was bothered not by its high human cost but by the fact that it did not seem to be working. One reason the plan did not work was the excessive amount of indiscriminate violence and brutality Stalin employed. Not only were the kulaks murdered or exiled, but whole communities of peasants were uprooted. Stories spread through the countryside of how Stalin's agents, combating the harsh effects of the remorseless Russian winter with excessive quantities of vodka, had machine-gunned whole villages. Many Russian peasants deliberately burned their crops and killed their cattle rather than cooperate with Stalin's requisition squads. The result was predictable. Despite an all-out national effort, industrial production grew only slightly, if at all. In the meantime, a killer famine depopulated the countryside.

Nevertheless, Stalin did not admit to any personal failure. He simply ignored the hunger and deprivation brought on by his economic policies and fabricated statistics to "prove" that real progress was being made. No one dared to question these figures. In the words of one expert, "The Stalin regime was ruthlessly consistent: All facts that did not agree, or were likely to disagree, with the official fiction—data on crop yields, criminality, true incidences of 'counterrevolutionary' activities . . . were treated as nonfacts."[30]

But Stalin, concerned that his policies were creating new and hidden enemies, did become increasingly paranoid. In 1934, after the first Five-Year Plan had come to an unspectacular end, the Soviet dictator declared that he had uncovered a far-reaching conspiracy, orchestrated by foreign agents and counterrevolutionaries, to resurrect capitalism in Soviet Russia. This conspiracy theory gained credibility when Sergei Kirov, the dynamic young leader of the Leningrad party organization, was assassinated in December 1934. Harsh reprisals, numerous arrests, phony trials, summary executions, and large-scale deportations followed in the immediate wake of this incident. Many of the victims were loosely identified as members of the so-called Leningrad Center.

Of course, no "Leningrad Center" had ever existed, and there had been no plot to overthrow Stalin. (Communist party First Secretary Nikita Khrushchev hinted in 1956 that Stalin himself may have been behind the assassination of Kirov.) But the alleged plot furnished Stalin with a golden opportunity to undertake perhaps the largest blood purge of "disloyal" subordinates in history. Prominent members of Lenin's original circle of revolutionary leaders, the so-called Old Bolsheviks, were arrested and imprisoned as the purge swiftly gained momentum. During the first phase of what came to be known as the Great Terror—January 1934 to April 1936—Communist party membership fell by nearly 800,000, or approximately 25 percent. The Soviet press denounced these excommunicants as "wreckers, spies, diversionists, and murderers sheltering behind the party card and disguised as Bolsheviks."[31]

The second phase of the Stalin purges (1936–38) was highlighted by the infamous *show trials*, in which the Old Bolsheviks, along with many other top-ranking party leaders, were placed on public trial and forced to make outrageous "confessions." The trials, however, represented only the tip of the iceberg. Of the nearly

One of the most ruthless dictators of the twentieth century, Joseph Stalin (1879–1953) moved away from the Soviet model of an international communist revolution proposed by Marx and Lenin to focus on "socialism in one country." In pursuit of his aims, Stalin committed mass murders on a grand scale and enslaved millions in a vast system of gulags (forced-labor camps).

Sovfoto

2,000 delegates to the Seventeenth *Party Congress* in 1934, more than 1,100 (about 56 percent) would be shot between 1934 and 1938. Of the 1,827 rank-and-file delegates to that congress, only 35 percent would be present at the convening of the next congress, five years later. Seventy percent of the 139 members of the Party Central Committee elected in 1934 would be murdered by 1938. By 1939, the party apparatus had been thoroughly purged.

In the Red Army the results were much the same. The Great Terror wiped out 3 of the 5 marshals of the Soviet Union, 14 of 16 army commanders, all 8 admirals, 60 of the 67 corps commanders, and more than half of the 397 brigade commanders. In addition, of 81 top-ranking political commissars, all but 5 were purged.

Nor were the rank-and-file workers spared. Throughout the mid- to late 1930s, Stalin carried out a policy known as the *Estafette,* whereby the Soviet labor force was collectivized through the institution of forced-draft or conscript labor. Work units were structured along military lines, and strict labor regimentation was enforced. This policy gave birth to the so-called *gulag archipelago,* a network of desolate slave-labor camps maintained and operated by the Soviet secret police where social and political undesirables were forced to live. Through the gulag system, railroads, canals, and dams were constructed in remote and inaccessible areas where workers would not go voluntarily. Aleksandr Solzhenitsyn, the celebrated dissident writer who chronicled life in the labor camps, estimated that they held as many as 12 million prisoners at any given time, perhaps half of them political prisoners. "As some departed beneath the sod," he noted, "the Machine kept bringing in replacements."[32]

Finally, on the eve of World War II, Stalin stood alone at the top. Industrial development had been spurred, but the Soviet Union was anything but a worker's paradise. Terror had brought about great political changes, with many luminaries from the pages of Soviet Communist party history uncovered as traitors and placed on public trial. The list of the accused read like the honor roll of the October Revolution. The military high command had been sacked, the party rank and file cleansed of all political impurities, and the "toiling masses" reduced to a new level of industrial serfdom. Although he ruled until his death in 1953, Stalin (and the legacy of Stalinism) would be identified, above all, with the bloody purges of the 1930s.

Germany under Hitler

The overriding theme of National Socialist (Nazi) party ideology during the Third Reich (1933–45) was the elimination of the Jews and other "social undesirables" and the subsequent creation of a "racially pure" Aryan community created in the image of its founder, Adolf Hitler. Racism, which had obsessed Hitler throughout his political career, prompted him to attempt a drastic reformulation of German life. The means he countenanced are by now familiar: mass indoctrination of the public in the tenets of Nazi ideology; maintenance of the Nazi party, under his tight control, as the guiding force in German life; heavy reliance on the secret police, or Gestapo, to ensure public obedience; and centralized control over the economy, the military, and the mass media.

Through Nazi ideology and propaganda, the German people came to accept the persecution of the Jews, the necessity of an eventual war, and the radical transformation of society. Every aspect of German life became politicized both through the terror tactics of the Gestapo and the SS and through an officially sponsored "cultural revolution," which called for the purging of all artists, journalists, and academicians whose political opinions could not be trusted. New governmental agencies, including the Reich chambers for literature, press, broadcasting, theater, music, and fine arts, were created for the primary purpose of censoring or quelling potentially "dangerous" forms of written or artistic expression.

In the realm of music, German folk tunes were exalted over "decadent" modern music and classical music written by composers of Jewish lineage such as Felix Mendelssohn and Gustav Mahler. Modern art was likewise condemned, and the works of virtually every well-known contemporary artist were banned. Literature under the Nazi regime fared no better. According to Karl Dietrich Bracher, one chronicler of the Third Reich:

> Blacklists were compiled ceaselessly and literary histories were revised. . . . The "cleansing" of libraries and bookstores presented some problems, but the destruction and self-destruction of German literature was achieved within a matter of months through the substitution of second- and third-rate scribblers for first-rate writers and by inhibiting contacts with the outside.[33]

The Nazi attack on the arts was indicative of the lengths to which Hitler would go to ensure that Nazi values were propagated. But perhaps no part of German life more vividly demonstrated Hitler's commitment to a new future than the Nazi school system. As Bracher points out, "While National Socialism could substitute little more than ideology and second-rate imitators for the literature and art it expelled or destroyed, its main efforts from the very outset were directed toward the most important instruments of totalitarian policy: propaganda and education."[34]

Nazi educational policy was implemented in three principal ways. To begin with, educators and school administrators who were suspected of opposing Hitler, Nazism, or Nazi educational "reform" were promptly removed from their positions. Then all academic subjects were infused with ideological content. History became "racial history," biology was transformed into "racial biology," and so on. All subjects were revised to reflect Hitler's anti-Semitic racial theories. Day in and day out, students were bombarded with the noxious racial doctrines that justified the Nazi political order. Often these theories were intertwined with tales of military prowess; virtually every academic subject had as its moral the coming triumph of the Aryans over their racial inferiors. Finally, the Nazis established special schools to train a future party elite, including military leaders, party officials, and government administrators. Students were assigned to these schools according to age group and career orientation. The Adolf Hitler Schools, to cite one example, taught twelve- to eighteen-year-old students who wished to become high party functionaries. Generally speaking, all special schools taught certain basic core courses (such as racial history and biology) and emphasized military drill (for example, the training of the infamous Hitler Youth).

The Nazi educational program turned out to be all too successful. In the judgment of one authority, "Just as teachers and parents capitulated to the pressures of the regime, so on the whole did the indoctrination of the young succeed. The young, who were receptive to heroic legends and black-and-white oversimplifications, were handed over to the stupendous shows of the regime."[35] Education of the young was reinforced by carefully planned pomp and ceremony: "From earliest childhood, they were exposed to flag raisings, parades, nationwide broadcasts in the schools, hikes, and camps."[36] Indoctrination and propaganda, not terror, became the instruments by which the children of the Third Reich were initiated into the new order.

This program of mass indoctrination, perhaps more than anything else, made it possible for Hitler to carry out the murderous racial policies that culminated in the Holocaust. After seizing power, Hitler implemented his anti-Jewish policy in stages, each more radical than the one before.[37] First came the attempt to define who precisely was and was not a Jew. Then the regime launched a systematic campaign to isolate Jews from the mainstream of German life and to expropriate their property. Next all Jews who had not fled the country between 1933 and 1938 were forcibly removed from German society and sent to the infamous concentration camps. This mass deportation presaged the fourth and final step, the murder of every Jewish man, woman, and child within the reach of the Third Reich.

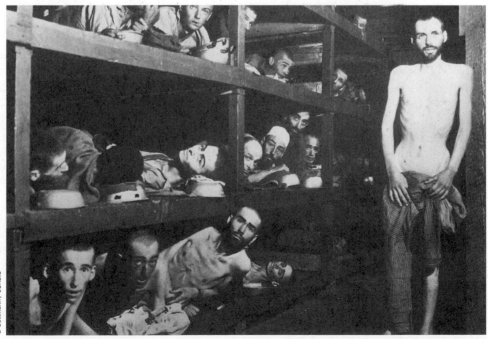

The overriding theme of Nazi party ideology was the elimination of the Jews and other "social undesirables" and the subsequent creation of a "racially pure" Aryan nation. Between 1933 and 1945, some 6 million European Jews perished in Nazi death camps.

As the anti-Jewish policies gained momentum in Germany during the 1930s, Hitler drew almost every element of German society into his murderous scheme. The bureaucracy composed anti-Jewish orders and planned the logistics of the annihilation process. German businesses benefited from the expropriation of Jewish property and from the use of forced labor in the concentration camps. As Germany conquered lands to the east, special units of the army became heavily involved in all aspects of the killing operations. Finally, the Nazi party hierarchy itself played a crucial role in planning and directing the whole annihilation program. The SS, the paramilitary arm of the party, actually supervised the killing operations in the death camps.

For Hitler, World War II represented an opportunity to spread his vision of a racially purified Aryan Germany to the whole of Europe. Unlike previous tyrants, who fought wars mainly for love of territory, power, or glory, Hitler was motivated by the dream of a radically new and revolutionary society. Thus, even when Germany's military fortunes plunged and the Third Reich was on the brink of defeat, Hitler moved ahead (and even accelerated) the liquidation of the Jews, pursuing a relentless and unstinting policy of genocide. In the end, some 6 million European Jews were murdered. Previous acts of racially motivated political persecution pale beside the barbarism of the Holocaust, whose architect, Adolf Hitler, sought to create a "master race" and build a brave new world in his own grotesque image.

China under Mao

Mao Zedong's rise to power in China is an epic example of revolutionary struggle—a true mass movement in a poor, peasant-dominated society. For more than twenty years (1927–49), Mao waged a bitter "war of national liberation" against the Kuomintang, headed by Chiang Kai-shek, as well as against the Japanese during World War II. In the mid-1930s, Mao was one of the leaders of the legendary Long March, a 6,000-mile trek, during which his ragtag band of guerrillas repeatedly evaded capture or annihilation by the numerically superior and better equipped forces of Chiang's Nationalist army. By 1949, when he finally won the last decisive battle and assumed command of the Chinese nation, Mao Zedong had been waging "class war" in the name of the Chinese masses for more than two decades.

Mao prided himself not only on his revolutionary exploits but also on his political thought. In time, the "thoughts of Chairman Mao," compiled in his "red book," attained the status of holy scripture in Chinese society. His vision of a new, classless state and of the exemplary communist cadres and comrades who would typify this morally reeducated society inspired the radical policies that have become known collectively as Maoism.

Although Mao's worldview was undoubtedly shaped by the basic tenets of Marxism, China in the 1920s was a preindustrial society without a true proletarian (industrial-worker) class or a "monopoly capitalist" class of the kind Marx had described in *Das Kapital*. The bane of China's peasant masses was not factory bosses but greedy landlords and bureaucratic officials preoccupied with the preservation of the status quo and of their own power and privilege. If the oppressed majority was to be liberated, those in power would have to be overthrown. To accomplish such a historic mission, Mao believed, violent revolution "from below" would be an unavoidable necessity. "Political power," he wrote, "grows out of the barrel of a gun."[38]

As part of his adaptation (or "Sinification") of Marxism, Mao glorified the long-suffering Chinese peasants, holding them up as models of communist virtue. The Chinese peasants, in his view, were "poor and blank." Because they had never been corrupted by "bourgeois materialism" and big-city decadence, Mao believed they could be molded into model communists more easily than their sophisticated urban cousins. In this way, Mao made the peasants the cornerstone of a utopian, classless society in which exploitation would no longer occur and the masses would live in harmony, equality, and abundance.

Armed with this glorious vision, Mao turned China, after 1949, into a kind of social laboratory. In the postrevolutionary years, the Chinese Communist party (CCP) and the Chinese army were used to carry out grandiose experiments in behavioral and environmental engineering. The first step involved mass campaigns to remove specific evils or to exterminate such undesirable social elements as landlords, counterrevolutionaries, and so-called bandits. Accompanying these "reeducation campaigns" was a sweeping land reform program that eventually culminated in the wholesale collectivization of Chinese agriculture. The often bitter pill of land reform was administered with massive doses of propaganda as well as physical force. In the early 1950s, a major push to industrialize China along Stalinist lines was also initiated.

Mao's rule was marked by alternating periods of freedom and repression. In 1956, for example, he announced the beginning of the *Hundred Flowers campaign,* which promised a relaxation of strict social discipline. As a high-ranking party official put it at the time, "The Chinese Communist party advocates [that] one hundred flowers bloom for literary works and one hundred schools contend in the scientific field . . . to promote the freedom of independent thinking, freedom of debate, freedom of creation and criticism, freedom of expressing one's own opinions."[39] It even seemed as though limited criticism of the party leadership would be tolerated.

What followed most likely caught Mao by surprise. Criticism of official policy poured in from all over the country. The spate of public protests and antiparty demonstrations was especially pronounced at Beijing University and on other campuses across China. Strikes and scattered riots ensued. Voices of dissent, cautious at first, grew bolder and more clamorous. Isolated physical attacks on party officials were reported. Instead of a hundred flowers, thousands of "poisonous weeds" had grown in the Chinese garden. To root them out, a vigorous antirightist campaign was launched. The official party newspaper, *People's Daily,* offered the face-saving (albeit plausible) explanation that the whole Hundred Flowers campaign had been a ploy to lure the enemies of the state into the open.

In retrospect, the Hundred Flowers episode was a mere warm-up for Mao's *Great Leap Forward* (1957–60). The Great Leap represented a spectacular attempt to catapult China to the stage of "full communism" by means of mass mobilization.

AP / Wide World Photos

Successful in his war of national liberation against the Chiang Kai-shek's Kuomintang, Mao's rule between 1949 and 1976 was characterized by periods of vast social experimentation as well as by violent periods of political repression.

Mao now launched a program of social transformation predicated on the belief that human willpower could triumph over objective conditions rooted in the poverty, illiteracy, and external dependency that plagued China.

According to John King Fairbank, a respected American student of China:

> The development strategy of the Great Leap Forward in 1958 was the sort of thing guerrilla warriors could put together. They had learned how to mount campaigns and mobilize the populace to obtain specific social objectives, much like capturing positions in warfare—indeed military terminology was commonly used. The whole apparatus of campaign mechanisms was now directed to an economic transformation, the simultaneous development of agriculture and industry, a strategy of dualism or as Mao said, "Walking on two legs," to achieve development in the modern industrial processes. . . . The CCP effort was to take advantage of China's rural backwardness and manpower surplus by realizing the Maoist faith that ideological incentives could get economic results, that a new spirit could unlock hitherto untapped sources of human energy without the use of material incentives.[40]

The most visible and dramatic symbol of the Great Leap was the establishment of innumerable communes—relatively large, self-contained, and self-sufficient social, economic, and administrative units. Private plots were absorbed into the communal lands, and private belongings, including pots and pans and other domestic items, were pooled. In addition, as Fairbank notes:

Many peasants for a time ate in large mess halls. All labor was to be controlled. Everyone was to work twenty-eight days of the month, while children went into day nurseries. This would bring large-scale efficiency to the village and get all its labor, including its womanpower, into full employment.[41]

Why were the unprecedented measures associated with Mao's grandiose concept instituted? In Fairbank's view, "The result, it was hoped, would be agricultural cities with the peasants proletarianized and uprooted from their own land"—with an overall view toward giving the state increased control over labor resources and changing the peasants' attitudes.[42]

The Great Leap Forward turned out to be an unmitigated disaster, both because it was ill-conceived and because nature proved to be uncooperative. In the late 1950s and early 1960s, China experienced severe food shortages and crop failures. In 1960 alone, the country's gross national product declined by as much as one-third. For the first few years of the new decade, Mao's power and influence seemed to decline. But this was only a short-lived period of retrenchment and reconstruction.

From 1966 to 1969, the *Great Proletarian Cultural Revolution* shook Chinese society to its very foundations. To the outside world, the Cultural Revolution still stands as one of the most bizarre events of the century. It represented Mao's most ambitious attempt to revitalize the spirit of the revolution and to eradicate all remaining vestiges of bourgeois capitalism and China's rich religious and cultural tradition.

The Cultural Revolution took shape in two distinct stages. The first stage was designed to wash away all that was "decadent" in Chinese life. To this end, Mao closed all schools and urged his youthful followers, called the Red Guards, to storm the bastions of entrenched privilege and bureaucratic authority. The spectacle of millions of Maoist youths rampaging through the country both bewildered and bemused the outside world for many weeks. Yet by the time the chaos and confusion had subsided, this phase of the revolution had accomplished much of what Mao intended—the Red Guards had "smashed most of the Republic's bureaucratic institutions and invalidated their authority and expertise."[43] Purges, public humiliations, executions, and orchestrated anarchy racked the nation. Temples and historical treasures lay in ruin, as did the party, the government, and the armed forces.

The second stage of the Cultural Revolution was predictably less successful than the first. Unlike the second stage, the first stage had been largely negative in that it sought the destruction of certain undesirable features of the existing social and political order. The succeeding stage, however, called for positive action to replace the previous order with a new and better one. Unfortunately, the economy, especially in urban areas, had been severely disrupted. And schools, having been shut down to make way for Mao's new revolutionary order, did not reopen for months or years. As a result, a whole generation of young Chinese failed to acquire the knowledge and skills the country's developing economy so sorely needed.

The ultimate cost of the Cultural Revolution is inestimable. One fact, however, is clear: Mao's untiring efforts to prove that human nature is infinitely malleable—and society, therefore, infinitely perfectable—foundered on the rocky shores of political reality. His death in 1976 closed a unique chapter in the political history of the modern world.

THE FACES OF TOTALITARIANISM

In addition to Stalin's Russia, Hitler's Germany, and Mao's China, there are other totalitarian states that deserve mention and study. Although these lesser totalitarian states have mostly disappeared or mellowed, the abuses they perpetrated in every case left deep scars in their nation's history, as well as a bitter legacy.

Pol Pot governed Cambodia (renamed Kampuchea) from 1975 to 1979. He and his followers sought to create a radically new society, based on the rustic and spartan life of peasant cadres. All vestiges of the old order, everything from the calendar to the family, were eradicated. Pol Pot proclaimed 1978 "Year zero," grotesquely appropriate, for at the end of his brief rule, some 2 million Cambodians (out of a population of 7.5 million) would be dead, the victims of purges, starvation, or persecution.

Another example of totalitarian rulers is Ethiopia's Mengistu Haile Mariam,

© Bettmann / CORBIS

Following its revolution in January 1979 and under the direction of Ayatollah Ruholla Khomeini (1900–1989), Iran was transformed into a theocracy governed by fundamentalist Shi'ite Muslim principles.

who ruled from the mid-1970s until May 1991. Mengistu attempted to reorganize the nation by physically relocating its people into regimented population and refugee centers for the purposes of permitting intensive governmental surveillance as well as encouraging systematic propaganda and indoctrination. His efforts destroyed the nation's agriculture, and a killer famine resulted. Although efforts were made by the West to feed the starving children of Ethiopia, the Ethiopian government appeared curiously detached. While his people went hungry, Mengistu staged lavish military parades, sold wheat to neighboring nations, and then used the money he received to buy weapons. In May 1991, with his regime under siege by a coalition of rebel forces, Mengistu fled the country.

Totalitarian rulers have come to power around the world. Fidel Castro, leader of Cuba since 1959, is the longest-lasting. Until July 1994, North Korea was ruled by the iron-fisted Kim II Sung and, after his death, it remained a totalitarian state. Elsewhere in Asia, other countries—China and Vietnam, for example—retain nondemocratic methods carried over from earlier totalitarian regimes.

As noted earlier in the chapter, totalitarian regimes assume a variety of forms, as is demonstrated by the fanatical right-wing rule of Iran's fundamentalist Islamic leader, Ayatollah Ruholla Khomeini (1979–89). Khomeini transformed Iran into a *theocracy,* a government based on religion and dominated by the clergy. Eventually, no aspect of life in Iran lay outside of governmental control. Teachers, textbooks, education, entertainment, the legal system, even courtship and sexual mores were made to conform to fundamental Islamic beliefs. The regime declared war on civil servants, intellectuals, professional and entrepreneurial elements of the middle class, and all others who had endorsed modern Western ways and culture.

Khomeini's Iran displayed most of the elements normally associated with totalitarian rule: an attempt to transform society; a dictatorship that demanded abject loyalty, obedience, and self-sacrifice; an all-encompassing creed that rationalized, explained, and justified state actions; press censorship; and secret police, show trials, summary executions, and holy wars. The Iranian case aptly demonstrates that totalitarian regimes, like democracies and traditional dictatorships, while sharing a single essence, can assume different guises throughout the world.

THE FACELESS VICTIMS OF TOTALITARIANISM

Totalitarian regimes embody a stark contrast between ends and means. If the goals of such states are often presented as divine, the means used to achieve those goals—institutionalized persecution, purges, and genocides—are diabolical. To many observers, the death camps of Nazi Germany and the labor camps of Stalinist Russia stand as the essence of twentieth-century totalitarianism. These horrors demonstrate how the unthinkable can become possible under totalitarian dictatorship because there is nothing to prevent the government from carrying its pursuit to the most violent and even self-destructive extremes.

One conservative estimate of the human cost of totalitarian repression can be found in a comparative study of Hitler, Stalin, and Mao written by the political scientist C. W. Cassinelli. Professor Cassinelli contends that "about 110 million people have died in the name of the three revolutions and [that] the amount of physical and mental suffering they have caused defies the imagination."[44] According to Cassinelli, these estimates, which include World War II casualties, may actually be low. Subsequent evidence has supported his intuition.[45] But even if we were to cut Cassinelli's estimated casualties in half, the numbers would still be staggering.

Cassinelli observes that Hitler's expansionist foreign policy can be blamed for the war-related deaths in the European theater during World War II. The war dead numbered "about 6 million for Germany and Austria, 20 million for the Soviet Union, and about 10 million for all other European countries, for a total of about 36 million.[46] Hitler's so-called Final Solution was estimated to have resulted in the deaths of an estimated 6 million European Jews, not to mention an indeterminate number of non-Jews whom Hitler considered "social undesirables." In addition, some senile senior citizens were killed before the war, and ordinary lawbreakers were sent to concentration camps, where some of them perished prematurely. All in all, perhaps 42 million people died directly or indirectly as a result of Adolf Hitler's policies.

The Russian Revolution of 1917 and its aftermath were hardly less costly in terms of human life. Between 1918 and 1923, approximately 3 million Soviet citizens died of typhus, typhoid, dysentery, and cholera, and about 9 million more disappeared, probably victims of the terrible famine that scourged the country in the early 1920s. Many of the latter perished because of a severe drought in 1920–21, but many others died of direct or indirect political causes.

In the late 1920s, during Stalin's titanic industrialization drive, the kulaks were annihilated as a class. In addition, another killer famine—at least partially self-inflicted—occurred in the early 1930s. When deaths associated with the early stages of collectivization are combined with deaths brought on by famine, the mortality figures for the period 1929–34 range well into the millions.

But the worst was yet to come. After 1934, Stalin's massive purges—perhaps the bloodiest reign of terror in history—resulted in the outright murder of perhaps 1 million Soviet citizens and the premature deaths of another 2 million "class enemies" in Siberian forced-labor camps. Nor did the end of the great purges in 1938 stop the political hemorrhaging that, together with World War II, drained Soviet society of so much of its vitality. Cassinelli estimates that 12 million prison and labor camp inmates may have died between 1938 and 1950 as a direct result of their harsh and inhuman environments. All in all, Stalin (and to a lesser extent, Lenin) may be held responsible for the demise of millions of innocent and defenseless citizens for whom "revolutionary justice" meant either the slow death of the labor camp or the sudden death of the firing squad.

The human cost of the Maoist revolution has received much less attention than that of the Nazi or Soviet revolution, yet between 1927 and 1949, an estimated 50,000 people perished in China. Many of these deaths were attributable to the routine liquidation of landlords and rich peasants in areas that came under communist control.

Between the time of the communist takeover in 1949 and the Great Leap Forward in 1957, several mass campaigns were launched to combat allegedly counterrevolutionary forces. According to Cassinelli:

The land reform program of 1949 to 1952 undoubtedly cost the lives of several million "landlords" and similar types; the 1951–52 campaign against counterrevolutionaries cost another million and a half; the bandit suppression campaigns, ostensibly to eliminate remaining pockets of physical resistance, disposed of many people from 1949 to 1956; the "three anti" and "five anti" campaigns of 1951–53 and the anti-rightist campaign to 1958–59 resulted in killings and other deaths; and, finally, the collectivization of agriculture from 1953 until 1967 was accompanied by a significant number of casualties. Accurate information is not available—and often even informed guesses are lacking—on the cost of the first decade of the People's Republic. An estimate of twelve million lives is modest but reasonable.[47]

These figures do not include deaths caused by hardship and privation, most notably those traceable to the dislocations that accompanied the Great Leap Forward in the late 1950s.

The Cultural Revolution (1966–69) was another bloody episode in Chinese history, although firm estimates of the number of casualties are impossible to make. A much heavier toll was probably taken by the Chinese gulag system; as many as 15 million may have perished as a direct result of inhumanly harsh labor camp conditions. When Cassinelli tallies the total number of politically related deaths—including "another million from miscellaneous causes"—he arrives at the astonishing figure of "about 33.5 million."[48] Though the figure cannot be verified, it is consistent with the available evidence. The mere fact that it is not implausible speaks volumes.

Totalitarian regimes typically refuse to concede that any goal, no matter how visionary or perverse, is beyond political reach. The compulsion to validate this gross misconception may help to explain the pathological violence that marks totalitarian rule.

THE LONGEVITY OF TOTALITARIAN REGIMES

Space does not permit a complete accounting of the atrocities and oppression associated with all twentieth-century totalitarian regimes. Yet it is important to recognize that in this most violent of all centuries, totalitarian states have been directly or indirectly responsible, through their participation in revolution, warfare, and systematic state terror, for an enormous amount of death and suffering.

Totalitarian regimes often loudly proclaim their longevity and vitality; Hitler, for example, termed his a thousand-year empire. Yet there is growing evidence that suggests totalitarian regimes are normally short-lived. They tend to burst on the scene dramatically, but soon thereafter they burn themselves out. At most, totalitarian regimes have lasted no more than several decades beyond the lifetime of their revolutionary leaders. Why might this be so?

Fatal wars with other nations, such as Hitler's defeat by the Allies in World War II, can bring a sudden end to totalitarian states. Alternatively, the death of a particularly charismatic or successful ruler—Mao or Stalin, for instance—can precipitate an extended downward spiral. Drab, indistinguishable successors who rule by coercion and terror rather than by consent may undermine the economic

---

GATEWAYS TO THE WORLD:
EXPLORING CYBERSPACE

http://www.historyplace.com/index.html

This site houses a twenty-four-chapter history on the rise to power of Adolf Hitler, as well as biographies of Adolf Eichmann, Rudolf Hess, and Reinhard Heydrich. There is also a photo-rich time line of the Holocaust.

http://www.marx2mao.org/Mao/Index.html

An excellent starting point for further research into Chairman Mao's personal and political life, this site provides a number of active links grouped by category (Historic Events, Theories and Writings, etc.).

http://www.marxists.org

The homepage of this site contains links to biographies, writings, and information about notable Marxists of the twentieth century, including Marx, Lenin, Stalin, and Fidel Castro.

---

efficiency, moral vitality, and political idealism on which legitimate political power ultimately rests. Thus, the collapse of the Soviet Union was preceded by both a prolonged period of economic disintegration and a widespread loss of faith in the regime and its political ideals, a period of "totalitarianism in decline."[49] A similar loss of faith in the official (communist) ideology today appears to be taking place in China.

Despite the fact that totalitarian rule lasted for some seventy years in the Soviet Union and is still somewhat intact in the People's Republic of China after almost five decades, these periods of time are historically brief. Unfortunately, however, experience has shown that totalitarian dictatorships need only a little time to do a lot of damage.

Summary

Totalitarian states attempt to realize a utopian vision and create a new political order. Like authoritarian states, totalitarian states are nondemocratic. Yet these two regime types differ in several important respects. In particular, totalitarian regimes seek total control over all aspects of their citizens' lives and demand active participation rather than passive acquiescence on the part of the citizenry.

The three major totalitarian states of the past century (Soviet Russia, Nazi Germany, and Maoist China) appear to have gone through several distinct stages of development. The first stage coincides with a period of violent revolution. The five major elements necessary for a successful revolution are charismatic leadership, ideology, organization, propaganda, and violence. During the second stage, which involves the consolidation of power in the hands of the totalitarian ruler, opposition parties are eliminated, the party faithful are put in charge, and real or imagined rivals within the party are killed. The third stage attempts to bring about the total transformation of society. In the Soviet Union, Stalin launched this effort in 1928 with the first Five-Year Plan. In Nazi Germany, Hitler's goal of "racial purification" provided the rationale for a totalitarian drive that culminated in World War II and the Holocaust. In Maoist China, the first attempt to transform Chinese society, the Great Leap Forward, failed miserably in the late 1950s and was followed by the Cultural Revolution (1966–69).

The human costs of totalitarianism have been staggering. Actual statistics often cannot be verified with any degree of precision, but even the roughest estimates suggest that the totalitarian experiments of the twentieth century have brought death or appalling hardship to many millions of people.

Totalitarian states appear in many guises, and there is no guarantee that new totalitarian states will not emerge in the future. Indeed, the recently ousted Taliban regime in Afghanistan qualified as a new form of totalitarianism that used a perverted form of a mass-based religion (Islam) as a political ideology.

Key Terms

totalitarianism	Kuomintang
mass movement	purges
rectification	Gestapo
islands of separateness	kulaks
true believer	collectivization
cells	Party Congress
Central Committee	gulag archipelago
partiinost	Hundred Flowers campaign
Gleichschaltung	Great Leap Forward
propaganda	Great Proletarian Cultural Revolution
salami tactics	theocracy

Review Questions

1. What sets totalitarianism apart from other nondemocratic forms of rule?

2. What is required for a successful total revolution to take place?

3. How do totalitarian states consolidate power?

4. What are the basic characteristics of the totalitarian system of rule?

5. What were the primary aims of Stalin's drive to transform Soviet society in the 1930s? What methods did he use?

6. How and why did Hitler try to reshape German society?

7. What was the impetus behind the Great Leap Forward and the Cultural Revolution? What methods did the Maoists employ? What kind of a society did they envisage?

8. What have been the costs of totalitarianism, measured in human terms?

9. "Totalitarianism passed away with the deaths of Hitler, Stalin, and Mao." Comment.

Recommended Reading

ARENDT, HANNAH. *Totalitarianism*. San Diego: Harcourt, 1968. A theoretical analysis of Nazi Germany and Stalinist Russia that spotlights totalitarian states' emphasis on terror, persecution, and mass murder.

BRACHER, KARL DIETRICH. *The German Dictatorship*. New York: Holt, 1972. A definitive study of Hitler's totalitarian state.

BROWNING, CHRISTOPHER. *Ordinary Men: Reserve Police Battalion 101 and the Final Solution in Poland*. New York: HarperCollins, 1992. This study of a civilian Nazi police force engaged in mass murder argues that human beings commit the most evil acts imaginable when faced with tremendous social pressure to conform.

BULLOCK, ALAN. *Hitler and Stalin, Parallel Lives*. New York: Knopf, 1992. A comprehensive and definitive account of the lives and character of these two tyrants.

CASSINELLI, C. W. *Total Revolution: A Comparative Study of Germany under Hitler, the Soviet Union under Stalin, and China under Mao*. Santa Barbara, Calif.: Clio Books, 1976. The writer argues that these regimes are fundamentally similar.

CHIROT, DANIEL. *Modern Tyrants: The Power and Prevalence of Evil in Our Age*. New York: Free Press, 1994. Hitler and Stalin are presented as the prototype of a new kind of ideological tyrant, who seeks to mold society according to specific "scientific" theories about how society should be constructed.

CONQUEST, ROBERT. *The Great Terror: A Reassessment*. New York: Oxford University Press, 1991. A detailed, carefully researched book that provides the definitive scholarly account of Stalin's bloodiest days.

———. *The Harvest of Sorrow: Soviet Collectivization and the Terror-Famine*. New York: Oxford University Press, 1987. A chilling account of Stalin's war against the kulaks and the Ukrainians.

FRIEDRICH, CARL, and ZBIGNIEW BRZEZINSKI. *Totalitarian Dictatorship and Autocracy*. New York: Praeger, 1965. A pioneering effort that attempts to classify and describe totalitarian states.

GOLDHAGEN, DANIEL JONAH. *Hitler's Willing Executioners: Ordinary Germans and the Holocaust*. New York: Knopf, 1996. A provocative and controversial argument that the Holocaust was predominantly carried out by ordinary citizens infected by a virulent anti-Semitism that was particularly rampant in Germany.

HOFFER, ERIC. *The True Believer: Thoughts on the Nature of Mass Movements*. New York: Harper & Row, 1951. A perceptive examination of individuals who form the nucleus of mass movements.

KIERNAM, BEN. *The Pol Pot Regime: Race, Power, and Genocide in Cambodia under the Khmer Rouge, 1975-79*. New Haven, Conn.: Yale University Press, 1996. This detailed examination of one of the darkest periods of human history makes the controversial argument that race, not ideology, motivated the Cambodian genocide.

MENZE, ERNEST, ed. *Totalitarianism Reconsidered*. Port Washington, N.Y.: Associated Faculty Press, 1981. A provocative collection of essays presenting different points of view on the usefulness of distinguishing between totalitarianism and other political orders.

MOSHER, STEVEN. *China Misperceived: American Illusions and Chinese Reality*. New York: Basic

Books, 1992. A controversial work that describes the reality of Mao's China and analyzes academic and journalistic misperceptions of it.

ORWELL, GEORGE. *Nineteen Eighty-Four.* New York: Knopf, 1992. The classic fictional caricature of Stalinist Russia that is full of insights regarding the nature of totalitarian societies.

PUNCHAUD, FRANÇOIS. *Cambodia: Year Zero.* New York: Holt, 1978. A chilling historical account of Pol Pot's rule in Kampuchea.

SELZNICK, PHILIP. *The Organizational Weapon: A Study of Bolshevik Strategy and Tactics.* North Stratford, N.H.: Ayer, 1980. A penetrating study of Soviet institutions under Lenin and Stalin.

SHAPIRO, LEONARD. *Totalitarianism.* New York: Praeger, 1972. An evenhanded and informative discussion of the scholarly controversy that surrounds the concept of totalitarianism.

SOLZHENITSYN, ALEKSANDR. *One Day in the Life of Ivan Denisovich* (trans. H. T. Willetts). New York: Farrar, Straus and Giroux, 1992. A description of the Soviet labor camps that became a cause célèbre in the Soviet Union during Khrushchev's de-Stalinization program.

WIESEL, ELIE. *Night.* New York: Bantam Books, 1982. A poignant autobiographical account of the suffering of the victims of totalitarian rule—in this case, the Jews under Hitler.

Notes

1. William Kornhauser, *The Politics of Mass Society* (New York: Free Press, 1959), 123.
2. C. W. Cassinelli, *Total Revolution: A Comparative Study of Germany under Hitler, the Soviet Union under Stalin, and China under Mao* (Santa Barbara, Calif.: Clio Books, 1976), 225.
3. The definition is Hans Buchheim's, as quoted in Leonard Shapiro, *Totalitarianism* (New York: Praeger, 1972), 104.
4. Carl Friedrich and Zbigniew Brzezinski, *Totalitarian Dictatorship and Autocracy,* 2nd ed. (New York: Praeger, 1966), 88.
5. Cassinelli, *Total Revolution,* 231.
6. Friedrich and Brzezinski, *Totalitarian Dictatorship,* 279-339.
7. Eric Hoffer, *The True Believer: Thoughts on the Nature of Mass Movements* (New York: Harper & Row, 1951), 104–105.
8. Ibid., 86.
9. Raul Hilberg, *The Destruction of the European Jews* (New York: Harper & Row, 1961), 12.
10. Cited in Cassinelli, *Total Revolution,* 16.
11. Karl Dietrich Bracher, *The German Dictatorship* (New York: Holt, 1972), 181.
12. Maurice Latey, *Patterns of Tyranny* (New York: Atheneum, 1969), 172.
13. Adolf Hitler, *Mein Kampf,* trans. R. Manheim (Boston: Houghton Mifflin, 1971), 179–180.
14. Ibid., 182.
15. Cited in David Shub, *Lenin* (Baltimore: Pelican, 1966), 62.
16. E. Kohr Bramstedt, cited in Hannah Arendt, *The Origins of Totalitarianism* (New York: Harcourt, 1951), 333.
17. Ibid.
18. Ibid., 335–336.
19. Quoted in Leo Strauss, *Thoughts on Machiavelli* (Seattle: University of Washington Press, 1968), 9.

20. Latey, *Patterns of Tyranny*, 100.
21. Cassinelli, *Total Revolution*, 103.
22. Ibid., 186.
23. Quoted in Bracher, *German Dictatorship*, 257.
24. Ibid., 272.
25. W. S. Allen, *The Nazi Seizure of Power: The Experience of a Single German Town, 1930–1935* (Chicago: Quadrangle Books, 1965).
26. Peter Drucker, "The Monster and the Lamb," *Atlantic* (December 1978): 84.
27. Ibid.
28. Friedrich and Brzezinski, *Totalitarian Dictatorship*, 374.
29. Ibid., 9–10.
30. Hannah Arendt, *Totalitarianism* (Orlando, Fla.: Harcourt, 1968), xiv.
31. See Stalin, *Mastering Bolshevism*, 10; cited in Merle Fainsod, *How Russia Is Ruled*, rev. ed. (Cambridge, Mass.: Harvard University Press, 1964), 435.
32. Aleksandr Solzhenitsyn, *The Gulag Archipelago, 1918-1956* (New York: Harper & Row, 1974), 595.
33. Bracher, *German Dictatorship*, 258.
34. Ibid., 259–260.
35. Ibid., 262.
36. Ibid.
37. Hilberg, *Destruction of the European Jews*, 31.
38. Mao Zedong, *Selected Works* (Beijing: Foreign Languages Press, 1960–65), 224.
39. Franz Michaels and George Taylor, *The Far East in the Modern World* (New York: Holt, 1964), 479.
40. John King Fairbank, *The United States and China*, 4th ed. (Cambridge, Mass.: Harvard University Press, 1979), 409.
41. Ibid., 413.
42. Ibid.
43. Cassinelli, *Total Revolution*, 195.
44. Ibid., 243. Of course, figures vary widely. For example, Rummel, using somewhat different criteria, postulates significantly different individual figures for Hitler, Lenin–Stalin, and Mao. Yet his total of almost 105.5 million people killed is remarkably close to Cassinelli's estimate. See R. J. Rummel, *Death by Government* (New Brunswick, N.J.: Transaction, 1996), 8.
45. For instance, almost 1.5 million pages of formerly classified documents (German messages intercepted by Britain during World War II as well as newly released Russian documents) revealed that Hitler probably murdered closer to 7 million Jews (as opposed to the 5–6 million Cassinelli and others have estimated). Also see comment in footnote 47.
46. Cassinelli, *Total Revolution*, 46.
47. Ibid., 186. Since Cassinelli published his book, new evidence indicates that these figures vastly understated the actual number of deaths during this period. According to one authority, a three-year famine between 1959 and 1962 *alone* caused at least 30 million Chinese deaths. The immediate cause of the famine was Mao's policy of taking property from Chinese peasants and relocating them in communes. See Jasper Becker, *Hungry Ghosts: Mao's Secret Famine* (New York: Free Press, 1997).
48. Ibid., 187.
49. Laqueur applies this concept to the Soviet Union, particularly in his chapter on totalitarianism. See Walter Laqueur, *The Dream That Failed, Reflections on the Soviet Union* (New York: Oxford University Press, 1994), 77-95, 84.

Jeremy Woodhouse / Getty Images

© Peter Turnley / CORBIS

© Earl & Nazima Kowall / CORBIS

PART II

ESTABLISHED AND EMERGING DEMOCRACIES

Jeremy Woodhouse / Getty Images

Chapter 6

PARLIAMENTARY DEMOCRACY

Great Britain: The Model

The Adaptability of Democracy: Five Cases

France: President against Parliament

Germany: Federalism against Militarism

Japan: Parliamentary Rule in the Land of Consensus

Parliamentary Rule in Unlikely Places

Presidents and Parliaments: A Comparative View

THE CONCEPT OF constitutionalism (or the rule of law) is deeply rooted in British history. However, the emphasis on a written constitution in the United States contrasts sharply with the unwritten British constitution, which is based on precedents, statutes, and traditions, as well as the famous principle of parliamentary supremacy.

If the American presidential system is based on architecture, the British parliamentary system owes its origins to horticulture—that is, rather than resulting from a blueprint devised by rational minds it simply grew from the fertile soil of British political life. In short, British political institutions were cultivated for centuries in the laboratory of an evolving civil society. The roots of the British "constitution" are thus very deeply embedded. The organic nature of the British parliamentary system raises an obvious question as to whether it can be easily transplanted to other societies, but before we explore that question let us take a closer look at this uniquely British form of representative democracy.

GREAT BRITAIN: THE MODEL

The American experiment in constitutional democracy represented a sharp break with the European autocratic tradition, one that necessitated the elaboration of a fresh political theory. By contrast, there is no British counterpart to *The Federalist*. Nonetheless, a sort of homegrown theory of British-style democracy can be found in the writings and speeches of Edmund Burke (1729–1797). Burke detailed Britain's long unbroken chain of political development, during which, significantly, gains in economic equality accompanied an expansion in the scope of political liberty. As the monarchy declined in power, British government became increasingly democratic, evolving into a *parliamentary system.* It was gradually established that the British monarch would automatically accept Parliament's choice of prime minister (PM). In time, the PM eclipsed the monarch as the chief operational officer in the government. Today, the British PM is the exclusive holder of executive power while the monarch is a mere figurehead.

A Mixed Regime

From the seventeenth century on, the British parliamentary system became a prime example of what Aristotle called a *mixed regime,* in which different institutions represent different classes. The ascendancy of Parliament over the Crown highlighted the fact that, throughout the nineteenth century, the two houses of Parliament reflected distinct class interests within British society. The House of Lords represented the interests of the traditional governing classes, whereas the House of Commons gradually came to represent the interests of the general electorate, as expressed through free elections and increasing suffrage.

Great Britain's mixed regime has historically promoted stability by providing representation for classes that otherwise might have become openly hostile toward one another and toward the political system as a whole. Today, things have changed. What is commonly called the British "welfare state" is actually an

SuperStock, Inc.

The elected House of Commons (pictured here) has eclipsed the largely hereditary House of Lords as the supreme legislative body in the modern British parliamentary system.

elaborate system of income redistribution aimed at creation of a large middle class. The emergence of a broad-based middle class has rendered the traditional representation of separate and distinct economic classes largely irrelevant, although the Conservative (Tory) and Labour parties continue to represent what remains of the old upper and lower classes, respectively. This trend is mirrored in the historical ascendancy of the popularly elected House of Commons over the aristocratic House of Lords. The House of Lords is composed of about 1,100 people holding aristocratic titles (gained, in most cases, through inheritance), but only about 300 of those who are eligible actively participate.[1] Its inferior status was ensured by the passage of the Parliament Acts of 1911 and 1949, which made it impossible for the House of Lords to defeat legislation passed in the House of Commons (at most, the Lords can delay a bill taking effect for one year).

Fusion of Powers

Under the British parliamentary system, the executive body—the prime minister and cabinet—is made up of the leaders of the majority party within the House of Commons. After an election, the head of the victorious party nominates the members (ministers) of the new cabinet, which is endorsed by Parliament and appointed by the Queen. In this fashion, a new government is formed. The government is responsible for formulating and initiating legislation. Although all members of Parliament, including those in the opposition party, are free to question and criticize, the government is assured of getting its legislative program passed because in the British system it always has a clear majority.

Most parliamentary systems operate according to the same basic principles as the British system, but in many such systems the government cannot count on a clear majority in the legislature (whatever it is named). The reason, as we will see later in this chapter, is that countries with parliamentary government have five or six competitive political parties, unlike Great Britain, which has only two major parties. Where there are multiple parties in the parliament, frequently no single party has enough seats to form a government. In this event, coalitions (two or more parties joining forces) are necessary. Sometimes coalition governments work fairly well and sometimes they do not. In the worst cases (Italy, for example), parliamentary rule can be unstable and even chaotic.

Indefinite Terms of Office

When Labour party's Tony Blair became Britain's new prime minister in May 1997, it was understood that he would serve a five-year term—or less. Here, too, the British and American systems differ significantly. U.S. presidential elections are held every four years, and all seats in the House of Representatives are contested every two years, as are one-third of those in the Senate. In the British system, terms of office are indefinite. Parliament is required to stand for election every five years, but the prime minister can call for elections earlier if it looks as though the mood of the electorate momentarily favors the ruling party. By the same token, Parliament can force the government to resign by a vote of "no confidence." In this event, either a new government is formed under new leadership or the Queen dissolves Parliament and calls new elections.

The authority to decide when to call new elections is an important prerogative in the British system, because it improves the ruling party's chances of remaining in power longer than five years. Prime Minister Margaret Thatcher made particularly shrewd use of this option. In 1983, for example, after serving in office for only four years, she capitalized on a surge of British patriotism spurred by the Falkland Islands crisis (which involved a brief war with Argentina) to renew her Conservative party's mandate to rule for another five years. In 1987, she again called for an election four years into her term and was reelected for five more years. Another reason a prime minister may serve less than a five-year term occurs when the political pressures mount, making a change of political leadership desirable. In 1992, Prime Minister Thatcher's popularity within the country fell as a result of her support for a poll tax that many Britons considered regressive and unfair. Thatcher came under intense attack within her Conservative party, and rather than be defeated, she resigned her position as party leader and prime minister, turning over the reins of government to her handpicked successor John Major. When Thatcher stepped down as prime minister, she had served continuously for over a decade—the longest uninterrupted tenure in that office in the twentieth century. The Conservatives headed by Major won a surprising, narrow nine-seat majority in the parliamentary elections held in April 1992, enabling the Tory government to continue until the Thatcher era in British politics was eclipsed by Labour's landslide win in the spring of 1997.

Margaret Thatcher's resignation as leader of her party was not unprecedented. Prime Minister Neville Chamberlain resigned in 1940, despite the fact that his party still commanded a majority in the House of Commons. So widespread was his unpopularity, and so severely had the ruling Conservative party's confidence in his leadership been shaken by his concessions to Adolf Hitler at Munich, that he felt compelled to step aside. No new elections were called because the Conservative party retained its large majority, and Winston Churchill, a prominent Conservative member of Parliament (MP), was able to rally the British people behind his personal leadership.

Other circumstances may cause a government to fall before its five-year term has expired. If the policy of the majority party becomes particularly unpopular, or if the government becomes embroiled in scandal, the opposition party may, as noted earlier, call for a vote of no confidence. Passage of a *no-confidence vote,* which usually requires the defection of disgruntled members of the majority party, forces the government to resign. As a rule, when the cabinet resigns, the prime minister asks the monarch to dissolve Parliament and call for new elections. This happens frequently in multiparty parliamentary systems, although in Great Britain it has been rare in recent times.

Finally, another way a government may change before a prime minister's five-year term expires is when the ruling party has only a thin majority and a minor third party holds the critical balance. This situation has prevailed in Germany, for example, for more than three decades. The government can teeter or even fall if its "junior partner" switches sides or withdraws its support on a crucial vote.

Disciplined Parties

Another characteristic of the British parliamentary system is the existence of *disciplined parties.* Such parties, characterized by their strong tendency toward united action and bloc voting, differ markedly from American parties, which are much more loosely organized, more decentralized, and far more driven by individual personalities. Thus, the Conservative and Labour parties in Britain maintain coherent party platforms that reflect differing philosophies and traditions—one conservative and business-oriented, the other socialist and labor-oriented.

In Parliament, the majority party receives a mandate to run the country, and once elected, it demands unstinting support from its members for programs it promised to put into effect. MPs who do not vote with their party on an important legislative matter run the risk of being "purged" from the party, which means not being nominated by the party in the next election. Few mavericks can survive without such party endorsement.

Strong party discipline does not mean that MPs never cross the aisle to vote with the opposition, however. Nor does it mean that disaffected MPs must always toe the line; they can abstain on an important vote, for example. Extremely disgruntled MPs can break away and form a new party. This rarely happens, but when it does, a major realignment of the party system can occur. In the early 1900s, for example, the Labour party eclipsed the old Liberal (or Whig) party as the rising trade union movement transformed the British working class into a powerful political force. And in the early 1980s, disenchanted Labour MPs broke away and formed the Social Democratic party (SDP), which then cooperated with and, in the summer of 1987, merged with the old Liberal party (to form the so-called Alliance) in an attempt to capture the political center. In 1990, the SDP voted to disband.

What role does "Her Majesty's loyal opposition," as it is called in Great Britain, play in the parliamentary system? Because the majority party in the British system can usually enact a legislative program on its own, minority parties play a limited, though not unimportant, role. They criticize the majority's policy initiatives and are occasionally able to influence the majority's actions. Even when an opposition party has little influence, however, its criticisms are usually responsibly stated, for it "usually thinks of itself as the next government, and a wise Opposition operates within those limits which it hopes its own opponents will respect when the tables are turned."[2] No stigma whatsoever attaches to the notion of opposition in the British parliamentary tradition. As the *loyal opposition,* members of the minority believe they have a duty to criticize the government. As one expert points out:

> It has become a tradition in British political life that there shall usually be a party which provides the Government, and another party which provides the Opposition and which is, in effect, an alternative Government. Organized opposition is not now considered subversive or treasonable. Indeed, since 1937, the Leader of the Opposition has been paid a special salary out of public funds, and people often talk about *"Her Majesty's* Opposition," because the existence of an Opposition is thought to be an essential part of the Queen's government.[3]

Are Two Heads Better Than One?

Unlike the United States, where one chief executive (the president) serves as both the head of state and head of government, Great Britain retains a *dual executive,* which separates these two functions. The British head of state is the reigning monarch. Queen Elizabeth II, "arguably the most famous person in the world," has occupied the British throne for five decades. As titular head of state, the monarch plays a largely ceremonial role—presiding over the pomp and circumstance usually associated with national celebrations, receiving ambassadors or other heads of state at diplomatic events, and representing the state at certain international events. The monarch is a national symbol and a source of unity—personifying the state but not wielding its powers.

The actual head of the government in Great Britain, the pivot of the parliamentary system, is the prime minister, who, in close consultation with key cabinet members (often called the *inner cabinet*), sets domestic and foreign policy. National policy emerges from this leadership core, which then presents it to the cabinet as a whole. Cabinet members who are out of step with the government on an important policy matter are expected to resign quietly.

The dual executive system of Great Britain is illustrated by its queen, Elizabeth II (left), *its national symbol head of state, and its prime minister, Tony Blair* (right), *the actual head of the country's government.*

Of course, not all parliamentary democracies function in exactly the same way as the British system. Most do not enjoy the long history or strong tradition that underpins British parliamentary rule. Lacking an equally supportive political culture, most countries with British-style democratic institutions must rely on the strength of a written constitution. Unfortunately, most written constitutions lack "the long history and strong tradition" that underpins American presidential rule. Consequently, one risk in using these two political systems to illustrate how the two major types of democracy work is that the reader will mistakenly associate democracy with governmental stability. In fact, many democracies—both presidential and parliamentary—are afflicted by recurring bouts of instability.

Can British Institutions Be Transplanted?

Most constitutional democracies in Europe have been patterned after the British system. Italy adopted parliamentary rule after World War II. France operated within a parliamentary framework from 1876 (the beginning of the Third Republic) to 1958 (the end of the Fourth Republic). Both countries have had a mixed experience with this form of government.

Politically, France and Italy came to be dominated by the political parties and the parliament. The leading role of the prime minister and the cabinet, so important in the British constitutional system, was thus diminished. Whereas the British people tend to be tradition-bound, deferential, and pragmatic, the French and Italians have deeper social divisions and have supported more extreme political parties. In both countries, intense partisanship spawned a multiplicity of parties and splinter groups. Under such circumstances, the political party system became fragmented, internal party discipline broke down, and the government fell victim to never-ending legislative skirmishes. Generally speaking, the more spirited and unruly the society in question, and the more numerous the factions on the political

The British Agenda: A Sampler

The Economy and the Electorate

The state of the economy has been a major political issue in Great Britain ever since World War II. The perennially superior performance of Germany, Italy, and France was a source of embarrassment and consternation. Under Labour leadership, Britain developed what sympathetic observers considered a model welfare state in the 1950s and 1960s. But the sagging British economy was stricken by "stagflation" (a worst-of-both-worlds combination of inflation and recession) in the 1970s.

Enter Conservative leader Margaret Thatcher, a vigorous opponent of big government. Taking the helm as prime minister in 1979, Thatcher set about reprivatizing state-run industries and systematically deregulating the British economy. Although economic performance improved under Thatcher's guidance in the 1980s, Great Britain was still plagued by relatively high unemployment, anemic growth, and a sluggish manufacturing sector. After Thatcher reluctantly stepped down in 1992, the Tories eked out yet another electoral victory and John Major, Thatcher's successor, kept the country on the same economic course. During Major's tenure, the British economy picked up steam, growing 2.2 percent in 1996 and 3.2 percent in 1997. Meanwhile, inflation was modest, holding at around 2.5 percent. Even the unemployment rate had decreased 6.2 percent by early 1997 (compared to an unemployment rate of over 12 percent in France, for example).

And yet, the British voters were in a foul mood, throwing the Conservatives out of office in May 1997 for the first time in eighteen years. One reason was that, despite the statistical evidence to the contrary, many members of the British middle class felt that the quality of life in Great Britain was steadily slipping. An important economic and political question facing newly elected Prime Minister Tony Blair was when, or if, to join Europe's Economic Union.

Taxes and Government Spending

When the Conservatives won the elections in 1979, taxes under the Labour party had reached roughly 40 percent of the gross domestic product (GDP). As prime minister, Thatcher kept her promise to reduce the tax burden, and by the early 1990s, taxes fell to a low of 34 percent of the GDP. But this sterile statistic did not translate into tax relief for the working classes. In 1994, treasury figures showed that, as a result of changes enacted by John Major's Conservatives, the average British taxpayer would surrender a larger slice of income in 1994–95 than in 1978–79 (the last year Labour was in power). Preelection polls showed that voters expected a new Labour government to raise taxes, but many were so angry with John Major that they intended to vote for Labour anyway. For his part, Tony Blair promised in Labour's election manifesto that there would be "no rise in income tax rates," and that he would cut the value-added tax (VAT) on heating.

Terrorism and Northern Ireland

Some 3,000 people have died in violent acts perpetrated by both Catholic and Protestant extremists since 1969. Before a 1994 cease-fire, the provisional Irish Republican Army (IRA) had carried out terrorist attacks in an effort to force the British to leave Northern Ireland. The IRA made bold attempts (one involving a bombing and another a mortar attack) to assassinate both Thatcher and Major. In 1990, IRA terrorists murdered Ian Gow, a Conservative MP and Thatcher confidant. Any lasting solution will have to take account of the claims of British-backed Protestants, who outnumber Catholics in Northern Ireland, and Catholics, who constitute an overwhelming majority in the Irish Republic. Hopes that such a lasting settlement had at last been reached were raised in April 1998 when interested parties agreed to a wide-ranging negotiated settlement. The agreement restored self-rule to Northern Ireland. It also created new political institutions designed to give minority Catholics a greater political voice and, at the same time, met Protestant demands that Northern Ireland remain a part of Britain. In 2001, however, tensions again rekindled the conflict and clouded the future.

scene, the more chaotic and deadlocked the government will become. In such a society, it is essential to have a forceful and energetic executive authority—a factor missing in both France (before 1958) and Italy (to this day).

Such conditions have led to political stalemate in both countries at different times. In France, during the entire Third and Fourth Republics, no single party ever won a majority of seats in the National Assembly. During this same period, no fewer than 119 governments with an average life span of less than a year ruled the country. Sometimes governments only lasted for a few short weeks or months. A similar volatility has plagued Italy, which had more than forty prime ministers between 1945 and 1986 (one per year on average).

But it would be false to assert that the parliamentary model cannot or does not work outside of British Isles. Indeed, for more than half a century, parliamentary government has performed admirably all over the Continent, from Scandinavia (Sweden, Norway, and Denmark) in the north to Iberia (Spain and Portugal) in the South, and in Germany, Austria, Belgium, the Netherlands, Austria, and Switzerland, as well. Finland, Ireland, and Greece also belong on the list of Europe's parliamentary democracies, as do Poland, the Czech Republic, Hungary, Slovakia, Slovenia, and several other former communist states in Eastern Europe. In a real sense, parliamentary government is Great Britain's gift to Europe.

THE ADAPTABILITY OF DEMOCRACY: FIVE CASES

How does parliamentary government work in other countries? Can it possibly work in countries with strong authoritarian traditions? What about societies prone to political instability and even revolution—can democracy possibly take hold in a volatile political culture?

The examples of France, Germany, Japan, India, and Israel suggest that democracy is far more adaptable than most theorists initially imagined. This is important because democracy has become the object of ritual praise almost everywhere. Virtually every government in the world today, no matter how tyrannical, tries to give the *appearance* of constitutionalism and claims to be democratic. In countries where the press is state-controlled, where foreigners' movements and contacts are restricted, and where ordinary people live in fear of police reprisals, nothing prevents the government from pretending to champion democracy and liberty at the same time as it persecutes, intimidates the citizenry, and suppresses all criticism.

There is no doubt that democracy has a broad (though not universal) appeal—many of the Muslim societies of North Africa, the Middle East, and South Asia are among the notable exceptions. Even the most brutal dictatorships often claim to be democracies. Is it not true then that democracy is the best form of government whether it is always recognized as such?

The answer is not so simple. Some nations have traditions that make democracy seem either unnatural or undesirable—for example, authoritarian political traditions. Other nations have customs and cultures that are not at all compatible with the individualism and egalitarianism inherent in the idea of democracy. Finally, nations plagued by overpopulation and chronic food shortages are apt to view constitutionalism as a vague and meaningless abstraction. For people living on the edge of starvation any government that can alleviate the misery of daily life is, by definition, good government.

Most countries have had to overcome formidable cultural, social, or ethnic barriers in order to establish representative governments. Until quite recently, extreme individualism and *incivisme* (lack of civility and civic consciousness) once raised serious doubts about the feasibility of democracy in France. Nonetheless, the Fifth Republic has now survived for over four decades—a remarkable record for a nation with a turbulent past. Similarly, many commentators attributed the failure of Germany's Weimar Republic, established after World War I, to an allegedly ingrained antidemocratic passion for order and authority among the Germans. But the success of democracy in former West Germany refuted that theory. By the same token, Japan had virtually no experience with democracy before World War II and its consensus-based patron–client culture appeared to be at odds with the basic principles of democracy. Yet Japan has been democratically governed for almost half a century. As we will see, India and Israel have functioned as democracies in the face of the most extreme diversity in one case and adversity in the other.

Are these nations exceptions that prove the rule? Or are generalizations about the irrelevance of democracy to many societies and cultures facile and false? The experiences of France, Germany, Japan, India, and Israel suggest that constitutional democracy is a surprisingly adaptable form of government.

FRANCE: PRESIDENT AGAINST PARLIAMENT

The U.S. presidential and British parliamentary systems represent two different approaches to democratic government. Under the Fifth Republic, France successfully combines elements of both systems.

The Fifth Republic: A Hybrid System

The Fifth Republic, created in 1958, represented an attempt to remedy the defects of previous republics. It was meant to overcome what its founder, Charles de Gaulle (1890–1970), understood to be the great nemesis of French politics: impotent executives dominated by fractious legislatures. Chronic governmental paralysis and popular disillusion had repeatedly led to the downfall of the constitutional system. As de Gaulle was fond of pointing out, France's first three experiments in republican government all ended in dictatorship. French history from 1878 to 1958 vividly illustrated what the authors of *The Federalist* understood very well: A rudderless government can become its own worst enemy.

Under the Fourth Republic (1946–58), governments lasted an average of six months. A profusion of political parties, some of fleeting duration, turned France's parliamentary system into a travesty. Worse, parties at the opposite ends of the political spectrum—Gaullists on the Right and Communists on the Left—both sought to undermine the constitution of the Fourth Republic. The only issue on which the two parties agreed was that the Fourth Republic was anathema, so they occasionally collaborated in bringing down governments. The two "extremist" parties had enough combined strength in the National Assembly to thwart initiatives and force the resignation of weak coalition governments (this has been called the negative veto).

Many in France hoped that the 1958 constitution would end the political instability. The new constitution was comparatively short and simple. Its provisions were guided by the political understanding of de Gaulle, who, in a famous address, presciently outlined its premises twelve years before its adoption:

> It is obvious that executive power should not depend on the Parliament, based on two houses and wielding legislative power, or else there will be a confusion of responsibilities in which the government will become nothing more than a cluster of party delegations . . . The unity, cohesion, and internal discipline of the Government of France must be sacred objects or else the country's leadership will rapidly become impotent and invalid. How can such unity, cohesion, and discipline be preserved if the executive power emanates from another body, with which it must be balanced, and if each member of a Government, which is collectively responsible before the national representative body, is but the emissary of his party? The executive power should, therefore, be embodied in a Chief of State, placed above the parties, elected by a body that includes the Parliament but is larger than it. . . .
>
> It is the role of the Chief of State to consider the general interest in his choice of men, while taking into account the orientation of the Parliament. It is his role to name ministers, and first of all, the Prime Minister, who will direct the policy and work of the Government. It is his role to promulgate laws and make decrees, for they obligate the citizens to the State as a whole. It is his task to preside over the Cabinet and, there, to defend the essential national continuity. It is his function to serve as an arbiter, placed above the political circumstances of the day, and to carry out this function ordinarily in the Cabinet, or, in moments of great confusion, by asking the nation to deliver its sovereign decision through elections. It is his role, should the nation ever be in danger, to assume the duty of guaranteeing national independence and the treaties agreed to by France.[4]

In sum, the centerpiece of the constitutional system, de Gaulle insisted, would be a strong executive branch to counterbalance the perennially divided parliament; the centerpiece of the executive branch, however, would be the chief of state (president) rather than the prime minister.

The Executive

The basic elements of de Gaulle's diagnosis are etched into nearly every provision of the 1958 constitution pertaining to the organization of public powers. In accordance with the parliamentary model, the French executive is divided. On paper, the prime minister (or premier) is the head of government, the president the head of state. Unlike the British monarch, however, the French president is democratically elected and wields considerable power. Indeed, the president, whose powers were specifically tailored to suit the ambitions of de Gaulle himself, is France's leading political figure. The French president is independent of the legislative branch, possesses a wide array of powers, serves a fixed term in office (seven years from 1962–2000, now five years).

The constitution positioned President de Gaulle as the arbitrator of conflicting interests and competing political parties. It also gave de Gaulle and his successors the upper hand in the realm of foreign policy. The French president can appoint

and dismiss the prime minister, dissolve the legislature and call for new elections, declare a state of emergency, issue decrees that have the force of law, and preside over cabinet meetings. In addition, the president can call for a national referendum on matters of extreme importance to the nation.

The 1958 constitution originally stipulated that the president was to be chosen by an electoral college composed of local and national officials in order to place the president above everyday politics. In 1962, de Gaulle imperiously placed before the French people a referendum calling for direct election of the president ("imperiously" because the constitution did not permit the president to bypass the

National Assembly in the amendment process). The referendum passed over-whelmingly, and from that point on French presidents have had a popular man-date to rule. De Gaulle knew that in a democracy nothing gives a political leader more legitimacy and authority than a direct endorsement by the voters.

Compared with the president, France's prime minister has generally exercised less power and influence, although there is a far greater balance between these two offices in recent years than there was in de Gaulle's time. The prime minister is cho-sen by the president and serves at his or her pleasure. As head of the government, the prime minister presides over the cabinet and is responsible to the legislature for public policy and national defense. The prime minister and his or her cabinet over-see the running of government and the bureaucracy. In general, however, the Con-stitution of the Fifth Republic did not clearly delineate which powers or functions belong to the president and which to the prime minister. Due to his unrivalled stature in French politics, de Gaulle enjoyed considerable latitude in interpreting the Constitution; thus, during his tenure, the presidential powers were elastic—de Gaulle could, and did, stretch them to fit the needs of the moment.

No president after de Gaulle would so dominate French politics. Although Socialist François Mitterrand served as France's president for fourteen years (1981–95), his reputation never matched that of de Gaulle. Still, during most of Mitterrand's rule, the balance of power clearly favored the presidency over the prime minister. France, under the Fifth Republic, did not have a prime minister who overshadowed or upstaged a president until 1988, when Jacques Chirac became the prime minister after his center-right party defeated Mitterand's Social-ist party in the 1986 national elections. In 1997, Lionel Jospin became prime minis-ter when his Socialist party turned the tables on Chirac, who had been elected president two years earlier (see page 144). In both these cases, the loss of a parlia-mentary election by the president's party resulted in a loss of face for the president and at least a temporary political advantage for the new prime minister (and head of the main opposition party).

Reduced Role of the National Assembly

If the presidency was clearly the big political winner under the Fifth Republic, the legislature was the loser. France's parliament is divided into two houses, the Sen-ate and the National Assembly. The French Senate, which has only limited pow-ers, is indirectly elected. The *National Assembly* is popularly elected from multimember districts in a double ballot (two-stage) election process. As the focal point of legislative power, the National Assembly must approve all proposed laws. However, the word *law* is rather narrowly defined by the 1958 constitution; many quasi-legislative decisions are left to the executive branch, which has the power to issue "decree laws."

The National Assembly is more interesting for the powers it does *not* have than for the powers it has. The executive sets the French parliament's agenda. Par-liament has a limited number of committees, it cannot meet for more than six months each year, and it has no power to introduce financial bills. If it fails to approve the government's budget by a certain deadline, the budget can be enacted by executive decree. Moreover, it can be compelled by the executive to cast a *package vote* on several pieces of legislation at once. Finally, the government can make any particular measure a vote of confidence; in such a case, a negative vote in the National Assembly forces the resignation of the government and gives the president the option of trying to form an alternative government or calling for new elections. Legislators may be reluctant to face new elections, especially if they have just incurred the wrath of a popular president.

De Gaulle went so far as to combine different provisions of the constitution in creative ways in order to gain even greater leverage over the parliament. At his direction, the government was not above calling for a package vote on some part of its overall program and then making the vote itself a matter of confidence. Since de Gaulle's departure from France's political scene in 1969, presidents have treated the National Assembly with greater deference.

Political Parties

France has a panoply of national political parties. As is the case in most European multiparty systems, French political parties are generally classified on a Left–Right continuum. The two most important parties of the Left (radical or liberal in orientation) are the Communist party and the Socialist party.

From the conclusion of World War II until the late 1970s, the Communist party generally received at least 20 percent of the popular vote. But over the past two

Jacques Chirac, a former neo-Gaullist prime minister, succeeded François Mitterrand, a Socialist, as president of France in May 1995. But in June 1997, President Chirac called for new parliamentary elections and was forced to name a Socialist, Lionel Jospin, to be the new prime minister when the center-right parties lost to the parties of the left. Jospin resigned after finishing last in a three-way presidential election in the Spring of 2002.

decades, there has been steady erosion of Communist party strength. The Socialist party has been the primary beneficiary on the Left. In fact, in 1981 it won a resounding victory at the polls and its candidate, François Mitterrand, was elected president. Although support for the Socialist party waned in the 1986 elections, it made a comeback in 1988 when Mitterrand was reelected and the Socialists again became the strongest party in parliament (although they did not have a clear majority).

For much of the 1990s, the popular tide ran with France's center-right parties. The center-right won in a landslide in 1993, retaking control of the National Assembly. Two years later, the neo-Gaullist candidate Jacques Chirac was elected president. Chirac's election, combined with the decisive center-right triumph in Senate elections the same year, put the forces of conservatism in the driver's seat—but not for long. The parliamentary elections called by President Chirac in June 1997, surprised everyone—especially Chirac, who had called the election early, expecting to receive a popular mandate for his economic austerity program. But the parties of the Left, again led by the Socialists, won overwhelmingly. Chirac had no choice but to name Lionel Jospin as the new prime minister.

The fact that Jean-Marie Le Pen's far-right National party won only one parliamentary seat in 1997 reflects the peculiar results of France's electoral system, in which a second round of balloting is required to elect delegates in voting districts where no candidate receives a majority in the first round. (However, it must be noted that Le Pen's strong showing in the first round of the 2002 presidential election gave the far-right new impetus.) Parties with similar political views are encouraged to form alliances between the two balloting rounds, agreeing to support one another's candidates in the districts where each is strongest. As a result, the influence of fringe or extremist parties is diminished.

Constitution under Pressure: Testing the Balance

In 1964, Prime Minister Georges Pompidou (who went on to serve as president from 1969 to 1974) described the delicate institutional balance of the Fifth Republic in terms that are still relevant today:

> France has now chosen a system midway between the American presidential regime and the British parliamentary regime, where the chief of state, who formulates general policy, has the basis of authority in universal suffrage but can only exercise his functions with a government that he may have chosen and named, but which in order to survive, must maintain the confidence of the Assembly.[5]

The Fifth Republic has brought stable democracy to France for nearly half a century now. The system created by the 1958 Constitution has worked far better than its predecessors, already lasting nearly four times longer than the Fourth Republic and exhibiting far less volatility than the Third Republic. De Gaulle's influence has extended well beyond his presidency. His successors have continued his emphasis on national pride and independence, his insistence on a major leadership role for France in a rapidly evolving Europe, his determination to enhance French prestige abroad (with an independent nuclear strike capability, among other things). Even de Gaulle's preference for a strong national economy that mixes a large role for the state (a French tradition) with a healthy respect for free-market principles remains firmly fixed as a part of his legacy.

Throughout this period, the National Assembly has also broadly supported these policies. The only (short-lived) exception came after 1981 when, for the first time, the Socialist party swept the presidential and parliamentary elections. In the exuberance of victory, the Socialists increased welfare programs and nationalized large pieces of French industry. But when the economy stalled in response to these market-busting measures, French voters punished the Socialist party at the polls, handing the center-right a victory in the 1986 elections. The message was clear: Leave well enough alone.

Ironically, while the president is arguably too far removed from public opinion, the French system as a whole is arguably too democratic for the society it serves. Since the president was elected every seven years until 2000 and a new parliament was elected at least every five years, frequent elections—and preparations for them—are a fixture of French politics. Indeed, legislative or presidential elections were held on fourteen separate occasions between 1962 and 1997. One authority suggested that "long-range programs gave place to expediency, and party alignments obeyed the logic of electoral tactics rather than policy making."[6] (Elections occur even more frequently in the United States, but off-year elections for the House and one-third of the Senate generally attract little voter interest.)

From the start of the Fifth Republic, France faced the potential danger of a *divided executive:* when the president and prime minister represent two different parties, embrace different ideologies, and advance different policies. Three such instances have occurred in the Fifth Republic, but the danger has thus far not posed an actual problem. In 1986, when rightist parties won national elections, Socialist President Mitterrand was compelled to invite the neo-Gaullist mayor Jacques Chirac to form a new government. In 1993, after President Mitterrand's Socialists were once again defeated by a right-of-center coalition, he reluctantly chose a center-right leader, Edouard Balladur, to be prime minister. Finally, in June 1997, President Chirac appointed Socialist Lionel Jospin to the office of prime minister after the center-right was defeated by parties of the left (led by the Socialists), but in 2002 Jospin himself suffered a humiliating first-round defeat when he challenged Chirac for the presidency.

The problem of the divided executive has led to the reality of *cohabitation*— a divided executive controlled by different parties living together uneasily. How well the president and prime minister work together is another matter. As noted, the formal demarcation of authority between these two executive offices is often murky, giving rise to the possibility of governmental deadlock. Nonetheless, past periods of cohabitation, while short, have not proved to be system threatening.

The Judicial System

The French judicial system is divided into two basic types of courts—ordinary courts and administrative courts—with different jurisdictions. Despite this rather routine distinction, there are some interesting and unusual innovations within the French legal system. For example, the High Council of the Judiciary, presided over

The French Agenda: A Sampler

Europe and World Trade

France cautiously continues to endorse expanded trade opportunities under the European Union (EU). Recent surveys indicate clearly, however, that a majority of the French believe a closer European union would call for "too many sacrifices." Under President Mitterrand, France backed the movement toward a single economy among the twelve (now fifteen) members of the EU. Nonetheless, many of France's traditional producers have felt threatened by competitors in Germany and other European countries. French farmers have been particularly vociferous in demanding protectionist measures, at times staging angry protests and demonstrations (for example, blocking major streets and roads with tractors). The proposal to establish a European Monetary Union (EMU) has caused a stir because large segments of French society have always vigorously resisted the idea of forfeiting national sovereignty to any supranational or international body. Furthermore, creating a single European currency depended on limiting the national budget deficit to 3 percent of a country's gross domestic product—a standard that motivated President Chirac to advocate budget-cutting measures. Those unpopular measures, in turn, were instrumental in enabling the Socialists and other parties of the Left to defeat Chirac's party in the June 1997 elections.

Unemployment and the Economy

Reasons for widespread disenchantment in French society today are not difficult to discern. In 1996, taxes and unemployment reached record highs, wages stagnated, and public spending was being cut, as were public-sector jobs; the national debt rose from 45.4 percent of the GDP in 1993 to an estimated 58 percent in 1997. The French economy grew at a sluggish pace of 0.9 percent in 1996, but accelerated to roughly 2.6 percent in 1997. However, unemployment was hovering above 12 percent, the second-highest rate in the EU, next to Spain. This persistent problem exacerbates the ever-tense relations between organized labor and the government in a country where workers often stage crippling strikes and demonstrations. Also, many French perceive a close link between unemployment and immigration, as immigrants willing to work for low wages crowd into cities and compete for scarce jobs.

Balancing Economic Security and Economic Growth

To reduce unemployment, the French desperately need to increase economic growth. But Prime Minister Lionel Jospin had promised during his 1997 election campaign to hire 350,000 more civil servants and reduce the work week from thirty-nine to thirty-five hours without reducing anyone's pay. Although these measures were popular for obvious reasons, they also placed France at a disadvantage in world economic competition, thus jeopardizing the long-term economic growth the French economy so badly requires.

Immigration and Society

The far-right National Front led by Jean-Marie Le Pen has taken up the immigration issue most stridently. More than 3 million Arabs, mostly from North Africa, plus a large number of newcomers from other former colonial areas in Africa and Asia, now live in France. Unemployment and urban decay have eroded traditional French hospitality toward political exiles, refugees, and asylum seekers. In response to popular pressures and complaints by the far right, the government has clamped down on illegal immigrants and treated claims of political persecution by seekers of asylum with greater skepticism. Foreigners, including tourists, are frequently heard to complain that they do not feel welcome in France. Le Pen's second-place finish in the first round of the 2002 Presidential elections shocked France (and all of Europe); although Chirac won in a landslide, Le Pen and his followers represent a serious challenge to mainstream parties.

by the president of the republic, considers issues regarding judicial promotions and discipline. Furthermore, the High Court of Justice is empowered to try the president of the republic for treason and members of the government for violations of criminal law resulting from abuses in office.

The Constitutional Council is composed of nine justices (three nominated by the president of the republic, three by the president of the National Assembly, and three by the president of the Senate), plus all the past presidents of the republic. This judicial watchdog plays several vital roles in the French system. It supervises presidential elections and can investigate and resolve contested legislative races. Under certain conditions, it can render opinions about the constitutionality of pending legislation and make similar determinations about laws that have been enacted. The cases that come before the Council are not the result of individual disputes or appeals (as in the United States). Rather they arise from special requests by the other two branches (executive and legislative). Typically, the issues it considers are political and deal directly with the constitutional powers exercised by different branches and offices of the government.

Does Democracy in France Work?

France has one of the two oldest democratic traditions in the world. The French Revolution occurred only a little more than a decade after the American Revolution and at almost precisely the same moment as the American Founders were meeting in Philadelphia to set up the first constitutional democracy in the modern world. Both revolutions enshrined liberty as the highest political good and both posited that political equality (another name for democracy) was the best, if not the only, way to safeguard liberty. But France's road to democracy was long and tortuous, compared to America's. Five times the French have tried "to get it right." By all appearances, they have gotten it right. Today, France has a robust economy (although it is now trouble-free), a strong civil society (with occasional protests by students, farmers, or labor groups), and a vibrant culture. France is a leader in the new Europe (the European Union or EU), a co-equal partner with its larger neighbor (and historical nemesis) Germany; and a key player in the Western alliance system known as NATO (the North Atlantic Treaty Organization). The overwhelming rejection of the xenophobic policies espoused by Jean-Marie Le Pen in the second round of the 2002 presidential election also can be taken as a positive sign of the maturing of the French electorate. By any reasonable measure, French democracy is working as well as can be expected in an imperfect world.

GERMANY: FEDERALISM AGAINST MILITARISM

Modern Germany came into existence in the latter part of the last century, bursting onto the European scene with two impressive military victories: over Austria in 1866 and France in 1871. To understand Germany's turbulent history in the twentieth century, it is necessary to examine an experiment in democracy that failed.

The Weimar Republic

Hitler's Third Reich grew out of the *Weimar Republic,* Germany's first experiment with constitutional democracy. According to many experts, the problem was not so much that the Weimar Republic failed but that it was never allowed to succeed. From the moment of its inception in 1919, it was associated with Germany's humiliating defeat in World War I and the harsh peace terms imposed under the Versailles Treaty. Burdened by punitive reparations to the victorious Allies that caused severe economic dislocations, the German people endured high unemployment, widespread business failures, and rampant inflation that sent periodic shock waves through the Weimar Republic. In the face of such turbulence, German society became increasingly polarized between the extreme Right and the extreme Left. The emergence of extremism in turn prompted governmental crises. In the words of one expert, "Stable democratic government was in jeopardy throughout the life of the Weimar Republic. The country was governed . . . by unpopular minority cabinets, by internally weak Grand Coalitions, or finally, by extra-parliamentary authoritarian Presidential Cabinets."[7]

Looking back, the collapse of the Weimar Republic was almost inevitable. Few democracies, it has been argued, could have survived such adversity. Whether democracy could have survived in post–World War I Germany even if political and economic conditions had been more favorable is anybody's guess. After all, the Germany ruled by Chancellor Otto von Bismarck (1871–90) and William II (1888–1918) was anything *but* democratic. Under those authoritarian rulers, free expression, political participation, and party politics had been repressed. In fact, obedience to authority was a German trademark. As a society, then, Germany appears to have been ill prepared for democracy in 1919, but the shortsighted, punitive policies dictated by the Versailles Treaty certainly did not help. Given this background, the founding of the Federal Republic of Germany in 1949 posed a crucial question. Could democracy *ever* work in a country that had only recently bowed to a brutal tyrant (Hitler), served a totalitarian state (the Nazi regime), and looked the other way while millions of innocent people (including children) were murdered in gas chambers?

Divided Germany: The Cold War in Microcosm

Understanding the origins of the Federal Republic of Germany (formerly known as West Germany) is important to evaluating its performance and its prospects. World War II destroyed Germany; the nation and its capital, Berlin, were subsequently divided among the Allies—the United States, Great Britain, France, and the Soviet Union. The intention was to merge the zones of occupation to prepare the way for self-government, but the Soviet Union refused to relinquish control of its portion of Germany, which declared itself the German Democratic Republic (GDR), or East Germany, when the other sectors united to form West Germany. From 1949 to 1990, Germany remained a divided nation. Berlin, the historical capital that was also divided, became a flash point during the *Cold War* between the United States and the Soviet Union. The very existence of a divided Germany reminded the world of the sharp political division between East and West—a division that threatened its very future.

Although East Germany became the most prosperous communist state in Eastern Europe, its economic performance paled by comparison with that of West Germany. The West German economy was hailed as a miracle after it made a spectacular recovery from the devastation of World War II. In the 1960s, West Germany became the keystone of the newly established Common Market, which subsequently grew into the world's largest trading bloc and is evolving into a single continental economy now called the EU. Meanwhile, the West German economy has continued to be the most dynamic force in Europe.

Equally impressive, democracy took hold in West Germany, in stark contrast to its communist neighbor, the GDR. The dramatic difference between the two Germanys was highlighted by the building of the Berlin Wall in 1961 to keep East Germans (and other East Europeans) from escaping to the West through West Berlin. The Berlin Wall not only divided East and West Berlin but also symbolized the political and economic differences between them.

Thirty years later, Germany was reunited. Pressure had long existed because East Germans, who endured far lower living standards than West Germans, had not been allowed to emigrate or even to visit the West. It was Mikhail Gorbachev (1985–91), the paramount leader of the Soviet Union, who provided the spark. The unpopular and insolvent communist regimes the Soviet Union had created in Eastern Europe after World War II were becoming major liabilities. Under Gorbachev (1985–91), the Soviet Union was no longer willing or able to prop up these failing economies and foundering states. East Germany's end came at a time when rebellion was rife in Central and Eastern Europe: Poland and Hungary had already taken giant steps toward dismantling communist rule, and Czechoslovakia, Romania, and Bulgaria were not far behind.

For East German communism, the unraveling started with a mass exodus. Hundreds of thousands fled through Hungary, Poland, and Czechoslovakia, where the communist leaders tried in vain to ride out the rising storm. At the same time, throngs of East Germans who chose to stay behind participated in large demonstrations in East Berlin, Leipzig, and elsewhere. What lay ahead was even more breathtaking—the bulldozing of the Berlin Wall following the collapse of the East German regime in late 1989.

United Germany: Democracy Triumphant

Within a matter of weeks, popular pressures brought down the hard-line regime of Erich Honecker, paving the way for the merger of the two German states. This union occurred faster than most experts had expected. In the democratic elections held in the former GDR in the spring of 1990, voters overwhelmingly rejected the East German Communist party. In October 1990, the two Germanys entered into a formal union, and Berlin was restored as the capital. With the collapse of Soviet power in Russia and the breakup of the Soviet Empire, Germany immediately became the dominant power in Europe.

Nevertheless, the remaking of Germany has carried a huge price tag. German reunification has cost tens of billions of dollars per year. West Germans have paid for the economic rehabilitation of East Germany with a 7.5 percent income tax surcharge and a higher sales tax. Unification was accompanied by social stresses as well—labor strikes, political demonstrations, an economic slowdown, high unemployment, hostility to immigrant workers, and the reemergence of far-right, neo-Nazi extremists. In the late 1990s, the unemployment rate in the east still stood at 21 percent, twice the rate in the west. It will take considerable time for Germany to become one economy and one society in the fullest sense.

German Federalism

Democracy is indeed thriving in Germany. Prior to 1989, the Federal Republic of Germany comprised ten states, or *Länder* (singular, *Land*), plus West Berlin. It encompassed an area about equal to that of Oregon. The merger of the two German states in 1989 enlarged the nation's territory and population and added six new *Länder* to the federal structure. Even so, no fewer than twenty-five countries the size of the new Germany would fit comfortably into the territory of the United States. The main reason for German federalism is political rather than geographic, to serve as a permanent check on the power of the center.

The Allied occupying forces drew the actual boundary lines of the *Länder* after World War II, but in most cases they correspond to earlier *Länder*. Although the country's geographic compactness may suggest a lack of regional diversity, some significant differences are seen in customs, attitudes, dialects, and so forth. Some *Länder*, however, do not correspond to natural patterns of regional or local diversity. Not surprisingly, then, Germany's federal system has brought about a somewhat greater degree of standardization among the *Länder* than American federalism has.

The *Länder* are the building blocks in a system designed to ensure a high degree of political decentralization. *Land* governments have the primary responsibility to enact legislation in certain specific areas such as education and cultural affairs. They alone have the means to implement laws enacted by the federal government, to command most of the administrative personnel to accomplish this task, to exercise police powers, or to administer the educational system. Finally, they alone have the authority to place limited restrictions on the press.

However, the federal government is not a weak link in the German political system. The government in Berlin has the exclusive right to legislate in foreign affairs, citizenship matters, currency and coinage, railways, postal service and telecommunications, and copyrights. In other areas, notably civil and criminal law and laws relating to the regulation of the economy, the central government, and the *Länder* have concurrent, or shared, powers.

Germany is more federal than the United States; that is, its *Länder* are more powerful and receive a larger proportion of taxes than American states do. For example, individual and corporate income taxes are split between Berlin and the *Länder* in equal 40 percent shares; cities get 20 percent. The *Länder* also receive one-third of the value-added tax, the large but hidden sales (or turnover) tax used throughout Europe. As a result, while some additional funds are transferred from Berlin to the *Länder* and cities, they do not have to make repeated pleas as American states and cities do in beseeching Washington for money.[8]

The Executive

Germany has a parliamentary form of government with a divided executive. The most important government official is the *chancellor*, who, with parliamentary approval, appoints and dismisses those who serve in the cabinet. In case of a national emergency, the chancellor becomes commander in chief of the armed forces and is responsible for the formulation and implementation of public policy.

As the titular head of state, the president serves a largely symbolic function, except in the event of political stalemate in parliament. Like the king or queen of

Great Britain, the president alone can remain above party politics and thus represents continuity and stability. The president is chosen indirectly and serves a seven-year term. The head of the majority party in the lower house of parliament becomes the chancellor; if no one party enjoys an absolute majority, as often has been the case, a coalition government chooses the chancellor.

The Legislature

The legislative branch of the German government is divided into a lower house, known as the *Bundestag,* and an upper house, called the *Bundesrat.* In this bicameral setup, as in France and Britain, the lower house is the more important of the two. In Germany, however, the upper house is a far more important player than in France and Britain.

The Bundestag   The presiding officer of the Bundestag is always chosen from the leadership of the majority party. Procedural matters are governed by rules inherited from the Reichstag (the prewar legislature). Important decisions regarding committee assignments, the scheduling of debates, and other questions of day-to-day parliamentary policy are made through the Council of Elders. This body consists of the president of the Bundestag, the three vice presidents (representing the two major parties—the Christian Democratic Union and the Social Democratic party—and the smaller Free Democratic party), as well as several other members chosen by each of the parties.

Bundestag deputies are democratically elected to four-year terms, although, as in other parliamentary systems, those terms may be cut short by a vote of no confidence. In this event, the chancellor resigns and the president dissolves the parliament. In Germany, unlike most other parliamentary systems, the Basic Law requires a "constructive" vote of no confidence. The chancellor cannot be ousted by a no-confidence vote unless the Bundestag simultaneously chooses a new chancellor.

The most important components of the Bundestag are the *Fraktionen.* To form a *Fraktion,* a political party must win at least fifteen legislative seats. Under the rules and procedures of the Bundestag, only through this unit of parliamentary organization can deputies be assigned to committees and parties receive formal recognition. Because the most important work is done in legislative committees, it is especially vital that political parties gain enough seats to form a *Fraktion.*

The Bundesrat   The upper house must pass on any measure that would alter the balance of powers between the national government and the *Länder.* Bundesrat members are appointed by the *Länder* governments rather than elected, and must vote as a bloc. In this way, the German states are given a powerful weapon to protect themselves against federal encroachment. As a result, the *Bundesrat* is one of the most important legislative upper houses found anywhere in the world. Germany's states governments play a primary role in implementing federal policy as well as in helping to shape that policy in the concurrent areas designated under the Basic Law.

Political Parties

The political party system was consciously designed to keep the number of parties at a reasonable level and to prevent tiny extremist groups from playing a significant role in the political life of the country. Parties must receive a minimum of 5 percent of the national vote and must win seats in a minimum of three electoral districts to gain Bundestag representation.

Another factor strengthening the major parties is the mode of elections to the Bundestag. Each voter casts two votes, one for the individual, one for a *list* determined by the party. This method of election gives the major parties a significant role in determining the future of those who aspire to careers in politics and public service, because fully half of the members of the Bundestag are elected from party lists in multimember districts by proportional representation. (In proportional representation (PR) systems, the political party not only determines who will be on the ballot but also in what rank order—the first candidate on the party list is most likely to win a seat, the last is certain not to.)

Since 1949, the German Federal Republic had just two major parties: the center-left Social Democratic party (SPD) and the conservative Christian Democratic Union/Christian Socialist Union (CDU/CSU). In addition, the relatively small Free Democratic party (FDP) managed to stay afloat and, most of the time, to play a strategic role in government by striking a balance midway between the evenly matched other two parties. Because the two major parties have frequently been in almost perfect balance in the Bundestag, the Free Democrats often have held the decisive votes. As a result, the influence of this little party has been disproportionate to its small following, and it has enjoyed junior partner status in most coalition governments.

Recently the Green party, which started as a social protest movement emphasizing environmental issues, has emerged as a party of some consequence. In 1998, when the SPD defeated the CDU/CSU but failed to win a majority of the seats in the Bundestag, the Social Democrats led by Gerhard Schroder entered into a coalition with the Greens to form a center-left government. Schroder became the new chancellor and Joshka Fisher, the leader of the Greens, became the new foreign minister. Several other cabinet posts also went to the Greens. This development marked the first time the Greens had ever participated in a German government.

Meanwhile, on the extreme right there are several small (but shrill) parties who seek to rekindle German nationalism and who despise foreigners, as well as racial and religious minorities such as Jews and Muslims. These parties include the National Democratic party (NPD), the German People's Union (GPU), and the Republican party. So far the extreme right remains a kind of lunatic fringe in Germany but the emergence of any extremism—especially on the right—is worrisome given Germany's record as a perpetrator of horrors during the era of Hitler and the Holocaust.

The Judiciary

Like Germany's other federal institutions, the court system was designed to provide a barrier against abuse of power by the central government. The regular judiciary, headed by the Federal Supreme Court, operates alongside a set of four specialized tribunals, known as the Federal Labor Court, the Federal Social Court, the Federal Finance Court, and the Federal Administrative Court. From a political standpoint, the most important judicial structure is the Federal Constitutional Court, which deals exclusively with constitutional questions and has the express power to declare unconstitutional the acts of both federal and *Land* legislatures.

In contrast to the procedures used in the selection of federal judges in the United States, Germany chooses its highest-ranking judges (those on the Federal Constitutional Court) by legislative election. The Bundestag elects half of these judges and the Bundesrat the other half. Most judges, however, are chosen on the basis of competitive civil service–type examinations and are appointed for life by the minister of justice, who is assisted by nominating committees, which are in turn selected by the federal and *Land* legislatures. To move up the judicial hierarchy, a German judge must be promoted from within, much like any other government employee in the regular civil service. Judicial independence is ensured by the fact that judges serve indefinite terms. In general, the court system seems reasonably well equipped to act as a barrier against abuses of executive or legislative power and as a guardian of civil liberties.

The Basic Law and Civil Liberties

In the realm of civil liberties, as one student of German politics has declared, "the relevant historical experience was that of the Third Reich, with its oppressive flouting of all human liberties."[9] The first nineteen articles of the Basic Law are devoted to a careful elaboration of the unalienable rights of every German citizen. All forms of discrimination, including religious and racial discrimination, are expressly prohibited. Freedom of speech, movement, assembly, and association are guaranteed except when they are used "to attack the free democratic order." This last proviso was clearly aimed at the two extremes, communism on the left and Nazism on the right, which have so afflicted German life in the twentieth century. Doubtless it reflected most of the postwar preoccupation with communism that prevailed throughout the Atlantic community and was particularly pervasive in Germany.

However, fear of a right-wing resurgence has never been far beneath the surface. Indeed, in postwar Germany neo-Nazi activity has generally been interpreted as constituting an "attack on the free democratic order."

Does Democracy in Germany Work?

One of the principal purposes behind the Basic Law was to arrange the institutional furniture in the "new Germany" to preclude a repeat performance of the "old Germany." Limited government—more than any other facet of constitutional democracy—was central to the drafters of the Basic Law, who deliberately sought to create safeguards against the concentration of power that had caused such turmoil in modern German history.

The democratic performance of the Federal Republic in the half-century since World War II has been impressive. The experience of Weimar has not been repeated. Whereas the Weimar Republic was largely undone by severe economic distress, West Germany's rapid postwar recovery and sustained industrial growth after 1949 have frequently been proclaimed an economic miracle. The Federal

The German Agenda: A Sampler

The Economy and Reconstruction of the Former GDR

Reuniting Germany has been costly. The former East Germany was economically depressed relative to its western counterpart. The infrastructure was in disrepair, factories operated with obsolete equipment, workers lacked essential skills, unemployment was high due to plant closings, and petty bureaucrats with little knowledge of modern management—holdovers from the communist era—proved difficult to dislodge from their positions. An improving economy benefited the coalition government headed by Helmut Kohl. In October 1994, Kohl was elected to serve his fourth four-year term as chancellor. However, after growing at 7–8 percent per year from 1992 to 1994, the economy of the east rose only 3.5 percent in 1996 and was expected to increase a mere 1.0 percent in 1997. Thus, the lopsided German economy, in which the west still accounts for 90 percent of the total GDP, is not likely to change soon.

Foreign Workers, Illegal Immigrants, and the Neo-Fascist Reaction

High unemployment (around 21 percent in eastern Germany) has been especially galling to East Germans, who were accustomed to full employment, job security, and low consumer prices under communist rule. Furthermore, numerous temporary workers and illegal immigrants from eastern Europe, the former Soviet Union, and the Middle East moved to Germany in order to take advantage of its prosperity. This has led to political controversy, ethnic tensions, and even instances of xenophobic persecution by German citizens worried that their nation may be inundated with foreigners. Among the more worrisome signs are the persistence of neo-Nazis (including skinheads), the continued efforts of the neo-fascist Republican party, and numerous acts of violence against foreigners.

Boosting the European Union

The Kohl government continues to be a staunch supporter of the EU, including the creation of a new European Monetary Union. Germany favors the movement toward a common Europe because without such a legitimizing structure, the fear of a new German juggernaut like the one Hitler launched in the 1930s would likely be raised anew. Another reason is that Germany knows it will be the dominant power in a united Europe; its strong economy ensures that it will have political clout and a competitive edge over other member states.

Investing in the East

Although western Germany's primary aim is to rebuild the eastern part, the Germans are also inclined by history and geography to look to central Europe for markets, raw materials, and investment opportunities. Germany is a natural trading partner for neighboring Poland and the Czech Republic and has a major interest in expanding trade with the republics of the former Soviet Union.

Redefining Its Role in Europe and the World

Germany today is in transition. Its importance and dynamism dictate that it will play a leadership role in Europe and beyond, but the precise nature of this role is unclear. When it participated in the UN peacekeeping mission in Bosnia in the mid-1990s, it was the first time German soldiers had been sent abroad since World War II. Germany will not continue to accept all the military restraints of the past half-century forever. Precisely how the new Germany will define its role in Europe and the world remains to be seen.

© Reuters NewMedia Inc. / CORBIS

German chancellor Helmut Kohl played a leading role in uniting Germany in 1990 and has been a strong advocate of European unification.

Republic became the leading industrial nation in western Europe and the third largest economic power in the "free world," trailing only the United States and Japan. This is one reason democracy succeeded where the Weimar Republic failed. Spurred on by a dynamic economy, the present generation of Germans has given democracy a new lease on life in a land where it was once thought to be unworkable. It was this very success more than any other single factor that led to the downfall of communism in East Germany.

It is too soon to say what long-term implications German unification will have for Europe and the world. Germany is now firmly committed to representative democracy and its economy is anchored in the burgeoning EU. Today there is little doubt that the new Germany will be a driving force in any future economic and political arrangements in Europe. Nor is there serious reason to doubt that German democracy will continue to flourish, having overcome the formidable challenge of converting the former East Germany from languishing dictatorship to full partnership in democracy.

JAPAN: PARLIAMENTRY RULE
IN THE LAND OF CONSENSUS

Like other Asian societies, Japan had no democratic traditions prior to 1947. In fact, its history and culture often worked against Western democratic ideas. Yet today Japan is one of Asia's oldest parliamentary democracies (the other one, India, came into being at the same time but under very different circumstances). To see how this remarkable transformation came about, we must first sketch the historical background of Japan.[10]

Historical Background

Japan's feudal era lasted until the *Meiji Restoration* in 1868. At that time, under the guise of recapturing ancient glories, a new emperor (the Meiji dynasty) was crowned, and the modernization of Japan was begun. Although some lip service was paid to democracy, Meiji Japan remained an oligarchy. A group of elder statesmen, or *genro*, dominated the government. The role of the emperor was long thought to be largely symbolic, but recent scholarship suggests that this interpretation is wrong. Worshipped as a flesh-and-blood deity, the emperor personified national unity, but he apparently also played an active role in decision making at crucial times.[11]

Domestically, Japan made great progress during this period. Economic development was promoted, protected, and subsidized by a modernizing elite. Only the basic or strategic industries were government-owned. This program of economic modernization was modeled after that of the West. Despite periodic opposition from rural landowners, the government force-fed the economy with a program of capital development designed to promote heavy industry. Within a few decades, the leaders of the Meiji Restoration, according to one authority, "abolished feudal institutions, legalized private property in land, started a Western-style legal system, established compulsory education, organized modern departments of central and local government, and removed the legal barriers between social classes."[12]

With the conclusion of World War I and the departure of the Meiji leadership, Japan entered a new phase of political development. Nationalism, taught in the schools, became a kind of religion. Governments blossomed and withered in a rapid and bewildering succession. Attempts were made at instituting democratic reforms: In 1925, for example, economic qualifications for voting were removed, and the franchise was extended to all men over the age of twenty-five. During the 1930s, however, such tentative democratic reforms were submerged in a wave of militarism. Charging that effete politicians infatuated with democracy had kept Japan inferior, ultranationalists declared that only a strong military leadership could propel Japan to its rightful place in the world community. The militarists triumphed, but their victory led only to Japan's ignominious defeat in World War II.

The relative ease and speed with which democratic reforms were crushed in the 1930s reflected the fact that the Japanese had never really embraced the concept of constitutional government. Sovereignty, according to popular belief, issued from the emperor–deity, not from the people. Thus, prewar Japan dallied with democracy in form far more than substance.

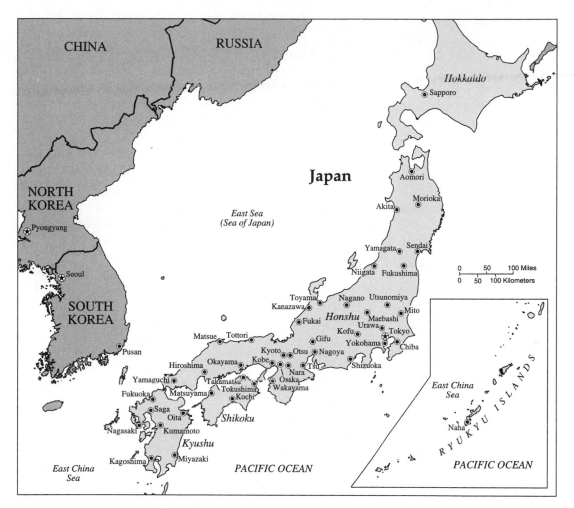

The New Constitution

The 1947 Japanese constitution, imposed by the United States after its victory in World War II, sought to remake Japan's political system. Henceforth, sovereignty would reside in the Japanese people, not in the emperor. The American influence on the new Japanese constitution is glaringly apparent, especially in its preamble:

> We, the Japanese people, acting through our duly elected representatives in the National Diet, determined that we shall secure for ourselves and our posterity the fruits of peaceful cooperation with all nations and the blessings of liberty throughout this land, and resolved that never again shall we be visited with the horrors of war through the action of government, do proclaim that sovereign power resides with the people and do firmly establish this Constitution. . . . Government is a sacred trust of the people, the authority for which is derived from the people, the powers of which are exercised by representatives of the people, and the benefits of which are enjoyed by the people.

Like weavers of an intricate tapestry, the framers of the 1947 constitution sought to construct an elaborate system of representative democracy. Among the fundamental rights guaranteed by the constitution were the right of citizens to an equal education and the right of workers to organize and bargain collectively. In another extraordinary feature, the Japanese constitution explicitly renounced war and pledged that "land, sea, and air forces, as well as other war potential, will never be maintained." (This provision has not, however, prevented the government from building limited "self-defense forces.")

Parliamentary Democracy: Appearance versus Reality

The constitution establishes a parliamentary form of government. The emperor remains the head of state, although merely as a ceremonial figure. The prime minister is the real head of government. The authors of the constitution, however, placed a preponderance of *formal* power in the new bicameral legislature. That body, called the *Diet*, was divided into a 511-member House of Representatives elected at least every four years (elections can be more frequent when the House is dissolved) and a relatively less powerful 252-member House of Councillors, who served six-year terms (half being elected every three years).

Originally, members of each house were elected by universal suffrage from multimember districts in which voters made only one selection. This system endured until 1994, when calls for election reforms led to redrawing district boundaries and altering the election process for the lower House (creating 300 single-seat constituencies and leaving the remaining 200 seats to be decided by proportional representation).

The constitution explicitly stated that popular sovereignty was to be expressed through the Diet, the only institution of the government empowered to make laws. Whereas in the past the prime minister and cabinet had been responsible to the emperor, they were now made responsible to the Diet, the "highest organ of state power." Japan's Supreme Court was empowered to declare laws unconstitutional (which it rarely does), and justices were to be approved by the voters every ten years after their appointment (which has become virtually automatic).

As we shall see, however, the Japanese have adapted Western institutions to fit their own highly resilient cultural traditions. The result has been a unique system that combines the new (democratic politics and market economics) with the old (political hierarchy, economic centralization, and social discipline).

The Party System

The Liberal Democratic party (LDP) dominated Japanese politics from 1955 to 1993. Although sundry smaller parties existed, they remained largely ineffectual. Among these opposition parties, the Socialists and Communists occasionally garnered significant numbers of votes, but the legislative role of both of these parties was one of parliamentary opposition. For four decades, the actual governing of the country fell almost exclusively to the LDP.

When a single party retains a majority of seats in a freely elected legislative assembly over an extended time span, it usually means that the party has satisfied a broad range of social interests. In Japan, the LDP succeeded because it sacrificed narrow party fervor for broad popular appeal, catered to powerful special interests, had an enormous advantage in financial and organizational resources, and benefited from the sheer force of political inertia. According to two authorities:

> The reasons for the long period of conservative domination are not too far to seek. In the first place, it was the conservatives who carried out the reforms and helped to see to it that there was not a complete discontinuity with the past. When independence came, they accepted the land reform. The changes they made toward a more strongly centralized system of government corrected some of the most obvious mistakes of the Occupation. The Liberal Democratic party, being in power, also controlled a considerable amount of patronage and had the advantage when seeking the support of economic and professional interest groups. With the support of the majority of the rural vote and access to the resources of the business community, the party was in a strong position. It was on intimate terms with the bureaucracy. The significant thing, however, was that close ties with the bureaucracy and with the business world and the control of patronage were not sufficient. Beginning in 1955, the Liberal Democratic party attempted to build up a national organization with mass membership. This was a surprisingly difficult thing to do in Japan where, on the local scene, groups based on personal loyalties, often around one individual, were more acceptable than branch units of a national party.[13]

The LDP's consensus-building role as Japan's invincible umbrella party—a loose-knit coalition of various interest groups rather than a cohesive voting bloc—became a defining feature of Japanese politics. The person chosen to lead the party before a national election automatically became the prime minister prior to 1993. But the LDP's party conference is not a monolithic body. The outcome of the vote for party president is the result of intense bargaining by party factions, each of which had its own leader, its own constituencies to protect, and its own projects to promote.

Japan's stable, one party–dominant system was shattered by the defeat of the LDP in the historic 1993 national elections. What really happened was that the LDP self-destructed. That is, it splintered in the early 1990s, when several LDP faction leaders quit the party after a series of highly embarrassing political scandals involving top LDP leaders severely tarnished the party's image. These scandals, however, only indirectly led to the collapse of Kiichi Miyazawa's government in the summer of 1993: A rising tide of social discontent over the rigors of daily life, high prices, long workdays, and the like also contributed to the party's undoing.

The ruling party's defeat did not produce a clear-cut alternative; the LDP was the clear loser but there were no clear winners. A shaky coalition of eight centrist, center-left, and leftist parties chose a newcomer to the political scene, Morihiro Hosokawa, as the new prime minister. Hosokawa was the head of the tiny New Japan party, which won only 35 seats, putting it in fifth place in parliamentary representation behind the LDP (223 seats), the Social Democratic party (70 seats), the Japan Renewal party (55 seats), and the Clean Government party (51 seats). Although all eight parties in the coalition opposed the LDP, that negative consensus was not enough to support Hosokawa's leadership for long.

The Hosokawa government lasted less than a year, and its successor, a government headed by Tsutoumo Hata, remained in power a scant two months. Like

Hosokawa, Hata was also an ex-member of the LDP who broke away to form a new party. When his fledgling New Frontier party proved to have a short political shelf life, Hata created yet another political vehicle, the Nationalist party. The simultaneous appearance of other new parties suggested that a kind of political transformation was occurring in Japan. The once highly stable Japanese party system had suddenly become fragmented and unpredictable. Japan appeared to be in the process of party realignment, but the final result of that process was not at all clear.

Japan's political volatility would continue. In June 1994, a Socialist party leader was chosen by an LDP-led coalition to head another new government—a political arrangement that would have been unimaginable a year earlier. Eighteen months later, Ryutaro Hashimoto, the head of the LDP, became the fifth Japanese prime minister in less than three years. In the meantime, the Liberal Democrats' rehabilitation was confirmed by the October 1996 elections, when voters handed the LDP a victory (although not quite a majority) in the Diet. Nonetheless, the party remained in the hands of a change-resistant old guard and again fell out of favor with the public as the economy continued a downslide throughout the 1990s.

In the spring of 2001, Junichiro Koizumi, a charismatic reformer won a hard-fought campaign to become the party's new president. Koizumi ran against the LDP's elders and against the conservative cronyism they represent. He did not enjoy the support of his own parliamentary party, but the party rank and file (and the public in general) responded enthusiastically to his personal charm, fresh ideas, and candor. He promised reform "without any sacred cows." Japan's political-economic structure is a haven for sacred cows. Its impenetrable and closed economy is in urgent need of structural reform as evidenced by a prolonged economic slump, a dismal stock market (reflected in the Nikkei index), and a sharp drop in asset prices (some property values have fallen by as much as 80 percent since the early 1990s). Before Koizumi can turn Japan around economically, he will have to tackle the political-economic reforms initiated after 1993, which have subsequently stalled. In tradition-bound Japan, this task amounts to a very tall order.

The Obstacles to Political Change

Contemporary Japanese democracy combines a unique blend of native culture and imported democracy. In particular, the Japanese democracy founded in 1947 retains elements of Japan's traditional patron–client system that had long characterized Japanese politics. The patron–client system comprises factional leaders and loyal followers. Personal loyalty is the basis of financial support, intraparty power, and the prestige of individual leaders within the LDP. To what extent the fragmentation of the LDP and the 1994 passage of electoral and anticorruption reforms have perhaps undermined this system of patron–client politics is difficult to determine. Nonetheless, with a fragmented party system and a less stable government, political power has become somewhat more diffuse and fluid, but it is unclear whether or to what degree it has disrupted the traditional behind-the-scenes collusion among government, bureaucracy, and the business elite.

Another tradition that may be slowly undermined by the stark political changes within Japan is the nation's preference for arriving at decisions by con-

© AFP / CORBIS

Prime Minister Junichiro Koizumi, leader of the Liberal Democratic party, celebrates his party's impressive victory in the 2001 election for the upper house. Koizumi has led the LDP back to a position of dominance in Japanese politics.

sensus (as opposed to adopting, say, the British notion of the loyal opposition). According to one expert:

> This method rests on the premise that members of a group—say, a village council—should continue to talk, bargain, make concessions, and so on until finally a consensus emerges. . . . Despite the spread of democratic norms, this tradition of rule by consensus still has its appeal and sometimes leads to cries against the "tyranny of the majority"—for example, when the ruling party with its majority pushes through legislation over the strong protests of the opposition.[14]

Like the remnants of patron–client ties that still remain in Japan, consensus seeking is also deeply rooted in Japan's political culture and unlikely to disappear soon. Yet, there is little doubt that multiple parties and increased political instability complicate, and perhaps undermine, the society-wide consensus-building process and incline those in the political system to direct their efforts toward direct opposition, in contrast to quiet cooperation and negotiation.

The Judiciary and Japanese Culture

The Japanese judicial system displays a curious combination of American and European influences. The American influence is evident in the name of Japan's highest judicial body, the Supreme Court. The chief justice is appointed by the emperor but nominated by the government; all other justices are appointed by the cabinet without the pretense of a bow to the Emperor. The Supreme Court, like its American counterpart, enjoys the power of judicial review (meaning it can declare acts of the legislature unconstitutional). Although an arrangement of this kind is not surprising to most Americans, it is, in fact, extraordinary to give a few appointed officials the power to undo the acts of more than 750 elected ones. Indeed, most constitutional democracies do not permit judges to second-guess legislators.

The legal system as a whole is modeled after the European civil law system, but again with some American influences. Culturally, the Japanese are far less prone than Americans to sue each other, to resort to the courts as a means of set-tling civil disputes, or to seek redress for alleged injuries and injustices. In Japan, social rather than judicial remedies are still the norm. Often, successful interven-tion by a respected member of the community, the head of the family, or a supervi-sor at work makes legal action unnecessary.

Does Democracy in Japan Work?

Despite the jarring economic and political bumps Japan has experienced in the past decade or so, Japanese democracy has been steady and stable during most of the post–World War II period. In view of Japan's lack of prior experience with popular self-government, this achievement is all the more impressive. As in the case of Germany, economics has played a key role in sustaining democracy in Japan. Its economic revival after World War II was swift and dynamic, as bombed-out cities (symbolized, of course, by Hiroshima and Nagasaki) were turned into models of efficient and innovative industrial production. Deliberate planning by a modernizing entrepreneurial elite was important to Japan's resurgence; a rising vol-ume of world trade and massive American purchases during the Korean War (1950–53) were also crucial. Within two decades, an export-oriented, mercantilist economic strategy produced huge advances in heavy industry—notably automobile manufacturing, robotics, and consumer electronics. Today Japan stands as a global economic power, despite "the loss of 52 percent of Japan's prewar territories, the return of five million persons to a country about the size of California, the loss of 80 percent of Japan's shipping, and the destruction of one-fifth of [its] industrial plants and many of [its] great cities."[15]

In the mid-1980s, the success of the Japanese market economy was clearly apparent in Japan's massive multibillion-dollar trade surpluses with the United States, which had become a market for over one-third of Japan's exports. This led to sharp criticism of Japanese trade practices in the United States. Japanese offi-cials countered that Americans look for "made in Japan" on the products they buy because American products are inferior in quality. The strains between the two nations have been evident for over a decade and could be detected in the rise of nationalism within Japan and the rise of anti-Japanese, "buy American" sentiment in the United States.

Japan has emerged as the dominant economic force in the Asian Pacific and the world's second-largest economy, but recent experience shows that even Japan's robust economy is not recession proof. Beginning in the early 1990s, the Japanese economy stagnated as its growth rate slowed dramatically under the impact of four recessions in a dozen years. After 1996, the Japanese banking sys-tem came under pressure as demands for government intervention or assistance mounted and many Asia economies (beginning with Thailand's) plummeted due to profligate bank lending and woefully inadequate regulation of financial institu-tions. Japan's economy continued to spiral downward in the early years of the new century led by a troubled banking system trapped in circumstances of its own making—industries such as construction, real estate, and retail trade in Japan

The Japanese Agenda: A Sampler

Restoring Governmental Continuity

In the 1990s, the most pressing political issue facing Japan is institutional in nature: Now that the LDP's monopoly has been broken, can Japan regain the political stability it enjoyed under LDP rule and without which its post–World War II "economic miracle" might not have happened? Or will Japan's democracy continue to be buffeted by the uncertainties that resulted from a steady succession of weak coalition governments incapable of mustering broad popular support or achieving consensus in a society that has always prized consensual decision making?

Retaining a Competitive Edge

Of late, Asia has proved to be economically volatile. Still, long term, Japan's dominant trade position in Asia is being challenged on several fronts. One group of challengers comprises the so-called newly industrialized countries (NICs)—South Korea, Taiwan, and Singapore. (Hong Kong was part of this group until it reverted to Chinese control in 1997, and its fate as an independent actor in the world economy remains uncertain.) A second wave of developing Asian countries, led by Thailand and Malaysia, is also changing the face of regional economic relations in Asia. But by far the biggest Asian challenge to Japanese mercantilism in the long run is posed by the rapid emergence of China as a major force in the global economy.

Maintaining Close Relations with the United States

The United States is Japan's most important ally and trading partner. As Japan's largest market and favorite place to invest, the United States is vital to Japan's economic health (and vice versa). The U.S. military presence in the western Pacific, as well as the American nuclear umbrella (which, in theory, protects not only the United States but also America's closest military allies from nuclear attack), have enabled Japan to concentrate on development of high-technology consumer industries and overseas markets, while spending less than one percent of its gross domestic product on defense. However, strains in the relationship have occurred because of long-standing disputes over trade issues, as well as differing views on the proper response to the threat posed by North Korea's nuclear weapons development program. According to the U.S. government, the perennial American trade deficit vis-à-vis Japan is caused by Japan's protectionist policies and an insular culture that often makes it all but impenetrable to potential foreign competitors.

Sustaining a High Standard of Living

Despite the prolonged economic downturn plaguing the country since the early 1990s, Japan remains an affluent society. But it is also a small country with a large population; most of its land is mountainous and unsuitable for settlement. The problems associated with overcrowding—air and noise pollution, traffic congestion, high land prices—are all prevalent in Japan. Modern technology has not yet provided Japan, or any other country, with solutions to the negative aspects of economic overdevelopment.

Balancing Tradition and Modernity

Japanese culture still exerts a powerful force beneath the surface of Japanese society. To the casual observer, Japan appears to be the epitome of modernity. But in reality, most Japanese are steeped in traditional values and attitudes, tenaciously clinging to the past. This makes it very difficult for outsiders to gain access, including those seeking to do business in Japan. An ongoing debate focuses on the tradition-versus-modernity issue. Some argue that Japan should open its doors to other nations, whereas others fear that Japan has already allowed in too much foreign influence that may jeopardize Japanese culture. Japan's economic downturn intensified this argument, causing some to argue that Japan's economy urgently required modernization and fundamental structural reform.

are riddled with deeply indebted businesses that overborrowed from banks all too willing and eager to collude while the government looked the other way.

After the economic miracle that coincided with Japan's first few decades of democracy and the economic surge of the 1980s, is Japan's parliamentary democracy in jeopardy now that the country has gone from boom to bust? The answer is no. Despite the severe setbacks of the 1990s, public opinion is still positive: some 60 percent of Japanese continue to be satisfied with life in general—a figure that has hardly changed since the "good old days" when Japan was the envy of Asia and the world. The persistence of this reservoir of optimism in the face of hard times is but one reason to believe that Japan's democracy is here to stay. Moreover, nothing succeeds like success. It is no accident that Japan's economic success has undergirded a political system that places civil liberties above unquestioned authority and military conquest.

PARLIAMENTARY RULE IN UNLIKELY PLACES

Even if parliamentary rule works in Europe and Japan (where it was imposed from the outside after Japan's defeat in World War II), can it work in other nations and regions where democracy has no roots in native traditions or even in a country that finds itself in a perpetual state of war with its neighbors? The experience of India and Israel is suggestive, if not conclusive: The answer is a pleasant surprise to admirers of parliamentary democracy.

India: A Parliamentary Miracle

India is home to an ancient Hindu civilization and great empires, including that of the *Moghuls* (Muslim conquerors). It was reduced to a colony of Great Britain in the nineteenth century, but regained its independence after World War II. Two large and distinct populations—one Hindu (the larger of the two) and other Muslim—inhabited the territory of historical India prior to World War II. The heaviest concentration of Muslims was in the northwestern and eastern parts, while the vast lands in between—constituting the bulk of the territory under the *British Raj* (colonial rule)—were dominated by Hindus. To avoid conflict between these two religiously distinct communities, the retreating British created two states: India and Pakistan. The western part of Pakistan was separated from the eastern part with India in the middle.

This geographic anomaly, however, was only one of the future problems the British left unresolved. Another was the Hindu–Muslim split within India: Although most Muslims inhabited the territory of Pakistan, a large Muslim minority remained within the territory of the newly independent state of India. Even more problematic for its future as a democracy was the fact that India is a mosaic of diverse ethnic and cultural minorities speaking a babble of different and mutually incomprehensible languages, not to mention several religions, including Sikhism, Jainism, and Christianity, as well as Hinduism and Islam.

Finally, no account of contemporary India is complete without mentioning

GATEWAYS TO THE WORLD: EXPLORING CYBERSPACE

http://library.byu.edu/~rdh/wess/fren/polygov.html

This site from the Association of College and Research Libraries is an excellent starting point for further information on French government and politics, including the political parties, at the national, regional, and local levels.

http://www.germany-info.org/

A general information site on Germany, including a collection of contacts' addresses and phone numbers from various levels and sectors of the German government, vital statistics on Germany, and links to other sites. Some of the referenced sites are available only in German, whereas others have an English translation.

http://darkwing.uoregon.edu/~felsing/jstuff/gov.html

This site contains links to a variety of text and multimedia pages grouped by category. Some of the links on this page are to sites available only in Japanese.

http://www.mofa.go.jp/

This is the official Web site of the Ministry of Foreign Affairs of Japan. It is updated daily with press releases, news, and other information related to the government and foreign policy of Japan. There are links to general information sites as well.

---

poverty and the population explosion. These two problems go hand in hand in many parts of the so-called developing world. India was (and remains) the second most populous country in the world (only China is larger). Today, India has more than one billion inhabitants. Tens of millions are illiterate and hundreds of millions are very poor, living in villages that continue to be home to the vast majority of the population.

India has experienced a great deal of political turmoil and has fought several wars with its neighbors—both China and Pakistan. The conflict with Pakistan, which involves the disputed territory of *Kashmir*, is especially troublesome. Both India and Pakistan have advanced nuclear development programs and both are thought to have operational nuclear weapons. The tensions between India and Pakistan have led to armed conflict on several occasions, most recently in the spring and summer of 2002. One of the most dangerous moments came in the early 1970s when East Pakistan broke away and became the present state of Bangladesh. In addition, communal conflict (involving Hindus, Muslims, and Sikhs) and ethnic violence have posed a major threat to India's survival and stability.

And yet, there it is: a parliamentary democracy functioning for more than half a century in a society faced with staggering challenges presented by such extremes of size and diversity that its very existence for five decades as a single state under a single form of government—*any* form of government—is nothing short of miraculous. Except for one brief interlude in the late 1970s (when then Prime

Minister Indira Gandhi declared a state of national emergency and assumed dictatorial powers), India's leaders (starting with the great Jawaharlal Nehru) have operated within the framework of a British-style parliamentary democracy.

India is a federal system with an indirectly elected president who plays an essentially ceremonial role in the government. The real power resides in a freely elected parliament and a prime minister who is the leader of the majority party (as in other parliamentary systems). The prime minister chooses a cabinet that is presented for approval to the *Lok Sabha* (lower house) parliament. The *Rajya Sabha* (upper house) is indirectly elected; it plays "second fiddle" to the lower house but debates—and can delay—passage of legislation, thus giving its members a real voice in the policy- and law-making process.

Israel: A War Republic

Like India, Israel came into being after World War II. Unlike India, Israel was a nation of newcomers rather than native-dwellers; also in stark contrast to India, Israel's population and territory were tiny—the problem Israel faced was being too small, not too large. From its inception as a state, Israel was awash in controversy and surrounded by hostile Arab neighbors. In fact, Israel's very birth was violent, involving a bitter and prolonged struggle with the indigenous population of *Palestinian Arabs*.

Israel is a secular state but it is a Jewish society. The great influx of Jews into *Palestine* followed on the heels of Hitler's rise to power in Germany in the 1930s; however, the movement for a Jewish state in the modern era dates back to the 1890s. *Zionism* (as this movement was called) gathered momentum in 1917 (World War I) with the famous *Balfour Declaration*, named for the then British foreign minister who authored the first official endorsement of the idea of a Jewish state (at the time, Palestine was a virtual colony of Great Britain). In a real sense, Israel is a child of the Holocaust (see Chapter 5) that occurred in Nazi Germany (1939–45). With a battle cry of "never again" and the support of two major powers, Israel's founders triumphed in 1947 against considerable odds.

Israel was forged in the fires of war and tragedy, but Israel enjoyed the legitimacy that accompanies acceptance by three "united" forces in the early postwar world—the United States, Great Britain, and the United Nations (successor to the League of Nations). The original idea was to create two states in Palestine, one for Jews and the other for Palestinian Arabs and to make Jerusalem (sacred to three religions) an international city under the auspices of the United Nations. That idea was stillborn when the Palestinian Arabs rejected the deal they were offered (Israel accepted). Most Palestinian Arabs were displaced then, living in squalid refugee camps in the Gaza Strip, the West Bank of Jordan, and Lebanon. Some fled to other Arab countries farther away.

This situation left a legacy of bitterness and despair, one that has inscribed itself in Middle Eastern history for all time. Israel fought and won three wars with Egypt: the 1956 Suez War, the 1967 Six-Day War, and the 1973 Yom Kippur War. In the 1967 war, Israel seized control of the Gaza Strip and the Sinai desert from Egypt, the West Bank from Jordan, and the Golan Heights from Syria. In the 1973 war, Israel was in a position to conquer all of Egypt but, under heavy diplomatic pressure from the United States, decided against doing so. In 1978, President Jimmy Carter brokered the *Camp David Accords*—a peace treaty between Egypt and Israel. This historic deal involved large U.S. subsidies to both parties, but it worked: Egypt and Israel have not exchanged blows now for almost three decades (since 1973).

Sadly, the history of the Middle East in general and Israel in particular since 1978 has been turbulent and violent. Israel has been in the middle of a maelstrom most of the time. Lebanon, Libya, Syria, Iraq, and Iran have been among the chief antagonists (and belligerents) in this never-ending tale of woe. In the 1980s and 1990s, a protracted Palestinian uprising—called the *intifadah* in Arabic—in the occupied territories caused many deaths and much suffering on both sides. Although it is customary to speak of two such uprisings, it is really one that was interrupted for several years during the 1990s when the hope of peace settlement hung in the balance. Peace has proven elusive and at the time of this writing Israel remains at war with the Palestinians in the occupied territories, while the Palestinians continue to carry out suicide bombings in Israel.

Despite all this turmoil, Israel has been governed as a parliamentary democracy without interruption since its founding. Like Great Britain, Israel does not have a written constitution, putting these two countries in a class by themselves. The reason Israel does not choose to put constitutional principles down on paper is also the basis for an important caveat to parliamentary rule in Israel: The perceived need for extreme security measures has led to restrictions on civil liberties and systematic discrimination against the roughly 600,000 Palestinian Arabs who are citizens of Israel, compared to roughly 5.1 million Jews. Nonetheless, Israeli citizens have the right and opportunity to vote in free elections on regular occasions.

Indeed, Israel is perhaps too democratic for its own good: elections based on a wide-open PR system in which even small upstart parties can often win a few seats means Israel's *Knesset* (parliament) is a free-for-all that is often confusing and chaotic. Governments are forged from coalitions of the Left or Right depending on the mood of the country, the state of relations with Arab neighbors, and the outcome of the last election. The occurrence of one crisis after another has probably saved Israel from the consequences of a contentious political culture and a chaotic party system, including a great deal of governmental instability.

Nonetheless, Israel remains a marvel of economic and political survival in an environment that has been inimical to its existence from the start. If Israel can function as a parliamentary democracy, albeit with enormous public and private support from the United States, any society with the necessary cultural supports can. It must be said, however, that these "cultural supports" are a product of Israel's origins in the West.

To a certain degree, the influence of the West (in particular, Great Britain) also helps to explain the success of democracy in India, but not to a *sufficient* degree. Taken together, the experience of these two countries as operational parliamentary democracies under extremely adverse circumstances does not prove that popular self-government can work everywhere but does prove that it can work in some very unlikely places.

PRESIDENTS AND PARLIAMENTS:
A COMPARATIVE VIEW

How do the two main types of democracy—presidential and parliamentary—stack up against each other? The United States and Great Britain will serve as the two "models" in this section, for simplicity's sake.

The Legislature

The purpose of a legislature in any constitutional democracy is to enact laws. Beyond that general similarity, however, the British legislative branch is surprisingly unlike its American counterpart. Perhaps the most fundamental difference is one of principle. In the British tradition, Parliament is sovereign. According to Sir William Blackstone (1723–1780), the famed British jurist, Parliament can do "everything that is not naturally impossible." In the words of another authoritative writer, "This concept of *parliamentary sovereignty* is of great importance and distinguishes Britain from most other democratic countries. Parliament may enact any law it likes, and no other body can set the law aside on the grounds that it is unconstitutional or undesirable."[16] In contrast, the American system places the Constitution above even Congress. Ever since the 1803 case of *Marbury v. Madison*, the U.S. Supreme Court has successfully asserted its right and duty to overturn any law passed by Congress it deems unconstitutional.[17]

Nonetheless, certain functions performed by the legislative branches under both systems are essentially the same. Both elective legislative bodies, for example, can pass or defeat proposed new laws, both confirm new cabinet ministers, and both have the power to question and investigate the chief executive and cabinet members, although this function is performed more directly and dramatically in the British Parliament than in the U.S. Congress. Also, both serve as forums in which the burning issues of the day are openly debated.

Unlike Great Britain, however, other countries with parliamentary systems (except for Israel) have written constitutions. Typically, parliaments created under a formal constitution cannot violate or tamper with that charter. Amendments are possible, of course, but the process is generally cumbersome and often controversial. The constitution frequently sets up a special constitutional court, as is the case in Germany, France, and Spain (to cite but a few examples) with the power to declare any law or government decree unconstitutional.

Legislative Independence   Although congressional powers are limited by the Constitution, U.S. legislators have far more latitude for independent action than do British MPs because U.S. representatives and senators are elected as individuals rather than on party tickets, Congress is an assembly of over 500 potential prima donnas. Political parties wield some influence, but in the United States they are far too weak to enforce discipline. Also, the possibility that one political party may dominate the Senate and the other the House of Representatives makes compromise across party lines imperative, thus further eroding any sense of strict party discipline or loyalty. By the same token, the Democrats may control the Congress and the Republicans the White House (a frequent occurrence in the United States), which has the same effect.[18] Finally, House members and senators tend to be oriented toward special interests and local rather than national constituencies. They are elected to advance local interests and are usually beholden to powerful special interests that contribute generously to the campaign coffers of virtually all incumbents. Former Speaker of the House Tip O'Neill's famous quip that "All politics is local" was probably true at one time. But in the Washington of today all politics no matter how "local" in appearance is largely financed by PAC (political action committee) money from out-of-state. It is money more than party affiliation that dictates how most legislators vote on most issues most of the time.

Most parliamentary systems display far greater party discipline than is found in the United States—especially in countries with electoral systems based on proportional representation (PR). In these countries, legislators are chosen in multi-member districts from party lists. In order to get elected, therefore, the candidate must be on good terms with the party, whose power brokers decide whether to put him or her on the ticket and in what position (first, last, or somewhere in between). The candidate at the top has the best chance of winning a seat.

Structural Complexity   The fragmentation of authority and power in Congress makes its structure notably more complex than that of Britian's Parliament. Significantly, there are only six standing committees in the entire House of Commons. These committees (comprised of twenty to fifty members!) are not specialized and consider bills without reference to subject matter. They do not have the power to call hearings or solicit expert testimony, and they cannot table a bill; at most, they can make technical adjustments in its language. Committee work in Parliament tends to be unexciting and uneventful, and committees afford special interests relatively limited opportunities to lobby.

Parliament's committee system is thus quite different from that of the U.S. Congress. Both in the House and in the Senate, more than fifteen specialized committees dominate the political landscape. These committees have numerous subcommittees, each of which is charged with even more specialized tasks. Moreover, committees and subcommittees have the power to hold hearings and subpoena witnesses as part of routine investigations into executive branch programs and operations. This elaborate committee system shapes legislative behavior. Because legislators cannot possibly become competent in all areas of policy, they tend to specialize in various areas—agriculture, foreign affairs, labor relations, and so forth. Expertise requires time to develop. Political scientists have long pointed to a kind of apprentice system in the two houses. Generally, the most effective legislators are those who remain in office for some time and become familiar with a particular facet of public policy; when they speak on that subject, other legislators tend to listen.

The watchdog role of Congress takes various forms. Oversight can occur at many points in the legislative process (during the authorization and appropriation phases of the budgetary process, for example, or by means of investigations and hearings). Legislators who have large professional staffs regularly conduct program evaluation and policy review. These staffers are often powerful behind-the-scenes operators on whom legislators rely for advice and counsel.

The British parliamentary system stands in sharp contrast. Generally, the most significant mechanism of accountability is the *question hour*, held several days a week, when individual ministers respond to questions submitted by MPs. The questions, which run the gamut from the trenchant to the trivial, are aimed at fixing governmental responsibility, focusing public attention, and eliciting additional information. By contrast, the specialization characteristic of the U.S. Congress is largely absent from the parliamentary system of accountability.

The Executive-Legislative Nexus   Another key difference between the two political systems lies in the extent to which the legislature is involved in determining the makeup of the executive branch. As noted earlier, Parliament plays a key role in determining the composition of a new administration (the cabinet). The prime minister heads the majority party in Parliament, and the cabinet is composed of parliamentary leaders. Because the parliamentary system blurs distinctions between legislative and executive powers, it is often difficult to determine where the authority of one branch begins and that of the other leaves off.

No such fusion of powers exists under the presidential system of government. Unlike senators and representatives, presidents enjoy a *national* popular mandate, and the presidency derives its powers from a separate section of the Constitution. Nonetheless, Congress does have some influence over the staffing of the executive branch, because the Senate must confirm all cabinet and many other high-level appointments. And if the conduct of those in the executive branch evokes suspicion or controversy, the appropriate legislative committee acting in its constitutional watchdog capacity can subpoena government officials and other witnesses to testify. Thus, there is constant interaction between the legislative and executive branches. Unlike the British Parliament, however, Congress does not have the power to bring down the executive by a no confidence vote. Even if Congress votes down a key program proposed by the White House, the president will remain in office for a full four-year term (barring extraordinary events such as impeachment, death, or resignation).

The Executive

The executive branch of government consists of the head of government and the head of state, the cabinet, and the bureaucracy. Pronounced differences, along with some important similarities, mark the executive structures of the two political systems we are examining. First, the U.S. president is the actual head of government *and* the chief of state whereas Britain's executive, as we have seen, is divided between the monarch and the prime minister. The combined duties of the American presidency make that office both more influential and more prestigious than the position of prime minister. The president not only leads the government and speaks for the state, but also, unlike the British prime minister, is *personally* elected by a national majority.

The president of the United States also enjoys the security of a fixed term. By contrast, the British prime minister's position depends on his or her ability to retain the confidence of a majority in the House of Commons. Prime ministers frequently are forced to step down either because public opinion turns against them or because they lose on a key vote in Parliament.

Only the voters can force a sitting president out of office, except in the most extraordinary circumstances. No American president has ever been removed from office by being impeached. (Andrew Johnson and William Clinton were both impeached by the House of Representatives but neither was convicted by the Senate.) It is likely that Richard Nixon would have been impeached and convicted, but he resigned before that happened.

Yet another comparative advantage of the presidency is its greater autonomy in decision making. U.S. cabinet officials are basically administrators and advisers—subordinates whom the president may or may not consult before reaching a decision. The British prime minister, on the other hand, acts as the "first among equals" in the cabinet to a far greater extent. Although this tradition has been eroded somewhat in modern times, prime ministers still make most executive decisions collegially. By the same token, however, the principle of *collective responsibility* virtually guarantees that cabinet-level officials in Great Britain will not publicly criticize any aspect of government policy or betray an inner-cabinet confidence.

Finally, the president is the nation's commander in chief, chief legislator (not only because of the veto power but also because of the significant amount of legislation presidents propose), and chief diplomat. As such, the U.S. president occupies a position whose power, authority, and prestige are unsurpassed among democratically elected chief executives.

In at least one area, a prime minister's authority exceeds that of a president. Although U.S. presidents are also party leaders, this responsibility is submerged in a system that features decentralized, loosely structured political parties. The British prime minister, however, is more than the titular head of the ruling party. Party leadership in Great Britain represents a major duty, for success of the party's policies and programs depends on it. Only through the party can a British prime minister govern. And while American parties may exert some influence over the actions of individual representatives or senators, British parties exercise a high degree of control over the voting behavior of most MPs in the House of Commons. Most other democracies more closely resemble the British system in this regard than the American one.

The Judiciary

Despite significant differences in the structures of their court systems, both the United States and Great Britain share what is generally known as the *common law* tradition. Common law is based on decisions made by judges rather than laws promulgated by legislatures. The idea dates back at least as far as the twelfth century, when Henry II sought to implement a system by which judges were charged with enforcing the king's law while taking into account local customs. In the process of resolving disputes, each judge made and sent to London a record of the legal proceedings. Over the years, certain common themes and legal principles emerged from these records. As this *law by precedent* evolved over the centuries, it was enhanced by certain celebrated judicial decisions. In time, these precedents and

© AFP / CORBIS

As both head of the government and the state, the president delivers the annual State of the Union address to members of Congress and the American people.

decisions were codified by judicial commentators, the most famous being William Blackstone, and carried to all corners of the globe, including the American colonies.

Notwithstanding this shared common law background, the legal systems of the United States and Great Britain differ with respect to selection of judges, organization of the judiciary, powers of judicial review, and other key structural matters.

Selection of Judges   Great Britain has two kinds of law schools. In the lower-level law schools, one studies to become a *solicitor,* a legal counsel who prepares cases for court, advises clients, and draws up contracts, wills, and other legal documents. More exclusive law schools produce *barristers,* who can do everything solicitors do but can also enter a court and plead cases. Judges are appointed only from the ranks of barristers. Furthermore, to be recommended for a judgeship (which, like federal appointments in the United States, carries a life term), a barrister must have achieved a high-class rank in law school and performed several years of outstanding legal service.

American judicial selection is much more political. A judge may be appointed on the basis of high marks at a prestigious law school or years of distinguished legal practice, but that is not necessarily the case. More often, appointments to the federal bench are based on transparent political calculations—to reward an individual for favors; to appease a powerful senator, representative, or local party boss; or to achieve a certain geographic balance in the distribution of judgeships. At the state and local levels, judges are sometimes elected.

Federal versus Unitary Courts   The American judicial system is organized on a federal basis; that is, it comprises fifty-one separate court systems. The federal court system adjudicates legal questions in which either the federal government is one of the parties or a federal law is involved. The federal judiciary is subdivided into *district courts,* in which most cases originate; *appellate courts,* which review cases on appeal from district courts; and the *Supreme Court,* which acts primarily as a court of last resort, settling cases that raise particularly troublesome questions of legal interpretation or constitutional principle.

Coexisting with this federal court system are fifty state court systems, most of which also feature a three-tier structure. The state courts are not completely separated from the federal courts in the U.S. judicial system. The U.S. Supreme Court frequently accepts cases on appeal from the highest courts of the various states when legal questions raised in state courts have constitutional implications.

In comparison with the American federal system, the British court system is more streamlined—reflecting Britain's unitary government. The absence of state courts means that many of the jurisdictional and procedural complexities that plague the American judiciary are absent in Great Britain.

Judicial Review   Perhaps the most important *political* difference between the two judicial systems involves *judicial review:* the power of the courts to uphold or strike down legislative or executive actions. In the United States, both state and federal courts review the acts of the other branches of government—state courts on the basis of state constitutions and federal courts on the basis of the U.S. Constitution.

This power of judicial review is greatly enhanced by the existence of written constitutions, which often provide a highly authoritative yardstick by which to measure ordinary (statutory) law. To some extent, the mere existence of federalism made judicial review necessary in the United States. If state courts could decide for themselves how to interpret federal law, no national body of jurisprudence would have much meaning.[19] The need for legal uniformity and the belief that there are certain higher principles of law to which governmental action at all levels must conform lie at the core of the concept of judicial review not only in the United States, but also in most other constitutional democracies.

In contrast, British judges play only a limited role in governing the nation. Whereas the question of constitutionality hovers over every legislative and executive act in the United States, in Great Britain the judiciary does not possess the power to overturn an act of Parliament. Nor do British judges act as constitutional guardians of civil liberties, as American judges do whenever they assert the primacy of individual rights over legislative acts. Only rarely do British judges rule that the executive branch has overstepped its legal bounds. In the words of one authority:

> The powers of the British government are constrained in spite of rather than because of formal institutions of the laws. Englishmen voice fewer complaints about the denial of

civil liberties or due process of the law than do citizens in many countries with written constitutions, bills of rights, and established procedures for judicial review.[20]

The U.S. Supreme Court is an independent body, deliberately insulated from the pressures of political life. The British court system is headed by a member of the cabinet, known as the lord chancellor, who presides over the House of Lords and makes recommendations on judicial appointments. Theoretically, the high court of Britain *is* the House of Lords, though in actual operation it comprises only a small number of lords with distinguished legal backgrounds. The fusion of powers characteristic of the British parliamentary system thus involves the intermingling of legislative and judicial powers in the upper house just as it meshes the legislative and executive powers in the lower house.

Strengths and Weaknesses of the Two Systems

According to one American academic, "The parliamentary system is a Cadillac among governments." The same author referred to the American presidential system as a "Model T."[21]

Parliamentary systems are often credited with being highly responsive to voters. Political parties campaign on distinct and well-defined platforms. If the election outcome results in a strong mandate for one party, the resulting government is likely to succeed in pushing its program through the parliament. If government policies prove unpopular or impracticable or if the government falls into disrepute for any reason whatsoever, the prime minister or the ruling party can be replaced with no major shock to the political system as a whole. Finally, some observers believe that the British parliamentary system's greater party discipline makes it more efficient than the presidential system.

The U.S. presidential system, critics have asserted, is too often marked by deadlocks stemming from the checks and balances built into its tripartite structure. Too often, one party controls the presidency and another controls the Congress. Moreover, it is very difficult to remove an incompetent or unpopular president from office. In addition, an ossified two-party system leaves many groups and interests underrepresented in the Congress. Finally, the so-called popular election of the president is a farce: in fact, the American president is typically elected by only about 25 percent of the people eligible to vote in the United States. In the critics' view, the archaic practice of choosing electors on a winner-takes-all basis means that the will of the majority may not carry the day—witness the 2000 election in which Al Gore won the most votes nationally but George W. Bush was declared the winner.

Defenders of the presidential system point out that there *are* times when things do get done in the nation's capital (consider the early legislative successes of Presidents Lyndon Johnson and Ronald Reagan, for example). Defenders of the presidential system have also argued that the legally defined term in office for presidents is by and large an asset. Although sometimes a drawback (consider how difficult it was to remove Richard Nixon, even after his abuses of power had become widely apparent), this guaranteed tenure in office often proves to be a blessing. Harry Truman, for example, who is now considered by many to have been one of the greatest U.S. presidents, was quite unpopular during much of his

GATEWAYS TO THE WORLD: EXPLORING CYBERSPACE

http://thomas.loc.gov/

Thomas is the site for the U.S. Congress on the Internet. This is the definitive resource on the American legislative branch, with categories ranging from information on specific members of Congress, to historical documents relating to Congress, to up-to-date reports from the floor of the House and Senate.

http://www.whitehouse.gov/WH/Welcome.html

This is an excellent starting point for information on the executive branch of the U.S. government. You will find information on the president and vice president, including updates on the presidential agenda, a search function for locating White House documents, photos, and audio files of speeches, and many other useful features.

http://www.ukpol.co.uk/

Titled "The British Politics page," this site takes an extensive look at British political parties and government, including information about individual members of Parliament, party platforms and manifestos, election results and analysis, and links to other sites. You may also want to search by entering the name of a government figure in Great Britain or the United States. For instance, there are a number of news articles and profiles on British Prime Minister Tony Blair, as well as U.S. President George W. Bush. Unfortunately, this Web site is available only to subscribers. Two other places to go for unrestricted access to news and information on British politics are *http://ourworld.compuserve.com/homepages/timb/* (available to non-Compuserve users) and *http://news.knownhere.com/ukpolitics.htm.*

term. Presidents have sufficient constitutional leverage to sustain effective leadership in times of national crisis, even when the public interest may require them to implement unpopular measures. This can be regarded as a clear advantage of the presidential system.

Constitutions and Contexts

The mixed results of experiments in parliamentary government serve to illustrate a point first made by Aristotle—that the study of politics can become too abstract. The question to ask, Aristotle tells us, is not what's best but rather what's possible *under the prevailing circumstances.* Under some circumstances, parliamentary government works very well indeed; under others, it founders. Aristotle's insight is still apt:

> We have not only to study the ideally best constitution. We have also to study the type of constitution which is practicable [that is, the best for a state under actual conditions]—and with it, and equally, the type which is easiest to work and most suitable to stages generally. . . . The sort of constitutional system which ought to be proposed is one which men can be easily induced, and will be readily able, to graft onto the system they already have.[22]

Summary

The British parliamentary model features a fusion of powers, indefinite terms of office, disciplined parties, and a dual executive. This model of constitutional democracy has been imitated more widely (except in Latin America) than the American model. It is especially influential in Europe where it has inspired most of the constitutional democracies in existence.

France is a hybrid form of constitutional democracy combining features of both the American and British systems. Germany features a parliamentary system, but differs from both France and Great Britain in that it is federal (comprising states called *Länder*) rather than unitary. Japan is also a parliamentary democracy; politically it differs from Europe in its political culture rather than its political structure. Japan has incorporated a consensus-based society with informal, highly personal networks of political power based patron–client relations into a set of political institutions that on the surface appear to be made in Europe (actually, they were made in America during the U.S. occupation after World War II).

India and Israel are two unlikely candidates for republican rule, yet they have both survived as parliamentary democracies for over half a century. The examples of India and Israel suggest that the British model has wide application even in places that appear to be too troubled or turbulent for elections to occur or stable governments to endure.

The American and British systems invite comparisons and offer provocative contrasts in the legislative, executive, and judicial areas. It is difficult to say which system is better in the abstract; the answer must be sought within the specific context and circumstances of each nation.

Key Terms

parliamentary system	Rajya Sabha
mixed regime	Palestinian Arabs
no-confidence vote	Palestine
disciplined parties	Zionism
loyal opposition	Balfour Declaration
dual executive	Camp David Accords
National Assembly	intifadah
divided executive	Knesset
cohabitation	parliamentary sovereignty
Weimar Republic	question hour
Cold War	collective responsibility
Bundestag	common law
Bundesrat	solicitor
Meiji Restoration	barristers
Moghuls	district courts
British Raj	appellate courts
Kashmir	Supreme Court
Lok Sabha	judicial review

Review Questions

1. Why is the British political system often considered a model of parliamentary democracy?

2. What are the basic operating principles of the parliamentary system?

3. How can the British manage without a written constitution?

4. When did the current French republic come into being and under what circumstances?

5. Compare and contrast democracy in France with democracy in the United States and Great Britain? (Trick question: Which country did France model its own political system after?)

6. When did Japan adopt the parliamentary system and under what circumstances?

7. Compare and contrast democracy in Japan with democracy in France and Great Britain.

8. Comment on the significance of parliamentary democracy in India and Israel.

9. Compare the strengths and weaknesses of parliamentary versus presidential rule.

Recommended Reading

BAILEY, SYDNEY. *British Parliamentary Democracy.* 3rd ed. Westport, Conn.: Greenwood, 1978. A comprehensive introduction to the functioning of the British democracy.

BIRCH, ANTHONY. *The British System of Government.* 9th ed. New York: Routledge, 1993. A good reference to British government.

DIAMOND, MARTIN, WINSTON FISK, and HERBERT GARFINKEL. *The Democratic Republic: An Introduction to American National Government.* Skokie, Ill.: Rand McNally, 1970. An introductory text that contains an extraordinarily insightful discussion of the relationship between the American Founders and political institutions.

DICEY, A. V. *Introduction to the Study of the Law of the Constitution.* Indianapolis: Liberty Fund, 1982. A classic account of the British political tradition.

ROSE, RICHARD. *Politics in England: Change and Persistence.* 5th ed. Reading, Mass.: Addison-Wesley, 1989. An examination of the British political system and how it formulates political decisions.

Notes

1. The Life Peerage Act of 1958 enables the monarch, upon the advice of the prime minister, to confer nontransferable titles for life on commoners. The rationale for the legislation was to ensure party balance and to increase the number of working members in the House of Lords. Approximately one-quarter of all Lords (and a higher percentage of working members of the House of Lords) are appointed in this way.

2. Sydney Bailey, *British Parliamentary Democracy*, 3rd ed. (Westport, Conn.: Greenwood, 1978), 130.

3. Ibid., 131.

4. Suzanne Berger, *The French Political System*, 3rd ed. (New York: Random House, 1974), 368.

5. Berger, *French Political System*, 368.

6. Roy Macridis, ed., *Modern Political Systems: Europe*, 6th ed. (Englewood Cliffs, N.J.: Prentice-Hall, 1986), 120.

7. Karl Dietrich Bracher, *The German Dictatorship* (New York: Holt, 1970), 75.

8. Michael Roskin, *Countries and Concepts: An Introduction to Comparative Politics* (Englewood Cliffs, N.J.: Prentice-Hall, 1982), 190.

9. Guido Goldman, *The German Political System* (New York: Random House, 1974), 56.

10. See John W. Dower, *Embracing Defeat: Japan in the Wake of World War II* (New York: Norton, 2000).

11. See Herbert P. Bix, *Hirohito and the Making of Modern Japan* (New York: HarperCollins, 2000).

12. Franz Michael and George Taylor, *The Far East in the Modern World* (New York: Holt, 1964), 263.

13. Ibid., 607.

14. Nobutaki Ike, *Japanese Politics: Patron-Client Democracy*, 2nd ed. (New York: Knopf, 1972), 17.

15. Michael and Taylor, *Far East in the Modern World*, 603

16. Ibid., 5.

17. *Marbury* v. *Madison*, 1 Cranch 137 (1803).

18. Ronald Reagan's presidency, from 1981 to 1987, is an example of a split between the two houses of Congress, with the Republicans controlling the Senate, and the Democrats controlling the House; however, a split between the executive and legislative branches is more common. Generally, the Democrats have controlled the legislative branches even when the president was a Republican, but in the 1994 midterm elections, the Republicans won control of both the House and the Senate only two years after Democrat Bill Clinton was elected president.

19. See *Martin v. Hunter's Lessee*, 14 U.S. 304 (1816).

20. Richard Rose, "Politics in England," in *Comparative Politics Today: A World View*, ed. Gabriel Almond (Boston: Little, Brown, 1974), 148.

21. Edward Courtier, *Principles of Politics and Government* (Boston: Allyn & Bacon, 1981), 84.

22. Aristotle, *The Politics*, trans. and ed. Ernest Barker (New York: Oxford University Press, 1962), 1288b–89a, 155–56.

© Peter Turnley / CORBIS

Chapter 7

STATES IN TRANSITION

NEW DEMOCRACIES AND EMERGING MARKETS

ON THE LAST day of December 1991, the Soviet Union, one of two superpowers that had dominated world politics for nearly half a century, ceased to exist. The demise of this communist behemoth stands as one of the most momentous political events of the twentieth century. Although the end came as a surprise, it was not without warning signs; on the contrary, the Soviet Union had been going through a fascinating but turbulent period of change since 1985, when Mikhail Gorbachev, the country's charismatic new leader, launched a series of bold reforms.

The disintegration of the Soviet order ushered in a new era in world politics. It also drew attention to the problems of transition facing the defunct (or dysfunctional) political economies in Eastern Europe. The problems of transition in these countries are also, to some extent, problems of political and economic redevelopment. Transition and development (discussed in the following chapter) are closely related; the issues facing societies in transition intersect with development issues at many points. Moreover, as we will see, the whole concept of "states in transition" applies to many countries in virtually every region of the world today. Following a look at the problems facing the former communist countries, we take a brief look at several Asian and Latin American countries in various stages of transition toward market-based liberal democracy.

THE COLLAPSE OF COMMUNISM

What was once called "the communist world" no longer exists; communism as a political force on both the national and international levels has receded nearly everywhere in the world with a few notable exceptions. In 1988, before the end of the Cold War, fifteen states could be classified as communist. By 2002, the number shrank to only five or six states (China, Cuba, Laos, North Korea, Vietnam, and perhaps Cambodia), each pursuing relatively independent policies— indeed, it no longer makes any sense to talk about a "communist bloc." What happened? Eastern Europe abruptly abandoned communist rule in 1989, ahead of the collapse of the Soviet Union in 1991. Since then, democracy and privatization (turning formerly state-run enterprises over to the private sector) have advanced in Poland, Hungary, and the Czech Republic. This process has been accompanied by political zigzags, especially in Poland and Hungary, where voters reinstalled former communists in power while rejecting centralized planning in favor of Western, market-oriented policies. In Romania, Slovakia, Bulgaria, and Albania the movement toward democratization has been far slower but not entirely absent. The former East Germany is a special case, having merged with West Germany in 1990.

In Asia, communist regimes have been more resilient. The People's Republic of China softened its totalitarian rule and liberalized its economy after Mao's death in 1976, but remains a repressive state. It continues to pursue market-friendly reforms, which have stimulated rapid economic growth, especially in its southern coastal region. North Korea, true to its long-standing reputation for Stalinist rigidity, displays a familiar tendency toward xenophobia, extreme secrecy, and self-imposed isolation. Vietnam and Laos remain under communist rule, but in contrast to North Korea, both have relaxed international controls and sought greater acceptance in the international community. Finally, in Cambodia, a July 1997 coup engineered by Hun Sen defeated a long and costly effort by the United Nations to promote democracy, establishing a dictatorial government.

In Cuba, Fidel Castro clings to political power, as the dictator struggled to replace the lost Soviet aid while combating the effects of an ongoing economic boycott imposed by the United States. Periodic public demonstrations, carried out in the face of a police state notoriously intolerant of dissent, reflected a strong undertow of popular discontent with Castro's rule. The historic visits to Cuba of Pope John Paul II in January 1998 and former President Jimmy Carter in 2002—both firsts since the Cuban revolution—were interpreted as possible steps toward greater religious and political freedom and a sign that the aging dictator was mellowing. However, other observers cautioned that meaningful reforms would unlikely follow and all that mattered to Castro was maintaining power in the face of mounting political problems.

RUSSIA: TURBULENCE AND TRANSITION (OR JUST TURBULENCE?)

As the 1990s began, the Soviet Union stood as one of the last of the world's great empires. It presided over conquered peoples and cultures, but not without great internal stresses and strains. Can such empires endure at all in a world increasingly governed by the ideas of nationalism, egalitarianism, and a belief in self-determination? Or are all such empires forever doomed?

The Stalinist state that stayed in place until 1991 displayed all the characteristics of totalitarian rule, including centralized control over the armed forces, the mass media, and the economy; a dominant monopoly party; an official ideology; and a systematic program of terror against suspected political opponents and the mass murder of innocents deemed unworthy (or dangerous) by the regime. The story of how the Soviet Union emerged from totalitarianism provides the essential background for understanding the nature of Russian politics today.

After the collapse of the old Soviet regime in 1991, a new downsized Russian state emerged. The post-Soviet government, headed by Boris Yeltsin, broke sharply with the past, initially seeking to establish a constitutional democracy. It then created a very loose confederation, the *Commonwealth of Independent States (CIS)*, which included Russia and the former Soviet republics minus the Baltic states of Estonia, Latvia, and Lithuania (see Figure 7-1).

1. ESTONIA   3. LITHUANIA   5. BELARUS   7. GEORGIA   9. AZERBAIJAN   11. TAJIKISTAN
2. LATVIA   4. RUSSIA   6. MOLDOVA   8. ARMENIA   10. KYRGYZSTAN

FIGURE 7-1   Russia and the Republics
SOURCE: Based on Milton F. Goodman, *Global Studies: Russia, Eurasia, and Central/Eastern Europe,* 5th ed. Copyright © 1994, the Dushkin Publishing Group, Inc., Guilford, Conn. All rights reserved. Reprinted by permission.

The Gorbachev Transition

In 1985, Mikhail Gorbachev, at age fifty-four, became one of the youngest general secretaries of the Communist party in Soviet history. He faced no shortage of political and economic problems. Gorbachev became convinced that these problems could not be surmounted without significant political and economic reforms, and because the political system was little more than a reflection of the power and influence of the Communist party, he made a fateful and momentously important decision to reform communism and the party in order to preserve each. Gorbachev therefore undertook policies that became famous in the West: perestroika, glasnost, and *demokratizatsiia.*

Why Gorbachev Risked Everything   From the time Lenin had assumed power in 1917, the Soviet Union featured a *planned economy,* also known as a *command economy,* in which all-important economic decisions (what and how much was to be produced, and so on) were made at the uppermost level of the Communist party. Competition, the pursuit of profits, and most forms of private ownership were forbidden as inconsistent with the tenets of communism.

This system of central planning succeeded in making the Soviet Union a first-rate military power, but at the cost of large budget deficits. Additionally, by the mid-1980s, it was apparent that central planning had also resulted in economic stagnation that placed the Soviet Union at a competitive disadvantage with industrial, democratic nations such as the United States, Japan, and several European nations.[1] By 1985, the nation's economic growth rate had declined to 2 percent, about half what it had been a decade earlier. One out of every nine industrial enterprises and nearly a third of state farms were losing money. Food, housing, medicine, and transportation were woefully inadequate in both quality and quantity.

Most Soviet citizens led relatively austere lives with few of the conveniences Westerners took for granted. Often stores were poorly stocked or not stocked at all. Spare parts in particular sizes sometimes simply could not be obtained. According to one estimate, the accepted norm was that women spent an average of two hours in line, seven days a week.[?] By the end of the 1980s, an estimated 28 percent of the Soviet population lived below the official Soviet poverty line.[3]

In the realm of agriculture, food production barely kept pace with population growth, and despite lavish investment in agriculture, the government continued to spend heavily for imported meats and grains. Meanwhile, the USSR's investment priorities in agriculture reflected terrible planning. Farm-to-market roads and facilities for storage, food processing, packaging, and retailing were woefully neglected. Soviet economists estimated that about one-fourth of all grain harvested each year was lost before it got to the market, and then-President Gorbachev said that losses equaled the value of Soviet grain imports—$4 billion in 1988. As a result, meat and dairy product consumption for the average Soviet citizen had declined 30 percent in less than two decades.[4]

While the Soviet economy decayed and the quality of life for the general populace deteriorated, worsening social problems simultaneously threatened the very fabric of Soviet society. Among the worst problems were alcoholism and corruption. Alcoholism long had been the Soviet Union's most persistent and costliest problem. Drinking adversely affected the drinker's health and family life, reduced labor productivity and job performance, produced a high infant mortality rate (due to drinking during pregnancy), decreased life expectancy, and aggravated juvenile delinquency. Meanwhile corruption also flourished, as the chronic absence of consumer goods and extremely high state-set prices caused a flourishing black market. Because so much of Soviet life was bureaucratized and required official state approval, an unofficial system involving unlicensed agents (tolkachi) and influence peddling (blat) developed. To speed official approval or receive favored treatment, it was common for Soviet citizens to use whatever means were necessary.

Another critical problem was the technology gap, which widened during the 1970s and 1980s, when the computer revolution eluded the Soviets while it transformed their economic competitors. There was little encouragement for managers to invest in this new technology, and the party feared that its widespread use could empower political dissenters. The consequence was an inability to modernize Soviet industry and infrastructure.

At the root of most of these problems was central planning, which discouraged initiative because plant managers and directors of government-run farms remained tied to a central plan that imposed rigid quotas on factory and farm production. Plan fulfillment was the highest priority for all Soviet economic administrators. The Stalinist system sacrificed quality for quantity, and there was insufficient incentive or opportunity for management, operating on instructions from above, to introduce new technology. Bottlenecks due to unanticipated interruptions in the flow of essential materials and equipment frequently delayed building projects and impeded factory and farm production. Because of relentless pressures to meet overly ambitious production quotas, managers often took shortcuts and used subterfuge to avert or conceal failures.

The cynicism of the managers was matched by the low morale of the Soviet workers, who were underemployed, unhappily employed, or simply not motivated to work. The result was appallingly low productivity caused by the absence of dependable and efficient workers. Prevailing worker cynicism was commonly reflected in popular Soviet sayings, such as "the party pretends to pay us, and we pretend to work." This cynicism was fed by the hypocrisy of high party officials who espoused egalitarian ideals but lived in secluded luxury while the proletariat they glorified had to stand in long lines to buy bread and other staples. Most worrisome of all: Many in the Soviet Union had lost faith in their political system.[5]

Hardliners, Nationalists, and the *Nomenklatura* Earlier we noted that individuals who occupied positions of power and authority within the Soviet system were called the ***nomenklatura***, and that these individuals constituted a privileged, entrenched elite class in the former Soviet Union.[6] They included members of the political bureaucracy *(apparatchiki)*, senior economic managers, and scientific administrators, as well as certain writers, artists, cosmonauts, athletes, and generals who represented the Soviet state and enhanced its reputation.

The existence of the *nomenklatura* proved significant for two reasons. First, the elaborate, exclusive, and largely concealed infrastructure of luxury apartments, specialty shops, vacation resorts, hospitals, clinics, health spas, and schools it used did not merely set it apart from ordinary Soviet citizens but stood in sharp contrast to the Marxist and communist ideals of equality and justice that Soviet leaders had so frequently proclaimed. Second, though not always outrightly corrupt, it nonetheless proved unresponsive and smug, much more concerned with perpetuating its power than with implementing official policies. In the mid-1980s, no one was more concerned about the capacity of this entrenched elite to block economic progress than the Soviet Union's new leader, Mikhail Gorbachev.

The Politics of Reform Gorbachev's three reform programs—perestroika, glasnost, and *demokratizatsiia*—attempted to salvage communism, not scuttle it. The goal of ***perestroika*** (literally "restructuring") was to revitalize the ossified system of central planning. Gorbachev hoped to accomplish this ambitious goal by attacking the political and social causes of the country's economic problems—that is, by reducing the power of the *nomenklatura* and the *apparatchiki* while simultaneously improving the efficiency of Soviet workers. Ironically, either Gorbachev did not understand or refused to face the need for radical change in the nation's underlying economic structures. Hence, the idea of perestroika was more a catchy political slogan than a coherent economic policy.

To his credit, Gorbachev did attempt to enact certain piecemeal reforms aimed at encouraging individual initiative by tying wages to job performance, reforming the system of pricing and distribution, and limiting the power of upper-level bureaucrats while supporting more local managerial discretion of state enterprises and encouraging worker-owned enterprises, or cooperatives. Other cautious market-oriented reforms were also undertaken. None of these reforms, however, fundamentally altered the economic system from one of state ownership of the means of production and central planning to one of private ownership and individual initiative.

Shown here visiting Finland in 1989 with his wife, Raisa, Mikhail Gorbachev instituted radical political and economic policies to reform communism and the Communist party during his period of leadership from March 1985 until August 1991. Ultimately, these initiatives exacerbated the erosion of the Stalinist state and helped precipitate the downfall of communism throughout Eastern Europe.

By 1989, the Soviet economy was rapidly disintegrating, and within two years it had plunged into a depression; by 1991, the Soviet Union's economy was shrinking at the rate of 10 percent each year. So what was to be done? The top leadership was deeply divided. Radical reformers favored a sharp transition away from central planning and a command economy to a market system. Old-line conservatives (especially those associated with the military and the secret police) abhorred such revolutionary changes. The Soviet leadership struggled to meet the mounting economic crisis but, unlike China under Deng Xiaoping (see p. 201), never articulated a clear vision for the future or united behind a comprehensive reform package.

Amidst all this turmoil, Gorbachev's own economic views remained unclear. During his last months in office, it became clear that perestroika (designed to revitalize central planning and communism) was dead, and revolutionary economic change (which, ironically, had been unleashed by perestroika) was accelerating. Private ownership and economic incentives proliferated as events undertook governmental policy, while economic confusion and desperation abounded.

Glasnost Gorbachev's much heralded policy of *glasnost* ("openness") reinforced perestroika and constituted the most extensive relaxation of media censorship in Soviet history. For a time, this policy won great sympathy for Gorbachev and distracted public attention from the dislocations entailed by economic reform.

It also had a wide appeal beyond Soviet borders, making Gorbachev the darling of the world press and a popular figure in many Western countries.

Despite its foreign policy advantages, glasnost was primarily an instrument of domestic policy. Its initial intention was to expose the official corruption and incompetence that Gorbachev blamed in part for the Soviet Union's economic malaise. He wished to shake up the massive, change-resistant Soviet bureaucracy, and hoped to goad the working class into working. Having neither the incentive to work nor the right to strike, Soviet workers had retreated into lethargy and alcoholism. In fact, the latter was a problem of epidemic proportions—a tragic symptom of a society in decay.

Glasnost was closely linked to perestroika: It was a means to reinvigorate a communist society that had lost its drive and sense of purpose. A policy of political *liberalization* could create a climate of excitement that would energize society by permitting criticism of the old, ineffective patterns of work and governing. In breathtaking fashion, glasnost quickly assumed a life of its own, as previously censored books and movies flourished. Perhaps most astonishing was the transformation of the Soviet mass media from a pliable instrument of state power to gadfly and social critic. Popular new television programs exposed official corruption and abuses of power while Soviet newspapers and magazines published scorching articles challenging time-honored political principles and precepts. The Soviet Union had transformed itself virtually overnight from a country that permitted no criticism, to one where criticism was rapidly undermining the legitimacy of both the Communist party and the political system that had long served as the instrument of its rule.

Demokratizatsiia   As with perestroika, it was not exactly clear what Gorbachev meant by this Russian-language equivalent for *democratization*. At a minimum, *demokratizatsiia* implied a political system in which elections would be opened up, although just how much remained uncertain. This vision was reflected in the 1989 nationwide legislative elections that allowed voters to register opposition to the government by voting against Communist party candidates for the first time in Soviet history. By the same token, Gorbachev ruled as the Soviet president (an indirectly elected position he had reinvented as part of his political reform package), not as general secretary of the Communist party. Related political changes wrought by *demokratizatsiia* were equally breathtaking and pointed to a more democratic future. They included:

- Emergence of opposing parties and influential noncommunist and anticommunist individuals and parties, some of whom were elected to the national legislature
- Significant weakening of internal Communist party discipline (and a concomitant increase in acrimony and disagreement within its ranks), while its membership declined throughout the Soviet Union
- Increase in power and influence of the republics at the expense of the power and prestige of the central government
- Reforms wherein the government, run by elected officials and headed by an executive president rather than the general secretary, would exercise actual power independent of the Communist party

The Failure of Reform: The System Disintegrates

Gorbachev's concerted efforts to reformulate the political and economic system of the USSR failed. Virtually every social, political, and economic problem present when he had assumed power worsened by the time he stepped down, a little over six years later. Popular expectations rose at the same time living standards fell dramatically, creating a politically volatile situation. Disconcerting new problems such as galloping inflation further undermined confidence in the government. Popular unrest was evidenced by a phenomenon new to the USSR—labor strikes. As social unrest escalated, Gorbachev's popularity plummeted and his power base within the party and state bureaucracies eroded.

An age-old nationality problem was a primary source of internal instability during the Soviet regime's final days. The seventeen largest nationalities accounted for more than 90 percent of the Soviet population, with the Russians at slightly over 50 percent and the Ukrainians at just below 16 percent accounting for some two-thirds of the total population of 294 million people in 1991. Furthermore, some twenty ethnic groups numbered over 1 million people. Among the larger ethnic groups were the fifteen nationalities for whom the union republics are named plus the Tatars, Poles, Germans, Jews, Chuvashes, Bashkirs, and Mordvinians, among others (see Table 7.1). In total, more than 100 different nationalities coexisted in the former USSR, speaking some 130 languages.

Historically, the Soviet government used force to assimilate non-Russian groups. In addition, one of the primary instruments of state policy was the education system: All schoolchildren were required to learn Russian. As a result, bilingualism was common in the Soviet republics—most non-Russians could speak fluent Russian. But

TABLE 7-1

Major Nationalities in the Soviet Union at the Time of Its Demise (1989)

Nationality	Percent of Total Population[a]	Nationality	Percent of Total Population[a]
1. Russian	50.78	11. Moldovan	1.17
2. Ukrainian	15.47	12. Lithuanian	1.07
3. Uzbek	5.84	13. Turkish	0.95
4. Belarusian	3.50	14. Kirgiz	0.85
5. Kazakh	2.84	15. German	0.71
6. Azerbaijani	2.38	16. Chuvash	0.64
7. Tatar	2.32	17. Latvian	0.51
8. Armenian	1.62	18. Jew[b]	0.50
9. Tajik	1.48	19. Bashkir	0.50
10. Georgian	1.39	20. Polish	0.39

[a]The figures are adapted from the last official census of the Soviet Union.
[b]The former Soviet Union classified Jews as a nationality.
SOURCE: *Population Today*, November 1991, Population Reference Bureau. Reprinted by permission.

Boris Yeltsin: Post-Soviet Russia's First President

Bill Burke / PageOne

In June 1991, Boris Yeltsin became the first popularly elected leader in Russian history, winning a landslide victory to become president of the Russian Republic. Two months later, in August 1991, Yeltsin faced down hard-liners who ousted Mikhail Gorbachev, president of the Union of Soviet Socialist Republics (USSR), in an attempted military coup. At a dramatic moment, when the outcome was still uncertain, Yeltsin climbed onto a tank and read a now-famous manifesto declaring the coup illegal and demanding the restora-

Russian Republic leader Boris Yeltsin represented a new breed of postcommunist political leader, having proclaimed a desire to establish democracy and a new market-based economic system.

tion of constitutional order, including the return of President Gorbachev to power.

There was great irony in this situation. Boris Yeltsin owed his meteoric rise in Soviet politics to Mikhail Gorbachev. Yeltsin was an obscure party functionary in Sverdlovsk in the mid-1980s when Gorbachev, who had just become the top party leader, brought him to Moscow to head the local party organization. But Yeltsin soon broke with Gorbachev, charging Gorbachev with foot-dragging on real reforms and advocating more radical liberalization policies than Gorbachev was willing to countenance. Incensed at Yeltsin's sharp and highly public criticisms, Gorbachev removed the maverick Yeltsin from the Politburo in 1987.

But Yeltsin did not surrender. Instead, he built a popular following in his native Russia. With his election in 1991, Yeltsin upstaged Gorbachev, who had never been popularly elected and therefore lacked the kind of mandate Yeltsin could claim.

repeated, often heavy-handed Soviet efforts to instill cultural dominance led to bitter resentment. Ethnic Russians dominated the upper levels of the Communist party, accounting for as much as 70 percent of its elite leadership—a fact that further aggravated the national minorities. The failure of the Soviet state to assimilate fully its many national minorities undermined one of the world's last great empires.

Moscow had good reason to fear that the "nationality question" might sooner or later be the Soviet Union's undoing. Ironically, it was Gorbachev's reforms that created the climate in which the non-Russian nationalities could dare to strive for self-determination and independence. Glasnost, in particular, encouraged a climate of local criticism of the central government and Communist party. Gorbachev's fateful decision to allow the former "satellite states" (Poland, East Germany, Czechoslovakia, Hungary, Bulgaria, and Romania) to leave the Soviet fold was also crucial. The independence movement surged in the Baltic states first, where Lithuania, Latvia, and Estonia (which had been independent for a time before they were seized by Stalin under his infamous 1939 pact with Hitler) pushed the pace of reform farther and faster than Gorbachev intended. The Baltic states, led by Lithuania, were the first to break away. Nationalistic demonstrations, riots, and rebellions rumbled across the Soviet empire, as republic after republic declared its independence.

But it was Yeltsin's heroics in August 1991, including his key role in saving Gorbachev from an uncertain fate, that finally put Yeltsin in a dominant position vis-à-vis Gorbachev, whose credibility and prestige—and thus, his power—evaporated after the coup attempt. In the end, Gorbachev not only felt compelled to resign his chairmanship of the Communist party and to separate the party from the government, but also found it necessary to accept the dissolution of the Soviet Union. Gorbachev resigned his position as president on December 25, 1991.

Yeltsin remained in charge of the Russian government, but he faced intense opposition in parliament due to the deepening economic and social crisis. Yeltsin's inept and brutal handling of the war in the breakaway republic of Chechnya did not improve his tarnished image, at home or abroad. His popularity, which made him invincible in the early 1990s, fell to a dangerous low in 1996, as a new presidential election loomed in June. Yeltsin was forced into a runoff with communist candidate Gennady Zyuganov, but won in the second round by a landslide. His moment of triumph, however, was cut short by life-threatening health problems. In late 1996, Yeltsin underwent heart bypass surgery. He recovered in 1997, but was no more effec-

Vladimir Putin is Russia's second president since the fall of Soviet Communism. When Boris Yeltsin named him premier in 1999, he was an obscure figure, having served for many years as a KGB (secret police) recruiter. In 2001, this former Soviet spy became an important U.S. ally in President George W. Bush's campaign against international terrorism and later (in May 2002) agreed to a major nuclear arms reduction treaty with the United States.

tive after that time than he had been before. In 2000, Vladimir Putin was elected to succeed him. Putin faced daunting challenges, including a sick economy, a society riddled by corruption and violent crime, and a smoldering war in Chechnya.

At the end of 1991, the Soviet Union self-destructed. Despite his best efforts, Gorbachev's attempt to solve the Soviet Union's fundamental political and economic problems had failed. In August 1991, Gorbachev himself was overthrown by a group of eight hard-line Communist party traditionalists with ties to the army and the KGB (the secret police). But the coup failed when Boris Yeltsin (championing the causes of democracy and market reforms) led the resistance to the coup, remaining in the besieged Russian parliament building in Moscow and exhorting huge crowds in the street to fight for democracy. With Yeltsin's urging, Gorbachev resumed his former position until the Soviet Union's formal dissolution at the end of 1991, but Russia had a new national hero.

Contemporary Challenges

Boasting 75 percent of the total landmass, about 50 percent of the population, and approximately 60 percent of the GNP of the former Soviet Union, Russia remains Eurasia's dominant power. Russia's great influence over the CIS raises a fundamental question: Will the Commonwealth be a means by which newly independent republics establish their independence or will it be a structure used by Russia to reestablish its lost empire? By the mid-1990s, there were clear signs that the second scenario was more likely, as Moscow sought to regain its influence within the territory of the Old Russian Empire and across the whole of the Slavic Europe.

Russian troops were stationed in many of the former Soviet republics, including Latvia, Estonia, Moldova, Georgia, Azerbaijan, and Tajikistan. In conflict-ridden states such as Azerbaijan, Tajikistan, and Georgia, Moscow undertook or justified military intervention on "peacekeeping" grounds as both internal and external disputes raged within and among a number of the newly independent republics.

Of greater concern to the rest of the world was that Russia, Ukraine, Kazakhstan, and Belarus all fell heir to the nuclear weapons that the former Soviet government had deployed on their territories. As a result, the world suddenly had several new nuclear powers, while the weapons heightened tensions among the newly independent nations. As a matter of policy, Russia sought to gather all the nuclear arms of the former Soviet state into its own arsenal. Both Ukraine and Kazakhstan promised to relinquish control of these inherited weapons but also sought economic and financial concessions from Moscow, as well as security guarantees from the West, before doing so. By 1996, all nuclear weapons reportedly had been removed to Russia, including those in Belarus. The security of Russia's huge arsenal of chemical and biological weapons of mass destruction was also a matter of great concern in the West. After the September 11, 2001, terrorist attacks on the United States this concern grew as the possibility that some of these lethal materials (including anthrax) might fall into the hands of international terrorists based in Afghanistan and elsewhere.

Russia is a political and economic work in progress. Although it is impossible to predict its future prospects, there is no doubt that Russia remains an important and powerful nation. Russia's success will depend on its ability to surmount at least three fundamental challenges: economic dislocations, ethnic fragmentation, and state building.

Economic Dislocations   Persistent economic problems plagued the Commonwealth countries after the breakup of the Soviet Union. Russia was no exception: Its failing economy presented a terrible hardship to the everyday lives of ordinary citizens. Like most of the Commonwealth nations, Russia experienced an extraordinary collapse in industrial production, retail sales, and national income after 1991. Budget deficits soared. Initially, these economic failures were accompanied by widespread, severe inflation.

Since then, signs of economic revival have been slow to appear. As a result of dislocations associated with the collapse of Soviet power and the Yeltsin government's failure to implement a consistent and rigorous program of economic reform, output in Russia by the mid-1990s had dropped by one-third.[7] But there were some positive signs: progress in converting to a market economy by freeing prices, cutting defense expenditures, discarding the old centralized distribution system, carrying out a large-scale voucher privatization program, establishing private banks, and demonopolizing foreign trade.

By 1996, Yeltsin had also succeeded in cutting inflation and stabilizing the ruble. Despite these steps, however, the economy was still failing. Both the GDP and industrial output declined by more than 6 percent.[8] (The decline, however, was slower than two years earlier, when it fell 15 percent.) The relatively slow pace of privatization in Russia (compared to more successful transitional economies in Poland, Hungary, and the Czech Republic) is perhaps at least partially to blame, but the failure to develop a solid legal framework to support a market economy and encourage foreign investment is also responsible. Other missing ingredients are clearly defined stockholders' rights, laws to encourage development of land markets, and a social safety net that would relieve enterprises of the burden of providing benefits to workers.

Significant economic problems invariably have important social consequences. Most Russians today perceive that they are worse off with each passing year. Widespread health problems (partially caused by government's failure to support public health programs), falling real wages (due to inflation), a large rise in wage arrears (workers owed back pay), and the widespread danger of increasing unemployment remain sources of anxiety for Russians (see Figure 7-2). In the mid-1990s, about 36.6 million Russians, or one-fourth of the population, were living below the poverty level. One of the only bright spots was the falling inflation rate—down to 10.2 percent at the beginning of 1998. In 2001, inflation was on the rise again (about 20 percent), but the Russian economy, under President Alexander Putin's strong leadership, was showing signs of recovery, including a positive overall growth rate of 5 percent.[9]

Ethnic Fragmentation   The Soviet breakup in 1991 was accompanied by civil war, religious persecution, and ethnic strife in many parts of the old empire. Russia remains an ethnically diverse state still trying to overcome the powerful centrifugal force of conflicting ethnic groups, some of which have sought sovereign independence. Integrating these groups successfully into the Russian state remained unfinished business at the advent of the new millennium.

Ethnic groups form the basis for the twenty-one republics in the new Russian Federation under the 1993 constitution. These federal units (similar to state governments in the United States) are represented as *republics* in the upper house of the Russian legislature. Still, no constitution can resolve the issue of ethnic tension within Russia—time, mutual respect, and economic success are among the ingredients in any recipe for long-term stable relations between the dominant Great Russians and the nationalities on the periphery (both inside and outside Russia's borders).

Compounding the difficulty of integrating differing nationalities into the political state is another complication: Traditionally, the Soviet Union was governed bureaucratically from Moscow through regional administrative entities *(oblasts)* as well as the ethnic (or national) republics. This system of separate dual jurisdictions continued in Russia after the USSR's demise. But the power of the central government shrank after the demise of communism, while the power of the regions increased. Pent-up ethnic pride and resentment of Russian domination in the republics fueled rivalries between various nationality groups and the central government. At the same time, the republics also competed with the *oblasts* for power and influence within the Russian political system.

The political problem posed by Russia's ethnic republics came to the fore in December 1994 when Russia attacked Chechnya, a Connecticut-sized, ethnic Muslim republic within its borders, situated in the north Caucasus between the Black and Caspian seas. Previously, Chechnya had declared independence from Russia. Determined to end Chechnya's defiance, Russian President Yeltsin sent in Russian troops to put the rebellion down. In the course of the war that ensued, Russian warplanes heavily bombed the Chechen capital of Grozny. The Chechen troops were highly motivated while the Russian troops, reflecting the widespread public skepticism, were more reluctant to go into battle (perhaps mindful of the disastrous war against Afghanistan in the 1980s) and suffered heavy casualties.

Following a protracted "dirty" war, a chastened Russia, in effect, sued for peace. The truce signed in late 1996, virtually conceded victory to the separatist rebels. It gave Moscow until the year 2001 to decide how to handle Chechnya's claim to independence. Meanwhile, haunting questions remained:

- Would the cease-fire hold?
- Would Moscow allow Chechnya to break away (equivalent to Washington allowing, say, West Virginia to secede)?
- How many more ethnic minorities in Russia would imitate the Chechens and make a bid for independence?
- Would a Russia brimming over with weapons of mass destruction be plunged into anarchy?

The maintenance and *internal* administration of a Russia rife with ethnic differences is one problem; however, ethnic tensions that influence the foreign policies and political ties between Russia and many of the newly independent republics of the former Soviet Union raise a different set of problems. For example, although Russia and Ukraine are both members of the Commonwealth of Independent States, they have at times been at odds. Part of the problem is historical. Ukraine (specifically Kiev) is the historical birthplace of Russia (the Kievan Rus). It is one of the largest countries in Eastern Europe with a population of 40 million (roughly the size of neighboring Poland). Within Ukraine, situated on a strategic peninsula, is an important piece of real estate on the banks of the Black Sea known as the Crimea. Crimea's current inhabitants are Great Russians who replaced the indigenous population after Stalin sent the Crimean Tatars (famous as formidable warriors) into internal exile to Siberia in the 1930s. When in January 1994 a pro-Russian nationalist was elected president of Crimea, he threatened to hold a referendum on "independence"—in effect, a vote for secession from Ukraine and for union with Russia. Although the referendum did not take place, the possibility that Ukraine may divide into western (Ukrainian) and eastern (Russian) halves cannot be dismissed.

A successful case of crisis management in the mid-1990s involving control of former Soviet naval facilities and forces at Sebastopol, a port city in southern Ukraine (on the Crimean Peninsula), points to the possibility of future conflict between Russia and the Ukraine. The crisis arose from the ambiguities and conflicting interests of these two former partners over the disposition (ownership) of the Black Sea naval assets of the former Soviet Union. Although the dispute was resolved peacefully in 1997 (Russia got 80 percent of the fleet but conceded that the port itself belongs to the Ukraine), it is a reminder that these two large Slavic states are now rivals rather than brothers in arms (even though from the standpoints of history and ethnicity they can only be viewed as two branches of one and the same family tree).

There are numerous other examples of this sort of actual or potential conflict. For instance, in 1997 Kazakhstan (which borders Russia) was 51 percent Kazak and 32 percent Russian. The tension between the two groups threatens Kazakhstan's social peace as the possibility of Russian intervention looms. Ethnic and political strife has occurred within Moldova, a state bordering Romania on the western border of the old Soviet Union. Russia's support of internal territorial claims made by ethnic Russians within Moldova (representing some 13 percent of the population) has led to internal dissension between Russians in Moldova and native Moldovans (who represent 65 percent of the population), as well as to tensions between the Russian and Moldovan governments.

The case of Moldova illustrates the complexities of ethnic politics in Russia. It is clearly not true that the internal ethnic republics are composed of only one ethnic group; on the contrary, in most (fifteen out of twenty-one), the titular nationality is in the minority.[10]

State Building   After the demise of the Soviet Union, new governmental structures and governments were immediately required to replace the discredited Communist party. Not only did newly created nations need to be governed, but they also had to be governed amidst the hostile environment of economic disintegration and ethnic tension.

Russia must solve serious state-building problems in order to secure future political stability. Although nationwide legislative elections were held at the end of 1993 and 1995, and a presidential election took place in 1996 and 2000, democracy in Russia is still in its infancy. The state-building challenges Russia must surmount in order to establish political stability include:

- *A Fragile Constitution.* Adopted in 1993, the Russian constitution strengthened the presidency vis-à-vis the legislature, helping Yeltsin to overcome parliamentary opposition. As such, it is widely understood to be a political (i.e., partisan) document, and does not yet receive the normal respect or reverence accorded such fundamental government documents.

- *A Fragmented Party System.* The Russian party system is highly fragmented; forty-two parties appeared on the ballot in the December 1995 election to the *Duma,* the lower house of the *Federal Assembly,* Russia's national legislature. These parties represented a remarkable breadth of professional, ideological, and ethnic interest; some of the more interesting ones are the Ecological Party, the Women of Russia, the Muslim Movement, the Association of Lawyers of Russia, and even the Beer Drinker's Party. Russia's leading parties represent two political extremes—the nationalists, advocating a revival of the Old Russian Empire, and the communists, championing a slowing or repeal of economic and democratic reform. Such divisions help promote political deadlock and immoderation—each a cause for political concern.

- *An Uncertain Federalism.* Russia's formal name is the Russian Federation, referring to a division of power between the central government and local governments. The constitution does not clearly delineate the powers between the center and members of the Federation. Some observers argue the balance of power is moving away from the central government. The adoption of the 1993 constitution and a subsequent law requiring the election of local leaders, who sit in the **Federation Council** (the upper house of the Federal Assembly), have helped create regional power bases headed by powerful bosses. No longer can Moscow oust insubordinate local governments; now it will have to negotiate with leaders on lower levels.[11]

- *The Rise of Organized Crime.* The need for state building is reflected by the rise of competing organizations willing to perform quasi-governmental functions, either independently or by operating through existing governmental structures (such as providing jobs and job security, and enforcing law and contracts). According to one estimate, organized crime today employs some 3 million people and has infiltrated the Russian police and bureaucracy, as well as those of other republics. The mob's influence is everywhere; it "intrudes into every field of Western concern, the nascent free market, privatization, disarmament, military conversion, foreign humanitarian relief and financial aid, and even state reserves of currency and gold."[12] In March 1995, after the mafia-style killing of a prominent journalist, Yeltsin declared that organized crime posed a serious threat to Russian political stability. Western governments have expressed concern that the Russian Mafia or government scientists, engineers, and technologists who have been hard hit by layoffs and IOUs in monthly pay envelopes may sell stolen nuclear, chemical, and biological weapons to terrorist organizations and maverick states on the black market (illegal international trafficking in arms and drugs is big business).

- *An Increasing Disrespect for Law.* The rise of organized crime, the emergence of localized political bosses, the prevalence of corruption, and a broad spectrum of social ills such as ordinary crime, prostitution, and drug abuse, all eat away at the social fabric. Widespread lawlessness also reflects government's inability to maintain law and order. One consequence of these problems is a disrespect for the very idea of law, which for good reason has been called "Russia's biggest blight."[13]

A Leader at Last?

In August 1999, then-President Boris Yeltsin named Vladimir Putin, a former KGB officer and political unknown, to be his new prime minister. None of Yeltsin's first four prime ministers had lasted long in office, so Putin's sudden elevation to this post might have been no big deal. In fact, it was a big deal: eight months later Putin was the newly elected president of Russia.

If Yeltsin's plan was to position Putin for succession to the presidency, the December 1999 parliamentary elections were critical. Putin, for his part, did two things that bolstered his standing with the voters. First, he quickly won over many Russians with a get tough approach to the conduct of the war in Chechnya after a long period of indecision on the part of his predecessors (and, of course, President Yeltsin). Second, he boldly endorsed two upstart political parties—Unity (also called Medved, which means "bear"), a last-minute coalition with no known program, and the Union of Right-Wing Forces, a party of liberal reformers. Unity nearly finished in first place, only slightly behind the front-running Communists, while the Union of Right Forces finished a respectable fourth. Together these two parties garnered about one-third of the popular vote and just a few seats fewer than the Communists in the new Duma. For the first time, the Russian parliament had two blocs—one left of center and one right of center—facing each other. Was the Russian political party system at long last becoming less chaotic, perhaps even normal?

Not exactly. At the first meeting of the newly elected Duma, the Communists and Unity (the main pro-Putin party) formed an alliance of odd bedfellows, dividing up the chairmanships of the key committees between them. The Communists came out best, retaining the post of Duma speaker (leader) and getting nine committee chairs, but in return pledged to support the new government—in other words, to accept Putin's choice of prime minister and reform program. The opposition parties cried foul (one former prime minister, Yevgeny Primakov, called the deal a "desecration"). Nonetheless, the arrangement was a first for Russia's young democracy: never before had the government (executive branch) enjoyed a clear majority in the Parliament.

In retrospect, Yeltsin's decision to make Putin prime minister in 1999 was the first scene in the final act of a drama that had begun almost a decade earlier. Once in office Putin quickly moved to put his personal stamp on Russia's domestic and foreign policies. At home, he moved against organized crime and Russia's notorious "oligarchs" (wealthy tycoons who gained control over gigantic pieces of the old Soviet economy during the Yeltsin era); abroad, he gave Russia's foreign policy a new look, reducing tensions with former Soviet republics, closing a Russian listening post in Vietnam and a naval base in Cuba, renewing Moscow's bid for membership in the World Trade Organization, and strongly backing the U.S. campaign against terrorism in the fall of 2001.

Putin also paid tribute to economic reforms, including changes in the tax laws and creation of a financial intelligence service to fight money laundering. Buoyed by high oil prices in the late 1990s Russia's economy appeared to revive following a much-needed devaluation of the ruble in 1998. But the basic structures of Russia's protectionist, cartel-dominated, red tape–ridden economy remain unchanged, including such key sectors as utilities, banks, and state-owned enterprises. Nor has the political landscape changed fundamentally: The regions are still cauldrons of intrigue and corruption, the bureaucracy is imperious and impenetrable, the independent press gets little or no protection from the state (threats against investigative reporters and media personalities are not uncommon and cannot be taken lightly).

In sum, a decade after the veil of communist rule was lifted, Russia is still a riddle to the West and the world it seeks to join. Putin's meteoric rise to power and firm leadership attest to both the unpredictability and the promise of Russia's experiment in democracy.

Future Prospects

Does Russia represent the remains of a great empire inexorably caught in the process of decay, disintegration, and anarchy, or can it stabilize and reemerge as a major world power and empire? Will Russia end its transition period as democratic or authoritarian state? These two questions frame any consideration of Russia's future.

In the midst of economic, ethnic, and political turmoil, Russia suffers from a crisis of identity, a spiritual crisis of sorts. What system of beliefs will provide meaning to people's lives, especially as they survive under adverse economic and political conditions? Communism, which steadily had lost credibility since Stalin's death, has largely collapsed as an influential belief system. Meanwhile, the Russian Orthodox church offers solace to many, but even with the fall of communism it still struggles to establish independence from pervasive political influences. As we have seen, the Russian Mafia offers the lure of power and self-aggrandizement to some. But perhaps the most powerful vision is that of a restored, powerful, imperialist Russia, motivated by a widespread nostalgia and by a love of the homeland rooted deep in Russian history. Putin appears to have appealed to this innate sense of patriotism and national pride without resorting to demagogic slogans or pandering to the extreme right.

Democracy in Russia always has been an uncertain prospect, given centuries of despotism and centralized rule. Still, in the early 1990s, optimists had believed that Russia was moving toward democracy and a free enterprise economy. Later in the decade, having encountered enormous cultural, political, and economic obstacles, political and economic liberalization seemed a more distant hope. Then came Putin and things started to change, apparently for the better.

While Russia's future hangs in the balance, democracy remains fragile in the face of various political factions for whom ethnic intolerance and nostalgia for the past were common denominators. But now, for the first time, Russia has a dynamic (and healthy) president. Russia's liberal-democratic constitution looks sound enough on paper. The real test, however, is not how a constitution looks on paper but how it works in practice. It is a safe bet that democracy in Russia will continue to be put to a series of severe tests in the years to come. If Russia is destined to complete the transition to an open and liberal society it will be due to wise and courageous leadership on the one hand and prodigious amounts of popular perseverance on the other.

We turn next to a brief look at Eastern Europe, a region of nations in transition. No two countries have approached the problems of political and economic reform in exactly the same way and there is a widening gap between the most and least successful countries.

EASTERN EUROPE: TRANSITIONAL CROSSROADS (WILL OLD HABITS EVER DIE?)

Without exception, the newly independent states of this region were communist-ruled during the Cold War era, which lasted for more than four decades. They were all saddled with centrally planned economies patterned after that of the

Soviet "Big Brother." Just as central planning did not work in the long run in the Soviet Union, so it did not work anywhere else. When communism was finally swept away, the long-suffering peoples of Eastern Europe rejoiced in the expectation of better times ahead. These high hopes were soon dashed nearly everywhere, and disappointment replaced euphoria. This phenomenon has been universal throughout the region, but the breadth and depth of mass disillusionment varies in direct proportion to state of the economies around the region.

The most dynamic economies in Eastern Europe are also the ones in which the boldest reforms have been implemented—namely Poland, the Czech Republic, and Hungary. Poland dived headlong into economic reforms after 1989, launching a set of policies called "shock therapy" that were designed to create functioning markets and to privatize the notoriously inefficient state enterprises that were a legacy of communist rule. Though Poland had a small private sector even under communism, today there are some 2 million registered businesses there.

Poland's tough approach to reform yielded impressive results in the 1990s. Unlike most emerging markets in the region (including Hungary and Czech Republic), Poland avoided recessions and currency crises (devaluations). At the same time, Poland's economy grew faster than that of its ex-communist neighbors, averaging over 5 percent a year between 1995 and 2000. Poland also managed to tame the beast of inflation, a major threat to social and economic stability throughout much of the region. As a direct result of these economic strides, foreign investment has flowed into Poland in sizeable amounts in recent years.

On the other hand, rising unemployment was a problem, especially in a country where jobs were guaranteed to all adults during more than four decades of communist rule. A growing disparity between rich and poor and between rural and urban dwellers was also an increasingly serious issue as the relatively impoverished rural population fell farther and farther behind the burgeoning middle class in the cities. Many of Poland's "dirt-poor villagers" still live and work on one of the 2 million family farms there.[14] It is important to note here that Polish agriculture was never collectivized.

In Poland as elsewhere in the region, there is a troubling relationship between inequality and poverty on the one hand and crime on the other. Surveys show that most Poles no longer consider Poland to be a safe place to live. Furthermore, official corruption has undermined public confidence in government. Small wonder then that three out of four Polish voters and taxpayers do not think the country is currently going in the right direction.

In the Czech Republic, Prime Minister Vaclav Klaus extolled the virtues of the marketplace and implemented an ambitious coupon redemption scheme that theoretically gave all Czech citizens shares of newly privatized (formerly state) enterprises. But the distribution was done without adequate safeguards and thus failed to accomplish one of its primary aims—to give Czechs a stake in the new market economy. In fact, crooks and insiders (a distinction without a difference in Czech politics) grabbed up the high-quality stocks (most of which were never made available to the public) and used connections to get operational control of the hottest properties. Ironically, this bungled attempt at reform soured ordinary Czechs toward democracy and capitalism rather than solidifying popular support as it was intended to do. Inflation, fear of job losses, corruption in high places, a growing gap between the nouveaux riche and the majority, and a heightened awareness of how far behind the West East Europeans in general and Czechs in particular had fallen all contributed to a deepening disillusionment with the shady entrepreneurs and self-aggrandizing politicians who became synonymous with "the system" in the eyes of the people.

Despite widespread popular dissatisfaction with "politics" and the pace of improvement in the general standard of living, the Czech Republic is again a true republic (Czechoslovakia came into being after World War I as a full-fledged parliamentary democracy—the only instance of popular self-government in Eastern Europe prior to 1989). In addition, the Czech economy, having stumbled along for most of the decade, made a strong recovery following the recession of 1997–99. Structural reforms (for example, in the banking sector) helped achieve this result.

Nonetheless, what is true of Poland is also true of the Czech Republic: The majority of Czechs are not satisfied with the direction the country is going. At the same time, the level of dissatisfaction, while worrying, is not so high that most people would prefer to go back to the days of communism, central planning, and the totalitarian state.

Hungary was the first country in Eastern Europe to launch economic reforms and did it well before the fall of communism. In 1968, the same year as the tumultuous Prague Spring in Czechoslovakia, the communist government of Hungary launched the New Economic Mechanism (NEM) aimed at limited decentralization of the economy and other market-oriented reforms. The initial phase of the NEM was a modest success. Production of consumer goods (always a low priority in Soviet-type economies) rose and the quality of life for Hungarians generally improved. But hard-line communists at home and abroad (particularly in the Soviet Union) opposed these reforms. In the 1980s, the NEM was abandoned. Even so, as the economy declined steadily during this time, Hungary turned to the West for trade, aid, and investment. The liberalization that accompanied this policy included a new tolerance of private businesses and partnerships with foreign multinational companies. Thus, Hungary's reform efforts, though limited in scope and scale, gave it a head start when communism self-destructed at the end of the 1980s.

After 1989, Hungary's new liberal-democratic government accelerated the pace of free-market reforms. In particular, as the leading emerging market in the region, Hungary attracted more than half of all direct foreign investment in Eastern Europe even though Hungary's population (about 10 million) was a mere 25 percent of Poland's (40 million) and a tiny fraction of Russia's (147 million). Postcommunist Hungary moved swiftly to break up and privatize its huge state-owned enterprises; by 1993 the private sector's share of GDP was about 50 percent. The pace of privatization slowed temporarily when the socialists gained a majority in the parliament in 1994, but the following year the same parliament passed legislation to speed the sale of state-owned enterprises and prepare to sell off public utilities and strategic industries such as steel and electricity. Despite these bold restructuring efforts, Hungary has suffered high levels of inflation and unemployment unknown in communist times.

On the positive side, Hungary is now firmly in the liberal-democratic category of European states. In three free elections since 1989, a different party has won control of the government each time—a sign of party competition and political pluralism at work. Moreover, these changes have not led to sharp lurches to the Left or Right and have not proved to be destabilizing for the political system as a whole. Finally, Hungary's economy appears to be on a glide path of steady (if less than spectacular) growth.

If the transitions in the three countries showcased here are incomplete, many of the ex-communist countries including Ukraine, Bulgaria, and Romania are worse off by far. Slovenia, formerly part of the Yugoslav federation, is the one notable exception, outshining all the others (including Poland, Hungary, and the Czech Republic). In general prosperity, Slovenia outranks two members of the European Union, Greece and Portugal, and is only slightly below another one, Spain. Slovakia (formerly part of Czechoslovakia) and Croatia (also part of Yugoslavia before the breakup) are close behind the three leaders and well ahead of the laggards. Belarus, Moldova, Macedonia, and Albania are among the losers in this region. Serbia and Montenegro (what remains of the old Yugoslavia) are discussed in Chapter 8.

Two subregions on the fringes of Eastern Europe deserve brief mention in this section. The Baltic states of Latvia, Lithuania, and Estonia fall somewhere between the leaders and the laggards. The three trans-Caucasian states—Georgia, Armenia, and Azerbaijan—occupy a geographic and cultural twilight zone between Slavic Eastern Europe and the Turkic Near East and Central Asia. In the transition race, they are near the back of the pack, but the rich oil deposits in the Caspian Sea give this region a strategic value beyond what it would otherwise have. Of course, the peoples of the Baltic and trans-Caucasus are not Slavic (neither are Hungarians and Romanians for that matter).

In sum, communism has largely disappeared from the map of Europe, although communist parties (often with new names) are still around. Free and fair elections are held nearly everywhere and genuine parliamentary democracy is by far the most common form of government. But these countries have all discovered that it is far easier to bring about political change on an institutional level than to change a political culture. They have also learned that holding elections is easier than holding the line on inflation or deficit spending, and that changing political structures is easier than changing economic structures. Even where the transitions to political pluralism and the marketplace have gone the farthest, people express general (and growing) dissatisfaction with the pace and direction of reforms. The story of communism's demise is thus full of suspense. It remains only half-written, its ending a mystery until the transitions to viable postcommunist order are completed—in other words, for many years to come.

We turn next to the transition in Communist China. There, the question of political change has been set aside in favor of economic transformation. The results have been nothing short of spectacular, but they are less than satisfying in the eyes of the West.

CHINA: TRANSITION TO GUIDED CAPITALISM (AND THEN WHAT?)

Now that the Soviet Union and the "world socialist system" (as Moscow called it) have passed into history, China is the only major communist state left. Although it remains a poor country compared to Japan, South Korea, and Singapore, China has a vast supply of cheap labor (its population is 1.3 billion) and a robust economy—two reasons for cautious optimism. And while most observers would agree it has shed its legacy of Maoist totalitarian rule (see Chapter 5), few would dispute that it remains a repressive, authoritarian state.

The path to power for Mao Zedong's Chinese Communist party (CCP) differed sharply from that taken by Lenin's Bolsheviks. Because Mao's victory followed a protracted guerrilla war against the Japanese and the Chinese Nationalist government of Chiang Kai-shek, the army played a much greater role in Mao's theory and practice of revolution than in Lenin's. When the Chinese Communists came to power in 1949, the army and the party were fused into a single organization. Acting as a virtual government, the army was charged not only with fighting but also with administration, including maintenance of law and order, construction and public works, management of the economy, and education and indoctrination. In effect, the army became the nucleus of the People's Republic, the new government of China.

Mao in Command

In the early 1950s, the People's Republic of China (PRC) was heavily dependent on political, economic, and military assistance from the Soviet Union, a dependency heightened by the Korean War (1950–53). The USSR, ruled by the aging Stalin, insisted that the fledgling Communist government in Beijing emulate the Stalinist model. Thus, the political structures of the Chinese state, as well as the thrust of Chinese economic and foreign politics, closely resembled those of the Soviet Union. Everything from collectivization of agriculture and a lopsided emphasis on industrial investment to the Soviet educational system was borrowed almost without modification.

The turning point came when Stalin's successor, Nikita Khrushchev, made his famous speech at the Twentieth Party Congress in 1956, in which he denounced the crimes of Stalin and proclaimed the advent of peaceful coexistence with the West. From that point on, the Chinese Communists, under Mao's erratic leadership, went its own bizarre way.

The Great Leap Forward, launched in 1958, represented Mao's declaration of independence from the Soviet model of industrial development. In place of the Stalinist emphasis on heavy industry, especially large-scale mining and metallurgical complexes, the Great Leap stressed decentralized industrialized production to take advantage of China's greatest natural resource—human labor. Numerous small-scale backyard steel furnaces became the symbol of this labor-intensive approach.

Mao's *mass line*, holding that everything could be achieved through the inspired efforts of the peasant masses, replaced the Soviet party-state bureaucracy as the driving force behind the revolutionary transformation of society. The Great

Proletarian Cultural Revolution, the Mao-inspired reaction against all bureaucracy, was the culmination of this approach. For China, the Soviet system had become a model of counterrevolution.

Changing of the Guard

The deaths of Zha Enlai and Mao Zedong, the People's Republic's two great founders, made the year 1976 a watershed in modern Chinese history. According to one China scholar, "Mao's death marked the end of an era; what was not clear was who would lead China and in what direction in the era to come."[15]

After two years of halting reforms, the nation's post-Mao leadership under the direction of Deng Xiaoping (who had twice been purged by Mao for his alleged lack of revolutionary zeal) "mounted a major campaign to abandon ideological dogma and to adopt pragmatism—symbolized by the slogans 'practice is the sole criterion of truth' and 'seek truth from facts.'"[16] Economic development replaced class struggle, and a welcome mat replaced the "no trespassing" sign that had impeded China's trade relations with the West for nearly three decades. Banished were the mass campaigns, crash programs, hero worship, and ideological fanaticism that had been the hallmarks of Maoism.

Expanding trade, especially with the industrial democracies, became a principal aim of Beijing's diplomacy. Deng's economic reforms were implemented gradually between 1978 and 1982, as he carefully and patiently consolidated his power within the ruling *Politburo.* By the fall of 1982, the reform-minded Deng was in full command.

Deng remained China's paramount ruler until his death, at the age of ninety-two, on February 19, 1997. Initially, he was replaced by a collective leadership of four former Deng associates, out of which Jiang Zemin emerged triumphant, becoming the general secretary of the Communist party and state president. An engineer by training, Jiang had been the mayor of Shanghai prior to his elevation to the Communist party leadership in 1989. After assuming his nation's leadership, Jiang gave every indication of continuing Deng's political and economic policies and institutions. The distinguishing characteristics of those policies and institutions are highlighted in the following section.

A Dominant Party

The Communist party continues to govern China. It claims some 57 million members—approximately 5 percent of the total population. Party members are a political elite who enjoy special privileges. In addition, high ranking in the party remains a prerequisite to the exercise of political power.

Throughout his rule, Deng attempted to bolster the Communist party. Unlike Mao, who frequently sought the limelight and whose social and political upheavals had uprooted the CPC, Deng quietly stayed in the background performing his dual role as the great stabilizer of the state and the protector of the party. His successor, Jiang Zemin, followed closely in Deng's footsteps. Thus, at a time when some observers argue that China is becoming a more complex nation, increasingly difficult to rule, the Communist party is able to retain its tight hold on China's politics and policies.[17]

The Decline of Ideology

Before 1978, Mao's adaptation of Marxism was the official ideology of China. After 1978, Deng's pragmatic view prevailed—that economic growth, not class struggle, ought to be the main measure of success for both the party and the state. No longer would the party invoke Marxist ideology to justify its programs or policies, or to legitimize the party's rule.[18]

A Communist party that distances itself from communism presents a curious picture, indeed. Rather than moral reliance on utopian promises, the CPC now defines its role in pragmatic terms: to protect a stable political order and promote a flourishing economy. Few trends are more noteworthy than China's deemphasis on communist ideology (and its concomitant resort to traditional ideas, institutions, and leaders) as a basis for political legitimacy or to justify its often harsh rule.

Market-Oriented Reforms

As already noted, Deng's decision to stress economic development after Mao's death represented a remarkable change that radically departed from the Marxist model—an emphasis on relatively free markets, private ownership of businesses, and market incentives, including profits. In order to implement these policies, Beijing boldly sought foreign loans and direct foreign investment, primarily from the West (thus violating a long-standing ideological taboo). China's new "open door" approach to relations with the West was designed to modernize the nation's economy (both agriculture and industry) as rapidly as possible. The approach worked, as Western investment and loans poured into the country in the 1980s and 1990s, providing much-needed capital for China's modernization drive (see Figure 7-2).

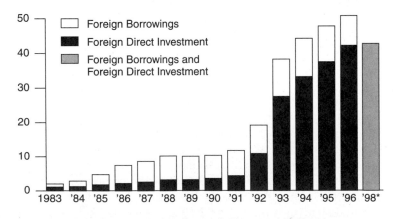

FIGURE 7-2   Foreign Capital Inflows (billions of dollars)
*1998 total of $42.6 billion includes both foreign borrowings and foreign direct investment.
SOURCE: *Economist*, February 22, 1997, 22; *2000 World Bank Atlas* (Washington, DC: World Bank, 2000), 56.

At the same time, agriculture underwent a major transformation. The watchword was *decollectivization*—rejection of state ownership of agriculture and a return to family-based farming. After considerable experimentation, the regime settled on a system whereby the state made contracts with individual households to purchase specified products. The reforms proved remarkably successful as farmers produced record harvests and sold them in private markets. In industry and commerce, too, China moved toward a greater reliance on market forces. One statistic is remarkably revealing. In 1978, there were no privately owned businesses in China; within twenty years approximately one-third of all businesses were privately owned (see Figure 7-3).

The results of China's agricultural and industrial revolution have been impressive. After decades of induced turmoil under Mao, China's economy has revived. In fact, China boasts one of the world's fastest growing economies at present, but it is still poor measured by the per capita wealth. China's gross domestic product is half the size of Germany's, for example, yet Germany's population is only about one-sixteenth the size of China's. Even so, between 150 and 200 million people (equal to half the population of western Europe) have escaped debilitating poverty, according to some estimates. While three-fourths of Chinese who live off the land do remain poor, farm incomes rose sharply since agricultural reforms were put in effect.[19]

Despite huge strides in the quarter-century after Mao died, China remains a poor country. (For comparative figures, see Table 7-2.) Although China officially acknowledged 80 to 100 million people living in poverty in the late 1990s, other estimates, such as those made by the World Bank, placed the figure at 350 million people.[20] By most measures of aggregate income, as well as the quality-of-life indicators of citizens' health and welfare (such as infant mortality rates), China is usually classified as a developing nation or as an emerging market.

There have been other economic challenges as well. High inflation has at times hobbled the nation's economy. In addition, enormous income disparities exist within China. One very large disparity exists between many of the poor

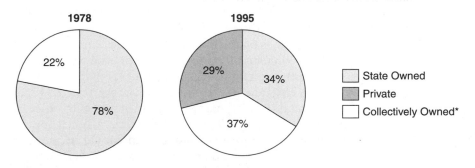

FIGURE 7-3   An Emerging Private Sector

Private ownership of business in China has increased dramatically.

*Partly government owned.

SOURCE: Newsweek, March 3, 1997, vol. cxxxix, no. 9, 27. The research is attributed to the Heritage Foundation and IMF, conducted by Anna Kuchment and Dante Chinni. © 1997 Newsweek, Inc. All rights reserved. Reprinted by permission.

TABLE 7-2

China and the United States—Comparative Standard-of-Living Indicators

Standard-of-Living Indicators	China	United States
Population	1,203,097,268	284,796,887
Annual population growth	1.04%	1.02%
Urban population	30%	76%
Life expectancy (years)	68.08	75.99
Infant mortality (per 1,000 births)	52.1	7.88
Fertility (children per woman)	1.84	2.08
GDP per capita (1998)	$3,051	$29,240
Stock market capitalization (1998)	$330 billion	$13.451 trillion
Electricity consumption per capita in kwh (1998)	714	11,822
Literacy	78%	97%
People per telephone	36.4	1.3
People per television set	6.7	1.2
Personal computers per 1000 (1998)	8.9	458.6

SOURCES: *Newsweek,* March 3, 1997, vol. cxxxix, no. 9, 27 (the research is attributed to the Heritage Foundation and IMF, conducted by Anna Kuchment and Dante Chinni); © 1997 Newsweek, Inc. All rights reserved. Reprinted by permission. *2000 World Bank Atlas* (Washington, D.C.: World Bank, 2000), 50–51; U.S. Census Bureau, www.census.gov, accessed May 13, 2002.

peasants in rural areas and a growing number of relatively affluent urban Chinese (including the wealthy entrepreneurial elite), in several of China's booming coastal cities. The rising new class exists side-by-side with China's "floating population" of 100 million unemployed or marginally employed people who have migrated from the provinces to the cities in search of good jobs and a better life. The coastal provinces of the east are growing much faster than those in central and western China and, according to official statistics they now produce between two to four times the incomes of the interior provinces.[21]

Shanghai is a particularly striking example of economic expansion—in 1997, it had one of the highest economic growth rates of any of the world's major cities. An ancient seaport city located near the mouth of the Yangtze River in east central China, Shanghai is taking advantage of its direct access to other important Asian ports, rapidly transforming itself into a worldwide financial and trading center.

In sum, free-market principles and guided capitalism have stimulated both incomes and inequality in contemporary China. However, an important question remains: How far can China's embrace of free enterprise go? Although China is privatizing little by little, China's largest firms—inefficient, heavily subsidized, and debt-laden—are still owned by the government. Nor is it likely that the government will relax its grip on the most strategic of those industries, including machine-building and weapons-manufacturing companies. Still, China has made halting progress toward privatization (see Figure 7-3). A decade earlier, it would have been unimaginable that shares in Chinese companies would be traded on the New York Stock Exchange (as they now are). In response to China's turn toward a more liberal economy, the United States dropped its opposition to Chinese membership in the World Trade Organization (WTO); China formally joined the WTO in 2001. According to the *Economist*, "China's accession to the WTO . . . is its biggest step since communist rule began more than 50 years ago toward the integration of its economic system with that of the capitalist West."[22]

Expanded Personal Freedoms

One mark of totalitarianism's demise in the PRC is that China "has become freer in terms of daily life for large numbers of people."[23] People can now change jobs, move from one part of China to another, exhibit greater individuality in dress and expression, and exercise free choice in such important personal matters as whom to marry and divorce—individual liberties scarcely imaginable in Mao's China. These new freedoms, however, stop far short of constitutional rights common in the West—for instance, couples are still limited by the government to having only one child. And, as we shall see, political and religious freedoms are nonexistent.

New Social Disorders

Oddly, China suffers from some of the same problems that are affecting Western democracy. According to one expert, "as a result of the loosening of more traditional forms of authority, China has begun suffering from an increasing crime wave."[24] Theft and robbery have been particularly bad in the cities, while drug-related crimes and prostitution are also on the increase—all represent the underside of China's economic expansion.

Corruption has become a way of life in China. With the blurring of the line between the public and private spheres, and vast amounts of money circulating through China's burgeoning economy, business and politics have become tainted by routine acts of bribery, nepotism, and "unofficial favoritism."

Political and Religious Repression

Despite liberalization in the economic and social spheres, political and religious persecution continues unabated in China. China's current rulers give no indication of straying from this seemingly inconsistent course, originally set by Deng Xiaoping.

Early in Deng's rule, there was a brief moment when it appeared that things might be otherwise. In 1978, a phenomenon known as the *Democracy Wall* captured worldwide attention. On this wall, located in the heart of Beijing, opinions and views at variance with the official line—including blunt criticisms of the existing system and leaders—were displayed with the tacit approval of the government. In addition to this unprecedented freedom of the "press," a newfound freedom of speech also blossomed around the Democracy Wall. But then, in 1979, the government clamped down on dissent. Subsequent arrests and show trials,

Reuters NewMedia Inc. / CORBIS

Under the shadow of Mao's portrait, tens of thousands of striking Beijing University students and supporters demonstrated in Tiananmen Square from April 17 to June 4, 1989, in a call for democratic freedom and government reforms. Many of the protesters camped out in tents and participated in hunger strikes for the duration of the protest as a sign of devotion to their cause.

The protest movement ended in a bloodbath in which an estimated 1,500 people died and as many as 10,000 were wounded. Before leaving the square, the demonstrators erected a statue to symbolize democracy and liberty, the "Goddess of Freedom," modeled after the Statue of Liberty.

plus other all-too-familiar forms of political repression, indicated clearly that the Chinese Communist party was not about to loosen its iron grip on the levers of political power.

A decade later, the **Tiananmen Square massacre** came to epitomize the Chinese government's persistent hostility to human rights. In May 1989, students and workers staged a mass march in Beijing to protest party privilege and corruption and to demand democratic reforms. The protest grew as throngs of demonstrators camped in Tiananmen Square, making speeches and shouting slogans. The rest of the world watched in rapt attention as the drama unfolded before Western television cameras. The fact that Mikhail Gorbachev, the father of "reform communism," visited Beijing that same month (the first Sino-Soviet summit in three decades) only added to the sense of high drama. When the unrest spread throughout the country, Beijing declared martial law—to no avail.

Army troops entered the Chinese capital with tanks and armor on June 3; it soon became apparent that the show of force was not a bluff. The crackdown that ensued brought the democracy movement to a bloody end. Hundreds (possibly thousands) of protesters were killed or injured, and many more were arrested. Subsequently, security forces rounded up thousands of dissenters, and at least thirty-one were tried and executed. The atrocities against unarmed civilians in the Tiananmen Square massacre proved clearly that China was still at its core a repressive state.

The Tiananmen Square massacre has come to symbolize China's persecution of critics and dissidents, especially those who dare to castigate the party's top leadership. A related issue is the way political prisoners are treated. Many are worked to death as slave laborers in factories that export cheap goods and products for foreign trade.

Another problem has been the Chinese government's persistent persecution of religious groups. To some extent, the government's imprisonment of religious followers is a remnant of Marxism's ideological mistrust of, and hostility to, religion. To a further extent, it represents the party's continuing perception that religion poses a political threat to the continuity and health of the regime.

For the most part, the government controls religion by licensing and monitoring religious institutions (churches, monasteries, mosques, etc.). Buddhists, Muslims, and Christians have been jailed for little more than practicing their religious faith. The Chinese have been particularly ruthless in Tibet, where they have closed Buddhist monasteries, jailed and executed worshippers, and exiled Tibet's religious leader, the Dalai Lama. In early 1997, anti-Chinese riots in the predominantly Muslim province of Xinjiiang in northwestern Tibet triggered reprisals by the Chinese government.

China's dismal human rights record has not gone unnoticed in the United States. Organizations such as the Christian Coalition have been particularly critical of the persecution of Christians in China. China's abuse of human rights became a central argument in the U.S. Congress by those opposed to renewing China's most favored nation (MFN) status, which extends to Chinese exports to the United States the same relatively low tariffs available to America's "most favored" trading partners.

Ironically, at the core of the debate over the MFN renewal was a dispute between idealists and pragmatists in the United States. Opponents contended that economic pressure would most clearly express moral disapproval and at the same time make China pay a real price for continued human rights violations. Supporters of MFN countered that only American businesses would be harmed by such a stance, as other businesses around the globe would happily take the U.S. market share. Supporters also asserted that trade, not economic isolation, would, in the long run, help to alleviate political persecution. In September 2000, the U.S. Congress voted to end the practice of making MFN status for China dependent on the outcome of an annual review—since then Chinese imports no longer face the recurring threat of tariff discrimination in the huge U.S. market.

The Threat of Political Fragmentation

Although the Communist party has kept a tight grip on society, China has not been free from internal problems.[25] One difficulty is tensions among China's far-flung regions. Another difficulty is terms-of-trade disputes between inland provinces rich in natural resources and coastal provinces that produce and sell finished goods. A somewhat different problem is that China's provinces and counties have, from time to time, set up trade barriers and enacted tariffs for the purpose of protecting local industries from competition. For example, in 1997 Shanghai's municipal government set new standards (engine size, luggage space, and so on) for cars serving as taxis that favored cars built by the city's local automaker, Shanghai Volkswagen. China continues to rotate local leaders throughout the country to prevent them from establishing local sympathies and loyalties.

An Emerging World Power

Over the past decade, China has become a dominant regional power and is fast becoming a global power as well. With the world's largest population, the PRC has no difficulty finding conscripts for its armed forces, which total 3 million troops. Since the late 1970s, China has sought to modernize its military capabilities. Today, it has the fastest-rising arms expenditures of any major world power. China has also garnered worldwide attention by continuing to test nuclear weapons and by selling high-tech armaments on the international market (in some instances, to customers the U.S. government regards as a threat to peace and order).

Nor has China's growing military power gone unnoticed in Asia or elsewhere around the world.[26] Thus, India's reluctance to forgo its nuclear weapons programs can be traced in part to its wary attitude toward China. By the same token, Japanese leaders have viewed China's military modernization with ill-concealed alarm. The Vietnamese have not forgotten the border war with China in 1979 and

---

American Trade with China: Problem or Opportunity?

Trade between the United States and China is surrounded by controversy. American business long viewed China as one huge, undeveloped marketplace: over 1 billion Chinese eagerly waiting to buy American goods. Many American multinational corporations have exerted influence to facilitate international trade by lobbying the American government to maintain good relations with China.

But an interesting trend has developed. The United States has been running a high balance-of-trade deficit with China (that is, the United States buys far more goods from China than China buys from the United States). In the late 1990s, the U.S. trade deficit with China ran neck and neck with that of Japan (with whom the United States has had the largest balance-of-trade deficit), and some economists predicted that China would soon permanently surpass Japan. China possesses an enormous advantage in international trade: Its goods are inexpensive to pro-

duce because of the low wages paid to Chinese workers.

Will the same sort of trade tensions that have strained U.S.–Japanese relations now cloud relations between the United States and China? Perhaps not, say some experts. Except for textiles, Chinese goods do not compete directly with U.S. goods; China's products are low-tech (for example, clothing, textiles, toys, and raw materials) while Japan manufactures high-tech products (such as cars, computers, electronics, and telecommunications equipment). Furthermore, unlike Japan, not all goods coming from China are Chinese, meaning that the balance-of-trade figures are somewhat unreliable. Why? Because some 50 percent of the goods exported from China are made in factories that are either co-owned or managed by non-Chinese. Apparently, the low costs that make Chinese exports attractive in the United States also make business opportunities in China attractive to non-Chinese entrepreneurs and businesses.

have periodically sought a Southeast Asian security alliance against the colossus to the north. The Philippines, long a staunch American ally in the Western Pacific, have an unresolved dispute with China over potentially oil-rich islands in the South China Sea. But the most dangerous situation involves Taiwan, which Beijing still regards as part of China and which it wishes to "reunify" with China.

Periodic Chinese naval exercises have reinforced this point, although Taiwan has continued to hold firm, buttressed by the U.S. Navy. Another potentially explosive issue was resolved without incident when the United Kingdom formally returned Hong Kong to Chinese control in 1997. This act, which ended nearly a century and a half of British rule over that bustling international commercial and financial center, was celebrated in Beijing as a sign of China's new stature in world politics.

China is an emerging world power, not simply an economic power, but a military one as well (see Figure 7-4). Some observers postulate that China may even rival the United States in the twenty-first century. Thus, from an American perspective, an important question looms: Will China and the United States cooperate and stay on good terms, or are they destined to be rivals, or perhaps even enemies?

ASIA: ECONOMIC TRANSITION (AND FREEDOM TOO?)

China is the giant of Asia, but the most impressive economic achievements in the region are found elsewhere. Following Japan's lead, South Korea, Taiwan, Hong Kong (a semi-autonomous part of China since 1997), and Singapore pursued highly successful export-oriented economic development strategies. The success of these four states, sometimes called the Four Little Dragon's or the Asian Tigers, gave rise to a new category, the *new industrial countries (NICs)*, discussed at greater length in the following chapter. Other transition-minded Asian

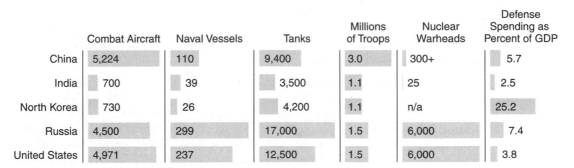

	Combat Aircraft	Naval Vessels	Tanks	Millions of Troops	Nuclear Warheads	Defense Spending as Percent of GDP
China	5,224	110	9,400	3.0	300+	5.7
India	700	39	3,500	1.1	25	2.5
North Korea	730	26	4,200	1.1	n/a	25.2
Russia	4,500	299	17,000	1.5	6,000	7.4
United States	4,971	237	12,500	1.5	6,000	3.8

FIGURE 7-4   The Chinese Military
Modernizing the armed forces was one of Deng's priorities, creating concerns that a "rising China" could tip the military balance in Asia.
SOURCE: Newsweek, March 3, 1997, vol. cxxxix, no. 9, 28. The research is attributed to the Heritage Foundation and IMF, conducted by Anna Kuchment and Dante Chinni. © 1997 Newsweek, Inc. All rights reserved. Reprinted by permission.

countries, including Thailand, Malaysia, and Indonesia, have also adopted free-market reforms aimed at attracting foreign investment and promoting exports. We put South Korea and Taiwan in the spotlight here, because they are now competing with Japan for export markets and also because they have taken steps toward political liberalization as well. In that respect, they differ sharply from China, which as we have seen, remains highly resistant to fundamental political change.

South Korea

The economic transformation of South Korea from a poor country dependent on agriculture to a modern industrial state powered by a technologically advanced manufacturing sector was an accomplished fact at the turn of the twentieth century. South Korea's per capita national wealth (or GDP) places it at roughly the same level as Portugal and Greece, both members of the European Union. Of course, the latter are among the poorest of the rich countries in Europe. To put South Korea's achievement in even better perspective, it is only necessary to note that South Korea's GDP per capita is larger than that of Argentina, the richest country in Latin America, and more than twice that of Brazil, Chile, Mexico, and Venezuela, four of the region's leading transitional states.

In the 1990s when South Korea's economy began to sag, the government under the leadership of President Kim Dae Jung launched a program of bold reforms. Traditionally, huge industrial conglomerates and largely unregulated big banks in South Korea dominated the economy; because these special interests had become so powerful and entrenched, the effect was to stifle competition. Asia's financial crisis of the late 1990s, also known as the *Asian flu,* did not start in South Korea but it had a devastating impact there. Big banks had lent money to big business without regard to the underlying financial condition of the borrowers. This situation, and the general need to revitalize the country's economy, compelled the popularly elected president to undertake aggressive state intervention—not to put the government in control of the economy but to give greater play to free-market forces. In effect, South Korea's government launched a second major transition in the late 1990s, including a restructuring of several huge industrial conglomerates and banking reforms, with very positive results. In 2000, South Korea's economy experienced a strong recovery and low inflation.

To what extent was this second transition political as well as economic? No doubt, politics played an important role. Like most other Asian societies, Koreans have always been ruled by an authoritarian state. North Korea was (and is) communist ruled after World War II, while South Korea, a close ally of the United States, was anticommunist. Even so, South Korean "democracy" was nothing more than facade for a pro-Western police state. But in 1997, after two previous unsuccessful bids for the presidency, Kim Dae Jung became the first opposition candidate ever elected in South Korea. (Similarly, Vicente Fox became the first opposition candidate to be elected in Mexico, another country previously dominated by a single party, three years later.) Electing an opposition candidate president is a breakthrough in any country undergoing a political transition toward liberal democratic rule. As we are about to see, this sort of breakthrough occurred in at least one other place in 2000.

Taiwan

Taiwan became an independent state after World War II when the Chinese Communists led by Mao Zedong defeated Chiang Kai-shek's Nationalists (Kuomintang). Until 1972, the United States recognized Taiwan as the legitimate government of China, although it was clear that the Communist regime in Beijing was in control of the mainland. Since 1972, Taiwan has remained independent, but no longer enjoys recognition as a permanent sovereign state. The reason for this unique state of affairs is that the People's Republic of China has successfully pressed its claim that Taiwan is part of China, there is only one China, and Beijing is the capital of China.

Nonetheless, Taiwan continues to enjoy the military protection and diplomatic goodwill of the United States, along with close economic ties. Taiwan's economy is one of the most dynamic in Asia, outpacing South Korea's by a wide margin. Indeed, if Taiwan were in Europe it would rank well above Portugal and Greece, in the same league as Spain, in terms of per capita national wealth. This "economic miracle" is nothing new, but Taiwan's recent moves toward a more liberal social and political order *is* new.

In 1988, Lee Teng-hui became the first native Taiwanese leader to assume the office of the presidency and the first popularly elected president in Taiwanese history. Lee instituted sweeping political reforms during his twelve-year tenure as president, continuing a process that had been initiated in the mid-1980s by his predecessor, Chiang Ching-kuo (Chiang Kai-shek's son). The gradual relaxation of the Nationalist party's iron grip on the government culminated in the election of opposition candidate Chen Shui-bian in 2000, another first in Taiwan's political history.

Asia's Holdouts

The political liberalization evident in South Korea and Taiwan today came long after economic changes had started to transform these two societies. This pattern of economic liberalization without significant political change is common throughout much of Asia. In fact, Asia's most successful economy is that of Singapore, a city-state whose leadership has been firm and unabashed in rejecting Western-style liberal-democratic institutions. Both the Philippines and Thailand, and to a lesser extent Malaysia and Indonesia, have adopted liberalizing reforms to varying degrees. But countries such as North Korea, Vietnam, Laos, and Myanmar remain mired in structures and systems that have kept fundamental economic and political change at bay.

Whereas Asia's transitional states started with economic reforms, Latin America's led with political change. The democratization of Latin politics in the 1980s was swift and certain, but Latin America remains a region in search of a recipe for economic revitalization.

LATIN AMERICA: POLITICAL TRANSITION (AND PROSPERITY TOO?)

Military-bureaucratic rule has been a tradition in Latin America for centuries since the independence era in the first quarter of the nineteenth century. The states of Latin America (formerly colonies of Spain or Portugal) became independent long before the European colonial empires were dismantled elsewhere in the world. Military dictatorship in practice coexisted with liberal-democratic values in theory. Only in a few countries, such as Colombia, Venezuela, and Costa Rica, however, had popularly elected civilian government ever struck roots in the region prior to the 1980s. But then things changed—not everything, of course, but enough to usher in a whole new age in Latin American history, a new page in Latin American politics, and perhaps a new stage in Latin American economic development.

The ABC's of Reform (Argentina, Brazil, Chile)

In the 1980s, one military dictatorship after another stepped aside in favor of democratically elected civilian governments. Today, virtually every government in the region qualifies as a liberal democracy. The political transitions coincided, suggesting that Latin America was ripe for a political reform. Ironically, what powered the political change was the need for economic reforms, evidenced above all by the huge foreign debts that many countries in the region had amassed. The burden of these debts, combined with outmoded economic structures and uncompetitive (protected) industries, high inflation, mass unemployment, widespread poverty, and shocking inequality between the rich and poor, plunged the region into a crisis of self-confidence and underconsumption (millions of people, especially *campesinos* in rural areas, struggle to survive at a bare subsistence level).

Chile has led the way in reforming its economy. In fact, Chile is an exception to the rule in Latin America, because the country instituted market reforms *before* it democratized its political system. Under Augusto Pinochet (1974–90), Chile was one of the harshest military dictatorships in the region, but the Chilean economy, spurred by market forces, came to life. No such thing happened anywhere else in Latin America, which helps to explain the downfall of military rule in the 1980s.

In Brazil, military rule gave way to civilian government in 1985, and three years later Brazil adopted a new constitution that provided for direct election of the president. The current president, Fernando Henrique Cardosa, is an economist by training. He is attempting to reform and restructure Brazil's economy, so far with mixed results at best. The country is plagued with heavy external debts, chronic budget shortfalls, extensive rural poverty, and glaring inequality. Brazil desperately needs a social security overhaul and tax reform to get its public accounts in balance. But these measures are political hot potatoes in a country where constitutional democracy is still in its adolescence (if not infancy).

Argentina's military rulers bowed out after the country's humiliating defeat by the British in the Falklands War (1982). A presidential democracy, Argentina is the richest country in South America measured by per capita GDP. However,

Argentina's economic performance has also been disappointing. In order to hold down inflation and budget deficits, Argentina's debt-burdened government has opted for fiscal austerity (high taxes and spending restraints). As a result, unemployment has hovered around 15 percent in recent years. But by taking the foot off the brake, so to speak, the government fears foreign investors would turn away.

The problems facing Brazil and Argentina are fairly typical of the whole region. In Latin America, political reform (democratization) has proved to be considerably easier than economic reform and revitalization. The reasons are many and varied; the most intractable problems, however, are essentially social and cultural. Latin American society has long been exceedingly elitist and unjust. Inequalities are so great and wealth is so highly concentrated that the majority of the people do not have enough purchasing power to be *consumers* in any meaningful sense of the word. Economies that achieve sustained growth are almost always associated with a phenomenon called mass consumption. In Latin America the masses too often do not have good jobs or steady income and therefore cannot engage in the kind of consumption that, along with exports, drives rapid economic development (as we will see in the following chapter). So "sharing the wealth" is not only a moral imperative, it is also an economic one—without a constant circulation of wealth involving the whole society it is difficult if not impossible to complete the transition from a rural-based, slow-growth, inward-looking protectionist economy to a modern, market-based, urban-industrial, export-oriented economy. That appears to be Latin America's destiny, but for the region's impoverished masses it is taking way too long to get there.

Mexico

Last, we turn to Mexico, the United States' "distant neighbor" to the south. Mexico is a good example of the historical contradiction found in so many Latin American countries—a romantic attachment to democratic ideals coexisting with an authoritarian regime disguised as a republic. Mexico has been a liberal democracy on paper since World War I. In reality, however, there has rarely been anything resembling genuinely competitive elections in Mexico—until 2000. Finally, after decades of one-party rule under the *Institutional Revolutionary party (PRI)*, Mexican voters were given a real choice and a real chance. The choice was between the PRI's candidate and several other candidates representing the opposition. The chance was a first in Mexico—a free and fair election (no ballot-box stuffing, no intimidation at the polls, etc.). The result was a bombshell: Opposition candidate Vicente Fox, representing the *National Action party (PAN)*, won in a runoff.

At the beginning of the 1990s, Mexico joined with the United States and Canada in the *North American Free Trade Association (NAFTA)*, which instantly boosted Mexico's economic prospects. But internal market reforms are difficult due to inefficient state-owned companies (for example, PEMEX, the oil monopoly), entrenched interests, and a corrupt bureaucracy fearful of losing its privileges. Membership in NAFTA gives Mexico easy access to U.S. markets but it also gives the United States leverage to pressure the Mexican government into accelerating economic reforms.

President Fox came into office vowing to do just that. It will not be any easier in Mexico than it has been in the rest of Latin America, but Mexico has little choice if it expects to compete as an equal NAFTA partner with the United States and Canada.

Throughout the region, Latin America has made a sharp turn toward political pluralism and liberal democracy. But the economic benefits of liberalization have yet to be realized and await at least two things: First, bold reforms involving friction between the top leadership and the entrenched bureaucracy on the one hand and conflict between the agents of change and the wealthy land-owning elite on the other; second, mobilization of a newly enfranchised and empowered underclass who for the first time have a stake in the system.

Summary

Communist power has disintegrated nearly everywhere in the world. The demise of the Soviet Union is the most prominent example of this phenomenon. Nonetheless, a few scattered nations—most notably China—continue to be communist-ruled. The collapse of communism focuses attention for the first time on the problems of transition in the former Soviet bloc states. Other countries such as South Korea and Taiwan in Asia and Argentina, Brazil, and Chile in Latin America are also undergoing political and economic transitions.

Traditionally, the Soviet system was totalitarian, created in the image of Stalin. Before Mikhail Gorbachev, only Nikita Khrushchev attempted to soften it. In the Soviet system, the Communist party ruled, and ranking in the party was the best indication of a person's political power. When Gorbachev rose to the top post in the Communist party in 1985, he faced both acute economic problems and associated social problems, each related to the failure of central planning. Additionally, he had to overcome the complacency and opposition of the Soviet elite, the *nomenklatura*. In attempting to reformulate the communist system, Gorbachev undertook economic reforms (perestroika), political liberalizations (glasnost), and democratic political reforms (*demokratizatsiia*). These measures proved inadequate to save the former Soviet Union.

Russia (under Boris Yeltsin), and the Commonwealth of Independent States, succeeded the Soviet Union. Yeltsin, too, faced daunting political challenges, including persistent economic dislocations, ethnic fragmentation, and the need for state building. How successfully Russia meets these challenges will help determine its future, particularly the question of whether it will be democratic.

China remains a communist country, yet it has changed considerably since Mao's passing. Although China has instituted meaningful free-market reforms, allowed citizens a greater degree of personal freedom, and downplayed much of its communist ideology, it remains a country headed by a single party that brooks no political or religious dissent. As China modernizes its armed forces and attempts to become a world power, it faces increasing social problems as well as economic and border tensions among its provinces.

South Korea and Taiwan are two other examples of Asian societies in transition. Both countries made the transition to market-based (though semi-protectionist) economies first and only much later turned to political reforms. South Korea recently launched a new reform program aimed at ending monopolistic structures and practices that have hampered growth. Taiwan has one of the most dynamic economies in Asia, but until recently it was a one-party dictatorship under the Nationalist party. Political reforms led to the election of an opposition candidate, Chen Shui-bian, in 2000.

The transition process in Latin America is the reverse of what we find in Asia. Argentina, Brazil, Chile, and Mexico are four key countries in the region. The transition to liberal democracy in these countries came before the implementation economic reforms, except in the case of Mexico. Latin America illustrates the blurred line between "transitions" and "development" in the theory and practice of political economy. Until the countries of Latin America can complete the transition from societies divided into the very rich (the few) and very poor (the many), economic development is likely to lag.

Key Terms

Commonwealth of Independent States (CIS)
nomenklatura
perestroika
glasnost
liberalization
demokratizatsiia
Duma
Federal Assembly
Federation Council

mass line
Politburo
Democracy Wall
Tiananmen Square massacre
new industrial countries (NICs)
"Asian flu"
Institutional Revolutionary party (PRI)
National Action party (PAN)
North American Free Trade Association (NAFTA)

Review Questions

1. What problems did the Soviet Union face in 1985?

2. How did President Gorbachev respond to the Soviet Union's problems? How successful was he? Explain.

3. "One of the most important questions facing Russia today is whether it can become a stable democracy." Comment on the problems of transition facing Russia today.

4. What countries have made the most successful transitions so far?

5. Comment on the transition in China since Mao's death.

6. Compare and contrast the transitions in Eastern Europe on the one hand and Latin America on the other.

7. Compare and contrast the transitions in Asia on the one hand and Latin America on the other.

Recommended Reading

BERNSTEIN, R., and R. H. MONROE, *The Coming Conflict with China*. New York: Knopf, 1997. A warning about the dangers posed by China's rapid rise.

COTTEY, ANDREW. *East-Central Europe after the Cold War: Poland, the Czech Republic, Slovakia and Hungary in Search of Security*. New York: St. Martin's Press, 1995. A solid study of the political, economic, and social transition taking place in the core countries of east-central Europe.

GORBACHEV, MIKHAIL. *Perestroika: New Thinking for Our Country and the World*. New York: HarperCollins, 1987. The theoretical underpinnings of the Soviet reform movement in Gorbachev's own words.

HAHN, JEFFREY W., ed. *Democratization in Russia: The Development of Legislative Institutions*. Armonk, N.Y.: M. E. Sharpe, 1996. A careful look at the often chaotic process and nettlesome problem of lawmaking in the new Russia.

HOUGH, JERRY. *Russia and the West: Gorbachev and the Politics of Reform*. New York: Simon & Schuster, 1990. An incisive analysis of the historical and political dimensions of perestroika by a highly respected Sovietologist.

HUSKEY, EUGENE. *Presidential Power in Russia*. Armonk, N.Y.: M. E. Sharpe, 1997. This book focuses on the key role of the president in Russia's still evolving political system.

KULLBERG, JUDITH S. *Legislative Politics in Russia: From Soviets to Parliaments*. Armonk, N.Y.: M. E. Sharpe, 1997. An interesting look at the attempt to establish legislative norms and practices in a society with virtually no parliamentary tradition.

LAQUER, WALTER. *The Dream That Failed: Reflections on the Soviet Union*. New York: Oxford University Press, 1994. Penetrating insights from a thoughtful student of Soviet affairs.

LEONG, LIEW. *The Chinese Economy in Transition: From Plan to Market*. Brookfield, Vt.: Ashgate Publishing, 1997. A good adumbration of how the Chinese converted from a command economy to one based primarily on free-market principles.

MALIA, MARTIN. *The Soviet Tragedy: A History of Socialism in Russia, 1917–1991*. New York: Free Press, 1994. Views the actions of the USSR as directed by utopian ideology, not by an effort to overcome historical backwardness.

MEISNER, MAURICE. *Mao's China & After*. New York: Free Press, 1997. A fresh look at contemporary China from the perspective of recent history.

NOGEE, JOSEPH L. *Russian Politics: The Struggle for a New Order*. Englewood Cliffs, N.J.: Prentice-Hall, 1996. A good introduction to contemporary Russian government and politics.

RA'ANAN, URI, ed. *Russia: A Return to Imperialism?* New York: St. Martin's Press, 1996. A distinguished Russia-watcher assesses the danger of Great Russia nationalism.

ROBERTS, PAUL CRAIG, and KAREN LA FOLLETTE. *Meltdown: Inside the Soviet Economy*. Washington, D.C.: Cato Institute, 1990. The final days of the woebegone Soviet economy and the outmoded communist system.

SLIDER, DARRELL L. *The Politics of Russia's Regions*. Armonk, N.Y.: M. E. Sharpe, 1997. A timely study that focuses on what some close observers consider to be an extremely important new frontier in Russian politics.

SMITH, HEDRICK. *The New Russians*. New York: Random House, 1990. A revealing, updated examination of life in Russia.

———. *The Russians*. New York: Times Books, 1983. A best-seller when it appeared, this book is an entertaining and extremely informative look at the reality behind the Soviet Union's pre-Gorbachev utopian facade.

VOSLENSKY, MICHAEL. *Nomenklatura: The Soviet Ruling Class*. Garden City, N.Y.: Doubleday, 1984. A biting description and analysis of the Soviet elite.

WATERS, HARRY J. *China's Economic Development Strategies for the 21st Century.* Westport, Ct.: Greenwood Publishing, 1997. A forward-looking analysis of China's economic problems and prospects.

YERGIN, DANIEL, and THANE GUSTAFSON. *Russia 2010.* New York: Random House, 1993. An intriguing description of different scenarios outlining Russia's future.

Notes

1. Thomas M. Magstadt, *Nations and Governments: Comparative Politics in Regional Perspective* (New York: Bedford/St. Martin's, 2002), 226–235.
2. Hedrick Smith, *The Russians* (New York: Time Books, 1978), 83.
3. See Susan Dentzer, Jeff Trimble, and Bruce Auster, "The Soviet Economy in Shambles," *US News & World Report,* November 20, 1989, 25–29, 32, 35–37, and 39.
4. Ibid., 25 and 26.
5. Walter Laquer, *The Dream That Failed* (New York: Oxford University Press, 1994), 71–73.
6. See Milovan Djilas, *The New Class* (New York: Praeger, 1957); and Hedrick Smith, *The Russians* (New York: Times Books, 1978), 30–67.
7. "Russia," *World Factbook* (electronic edition), Central Intelligence Agency, 1996, 6.
8. "Emerging Market Indicators," *Economist,* March 15, 1997, 108.
9. See "Emerging Market Indicators," *Economist,* April 13, 2002, 104.
10. Vera Tolz, "Thorny Road toward Federalism in Russia," *Radio Free Europe/Radio Liberty Research Report* 48 (December 1993): 1.
11. "Russia's Regions: Fiefs and Chiefs," *Economist,* January 25, 1997, 47.
12. Claire Sterling, "Redfellas: The Growing Power of Russia's Mob," *New Republic,* April 11, 1994, 19.
13. Xan Smiley, "Russia's Wobbles Ahead," *The World in 1997* (an annual publication of *Economist*), 39.
14. See Matthew Valencia, "Limping Towards Normality: A Survey of Poland," *The Economist,* October 27, 2001, 3–16.]
15. A. Doak Barnett, "Ten Years after Mao," *Foreign Affairs* (Summer 1986): 38.
16. Ibid., 39.
17. See Peter Ferdinand, "Social Change and the Chinese Communist Party," *Journal of International Affairs* 49, no. 2 (Winter 1996): 478–492.
18. "Deng's China," *Economist,* February 22, 1997, 21.
19. Ibid. Also see Johanna McGeary, "The Next China," *Time,* March 3, 1997, 52–53.
20. These are 1996 figures. The difference is explained by the fact that the World Bank uses earnings of $1 per day as a standard of worldwide poverty. The lower Chinese standard classifies how many Chinese are poor according to the Chinese standards of welfare and entitlement. See *World Bank News,* October 25, 1996, 5. Also see World Bank press release no. 96/41 EAP.
21. "China's Feuding Regions," *Economist,* April 20, 1996, 27.
22. "China Learns the World's Rule," *The World in 2001* (London: The Economist Newspaper Limited, 2000), 85–86.
23. Ferdinand, "Social Change and the Chinese Communist party," 483.
24. Ibid., 478.
25. This discussion is heavily dependent on "China's Feuding Regions," 27–28.
26. See "Charting the Deng Revolution," *Newsweek,* March 3, 1997, 26–27.
27. Robert G. Wesson, *Communism and Communist Systems* (Englewood Cliffs, N.J.: Prentice-Hall, 1978), 172–173.

© Earl & Nazima Kowall / CORBIS

Chapter 8

DEVELOPING COUNTRIES

DEMOCRACY OR DICTATORSHIP?

NOT UNTIL THE twentieth century did the United States emerge as both a modern nation-state and a great power. Geographic isolation, an energetic people, abundant natural resources, and a vast frontier allowed for its development; wise founders and good fortune contributed to its eventual ascent to world leadership. Economically, it is relatively wealthy, industrialized, and scientifically advanced. Socially, a meaningful percentage of the American people share in its wealth, are literate and competently educated, and, to an important extent, feel themselves to be a part of the larger society. Politically, its government is well established, effectively provides for transitions in political power, and assures public services and individual safety.

By contrast, *developing nations* (also called *less developed countries, modernizing nations,* or *Third World nation-states*) fail one or more of these criteria, often in dramatic ways. The consequences of such failures are often painful and include endemic poverty; a high level of ethnic, religious, or tribal conflict; widespread illiteracy; political turmoil; and significant class cleavages. Today, many African, Asian, and Latin American nations aspire to the level of prosperity and stability now enjoyed by the developed countries of Europe and the Pacific Rim (Australia, New Zealand, and Japan) as well as the United States and Canada. These so-called developing states face great obstacles on the often perilous path to full political, economic, and social development. In the worst cases, the economy goes into a tailspin, the government fails utterly, societies break apart, and entire populations are plunged into a nightmarish civil war of the kind envisioned by the English political philosopher Thomas Hobbes in the seventeenth century—"a war of everyman against everyman." This chilling possibility has become a reality in places like the former Yugoslavia, Afghanistan, and parts of sub-Saharan Africa (including Somalia, Rwanda, the Congo, and Sierra Leone). To understand better the extreme challenges developing countries face, we need to take a closer look at the context of politics in the so-called *Third World*—a term that is still convenient but no longer appropriate.

CLASSIFYING DEVELOPING COUNTRIES

People often employ shorthand terms or jargon as a kind of semantic convenience in everyday conversation. Although these terms become commonplace, they are not necessarily helpful. Such is the case when developing nations are labeled "Third World." This term grows out of a classification scheme popular during the Cold War when the *First World* comprised the advanced industrial democracies of North America, Western Europe, Japan, Australia, and New Zealand and the *Second World* encompassed communist countries, including the former Soviet Union, the former satellite states of Central and Eastern Europe, various communist states in Asia, Cuba, and (usually) China. What remained was the *Third World*—countries that were neither economically well off nor communist. However, with the collapse of communism, and the transformations occurring in the former communist states (see Chapter 7), the three-world distinction no longer makes any sense—if the Second World has vanished how can there be a third (or has the Third World suddenly moved into second place even though the Second World has still not merged with the First World)? Nonetheless, the term continues to be used, although it is becoming a rarity.

Developing nations have also been called "the South," which highlights the great disparities between the industrially developed states north of the equator and less developed states to the south. Some observers believe that the rich nations of the North have economically exploited the poor nations of the South, going so far as to talk about a "North-South Conflict." But lumping developing nations into one category obscures more than it explains. A literal application of the North–South distinction consigns not only economically poor states to the South, but also includes Australia and New Zealand—two countries that clearly belong in the same category as the affluent liberal democracies of Western Europe. In terms of national wealth, political institutions, and international status, countries as different as Saudi Arabia, South Africa, and Brazil—to mention but a few—do not fit into the North–South paradigm. Neither do South Korea, Taiwan, Hong Kong, and Singapore.

We look next at the developing world and ask the "who" question: Who are the nations of the world going through the throes of development? In truth, all nations are either developing or decaying. What is commonly meant by the term *developing countries* is simply this: Most of the world's peoples (nations) do not enjoy the opportunities for education, employment, recreation, travel, or conspicuous consumption that are the hallmarks of "modern" living in the Westernized world (not only the "West" but also Japan, Australia, New Zealand, and a few others). Moreover, most nations are not blessed with good government—that is, governments that are accountable, stable, and clean (as opposed to corrupt). In sum, when we say a country is developing what we mean is that it is not *yet* truly modern (resembling the Westernized world) and we assume that as (if) these countries develop they will look increasingly like we do (that is, urbanized, secularized, materialistic, and technology-dependent).

UNDERSTANDING DEVELOPING COUNTRIES

Developing nations defy simple generalizations. There is no easy way to categorize countries that account for over half the world's surface and comprise well over 60 percent of the world's population (see Figure 8-1).[1] By most counts, over 115 of the roughly 190 nations on the globe can be classified as developing; almost 40 percent are in sub-Saharan Africa, slightly under 25 percent in Latin America, and the rest divided almost equally between the Asian Pacific and the Arab worlds (the Middle East and North Africa). Indeed, diversity is one of the most striking characteristics of developing countries. Some of them are huge—Brazil has a territory of 3 million square miles (larger than the continental United States) and a population of 160 million; India's territory of 1 million square miles supports a population of more than 1 billion.

Contrast these giants with such tiny island states as Barbados (territory, 166 square miles; population, 252,000) in the Caribbean, and Kiribati (territory, 266 square miles; population, 61,000) in the Pacific. The Pacific island of Nauru may win the "pygmy" prize: It has 8,000 people living on eight square miles of land. Nauru may be small, but it is not poor: Phosphate exports push annual per capita income above $20,000.

Nauru is an exception in the developing world—poverty is the rule. Most developing economies depend primarily on agriculture, yet a few, such as the oil-rich states of the Persian Gulf (Bahrain, Kuwait, Oman, Qatar, Saudi Arabia and the United Arab Emirates), rely largely on mineral resources.

With few exceptions, developing nations have the world's highest population growth rates. (The world's population is increasing at an annual rate of about 1.48 percent; at that rate, it will double within forty-eight years.) Rapid population growth can place an enormous burden on economic, social, and political structures and impede their development.

But comparisons often yield surprises. The population of Mexico, for instance, is growing approximately as fast as that of India. Asia, the most densely populated region of the world, has roughly 60 percent of the world's population but only about 18 percent of its landmass. Apart from Asia (and a few exceptions such as Egypt, whose population is clustered around the Nile River), population density in the developing countries is relatively low. Africa's average population density is only 24 per square kilometer, as opposed to India's 296 and Singapore's 5,571. (Israel has almost exactly the same population density as India, yet Israel welcomes immigrants.) Although such figures do not take into account what part of the land area is habitable or the distribution of population (for example, the extent of urbanization), it is noteworthy that Africa also has more arable land per capita than any other developing region. At the same time, however, population growth rates in parts of sub-Saharan Africa (including Somalia, Uganda, Congo, Niger, Angola, and Burkina Faso) are among the highest in the world. Surprisingly, the fastest growing population in the world is in the Israeli-occupied territories of the West Bank and Gaza; Yemen and Afghanistan are in second and third place respectively. In general, Islamic and Arab populations are experiencing something of a population explosion. The number of Muslims in North Africa, the Middle East, and the southern sub-regions of Asia, according to some estimates, is close to 1.5 billion.

Developing nations are not the only places where social, economic, and political development is occurring. Indeed, development and decay are constants everywhere in the world—societies are always rising or falling, none is static. But development takes place unequally; some nations, such as Afghanistan, Bangladesh, Burundi, Chad, Congo, Eritrea, Ethiopia, Guinea-Bissau, Mali, Malawi, Myanmar, Rwanda, Sierra Leone, Somalia, and Sudan, are all extremely poor and mired in misery. (Note how many of the countries on this "poorest of the poor" list are located in sub-Saharan Africa). This global inequality is a potential source of conflict and violence, as well as a moral issue of major dimensions.

Why are poor countries poor? Do they lack resources? Is it Nature's cruel joke? Or is the West (colonialism and neocolonialism) to blame? These questions are examined in the following section.

THE LEGACY OF COLONIALISM

Only 23 countries among the current United Nations membership were independent in 1800. More than half of these states were in Europe; Afghanistan, China, Ethiopia, Japan, Iran, Nepal, Oman, Russia, Thailand, Turkey, and the United States rounded out the list.[2] Since then the number of independent states has increased more than eightfold. The Second World War (1945–49) was a watershed because it led to the rapid deconstruction of the European colonial empires. More than half of the countries existing today thus came into being during the last three decades, and most of them can be classified as developing countries.

The breakup of the Soviet Union led directly to the creation of many new independent states in Eastern Europe, the trans-Caucasus and Central Asia. A second wave occurred with the disintegration or division of some of these independent nation-states (for example, Czechoslovakia and Yugoslavia). By 1994, this process of disintegration had led to the creation of nearly twenty-five new independent states.[3] For centuries, the Great Powers of Europe had competed for colonial holdings, ruling and administering over weaker and technologically less-advanced peoples and territories located in faraway places around the globe. These colonial empires were not only a source of prestige but also (and more importantly) were economically advantageous. For various reasons, Africa was especially ripe for colonization and the European powers carved up and claimed

Reuters NewMedia Inc. / CORBIS

Ethnic warfare between the Hindu Tamils and Buddhist Sinhalese in Sri Lanka, which began in 1983 when Tamil rebels demanded independence for the Sri Lanka northeast, to some extent reflects the imposition and policies of Britain's colonial rule. Ethnic strife is an all-too-common legacy of colonialism and remains a problem for many developing nations throughout the developing world.

virtually all of Africa by the end of the nineteenth century. At the beginning of the twentieth century, Britain, France, Belgium, Germany, Portugal, Holland, Italy, and Spain (as well as Turkey) were all wedded to *colonialism* or imperialism. Regardless of its name, this Eurocentric system became synonymous with subjugation and exploitation at the hands of pale-faced foreigners in the minds of the native peoples of Africa, Asia, and Latin America.

There is little dispute that colonialism was all about Europeans dominating native peoples and that it was based on implicit or explicit notions of racial superiority and religious zeal. However, there were great differences in the methods and means employed by the colonial powers. For instance, the British approach stressed the rule of law and was far milder than Spanish colonial governance, which was known for its cruelty. The Portuguese and French tried to assimilate colonized peoples (the French, for example, granted Algerians seats in the national legislature and positions in the national cabinets), while the Dutch in Indonesia allowed native rulers to remain in power. Britain pursued both strategies, depending on local authorities to maintain law and order while allowing talented members of the indigenous populations to pursue careers in public administration, attend British schools and universities, and the like.[4]

Nonetheless, the idea of being governed by a distant country was repugnant to most colonial peoples. In many instances, they finally gained independence by resorting to various forms of violence. In India, Mahatma Gandhi led a nationwide mass campaign of *nonviolent resistance* (*Satyagraha*)—this approach, also called *civil disobedience,* was later adopted in the 1960s by Martin Luther King, Jr., the great leader of the Civil Rights movement in the United States. (Ironically, both Gandhi and King were assassinated.)

Colonialism's ultimate legacy remains controversial. From a positive perspective, Europeans did introduce some elements of modernization, including modest advances in health (hospitals), education (schools), and transportation (roads). However, these changes were often quite limited in impact and came at the expense of economic and political self-sufficiency, as well as traditional ways of life. In addition, any gains have to be measured against the losses, namely the humiliation, oppression, and diseases (epidemics introduced by Europeans into populations with no resistance to new germs) associated with colonial rule.[5]

The extent to which developing nations *after* independence were still exploited by rich Western countries also remains controversial. For instance, so-called *dependency theorists* have maintained that the underdevelopment was not a natural occurrence but one caused by Western exploitation. They contend that by obtaining natural resources cheaply, and using scientific and technological advances to turn these resources into high-priced manufactures, industrialized nations not only exploited developing countries but also deliberately kept them weak and impoverished. Other scholars reject this explanation, blaming the plight of developing countries on endemic factors such as climate and natural resources, arable land, population size and growth, epidemics, ethnic rivalries, and cultural values.

The effects of colonialism continue to haunt the contemporary world. Colonial empires were created without regard to the preexisting ethnic identities, territorial boundaries, and loyalties of native populations. When the European powers withdrew, they typically created a crazy quilt of new states with borders that made no sense because they cut across traditional religious, ethnic, and tribal territorial lines. The result was predictable: chronic political instability, coups, revolutions, civil wars, and even genocide. This bitter legacy of colonialism has afflicted many developing countries in recent years, including Angola, Burundi, Cambodia (formerly Kampuchea), Congo (formerly Zaire), Ethiopia, Liberia, Nigeria, Rwanda, Sierra Leone, and Sri Lanka.

POLITICAL DEVELOPMENT: FOUR CHALLENGES

Countries that pursue modernizing strategies seek to establish a stable government, provide basic public services (police and fire protection, education, health, and sanitation), and put a legal system (laws and courts) in place. These elements of *political development* are prerequisites to social and economic progress and appear to be modest goals. However, achieving these goals in the context of pervasive corruption, poverty, illiteracy, and disharmony is a challenge that very few developing countries have met.

Because the development process is intrinsically unsettling, the governments of many developing nations are often chronically unstable. These governments, almost always authoritarian, are prone to coups and beset by crises. Developing countries typically face four fundamental challenges: nation building, state building, participation, and distribution.[6]

The most basic of these challenges is *nation building,* the process by which all the inhabitants of a given territory—irrespective of individual ethnic, tribal, religious, or linguistic differences—come to identify with the symbols and institutions of the state and to share a common sense of destiny. In theory, a new sense of nationhood—that is, a new nation—eventually emerges but in practice this goal is extremely elusive because of the great diversity that is so often found in developing countries.

Some developing countries have not been able to meet this challenge and as a result have experienced wrenching civil wars and even dismemberment. Examples of the latter include Pakistan (what is now Bangladesh was East Pakistan prior to 1971) and the Congo (formerly Zaire). Civil wars have also torn asunder the societies of Nigeria, Chad, Angola, Rwanda, and Somalia, to name but a few.

Political leaders have frequently blamed colonialism and imperialism for this striking propensity toward internal strife; often the struggle for independence is itself exploited as a way to unite the new nation in a common cause. Flags, celebrations, and even a national airline (which may consist of only one or two passenger jets with the country's name and colors emblazoned on the sides) can help instill a sense of national identity. Threats from a neighboring state—real, imagined, or manufactured—can also be useful. Finally, the presence of a charismatic national leader appears to be one of the most important variables of all. Notable examples include Egypt's Gamal Abdel Nasser (who ruled from 1954 to 1970), Kenya's Jomo Kenyatta (1963–78), India's Jawaharlal Nehru (1947–64), Indonesia's Achmed Sukarno (1949–65), and Libya's Muammar Qaddafi who is still in power.

Another important facet of political development process is *state building,* the creation of political institutions—in particular, a central government—capable of exercising authority throughout the length and breadth of society. This type of *political penetration* promotes economic development and social unity by such mundane means as creating the infrastructure (roads, bridges, telephone lines) necessary for an integrated national economy. Similarly, to finance the creation of this type of infrastructure, the government must at a minimum be capable of levying and collecting taxes (a hallmark of effective government). But governments in developing countries often cannot raise adequate revenues through taxation for the simple reason that there is nothing (or not enough) to tax. It is a vicious circle that can only be broken with infusions of foreign capital (trade, aid, and, above all, investment). But foreign investment (an external variable) depends on political stability (an internal variable). In developing countries, there are all sorts of vicious circles.

Yet another challenge facing developing countries is *participation.* For new societies to prosper and grow economically, the people must be actively engaged in the development process. As part of any well-conceived development strategy developing countries need to mobilize people—literally to move the society in a single direction. But mobilization gives rise to a political dilemma: As people become more actively involved and feel the effects of government (good or bad), they begin to demand a greater voice in determining who governs and how. Yet if popular demands for participation outstrip the development of institutions and the capacity of government to respond positively, the state will be faced with a serious threat of episodic or even chronic instability. Hence the challenge of participation: how to harness popular energies without setting in motion the forces of political disintegration or revolution.

Meaningful participation requires political organization. Preexisting patterns of popular participation in agrarian societies are often based on kinship ties or, especially in Asia, *patron–client relations.* In the latter, patrons are influential figures who use their status, wealth, and political connections at the national and provincial levels to secure material benefits (jobs, schools, roads, and the like) for clients at the local (village) level. In return, clients give patrons the support they need to operate politically, including loyal support, physical protection, in-kind payments (for example, volunteer labor), and votes. Since the social system is hierarchical, patrons at one level become clients at another. What develops is an intricate network of interrelated personal loyalties based on kinship and cultural or geographic ties. In this way, exclusive in-groups are created through which political demands, instructions, and decisions can be transmitted both vertically and horizontally. Actually, because of the exclusive and particularistic character of patron–client relationships, a system of networks develops in which each network forms a political "machine" of sorts. Out of these structures the prototype of a modern political system can emerge (albeit one based on principles quite opposite to the legalistic political cultures of the West).

A fourth major development challenge for governments of developing countries involves distribution—how to ensure against the overconcentration of wealth, property, and power that often characterizes traditional and transitional societies. This overconcentration of resources can lead to a pervasive sense of injustice and, in turn, to mass revolt (see Chapter 14). This sense of injustice is often rooted in a feeling that the fruits of society are not being apportioned fairly—that the rich exploit the poor—and that revolution is the only way to bring about real change. The influence of Marxist theory and ideology has frequently been felt not only in Communist China or Vietnam but also in places as far apart and unexpected as Yemen, Angola, Ethiopia, Cambodia, Laos, Indonesia, the Philippines, Chile, Cuba, Nicaragua, El Salvador, and Colombia (even this long list is incomplete). Governments sometimes address the challenge of distribution through land reform initially. Later they readjust tax burdens and may even enact social welfare legislation, but steps of this sort depend on a measure of economic success that often eludes the former colonies.

DEMOCRACY AND DEVELOPING COUNTRIES

As we have seen, political development often leads to wider political participation. But does it also necessitate a democratic form of government? In other words, do development and constitutional democracy necessarily occur together? Is democratic government itself a sign of political development? As we suggested in Chapter 3, accountability is hallmark of constitutional democracy. But democratic states are limited in what they can do by some idea of rights, rules, laws, and, of course, public opinion. Thus, democracy and development often do not easily coexist.

The governments of most developing countries are neither democratically elected nor avid protectors of civil liberties. Most emerging nations are governed or controlled by the military. Civilian governments are typically authoritarian and often revolve around a (founding) father figure such as Jomo Kenyatta (Kenya), Joshua Nkruma (Ghana), Gamal Abdel Nasser (Egypt), Jawaharlal Nehru (India), and Achmed Sukarno (Indonesia).

Western observers tend to assume that democracy is a sign of political development. Not all democracies are developed nations, although almost all are; nor are developed nations necessarily democratic, although most are. But the fact remains that representative democracy is one characteristic among several often present in politically developed countries.

The Correlates of Democracy

Creating a stable government capable of ruling effectively is no easy task; establishing a democratic government is particularly daunting in societies facing the challenges of modernization. To be viable, democracy requires the existence of certain important characteristics. One way to gauge a developing nation's potential to achieve democracy is to focus on *democratic correlates*. Where these correlates exist in the greatest number and measure, the probability of democracy is greatest; conversely where they are largely absent democracy has the smallest chance of succeeding.[7]

Economic correlates are perhaps the most important:

- *National Wealth*. Prosperity generally correlates with democracy. Conversely, poverty is not conducive to democracy. But if democracy is a luxury that poor nations cannot afford, how does one explain India, which has been democratic, extremely diverse, and very poor since independence?

- *A Market or Mixed Economy.* Market economies allow both public and private ownership of the means of production and distribution, and have the flexibility to combine elements of a market economy with varying types and degrees of governmental intervention. Most important is what such economies do not allow: Economic decisions, especially those involving the production and distribution of products and services, are left primarily to private enterprises and consumers. Large-scale centralized state planning of the economy is excluded.

- *A Middle Class.* This correlate stresses the distribution of wealth in society rather than its distribution. Sharp class differences are not conducive to a stable democracy.

   Political correlates include the following:

- *Freedom of Communication.* Because democracy requires transparency (no more secrecy than is absolutely necessary) in government, the open airing of views, freedom of the press, and the free flow of information are important correlates of democracy. Conversely where press censorship occurs and journalists are imprisoned or threatened democracy cannot thrive.

- *A Stable Party System.* This political correlate stresses the need for a political party system to represent the political opinions of individuals and groups. To be effective, such a system must involve more than one political party and each party must be free to operate without intimidation or state interference.

- *Civilian Control Over the Military.* Because the military frequently seeks (and seizes) political power in developing countries, it poses a real and present danger to civilian rule.

- *A Strong, Independent Judiciary.* Essential to the effective functioning of any democracy is the protection of civil liberties and minority rights which in turn depends on the existence of an independent judiciary.

- *Political and Social Pluralism.* Although sharp social or political divisions within a country may actually inhibit or endanger democracy, it is often thought that the existence of a variety of such groups and voluntary associations (unions; business and trade associations; intellectual, educational, and religious institutions; cooperatives; citizen groups committed to popular civic education and government accountability) must be regarded as legitimate, thus requiring their representation for the necessary give-and-take of representative democratic politics to take place.[8]

   Two important psychocultural correlates are:

- *Tolerance of Individual and Group Differences.* If democracy requires acceptance of the rights of others, then respect for social and cultural diversity becomes an important correlate of democratic government. Conversely, it is difficult for a democracy to develop and survive amidst widespread societal distrust stemming from pronounced ethnic, religious, or tribal differences.

- *Pervasive Belief in Democracy.* This one requires no explanation: People cannot be forced to be free.

  A final pair of correlates is historical, or circumstantial:

- *Previous Democratic Experience.* Some countries such as Chile, Ecuador, and Uruguay had democratic governments interrupted by periods of authoritarian rules. Where democracy is part of the collective memory of society, the likelihood that democracy will succeed goes up.
- *Existence of Democratic Neighbors.* The form of government in successful neighboring states can exert a positive influence. The former authoritarian governments in Spain and Portugal are frequently cited as examples of nations whose political future was influenced by the presence of flourishing democracies on the Continent.

One political scientist has advocated a comprehensive theory of democratic correlates called the *distribution of power resources.*[9] This index encompasses six specific correlates intended to measure the distribution of economic and intellectual (educational) resources within any nation (the assumption being that the greater this distribution, the more likely that democracy will succeed). One such measurement is tied to percentage of urban to rural population; in theory, the higher the rate of urbanization, the more diversified the economy, job opportunities, and skills, and the more widely distributed income will be. Another measure positively associated with the desired distribution of economic resources is the percentage of family farms. A more complicated measure gauges the decentralization of the nonagricultural economy. Finally, per capita school enrollment and the literacy rate are used to measure the distribution of intellectual resources.

Democratic Strategies

Establishing democratic rule in developing nations is no clearly easy task. What strategy should a nation lacking democratic traditions pursue? The former communist states faced the same question in the early 1990s. Specifically, should emphasis be placed on liberalizing political reforms to be followed by economic restructuring to a greater market economy, the so-called *glasnost-first model,* or should the economic reforms come first, as the *perestroika-first model* suggests?[10] The extreme economic and social difficulties encountered by the former Soviet Union, having pursued the strategy of political change first, and the relative success of countries such as Mexico, Chile, South Korea, China, Taiwan, Singapore, Thailand, and Malaysia argues for a strategy of economic change first. Why? Two reasons spring to mind: First, meeting basic economic needs is a more fundamental obligation of government than guaranteeing political liberties—civil rights are irrelevant to people who are starving, sick, or homeless. Second, a vibrant economy is more likely to have an immediate impact on the quality of life, social services, infrastructure, and educational opportunity than changes in political structures.

Democracy in Developing Countries: Trend or Illusion?

Between 1974 and 1990, more than thirty countries in southern Europe, Latin America, East Asia, and Eastern Europe replaced authoritarian with democratic governments. One noted political scientist has proclaimed this a global revolution and "probably the most important political trend in the late twentieth century."[11] The most dramatic changes occurred in Latin America, where one military dictatorship after another gave way to popularly elected governments and multiparty democracy in the 1980s, when Brazil, Argentina, and Chile, among others, made the switch. In Nicaragua and Panama elected governments have replaced dictatorships. In Mexico, where the Institutional Revolutionary Party (PRI) totally dominated the political scene for many decades, the voters elected Vicente Fox to the presidency in 2000; President Fox is the first opposition candidate to lead the country in seven decades.

Will development and democracy be able to coexist more easily in the future? It is too early to proclaim the final triumph of democracy in Latin America, where civilian governments in some cases still face an uphill battle. Instability of one kind or another still plagues most governments in this region. In addition to a heavy foreign-debt burden, they continue to be hit by high unemployment, inflation, currency crises, and other woes. In the 1990s, terrorism continued to plague Peru and also caused political tremors in Mexico. Colombia, with a longer democratic tradition than most other Latin American states, faces major uncertainties due to the power of its drug kingpins and continued attacks by left-wing guerrilla groups.

History is also cause for some caution about the future of Latin American democracies. The military has played a dominant role throughout the region until recently; prior to the early 1980s, few Latin American countries had ever experienced genuine democracy. More often, popular elections have taken the form of plebiscites in which a *caudillo* (strongman) seeks a mandate to rule autocratically. Another familiar pattern involves a military coup d'état in which a clique of senior officers simply cancels the results of an election or seizes control of the government.

In the early 1990s, the democracy "bug" spread to sub-Saharan Africa.[12] In 1990 and 1991, at least nine sub-Saharan African countries, including Benin, Cape Verde, and Gabon in west Africa, held free elections—in most cases, for the first time ever. In March 1991, Benin's president, Brigadier General Mathieu Kerekou, became one of the first African leaders ever to be voted out of office. Other countries in the region—including Mozambique and Congo—adopted reforms designed to usher in democratic governments. In the 1990s, South Africa witnessed stunning changes, as black majority rule supplanted the white-supremacist rule of the Boers (Dutch). By 1997, Benin, Botswana, Guinea-Bissau, Madagascar, Mali, Namibia, and Sao Tome, as well as South Africa, were true multiparty states where respect for human rights and the rule of law were taking hold.[13]

Sub-Saharan Africa's romance with democracy has been tempestuous and extremely untidy. Nigeria's military rulers rescinded election results in 1993 when they disapproved of the outcome and Cote d'Ivoire's government did the same thing. (Nigeria finally took a step in the right direction in 1999 when Olusegun

Wars, civil wars, and ethnic rivalries cause widespread human misery while threatening the democratic future of numerous countries. Pictured here are refugees escaping from a bloody civil war that consumed Rwanda in 1994.

Obesanjo became the country's first democratically elected president since 1983.) The 1992 and 1993 elections in Kenya, the Cameroon, and Gabon were marred by irregularities and corruption. Rwanda was the scene of genocidal violence in 1994. In 1996, military governments in Chad, the Gambia, and Niger rigged the national elections to achieve the outcomes they desired. Nor are the underlying societies of many African states particularly stable (and, therefore, conducive to democracy). Liberia and Sierra Leone have had particularly bloody civil wars and the Democratic Republic of the Congo (formerly Zaire) descended into a state of anarchy in the late 1990s. Indeed, clan or tribal tensions threaten domestic tranquility in much of sub-Saharan Africa, where any trend toward democracy has been met by powerful countertrends.[14]

THE DEVELOPMENT PUZZLE

Political development, including efforts to secure a democratic government, is part of a modernizing, yet painful and turbulent, process. Traditional bonds among people are undermined, people are uprooted, and culture is altered, often irreversibly. Food shortages and social discontent frequently accompany industrialization. Why then are leaders of developing countries willing to accept the political risks associated with modernization?

Motives for Development

Developing countries often have little choice but to modernize. Very few are as fortunate as, say, Qatar (on the Arabian peninsula), which has an abundance of oil and a small population. Venezuela, too, has been blessed with large oil deposits. But to capitalize on these natural resources, even Venezuela and Qatar have had to drill wells, build roads, train petroleum engineers, construct refineries and storage facilities, lay pipelines, establish a banking system, and develop export markets—in other words, to modernize.

For less fortunate developing countries, economic development offers the only hope of escaping pervasive poverty. Most of these nations are poor; the poorest of the poor—sometimes called the least developed countries—have an average yearly per capita income of less than $250. Even nations that are comparatively prosperous suffer from widespread poverty. Thus, in the mid-1990s, few countries in Africa or Asia had surpassed $1,000 in annual per capita income.

Another incentive for development is the desire to fulfill the nation's destiny by obtaining modern armaments at any cost. Nearly every war since World War II has been fought in the Third World.[15] Examples of major Third World rivalries include those between Iran and Iraq, Pakistan and India, Vietnam and China, Libya and Chad, and Ethiopia and Somalia. Many Latin American countries, too, have long-standing disputes and rivalries involving neighbors. Chile, for example, has engaged in military clashes with all three adjacent states: Argentina, Bolivia, and Peru. In addition, Peru has had a smoldering border dispute with Ecuador. Relations between Colombia and Venezuela have been tense at times because of questions over an unresolved border. Of course, warfare can interrupt—and even defeat—a nation's development efforts by diverting the government's attention and sapping its limited resources.

The very existence of developed countries provides a final incentive for development. Modern global communications, transportation systems, and an increasingly interdependent world make the power and wealth of these nations more conspicuous. Thus, the success of many industrialized nations has given rise to what is commonly called the *revolution of rising expectations,* a revolution whose goals can only be achieved through development.

Precisely what problems must developing nations address to undertake development successfully on a large scale? In addition to the political challenges examined earlier, there are also social, psychological, and economic impediments to development.

Social Barriers to Development

Many developing countries were carved out of former colonial holdings with little concern for the geography or history of the area or indigenous ethnic, religious, tribal, or linguistic patterns. As a result, cultural diversity is a salient feature of many Third World countries. Sometimes this diversity has been subsumed into a new "national" political culture; more often, it has led to interethnic strife and even civil war.

In every case, development poses daunting problems. With fragmented populations, what drops out of the concept of the nation-state is the idea of a nation; one key element in successful development lies in forging a single national identity and the sense of a shared political destiny. Furthermore, some militant groups or movements may be hostile to social integration and peaceful modernization. For example, Islam is generally thought to be an impediment to modernization, because its emphasis on piety, devotion to Allah, and daily prayer (five times each day), as well as its strict rules of moral conduct place the religion at odds with secularization, the sexual revolution, materialism, and self-gratification that have accompanied social change in Europe, North America, and elsewhere. Finally, in the face of pronounced ethnic, religious, tribal, or linguistic differences, it is unlikely that a significant majority of the people in a given developing country will view the existing government as legitimate.

Specific examples best illustrate the practical problems associated with diverse populations. Nigeria and India are both developing countries with very diverse populations.

Nigeria   This large country in West Africa comprises several distinct ethnic groups that predominate in different parts of the country. In addition, there are many smaller tribes and a multitude of tongues are spoken (nearly 400 mutually unintelligible languages).[16] Also, there are simmering tensions between Christians and Muslims. Regional animosities exacerbated by religious, ethnic, and linguistic differences erupted in a bloody civil war in 1967 when eastern Nigeria seceded as the independent state of Biafra. The war, which lasted about three years and ended in defeat for the Biafrans, claimed at least 600,000 lives.

For most of the period after 1967, corrupt military regimes ruled Nigeria. Despite large state-owned oil reserves that produced a steady flow of export revenues, Nigeria's economy sank deeper and deeper into a morass and the vast majority of Nigeria's population (106 million in 2000) was forced to live from hand to mouth. The average per capita income in Nigeria (a paltry $300) is only half that of Indonesia, where the national income is measured against a total population twice the size of Nigeria's. By any standards, Nigeria has been an economic basket case.

Why? Quite simply, bad government was the number one cause. Corrupt military regimes ran the country almost continuously after 1967. The military dictator du jour would promise (and sometimes stage) national elections, but either the outcome was rigged ahead of time or the results (if they did not please the generals) were cancelled, which happened as recently as 1993. Nigeria's generals were so corrupt, brutal, and negligent that the country became an international pariah only a notch or two above such widely blacklisted states as Iran, Iraq, and North Korea in the 1990s. International pressure no doubt played a large role in compelling Nigeria's military rulers to allow free elections in 1999 and to permit the results—election of the first popular presidential candidate in nearly 20 years—to stand.

India This country, too, encompasses a plethora of distinct ethnic groups that speak many different languages. India is the second largest country in the world (population: 1 billion). It is also one of the most diverse. The Indian constitution recognizes sixteen languages, but census data indicate that there are over 1,500 languages spoken in India, including dialects. The "big three" official languages are English, Hindi, and Urdu. Hindi is spoken by about one-third of all Indians. English is the elite language, spoken by all university-educated Indians. Urdu is the language of Indian Muslims, the nation's largest minority group.

Besides distinct ethnic and linguistic groups, Indian society is deeply divided by religion. Hinduism is the religion of India's majority, but there is also a large Muslim population (about 11 percent of the total) as well as other significant religious minorities (Sikhs, Jains, Parsees, Buddhists, and Christians). Since Indian independence in 1947, communal clashes involving rival religious communities have erupted from time to time. In some instances, members of one religious group have massacred members of another. Sometimes these encounters have pitted Hindus and Muslims against each other, sometimes Hindus and Sikhs. In 1984, Sikh bodyguards assassinated Prime Minister Indira Gandhi (a Hindu). In 1991, Indira Gandhi' s son, former Prime Minister Rajiv Gandhi, was assassinated while campaigning to regain office. This violent past leaves a legacy of bitter feelings that complicates future efforts at reconciliation and compromise.

In India's case, the traditional caste system created another barrier to development. Under this system, everyone is born into a particular socioreligious caste and remains there for life. Obviously, this rigid framework greatly impeded social mobility—the very mobility needed to transform a traditional society into a modern one. A vast underclass—the untouchables—had no rights or opportunities in traditional India. The Indian government has outlawed untouchability now but old attitudes die slowly, especially in tradition-bound rural societies like India (75 to 80 percent of the population live in small villages).

At least one more feature of India's diverse society is noteworthy: Societal divisions tend to be reinforcing rather than crosscutting. Thus, not only do Indian Muslims practice their own distinct religion, but they also live in their own insular areas, have a distinct ethnic heritage, and speak their own language. Much the same can be said of Sikhs, Jains, and other groups. As a result, a multitude of factors conspire to make India's social groups acutely aware of their communal separateness while undermining the central government's efforts to create a sense of national unity. Sometimes these divisions can lead to calls for separatism, much in the way the Sikhs have called for an independent state in northwestern India (where they are concentrated).

Although we have focused on India and Nigeria, many other developing countries face similar problems. Sri Lanka, for example, is split between the majority Sinhalese (74 percent), who are mostly Buddhist, and the Tamils (18 percent), who are mostly Hindu and predominate in the northern and eastern parts of the country. (Moors, Europeans, and Veddah aborigines constitute the remaining 8 percent of the population.) Militant Tamil groups seeking to secede have carried out terrorist acts and conducted guerrilla warfare against the central government since 1983, when an outbreak of communal riots left at least 2,000 Tamils dead.[17]

Thus, Sri Lanka, like India, displays a pattern of cultural diversity characterized by reinforcing societal divisions.

Most countries in Africa and many countries in Asia and Latin America reveal a startling degree of sociocultural diversity. One survey of 132 nations found that 53 of them (or 40 percent) had populations divided into more than five major groups.[18] Thus, *mosaic societies* are quite common in the Third World. This diversity frequently poses significant social barriers to development.

Psychological Barriers to Development

An individual's relationship with a social group and that group's status in society both play important roles in determining personal identity. These relationships also help to determine whether people will identify with the national government and acknowledge its right to rule (its legitimacy). Attitudes and beliefs grounded in specific cultures also play a key part in this process. For development to succeed, the psychological state and moral values of individuals in developing countries have to change. Let us see why.

Most Americans think in modern terms. As a result, it is often difficult for Americans to understand people from other cultures, especially those living in developing nations. For example, people in such *traditional societies*, by defi-

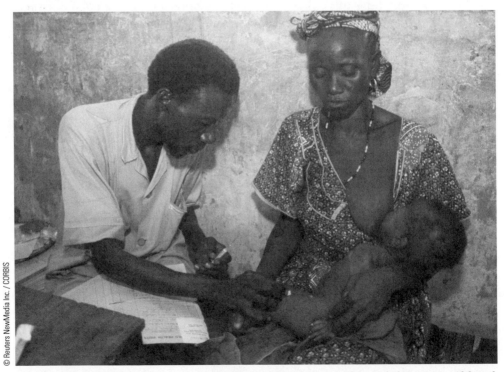

© Reuters NewMedia Inc. / CORBIS

Traditional people tend not to trust strangers and often do not understand their ways. Although such reactions are natural, they can impede modernization.

nition, depend heavily on old ways for guidance in everyday living. Americans (even more than most Westerners) tend to scoff at tradition.

Villagers living in traditional ways are typically ill disposed to change because familiar ways are considered safe and reliable, whereas new and untested ways are often feared. This tendency to avoid uncertainty and to fear the unknown is understandable when so much about the environment is uncertain, uncontrollable, or fraught with danger. Traditional people view nature with awe and reverence; they tend to approach nature's whims with resignation.

Traditional people tend not to trust strangers (that is, anybody they do not know well). Of course, they seldom have to deal with strangers; generally, social interaction is confined to family, clan, or village members. Fear of the unfamiliar, fatalism in the face of nature's accidents, and a low sense of personal efficacy combine to make traditional peasants and villagers loath to take risks. It takes little imagination to see how such attitudes would stand in the way of modernization. Individuals who are cautious and conservative are unlikely to try new things, whether it means planting a new crop or learning about a new agricultural technology. Frequently, they experience great adjustment and identity problems, such as when the development process requires them to move to cities and to leave the villages where they and their ancestors have spent their whole lives.

Other traditional attitudes can impede development as well. Traditional people are less conscious of time, less likely to plan ahead, and less inclined to believe that they can shape their own destinies than people accustomed to modern ways of life. The concepts of individual achievement, personal rewards and satisfactions, and "moving up the ladder" are alien to those bound by traditional values and folkways. All of this is a reflection of traditional societies' tendency to be *ascriptive societies* (the Indian caste system having been an extreme example)—that is, status and position are ascribed by society on the basis of religion, age, and the like. Status and position are also largely determined by gender; male social and political dominance is much more evident in developing nations, where a low level of applied technology, ranging from a lack of heavy machinery to an absence of birth control devices, combines with high infant mortality rates to reinforce traditional gender roles and attitudes. Thus, in developing nations, notions of personal freedom and individual aspiration are often precluded by the customary and communal nature of most traditional societies.

Obstacles to Economic Development

Despite significant differences in economic development and national wealth, most developing nations remain poor. As noted earlier, poverty, more than anything else, motivates these countries to undertake development. Contributing to the poverty in most developing nations are unfavorable terms of trade, rising foreign debt, a rapidly increasing population, a low level of technology, an entrenched land tenure problem, illness and malnourishment, a low level of education, and an unforgiving environment. Although exceptions exist, these problems are endemic. As such, they both cause national poverty and impede the economic development that could ameliorate that poverty.

Developing economies are still based on agriculture and mining, despite rapid (and accelerating) migrations of the rural poor to the cities. As a result, improvements in living standards have been, at best, painstakingly slow, and widespread economic disparities still exist (see Table 8-1).

Severe problems accompany excessive dependence on agricultural commodities and raw materials. Some developing countries raise only one major crop (a practice called *monoculture*). Bangladesh, for example, produces nothing but jute for export. When the price of jute declines, Bangladesh—one of the poorest developing nations—has nothing to fall back on. Ethiopia's economy is heavily dependent on coffee, Cuba mainly produces sugar for export, Honduras exports bananas, and so on. Some developing countries are economically addicted to illegal cash crops: peasants in Colombia, Ecuador, and Peru, for example, produce coca (cocaine) for export; Afghanistan is the world's primary source of heroine (a derivative of the opium poppy plant). Though most developing countries have more than one crop or mineral resource, few are diversified enough to have a healthy mix of agriculture and industry.

To modernize, developing countries need to import industrial goods; to pay for manufactures, they need to export food, fiber, and minerals. But the terms of trade work against them: The price of industrial goods is high, while the price of agricultural products and raw materials is often low. Furthermore, the prices of commodities on the world market fluctuate wildly, creating terrible uncertainties and mounting foreign debt.

Some developing countries also face a serious population problem. The industrial democracies have population growth of less than 1 percent, and several western European countries reached zero or negative population growth by 1990. By contrast, most developing countries have growth rates of 2 to 3 percent annually (see Figures 8-1 and 8-2 on pages 238 and 239). In some countries, such as Niger, Ethiopia, and Angola, populations are increasing at a much faster rate.

Typically, population pressures have the greatest impact in urban areas. Rural poverty and governmental policy encourage migration to cities. Rapid urbanization is particularly nettlesome because developing nations do not have the resources to support public services and create new schools, hospitals, housing complexes, and, most important, jobs. In the face of such population increases and dislocations, it becomes increasingly difficult, even under optimal climatic and economic conditions, for farmers in developing countries to expand food production fast enough to keep pace with population growth. Despite the *green revolution*—the dramatic rise in output that has occurred in a number of countries (including India, Mexico, Taiwan, and the Philippines) when high-yield strains of wheat, rice, and corn are combined with modern irrigation systems and synthetic fertilizers—developing countries continue to face difficulty.

In addition to unfavorable terms of trade, rising foreign debt, and a population explosion, developing countries face three other key obstacles to successful development: a low level of technology, a significant land tenure problem, and an unforgiving environment. The green revolution is possible only where advanced agricultural technologies—including improved seeds, pesticides, herbi-

TABLE 8-1

Per Capita GNP, by Region

Region	Per Capita GNP (U.S. dollars)
Africa	$1,790
Sub-Saharan Africa	1,370
Northern Africa	3,070
Western Africa	1,000
Eastern Africa	850
Middle Africa	—
Southern Africa	8160
North America	31,260
Latin America and the Caribbean	6,460
Central America	6,900
Caribbean	—
South America	6,730
Asia	3,930
Asia, excluding China	4,130
Western Asia	4,810
South Central Asia	2,250
Southeast Asia	3,210
East Asia	5,750
Europe	14,970
Northern Europe	21,460
Western Europe	23,480
Eastern Europe	6,770
Southern Europe	16,520
Oceania	17,880

SOURCE: *2001 World Population Data Sheet 5,* Population Reference Bureau, www.prb.org, accessed May 16, 2002.

cides, synthetic fertilizers, irrigation, animal husbandry, farm-to-market roads, and storage facilities—are available. This availability in turn presupposes access to investment capital and foreign reserves, both typically in short supply.

Land tenure also poses a significant problem in many developing countries. Land ownership patterns vary from one country (and region) to another, but few developing nations have dealt effectively with their own particular land tenure problems. Because tradition is most resistant in rural settings, established patterns and practices there are slowest to change. The most basic problem centers on the inappropriate or economically unsuitable size of landholdings. In some areas, land ownership (and local power) is highly concentrated; in others, land is fragmented into parcels too small to be profitable. In Latin America these two problems exist side by side—huge estates (known as *latifundia*) coexist with tiny parcels (or *minifundia*). Egypt has a similar problem. Moreover, in many developing countries, it is common for peasants to be landless tenant farmers subject to the whims of absentee landlords.

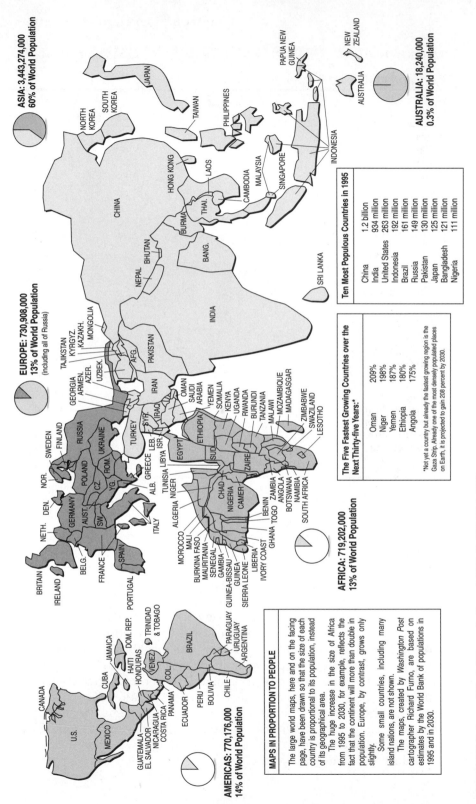

FIGURE 8-1 World Population, 1995: 5,692,210,000.
© 1997 The Washington Post. Reprinted with permission.

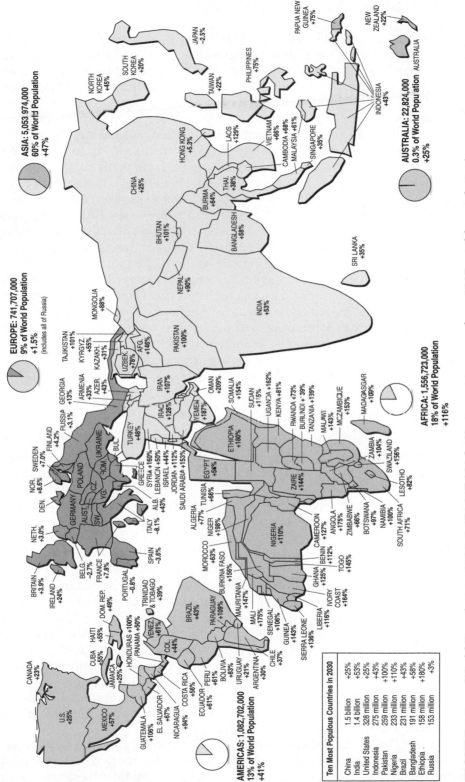

FIGURE 8-2 World Population, 2030: 8,474,017,000 (a 49 percent increase from 1995 world population)

Maps 8-1 and 8-2 show the projected change in population growth between 1995 and 2030. The maps are drawn so that each country's size is proportional to its population. The maps emphasize that much of the projected population increases will occur in developing nations.

SOURCE: Boyce Ransberger, "Damping the World's Population: Birthrates Are Falling Now but More Needs to Be Done in the Long Term," *Washington Post National Weekly Edition.* September 12–18, 1994, 10–40. © 1994 The Washington Post. Reprinted with permission.

239

In Africa, communal ownership of rural land is widespread. Here a different set of problems arises. Villagers are assigned parcels of land and share the crops, most of which are consumed rather than sold. Commercial plantations are now encroaching on village land; increasingly, cash crops are replacing traditional food crops. Worse still, young men are forced to leave their villages in a futile search for jobs; many become migrant farm workers and sink deeper into poverty and hopelessness. In Asia, the patterns are somewhat different, but the land tenure problems have the same effect: They impede government efforts to spur overall growth by revitalizing and modernizing the still predominantly rural economy.

Finally, the environment frequently makes for the most devastating obstacle to economic development. The worst tragedies tend to combine natural disasters with human folly. Thus, for example, overgrazing exacerbated a terrible drought across much of Africa's midsection in the 1980s. Similarly, floods in some developing nations have been caused at least in part by upstream deforestation, prompted by a search for wood used in cooking and heating. The most common result of such disasters is pervasive and debilitating hunger. Even without these environmental tragedies and the epidemics that frequently accompany them, undernourishment continues to afflict hundreds of millions of people in developing countries, especially in Africa. People who subsist on severely limited diets do not have the energy to be productive, leaving many developing nations caught in a vicious cycle: They are poor because they are not productive enough, and they are not productive enough because they are poor.

When Development Fails

Nations become developed as the result of a complex process with political, psychological, social, and economic dimensions. Yet it would be a mistake to assume that development is continuous or that, once set in motion, the wheels of progress are irreversible. Nation-states and societies at all levels and stages of development can fall victim to forces of instability and decay. No student of the American Civil War, or of the recent history of such disparate nations as Somalia, the former Yugoslavia, and contemporary Egypt, can ignore the perils of disintegration that can threaten developing and advanced industrialized nations alike.

What causes disintegration? Interestingly, political decay often stems from a nation's inability to solve the very problems that initially blocked development. Governments that cannot surmount the social disturbances arising from tensions among religious, ethnic, racial, or cultural groups often show marked signs of decay. In the mid-nineteenth century, the United States faced enormous stress from the unresolved issue of slavery. Today, there are countless variations on this theme. The Egyptian government's ability to govern has been significantly undermined by the opposition of fundamentalist Muslims. Sri Lanka (formerly Ceylon) has been beset by periodic violence between the Tamil minority and the Sinhalese majority. Rwanda has disintegrated into periodic civil war and violence as a result of the bloody conflict between Hutu and Tutsi tribes.

Similarly, economic dislocations may lead to social and political decay. Not only is the state of a nation's internal economy a source for concern, but worldwide, macroeconomic influences can also be particularly important. An extreme but historically important example took place in the 1970s, when many struggling Third World nations with meager resources and export earnings suffered tremendous hardship as oil prices skyrocketed. Political dislocation and social unrest followed the austerity measures forced on many Third World governments. Subsequently, rising external debt and economic instability existed throughout much of Africa, Asia, and Latin America for almost two decades.

Finally, disintegration can be caused by inadequacies in the political system. As noted earlier, when a government fails to forge a widely diffused sense of national identity, to promote political participation, or to distribute wealth across the entire society, political development will fail. In addition, as political scientists have long recognized, development can fail even when a government *is* able to promote such goals (for instance, by improving literacy, mass communications, voting participation, and urban life), but lacks the institutions, traditions, or wherewithal to deal effectively with political change.[19] In such cases, political decay can become the dark side of development. "Modernization," notes political scientist Samuel Huntington, "in practice always involves change in and usually the disintegration of a traditional political system, but it does not necessarily involve significant movement toward a modern political system. . . . Yet the tendency is to think that because social modernization is taking place, political modernization must also be taking place."[20]

DYSFUNCTIONAL STATES

In recent decades, the world has witnessed the spectacle of several societies self-destructing, destabilizing neighboring states in the process, and even threatening world peace. Dysfunctional states are wretched places where extremes are the norm—where government is extremely repressive or extremely weak, too weak to maintain a modicum of law and order. Under such circumstances, the most violent elements in society take over. Both criminal and political violence stalk city streets and threaten villages unprotected by police or a vigilant free press. The world is not watching and atrocities can go unnoticed for days, weeks, even months. If this image is disturbing, it is all too real in too many places. In this section, we look at four examples of political systems that are (or were) dysfunctional—sadly these examples by no means exhaust the list of candidates. A complete list would include the former Soviet Union (see Chapter 7).

Somalia

The Horn of Africa is home to several of the poorest countries on earth, including Sudan, Somalia, Eritrea, and Ethiopia. In the 1980s and 1990s, this region was afflicted by drought, famine, international conflict, civil wars, and all manner of violence. In the early 1990s, the most critical food shortages occurred in Somalia, where civil war and drought conspired to cause terrible human suffering. In August 1992, the United Nations Children's Fund (UNICEF) triggered a massive international relief effort when it warned that 2 million Somalis (out of a total population of slightly over 8 million) faced starvation within six months.

Against this backdrop of violence and misery, rebels ousted Somalia's long-time dictator, Siad Barré, in January 1991. Fighting and famine followed, leaving 300,000 people dead and millions at risk of starvation. A near-total breakdown of law and order plunged the country into anarchy and placed women and children at the mercy of armed bandits who disrupted relief efforts by international agencies, stole food intended for starving children, and murdered relief workers. At the end of 1992, outgoing U.S. President George Bush (the father of President George W. Bush) ordered a military intervention to safeguard relief supplies and workers. The scene was so chaotic that restoring law and order proved impossible. Long after the American-led UN forces departed in March 1995 (following the brutal killing of several American soldiers), Somalia remained a country without a national government; maps showing what areas were controlled by what factions looked more like a jigsaw puzzle than a political configuration.

Somalia remains one of the poorest countries in Africa, with a per capita GNP of less than $500 and an illiteracy rate of more than 75 percent in the 1990s. Moreover, Somalia is underdeveloped politically as well as economically. The structure of Somali society is based on kinship ties, or clans, and the civil war was in fact a clan war. If Somalia cannot find a formula for political stability, it cannot rebuild its economy. The reverse is also true: stability depends on economic and social progress. Whether Somalia will find a recipe for ruling the country effectively remains to be seen. Somalia's reputation as a dysfunctional state will not change until Somalia changes.

Yugoslavia

This country, in truth, no longer exists except in name. After surviving as a relatively independent state for most of the Cold War, it broke apart as the disintegration of the former Soviet Union transformed the geopolitical map of Europe in the 1990s. The former Yugoslavia's disintegration gives rise to what some observers are calling the "nightmare scenario," the prospect of political collapse fueled by ethnic hatreds that, in varying degrees, threatens many former communist states.

The Balkan Crisis in Historical Perspective   Yugoslavia's relationship with the USSR after 1945 grew out of specific circumstances at the end of World War II. Unlike the other Eastern European nations, which were liberated from German occupation by Stalin's armies, Yugoslavia was liberated by the partisan forces of Marshal Josip Broz Tito. Because of his role in the Yugoslav resistance movement, Tito emerged as a national hero and eventually became the symbol of a new Yugoslav nationalism.

In the immediate postwar era, Tito refused to take orders from Moscow, and Stalin retaliated by excommunicating Yugoslavia from the socialist commonwealth. Shortly thereafter, Tito began to take definite steps to popularize his rule, first by slowing the pace of agricultural collectivization and then by totally abandoning it. However, Yugoslav Communism made its most distinctive mark in the realm of industrial relations. Rejecting the extreme centralization that had been practiced in the former Soviet Union, Tito proclaimed the advent of a new form of socialist economic organization based on the concept of *self-management*. This granted a

FIGURE 8-3   Division of Former Yugoslavia
SOURCE: Adapted from former Yugoslavia, map no. 728104, CIA 1993, and Bosnia and Herzegovina (political) map no. 802474, CIA 1997.

large measure of regional autonomy—at least in principle—to the six republics in the Yugoslav federation. More significantly, it led to the creation of workers' councils in economic enterprises. Elected by factory or enterprise workers, these councils in turn elected management committees, and the management committees, meeting as regional associations, chose the directors of the various enterprises, subject to approval by the party. In 1950, workers gained the right to strike, trade unions were declared independent, and direct economic planning was replaced by the less coercive policy of "planned guidance." The 1970s saw a general tightening of controls over the Yugoslav economy and society, as the government sought to discourage dissent and resuscitate the sluggish economy.

Even so, Yugoslavia was unique among communist regimes. One scholar sketched the following picture of how the nation had, for the most part, been governed under Tito:

Most art and literature are apolitical, and artists and writers are free to create so long as they do not criticize sharply. There is no prior censorship, only the possibility of subsequent ban by court order; and private publishers produce nearly as many titles as official publishing houses. Newspapers are nearly uniform, but they are very informative in comparison with those of other East European Communist states, not to speak of the Soviet Union. The foreign press is freely available. Party spokesmen denounce Western influences in the press, but magazines continue to carry sensationalism and nudes, quite contrary to Communist morality. Perhaps fifteen million persons cross the borders yearly. There is freedom of association as long as it is not anti-party. Tito has never shot and seldom jailed his opponents.[21]

During the 1980s, the power and authority of Yugoslavia's central government declined rapidly. Yugoslavia was an artificial state composed of peoples of significantly different ethnic, cultural, and religious backgrounds—Greek Orthodox Serbs and Montenegrins, Roman Catholic Croats and Slovenes, a Muslim minority in Serbia, and mixed Bosnians, Herzegovinians, and Dalmatians. The glue that held them together was Tito's prestige and authority. When Tito died in 1980, fissures that had existed all along turned into conspicuous cracks in the structure of Yugoslav unity. The fall of communism in Eastern Europe accelerated the process of disintegration. By 1990, democracy and free elections had replaced communism. They did not last long. In the early 1990s, the economy was battered by heavy foreign debt ($16 billion), skyrocketing inflation (100 percent), and high unemployment (20 percent). Yugoslav society resorted to long-simmering ethnic rivalries and animosities, and the central government was increasingly paralyzed by conflict between the republics. Politically prosperous Slovenia and Croatia were at odds with the traditionally dominant Serbs over the future of the nation.

Serbia's hard-line president, Slobodan Milosevic, wanted to perpetuate Yugoslavia's Communist-led centralized federal system, while the center-right governments of Slovenia and Croatia favored a loose-knit confederation and a free-market economy. In the end, the forces of nationalism prevailed. In June 1991, both Slovenia and Croatia declared independence and a bloody civil war between Serbia and Croatia ensued, claiming an estimated 10,000 casualties. The efforts of these republics proved largely successful, and by January 1992 both were widely recognized as independent nation-states.

The Bosnian Tragedy   No sooner had the smoke cleared in the conflict between Serbia and Croatia when another tinderbox—the republic of Bosnia-Herzegovina—burst into flames. Bosnia is a society rife with ethnic tensions, with its population divided among three major ethnic groups—Serbs, Croats, and Bosnian Muslims. While the latter are the largest group, they have been squeezed into the smallest amount of territory. Ethnic cleavages are reinforced by religious differences (Croats are Catholic, Serbs are Eastern Orthodox) and historical animosities that have grown out of the abuses these groups have inflicted on each other.

The conflict, involving a scramble for territory and the settling of old scores, has been a three-sided affair: Serbs against Croats, Muslims against Croats, and, most notably, Serbs against Muslims. The war between Serbs and Muslims in Bosnia has been a particularly brutal and unequal contest. The Serbs gained a great amount of territory. They also engaged in wholesale *ethnic cleansing,* the unconscionable practice of rape, pillage, and mass murder, which led to clearing

Time Magazine / Black Star

Sparked by the collapse of the Yugoslav Communist party in January 1990, ethnic struggles between the Serbs and other republics resulted in a bloody civil war, which dragged on until 1996 despite the efforts of the European Union and the United Nations. Most reprehensible was the genocidal "ethnic cleansing" that claimed tens of thousands of lives in Bosnia.

all Muslims and non-Serbs out of towns and villages in areas the Serbs had conquered and wished to absorb into a separate Bosnian Serb state called Serbska. In 1993–94, the Bosnian Serbs, backed by Serbia proper, carried out a long siege of Sarajevo, the Bosnian capital, as well as several major Muslim towns. The siege of Sarajevo ended only when NATO and the United Nations intervened; elsewhere, the siege continued in defiance of an ineffective UN resolution declaring these endangered towns "safe havens." The United Nations denounced Croatia for its part in fanning the conflict in Bosnia. It also threatened the Bosnian Serbs with NATO air strikes. These measures, combined with intense mediation efforts (especially by Russia), yielded results.

In February 1994, the Serbs agreed to withdraw their heavy weapons from Sarajevo, and a week later the Bosnian government and Bosnian Croats signed a cease-fire agreement. In March 1994, prospects for peace temporarily brightened when the Croatian government and local Serb authorities also signed a cease-fire, ending hostilities.

Peace proved to be a mere illusion, however. UN troops had been sent to Bosnia to bring humanitarian aid. However, Bosnian Serbs promptly attacked them and resumed the offensive. NATO air strikes, launched in April 1994, November 1994, and May 1995, were ordered to protect the lives of UN peacekeepers. Once again, Bosnia was sinking into bloody anarchy.

But, at long last, a revised peace plan proposed by the United States became the basis for a settlement. All warring parties endorsed the plan at Dayton, Ohio, in November 1995, and a peace agreement—the *Dayton Accords*—was signed in

Paris on December 14. The agreement gave 49 percent of Bosnia to the Bosnian Serb Republic and 51 percent to the Muslim-Croat Federation. Sarajevo remains the capital inside the territory of the Muslim-Croat Federation. A central government comprised of a collective presidency and a parliament would deal with foreign policy, the economy, and finances, among other things. Each half of Bosnia would handle its own defense and internal affairs.

An international force of 60,000 troops under NATO command was sent to the scene to monitor the peace settlement. Amid reports of irregularities, elections were held throughout the country in September 1996. But few expected the Dayton Accords to hold. Already by mid-1997, nationalist Serbs and Croats in Bosnia envisioned carving Bosnia into ethnically "pure" territories. In March 1998, Serbian-sponsored violence against the Albanian majority in the autonomous province of Kosovo rocked the region. In the face of such territorial ambitions and undiminished ethnic emotions, it seemed improbable that Bosnia could long endure as a single multiethnic, multireligious state.

A full-scale civil war broke out in Kosovo in the late 1990s. The war was sparked by a dispute over the question of autonomy—the Kosovars demanded it and Belgrade said no. Serbian forces showed no mercy to civilians, systematically driving Kosovars (Albanian Serbs) out of the country (out of Kosovo, that is). By the time NATO's intervention finally brought the Milosevic government to its knees, well over a million Kosovars (roughly three-fifths of the entire ethnic Albanian population) had become refugees. An uneasy peace returned to Kosovo only after fierce fighting led on the rebel side by the Kosovo Liberation Army (KLA) and only as a result of intervention by the United States and the international community.

The joyless end of the fighting was accompanied by an imposed "peace." The United Nations put its own "interim administration" in charge, with NATO troops serving as a kind of police force. The declared aim was "substantial autonomy and self-government" for the province, whatever that meant. The UN–NATO regime disarmed the KLA and promised to protect the tiny (5 percent) Serbian minority in Kosovo against recriminations by angry ethnic Albanians. It was a promise not perfectly kept, as many Serbians in Kosovo were attacked or threatened.

In sum, nothing was settled. There was no end in sight for the UN protectorate so long as Milosevic was in power. For all its good intentions, the United Nations once again proved itself ill-equipped to govern. UN administrators were unfamiliar with local customs and struggled with a baffling language barrier. NATO forces, now in the odd role of protecting Serbians, met with hostility from the outraged Kosovars. Meanwhile, there was an institutional and legal vacuum with neither laws, nor courts, nor local police to fight ordinary (and not-so-ordinary) crime.

The bloody dictator Milosevic was finally ousted in the presidential elections of 2000 (he tried to steal the election but was swept away by a tidal wave of popular opposition). Only time will tell whether Milosevic's successor(s) will be able to restore political order and international respectability to this divided nation with a ruined economy.

Sierra Leone

As noted earlier, democracy is not at all common in sub-Saharan Africa. Even where it looked like it was working, it has failed—in some cases, miserably. Nowhere has it failed more miserably than in Sierra Leone.

When legislative elections were held in Sierra Leone in 1986, the aptly named All Peoples party approved 335 candidates to contest 105 elective seats. The party typically offered at least three contestants for each seat, a common practice among one-party states in sub-Saharan Africa. So voters in Sierra Leone actually had more choices—relative to personalities at least—than voters do in most U.S. legislative races.

Nonetheless, Sierra Leone began a steady descent into anarchy in the 1990s. Between 1996 and 1998, the government changed hands four times. Then all hell broke loose, and rebels (members of the so-called Revolutionary United Front) began chopping hands off right and left. They chopped off heads, too. They recruited (kidnapped) small boys and turned them into sex slaves and killers. There is no way—or need—to describe the horror of Sierra Leone in words. Neither the civil institutions nor the political culture necessary to support and sustain democracy were developed in Sierra Leone. For several decades, the appearance of democracy has masked the reality of a society capable of erupting into volcanic civil violence at any moment.

Afghanistan

Finally, we turn to Afghanistan, where the United States, with the backing of the international community, intervened with military force in 2001 following the September 11 terrorist attacks on the World Trade Center and the Pentagon. In a single day, Afghanistan went from being "off the map" for most Americans to being the most talked-about country in the world. What most Americans quickly learned was that a brutal bunch of thugs comprising a totalitarian regime called the Taliban ruled an oppressed and desperately poor country in the name of a twisted version of Islam. What they (we) also learned was that the Taliban was providing safe haven to Osama bin Laden and his terrorist network, al Qaeda. What few understood fully at the time was the historical background: Afghanistan had been one of the world's most dysfunctional states for some three decades prior to the events that led directly to the landing of U.S. Special Forces on Afghan soil. Even prior to the 1970s, Afghanistan was one of the poorest countries in the world; things deteriorated rapidly in the decades after the overthrow of the monarchy. In 2001, the entire country was in a shambles and millions of people—especially women and children—were living on the very edge of a precipice.

Afghanistan is home to many ethnic groups reflecting the disparate populations around the periphery of the country—Pakistan, Iran, Turkmenistan, Tajikistan, Uzbekistan, and China. The largest group, the Pashtuns, constitute about 40 percent of the total population (about 26 million in 2000). Thus, there is no majority group in the country; there are only minorities of different sizes. Roughly 99 percent of all Afghans are Muslims; about 15 percent are Shi'ite Muslims (as are most Iranians).

Afghanistan was a monarchy from 1747 to 1973. Then the country came apart at the seams, and it soon became painfully evident that there were lots of seams in this patchwork society. Various factions fought for supremacy after 1973 until the Soviet Union made the fateful decision to intervene on behalf of its favorite thug (a communist) in 1979. A brutal and protracted war ensued; the Soviet Union finally withdrew in defeat in 1989 after a decade of debilitating (and humiliating) warfare. Opponents overthrew the communist regime and seized power in 1992. The new strongman refused to relinquish power when his term officially expired but Taliban forces assaulted the capital and ousted him in 1996. The new regime instituted a totalitarian system of rule couched in the language and concepts of Islam, but based on a perversion of the Koran (Holy Scripture) and Sharia law (based on the teachings of Muslim clerics or mullahs). Women and girls were forced to wear *birkas* (a one-piece, head-to-toe garment) in public, and were not allowed to work outside the home, to go to school, or to express opinions at variance with the government. The government banned television, movies, music, dancing, and most other forms of "decadent" entertainment. There were even restrictions on children's games and activities (according to press reports, for example, kite flying was forbidden).

Afghanistan is only the best-known example of a dysfunctional state in recent times; it is not the only one. As the history of Afghanistan in the past three decades illustrates, dysfunctional states can become a threat to regional stability and even to world order. The solution is as obvious as it is difficult to bring about: economic and political development leading to a better life for societies afflicted by violence, hunger, disease, and despair.

DEVELOPMENT THEORY: A BIASED DISCUSSION?

Development and *democracy* are often viewed as synonymous in the West and all aspects of development are assumed to be desirable. The language of political science and the literature of development reveals as much. Implicit in this language and literature is the basic (but generally unstated) assumption that it is better to be developed than not developed. Consider the antonyms: *underdeveloped, less developed, developing, traditional,* or even *backward.* Sometimes in an effort to be politically correct, political scientists use the term *premodern* to describe societies that are in an early stage of development.

Development theory thus assumes that development is good. Perhaps one reason is that the least developed and least modern countries are also usually the poorest. Sometimes, too, as we have seen, economic development and social modernization are associated with political democracy.

Is it necessarily true, however, that modern-day citizens in an industrially developed nation-state are happier than members of an African tribe who lead a relatively simple life, whose needs are supplied by the tribe (their immediate community), and whose religious and metaphysical questions are answered by a clear-cut set of beliefs passed down from one generation to the next? To most sophisticated Westerners, such an existence seems primitive and backward. According to this view, superstition, mythology, and the "dead hand of the past" block the development of both individuals and society.

But some critics point out that discussions of development often amount to little more than the praising of Western-style development and imply that Western experts on the subject are guilty of ethnocentrism.[22] Actually, Western philosophers have long struggled with this problem. In 1750, the French philosopher Jean-Jacques Rousseau declared, "our souls have been corrupted in proportion to the movement of our sciences and arts towards perfection."[23] Indeed, much of Rousseau's political philosophy is rooted in the notion that modern civilization has eroded rather than enhanced our humanity. Undoubtedly, many people in developing countries who have been forced to forsake their villages for the vicissitudes of city life (often in squalid slums) would agree.

OVERDEVELOPMENT: CAPITALISM'S DIRTY LITTLE SECRET

At the outset we suggested that development is not something that happens only in certain countries beyond the boundaries of the Western world. All societies are in a constant state of flux, they are either rising or falling, but one thing is certain: they are never standing still. Societies develop in different ways, at different rates and different times. In the modern era, Western societies led the way—they developed economically and technologically along lines congruent with the political institutions that were evolving at the same time. In this sense, development as it is defined in the contemporary world was a natural process that originated within these societies. For developing countries, it is often just the opposite: development is an alien process that originates from the outside (that is, from world market forces, IMF pressures, foreign capital looking for cheap labor, and the like).

Development was thus less disruptive, generally speaking, in the West than it has been in many Third World countries. But the story of development does not end with the arrival of the postindustrial state. Western countries have developed beyond the agricultural stage, beyond the industrial stage, and are high-tech economies now offering a vast array of commercial and financial services. (Of course, these countries are still involved in agriculture, mining, and industry, but these sectors of the economy have been eclipsed in importance by high-tech goods such as computer software, science- and research-based products such as pharmaceuticals, and financial services, among other things.) These new products bring a higher quality of life to consumers who can afford them, but they come with a hidden price tag—traffic congestion, urban crowding, air and noise pollution, stress-related illnesses, high divorce rates, illegal drug use, a surge in violent crime, overconsumption, urban sprawl, energy shortages (consider California), mounting waste disposal problems, ground water contamination, acid rain, possible global warming, depletion of the ozone layer, extinction of countless plant and animal species, and many other maladies commonly associated with development.

Listing even some of the problems facing postindustrial societies is sufficient to underscore the point that late-stage development is not free from challenges any more than early-stage development. The challenges are different, but they are no less daunting. *Overdeveloped countries*—where development has outrun society's capacity to deal with undesirable side effects of rapidly accelerating technological and social change—would do well to focus more attention on solving the problems *they* are facing and less on telling supposedly *underdeveloped countries* what to do and how to do it.

Summary

Developing countries are so named because they are less developed economically and less modernized socially than Western liberal democracies. Although some generalizations about developing countries are possible (for instance, most are poor, have high population growth, and rely on agriculture), these nations are highly diverse. The historical legacy of developing nations—especially European colonialism—has led to political resentment in the poor South against the rich North. Part of that legacy is a political map that makes little sense: borders that do not reflect indigenous ethnic, religious, and tribal patterns and thereby have fostered political instability, including riots, rebellions, civil wars, and even genocide.

Political development requires that leaders effectively unify the population (nation building), provide for government institutions that respond to people's needs (state building), encourage citizen participation, and ensure an adequate distribution of wealth, power, and property. Specifically, political development requires a government that can govern effectively and transfer political power smoothly. Usually, political development also assumes movement toward democratic government. Democracy in developing countries correlates with the existence and distribution of certain identifiable economic, political, social, and attitudinal variables. To institute democratic reforms, a nation may start with either political or economic reforms, but an economy-first strategy provides the more likely prospect for success. From 1974 to 1990, many developing nations became democratic, but this trend is reversible.

Development can be an arduous task. Developing nations are motivated to undertake development programs by economic hardships, political rivalries, and rising expectations; however, in the process, they encounter significant barriers. Socially, populations are often fragmented. Psychologically, individuals are heavily dependent on tradition and frequently oppose change. Economically, the problems range from unfavorable terms of trade and high foreign debt to rapid population growth, a low level of technology, entrenched land tenure problems, and environmental difficulties. When leaders cannot successfully meet the social, economic, and political demands of development (for any number of reasons), development fails and nations disintegrate.

Some societies decline, decay, and disintegrate rather than develop. Recent examples include Somalia, Yugoslavia, Sierra Leone, and Afghanistan. The Soviet Union was a spectacular example; there are many others.

Overdevelopment (the opposite of underdevelopment) is a problem that afflicts many Western societies. Contemporary discussion of development tends to assume its desirability. This assumption, however, can be disputed.

Key Terms

developing nations	patron–client relations
First World	democratic correlates
Second World	glasnost-first model
Third World	perestroika-first model
colonialism	revolution of rising expectations
nonviolent resistance	mosaic societies
civil disobedience	traditional societies
political development	ascriptive societies
nation building	green revolution
state building	ethnic cleansing
political penetration	Dayton Accords
participation	

Review Questions

1. What are the salient characteristics of the so-called Third World? How do these relate to the development process?

2. Elucidate the correlates of democracy. How compelling is this line of analysis? Comment.

3. What are the incentives for modernization? What sources of resistance can you identify?

4. Does development always lead to democracy? Is the reverse true? Can you think of examples?

5. What are the barriers to development? If development is so difficult, why do nations undertake it?

6. How are development and decay related? Are states and societies ever static? Comment.

7. Name four dysfunctional states and use one as an example to illustrate the nature of this type of state.

Recommended Reading

ALLEN, JOHN. *Student Atlas of World Politics.* Guilford, Conn.: Dushkin, 1994. An extremely valuable resource emphasizing historical, economic, population, military, and environmental information. Excellent introductions.

BINDER, LEONARD. "The Crises of Political Development." In *Crisis and Sequences in Political Development*, edited by Leonard Binder et al. Princeton, N.J.: Princeton University Press, 1971. A groundbreaking analysis that identifies five "crises of development": identity, legitimacy, participation, distribution, and penetration. The book is seventh in a series titled *Studies in Political Development*.

CAMMACK, PAUL, DAVID POOL, and WILLIAM TORDOFF. *Third World Politics: A Comparative Introduction.* 2nd ed. Baltimore: Johns Hopkins University Press, 1993. A basic book recommended for students interested in comparative politics beyond Europe and North America.

CASPER, GRETCHEN. *Fragile Democracies: The Legacies of Authoritarian Rule.* Pittsburgh: University of Pittsburgh Press, 1995. Relying on numerous examples from developing countries, the author suggests reasons why democracy "remains problematic" in such states.

CHANG, HA-JOON and ROBERT ROWTHORN. *The Role of the State in Economic Change.* Oxford, England: Clarendon, 1995. A collection of advanced essays that focus on the positive role the state has played in national economic development.

CLARK, ROBERT. *Power and Policy in the Third World.* 4th ed. New York: Macmillan, 1991. A good survey of developing nations. The discussion of colonialism in the first chapter is especially incisive.

GRINDLE, MERILEE S. *Politics and Policy Implementation in the Third World.* Princeton, N.J.: Princeton University Press, 1980. A comparative exploration of the political, economic, and ideological foundations of the major national policies for economic and social development in the Third World.

HUNTINGTON, SAMUEL P. "How Countries Democratize." *Political Science Quarterly* 106 (1991–92): 578–616. Examines how various nondemocratic regimes (classified as one-party systems, military regimes, and personal dictatorships) democratized between 1974 and 1990, with an emphasis on Third World nations.

————. "Will More Countries Become Democratic?" *Political Science Quarterly* 99 (1984): 193–218. Articulates the economic, cultural, and social factors assumed to be associated with democracy.

KARAHASAN, DZEVAD. *Sarajevo, Exodus of a City.* New York: Kodansha America, 1994. An insider's view of the siege of Bosnia's ancient capital.

LIPSET, SEYMOUR. *American Exceptionalism: A Double-Edged Sword.* New York: Norton, 1996.

————. *Political Man: The Social Bases of Democracy.* Rev. ed. Garden City, N.Y.: Doubleday, 1983. A wide-ranging discussion of politics and nation-states that argues compellingly that national wealth is the most reliable predictor of democracy.

MAYER, LAWRENCE, JOHN BURNETT, and SUZANNE OGDEN. *Comparative Politics: Nations and Theories in a Changing World.* 2nd. ed. Englewood Cliffs, N.J.: Prentice-Hall, 1996. A sophisticated text covering a broad range of topics and nations. Its discussion of developing nations is particularly germane.

MEIER, GERALD M. *Emerging from Poverty: The Economics That Really Matter.* New York: Oxford University Press, 1985. An excellent survey of the basic issues of development economics in which the author argues that one cause of persistent poverty is "the underdevelopment of economics itself."

REYNOLDS, LLOYD G. *Economic Growth in the Third World, 1850–1980.* New Haven, Conn.: Yale University Press, 1985. Traces the growth and development of forty-one large developing countries and examines the economic impact of colonialism, the persistence of poverty, the gains from exporting (and the resulting dependency), and the proper functions of government in promoting growth.

ROSTOW, WALT WHITMAN. *The Stages of Economic Growth: A Non-Communist Manifesto.* 3rd ed. Cambridge, England: Cambridge University Press, 1991. A provocative study which posits that all developing economies go through basically the same stages, beginning as traditional societies and progressing through self-sustaining growth to the age of mass consumption. The theory suggests that eventually all societies will become industrialized, capitalist, and democratic.

VANHANEN, TATU. *The Process of Democratization: A Comparative Study of 147 States, 1980–1988.* Bristol, Pa.: Taylor & Francis, 1990. A carefully researched study that argues the widespread distribution of economic and educational resources within a developing nation-state is the key to its ultimate democratization.

Notes

1. This is true according to almost any classification system, although whether China is considered a developing nation significantly affects the precise numbers. Our figures include it.

2. John Allen, *Student Atlas of World Politics* (Guilford, Conn.: Dushkin, 1994), 16. Thailand was then called Siam and Iran was named Persia.

3. Ibid., 17. However, given the fluidity of contemporary politics, especially in former Yugoslavia, this number is highly unstable.

4. As pointed out by Robert Clark, *Power and Policy in the Third World*, 4th ed. (New York: Macmillan, 1991), 26.

5. See Jared Diamond, *Guns, Germs, and Steel: The Fate of Human Societies* (New York: Norton, 1997).

6. These points are generally emphasized in the literature. See James A. Bill and Robert L. Hardgrave, Jr., *Comparative Politics: The Quest for Theory* (Websterville, Ohio: Merrill, 1973), 70–71.

7. For instance, see Seymour Lipset, *Political Man: The Social Bases of Democracy* (Garden City, N.Y.: Doubleday, 1983); Tatu Vanhanen, *The Process of Democratization: A Comparative Study of 147 States, 1980–1988* (Bristol, Pa.: Taylor & Francis, 1990); and Samuel P. Huntington, "Will More Countries Become Democratic?" *Political Science Quarterly* 99 (1984): 193–218. Also of interest is Thomas Scanton, "Democracy's Fragile Flower Spreads Its Roots," *Time*, July 13, 1987, 10–11. An optimistic outlook for democracy, based on such correlates, is offered by Carl Gershman, "Democracy as the Wave of the Future: A World Revolution," *Current* (May 1989): 18–23. See also Morton Kondracke, "Freedom Bummer," *New Republic*, November 26, 1990, 21–24.

8. Gershman, "Democracy as the Wave of the Future," 23.

9. Vanhanen, *Process of Democratization*, 51–65.

10. See Kondracke, "Freedom Bummer," 23.

11. Samuel Huntington, "How Countries Democratize," *Political Science Quarterly* 106 (1991–92): 579.

12. See, for example, Robert M. Press, "Africa's Struggle for Democracy," *Christian Science Monitor*, March 21, 1991, 4; and Kenneth B. Noble, "Despots Dwindle as Reform Alters Face of Africa," *New York Times*, April 13, 1991, 1.

13. As Thomas R. Lansner pointed out in "Out of Africa," *Wall Street Journal*, December 10, 1996, A18.

14. Huntington, "How Countries Democratize," 12.

15. Usually by Third World nations. A recent and important exception was the war between U.S.-led United Nations forces and Iraq, fought in early 1991.

16. Jean Herskovits, "Nigeria: Power and Democracy in Africa," *Headline Series* 527 (January–February 1982): 8.

17. Vyvyan Tenorio, "Sri Lanka Peace Process at Delicate Point," *Christian Science Monitor*, September 2, 1986, 11.

18. Robert E. Gamer, *Developing Nations: A Comparative Perspective*, 2nd ed. (Dubuque, Iowa: William C. Brown, 1982), 312–314.

19. Samuel Huntington, "Political Development and Political Decay," *World Politics* 17 (April 1965): 386–430.

20. Samuel Huntington, *Political Order in Changing Societies* (New Haven, Conn.: Yale University Press, 1968), 35.

21. Robert G. Wesson, *Communism and Communist Systems* (Englewood Cliffs, N.J.: Prentice-Hall, 1978), 172–173.

22. See, for instance, Bill and Hardgrave, *Comparative Politics*, 58–59.

23. Jean-Jacques Rousseau, "The First Discourse," in *The First and Second Discourses*, ed. Roger D. Masters (New York: St. Martin's Press, 1964), 39.

© Steve Chenn / CORBIS

© Hulton-Deutsch Collection / CORBIS

Getty Images

PART III

POLITICS BY CIVIL MEANS

255

© Steve Chenn / CORBIS

Chapter 9

POLITICAL SOCIALIZATION

THE MAKING OF A CITIZEN

THE YEAR IS 1932. The Soviet Union suffers a severe shortage of food, and millions go hungry. Joseph Stalin, leader of the Communist party and head of the Soviet government, has undertaken a vast reordering of Soviet agriculture that involves the elimination of a whole class of landholders (the *kulaks*) and the collectivization of all farmland—henceforth, every farm and all farm products belong to the state. To deter theft of what is now considered state property, the Soviet government enacts a law prohibiting individual farmers from appropriating any grain for their own private use. Acting under this law, a young boy reports his father to the authorities for concealing grain. The father is shot for stealing state property. Soon after, the boy is killed by a group of peasants, led by his uncle, who are outraged that he would betray his own father. The government, taking a radically different view of the affair, extols the boy as a patriotic martyr.

THE GOOD CITIZEN VERSUS THE GOOD

Stalin considered the little boy in the story a model citizen, a hero. That a child who betrayed his own father could be considered a good citizen points to a distinction originally made by Aristotle: The good citizen is defined by laws, regimes, and rulers, but the moral fiber (and universal characteristics) of a *good person* is fixed and transcends the expectations of any particular political regime.[1] Thus, good *citizenship* involves behaving in accordance with the rules, norms, and expectations of one's own state and society. But the actual requirements of good citizenship can (and do) vary widely among nations. A good citizen in 1930s' Soviet Russia would have been a person whose first loyalty was to the Communist party. The test of good citizenship in a totalitarian state is this: Are you willing to subordinate all personal convictions and even family loyalties to the dictates of political authority and to follow the dictator's whims no matter where they may lead? In marked contrast are the standards of citizenship in constitutional democracies, which prize and protect the civil and political rights of individuals to follow their conscience and to express their convictions.

Where the requirements of the abstract good citizen (always defined by the state) come into conflict with the moral compass of real people (citizens as good and compassionate human beings), and where the state seeks to obliterate the difference between the two, a serious problem arises in both theory and practice. At what point do people cease to be real citizens and become mere subjects or even slaves? Does one obey the state or the dictates of one's own conscience?

Throughout history, people of diverse moral character have claimed to be models of good citizenship for society. The relationship between the moral character of citizens and different forms of government underscores Aristotle's observation that the true measure of a political system is the kind of citizen it produces. According to this view, a good state is one whose model citizen is also a good person; a bad state is one whose model citizen obeys orders without regard for questions of good or evil. Simple though this formulation may sound, it offers striking insights into the relationship between governments and citizens, including, for example, the fact that civic virtue (or public morality) cannot be divorced from personal integrity (private morality).

Contrasting Definitions

It is little wonder that different political systems embrace different definitions of citizenship. In many authoritarian states, people can be classified as citizens only in the narrowest sense of the word—that is, they reside within the territory of a certain state and are subject to its laws. The relationship between state and citizen is a one-way street. As ordinary citizens, they have no voice in deciding who rules or how (even if they have a vote). Generally, the government leaves them alone as long as they acquiesce in the system.

By contrast, in totalitarian states, where the government seeks to transform society and create a new kind of citizen, people are compelled to participate in the political system. From the standpoint of citizenship, however, this kind of participation is meaningless because it is not voluntary and stresses duties without corresponding rights. Loyalty and zealotry form the core of good citizenship, and citizens may be forced to carry out orders they find morally repugnant.

In democratic societies, people define citizenship very differently. In elementary school, the good citizenship award typically goes to a pupil who sets a good example, respects others, plays by the rules, and hands in assignments on time. Adults practice good citizenship by taking civic obligations seriously, obeying the laws, paying taxes, and voting regularly, among other things. In democracy, the definition of *good citizenship* is found in the laws, but legislators who are freely elected by the people write the laws—in other words, a true republic at its best erases (or at the very least eases) the tension between citizenship and moral conscience.

Many individuals, including civil libertarians, emphasize that the essence of citizenship lies in individual rights or personal liberties. The formal requirements of citizenship in the United States are minimal, even though people the world over envy the rewards (hence the steady flow of immigrants into the United States compared to the trickle of U.S. citizens emigrating to other countries). According to the Fourteenth Amendment, "All persons born or naturalized in the United States, and subject to the jurisdiction thereof, are citizens of the United States, and of the State in which they reside." Note that in this country citizenship is constitutionally defined.

Note also that citizens of the United States are distinguished from noncitizens not on the basis of how they act or what they have done but simply by their place of birth. The underlying presumption here is once a citizen, always a citizen, barring some extraordinary misdeed (such as treason) or a voluntary renunciation of citizenship. In the United States, in peacetime, the demands of citizenship are usually quite limited.

A Classical View

Our minimal view of citizenship may provide a convenient way of distinguishing "insiders" from "outsiders," but it obscures the true significance of a concept that has long been honored in Western civilization. To the ancient Greeks, the concept of citizenship was only partly related to accidents of birth and political geography; responsible and selfless participation in the public affairs of the community formed the vital core of citizenship. Aristotle held that a citizen "shares in the administration of justice and in the holding of office."[2] The Athens of Aristotle's time was a small political society, or city-state, that accorded a proportionately large number of citizens significant decision-making power in the community at any given time. Citizenship was the exalted vehicle through which public-spirited and properly educated free men could rule over, and in turn be ruled by, other free men and thereby advance civic virtue, public order, and the common good.

In eighteenth-century Europe, the Greek ideal reemerged in a modified form. *Citizen* became a term applicable to those who claimed the right to petition or sue the government. Citizens were distinguished from slaves, who had no claims or rights and were regarded as chattel (property). Citizens also differed from subjects, whose first and foremost legal obligation was to show loyalty to and obey the sovereign. According to the German philosopher Immanuel Kant (1724–1804), citizens, as opposed to slaves or subjects, possessed constitutional freedom; that is, the right to obey only laws to which they had given their consent. Kant also contended that citizens possessed a civil equality, relieving them from being bound by law or custom to recognize any superior among themselves, and political independence, meaning that a person's political status stemmed from fundamental rights rather than from the will of another.[3]

Clearly inherent in the evolving conception of citizenship was the idea of individual dignity. Citizens were to be treated as free and equal individuals, capable of determining their own best interests. No longer were they to be ruled arbitrarily by others; as intelligent human beings, they deserved to be treated with respect. Republican government came the closest to this ideal of citizenship. In the final analysis, as Kant and other eighteenth-century thinkers recognized, the freedom and dignity inherent in citizenship could flourish only under a republican government, and such a government could function only if its rank-and-file members understood and discharged the responsibilities of citizenship.

In modern times, many more people can legally claim the title "citizen" not only in the world as a whole but also within particular countries. In the United States, for instance, it took many years for racial minorities, women, and individuals without property to gain the right to vote and the right to protection under the law in the exercise of their civil rights. Yet this expansion of meaningful citizenship has not been without pitfalls. As the number of citizens (and of people generally) has risen, effective political participation for individuals has become more difficult, and governments have been hard-pressed to provide the civic education and social environments needed to ensure that all citizens exercise their rights in a responsible manner. In ancient Athens, any citizen could hold public office and play an active role in formulating laws and policies because of the city's relatively small size and small number of citizens (slaves and women were excluded). In sprawling nations with millions of inhabitants, in which almost all adults are classified as citizens, meaningful and effective participation is often an elusive ideal.

POLITICAL SOCIALIZATION

Though the proper definition of citizenship may be disputed, it is generally agreed that good citizens are made, not born. Children grow up to be responsible citizens through the interplay of various influences and institutions—including family, religion, school, peer groups, the mass media, and the law—that help to shape their sense of civic duty and political self-confidence. The process of being conditioned to think and behave in a socially acceptable manner is called socialization.

Political socialization is the process whereby citizens develop the values, attitudes, beliefs, and opinions that enable them to support the political system.[4] Every self-sustaining society inculcates in its citizens certain basic values. Unquestionably, shared beliefs are the necessary building blocks of any state. Even as staunch an individualist as the British philosopher John Stuart Mill (1806–1873) acknowledged that the sense of citizen loyalty or allegiance "may vary in its objects and is not confined to any particular form of government; but whether in a democracy or in a monarchy its essence is always . . . that there be in the constitution of the state something which is settled, something permanent, and not to be called into question; something which, by general agreement, has a right to be where it is, and to be secure against disturbance, whatever else may change."[5]

It follows that no government, however legitimate, can afford to ignore the way its citizens develop their political beliefs. This process begins with the family.

The Family

The family exerts the first and most important influence on the formation of individual values. Different political regimes view the family in different ways. Some governments support and nurture the family; others choose to remain indifferent toward it; a few seek to undermine it, regarding the love and loyalty that flow from family ties as subversive to the state. Despite these varying reactions, all governments recognize the importance of the family in the socialization process.

Even nations that publicly proclaim the value of the traditional family, however, may not be able to ensure its success in society. The number of children living in single-parent households in the United States, for example, has risen dramatically since the 1960s, in response to a rising divorce rate and increases in the rate of births to unmarried women (see Figure 9-1). Whereas in 1970 about 12 percent of all children were born to unmarried women, by 1996 that figure approximated 33 percent. In some cases, the mother, abandoned by the baby's father, is left with the overwhelming tasks of child rearing and providing for the family's needs. Teenage pregnancy, poverty, and a lack of education have been associated with these fragmented families. The problem contributes to high social welfare expenses, such as Temporary Assistance to Needy Families benefits and food stamp programs.

The future economic and social toll posed by the problem may be far greater. Studies confirm that children raised in single-parent families are at greater risk than those in two-parent families to drop out of school, to be involved with crime

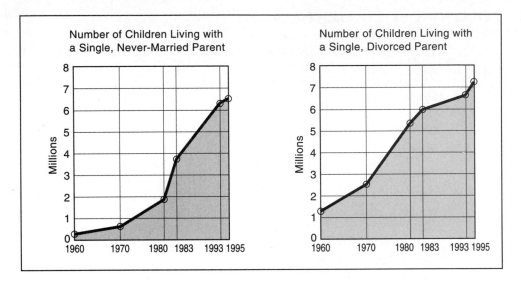

FIGURE 9-1   U.S. Children Living in Single-Parent Households, 1960–95
SOURCE: "Keeping Track," *New York Times,* July 20, 1994, A7.

and illegal drugs, to be unemployed (or underemployed) and poor, and to have failed marriages and personal relationships as adults.[6] Of course, single-parent families are often successful and many children raised by single parents become well-adjusted adults. If one parent is physically or emotionally abusive, it is often better for a child to be nurtured (and protected) by the parent who is not.

Children are first socialized at home within the family structure, learning what is and what is not permissible, with rewards and punishment to reinforce daily behavior. In this manner, the obligations of children to the family and to others are made clear. Slowly they become citizens of the family, often with clearly defined responsibilities and occasionally with rights or privileges. Moral ground rules are emphasized even if the reasons for them are not always specified ("Do it because I said so"). Trust, cooperation, self-esteem, respect for others, and empathy, each rooted in family relations, bear on the behavioral and moral development of individuals.[7]

The family also helps to determine the direction that the ultimate political socialization of children takes and how successful it will be. Party orientation and even affiliation often derives from the family, especially when both parents belong to the same party. In addition, the family exerts a powerful influence on religious persuasion, which tends to correlate highly with party affiliation as well as with certain political opinions (fundamentalist Protestants tend to oppose abortion; Jews tend to support Israel; and so on).[8] In the United States, about 70 percent of children whose parents have the same party affiliation favor that party too.[9] However, studies indicate that when it comes to opinions about more abstract political issues, parental influence is quite limited.[10] And as adults we often find ourselves at odds with our parents' ideas about politics (among other things), a fact often attributed to "generational" differences.

Social Class and Minority Status   Several studies indicate that patterns of political socialization vary only slightly with the social class of the parents.[11] Middle- and upper-class children are most likely to become actively involved in politics since a family's interest in politics is believed to increase with social standing. Children from lower-class families, by contrast, tend to be uninformed about politics and to participate less often in political activities.[12]

Within families, minority status can play a significant role in political socialization. For example, some researchers have found that in the United States, African American children tend to place less trust in government than white children. These children tend also to be less confident of their ability to influence government.[13] Not surprisingly, such attitudes correlate with political opinions; thus, black Americans (holding class differences constant) tend to be more politically liberal than white Americans on most economic and foreign policy issues (although not necessarily on all political issues; for example, crime). Similarly, Asian Americans, given their general deference for authority and traditional family structure, tend to resemble white ethnic groups more closely than black groups, particularly on domestic social issues. Hispanic Americans tend to fall between blacks and whites, although the effects of family socialization and the transmission of political beliefs have exerted an influence on Cuban Americans, who as a group tend to be more hard-line conservative (especially on foreign policy questions) than other Hispanic-American groups, including Mexicans and Puerto Ricans. One reason is that after Cubans fled to the United States at the time of the Cuban Revolution, Cuban leader Fidel Castro confiscated their property and persecuted family members they had left behind.

Gender and Politics   In American politics, men and women sometimes tend to view government and politics in different ways. Like class and race, gender differences can be important independent correlates of political behavior and opinions. In the United States, it appears that a *gender gap*—differences in the ways men and women think and vote in the aggregate—may exist on some political issues. For instance, in the 1996 general elections, 54 percent of women voted for Bill Clinton while 37 percent voted for Bob Dole, a far different voter profile than that exhibited by men, who split their vote almost evenly between Clinton and Dole (each received 44 percent of the vote). In that same election, 55 percent of women voted Democratic while 54 percent of men voted Republican in House races nationwide.

How can this phenomenon be explained? Some researchers tie gender differences to early family experiences and expectations; others contend that there are innate differences in the way men and women develop moral and political awareness. One theory postulates that due to some combination of socialization and biology, women—as mothers and the primary caregivers for children—tend to develop a moral and political perspective that emphasizes compassion and the protection of human life.[14] An alternate theory holds that gender-based political differences are rooted in *some* women's later life experiences; one recent study on voting patterns found that "married women, and especially married women who never had children, voted very much like men, while single and divorced women formed almost a left-wing proletariat."[15]

Whatever the source of difference, it does not arise primarily from gender-related issues—for example, public opinion surveys have found no differences between men and women regarding civil liberties controversies or other issues of equal rights. One important political difference between the sexes tends to revolve around the government's use of force. Generally, women tend to be more reluctant to support war, more opposed to capital punishment, and more inclined to support gun control. Women also tend to give more support to social welfare programs intended to help families, the working poor, and the economically disadvantaged. These differences help explain why the gender gap has aided Democrats in recent years.

Religion   Either the church or the state may present itself as the true source of moral authority, which makes religion particularly important in the socialization process. And just as religion can influence a young person's developing political opinions, so can politics decisively shape the role of religion within the family and the place it ultimately occupies within the larger political order.

Sometimes religion can legitimize existing practices and lend stability to a society in transition. Hinduism in India, for instance, has proved compatible with changing political institutions. Described by one expert as "a multi-layered complexity allowing for the existence of many gods, many incarnations, many layers of truth,"[16] Hinduism has tended, historically, to support the status quo. Even when the status quo involved systematic discrimination against a lower, "untouchable" class, Hinduism counseled patience and perseverance in anticipation of future lives to come. In other parts of the world, religious doctrine has ignited aggressive policies. In Libya and Iran, for instance, Islamic fundamentalism has helped fuel belligerent foreign policies and contributed to a periodic fervor for war.

Religion and politics sometimes conflict. For example, the Nazi government steamrolled the Lutheran and Catholic churches in Germany. In the former Soviet Union, the regime allowed the historically entrenched Russian Orthodox Church to continue functioning but restricted and monitored its activities, frequently persecuting believers.[17]

In the United States, religion and politics reinforce each other at a number of levels. Although the Supreme Court has interpreted the Constitution to prohibit government from directly supporting religion, the First Amendment also clearly prohibits government from denying an individual's free exercise of religious beliefs. Religion continues to flourish in the United States. "More than 90 percent of all Americans identify with some religious faith, and on any given Sunday morning more than 40 percent are to be found in church." Furthermore, by "most measurable indices the United States is a more religious country than any European nation except Ireland and Poland."[18] Although religion plays a smaller role in the lives of many Americans than it once did, it is still a major force in American society, culture, and politics (see Figure 9-2).

The Judeo-Christian tradition continues to be dominant in the United States, yet there is significant diversity within that tradition. Mainstream Protestant denominations constitute about 30 percent of the population; Roman Catholics, 25 percent; white evangelical Protestant churches, 20 percent; black Protestant churches, 8 percent; and Jews, 3 percent. After the terrorist attacks of September 11, 2001, both the public reaction and the mass media focused attention on the fact that there is also a substantial Muslim minority in the United States.

Some important political differences correlate with these differences in religious orientation, even arising from the religious doctrines themselves. Thus

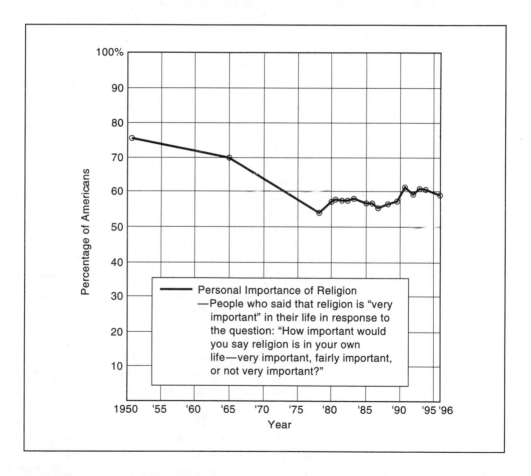

FIGURE 9-2   The Continuing Importance of Religion to Americans, 1952–96
SOURCES: "Influence, Relevance of Religion in Today's Society" (March 28–30, 1994; Survey GO 422041), in *Gallup Poll Monthly,* April 1994, 2–4 and "Importance of Religion," Gallup Poll (November 21–24, 1996).

Quakers and Mennonites tend to be pacifists, while, as previously mentioned, fundamentalist Protestants tend to oppose abortion and Jews generally favor Israel. By the same token, members of black Protestant churches tend to be more politically liberal than Protestants who affiliate with mainstream churches, and members of mainstream churches tend to be more politically liberal than their evangelical Protestant counterparts. More generally, on a scale measuring political conservatism and liberalism, Protestants tend to be somewhat more conservative than Catholics and much more conservative than Jews. Jews and Catholics have historically identified more with the Democratic party, while Protestants have leaned toward the Republican party, though the correlation between religion and party affiliation appears to be weakening.

Arguably, religion also has a utilitarian political value in the United States. In this view, religion benefits public life by providing, in George Washington's words, an "indispensable support" for representative government. By teaching that everyone is equal in God's eyes, religion inculcates a private morality that can elevate public life.

Sometimes political leaders draw on religious imagery to unite citizens in a common understanding of the present or point them toward a more noble vision of the future.[19] For example, the famous American clergyman and civil rights leader Martin Luther King, Jr., inspired the nation with his dream of a day "when all of God's children, black men and white men, Jews and Gentiles, Protestants and Catholics, will be able to join hands and sing in the words of the old Negro spiritual 'Free at last! Free at last! Thank God Almighty, we are free at last.'" The tragic assassination of King, like the assassination of Abraham Lincoln a century earlier, helped to rally the American people to the cause of racial equality.

Osama bin Laden and the al Qaeda terrorism network provided a contemporary example of the dark side of religion and politics in the fall of 2001 when they attempted to unite the world's 1.3 billion Muslims against the "Crusaders" (Christians and Jews) in a *jihad* (holy war). This effort failed, but the fact that bin Laden tried to use religion as a political ideology and as the basis of his movement's propaganda campaign against the West (mainly the United States) is instructive. It demonstrates anew that religion can be placed in the service of the noblest aims or the most evil ones imaginable.

Schools   Schools play a vital role in transmitting *civic education*, the inculcation of fundamental values and beliefs of society, to the young. Through public education, states seek to influence young people before their moral character is fully formed.

All countries use schools as a means of political socialization. Some governments merely prescribe one or two courses in civics or history, require students to salute the flag, and hang pictures of national heroes on school walls. Other governments dictate the entire school curriculum, indoctrinate the children with slogans and shibboleths, heavily censor textbooks and library acquisitions, and subject teachers to loyalty tests.

All states attempt to perpetuate certain core values, but the substance of these values, as well as the methods used to instill them, may vary enormously. Different regimes inculcate different values. Under some regimes (for example, the Soviet Union in the 1930s), blind obedience to authority is the norm. In others, patriotism is encouraged, but so is the habit of critical and independent thinking.

Socialization studies have revealed much about the way children learn politically relevant values in American public schools.[20] During the elementary school years, American children tend to develop positive emotional attachments to key political concepts such as liberty and democracy and respect for others. Also, small children typically think of the government in terms of an authority figure— a police officer, the president, and so on.

As children mature, they begin to react less emotionally and more cognitively, grasping the subtleties of abstract concepts such as democracy. During adolescence and early adulthood, students' attitudes toward government often change radically. As parental supervision recedes and independence grows, children cease to obey authority without question. Increasingly, they want to decide things for themselves—a sentiment that is readily transferable to the political realm.

While some observers consider the typical high school civics class the most important formal training ground for good citizenship, a number of studies have indicated that civics classes are less important than the total context of the student's educational experience.[21] Influential factors include teachers' attitudes toward democracy; the focus of textbooks in presenting positive or negative lessons about the nation's history, culture, economic system, and so on; the overall curriculum; and formal rituals such as reciting the Pledge of Allegiance and singing patriotic songs. Extracurricular activities such as music and sports can convey the importance of responsible participation and working toward a common goal. Work on the school newspaper can highlight the role of the media in public affairs. Debate clubs can familiarize students with political, social, and economic issues and teach them that there are at least two sides to every issue. Finally, participation in student government can introduce students to the fundamental rules of the political process.

In general, the higher the level of education, the greater a student's interest will be in keeping informed about and participating in politics. More precisely, a positive correlation tends to exist between the amount of education and a student's awareness of the impact of government on the individual, interest in following the news, overall knowledge and range of opinions about politics, and desire to discuss politics and to do so with a great number and variety of people. Finally, a high level of education is associated with a strong tendency to believe that one can influence government and with strong feelings of personal self-confidence and trust in others.[22]

The Impact of Higher Education   It is difficult to determine how much higher education affects political socialization. In the United States, the college curriculum often represents a blend of vocational training and liberal arts, the latter (which includes literature, philosophy, science, history, and linguistics) placing great emphasis on the development of critical thinking.[23] Supporters of a *liberal arts education* (combining the study of literature, philosophy, history, and the sciences) emphasize that students are challenged to think clearly, write precisely, and speak correctly. They are also exposed to perennial questions and great ideas in the arts and sciences, and are encouraged to reexamine the moral and material values that comprise the conventional wisdom of the day. Proponents of this view argue that liberal arts students gain the intellectual tools they will need to assume the responsibilities of democratic citizenship.

Some conservative critics of American higher education charge academicians with exhibiting predominantly left-of-center political opinions that affect the content of what is taught and learned. There is some evidence that students' political opinions are influenced by exposure to intellectually challenging books, ideas, and teachers in college; however, it is not clear if the college experience leads directly to more liberal thinking. What it does at its best is to produce adults capable of critical thinking. That said, American college graduates are more prone to support civil liberties and government-sponsored social programs.[24]

The ideal of liberal education fits easily into the scheme of constitutional democracies that protect the right to question authority. Simultaneously, higher levels of education seem most likely to encourage citizens to participate meaningfully in politics.[25] Citizens do not develop the habits or skills of political participation in countries where unquestioning obedience to authority is paramount. Liberal education aims at producing citizens who possess such skills, especially those based on critical thinking. A good citizen in a democratic society praises government when it deserves praise and criticizes government when it warrants criticism. Only in a democratic society, therefore, are independent thinking and public dissent not considered subversive. Recall that the Greek philosopher Socrates was considered subversive and sentenced to death (by self-poisoning) not for teaching his students what to think but for teaching them how to think.

Peer Groups

Most people acknowledge that peer groups exert considerable influence over one's political activities and beliefs, but at least two points must be clarified. First, there is an inherent ambiguity in the meaning of the term. A *peer group* can refer either to a group of people who are friends or to people of similar age and characteristics. In either case, the term focuses on "the tendency for individuals to identify with groups of people like themselves."[26]

A second, more serious, difficulty is that there has been little research in this area. For example, a 1930s study of the effect of peer-group pressure on the political attitudes of women enrolled at Bennington College concluded that the group's influence caused its members to become more liberal. In another example, a 1965 study of high school students compared peer-group and parental influences on different kinds of political issues and found that parental influence was higher on specific political issues—for instance, what party to identify with and whom to vote for in the presidential election. These studies raise as many questions as they answer.[27]

Gender is another peer-group puzzle. We know that young boys tend to associate with other young boys and young girls with other young girls, and we suspect that there are political differences between such groups. For example, third- to eighth-grade boys are thought to have a more mature and less idealistic concept of the presidency than girls of similar age, yet there is no research to support (or refute) this notion.[28]

The relationship between the development of antisocial attitudes by adolescent male lawbreakers and their association with like-minded peer groups (and gangs) is especially interesting in that it points to the difficulty of determining exactly what influence peer groups exert on individual attitudes and beliefs. Here, too, there have been relatively few studies.[29] And although it might seem that the concept of peer groups and gangs is especially important in understanding teenage crime, it is still not clear whether "good" boys (and girls) join the "wrong crowd" and become corrupted by antisocial attitudes among their peers, or whether youth gangs primarily attract criminal types who harbor antisocial attitudes when they join. A close peer-group association, and especially membership in a gang, increases the frequency with which the average teenager commits crimes. Peers and gangs "can affect the value a person assigns to the rewards of crime (by adding the approval of colleagues to the perceived value of the loot or the direct gratification of the act)."[30]

Psychologically, peer groups fulfill a member's need for approval, which affects the formation of political attitudes and beliefs. Generally speaking, peer groups are formed voluntarily and informally. If we expand the peer-group concept to encompass such organizations as the Girl Scouts, the Young Democrats, or a high school journalism club—and then of similar organizations that operate in other political contexts—we make an important discovery. In totalitarian states, where governments attempt to transform the political order by radically reshaping attitudes and beliefs, peer-group structures can be created by the state for the youth as well as adults. These involuntary associations are designed to spread the regime's message and to educate or reeducate citizens. This phenomenon is illustrated in Figure 9-3, which shows how the hierarchy of the Nazi party (designated as PO) was able to direct a large-scale social movement whose ultimate aim was to transfigure German society. Under the National Socialist (NS) party, German life was organized through an elaborate network of centrally controlled "peer groups" to ensure that every German would, in time, adopt "correct" political attitudes and be properly socialized into the new Nazi state. Similarly, the Communist party of the Soviet Union created an all-encompassing set of centrally controlled social organizations (in the guise of clubs and civic associations).

The Mass Media

The mass media also play a significant role in the political socialization, and continuing education, of citizens. In nondemocratic states, the *mass media* (television, radio, newspapers, and large-circulation magazines) are almost always owned or controlled by the state. Even some democratic governments monopolize radio and television broadcasting (as in Denmark) or own and operate television networks (as in Great Britain). In such cases, the principal difference between nondemocratic and democratic states is that democratic states pass laws or adopt

FIGURE 9-3   Organizations in the Nazi Movement

SOURCE: Mark N. Hagopian, *Regimes, Movements, and Ideologies,* 2nd ed. (White Plains, N.Y.: Longman, 1984).

procedures designed to ensure the fairness and objectivity of the media. And in the United States, where almost all television and radio networks and most individual stations are privately owned, the Federal Communications Commission, a regulatory agency charged with determining policy for the national licensing of radio and television stations, has from time to time promulgated regulations to guarantee evenhandedness in political broadcasting. Rules designed to discourage undesirable or unhealthy behavior have been promulgated as well. For that reason, television stations in the United States are not permitted to broadcast commercials for cigarettes.

In highly industrialized nations over the past several decades, the so-called electronic media (radio and television) have gained ascendancy. Controversy rages in the United States over the growing influence of television. Some Americans, including some congressional representatives, worry about excessive television violence and its influence on citizen behavior. Other critics point out that television is mindless, vulgar, or too sexually explicit.

Yet another troublesome area is the use of mass media in the political process. For instance, television political advertising has become increasingly important as Americans read fewer newspapers and attend fewer political party functions.[31] The high cost of such advertising, the number of challengers discouraged by it, its effectiveness, and the extent to which its content is determined by media considerations and media consultants are important issues because they can (and often do) affect the quality not only of the campaigns but also of the candidates.

Equally worrying is the content of the commercials themselves. Since the mid-1970s, American political campaigns have become increasingly dominated by short, emotional, attack-style advertisements (as opposed to the documentary-style ads more common earlier); almost always they are simple, symbolic, and personalized. Frequently, they feature dark colors, foreboding music, deep voices, and negatively perceived individual or group symbols. They typically attack the integrity, motives, or record of political candidates.

The way news is presented, particularly on television, is also highly suspect. Some conservative critics contend that television news (and the media generally) often reflects the political agenda or ideas of the journalists and broadcasters, who are predominantly liberal. Also, radio and television are often exceedingly superficial and sensationalistic. They look for bad news rather than important news. Television coverage of election campaigns, for example, stresses candidates' attempts to gain strategic advantage instead of focusing on the policies and ideas they stand for, often singling out inconsistencies and blunders—a president stumbling and falling down the steps of the presidential helicopter or getting sick and vomiting at a formal state dinner in Japan. Meanwhile, anyone can exploit the new Internet technology, establishing Web sites that sometimes spread gossip while speculating about the private lives of public officials. It is little wonder that the media is blamed for the sharp rise in public cynicism over the past four decades. Indeed, one mainstream political scientist believes "that the United States cannot have a sensible campaign as long as it is built around the news media."[32]

Because network and cable television is a business whose profits depend on maintaining high audience ratings, television news tends to emphasize entertainment and drama at the expense of substance. For instance, it is not uncommon for the evening news to show a spirited exchange between a key witness and a Senate committee chair while glossing over the substance of the testimony. This is a conscious corporate decision. Television executives know that conflict and confrontation are entertaining and that, as a rule, bad news makes good ratings. For this reason also, television almost always emphasizes the "horse race" aspect of presidential elections, dwelling on who is ahead, who gained, and who lost because of this gaffe or that revelation. The networks compete vigorously to call the election minutes ahead of other networks. For many citizens, therefore, the race itself now takes center stage in presidential campaigns and elections rather than the issues.

Moreover, in its nightly news programs, television stations today communicate less and less information about American political leaders. In one study of network news coverage conducted between 1968 and 1988, the average length of presidential quotations decreased from forty-five seconds to nine seconds.[33] A

Negative Advertising—Fair or Foul Play?

Increasingly, the mass media broadcast negative political advertisements. These ads may or may not be entirely truthful, but they are often very effective. Sometimes viewed as a kind of political ambush, they are the product of extensive research into the backgrounds of political opponents and are aired at strategic times during the campaign.

Consider the case of Sandra Schultz Newman, who sought election to a Pennsylvania judgeship in the fall of 1993. Newman, an attorney from a Philadelphia suburb, had no prior political experience, but she hired a father–son political consulting team. Her opponent, Joseph Mistick, was better known. He was a Pittsburgh attorney who had worked in the mayor's office and had been a member of local zoning and planning boards.

Newman's consulting team employed researchers to investigate Mistick's past record. The researchers uncovered a six-year-old story from a defunct Pittsburgh newspaper. The story suggested that when Mistick served on the Pittsburgh zoning commission, he may have ruled as many as forty times in favor of his business partner's interest. Newman's campaign team then prepared a thirty-second commercial charging Mistick with political impropriety. The commercial was not aired until several days before the end of the campaign, leaving Mistick with little time to respond. Newman won the election, while Mistick, in defeat, denied that he had done anything wrong as a member of the zoning panel.

SOURCE: Adapted from James M. Perry, "Young Guns: A Second Generation of Political Handlers Outduels Forebears," *Wall Street Journal*, January 10, 1994, A6. Reprinted by permission of the *Wall Street Journal*, Copyright © 1994, Dow Jones & Company, Inc. All rights reserved worldwide.

short introduction from the reporter and a relatively long presidential pronouncement was reversed as the reporter's introduction and comments significantly overshadowed the president's comments. Television stations at the local level now follow this same practice (they also depend heavily—too heavily—on network feeds for reporting national news). Candidates and campaign managers, aware of this shift in news coverage, now routinely prepare clever quotations, called sound bites, in an attempt to capitalize on the media's superficial and often glitzy news coverage. In-depth analysis, critics say, has become a casualty of Madison Avenue marketing techniques, the Nielsen ratings, and outright manipulation by highly paid professionals—political gurus, media consultants, and spin-doctors (public relations specialists).

Another disturbing trend evident in recent television news coverage is the drift toward so-called tabloid journalism. The media's emphasis on rumor and innuendo, often used as a vehicle to discuss the sleazier elements of stories, as well as its seeming emphasis on the perverse and unusual—especially regarding highly publicized trials—has blurred the difference between sensationalist weeklies and straight news. This type of coverage, pandering to the most prurient of viewer interests, may even crowd out the more legitimate, complex news from the airways.

Although such criticisms have merit, they need to be tempered. Television is a highly competitive industry profoundly influenced by consumer tastes and preferences. Thus, the news is entertaining because viewers want it to be entertaining. Moreover, because the average viewer has a short attention span, television news

GATEWAYS TO THE WORLD: EXPLORING CYBERSPACE

http://www.politicsol.com/quiz.html
http://www.cnsnews.com/cnsquiz/welcome.asp

Did this chapter make you think about how you have been socialized? How politically knowledgeable a citizen are you? These two sites provide a political I.Q. Quiz geared specifically to American politics. The quizzes are offered as enticements to visit the home pages, an increasingly common practice on the Web. When you take the quizzes, spend a little time checking out the information found at each of the locations.

http://www.icpsr.umich.edu/GSS

This site provides access to public opinion data from the General Social Survey. Here, students can examine—and even perform calculations on—actual data from the archives at the Inter-University Consortium for Political and Social Research [ICPSR] housed in Ann Arbor at the University of Michigan.

http://www.umich.edu/~nes/nesguide/nesguide.htm

Also from ICPSR, this site from the National Elections Studies provides an excellent source of information about the demographic and behavioral aspects of the American electorate and its development over time.

---

directors spotlight the razzle-dazzle of video technology, flashy computer graphics, and fast-paced interviews, and rapidly change stories, locations, and camera angles. Television executives understand that viewers prefer the news in predigested snippets. After a hard day's work, most viewers are not in the mood for a debate over some complex political issue, and political issues tend to be complex.

The media's tendency to focus on negative news serves as a reminder that freedom of speech and criticism of the government are protected rights in liberal democracies. Indeed, the content of newspapers and of radio and television news broadcasts in any given country is one indicator of how much freedom exists there. Where criticism of the government is allowed, freedom is usually the norm. In the final analysis, the mass media in democratic states are both gauge and guarantor of individual freedom.

The Law

Although the law in some societies reflects citizens' values and attitudes, it often helps to form them as well. Of course, some laws simply promote public order (driving on the right side of the street, for example). Other laws, however, prohibit behavior that society regards as inherently evil, such as laws against murder, pedophilia, theft, and racial discrimination. The passage and enforcement of such statutes sends a message to society (and especially to its youngest members, whose moral sensibilities are shaped by such rules) that murder, false advertising, theft, and racial discrimination are wrong in the eyes of the law and will be punished. To the extent that this message is received, understood, and acted on, it influences citizens' political socialization.

Key Political Values: Striking the Right (or Left?) Balance

A nation's political culture is underpinned by the fundamental values its people hold dear. These values need not be entirely consistent and may even conflict at times. In addition, individuals' day-to-day political beliefs and actions need not always conform to the standard (and often do not).[34] However, a coherent political culture requires that political values exist, be widely recognized, and serve as a yardstick for measuring the politics and policies of government. The mere existence of these shared values infuses a given society's version of civic virtue into the socialization of prospective citizens. This process also governs the pace at which the nation's basic political values evolve in light of changing circumstances (including science and technology). Above all, commonly held values are the best insurance a society has against chronic (or even episodic) instability.

In the United States, private values correlate highly with key public (or civic) values.[35] Americans profess a strong belief in such fundamental liberal values as personal freedom, political equality, private ownership of property, and religious tolerance. Not only are these values expressed in the nation's fundamental documents and writings, including the Declaration of Independence, the Constitution, and *The Federalist*, but they are also instilled in America's youth by a variety of socialization strategies.

In other democratic societies, the process of socialization works the same way and serves the same purposes as it does in the United States, but the *expression* of such core values as liberty, equality, security, prosperity, and justice (see Chapter 13), as well as the precise content and balance among them, will vary significantly from one country to another. For example, in the Scandinavian countries (and Europe in general), equality has a decidedly social (or class) dimension as well as a political one (civil rights). As a result, the state provides a much wider range of social services (for example, guaranteed universal health care for all) than is the case in the United States. By the same token, liberty in many European countries does not impede the police in criminal investigations the way it sometimes does in the United States, nor does it, for example, prevent the state from implementing tough antiterrorist measures (such as the use of heavily armed military personnel and professional screeners at major international airports).

WHEN POLITICAL SOCIALIZATION FAILS

When a multiethnic nation fails to socialize (politically) large numbers of citizens as members of a single community (in effect, a new nation), the consequences are far-reaching. If there are multiple communities there will be multiple processes going on and multiple political cultures being perpetuated. Members of the various subnational communities will not be successfully integrated into the political system, and they will not share the norms, rules, and laws of the society.

A breakdown of this kind can threaten the very survival of multiethnic or otherwise internally divided societies striving to become nation-states. The frequency of student protests around the world in recent decades suggests that the political socialization of young people may not be as effective in many societies as it once was. For example, students in South Korea since 1987 have staged mass protests, frequently involving violent clashes with the police. Many of these students have apparently rejected the entire system, not just particular policies. In the United States, race riots in Los Angeles in 1992 as well as more recent demonstrations against the World Bank (for example, in Seattle in 2000) conveyed a similar message of alienation and mistrust toward the U.S. government.

Some citizens may never become fully socialized politically. A political regime's failure to socialize its citizens may result from unequal or unfair government treatment of those citizens. In such cases, citizens may become angry, cynical, or embittered, or they may even turn to crime or revolution. In extreme cases of unjust, tyrannical government, citizens' "crimes" may be viewed as actions taken justifiably. Thus, while the failure of political socialization is always detrimental to the government in power, the moral and political implications of that failure are not always as easy to evaluate.

Summary

Different governments treat the concept of citizenship in different ways. All states demand adherence to their rules (laws) of course, and most treat birth in, or naturalization into, the political order as a sine qua non of citizenship. In democratic states, the concept of citizenship is also tied to the ideas of equality and liberty, as well as meaningful participation (periodic elections, for example) in politics. This ideal of democratic citizenship dates back to the ancient Greek city-states, which were small enough to permit direct democracy (self-representation of enfranchised adults through public assemblies and plebiscites).

How are citizens formed? Political socialization is the process by which citizens develop the values, attitudes, beliefs, and opinions that enable them to relate to and function within the political system. Specific influences on the developing citizen include the family, religion, public education, the mass media, the law, peer groups, and key political values. Political socialization is of paramount importance; if a nation fails to socialize its citizenry on a large-scale basis, the nation's political stability can be endangered.

Key Terms

citizenship
political socialization
gender gap
civic education

liberal arts education
peer group
mass media

Review Questions

1. Why has the concept of citizenship been of central importance to Aristotle and other political thinkers?

2. In what contrasting ways can citizenship be defined? Which definition best describes your understanding of citizenship? Explain.

3. It is sometimes argued that true citizenship can be found only in a democracy. What is the meaning of this statement?

4. What factors influence the political socialization of citizens?

Recommended Reading

ALMOND, GABRIEL, and SIDNEY VERBA. *The Civic Culture: Political Attitudes and Democracy in Five Nations.* Princeton, N.J.: Princeton University Press, 1963. An influential comparative study of politics and political culture in the United States, Great Britain, the former West Germany, Italy, and Mexico.

BENNETT, LANCE W. *News: The Politics of Illusion.* 2nd ed. White Plains, N.Y.: Longman, 1988. An intriguing analysis of television news which argues that everyday viewers tend to be more trusting and hence more frequently misled than less frequent and more skeptical viewers.

GLENDON, MARY ANN and DAVID BLANKENHORN, eds. *Seedbeds of Virtue: Sources of Competence, Character, and Citizenship in American Society.* Lanham, Md.: University Press of America, 1995. Thoughtful essays discuss the role of virtue and values in the contemporary formation of the American character.

HOLLOWAY, HARRY, and JOHN GEORGE. *Public Opinion.* 2nd ed. New York: St. Martin's Press, 1985. A thoughtful general introduction to the American political culture.

JAROS, DEAN. *Socialization to Politics.* New York: Praeger, 1973. A short description of the process of political socialization.

KERN, MONTAGUE. *Thirty-Second Politics: Political Advertising in the Eighties.* Westport, Ct.: Greenwood, 1989. A detailed and disturbing analysis of contemporary political advertising on television.

LIPSET, SEYMOUR MARTIN. *American Exceptionalism: A Double-Edged Sword.* New York: Norton, 1996. According to Lipset, American exceptionalism resides in its culture and its creed, including liberalism, individualism, egalitarianism, populism, voluntarism, and moralism.

PATTERSON, THOMAS E. *Out of Order.* New York: Vintage, 1994. The author makes a convincing case that the media has distorted and undermined the integrity of U.S. elections.

REICHLEY, A. JAMES. *Religion in American Public Life.* Washington, D.C.: Brookings Institution, 1985. The best discussion available of religion's historical influence in the United States.

ROELOFS, H. MARK. *The Tension of Citizenship: Private Man and Public Duty.* New York: Rinehart, 1957. A discussion of the development of various conceptions of citizenship.

WALD, KENNETH. *Religion and Politics in the United States.* 3rd ed. Washington, D.C.: C.Q. Press, 1996. A comprehensive account of the relationship between public life and religion in contemporary America.

WALZER, MICHAEL. *Obligations: Essays on Disobedience, War, and Citizenship.* Cambridge, Mass.: Harvard University Press, 1982. A collection of philosophical essays dealing with the meaning of citizenship by one of the United States' leading socialist thinkers.

WILSON, JAMES Q. *The Moral Sense.* New York: Free Press, 1995. How is it that people come to act morally? Wilson fuses theory and social science research in an attempt to come to an answer.

YERIC, JERRY L., and JOHN R. TODD. *Public Opinion: The Visible Politics.* 3rd ed. Itasca, Ill.: Peacock, 1995. A clearly written summary of public opinion research.

Notes

1. Aristotle, *The Politics,* trans. and ed. Ernest Barker (New York: Oxford University Press, 1962), 1276b, 101–102.
2. Ibid., 1274b, 93.
3. Immanuel Kant, *The Science of Right,* vol. 42 (Chicago: Encyclopaedia Britannica, 1952), 436.
4. The modern study of political socialization is closely tied to the Greek concern for character formation. One key difference between the two is that whereas behavioral political science focuses primarily on the process by which political opinions are formed, the Greek emphasis is on the traits of character that all good citizens should display.
5. John Stuart Mill, *A System of Logic, Ratiocinative and Deductive,* vol. 2 (London: Longmans, Green, 1879), 518.
6. Persuasive evidence is provided by Barbara Defoe Whitehead, "Dan Quayle Was Right," *Atlantic* (April 1993), 41. However, single-parent families are only one source of why some families fail. Note James Q. Wilson's comment that one way "the family has become weaker is that more and more children are being raised in one-parent families, and often that one parent is a teenage girl. Another way is that parents, whether in one- or two-parent families, are spending less time with their children and are providing poorer discipline." For a thoughtful review of two-parent families, in light of the academic debate on the subject, see James Q. Wilson, "The Family-Values Debate," *Commentary* (April 1993), 24–31. The quotation is from page 24.
7. See James Q. Wilson, *The Moral Sense* (New York: Free Press, 1995), 141–163.
8. Harry Holloway and John George, *Public Opinion,* 2nd ed. (New York: St. Martin's Press, 1985), 73–77.
9. Herbert Winter and Thomas Bellows, *People and Politics* (New York: Wiley, 1977), 120.
10. Dean Jaros, *Socialization to Politics* (New York: Praeger, 1973), 87–88.
11. Ibid., 83.
12. See M. Margaret Conway and Frank Fergert, *Political Analysis: An Introduction* (Boston: Allyn & Bacon, 1972), 106.
13. Holloway and George, *Public Opinion,* 79.
14. See M. Kent Jennings, "Preface"; Henry Kenst, "The Gender Factor in a Changing Electorate"; and Arthur Miller, "Gender and the Vote," in *The Politics of the Gender Gap: The Social Construction of Political Influence,* ed. Carol Mueller (Newbury Park, Calif.: Sage, 1987). Much of the political literature advocating natural differences between the sexes presumes the existence of scholarship in the field of developmental psychology; see Carol Gilligan, *In a Different Voice* (Cambridge, Mass.: Harvard University Press, 1982); and M. Belenky, B. Clinchy, W. Goldberger, and J. Tarule,

Women's Ways of Knowing: The Development of Self, Voice, and Mind (New York: Basic Books, 1986).

15. Michael Barone and Grant Ujifusa, *The Almanac of American Politics, 1994* (Washington, D.C.: National Journal, 1994), xxvii.

16. Ralph Buuljens, "India: Religion, Political Legitimacy, and the Secular State," *Annals of Political and Social Sciences* 483 (January 1986): 107.

17. James Billington, "The Case for Orthodoxy," *New Republic,* May 30, 1994, 26.

18. A. James Reichley, *Religion in American Public Life* (Washington, D.C.: Brookings Institution, 1985), 2.

19. This is not to deny, of course, that religion can be exploited by unscrupulous leaders for ignoble purposes.

20. This discussion builds on William Flanigan and Nancy Zingale, *Political Behavior of the American Electorate* (Boston: Allyn & Bacon, 1979), 184–187.

21. Kenneth Langton and M. Kent Jennings, "Political Socialization and the High School Civics Curriculum," *American Political Science Review* (September 1968): 851.

22. Conway and Fergert, *Political Analysis,* 110. Also see Judith Torney-Purta, "From Attitudes and Knowledge to Schemata: Expanding the Outcomes at Political Socialization Research," in *Political Socialization, Citizenship Education, and Democracy,* ed. Orit Ichilov (New York: Teachers College Press, 1990), 99.

23. Or so it would seem. Still it is important to determine not only what is studied but also how it is studied. See Albert Speer's comments on German education in Albert Speer, *Inside the Third Reich,* trans. R. Winston and C. Winston (New York: Avon, 1971), 35.

24. Robert Erikson, Norman Luttbeg, and Kent Tedin, *American Public Opinion* (New York: Macmillan, 1991), 113.

25. Ibid., 7.

26. This is commonly recognized. See James MacGregor Burns, J.W. Peltason, Thomas E. Cronin, and David B. Magleby, *Government by the People,* 17th ed. (Upper Saddle River, N.J.: Prentice Hall, 1998), 293.

27. Ibid., 49–50.

28. Richard Dawson et al., *Political Socialization,* 2nd ed. (Boston: Little, Brown, 1977), 62–63.

29. James Q. Wilson and Richard Hernstein, *Crime and Human Nature* (New York: Simon & Schuster, 1985), 293.

30. Ibid., 311.

31. This section builds on the analysis offered in Montague Kern, *Thirty-Second Politics: Political Advertising in the Eighties* (New York: Praeger, 1989).

32. Thomas E. Patterson, *Out of Order* (New York: Vintage, 1994), 25.

33. Daniel Hallin's study is cited as part of a wider discussion of the issue in Samuel Popkin, *The Reasoning Voter: Communication and Persuasion in Presidential Campaigns* (Chicago: University of Chicago Press, 1991), 228–229.

34. Hence the author of one famous behavioral study concluded, "the principles of freedom and democracy are less widely and enthusiastically favored when they are confronted in their specific or applied forms." See Herbert McCloskey, "Consensus and Ideology in American Democracy," *American Political Science Review* 58 (June 1964): 361–384.

35. Donald Devine, *The Political Culture of the United States* (Boston: Little, Brown, 1972), 187–230. Also see Seymour Martin Lipset, *American Exceptionalism: A Double-Edged Sword* (New York: Norton, 1996) for an extensive discussion of the values comprising the American creed.

Chapter 10

POLITICAL PARTICIPATION

THE PRICE OF INFLUENCE

IN CHAPTER 9 we learned that true citizenship involves meaningful participation in politics. To be meaningful, participation must *at a minimum* be voluntary and consequential. Although political participation might appear rather straightforward, a closer look reveals some ironies. For example, participation is pervasive in totalitarian societies, where it is meaningless, because the state commands everybody to participate, as by voting for the ruling party's hand-picked candidates in phony national elections. By contrast, political participation is hit-and-miss in democratic countries, where citizens are free *not* to participate.

Many Americans hold certain unexamined assumptions about democracy and political participation:

- The more citizens participate, the healthier the democracy.
- Participation is *natural*; that is, citizens want to participate.
- The average voter is *knowledgeable*; that is, participants know and understand the political choices they make.
- Public opinion matters.

We will take a closer look at these assumptions after examining the various ways in which citizens participate in the political process.

FORMS OF PARTICIPATION

Citizens who wish to participate in politics have two alternatives—they can engage in legal or illegal activities. Most citizens choose to participate legally or not at all.

Legal Forms

The most familiar types of political participation involve legal activities within the framework of existing institutions. Most citizens participate in politics in largely symbolic, passive, or ritualistic ways—for example, attending a political rally, responding to a political poll, writing a letter to the editor of the local newspaper, or putting a bumper sticker on their car.

Voting constitutes the most visible form of *conventional participation*. However, the effectiveness of voting as a measure of active citizen participation depends on a number of factors: the extent to which votes are counted fairly, the size of the electorate (the larger the number of voters, the less impact each individual vote has), and the availability of meaningful choices. Voting can convey an important message; it can even be a powerful or amusing form of peaceful protest. In 1959, for example, dissatisfied citizens of São Paulo, Brazil, elected a rhinoceros in the local zoo to the city council![1] Similarly, the past three decades have witnessed a proliferation of issue-oriented initiatives and referendums in the United States; during that time, state voters have judged the wisdom (or folly) of issues as divergent as reducing or freezing property taxes, determining the level of legal protection afforded homosexual men and women, and requiring the use of seat belts and motorcycle helmets.

Perhaps one-quarter of the citizens in the United States are more or less actively involved in politics.[2] Many of these political activists contribute time and money to a political party, belong to public interest groups (such as the American Civil Liberties Union, Common Cause, or the Sierra Club), and do volunteer campaign work for their favorite candidates. Also, many citizens serve on governmental bodies, especially at the state and local level. Often these citizens are unpaid. In fact, there are many local governments in the United States that have no salaried employees. Public service at the local level can function as a school for future political professionals, providing valuable firsthand experience in the procedures, norms, and practices of governing.

Political activists are fairly rare in the United States, but those who seek full-time careers in politics are even rarer. This group includes people who exercise authority through paid political positions or elective office (party officials, lobbyists, political appointees, staffers, legislators, and the like). Of course, not all public officials start out as professional politicians. Indeed, in democratic societies relatively inexperienced candidates occasionally get elected to high office.

Any form of political action that is legal but nonetheless considered inappropriate by a majority of citizens is *unconventional participation.* Of course, acceptable political behavior depends on the prevailing political culture and varies widely from one country to another. In the United States, where most citizens place a high value on law and order, the majority has traditionally disapproved of protests and demonstrations. This pattern changed somewhat during the turbulent 1960s and early 1970s, a period of upheaval marked by the racial strife of the Civil Rights movement and the widespread student protests against the Vietnam War. However, even after the Watergate scandal forced President Richard Nixon to resign in 1974, only 8 percent of the public endorsed demonstrations of any sort, whether as sit-ins, mass marches, rallies, or other attempts to obstruct government activity.[3]

In that same year, a study found that out of ten forms of unconventional political action, a majority of U.S. citizens approved of only three: signing petitions, engaging in lawful demonstrations, and supporting boycotts (such as not buying lettuce to show solidarity with underpaid migrant workers).[4] Only 2 percent of those surveyed believed that violence was justified to achieve political aims. Support for milder forms of unconventional participation is much higher so long as the action in question does not approach the line between legality and illegality.

Illegal Forms

Political regimes differ widely in what actions they classify as *illegal participation* and in how severely they punish such behavior. Authoritarian governments normally outlaw a great many more political activities than do democratic ones. For example, under democratic rule, few, if any, political parties are declared ille-

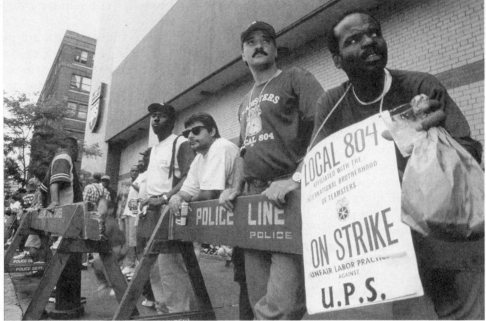

Michael Sofronski / Sipa Press

Lawful demonstrations are a form of political protest considered appropriate by most Americans. Pictured here is the 1997 strike against United Parcel Service.

gal, and citizens usually can affiliate with any party they choose. Under totalitarian rule, all parties except one are illegal. Moreover, authoritarian governments often define "political crimes" more broadly and punish the perpetrators of such crimes more harshly than their democratic counterparts.

Some illegal acts—in particular, those classified as *civil disobedience*—are intended to stir a nation's conscience (and, therefore, are more effective in some nations than in others). Civil disobedience involves breaking specific laws to demonstrate their injustice. Mahatma Gandhi (1869–1948) used civil disobedience in the struggle for India's independence from Great Britain; similarly, Martin Luther King, Jr. (1929–1968), advocated nonviolent protest in the push for racial equality in the United States.

Civil disobedience stresses nonviolence and encourages participants to accept their punishment as legitimate. At the other end of the spectrum stand political *terrorism,* using violence or threats of violence to demoralize, intimidate, and subjugate opponents; *subversion,* attempting to undermine a government, often with outside assistance; and *sedition,* inciting rebellious, antigovernmental acts. All are revolutionary actions. Depending on the regime, however, subversion or sedition can be defined as anything from attending an illegal meeting or joining an outlawed political party to publishing a pamphlet critical of the government or merely holding opinions at odds with official policy or ideology. In many authoritarian nations, any kind of opposition to the government can be considered subversive, even something as innocuous as writing a letter to a friend that includes implicit criticism of the regime in power.

Premeditated terrorist acts against the government are always revolutionary. Such acts are illegal even in countries ruled by self-styled revolutionary regimes (see Chapter 15).

DEFINING CITIZEN PARTICIPATION

Citizens in democracies participate in politics by expressing opinions and casting votes. Polls focus attention on public opinion and give it clear definition. We turn first to *public opinion.*

Public Opinion

Polls showing a clear preference or dramatic shift in public opinion can influence decisions, actions, and policies of government officials. In democracies, public opinion attains legitimacy from the fact that government is responsible to the voters. Public opinion derives its power to influence policy from the desire of politicians to get elected to office and then to hang onto it as long as possible. But when public opinion is divided, which is often the case, elected officials can often afford to ignore it.

Measuring public opinion and gauging its influence can be elusive. Its influence is maximized when: (1) a significant number of citizens actually hold preferences regarding particular issues and are not simply indifferent to them; (2) it is stable over time; (3) it is unevenly distributed or lopsided in a particular direction; (4) it is felt intensely; and (5) the issue it revolves around is salient; that is, voters consider it a high priority.

To what extent ought leaders look to citizen opinion when making important policy decisions? In pondering this question, keep in mind that public opinion often is less a distillate of rational judgment than a collection of inklings, hunches, and guesses made on the basis of prejudices, preconceptions, and scanty information by individuals who are not paying close attention most of the time.

Polls

All governments make some effort to assess and analyze public opinion. In democratic states, public opinion on a variety of issues is gauged and discussed freely, and efforts to identify the majority opinion on any particular issue are undertaken not only by public agencies but also by political parties and candidates, the media, various private organizations and research institutes, and inquiring scholars. To determine how the public stands on a given issue, organizations rely on *public opinion polling* (canvassing citizens for their opinions), which has become the most popular and accurate means of defining and charting changes in public opinion.

The first attempts to measure public opinion were the *straw polls* (unscientific opinion samples) developed by newspapers in the nineteenth century. These polls, however crude, often correctly predicted the winner. On the local level, newspapers, radio, and television still use straw polls today. The main problem with them is that there is no way of knowing whether the sample in such a poll is at all representative of the population as a whole. Usually it is not.

The *Literary Digest* poll that predicted Alf Landon would defeat Franklin D. Roosevelt in 1936 is the most famous example of how an unscientific survey can have disastrous results—in this case, for the magazine that published it. Where did this particular poll go wrong? The names in the sample were taken from the telephone directory and automobile registration lists—two very unrepresentative rosters at the time because only rich people could afford telephones and cars in the 1930s (during the Great Depression). Using this same sampling method, however, the *Literary Digest* had correctly predicted the outcome of the three previous presidential elections. In 1936, however, the poll missed by a mile: Roosevelt won by a landslide.

Incidentally, that was the end of the *Literary Digest*'s polling and, for all practical purposes, of the *Literary Digest* itself. In 1938, it went out of business.

Over the past few decades, public opinion polling has grown increasingly sophisticated. Most polls ask individuals whether they approve or disapprove of a statement or policy. Some polls ask citizens to identify their preferences from among various policy alternatives (though it is commonly recognized that this method tends to overstate the number of people who hold political opinions). Through such polling techniques, researchers predict the actions of a large population based on the answers given by a relatively small number of respondents. In the preferred method of polling, a ***random sampling*** of citizens is taken from among the entire population (or "universe") being polled. (Statisticians have determined that a sample of 1,500 respondents is ideal for polls involving large numbers of people.) In a cross-section of this kind, differences in age, race, religion, political orientation, education, and other factors will approximate those found within the larger population.

The Political Uses (and Abuses) of Polls

Traditionally, polls measured public opinion *after* political leaders took positions or enacted legislation. Increasingly in election campaigns, however, polling has become future oriented, used to determine what positions candidates *ought* to take, or how positions are to be advanced, or what political advertisements will project positive candidate images. This is sometimes called ***strategic polling***.

In order to gauge whether a political advertisement or position will be popular, ***focus groups,*** small numbers of people led by a professional communications expert, are employed to react to and discuss particular agenda items. More recently, electronic polling has involved ***dial groups***, where individuals are given a dial on which to register instant approval or disapproval.

Strategic polling, even among incumbents, has become a fact of political life since the presidency of Jimmy Carter. President Bill Clinton relied on polls extensively to determine what issues to emphasize and how to present them.

Because it is not always possible to conduct hundreds of separate interviews, pollsters sometimes use smaller, preselected samples based on such key characteristics as age, religion, income, and party affiliation. This method of polling is known as *stratified sampling*. Exit polling, which permits the television networks to predict political winners as the polls close, illustrates two levels of stratified polling. First, pollsters identify precincts that statistically approximate the larger political entity (a congressional district, a state, or the nation). Then those who conduct the exit interviews try to select a sample that reflects the overall characteristics of the precinct.

In *tracking polls*, often conducted by candidates for public office, the same voters are sampled repeatedly during the course of a campaign. Such polls seek to determine shifts in voter sentiment and correlate them with media strategy, changing issues, candidates' gaffes, and so forth. Tracking polls are designed to inform candidates which strategies are working (and which are not) in any particular campaign. This kind of strategic polling is frequently used in conjunction with focus groups and other campaign instruments.

Polls are usually quite accurate, but they are hardly infallible; even the best polls may contain errors. Generally, they have a margin of error of 3 percent at the .05 level of confidence, which means that 95 out of 100 times the error is no more than 3 percent in either direction. The exact wording of a given instrument is particularly important on issues where most people do not have well-formed opinions; given a choice between two policy alternatives (for example, "Should the federal government see to it that all people have housing, or should individuals provide for their own housing?"), some respondents can be so influenced by the order in which the policies are mentioned that a 30 percent variance between the two choices may result, depending solely on which policy alternative is given first in the question.[5] Furthermore, asking the same question in such a way that only one side of the issue is mentioned (for example, "Should the federal government see to it that all people have adequate housing?") is likely to produce a significantly greater level of agreement with the policy and the question than phrasing it to include policy alternatives.

The danger of drawing conclusions from the results of a single poll is nicely illustrated in Figure 10-1 ("Same Poll, Different Results"). This example also shows how polls can be used not only to *measure* public opinion but also to *influence* it. For instance, if respondents are asked a question which describes smoking in terms of freedom to exercise a personal choice it will yield a higher rate of approval than if they are asked a similar question which mentions the danger that smoking presents to the health of others. Candidates, corporations, and other organized interest groups of all kinds who wish to demonstrate the popularity of a given position or product can often obtain the results they want through careful phrasing of the questions. Unfortunately, stacking the deck in this way is a common practice in both the public and private sectors.

For better or worse, polling has played an increasingly prominent role in presidential election campaigns. During the 1996 election, CNN alone commissioned some 200 polls. Contrast this with the 1992 presidential election campaign, when all media outlets combined commissioned between 125 and 150 polls.[6] Over a

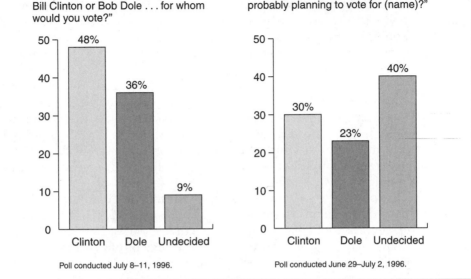

FIGURE 10-1   Same Poll: Different Results

These two polls were conducted at almost the same time, but the results are dramatically different, a fact attributable, at least in part, to differences in the wording of the question.

SOURCE: *The Polling Company National Survey,* reprinted from John H. Fund, "The Perils of Polling," *Wall Street Journal,* August 13, 1996, A12. Reprinted by permission of the *Wall Street Journal.* Copyright © 1996 by Dow Jones & Company, Inc. All rights reserved worldwide.

longer time period, the prominence of polling has grown dramatically. One authority noted that between Labor Day and Election Day in 1968, only 10 national polls asked voters the question "How would you vote if the presidential election were being held today?" By the 1996 presidential election, 300 national polls asked that question.[7]

Public opinion polling has become more reliable in recent years. For example, in the 2000 presidential race between George W. Bush and Al Gore, both the CNN/USA Today/Gallup poll and the CNN/Time poll on the eve of the election predicted a dead heat. In the end, Bush captured enough electoral votes to claim victory by carrying Florida in a contested and controversial election that was ultimately decided by the Supreme Court. Gore actually received more votes than Bush nationwide. The polls were vindicated even if the voters were not.

Still, polls are not always accurate, or equally accurate, as is demonstrated by Table 10-1. All political polling involves certain hazards. First, polls are only snapshots of public opinion, and public opinion is subject to rapid changes. Second, as polling has become more widespread and intrusive, citizens are becoming less cooperative. Third, there are important methodological differences among the

TABLE 10-1

Final Poll Projections, 1996 Presidential Election

Polling Organization	Clinton	Dole	Perot	Margin of Victory
CBS/*New York Times*	53%	35%	9%	18
Pew Research	49%	36%	8%	13
ABC News	51%	39%	7%	12
Harris	51%	39%	7%	12
NBC/*Wall Street Journal*	49%	37%	9%	12
USA Today/CNN/Gallup	52%	41%	7%	11
HOTLINE/Battleground	45%	36%	8%	9
Reuters/Zogby	49%	41%	8%	8
ACTUAL RESULTS	49%	41%	8%	8

SOURCE: From Everett C. Ladd's "The Pollster's Waterloo" in the *Wall Street Journal* (November 19, 1995), p. A–22. Data provided by the Roper Center for Public Opinion, University of Connecticut. Reprinted with permission of the author.

various polls. Polls conducted between elections can rival in importance the polls conducted during election campaigns. For example, a president's popularity, as measured in public opinion polls, helps to determine how much political influence the chief executive can wield on a wide range of political issues. The same holds true for relations between the president and Congress, especially when the opposing party has a majority in one or both houses.

Elections

Meaningful elections give polling its most important political justifications and uses. Without elections, the political uses of polls would be far more limited.

Functions of Elections   Surprisingly, elections serve different functions in different political systems. Under most military dictatorships, regular elections simply do not take place—a reflection of the minimal, or nonexistent, citizen participation in such regimes. If elections are held in totalitarian states, they exist as an empty political ritual, allowing rulers to legitimize their authority. In constitutional democracies, by contrast, elections act as the principal means by which citizens determine who will govern and, indirectly, what policies will be pursued.

Free elections are implicit in the concept of representation. Representatives, acting on behalf of voting citizens, make the legislative and executive decisions that voters in the aggregate could not possibly make for themselves, considering the sheer numbers of people involved. The very idea of modern constitutional government takes for granted that elections are essential to the functioning of a truly representative system.

Limitations of Elections   Ideally, elections should enable a democratic society to translate the preferences of its citizens into laws and policies. In reality, however, elections do not always produce ideal results. Among the inherent limitations of elections as vehicles of public choice are the following:

1. If public opinion on the most important issues of the day is ill defined or badly divided, newly elected officials may receive no clear mandate from the voters. And even if such a mandate is given, an elected official may regard public opinion on a particular issue to be misguided and either ignore it or try to change it.

2. The great expenditure of time and money required to run for public office may either discourage capable candidates from seeking office or give an unfair advantage to incumbents.

3. To attract as many voters or interest groups as possible, candidates for public office may waffle on an issue. This studied ambiguity can pose difficulties for conscientious voters interested in making an intelligent choice.

4. Candidates often make promises they cannot keep because they simply underestimate the forces of resistance. In the United States, political change is difficult because often the president's politics and policies differ from those of Congress and also because an incredibly convoluted budget process preoccupies and sometimes paralyzes Congress.

Betty Press / Woodfin Camp & Associates

Political representation is implicit in the very idea of modern constitutional government, with elections essential to the functioning of a truly representative system. Here a voter in Kenya casts her ballot.

5. After being elected to office, a candidate may simply have a change of heart about the desirability or feasibility of a particular policy. The influence of powerful special interests, access to more and better information, or the realization of the intricate relationships among various domestic and foreign policies can have a profound impact on a newly elected member of Congress.

Despite these limitations, elections work better than any other method of translating citizen sentiment into public policy, especially in a large and diverse society. In fact, there is good reason to believe that political promises are kept far more often than they are broken.[8] From time to time, elected officials may turn out to be disappointments, but they are seldom surprises. Voters usually have a fairly good idea of what to expect when they elect a particular candidate. Finally, when candidates do break election promises, they sometimes pay a heavy price.

Electoral Systems

Electoral systems can be structured in different ways. The winner-take-all and proportional representation schemes are by far the most widely utilized methods of electing representatives to office.

Winner-Take-All Systems   In the United States, members of Congress are elected by plurality vote in single-member districts; that is, in the *winner-take-all system,* only one representative is elected from each electoral district, and the candidate who gets the most votes in the general election wins the seat. Because a state's two senators are elected in different years, entire states function as single-member districts as well. Finally, the fifty states are each single-member districts in the presidential race, as *all* the electoral votes in any state are awarded to the electors of the presidential candidate who receives the most votes in that particular state.

The practical political implications of such a system are wide-ranging. In any election within a single-member district, if only two candidates are seeking office, one of them necessarily will receive a *simple majority*—defined as the largest bloc of votes. If three or more candidates are vying for a seat, however, the one who receives the greatest number of votes is elected: In a five-way race, for example, a candidate might win with 25 percent (or less) of the votes. As we shall see, this method of election strongly favors the emergence of a two-party system.

The effects of the winner-take-all—also known as *first past the post*—electoral system are graphically illustrated by the hypothetical U.S. congressional race depicted in Table 10-2. Notice that this system has at least one important advantage: It produces clear winners. A simple majority (or plurality) decides who will represent the district. In the example cited in the table, John Liberal is the clear winner. But there is a price to be paid for this convenient result—a majority (57 percent of the electorate) did not vote for Liberal. For all it mattered, they might as well have stayed home. Neither the policies advocated by candidates Jane Conservative and Ima Noparty nor the preferences of the majority in this congressional district will be represented.

The winner-take-all electoral system can also produce national political distortions. In our hypothetical race, Liberal won only 43 percent of the popular vote

TABLE 10-2

A Hypothetical Political Race

Party	Candidate	Votes Received	Percent of Vote
Democratic	John Liberal	25,800	43
Republican	Jane Conservative	24,600	41
Independent	Ima Noparty	9,600	16

in his district, but he gained 100 percent of its representation. His candidacy was no doubt aided by the superior organization and fund-raising advantages enjoyed by the two major American political parties. In addition, the two major parties have the benefit of inertia—voting out of habit rather than conviction.

Under this system, one of the two major parties in every election invariably gains representation disproportionate to the actual popular vote it receives *at the expense of the other party and any minor parties in the race.* Hence, a major party receiving 40 percent to 45 percent of the popular vote may win a clear majority of legislative seats as normally happens in British elections. This type of distortion is so pronounced in Great Britain that a major party receiving less than half the votes can sometimes win in a landslide (an election resulting in a huge parliamentary majority for the party getting the most votes).

In this way, the winner-take-all electoral system encourages the emergence of two major political parties and hampers the growth of smaller political parties and splinter groups. The advantage is greater political stability compared to many multiparty systems. In the view of some critics, however, such stability is achieved by depriving *representative* democracy of its very essence—that is, its emphasis on government that reflects the will (and preferences) of the majority. Because the winner-take-all system does not represent the total spectrum of voter opinions and interests, they point out, it tends to magnify the legislative power of the major party (or parties) and stultify the attempts of minor parties to secure a legislative toehold.

Proportional Representation Systems   The alternative to winner-take-all is an electoral system based on *proportional representation (PR),* designed to ensure that the representation of parties in the legislature approximates party support in the electorate. Usually, under this type of system, the nation is divided into *multi-member* electoral districts with several representatives elected in each according to a formula that divides the seats in accordance with the fractions of the vote the various parties receive in each electoral district.

Among the many countries around the world that have adopted this system are Israel, Italy, Belgium, Norway, and Ireland. Germany also uses a PR system to elect half the members of the Bundestag (lower house of parliament). Generally, candidates in a district win office if they receive at least a specified number of votes. The minimum number of votes required is determined by dividing the number of votes cast by the number of seats allocated. For example, let us assume in Table 10-2 that a proportional representation system is in place, that the district in question has been allocated three seats, and that a total of 60,000 votes have been cast. Under those circumstances, a representative will be elected for every 20,000 votes a party receives. According to this formula, candidate Liberal and candidate Conservative would each be elected because each received more than 20,000 votes. The district's third representative would be determined by a regional distribution, which works like this: 5,800 Democratic votes, 4,600 Republican votes, and 9,600 Independent votes would be forwarded to the region, where they would be combined with other districts' votes and reallocated. Where regional distributions fail to seat a candidate, a final *national* distribution may be necessary. In this manner, a proportional representation system guarantees that everyone's vote will count.

However, some countries have modified the PR system to prevent a proliferation of small, fringe parties. In these countries, minor parties must receive a certain minimum of the national vote to qualify for district representation. In Germany and Russia, this figure is 5 percent; in other countries, it can be 15 percent or even higher.

The *list system* is by far the most common method of proportional representation in use. Under this system, a party may run as many candidates as it wishes in any particular electoral district, but it must rank its candidates on the ballot. If the party receives enough votes in the district to win only one seat, the candidate ranked first on the list gets that seat; if the party garners enough votes to elect two delegates from that district, the candidate ranked second also gets a seat; and so on. The list system strengthens political parties significantly, because citizens vote primarily for the party (as opposed to the candidate) and the party controls the ordering of the candidates on the ballot.

The *Hare plan,* one alternative to the list system, is based on a single, transferable vote and emphasizes individual candidates or personalities rather than parties. Candidates compete freely for a given number of elective offices. A quota is set in advance, and all candidates who receive a stipulated number of votes are declared elected. But this system offers an unusual twist: Each voter indicates both a first and a second choice, and if there are any seats left unfilled after the first-choice votes have been counted, surplus votes are transferred to the remaining candidates on the basis of the voters' second-choice preferences.

Electoral Systems Compared   Proportional representation systems have certain advantages over the winner-take-all method of representation. Fewer votes are "wasted," in the sense that a broader spectrum of views can be represented and more parties can gain seats in the legislature, and these systems appear to be fairer and more equitable than winner-take-all systems because the available seats are apportioned according to the vote totals that each party actually receives.

However, proportional representation, especially under the list system, has several by-products, including a pronounced tendency toward party centralization, the emergence of single-issue splinter parties, more intense parliamentary factionalism, increased difficulty in forming a national consensus, and a de-emphasis on individual candidates in favor of political parties as the main vehicles of political choice. Some of these side effects may be desirable; however, most Americans are not inclined to trade the present winner-take-all system, whatever its defects, for a new system that is unfamiliar. Fear of the unknown is a major force in American politics.

Direct Democracy

Direct democracy means that the voters decide political questions for themselves. Perhaps the most easily recognized model is the New England town hall meeting. The Constitution, by providing for elected representatives, rejects the idea of a direct democracy in favor of a representative democracy.

Today, direct democracy coexists with representational democracy in many places. In some democracies, such as Switzerland and Australia, as well as a number of American states (see Figure 10-2), citizens can bypass or supersede the legislature by voting directly on specific questions of public policy. Generally, such an

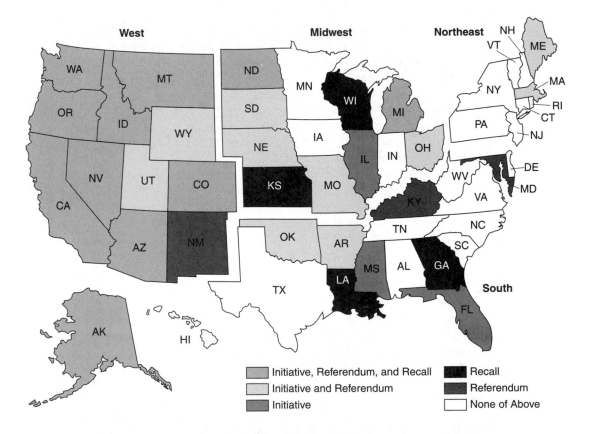

FIGURE 10-2 Citizen-Initiated Initiative, Referendum, and Recall at the State Level

SOURCE: Reprinted by permission of the publishers from *Direct Democracy: The Politics of Initiative, Referendum, and Recall* by Thomas E. Cronin (Cambridge, Mass.: Harvard University Press). Copyright © 1989 by the Twentieth Century Fund, Inc. Updated by Thomas Magstadt, 2002.

Initiative and Referendum

There are two types of initiative—direct and indirect; and there are two types of referendum—popular and legislative. Twenty-three states adopted statewide initiative or popular referendum between 1898 and 1959; four states have adopted statewide initiative or popular referendum since 1958.

- Twenty-seven states have some form of initiative or popular referendum.
- Twenty-four states have a form of initiative.
- Twenty-four states have a popular referendum.
- Forty-nine states have legislative referendum.
- The first state to hold a statewide legislative referendum to adopt its constitution was Massachusetts in 1778.
- The first state to adopt statewide initiative and popular referendum was South Dakota in 1898.
- The first state to place a statewide initiative on the ballot was Oregon in 1904.
- The first state to allow cities to use initiative and popular referendum was Nebraska in 1897.
- The first state to provide for initiative and popular referendum in its original constitution was Oklahoma in 1907.
- The last state to adopt statewide initiative was Mississippi in 1992.

SOURCE: Adapted from Initiative and Referendum Institute, http://www.iandrinstitute.org/factsheets/quickfacts.htm, accessed May 15, 2002.

election is called a *plebiscite.* In the United States, these direct democratic elections take three forms. A *referendum* occurs when a state legislature or constitution refers a question of public policy to its voters. In some instances, the vote taken is merely advisory (indicating the electorate's preferences); in other cases, voter approval is required before a ballot item can be enacted into law. In an *initiative,* the voters themselves put a measure on the ballot by filing petitions containing a stipulated number of valid signatures. The *recall* is a political device intended to remove an elected official from office. It works much like an initiative and is also placed on the ballot by obtaining the signatures of a predetermined number of citizens.

Notable instances of important political issues decided by this kind of direct vote have occurred in many democracies. In 1962, French President Charles de Gaulle used a referendum to amend the French constitution to provide for the direct election of the president (de Gaulle himself). In 1973, Great Britain held the first referendum in its history to decide whether the nation should join the Common Market. (A narrow majority voted in favor of joining.) The modern era of direct democracy in the United States can be traced to 1978 and California's passage of the famous Proposition 13, which not only cut property taxes by at least half but also spurred a large number and variety of initiatives and referendums throughout the nation.

Many direct democracy measures remain controversial. For instance, the California Civil Rights Initiative (CCRI), passed in 1996, limited affirmative action programs by amending California's constitution to prohibit the state from discriminating against, or granting preferential treatment to, "any individual or group on the basis of race, sex, color, ethnicity, or national origin in the operation of public employment, public education or public contracting." The battle between advocates and opponents of CCRI continued after its passage, when opponents successfully delayed its implementation by arguing in the courts that CCRI was unconstitutional. Judicial intervention in this case reflects something of a national trend, as courts discover constitutional issues in many direct democracy measures, thus slowing the implementation of direct democracy.

This debate is important because direct democracy measures have been championed as a means of enhancing democracy, by increasing government's responsiveness and accountability, improving voter participation, and addressing elected representatives who are corrupt, inept, or unresponsive.[9] Opponents of direct democracy argue that money and special interests may play a disproportionately larger role in these special elections than they do in the ordinary legislative process. They also contend that initiatives and referendums are often so complex and technical that the average voter cannot understand the issues involved. However, this view is not shared by a foremost student of these processes, who contends that experience "in the states suggests that on most issues, especially well-publicized ones, voters do grasp the meaning of the issues on which they are asked to vote, and that they act competently."[10]

Hence, negative evaluations of direct democracy measures have been overstated. Certainly, for opponents to argue that money is likely to distort the outcome of a plebiscite is disingenuous at best—money is a major factor (arguably *the* major factor) in virtually *all* American elections of any consequence today. Does this mean that the proliferation of initiatives and referendums is an unmitigated good? Not necessarily. Too much democracy can be a problem. The solution involves striking the right balance. Such measures often enhance self-government at the local level. But once these measures become too numerous, and the issues they involve so complex, the opportunity for special interests grows and the possibility of competent voter review diminishes. For these reasons, direct democracy is today understood as a supplement to, rather than a substitute for, representative democracy.

ASSESSING PARTICIPATION: WHY VOTE?

Underlying the debate over direct democracy is the assumption that citizen participation is natural—that citizens want to participate in their democratic government but can sometimes be shut out of the process. Such a belief is certainly plausible. Ordinary men and women have struggled to win the franchise in nations around the world because they prize free elections and voting rights so highly. Yet often rights that were so hard to gain for earlier generations are taken for granted by later ones. This is particularly true in the United States. The question is: Why?

Voting in the United States

The most important fact to understand about voting in the United States is that voting rates are low and appear to be in long-term decline. In 1960, in the

Kennedy–Nixon election, nearly 63 percent of the adult population voted. By 1996, the percentage had declined to approximately 49 percent and was only slightly higher in 2000 (50.4 percent). In the 2000 election, which George W. Bush (a Republican) won by the thinnest of margins in the Electoral College after losing the nationwide popular vote, a slightly larger turnout in Florida (where it was less than half the voting-age population) or any one of a number of other states would probably have tilted the election decisively toward Democratic candidate Al Gore.

Another measure of voting participation is midterm elections (when there is no presidential race). In 1962, that rate was 46.3 percent; by 1994, it stood at 38.7 percent (see Figure 10-3); in 1998, only 36 percent (barely more than a third) of the voters turned out at the polls. The turnout has not exceeded 45 percent since World War II. Compared to other democracies (in Italy, Austria, Belgium, Sweden, Greece, the Netherlands, Australia, Denmark, and Norway, for instance, an average of over 80 percent of the electorate participates in presidential elections or their equivalent), voter turnout in the United States is embarrassingly low.[11]

The low voter turnout is an enigma (and a stigma) because it has occurred against a backdrop of changes that ought to have produced the opposite effect. As

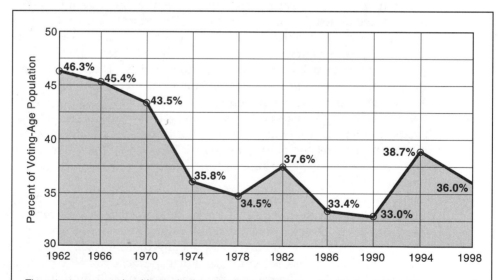

The voter turnout rate in midterm elections remains low. It fell abruptly after the voting age was lowered to 18 in 1971 and has trended downward, with a mild reversal in the recession year of 1982 and a significant upturn in 1994.

In Tennessee, Mississippi, and Louisiana (where only one district was decided in November), the turnout rate did not reach 20 percent. In only four states did a majority of the voting-age population participate in voting for the House: Maine (55.6 percent), Minnesota (54.8 percent), Montana (54.6 percent), and Alaska (52.5 percent).

FIGURE 10-3   U.S. Midterm Election Turnout, 1962–94, Based on House Votes Cast (percentage of voting-age population)
SOURCE: Adapted from *Congressional Quarterly Weekly Report,* February 23, 1991, 484.

two experts have pointed out, during this period of declining turnout much happened that in theory ought to have caused a *rise* in voter participation. For one thing, there were the changes over time in the law. Provisions designed to burden voter access to the ballot, such as poll taxes, literacy tests, and lengthy residence requirements, were largely done away with. The voting age was lowered to 18. In effect, the nation created (structurally and legally) the potential for a huge mass electorate consisting of virtually all adults, with only minor exceptions.[12]

Moreover, with the passage of the so-called *motor-voter law* in 1993, new voters can register while obtaining or renewing driver's licenses. Finally, low voting rates are also unexpected given that "broad changes in the population have boosted levels of education, income, and occupation, all associated with enhanced rates of turnout."[13] Perhaps the real question, then, is not "Who votes?" but rather, "Who does not vote?"

Patterns of Participation

It is axiomatic that only a minority of American citizens actively participates in politics. A pioneering study done in 1950 by Julian L. Woodward and Elmo Roper revealed that about 70 percent of the adult population was politically inactive.[14] A later study found that approximately 26 percent of the American population could be classified as activists and that the rest of the population limited participation to voting or avoided politics altogether.[15] Active participants can be readily identified: a higher percentage of middle-aged citizens than younger or older people vote, more white-collar workers than blue-collar workers, more married people than singles, more whites than blacks, and more blacks than Hispanics.

Those who participate in politics (at least by voting) generally have a greater belief that they can make a difference. Not surprisingly, this sense of *political efficacy* often reflects a mixture of innate ability, individual conditioning, and social circumstances. Yet the question remains: Why do so many Americans not even vote, and why, despite periodic upturns, has that rate decreased in the past three decades?

Some observers cite the lowering of the voting age to eighteen in 1971, pointing out the relatively low rate of voting among citizens eighteen to twenty-one years old. Increased citizen mobility, attitudinal factors, especially the falling rate of party identification, and a growing feeling that individual actions are ineffectual or that politics has become boring or superficial are all part of any comprehensive explanation. There is mounting evidence of a declining sense of civic duty in the general population. Finally, the lengthy political campaigns (especially for president) and the mind-numbing blitz of distasteful television advertisements tends to sour many voters on the whole process.

Individualism and Public Participation

Such factors may well explain the general decline in voter participation. But what accounts for the fundamentally low level of voter turnout? Some social scientists have argued that the relatively low level of political participation in the United States proves that *alienation* is widespread, meaning that Americans are disaf-

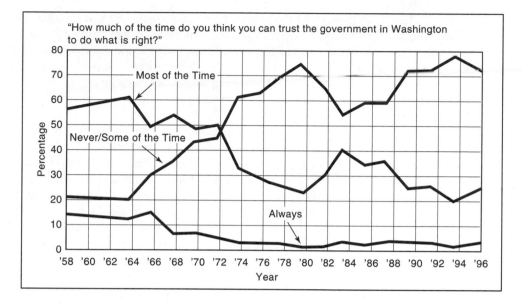

FIGURE 10-4   Growing American Cynicism
SOURCE: Wall Street Weighs the Election, by Thomas D. Gallagher. © Lehman Brothers. Reprinted with permission from Americans Talk Issues Foundation.

fected with government. But most Americans do not consider themselves either alienated or disaffected, even though they (we) have become much more cynical during the past forty years (see Figure 10-4). Mistrust of government only partially explains declining voter participation. We must look elsewhere for a more complete explanation.

A long time ago, French writer Alexis de Tocqueville (1805–1859) observed that wherever a widespread belief in equality exists, individuals tend to be morally self-reliant. The established sources of instruction in such matters—religion, family, monarchy, tradition, or even government—simply do not carry the weight that they did in more traditional societies.

Tocqueville regarded this social characteristic, which he called *individualism,* as the moral equivalent of selfishness. "Individualism," he wrote,

> is a mature and calm feeling, which disposes each member of the community to sever himself from the mass of his fellow creatures; and to draw apart with his family and friends; so that, after he has thus formed a little circle of his own, he willingly leaves the society at large to itself.[16]

In Tocqueville's eyes, Americans were so self-centered (and self-interested) that concern for the common good was in danger of extinction. To him, the will to succeed in a society where success is defined as "keeping up with the Joneses" condemned Americans to constant agitation arising from personal ambitions. Thus, he noted that "in America the passion for physical well-being . . . is felt by all" and that "the desire of acquiring the good things of this world is the prevailing passion of the American people."[17]

Tocqueville thought that the detrimental effects of individualism were counteracted to some extent by the fact that Americans were involved in an enormous number and variety of civic associations. These associations expanded the personal horizon of the average American while simultaneously reinforcing democracy's underpinnings by encouraging social cooperation, teaching the value of respecting other's opinions, and emphasizing the importance of regular procedure and majority rule.

Today, some experts believe that participation in groups and group activities of all kinds is decreasing in the United States. Observing that between 1980 and 1993 the number of bowlers in the United States increased 10 percent while league bowling decreased 40 percent, Robert Putnam concluded in an influential article that bowling had come to symbolize American life.[18] Reduced voter turnout is one political manifestation of this phenomenon. Putnam also pointed out that participation in religious services and church-related groups, labor unions, the PTA, traditional women's groups such as the League of Women Voters, and service clubs such as the Shriners and Masons, had declined during the last thirty years. So had volunteering for service organizations such as the Boy Scouts.

Americans today even spend less time with neighbors than they did thirty years ago. The implications are worrying: a withering of our sense of community and a diminished concern for others—two vital components of civil society.

Political Apathy: An American Disease?

As was observed, the United States is hardly free of political disaffection. Increasingly Americans express a pervasive distrust of politicians. But voter apathy in the United States does not arise primarily from a general belief that most elected officials are corrupt or that the political system has broken down and is beyond repair. Rather, one possible reason most Americans are so nonchalant about politics is that they do not usually feel threatened, oppressed, egregiously overtaxed, or otherwise victimized by government (and when they do voting turnout increases). Seen in this light, *political apathy* is a kind of luxury. Only in an affluent and satisfied society do people take the right to vote for granted or treat it as a trivial thing.

Furthermore, the common observation that widespread political apathy is a sign of political decay is not necessarily valid. To the contrary, American democracy has functioned as a stable political system in harmony with an ever-expanding economy in spite of high levels of political nonparticipation. When people who are normally apathetic suddenly begin to express high anxiety about politics, usually all is not well. Shortly before the Civil War, for example, political apathy almost disappeared amid the controversy over slavery and states' rights, yet the country was on the verge of disintegration. When there is a division of opinion so sharp that no compromise appears possible and when the issue involved is so important that large numbers of citizens are vitally affected, participation and instability tend to increase in tandem.

It would be wrong to conclude, however, that because American democracy can function in spite of apathy and because instability is often associated with increased participation, apathy is good and participation is bad. On the one hand, apathy that grows out of a deep sense of alienation is cause for serious concern; on the other, high levels of participation stemming from a genuine commitment to the public good represent the best antidote to excessive individualism. Finally, although high levels of participation are not necessary in a democracy, a minimal level of voter interest is essential if representative government is to work effectively.

ASSESSING PARTICIPATION: WHAT DO VOTERS KNOW?

Many adult Americans cannot identify the names of government leaders, are unfamiliar with election issues, and are ignorant of politics. Dead candidates are elected to state offices; accused felons, running for public office on a lark, get thousands of votes. Political consultants point out that in many races (particularly city and county races with long ballots), having one's name at the head of the ballot can be worth hundreds or thousands of votes.

A recent study discovered that four out of ten Americans could not correctly name the vice president, while two-thirds could not correctly identify the person who served in the House of Representatives from their legislative district. Nor did Americans do much better identifying elementary facts about how the U.S. government operates. Nearly half did not know that the Supreme Court has the final authority to determine whether a law is constitutional, while three out of four were unaware that senators serve six-year terms.[19] Given such a lack of knowledge, how can Americans make thoughtful or wise decisions? This state of affairs is troubling, if only because a healthy democracy would seem to require an informed and intelligent citizenry.

But perhaps the picture is not quite as bleak as some commentators make it out to be. First, where only a minority of the voting-age population (VAP) votes, those who do vote generally are better informed than those who do not. Second, while some citizens are appallingly ill informed, Americans as a whole know as much about politics as they did in the 1940s (and the country has survived quite well in the interim).[20] Third, that Americans do not know more is perhaps understandable. A well-recognized authority on American government, James Q. Wilson, believes the problem it is not "that the American people are ignorant, unstable or gullible, only that most Americans do not find it worth their while to spend the amount of time thinking about politics that they spend on their jobs, families and friends."[21]

Fourth, many U.S. elections are complicated, involving numerous obscure state and local candidates and issues (and, thus, are different from elections in some European nations, where citizens merely cast party votes). Fifth, many candidates have no clear political stance, while those who do take positions sometimes deliberately try to obfuscate them.

Finally, even if these polls and studies uncover widespread political ignorance they also demonstrate that Americans know something about government and politics. For instance, in the study quoted at the beginning of this section, it

Murderer Gets 33,000 Votes

Some voters don't seem to know, or care, whom they vote for. Consider the case of Leonard J. Richards, who in the 1990 DFL (Democratic Farm-Labor party) Minnesota primary received 33,004 votes, finishing third in the race. The winner, incumbent Michael McGrath, received 148,617 votes. Richards did not campaign, however, because he was in Hennepin County jail at the time, awaiting a second trial for murder. In 1987, Richards had been convicted in the shooting and stabbing death of his tax attorney, but was granted a new trial by the Minnesota Supreme Court because he had not been allowed to act as his own attorney. This enabled him to file for office, since technically it obliterated his only felony conviction. During the campaign, Richards's mug shot appeared in the newspaper voters' guide. His address was listed as 300 South 4th Street #36 (the county jail).

Reactions to the election results varied. "It's impossible for voters to know a lot about all the candidates," observed Secretary of State Joan Growe. "You have to remember that the primary is just one step along the way. That's one of the reasons we have all these steps, so we don't have these kinds of things, hopefully. It's not a perfect system, but it's understandable. It's the nature of what happens in a real, open democracy." The primary winner, McGrath, said "I have no theory about why anybody would vote for him." McGrath added, "I only said nice things about him." After the election, Richards was again tried, convicted, and sentenced to life imprisonment for the killing of his tax attorney. Then, in May 1994, he was convicted of murdering his half sister.

SOURCES: Adapted from Kevin Diaz, "Blind Ballots? 33,004 Voted for Candidate Who's in Jail," *Star Tribune,* September 13, 1990, 1A, 17A; and Margaret Zack, "Richards Convicted of Killing Half Sister: Case Has Been Long and Costly," *Star Tribune,* May 13, 1994, 1B, 4B.

was discovered that most respondents knew there was a limit on the number of terms a president can serve and that Richard Nixon was president during the Watergate scandal. And nearly nine out of ten were aware President Clinton was a member of the Democratic Party, while eight in ten knew Congress had passed a law requiring businesses to provide family leave after the birth of a child or in a family emergency. In fact, there is reason to believe that voters can make reasonable judgments about issues and candidates even though they are often poorly informed.[22]

Political scientist Samuel Popkin provides a good explanation of why so many voters lack information yet vote intelligently. He contends that voters exercise *low-information rationality* ("gut" rationality that is "by no means devoid of substance"), incorporating "learning and information from past experiences, daily life, the media, and political campaigns."[23] Voters may not know which party controls Congress or even the names of their senators, but they know about the economy, their children's schools, their retirement plans, their views on abortion, and so forth. Citizens use "shortcuts" (for example, if a candidate looks the part) and "simplifying assumptions" (party identification) to make political judgments.

Popkin's low-information voter is neither the idealized citizen who votes wisely on the basis of full information nor a complete fool. It is probably fair to say that many citizens devote roughly the same amount of time and energy to voting as they do to buying a car. Patently unwise election choices and foolish car purchases can result, but in general these are the exceptions rather than the rule. The critical difference, however, is that when voters go to the polls they have a far narrower range of choices than car buyers—this is a problem that can only be fixed by elected representatives, who unfortunately have a vested interest in *not* fixing it.

Finally, we need to explain why voters almost always vote for incumbents (that is, reelect individual members of Congress) while mistrusting Congress as an institution. Often, this may well be little more than a case of voters trying to maximize economic and political self-interest by electing representatives who are most capable of safeguarding those interests against the threats posed by representatives from other states. While this approach to electing officials is not terribly enlightened, it is rational on the local level. The dilemma for democracy arises from the fact that this type of "comfort zone" voting is not necessarily rational in the aggregate—that is, on the national level where the most important decisions, laws, and policies are made.

ASSESSING PARTICIPATION: THE REVOLVING DOOR

Some influential political theorists argue that a "power elite" controls the political process from top to bottom. The most popular version of this theory holds that ordinary citizens never exercise much influence, elections and public opinion polls notwithstanding. The political system is manipulated from above rather than from below. The manipulators are the power elite, a small group of individuals who go back and forth through a "revolving door" between the commanding heights of industry and the rarefied echelons of government, exercising enormous power over the destiny of the nation. The status, wealth, and power of this self-perpetuating political class ensure that access to the levers of government is monopolized by the few. The power elites use government to pursue private interests, not the public interest.

Elitist Theories: Iron Laws and Ironies

These theories hold that democracy is governed neither by the voters nor public opinion nor a variety of competing interests, but by a small number of wealthy individuals. It was propounded most influentially in the 1950s by sociologist C. Wright Mills.[24] Mills studied the ruling class in the United States, which enshrines the principle of political equality. By putting the "power elite" in the spotlight, Mills challenged the idea of "government by the people" and called into serious question whether it exists (or has ever existed) in America.

Robert Michels also advanced a theory of elitism, but his study applied to all modern bureaucratic organizations. His findings were distilled from an analysis of the German Social Democratic party, which before the outbreak of World War I was the largest socialist party in the world. Michels reasoned that because the party favored equality in wealth and status, it should have been sufficiently committed to democratic principles to internalize them in its own modes of operation.

He found, instead, that elite groups who derived their power and authority from well-honed organizational skills ran the party.

This discovery led Michels to postulate his famous *Iron Law of Oligarchy,* which holds that all large organizations, including governments, are run in the same fashion. He believed that however democratic organizations start out, they inevitably become more oligarchic, bureaucratized, and centralized over time as those at the top gain more information and knowledge, greater control of communications, and sharper organizational skills, while the great mass of members (or citizens) remain politically unsophisticated, preoccupied with private affairs, and bewildered by the complexity of larger issues. According to this view, the people, for whose benefit democratic institutions were originally conceived, are inevitably shut out of the political or organizational process as corporate officers or bureaucratic officials govern in the name of the rank-and-file shareholder or citizen.

In elitist theories, democracy is seen as a sham or a myth: It does not matter what the people think, say, or do because they have no real influence over public policy. If most people believe that public opinion matters, it is only because they are naive and do not really understand how "the system" works.

Most believe that "democracy for the few" violates the very essence of government by consent, but a few theorists have argued that the American political

AP / Wide World Photos

ACT-UP (AIDS Coalition to Unleash Power) staged a "die-in" in front of the New York Stock Exchange to protest the high cost of AZT. Eventually, manufacturer Burroughs Wellcome reduced the cost of the drug, making it more affordable to men and women living with HIV and AIDS.

system is dominated by the privileged few and that we are all much better off for it because the people as a whole are unfit to govern themselves. In this view, the "masses are authoritarian, intolerant, anti-intellectual, atavistic, alienated, hateful, and violent."[25] From this perspective the "irony of democracy" is clear: Allowing the people real power, permitting them to rule, will only result in the expression of antidemocratic preferences and policies.

Pluralists versus Elitists

The chief opponents of the elitist school of thought are known as *pluralists.* Pluralists and elitists alike accept that in any society there are gradations of power, and certain groups or individuals exercise disproportionate influence over particular policies. They disagree about the basic nature of the political system itself.

According to the pluralists, the American political system is intricate and decentralized. They concede that various organized interest groups, by concentrating all their energies, resources, and attention on one issue (or issue area), exert disproportionate influence in that specific policy area. They also admit that from time to time, certain disadvantaged or unpopular groups may not be adequately represented. Nonetheless, no single individual or group can exercise total power over the whole gamut of public policy. The political system is too wide open, free-wheeling, and institutionally fragmented to allow for any such accumulation of power. In the opinion of one prominent pluralist:

> The most important obstacle to social change in the United States, then, is not the concentration of power but its diffusion. . . . If power was concentrated sufficiently, those of us who wish for change would merely have to negotiate with those who hold the power and, if necessary, put pressure on them. But power is so widely diffused that, in many instances, there is no one to negotiate with and no one on whom to put pressure.[26]

Of course, that there are millions of Americans and only a small number of public offices does place some constraints on direct political participation. But because power is so diffused and there are so many opportunities to exert political pressure at the local, state, and national levels, pluralists argue that the public interest—defined as the aggregation of private interests—is generally better served under constitutional democracy than under any other system.

Pluralists do not deny that those who hold the highest positions in government and business tend to have similar backgrounds and characteristics: Without a doubt, many are males from well-to-do WASP (white Anglo-Saxon Protestant) families who have had Ivy League educations. But in the eyes of pluralists, the mere fact that wealth, status, and education correlate closely with political participation does not prove that the system is closed and public policy predetermined, nor does it demonstrate that democratic citizenship is a sham. Elitist theory is difficult to disprove. Nonetheless, public policies *have* been affected at times by public opinion. Widespread and steadily growing popular sentiment against the Vietnam War, for example, was instrumental in pressuring America to withdraw from that conflict. Public opinion in the United States may often be fragmented, but that does not render it nonexistent or irrelevant. Whether elections are still

GATEWAYS TO THE WORLD:
EXPLORING CYBERSPACE
WEB WATCH

http://www.umich.edu/~nes/nesguide/nesguide.htm

From the Inter-University Consortium for Political and Social Research (ICPSR), housed in Ann Arbor at the University of Michigan, this site from the National Elections Studies research group provides an excellent source of information regarding political participation in the United States.

http://www.interpolitics.com/interpol/index.html

This is the site of InterPolitics, which poses a question each day to its visitors. There is also an archive of previous results and an area for public discussion.

http://headlines.yahoo.com/Current_Events/Proposition_209

This site follows the events surrounding the California Civil Rights Initiative (Proposition 209). Beyond the implications for California politics and society, the articles and links here provide critical analyses and coverage of affirmative action in general.

meaningful, however, is a different question altogether (one taken up later in this chapter).

POLITICAL PARTICIPATION IN AUTHORITARIAN STATES

Unlike their democratic counterparts, in authoritarian states meaningful citizen participation in politics rarely exists. In authoritarian states, citizens are hardly ever involved in their nation's government. By contrast, in totalitarian states, the appearance of citizen participation is often encouraged or demanded. Mass rallies and frequent attendance at political or party meetings are the trappings of involvement, leading some observers to refer to totalitarian states in their most active stage as *mass-mobilization regimes.* In such states, citizens are involved in politics, but it is only for the sake of their indoctrination and control, rather than for the purpose of seeking their opinion, that their participation is demanded.

Authoritarian governments have no reason to permit private polling. Nor do they have much need to utilize polls (although during the last days of the Soviet Union, government-sponsored polls were commissioned). Some authoritarian states do permit elections, and sometimes even require citizens to vote, but the results are almost always rigged and therefore meaningless.

Most forms of meaningful citizen participation are illegal in authoritarian states. Thus, efforts to encourage citizen participation (and spur democratization) are usually regarded by the government as illegal and are punished harshly. Sometimes, meaningful participation can be interpreted as a protest against the government and can take the form of nonparticipation. Refusing to vote when voting is required but meaningless is one example. The ultimate form of citizen nonparticipation occurs when citizens emigrate from or flee their country. It is among the greatest ironies of such regimes that the most meaningful statement their citizens can make is to leave.

POLITICAL PARTIES

In modern mass societies, the voice of one individual is usually too weak to be heard in the public arena. To be noticed by society, the voices of the citizenry must be magnified many times. For this reason, the most effective forms of citizen participation involve the aggregation of individual interests and opinions. Political parties and interest groups are two types of structures that are capable of performing this aggregation function. The availability or effectiveness of these structures in a particular society depends in large part on the extent to which the government protects political and civil rights and is responsive to the demands of the people.

Broad-based political parties by definition bring a variety of special interests under a single umbrella. In recent years the influence of interest groups has increased in both the United States and Europe; at the same time, the role of political parties has declined. We now examine the reasons for this development and its implications for democratic government.

The purpose of a *political party* is to select, nominate, and support candidates for elective office. Political parties have become permanent fixtures in all liberal democracies, including the United States. Surprisingly, political parties were not part of the Founders' original plan. The emergence of a two-party system was a seminal development in U.S. history.

Historical Background

The Constitution makes no mention of political parties, and many of the Founders abhorred them. George Washington sought to avoid partisanship by forming a cabinet composed of the best available talent, including Thomas Jefferson as secretary of state and Alexander Hamilton as secretary of the treasury. The appointment of these two gifted but philosophically opposed individuals reflected Washington's belief that the public would best be served by calling on the nation's wisest and most public-spirited citizens to work together for the common good.

Unfortunately, Washington's noble attempt to avoid partisan politics ultimately failed. Personal animosities developed between Jefferson and Hamilton, in large part due to conflicting understandings of government and public policy, and the two became fierce rivals. In the late 1790s, Jefferson and his followers founded a loosely organized Republican party to oppose the strong anti-French policies of Federalists such as John Adams and Alexander Hamilton. Yet in 1789, Jefferson himself had written, "If I could not go to heaven but with a party, I would not go there at all."[27]

Why did so many statesmen of Jefferson's generation distrust political parties? In Jefferson's case, dislike of parties stemmed from a peculiarly American brand of individualism that has survived to this day. "I never submitted the whole system of my opinions to the creed of any party of men whatever, in religion, in philosophy, in politics, or in anything else, where I was capable of thinking for myself," he observed, concluding that "such an addiction is the last degradation of a free and moral agent."[28] Other Americans of Jefferson's generation, like some of their English counterparts, believed that political parties fostered narrow self-interest at the expense of the general or public interest. In this sense, political parties often were seen as the public extension of private selfishness.

Only gradually did partisanship lose this stigma. In England, the idea that parties embodying different political philosophies could be beneficial (for example, by providing policy alternatives) had begun to take hold by the late seventeenth century. The experience of the leading American statesmen a century later led to a similar, if grudging, recognition of the vital importance of political parties in the democratic process.

General Aims

Political parties typically strive to gain or retain political power; in practical terms, this means capturing control of the government. Since the right to rule in a constitutional democracy is determined by elections, political parties in democratic states concentrate on winning elections. They seek to build a broad-based consensus for their party platform, which is designed to offer an appealing alternative to the other party or parties.

Typically, the successful political party fashions a national consensus out of myriad economic, social, ethnic, and cultural interests. The party must appeal to various voter interests while reconciling and forging them into a workable majority. Even if a party has no hope of gaining a majority following, its influence and legislative strength usually depend on the size and distribution of its vote total, which in turn reflects its success in attracting voters across a relatively wide spectrum.

Candidates frequently appeal for votes by promising to be more responsive and energetic than their opponents in addressing the rank-and-file voter's everyday concerns—the so-called bread-and-butter issues. Sometimes, however, candidates and parties stress ideological issues or advance controversial domestic and foreign policy initiatives. Using these strategies, parties create political alternatives, frequently between liberal policies of the left and conservative policies of the right. This is especially true in Great Britain and in the continental European parliamentary and quasi-parliamentary democracies, where a number of parties often vie for votes and each can formulate distinctive national and international policy alternatives. In such systems, the political platforms of the major parties are much more important than the personal popularity of individual candidates because parties in a parliamentary system seek to capture and maintain a majority of seats in the parliament. Thus, the party that controls the parliament controls the government. As a result, political parties in a parliamentary system tend to be not only more disciplined, hierarchical, and centralized but also more policy-oriented and ideologically distinct than their American counterparts.

In the United States, where the legislative and executive branches are separated and candidates for national office are often selected on the basis of personal rather than political attributes, parties seldom present sharply defined policy alternatives. As a rule, the presidential candidate who is perceived to be closest to the political center is elected.[29] According to its admirers, the American two-party system produces stability and politically moderate candidates while discouraging strident ideology and political polarization.

Critics—especially those who admire the way parties function under the British parliamentary system or the multiparty systems found elsewhere—dismiss American presidential elections as mere popularity contests. Nonetheless, all parties in constitutional democracies seek to build consensus and provide alternatives by carrying out certain essential tasks: selecting or encouraging candidates, raising money, and launching media campaigns, including paid political advertising. In the party platform, proposals and policies are formulated in such a way as to appease key interest groups that in turn will support the party's candidates with money and votes.

Between elections, parties perform other important functions. The winning party or coalition organizes the government in a British-style parliamentary system; in presidential systems like our own, where the executive and legislative branches are separated, political parties help to coordinate the actions of the two branches, especially when the same party dominates both. Just as the winning party plays a prominent role in setting the nation's political agenda and facilitating governmental action, so the losing party performs a vital function by opposing and criticizing the current government and offering an alternative in the next election. Seldom can a party in power satisfy the electorate indefinitely (Japan under the Liberal Democratic Party is one notable exception); when inflation soars or unemployment climbs to an unacceptable level, voters will seek new leadership and new policies.

One-Party Systems

The focus to this point has been on constitutional democracies, where parties are called on to shape a national consensus and offer political alternatives in order to win elections. Political parties can also be found, however, in countries that do not hold free elections.

In authoritarian states, the party exists as much to discourage political alternatives as it does to build a popular consensus. Often, a mere tool of the ruling regime, it serves to enhance state power and suppress political opposition.

In totalitarian states, the party performs a wide range of functions, including political recruitment, indoctrination, mobilization, and surveillance. In Nazi Germany, as in most communist countries, the party became the government. As these states evolved, all vital functions of government came to be performed either by the party directly or by bureaucratic officials operating under the constant supervision of party leaders. The concept of the party as a vehicle for the expression of popular will was thus turned upside down as parties became instruments of centralized social control fully capable of suppressing all attempts at

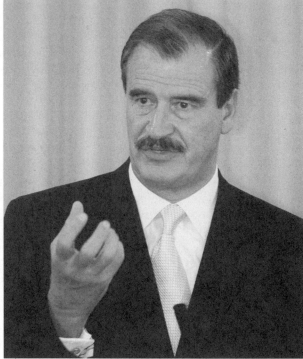

© Reuters NewMedia Inc. / CORBIS

In 2000, Vicente Fox became the first opposition candidate to be elected president in Mexico in some 70 years. Prior to Fox's historical victory, the Institutional Revolutionary Party (PRI) monopolized the presidency and controlled Mexico's government from top to bottom. Fox vowed to fight corruption and institute far-reaching economic and political reforms.

individual self-expression. As noted earlier, mass participation under these circumstances is little more than a charade designed to mask the antidemocratic nature of the regime.

Although most one-party systems are found in authoritarian states, some are embedded in more or less democratic politics. Until the early 2000s, for instance, Mexico's Institutional Revolutionary Party (PRI) dominated Mexican politics. In India, political power in the immediate postindependence period rested almost exclusively with the Indian Congress (a political party, despite the name). As already noted, the Liberal Democratic party has dominated Japanese politics since the mid-1950s. Even in the United States, which is not noted for one-party tendencies, the Democratic party dominated the South for nearly a century after the Civil War.

In the case of Mexico, the PRI maintained its dominant position by a combination of corruption, intimidation, and voting fraud. In India, Japan, and American South, these factors played a smaller role but corruption has not been absent in any of these cases, and intimidation and voting fraud were practiced in the South before the Civil Rights movement of the 1960s transformed the politics of that region.

Democratic one-party systems are relatively rare. Such parties are particularly susceptible to charges of corruption; a virtual monopoly political power encourages cozy arrangements among business leaders, bankers, entrenched bureaucrats, and top government officials. It is therefore not surprising that charges of corruption played a major role in interrupting (but not ending) single-party domination in Japan and Mexico in recent years.

Two-Party Systems

Under a two-party system, the vast majority of voters support one major party or the other, only major-party candidates for office stand much chance of being elected, and the opposition party is constitutionally protected from undue interference or intimidation by the government. One key advantage of two-party systems is relative governmental stability, because the majority tends to share basic political beliefs, to be comfortably situated in the middle-class, and to be culturally and ethnically homogeneous, a condition often absent in developing countries. To some extent, continuity is ensured by the system itself as the two major parties keep to the middle of the road to appeal to a broad range of interests. At the same time, there is the ever-present availability of a widely acceptable opposition party ready and able to take over the government.

Two-party systems are not legally or constitutionally limited to two parties. Minor parties can and do exist, although in the United States they have had precious little success. Commonly, a minor party comes into being through the efforts of a single political figure who has broken with one or both major parties (for example, Teddy Roosevelt's Bull Moose party in 1912 or Ross Perot's Reform party in the 1990s). In Germany, where there are two major parties that have alternated in power since World War II, the small Free Democratic party has enjoyed power and influence greatly disproportionate to its size until the late 1990s when the Greens became the junior partner in a "Red-Green" coalition government with the Social Democrats.

Multiparty Systems

A multiparty system operates where more than two political parties are strong enough to compete for a chance to govern. No one political party is always in the majority in such a system; in any given election, any one of several parties may emerge with the largest number of seats, although often with less than an absolute majority. Individual parties in *multiparty parliamentary systems* tend to eschew compromise during elections and to run on specific issues or programs. Only after the votes are counted do the compromises necessary to form a new government take place. As a rule, the strongest party attempts to form a ***coalition government***, an alliance with another party or parties, in order to create a governing majority. Once a coalition has been forged, it governs until a new election is called or mandated, or until the coalition falls apart. This process sounds strange to Americans, but it is so familiar as to be "second nature" to Europeans, Asians, and others living under parliamentary democracy.

The multiparty system offers as its chief advantage many choices for the voter. Its major disadvantage is that it sometimes leads to unstable governments—in some countries, this instability can become chronic. The process can feed on itself: Stresses bring about factious quarrels within the government, the general disarray at the political center leads to a "crisis of confidence," and that crisis in turn causes more stress. More than any other country in Europe, Italy has exemplified this phenomenon since the end of World War II.

The Determinants of Party Systems

What determines the number of political parties in a particular nation? First, the form of government is crucial—only in constitutional democracies do political parties compete for the chance to control the political system temporarily (until the next election).

Second, among democratic countries, the type of electoral system can influence the type of party system in use. The success of minor parties is discouraged in systems based on single-member districts, where any candidate with a one-vote advantage (a plurality) wins the only available seat. Smaller parties find it difficult to attract voters simply because their candidates have such a small chance of winning. By contrast, in proportional representation systems, where several candidates are elected from each district, smaller, minor parties enjoy a far greater chance of being elected. Thus, proportional representation, as opposed to the first-past-the-post system, is far more likely to produce a multiparty political system.

Third, the political party system, as well as its basic form of government, is sometimes prescribed by the constitution. Constitutions differ on how they treat political parties; some, like the U.S. Constitution, do not address the subject, whereas others refer to them explicitly or implicitly. Even so, there is always a clear distinction between the party, which helps to organize politics and government, and the bureaucracy, which is charged with administering the government—if there is little or no distinction, there is most likely little or no democracy.

Fourth, tradition influences a nation's form of government and the party system it adopts. Since most developing nations have authoritarian regimes and lack a democratic tradition, it is not surprising that single-party systems are common in the Third World. Two notable exceptions in Latin America are Venezuela and Colombia, both of which have developed impressive democratic traditions since World War II. Both these governments have been highly stable; and in Colombia, even a long-standing insurgency has not seriously threatened the system's survival.

Fifth, where deep social, economic, cultural, or religious splits exist, political life is likely to be polarized, infused with emotion, and ideologically charged. Such circumstances favor the development of multiparty rather than two-party systems.

Parties vary significantly from one democracy to another. In some, authority is highly structured and power is concentrated at the top. For instance, British political parties are more disciplined and centralized than the two major parties in the United States. Party centralization is important in a parliamentary system because, with the fusing of both legislative and executive powers, legislators must either "follow the party line" or risk bringing the opposition to power. A centralized party can best exert the political pressure necessary to enforce party discipline. Furthermore, because the party program, and not the personalities of individual candidates, counts most in a parliamentary system, planning, organizing, and financing campaigns at the national level works best.

Another important consideration is whether the political system itself is centralized or decentralized. In nations with federal systems, parties structure their national organization to mirror the federal structure of the government. A practical example illustrates this point. In the United States, vote totals in presidential elections are determined nationally but counted (and weighted) state by state in winner-take-all contests (the winner in each state receives all that state's electoral votes). Thus, as previously mentioned, George W. Bush won the 2000 election despite the fact that his opponent Al Gore received more total votes nationwide. To win, the political parties face the challenge of winning not one election but 50. In such a political environment, a decentralized structure is indispensable. Strong state-level party organizations help elect senators, representatives, and state and local officials. A similar system operates in other federal systems.

American parties are nonetheless comparatively weak. American political parties are not more powerful in part because they do not need to be. The United States is largely a middle-class society with a broad consensus on first principles in politics. This means that neither major party is dogmatic in its ideology or narrow in its appeal; each is more like a loose coalition of diverse groups and interests than a monolithic body of like-minded adherents. In the United States, presidents are far more important than political parties in directing and coordinating the operations of government; in parliamentary systems the political party (or a coalition of parties) form the vital core of each new government.

Political parties—using a liberal-democratic constitutional system to *destroy* the constitution—can become the basis for totalitarian movements (the National Socialist or Nazi Party in Germany between the two world wars is a classic example). Once in power, totalitarian parties transform to become the government. By contrast, the scope of authoritarian parties is narrower. These parties implement the ruler's edicts and policies but do not launch mass-mobilization campaigns, grandiose construction projects, or "revolution from above" designed to transform or purify society. Although both totalitarian and authoritarian parties are usually centralized and regimented, they are not necessarily efficient. Authoritarian parties are by no means exempt from the waste, stultification, and conflicting interests that can be found in large bureaucracies everywhere.

Prospects: Eclipse of Political Parties?

Many experts believe that political parties in the United States are waning. They cite opinion polls that point to an erosion of public respect: Parties are perceived as unable to keep elected officials responsive to the electorate, voters less often identify themselves as party members, and ticket splitting is commonplace. Political scientists tend to agree with public opinion: Political parties are ineffectual.

What accounts for this turn of fortune? Some observers contend that many contributors are choosing to give money directly to candidates rather than to political parties because they want future officeholders to "owe" them. Others suggest that many voters place unrealistic expectations on parties or that parties were the outgrowth of a class struggle between labor and business that has faded in importance.[30] Still others see them as part of a failed political process.

In the United States, the very idea of party politics has come into conflict with the ideal of democracy in recent decades. At both the state and national levels, Democrats and Republicans alike have tried to reduce the influence of party professionals in the candidate selection process. The unpleasant image of party bosses in smoke-filled rooms deciding who will run for what office goes counter to our concept of democracy. Real or imagined, this image has helped to spur movement toward election reform (although real election reform has proven elusive thus far).

Efforts to democratize the nomination process have been particularly popular. State primary elections, once the exception, have become the rule. States now compete to hold the earliest primaries. (The elections themselves have become a bonanza for some states, attracting revenue and wide media attention.) Other states hold party caucuses, where rank-and-file party members choose delegates who later attend state conventions, where they in turn select delegates pledged to support particular candidates at the party's national convention.

Such reforms make the average citizen at least *feel* more a part of the party's nominating process and diminish the power of both state and national party regulars. However, with more states holding primaries, American presidential campaigns have grown more arduous, costly, and prolonged; the presidential nomination and election process can last for well over a year. (By contrast, British parliamentary elections often last less than a month and cost a tiny fraction of what American elections cost.) Furthermore, fund-raising is now a full-time endeavor, not only for presidential hopefuls, but also for serious candidates in Senate and House races, prompting cynics to remark that in the United States, elections have become nonstop events.

This situation is unique to the United States. *No other liberal democracy in the world spends nearly as much time and treasure choosing elected officials.* Whether any democracy can continue to be responsive to all the people under such circumstances is an open question.

Parties still help candidates get elected, but they cannot come close to providing the level of funding now required in the United States. How is this gap filled? Where do candidates turn for financial backing? As we are about to see, interest groups have rushed in to fill the breach, but not without raising new questions about the implications for the nation's democratic ideals.

INTEREST GROUPS

Interest groups do not seek direct control over government nor do they recruit, nominate, and elect public officials. Instead, they concentrate on influencing legislation, policy, and programs in specific issue areas of special interest (hence the name *special interests*)—corporate taxes and subsidies (big business), banking regulations, farm subsidies, federal aid to education, or wildlife conservation, for example. We begin our discussion by examining the different types of interest groups.

Types of Interest Groups

The most commonly used classification scheme for interest groups was developed by Professor Gabriel Almond, who distinguishes among four basic types.[31] First are *associational interest groups,* the most familiar kind, which typically have a distinctive name, national headquarters, professional staff, and the like. Examples include the National Association of Manufacturers (NAM), the National Rifle Association (NRA), and the United Auto Workers (UAW).

Second are *nonassociational interest groups,* which do not have a name and lack formal structures but reflect largely unarticulated social, ethnic, cultural, or religious interests capable of coalescing into potent political forces under the right set of circumstances. Such interest groups are most common in the developing countries of Asia, the Arab world, Latin America, and sub-Saharan Africa.

Third, *institutional interest groups* exist within the government. The various departments and agencies of government have vested interests in certain policies and programs for which they lobby from the inside—often out of public view. Thus, the Pentagon joins defense contractors in promoting weapons programs, and departments such as Labor, Agriculture, and Education are frequently accused of being captives of the special interests most directly affected by the programs they administer.

Fourth, *anomic interest groups* sometimes develop spontaneously when many individuals strongly oppose specific policies. The nationwide student demonstrations against the Vietnam War in the late 1960s and early 1970s serve as an excellent historical example of this phenomenon. Almond suggests that street riots and even some assassinations also can be placed in this category.

Another way to categorize interest groups is to distinguish between ones that represent special interests versus the ones that represent the public interest. Common Cause, an organization founded by a former secretary of Health, Education, and Welfare, with a membership of more than 300,000, exemplifies this type of interest group.

Not only do interest groups differ in the issues they emphasize, but they also differ in focus. A fairly narrow focus characterizes most ethnic groups (the Italian-American Foundation, for example), religious groups (the American Jewish Congress), occupational groups (the American Association of University Professors), age-defined groups (the American Association of Retired Persons), and a variety of groups that cannot be easily categorized (such as the Disabled American Veterans). In each case, these **private interest groups** primarily seek to advance the self-interest of their members.

The focus of **public interest groups** is broader. They promote causes that they believe will benefit society as a whole. One example of such an organization, the Sierra Club, lobbies for strict environmental protection and comprehensive conservation policies. Although not everyone agrees with the Sierra Club's goals, no one can accuse its members of pursuing narrow self-interest; indeed, all citizens benefit from clean air and pure water.

Associational interest groups differ greatly in assets and attributes. The key differences relate to the amount of money they can raise, membership size and diversity, the access they enjoy to legislators and decisionmakers, the professional staffs they can afford to pay. Also, interest groups differ in the tactics they use, including face-to-face lobbying with government officials, political contributions, mass mailings, sponsoring lawsuits, organizing rallies and demonstrations, and funding studies of key issues.

Sources and Methods of Influence

Interest groups typically attempt to sway public policy by influencing elected officials and public opinion at the national or state level. They do so in three primary ways: (1) by seeking the election of representatives they trust; (2) by seeking access to elected officials; and (3) by mounting mass media campaigns. Interest groups prize access to decisionmakers, especially on a one-on-one basis. Many interest groups employ *lobbyists*, who attempt to gain credibility and influence with legislators in various ways. They testify before legislative committees on the basis of their expert or specialized knowledge, and arrange for intermediaries—close personal friends or constituents—to advance their viewpoint. Lobbyists also mount and then benefit from public relations, fax, telephone, telegraph, or Internet campaigns; coordinate and cooperate with other like-minded lobbyists for common legislative objectives; and work to increase communication opportunities between themselves and legislators (for example, by throwing a party or sponsoring a charitable event).[32]

Some interest groups are more successful than others, of course. Two factors are vitally important—money and membership. Organizations representing a large and distinct group of citizens with identical interests have a clear advantage. This edge is especially sharp when the issues involved are specific and keenly felt and when there are no competing or countervailing interest groups stressing the same issues. The American Association of Retired Persons (AARP) is a prime example of a lobby with a large number of like-minded members (totaling some 33 million members) and an issue monopoly (protecting and expanding governmental entitlement for senior citizens) that opposing organizations have seldom challenged successfully.[33] Forty-eight percent of all Americans over the age of fifty (some 20 percent of all voters) belong to AARP, making it the second-largest nonprofit organization in the country, trailing only the Roman Catholic church. Employing eighteen registered lobbyists and a staff of 1,700 people, maintaining a budget of nearly $500 million, and presenting itself as a protector and defender of America's elderly, AARP has become the nation's most influential lobby.

The National Rifle Association (NRA) is an example of a powerful single-issue special interest group, whose influence has declined somewhat in recent decades. The NRA's adamant opposition to any form of gun control has come under attack as firearms have been increasingly linked to violent crime in the United States in the public mind. Even less successful now are family farmers; they are an endangered species represented by a variety of organizations, which has produced a historically fragmented agricultural lobby.

Among the factors tied to interest group success are the number of citizens represented, strong member identification with the relevant issues, and the

Seeking to expand and preserve the government's support of America's elderly, members of AARP (formerly the American Association of Retired Persons) demonstrate to stress their concerns and political positions.

absence of multiple groups that can weaken efforts to exert concerted pressure on government. *But nothing is more important than money in American politics.* A relatively small number of affluent individuals can sometimes exert tremendous influence on the political process, for example by launching expensive media campaigns or contributing large monetary sums to political campaigns. In addition, the members of such groups are likely to have personal networks and political contacts that can be crucial in influencing how a representative or a senator votes on a particular issue.

Interest groups can sometimes gain advantage from close ties to a political party. In Western Europe, the giant trade unions maintain close ties with working-class political parties (for instance, the British Labour party and Trades Union Congress, which have the support of some 85 percent of organized labor in Great Britain). In the United States, by contrast, interest groups increasingly bypass political parties entirely, providing direct financial support to the candidates they favor. In some cases, interest groups hedge their bets by contributing to both candidates in the same race.

Soliciting funds through computerized direct-mail appeals is one key to interest-group success, but dynamic leadership is also important. Leaders of interest groups orchestrate and often personally spearhead lobbying efforts, attempting to persuade legislators or decisionmakers to support or oppose a particular measure in one-on-one meetings. How successfully interest groups operate often depends on the strength of the individual lobbyist's personality and reputation. With that in mind, interest groups frequently vie for former presidential advisers (and pay them handsomely) as special-interest representatives in Washington.

The Interest Group Explosion: Getting Ahead of the PAC

Although estimates differ significantly, experts agree that the number of interest groups in the United States, and the lobbyists they employ, has increased by at least 50 percent over the past three decades. Today, these associations comprise the third-largest industry in Washington, behind only government and tourism. One source estimated that in 1991 there were just under 6,000 registered lobbyists and about 80,000 people working for associations whose purpose was to lobby Congress.[34] Business and trade groups account for nearly two-thirds of all the lobbies in Washington. A particularly disquieting view was offered in 1994 by another observer:

> Consider, for instance, the number of groups listed in Gale Research's *Encyclopedia of Associations*. The listings have grown from fewer than 5,000 in 1956 to well over 20,000 today. They represent, of course, only a small fraction of America's universe of interest groups. Environmental organizations alone number an estimated 7,000, once you count local clean-up groups and the like; the *Washington Blade* resource directory lists more than 400 gay groups, up from 300 at the end of 1990. Between 1961 and 1982 the number of corporate offices in Washington increased tenfold. Even more dramatic was the explosion in the number of public-interest organizations and grassroots groups. These barely existed at all before the 1960s; today, they number in the tens of thousands and collect more than $4 billion per year from 40 million individuals, according to political scientist Ronald Shaiko of American University.[35]

Reasons for this interest-group explosion include the dramatic increase in governmental benefits, the declining influence of political parties, the increasing diversity of American society, and the empowerment of new socioeconomic groups which has given rise to a variety of single-issue interests groups.[36] At the same time, mass mailings and computer technology make founding such organizations relatively easy. Higher levels of education have increased individuals' interest in such associations, and relative prosperity has made them more able to pay dues.

In the early 1970s, a new kind of interest group known as *political action committees (PACs)* became prominent in the United States. In 1971, Congress attempted to curb election abuses by prohibiting corporations and labor unions from contributing directly to political campaigns. However, the law, as finally passed by Congress and interpreted by the courts, did not prohibit special interests from spending money indirectly through specially created committees. The number of PACs rose dramatically until the mid-1980s, as shown in Figure 10-5. Interest groups with large and influential PACs include the American Medical Association, the National Association of Realtors, the National Dealers Association, the National Association of Letter Carriers, the American Institute of CPAs,

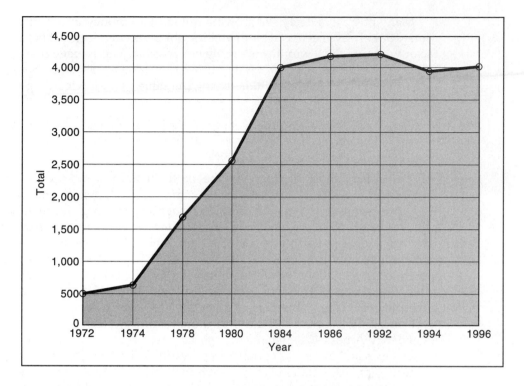

FIGURE 10-5   Growth of Political Action Committees, 1972–96
The number of PACs has remained fairly constant since 1984.
SOURCES: Adopted from Theodore L. Lowi and Benjamin Ginsberg, *American Government: Freedom and Power*, 3rd ed. (New York: W. W. Norton & Company, 1994), 345, and "Midyear and Year-End PAC Counts, 1990–1996," *Federal Election Commission Record*, vol. 27, no. 9, September 1996, 7.

the American Dental Association, and the American Federation of State, County and Municipal Employees.

PACs have played a key role in financing candidates and causes, at both the national and state level. At the same time, the cost of elections—increasingly dependent on television advertising—has escalated. Dianne Feinstein, a Democratic senator from California, raised $22,000 a day during the seven months before the 1994 election; if "Feinstein Inc. were a business, its projected revenue would place it among the top 5 percent of U.S. corporations."[37] Incredibly, Feinstein was outspent by her wealthy Republican opponent, Michael Huffington, who squandered approximately $29 million of his own money in a losing campaign against Feinstein. Another example of spiraling election costs was the 1996 Virginia senatorial election, in which the defeated Democratic candidate, Mark Warner, spent $11 million (an expenditure of $3.30 per voter, compared to Huffington's $2.03 per voter). Thus, while limiting PAC contributions has been a popular reform proposal, the length and high cost of today's political campaigns, coupled with the public's reluctance to pay for them, ensure that politicians will continue to have an insatiable appetite for PAC money.

Many observers decry the growing influence of money in American politics. Money has always been a factor in politics, but in recent decades it has become *the* factor without which winning is simply not possible. The average cost of winning a House seat jumped from $73,000 to 1976 to $680,000 in 1996; for a Senate seat, it rose from $595,000 to $3.8 million during the same period. According to the Pew Charitable Trusts,

> Simply put, money is the fuel that powers the current campaign system. In a circular fashion, interest groups, candidates and parties raise money to pay consultants to launch expensive television ad campaigns.[38]

The rise of interest groups in the parliamentary democracies of Western Europe has, in its own way, been no less impressive.[39] In some European countries, interest groups have been officially recognized by the government and have achieved quasi-governmental status. For instance, in Sweden and Norway, a ministry considering an administrative action is obliged to consult affected groups, thus directly involving interest groups in the policy process. In France, a national system of consultation between government and the private sector encompasses some 500 councils, 200 committees, and 300 commissions. Serving on each of these governmental bodies are representatives of both government and interest groups.

Thus, interest groups in the United States and Western Europe have gained ascendancy. Americans often refer to special interests in a derogatory manner. The rise of PACs and big money politics has contributed to this negative image. Interest groups are essential, but in the absence of any effective curbs on *soft money* (money given to political parties ostensibly for purposes other than campaigning and money spent independently on behalf of candidates or parties) they are increasingly drawn into a kind of systemic corruption for which there is at present no legal or political remedy.

Two decades ago, interest groups were careful to couch their activities in high-minded arguments. Today, one hears a far more frank political language spoken. Leaders of various private interest groups (representing middle-class taxpayers, apartment house owners, Hispanic Americans, senior citizens, and the like) unabashedly protest that they have not received a fair share of the public goods. Talk of the public interest is far less common now; more and more, American politics is viewed as a contest, with the winners—usually represented by powerful special interest lobbies—expecting to be rewarded by the officeholders they helped elect.

The cost in community spirit and public morality is difficult to calculate, but it is no doubt very high and will only gradually reveal itself. One thing is clear: Along with the growing power of interest groups has come an increased public acceptance of selfish interest as the motivating force in American political life.

Interest Groups in Democracies

Ordinary citizens tend to believe that politics ought to be above crass self-interest, often displaying an almost reflexive aversion to the term *special interests*. Nonetheless, pressure groups are part and parcel of democracies, for at least three reasons.

First and foremost, constitutional governments protect individual freedoms, including the freedom of expression and the freedom of association. Thus, interest groups can be considered both an essential part and an inevitable consequence of a free society. As James Madison, perhaps the preeminent political theorist among the Founders, pointed out in *The Federalist,* liberty is to factions (interest groups) as air is to fire: Factions can be suppressed, but to do so, liberty would have to be extinguished.[40]

Second, democratic societies tend to be more politically and economically complex than authoritarian ones. In democracies, where individuals are free to express and act on their opinions and interests, the interests themselves proliferate *because of* political freedom. For this reason, democracies characteristically generate a multiplicity of political, economic, and social interests. An example from economics illustrates this point. Western economies can be broken down into "such diverse business organizations as giant corporations, small businesses, heavy industries, service firms, unionized industries, non-unionized industries, agricultural firms, multinational corporations, and nationalized or state-owned industries—all having unique political needs and interests."[41]

The third reason interest groups prosper in constitutional democracies is because the government regularly distributes benefits. In the annual "battle of the budget," the allocation of benefits is up for grabs. Interest groups, vying for a

Steve Allen / Gamma Liaison International

Interest groups organize to publicize their concerns and influence public opinion. Often they recruit celebrities to draw greater attention to their efforts. Here actor Richard Gere protests Chinese repression in Tibet.

bigger share of the benefits, have proliferated with the rise of the welfare state in Western democracies. A profusion of benefits for young and old alike, ranging from subsidized Medicare payments to food stamps and school hot-lunch programs, have helped to incubate new interest groups. And, of course, the government agencies and corporate participants that provide the programs also have a vested interest in perpetuating and explaining these programs.

Eclipse of the Public Interest?

Often, when citizens complain about influential special interests, they mean lobbyists or pressure groups that advocate *other people's* interests; when they represent *our* interests we both approve and applaud. For instance, interest groups that advocate extending work-study and student loan programs are praised by some of the same people (e.g., educators) who lament the undue influence exercised by such groups in general.

What problems do interest groups objectively pose to the public interest? Some critics argue that the proliferation of interest groups in the United States and Western Europe imposes a particular hardship on the most disadvantaged segments of society. The poor have too little influence in the arena of interest-group politics, whereas the rich have way too much. In this view, the ascendancy of interest groups in democracies has produced a system that promotes the most powerful interests in society at the expense of the weak and downtrodden.

Critics also express alarm at the number of governmental officials who leave high positions to work (directly or indirectly) for companies with whom they previously had dealings, such as former Pentagon officials who are employed by defense contractors, or former presidential advisors who become lobbyists or media commentators, or obtain other high-salaried positions. In 1978, Congress banned high-ranking ex-government officials from any contact with the agencies for which they previously worked for a year and prohibited them from attempting to influence the government on policies for which they had "official responsibilities" for two years.

According to defenders of the existing system, the vast majority of citizens *are* adequately represented. Defenders also point to the profusion of interest groups as evidence that countervailing forces work to keep most of them in check most of the time.

Still, the growth of the welfare state, and its concomitant growth of entitlements, has caused alarm among some conservatives while the growth in the influence of PACs has alarmed liberals and reform-minded moderates alike. Political pressures (interest groups are also known as "pressure groups") accurately reflect the policy preferences of different segments of society, but that is precisely the problem. How can the government act responsibly when facing powerful interest-group pressures that accurately reflect an overwhelming public consensus? On the other hand, when a single-issue interest group champions a very specific regulation or law—one that most voters do not care about and pay no attention to—where is the incentive for lawmakers or bureaucrats to resist pressures from special interests? In a large country comprising numerous levels of government, it

GATEWAYS TO THE WORLD:
EXPLORING CYBERSPACE

To find out more about the political organization of a particular country, including Web sites for individual parties, enter the name of the country and *politics* or *government* as keywords. For instance, the following URL was found by using the keywords *Britain* and *politics*:

http://www.stm.it/politic/uk.htm

This site provides an index of British political Web pages, with links to parties, organizations, governments, and media.

To find out more about the political agenda and goals of a specific interest group, try entering the name of the interest group as a keyword in your search. If you wish to find out if an established interest group exists in a particular area of interest, enter a keyword that describes the issue or cause. For example, if you would like to find out how to get involved in an environmental cause, you could enter "environmental groups" as your search term. A recent search using this strategy returned a number of matches, including this URL:

http://www.seac.org/

This is the Web page of the Student Environmental Action Coalition, "a student run and student led national network of progressive organizations and individuals whose aim is to uproot environmental injustices through action and education."

http://www.pewtrusts.com/

This is the Web page of the Pew Charitable Trusts, a public interest foundation and policy think tank. Check out the links under "Investing in Ideas."

is hardly surprising that many obscure laws or policies are given routine consideration. When pressure groups lobby heavily on behalf of an issue for which there is little popular support and which bears little, if any, obvious relationship to the public interest, the policy process is likely to be corrupted.

Interest Groups in Authoritarian States

Interest groups do not flourish in authoritarian states because opposition is generally discouraged. Since many authoritarian states are in the early stages of economic development, individual interests are often expressed through groups based on kinship ties (tribes or clans). Generally, the military wields considerable influence, even when it is not in charge, because its support is essential for the government to retain power. In developing countries, "labor unions often become a part of political parties and become subordinate to them."[42] Organized labor is generally independent of political parties in the West.

The most significant lobbies in authoritarian states often are not interest groups representing citizens but bureaucratic cliques and intraparty factions that compete for priority treatment in the centralized allocation of limited budgetary resources.[43]

These are not interest groups in the normal sense, but they do introduce an element of pluralism into political regimes not otherwise tolerant of opposition.

Summary

Citizens can participate in the political system in a variety of legal ways: conventionally, by voting and taking part in public opinion polls; organizationally, by joining political parties or interest groups; or professionally, by working full-time for such organizations. Some types of political participation are unconventional, such as engaging in protests or economic boycotts. Illegal participation goes beyond unconventional means—from deliberately nonviolent actions (civil disobedience) to extremely violent acts (terrorism).

To influence government, citizens in constitutional democracies must be able to convert individual opinions and interests into group opinions and interests. Political scientists call this process interest aggregation. Public opinion can be expressed through polls, which have great influence in the political process. Elections, despite inherent limitations, represent the best means of translating mass preferences into public policy. Electoral systems vary, but the two major types are first-past-the-post systems (found in the United States and Great Britain) and proportional representation systems (used in most representative democracies). In democratic republics voters elect legislators, chief executives, and sometimes judges. Direct democracy instruments include referendums, initiatives, and recalls, intended to allow citizens to participate directly in the formulation of public policy.

Voting rates are low in the United States and have been declining, historically speaking. Voters are generally not very knowledgeable.

Some observers argue that political participation by the masses is more illusory than real and that power is actually concentrated in the hands of a small, elite group of influential people. This elitist theory is disputed by the advocates of pluralism, who argue that in a democratic society, power is diffused rather than concentrated and that political phenomena are too complex to be reduced to the simplistic terms of elitist theory.

In authoritarian states, meaningful participation is rare. When it occurs, it is for the purpose of indoctrination and exercising of the government's control, rather than for encouraging citizen participation.

In democratic states, citizens attempt to influence public policy through political parties and interest groups. In authoritarian states, parties are tools of the government rather than instruments for the expression of the popular will. Interest groups, to the extent that they exist in such nations, play a much more limited role than they do in democratic states.

In the United States, political parties were originally regarded as divisive and dangerous. Today they are generally understood to perform key functions in democratic states. They help to organize governments by building a national consensus and offering alternatives, especially during the election process. Political parties may operate in the context of one-party, two-party, or multiparty systems.

The scope and organization of parties can be influenced by a variety of factors within a nation, including its traditions, its constitution, and its cultural and economic diversity. Recently, political parties have declined in power.

Interest groups can be classified in several ways; one method is to distinguish private interest groups from public interest groups. A number of factors determine the effectiveness of these groups, including their size, the intensity of political opinions held by their members, their financing, and their leadership. In recent years, these associations have become more numerous and powerful. Some observers fear that they have become too influential, but others believe that their great number and diversity help to promote political stability and ensure the survival of free institutions.

Key Terms

conventional participation
unconventional participation
illegal participation
civil disobedience
terrorism
subversion
sedition
representative democracy
public opinion
public opinion polling
straw polls
random sampling
strategic polling
focus groups
dial groups
stratified sampling
tracking polls
winner-take-all system
simple majority
first past the post
proportional representation
list system
Hare plan

direct democracy
plebiscite
referendum
initiative
recall
motor-voter law
political efficacy
alienation
individualism
political apathy
low-information rationality
Iron Law of Oligarchy
pluralists
mass-mobilization regimes
political party
coalition government
interest groups
private interest groups
public interest groups
lobbyists
political action committees (PACs)
soft money

Review Questions

1. In what ways can citizens participate in the political process?

2. What are the different forms of electoral systems? Contrast their advantages and disadvantages.

3. Is apathy the enemy of the meaningful practice of citizenship in democratic nations? Explain.

4.   How do the elitist theories of democracy differ from the pluralist model? What political implications follow from the elitist theories?

5.   What assumptions are generally made about political participation in democracies? Are they correct? Explain.

6.   What are the differences among one-, two-, and multiparty systems? Discuss their implications.

7.   To what extent does the functioning of interest groups depend on the political system in which they operate?

8.   Why has the power of interest groups increased as the power of political parties has decreased? To what extent are these two phenomena related?

9.   What does the statement "Not all interest groups are created equal" mean?

Recommended Reading

ASHER, HERBERT. *Polling and the Public.* 3rd ed. Washington, D.C.: C.Q. Press, 1995. A solid introduction to polling and polling techniques.

BECK, PAUL ALLEN, and FRANK J. SORAUF. *Party Politics in America.* 7th ed. New York: HarperCollins, 1992. The latest edition of a comprehensive textbook on American political parties.

BEST, PAUL, KUL RAI, and DAVID WALSH. *Politics in Three Worlds: An Introduction to Political Science.* New York: Wiley, 1986. Chapters 8 and 9 contain an excellent cross-cultural study of political parties and interest groups around the world.

CIGLER, ALLAN, and BURDETT LOOMIS, ed. *Interest Group Politics.* 3rd ed. Washington, D.C.: C.Q. Press, 1991. A comprehensive account of the roles and influences of interest groups in contemporary American politics.

CONWAY, M. MARGARET. *Political Participation in the United States.* 2nd ed. Washington, D.C.: C.Q. Press, 1990. A good summary of the literature.

CRONIN, THOMAS. *Direct Democracy: The Politics of Initiative, Referendum, and Recall.* Cambridge, Mass.: Harvard University Press, 1990. A measured examination of the history, advantages, and disadvantages of direct democracy measures.

DAHL, ROBERT. *Democracy in the United States.* 4th ed. Boston: Houghton Mifflin, 1981. An introduction to American government that emphasizes a pluralist approach.

DYE, THOMAS. *Who's Running America?: The Clinton Years.* 6th ed. Englewood Cliffs, N.J.: Prentice-Hall, 1994. A detailed examination of the political and corporate elites who decisively influence American politics.

ERIKSON, ROBERT, NORMAN LUTTBEG, and KENT TEDIN. *American Public Opinion.* 5th ed. Englewood Cliffs, N.J.: Prentice-Hall, 1994. An excellent summary and discussion of the literature.

FLANIGAN, WILLIAM, and NANCY ZINGALE. *Political Behavior of the American Electorate.* 9th ed. Washington, D.C.: C.Q. Press, 1998. A general but comprehensive account of voting in the United States.

GAIS, THOMAS. *Improper Influence: Campaign Finance Law, Political Interest Groups, and the Problem of Equality.* Ann Arbor: University of Michigan Press, 1996. An advanced, empirical study that focuses on interest groups and PACs, and argues that business PACs in particular are able to exercise excessive influence.

GOLDWIN, ROBERT, ed. *Parties U.S.A.* Skokie, Ill.: Rand McNally, 1964. A stimulating collection of essays that presents important and contrasting interpretations regarding the theory and practice of American political parties.

HOFSTADTER, RICHARD. *The Idea of a Party System: The Rise of Legitimate Opposition in the United States, 1780–1840.* Berkeley: University of California Press, 1969. A historical examination of the origins of the American party system.

LIPPMANN, WALTER. *Public Opinion.* New York: Simon & Schuster, 1997. This book, written by a man often considered the greatest American journalist of the twentieth century, explores the relationship between public opinion and democracy.

MICHELS, ROBERT. *Political Parties.* Translated by E. Paul and P. Paul. New York: Free Press, 1966. The original study that produced the Iron Law of Oligarchy.

MILBRATH, LESTER. *The Washington Lobbyists.* Westport, Conn.: Greenwood, 1976 (reprint of 1963 ed.). An often-cited study of the methods and value of American interest groups.

MILLS, C. WRIGHT. *The Power Elite.* New York: Oxford University Press, 1959. The original formulation of the power elitist thesis.

NIEMI, RICHARD, and HERBERT WEISBERG. *Controversies in Voting Behavior.* 3rd ed. Washington, D.C.: C.Q. Press, 1992. The authors' introductions provide invaluable discussions of contemporary scholarly studies of voting.

POMPER, GERALD M., with SUSAN LEDERMAN. *Elections in America: Control and Influence in Democratic Politics.* 2nd ed. New York: Dodd, Mead, 1980. A persuasive argument that elections serve an important purpose in the American political system.

POPKIN, SAMUEL. *The Reasoning Voter and Persuasion in Presidential Campaigns.* Chicago: University of Chicago Press, 1991. An interesting and thoughtful explanation of how and why Americans vote.

RAUCH, JONATHAN. *Demosclerosis: The Silent Killer of American Government.* New York: Random House, 1995. Explains and details the increasing number and power of interest groups and the threat they pose to American democracy.

ROSE, ARNOLD. *The Power Structure: Political Process in American Society.* London: Oxford University Press, 1967. A pluralist refutation of Mills's power elitist thesis.

ROSE, RICHARD. *Electoral Behavior: A Comparative Handbook.* New York: Free Press, 1974. An examination of political participation in twelve Western nations.

TOCQUEVILLE, ALEXIS DE. *Democracy in America.* New York: Schocken Books, 1961. A classic study of American democracy in the nineteenth century.

WATTENBERG, MARTIN P. *The Decline of American Political Parties: 1952–1994.* Cambridge, Mass.: Harvard University Press, 1996. A scholarly study that examines the historical period in which the decline of political parties primarily occurred.

WILL, GEORGE. *Restoration: Congress, Term Limits, and the Recovery of Deliberative Democracy.* New York: Free Press, 1993. An argument for congressional term limitations.

Notes

1. M. Margaret Conway, *Political Participation in the United States* (Washington, D.C.: C.Q. Press, 1987), 10.
2. Later in the chapter we look more closely at voting patterns in the United States.
3. Conway, *Political Participation,* 52–53.
4. Ibid.
5. Howard Schuman and Stanley Presser, *Questions and Answers in Attitude Surveys* (Orlando, Fla.: Academic Press, 1981), 70–71. This study is illustrated in James Q. Wilson, *American Government,* 4th ed. (Lexington, Mass.: Heath, 1989), 99.

6. John L. Fund, "It'll Be Close," *Wall Street Journal,* November 1, 1997, A12

7. Everett Carll Ladd, "The Pollsters' Waterloo," *Wall Street Journal,* November 19, 1997, A22.

8. One study found that almost two-thirds of the promises made in major-party platforms were kept; see Gerald M. Pomper with Susan Lederman, *Elections in America: Control and Influence in Democratic Politics,* 2nd ed. (New York: Dodd, Mead, 1980), 161.

9. This discussion is indebted to Thomas Cronin, *Direct Democracy: The Politics of Initiative, Referendum, and Recall* (Cambridge, Mass.: Harvard University Press, 1989).

10. Ibid., 87.

11. The fact that voters in many democracies do not need to register is often cited as a reason their participation rate is higher. In several democracies (including Australia and Belgium), citizens who do not vote are subject to a fine.

12. Harry Holloway and John George, *Public Opinion: Coalitions, Elites, and Masses,* 2nd ed. (New York: St. Martin's Press, 1986), 161.

13. Ibid., 162–163.

14. See Julian L. Woodward and Elmo Roper, "Political Activity of American Citizens," *American Political Science Review* 44 (1950): 822–885.

15. Sidney Verba and Norman Nie, *Participation in America* (New York: Harper & Row, 1972), 79–80.

16. Alexis de Tocqueville, *Democracy in America,* vol. 2 (New York: Schocken Books, 1961), 18.

17. Ibid., 153, 159.

18. Robert D. Putnam, "Bowling Alone: America's Declining Social Capital," *Journal of Democracy* (January 1995), 65–78.

19. Richard Morin, "Who's In Control? Many Don't Know or Care," *Washington Post,* January 29, 1996, A6.

20. Ibid.

21. James Q. Wilson, *American Government,* 100.

22. Richard Niemi and Herbert Weisberg, *Controversies in Voting Behavior,* 3rd ed. (Washington, D.C.: C.Q. Press, 1992), 103.

23. Samuel Popkin, *The Reasoning Voter and Persuasion in Presidential Campaigns* (Chicago: University of Chicago Press, 1991), 212–216.

24. C. Wright Mills, *The Power Elite* (New York: Oxford University Press, 1956).

25. Thomas Dye and L. Harmon Ziegler, *The Irony of Democracy: An Uncommon Introduction to American Government,* 4th ed. (North Scituate, Mass.: Duxbury Press, 1978), 374.

26. Andrew Greeley, "Power Is Diffused throughout Society," in *Taking Sides: Clashing Views on Controversial Political Issues,* ed. George McKenna and Stanley Feingad (Guilford, Conn.: Dushkin, 1983), 23. Also see Arnold Rose, *The Power Structure: Political Process in American Society* (London: Oxford University Press, 1967), 483–493.

27. Thomas Jefferson to Francis Hopkinson, March 13, 1789, in *The Political Writings of Thomas Jefferson,* ed. Edward Dumbauld (Indianapolis: Bobbs-Merrill, 1955), 46.

28. Ibid.

29. A theory is presented in Harry Jaffa, *Equality and Liberty: Theory and Practice in American Politics* (New York: Oxford University Press, 1965), 3–32.

30. Paul Best, Kul Rai, and David Walsh, *Politics in Three Worlds: An Introduction to Political Science* (New York: Wiley, 1986), 271–272.

31. Gabriel Almond and G. Bingham Powell, *Comparative Politics: A Developmental Approach* (Boston: Little, Brown, 1966), chap. 4.

32.   This discussion is indebted to William Keefe and Morris Ogul, *The American Legislative Process: Congress and the States,* 8th ed. (Englewood Cliffs, N.J.: Prentice-Hall, 1992), 334.

33.   Thomas DiLorenzo, "Who Really Speaks For the Elderly?" *Consumers' Research* 79 (September 1996): 15, and Charles Morris, *The AARP: America's Most Powerful Lobby and the Clash of Generations* (New York: Times Books, 1996), 4, 10–11.

34.   Jeffrey Birnbaum, "Overhaul of Lobbying Laws Unlikely to Succeed Thanks to Opposition of Lobbyists Themselves," *Wall Street Journal,* May 30, 1991, A20.

35.   Jonathan Rauch, "The Hyperpluralism Trap," *New Republic,* June 6, 1994, 22.

36.   Ibid., 2–3.

37.   John Harwood, "Political Treadmill: For California Senator, Fundraising Becomes Overwhelming Burden," *Wall Street Journal,* March 2, 1994, A1. Feinstein's concerted effort to raise money was spurred by the fact that her 1992 election victory was for only a two-year term. Harwood estimated that her 1992 race and her failed 1990 gubernatorial race together cost about $30 million.

38.   See "Campaign finance reform" at the Pew Charitable Trusts Web site at *www. pewtrusts.com/ideas/.*

39.   This paragraph is based on Best, Rai, and Walsh, *Politics in Three Worlds,* 228–229.

40.   Alexander Hamilton, James Madison, and John Jay, *The Federalist* (New York: Modern Library, n.d.), no. 10, 55.

41.   Best, Rai, and Walsh, *Politics in Three Worlds,* 220.

42.   Ibid., 240.

43.   Gordon Skilling and Franklyn Griffiths, eds., *Interest Groups in Soviet Politics* (Princeton, N.J.: Princeton University Press, 1971).

Chapter 11

POLITICAL LEADERSHIP

THE MANY FACES OF POWER

True Leaders
The Essence of Statecraft • The Lure of Fame
• Four Model Leaders • The Eclipse of
Leadership?

Demagogues

Politicians
Legislators as Delegates • Legislators as
Trustees • Politicos • Appeasers

Citizen-Leaders

MORE THAN ANY other group in contemporary life—more than sports personalities, physicians, business leaders, or even entertainers—politicians tend to be lumped together and stereotyped. Nonetheless, whenever we make a campaign contribution or cast a ballot in an election, we express a preference for one candidate over another and thus betray an underlying belief that it *does* make a difference which candidate is elected. Just as airline passengers cannot afford to be indifferent to the skill of the flight crew, citizens cannot afford to be indifferent to the character and judgment of a nation's leaders.

The well being of nations often depends on the capacity of leaders to choose wisely and act prudently. President George W. Bush's decision to punish the perpetrators of the September 11, 2001, terrorist attacks on the United States was deemed necessary and appropriate by the vast majority of the American people. His father's decision to send troops to oppose Saddam Hussein's invasion of Kuwait in 1990 enabled the United States to safeguard access to oil worldwide at market prices, thus avoiding a severe gasoline shortage (but the decision to stop short of removing the Iraqi dictator from power was followed by years of tension and the intermittent threat of war between the two nations). President Richard Nixon's Watergate actions brought the nation to the brink of a constitutional crisis. And President Lyndon B. Johnson's decision to escalate the war in Vietnam by committing over 500,000 American troops had substantial consequences for the United States and the world.

Clearly leadership does matter. After World War II, President Harry Truman made a series of historic decisions—to rebuild Europe by means of the Marshall Plan, to create new military alliances such as the North Atlantic Treaty Organization (NATO), and to confront the Soviet Union's perceived expansionism with a firm policy of containment. In all likelihood, Warren Harding, for example, would not have adopted those strategies.

According to one eminent scholar, "Politics in essence is leadership or attempted leadership of whatever is the prevailing form of political community."[1] Every community and every country is profoundly affected by the quality of its political leadership. For instance, in May 1994, after years of imprisonment, Nelson Mandela, the former head of the antiapartheid African National Congress, was elected president of a multiracial South Africa. The seventy-five-year-old Mandela, self-taught, widely trusted, and much admired, had successfully led a peaceful transition to power, ending the former rule of the white supremacist government. Probably no one else could have accomplished this task. Still, leading a revolutionary struggle and heading a government are two different tasks; while Mandela possesses many of the attributes of a great leader, it is still too early to judge his actual leadership of the new South Africa.

In this chapter we consider four types of leaders—true leaders, demagogues, ordinary politicians and citizen-leaders—often differentiated according to their accomplishments, character, methods, and purposes. *True leaders* are the political architects who create new states, the peacemakers who resolve conflicts, and the orators who inspire in times of national crisis—they are yesterday's founders, today's pathfinders, and tomorrow's legends. *Demagogues* deceive and manipulate the people for selfish ends—they are schemers, rabble-rousers, and warmongers.

Ordinary politicians do no great harm or good and concentrate, above all, on getting reelected. *Citizen-leaders* hold no official public office but become actively involved in and can significantly influence a nation's politics.

Often these distinctions are easier to make in theory than to apply in practice. For example, one person may view Franklin Delano Roosevelt as an exceptional leader, whereas another may view him as an ordinary politician, a misguided leader, or even a demagogue. (Or as a representative of all four types—obviously, the same leader may fit into different categories at various times in a career in public life.) However, most people would agree that Adolf Hitler was a demagogue and that Winston Churchill was the architect of Great Britain's heroic defense in the darkest days of World War II.

TRUE LEADERS

True leaders practice *statecraft,* the wise use of state power. This leadership ideal has been around for a long time. Plato and Aristotle both examined it. Indeed, Plato depicts Socrates partaking in a dialogue about *statesmanship,* the term traditionally used to refer to a gifted leader. During this century, the title of *statesman* has been bestowed (rightly or wrongly) on a variety of world leaders, ranging from Josip Tito, the founder of Yugoslavia, to Golda Meir, the former Milwaukee, Wisconsin, schoolteacher who in 1969 became Israel's fourth prime minister.

Leaders who make a lasting difference are men and women of rare quality who display a firm commitment to peace, harmony, and the public good; who possess extraordinary political skills; and who exhibit practical wisdom. In addition, in times of crisis these men and women provide crucial leadership necessary for the nation's survival. An especially exalted place is often reserved for the founders of new nations, without whose vision, wisdom, and inspirational leadership a particular nation or government might never have existed at all. George Washington is a father figure in the founding of the United States; many other countries also have a father figure whom the people admire and remember on special occasions (for example, a national independence day).

The Essence of Statecraft

Defining the ideal leader is no easy task. At the core of all good leadership are elusive qualities such as intuition, inspiration, and good judgment. Other qualities, including intelligence and humility, are also essential. In *A Preface to Morals,* the late Walter Lippmann, a famed philosopher and syndicated columnist, attempted to isolate these qualities by contrasting enlightened leaders with run-of-the-mill politicians. Lippmann suggested that most politicians only work "for a partial interest." Examples include politicians who feather their own nests or slavishly follow the party line. The word *statesmanship,* in contrast, "connotes a [person] whose mind is elevated sufficiently above the conflict of contending parties to enable him to adopt a course of action which takes into account a great number of interests in the perspective of a longer period of time."[2]

Lippmann recognized that the line between an ordinary politician and a real leader is often blurred. Even true leaders cannot ignore special interests—in a democracy, all leaders must sometimes act like politicians. Nonetheless, a politician begins to look like a leader whenever he or she stops trying merely to satisfy the momentary wishes of the constituents. The better course is to persuade the people (voters) that the pursuit of the public interest is in everyone's interest and that private interests are not (and ought not to be) the primary concern of public policy.

Pursuit of the Public Good   A true leader is motivated by neither crass self-interest nor narrow partisanship but by considerations of the nonpartisan public good or the general welfare. By choosing what "the people will in the end find to be good against what the people happen ardently to desire," Lippmann contended that such leaders eschew immediate popularity. By refusing to promise the politically impossible, they choose honesty and moderation over flattery. Such a decision, he continues, requires the "courage which is possible only in a mind that is detached from the agitations of the moment," as well as the "insight which comes from an objective and discerning knowledge of the facts, and a high and imperturbable disinterestedness."

Although concern for the public good can be described in terms of moderation, detachment, insight, and honesty, it does not lend itself to neat generalizations. For instance, honesty is a virtue, but in political life there are exceptions. When the stakes are high, when complete honesty is an impediment to success, and when best interests of the nation are served by stealth or dissimulation, a true leader will sometimes resort to deception.

Extreme circumstances justify extreme measures. For example, both before and during the Civil War, Abraham Lincoln consistently downplayed the slavery issue, preferring to keep the political spotlight on the overriding importance of preserving the Union. Lincoln understood that emphasizing the slavery issue would alienate members of the precarious coalition on whose support his political popularity rested, ultimately harming the cause of both black emancipation and the Union.[3]

Practical Wisdom   True leaders possess what Aristotle called prudence or practical wisdom; a compelling vision of the public good is useless without a way of achieving it. They understand the relationship between immediate actions and ultimate consequences and can anticipate the reactions of friend and foe alike. Finally, they are able to distinguish between the enduring and the ephemeral, the fundamental and the frivolous, the possible and the unattainable. In sum, statecraft requires rare insight and an ability to both diagnose problems and prescribe remedies. In this sense, wise leaders bear a resemblance to physicians, whose success is ultimately measured not in dollars and cents but in the health of the community they serve.

Political Skills   It is not sufficient that a president, for example, have the national interest at heart; mustering support for proposed programs and policies is essential. In a democracy, law and policies (and in the case of elections, the leaders themselves) require the consent of the governed. Reconciling wisdom and consent in the often-turbulent public arena is one of the primary tasks of leadership in a democracy.

In the everyday world of politics, a leader must also be able to manage a vast bureaucracy and direct a large personal staff, to work with the legislature to ensure a majority for the passage of the administration's programs, and to rally public opinion behind the administration's policies. A successful chief executive must display skill in organization, persuasion, and other political abilities.

Political wisdom presupposes that the requisite leadership skills are put to good and proper use; political adroitness is commendable only when a political leader's abilities are directed toward the public good. If those abilities are used primarily to advance the career or line the pockets of the officeholder, then his or her success represents a failure of the democratic system. By the same token, even if the political leader's goals are praiseworthy, the methods used to achieve them may be repugnant. Political leaders who seek to remove obstacles to needed social reforms by ruining, jailing, or killing their opponents can hardly be praised for their actions, no matter how beneficial their policies might be.

Extraordinary Opportunities   Historians have frequently observed that great times make great leaders. To become a true leader, a person must live at a time when the actions and decisions taken can make a crucial difference in the history of society and perhaps the world. Such a leader may be genuinely concerned about the public good, have extraordinary political skills, and possess enormous practical wisdom, yet fail to make a great or lasting impact. During times of politics as usual, even the most capable leaders lack the opportunity to exercise their special talents.

Is it, then, the individual or the times that make for political greatness? Here an analogy with medicine is again appropriate. The doctor who receives the greatest acclaim is not the one who gives competent day-to-day health care advice but the one with a reputation for pulling patients through life-threatening illnesses or traumas. Like individuals, nations go through crises that may threaten their very existence. At such times, moral inspiration and political expertise are essential if the nation is to endure; such a situation is tailor-made for the exercise of statecraft.

Good Fortune   The final prerequisite of exceptional leadership is good luck. No political leader can be successful without a certain amount of good fortune. A turn in the tide of a single battle, a message thought about but not sent (or sent too late), or any number of other seemingly unimportant incidents or actions may prove decisive. Great leadership can never be attributed entirely to good luck, but considering the complex environment in which such leaders operate, good luck often makes the difference between success and failure.

The Lure of Fame

Often, political leaders (or aspiring leaders) assume positions of public responsibility at significant cost to themselves. They must endure long separations from family, relinquishment of more lucrative careers, and constant public criticism.

The question inevitably arises, why would men and women of outstanding ability devote the best years of their productive lives to the pursuit of political excellence? What would inspire such individuals to work for the public good, often at the expense of more obvious and immediate self-interests?

According to historian Douglass Adair, the Founders were motivated primarily by the idea of fame. For George Washington, James Madison, Alexander Hamilton, and Benjamin Franklin, narrow self-interest, defined in terms of personal power or wealth, was not an overriding concern. Nor was individual honor, which Adair defines as a "pattern of behavior calculated to win praises from [one's] contemporaries who are [one's] social equals or superiors."[4] Rather, the Founders' great motivating force was a desire for fame—a concept that, according to Adair, has been deeply embedded in the Western philosophical and literary tradition since the classical era. Applying this interpretation to the U.S. Founders, Adair writes:

> Of course they were patriots, of course they were proud to serve their country in her need, but Washington, Adams, Jefferson, and Madison were not entirely disinterested. The pursuit of fame, they had been taught, was a way of transforming egotism and self-aggrandizing impulses into public service; they had been taught that public service nobly (and selflessly) performed was the surest way to build "lasting monuments" and earn the perpetual remembrance of posterity.[5]

Just as not all (or even most) political leaders are wise, so too not all wise leaders are motivated by the desire for fame. Sometimes the simple desire to do a good job or to win public approval provides sufficient incentive. But it seems likely that the greatest leaders have been motivated principally by a desire for fame. Indeed, Alexander Hamilton observed that a love of fame is "the ruling passion of the noblest minds."[6] The desire for immortality is a powerful elixir.

Four Model Leaders

True leaders have appeared at many times and in many places throughout history. As the following political biographies of four world-famous leaders demonstrate, the backgrounds, qualities, and motives of leaders who have risen to the first rank of leadership display both remarkable similarities and wide disparities. Setting a good example is the best way to lead any organization, whether a Boy Scout troop or a political state, which is why we often use the term "exemplary" to characterize leaders we admire.

Rómulo Betancourt (1908–1981) In 1830, Venezuela became a nation. From then until 1959, when Rómulo Betancourt assumed the elected presidency of Venezuela, no democratic ruler had survived in office for even two years. Betancourt not only survived, battling seemingly insurmountable obstacles, but his public career also prospered, giving life to his country's fledgling democracy. Although he acted as a strong president, Betancourt made clear the difference between democratic leadership and dictatorial abuse of power. He encouraged a politics of moderation, compromise, and toleration; he heeded the rightful powers of the other branches of government, followed the constitution, respected the rights of citizens, and almost obsessively avoided using his power for material advantage (or permitting anyone under him to do the same).[7] And when his five-year term expired, Betancourt did what no Venezuelan had ever done before; as the constitution written during his term of office required, he turned over his office to his democratically elected successor.

For these reasons, Rómulo Betancourt can justly be considered the founder of democracy in Venezuela. As such, he differs markedly from other twentieth-century founders such as Pol Pot and Fidel Castro, who zealously undertook to establish and then exercise unlimited political power with insufficient regard (or contempt) for individual suffering. Furthermore, it appears that Betancourt sought power not for its own end but for the public good it might accomplish. For that reason, he was able to relinquish it willingly, understanding that great lesson of political leadership: Exceptional leaders deliberately make themselves dispensable by preparing the people to govern in their absence.[8]

Betancourt's political career began when he was still a university student and a military dictator named Juan Vicente Gómez (1908–35) ruled Venezuela. In 1928, at the age of twenty, Betancourt became a student leader in a failed revolution, eventually ending up in jail. Upon release from jail, he went into exile in Costa Rica for eight years, returning shortly after the death of the dictator. He became a prominent political figure in his native Venezuela, but from the mid-1930s until 1959, Betancourt was a political maverick, often on the run, active in the underground, and sometimes living in exile as he continued his opposition to the dictator of the day. During his early years in opposition he sympathized with the communists, but he moderated in time, favoring democratic socialism instead. Betancourt's most notable achievement during this time was laying the groundwork for what would become Venezuela's leading party, Acción Democrática. Throughout most of his opposition years, both Betancourt and his party consistently championed broad democratic participation for all citizens, agrarian reform, guaranteed universal education, national health care, and economic diversification (Venezuela was heavily dependent on oil exports).

Betancourt joined (and, according to some versions, headed) a group of military reformers in a coup d'état against Venezuela's military government in October 1945. Betancourt ended up as president, championing a foreign policy in which Venezuela refused to extend diplomatic recognition to dictatorships and urged other governments in the region to follow suit. Domestically, Betancourt decreed that the large oil companies in Venezuela turn over half of their income, enabling the government to undertake a far-reaching program to establish schools, hospitals, public water and sanitation facilities, and low-cost housing developments. He sponsored a new constitution in 1947, promoted elections, and declared that he would not be a candidate for office. The candidate who succeeded Betancourt lasted only nine months before being ousted by another military coup. It was not until Betancourt was elected president in 1959 that democracy returned to Venezuela.

During this five-year term as president, Betancourt pursued the progressive policies he had always advocated. Particularly notable were his efforts to encourage foreign investment and improve urban housing. Betancourt also initiated a program of land reform. His economic and political achievements were all the more remarkable because when he took office, his nation was facing an economic crisis, the military did not support his rule, and coup attempts from both the Left and the Right punctuated his term in office (Betancourt survived more than one assassination attempt).

Betancourt prevailed in the end and was beloved by his people. What accounted for his success as a democratic leader in a country with an autocratic tradition? Betancourt appears to have possessed an uncanny ability to judge the motives and character of others; almost unerring judgment as to when to stand firm and when to compromise; a capacity to listen to advice but to keep his own counsel; an ability to make difficult decisions; self-control; and great personal valor, both moral and physical. He combined all these qualities with a high degree of practical idealism—a clear vision of what he wanted to accomplish for his country, and a commitment to values which (together with ambition) had for several decades motivated him in national politics.[9]

Rómulo Betancourt was Venezuela's indispensable national leader, succeeding against difficult odds. One of his foremost biographers, Robert J. Alexander, has observed that "no other Venezuelan political leader of his time could have succeeded under all these circumstances."[10] The historian John Fagg has written, "If moral authority and high principles counted, Rómulo Betancourt loomed as a titan in the history of Venezuela."[11] Exemplary leaders have existed in many times and places, but they are fairly rare; Venezuela was fortunate to have had one.

Winston Churchill (1874–1965)   Until Churchill became the British prime minister in May 1940, he had a checkered public career. A colorful personality, Churchill was brilliant, charming, witty, controversial, cantankerous, and courageous. His public career reflected a steadfast devotion to the cause of political liberty. Furthermore, he was right at a very important time when freedom was threatened. Almost alone among the major political figures of the 1930s, he recognized and consistently pointed out the grave dangers posed by Nazi Germany. In discerning these dangers long before they became apparent to most of his contemporaries, Churchill proved himself the most perceptive political observer of his day.

Winston Churchill was born into a prominent English family that traced its lineage directly back to John Churchill, the first duke of Marlborough. Winston's father had been a distinguished member of Parliament and cabinet minister; his mother was an American. He himself was elected to Parliament at the tender age of twenty-five and almost immediately acquired a reputation as an eloquent and outspoken maverick. In 1911, he was appointed first lord of the Admiralty, a high office he held through the first year of World War I. He was forced to resign in 1915, after the dismal failure of an amphibious attack on Turkey, by way of the Dardanelles, which he had sponsored. Churchill's political prestige then fell to an all-time low, although he managed to recoup sufficiently to be appointed minister of munitions in 1917.

© Bettmann / CORBIS

A voice of determination and confidence in an era of despair, Winston Churchill (1874–1965) rallied the British nations with such words as "We shall not flag or fail. We shall go on to the end. . . . We shall never surrender."

Churchill remained a Conservative MP throughout most of the 1920s and even held the prestigious position of chancellor of the Exchequer (comparable to the U.S. secretary of the treasury) for an extended period. Despite a solid record of public service, he entered the 1930s as something of a political outcast, having alienated the leadership of his party. Even though the Conservatives held power, he was excluded from the government, and he found himself increasingly isolated in Parliament. At the age of fifty-six, he was facing a premature end to his political career.

But Churchill had the kind of clairvoyance that is rare in politics—he could see things clearly when others were lost in the fog. From the time of Hitler's ascent to power, he sought to alert the Western democracies to the Nazi danger, warning of the danger posed by Germany's rapid rearmament and the comparative weakness of Britain's armed forces—especially its air power. Many mainstream politicians and commentators ridiculed him as an alarmist. In the words of his foremost biographer, Churchill was a voice in the wilderness.[12]

As the 1930s progressed and Churchill's alarms began to arouse the nation, there still was no place for him in his party's cabinet. Only after Britain entered World War II was he asked to return to the government, at first in his former post as first lord of the Admiralty and then as the prime minister. His inspiring words and example proved decisive, as Britain for a time stood alone against the Axis powers. In Churchill's own words, "Alone, but up-borne by every generous heartbeat of mankind, we had defied the tyrant in his hour of triumph."[13]

Churchill had rare leadership qualities. He understood the darker side of human nature and thus grasped the danger Hitler posed to civilization. He had the courage of his convictions, never yielding to the pressures of public opinion—even if it meant being ostracized by his own party. His rhetoric inspired the nation in the face of a mortal threat and relentless bombardment. Above all, events proved him tragically right; right about the imminent threat; right about the malignant evil Hitler represented; right about the urgent need for military preparedness. His message (that another terrible war was coming unless Britain acted to prevent it) was one his compatriots did not want to hear, but he never confused what the nation wanted to hear with what it *needed* to hear. Churchill demonstrated the power of leadership to make a life-and-death difference in perilous times.

Abraham Lincoln (1809–1865)   Churchill rallied his nation against an external threat; Abraham Lincoln helped to save his nation from itself.

The pivotal political issue in Lincoln's time was slavery. Churchill conceivably could have changed British public opinion before World War II, but Lincoln had no chance of persuading the majority of Southerners that slavery should be abolished. The South's economic dependence on slavery, along with the persistence of racial prejudice in the North, guaranteed that no political figure who favored the immediate abolition of slavery could serve as chief executive of a truly united nation. This was the context in which Abraham Lincoln decided to run for president, a decision that culminated in his election to the nation's highest office in 1860.

Lincoln's politics were guided by a basic moral precept and a profoundly practical judgment. The moral precept, which he repeatedly voiced in his debates with Stephen Douglas during his 1858 campaign for the Senate, held that slavery was wrong in principle, everywhere and without exception. In declaring slavery unjust and immoral, Lincoln did not resort to abstract philosophy; rather, he based his judgment squarely on the Declaration of Independence, which states, ". . . all men are created equal." Thus for Lincoln, slavery violated the most basic principle of the American political order.

Lincoln exercised uncommon practical judgment in evaluating the conditions under which slavery might be eradicated in the United States. He believed above all that it was necessary to maintain the Union as a geographic entity, as well as preserve its integrity as a constitutional democracy. Only through a single central government for North and South alike could slavery be ended (although this was by no means inevitable). Conversely, any breakup of the Union would mean the indefinite extension of slavery, at least in the South.

Lincoln's belief in political equality and his conviction that such equality could only be achieved by preserving the Union help to explain the pre–Civil War stands he avoided taking, as well as the ones he adopted. Although he believed that slavery was morally wrong, he did not propose its immediate abolition; he knew that such a proposal would prompt the South to secede and ensure the survival of slavery in that region. Nor did he support Northern abolitionists who sought to disassociate themselves from the Union so long as it continued to countenance slavery. Here again, Lincoln recognized that such a policy would only entrench the very institution it was designed to eliminate. Finally, he opposed Stephen Douglas's formula of "popular sovereignty," under which each new state would be allowed to declare itself for or against slavery. The question of slavery, Lincoln believed, was too fundamental to be submitted to the vagaries of the political marketplace.

Rather than pursue any of these policies, Lincoln favored an end to the extension of slavery into the territories so that from then on, only free states would be admitted to the Union. In Lincoln's mind, this was the only antislavery policy that had any chance of gaining popular acceptance. The keys to his strategy were patience and perseverance. Adoption of his plan would ultimately bring about an end to slavery in the whole United States, as the relative weight and legislative strength of the slaveholding states diminished with the passage of time and the admission of new non-slaveholding states.

When it became evident that Lincoln's policy would not win the day, he accepted the Civil War as inevitable. Yet during the course of this conflict, his approach to the slavery question varied according to the circumstances of the war. As noted earlier, when the tide of battle ran against the Union and victory seemed to depend on not alienating several of the slaveholding border states Lincoln went out of his way to soft-pedal the slavery issue. The North needed military victories, not pious pronouncements, if the Union was to endure. It could not endure, he believed, if it remained "half slave and half free." In the final analysis, the reason Lincoln was willing to countenance civil war was, paradoxically, to preserve the kind of Union the Founders had intended.

Both before and during the Civil War, Lincoln's policies were aimed at achieving the maximum amount of good possible within the confines of popular consent. As commander in chief, he pushed his constitutional authority up to (and arguably beyond) its legal limits. But just as his ultimate political purposes were not undermined by the compromises he accepted to save the Union in time of peace, so too his moral integrity was not corrupted by the dictatorial powers he wielded in time of war. For all these reasons, Lincoln stands out as an exemplary political leader whose resolute actions and decisions under fire were instrumental in saving the Union.

Anwar el-Sadat (1918–1981)   The Middle East has long been among the world's most unstable and violent places. Miraculously, in late 1993, Israeli Prime Minister Yitzhak Rabin and Palestine Liberation Organization leader Yasir Arafat, bitter enemies, agreed to a deal that gave limited autonomy to the Palestinians in the Israeli-occupied West Bank and Gaza Strip. The agreement was potentially a big step toward peace, but it was not the *first* step. In fact, there was a preexisting precedent in the Middle East, one that suggested even the deadliest of enemies can live together in peace. Anwar el-Sadat was the political architect of that peace-making precedent.

Sadat became president of Egypt in 1970 and held that position until his assassination in 1981. He succeeded Gamal Abdel Nasser, the acknowledged leader of the Arab world and a prime mover in the post–World War II anticolonialist movement. Nasser was an autocratic ruler who governed Egypt with an iron fist and staunchly opposed the existence of the state of Israel. When Nasser died in 1970, Sadat automatically succeeded him. (As vice president Sadat was Nasser's hand-picked successor.) Under Egypt's constitution, Sadat was to hold office on an interim basis for only sixty days, during which time the National Assembly was required to choose a permanent successor. Ironically, this legislative body eventually endorsed Sadat in the belief that he would be noncontroversial and would adhere tightly to his predecessor's policies.

Indeed, there was little reason to expect anything else from Sadat, whose early political life was devoted to securing Egyptian independence from Great Britain. His anti-British activities during World War II included contacts with Germans aimed at collaboration against the British imperialists. For these efforts, Sadat spent two years in a detention camp. Later he would spend three more years (1946–49) in prison, charged with attempting to assassinate a British official. In pursuit of a nationalistic strategy that sought to capitalize on anti-British sentiment in Egypt, Sadat and Nasser cooperated closely. It was Sadat who publicly announced the overthrow of the Egyptian monarchy and the establishment of the new, independent republic of Egypt, under Nasser's leadership, in July 1952.

Given this history, it seemed inevitable that as president Sadat would continue Nasser's policies. Events seemed to bear out this expectation. In 1971, he

Egyptian president Anwar el-Sadat (1918–1981), shown here with Israeli prime minister Menachem Begin, was assassinated for his bold steps toward peaceful coexistence with Israel.

was instrumental in forging the Federation of Arab Republics, an alliance of Egypt, Libya, and Syria motivated by Nasser's policy of uniting the Arab world. The federation ultimately failed, but not for want of trying on Sadat's part.

In 1973, Sadat led Egypt in a war against Israel. Although Egypt was defeated, Sadat stressed that the Egyptian army had won a major battle at the outset of the war; this victory, he maintained, restored Egypt's national honor.

In the aftermath of the war, Sadat switched from belligerent Arab nationalist to committed advocate of peaceful coexistence. This transformation was capped by a precedent-shattering state visit to Israel, where Sadat delivered a memorable speech before the Israeli Knesset (parliament) on November 20, 1977. More important than the speech itself was the symbolic significance of his official presence in the Israeli seat of government: Egypt had become the first Arab country to recognize Israel as a sovereign state.

This dramatic act of conciliation by Sadat paved the way for the Camp David accords between Egypt and Israel the following year. The Egyptian-Israeli agreement at Camp David, Maryland, which set the stage for Israel's withdrawal from the Sinai peninsula, caught foreign observers by surprise and stunned the Arab world. Sadat was bitterly attacked by many of his fellow Arab rulers as a traitor to the Palestinian cause. To the Arabs, and to many of the most astute observers as well, Sadat's bold step toward a lasting Arab-Israeli peace was as unexpected as it was unprecedented.

Why did Sadat take this extraordinary step? Some experts have suggested that Sadat recognized that given the serious economic problems facing his impoverished, densely populated nation, Egypt simply could not afford a perennial cycle of war with Israel. Others have pointed to the fact that Israel had furnished Egypt with valuable intelligence about the activities of its increasingly hostile neighbor, Libya. Finally, it has been argued that Sadat was a pragmatist who concluded that the only way Egypt was ever going to regain the Sinai, which Israel had occupied since 1967, was by signing a peace treaty.

Although all of these factors may have figured into Sadat's calculations, they do not explain the intensity of his peace efforts or the magnitude of the personal and political risks he was willing to take. He knew that his actions would alienate most of the Arab world (including many of his fellow citizens). It seems likely that just as the young Sadat was moved by the ideal of a free and independent Egypt (which he helped to bring about), the older Sadat was inspired by an even more noble vision. As he himself expressed it on the occasion of the signing of the Camp David accords:

> Let there be no more wars or bloodshed between Arabs and Israelis. Let there be no more suffering or denial of rights. Let there be no more despair or loss of faith. Let no mother lament the loss of her child. Let no young man waste his life on a conflict from which no one benefits. Let us work together until the day comes when they beat their swords into plowshares and their spears into pruning hooks.[14]

The eradication of hatred, religious bigotry, and incessant warfare from a region where they had been a way of life for as long as anyone could remember would indeed be a great act of statecraft. The attempt to bring peace to the Middle

East may well have been Sadat's own personal bid for immortality. He may or may not have been aware of Alexander Hamilton's views on the subject of leadership, but through his actions Sadat bore out the truth of Hamilton's observation that love of fame is the "ruling passion" of history's most exceptional leaders.

Like Lincoln, Sadat was assassinated by one of his own countrymen. Oddly, such is often the fate of history's greatest peacemakers (for example, the twentieth-century's greatest apostle of nonviolence, Mahatma Gandhi, was also assassinated). A lasting peace in the Middle East has been elusive, but Egypt and Israel have been at peace for over two decades thanks to the treaty that stands as a fitting memorial to the wisdom and courage of Anwar el-Sadat.

The Eclipse of Leadership?

It may seem strange to devote such a large part of a chapter on political leadership to a discussion of exceptional leaders. After all, a well-known aphorism of American politics holds that a statesman is nothing but a politician who has been dead for a while. Like the proverbial prophet who is not honored in his or her own country, true leaders often are not honored in their own time. Full appreciation of such rulers, of course, may come only after enough time has passed for the practical results of farsighted leadership to become widely apparent.

Yet, in an age when political leaders are plagued by scandals, and increasingly fashion proposals and policies to reflect the results of focus groups and specially commissioned polls, courageous political leadership often seems like a distant ideal. But there is another, peculiarly modern reason why this kind of leadership is held in such low esteem in American political life: Its existence—if not its very possibility—has been cast into doubt. Just as American citizens tend to be highly suspicious of the public pronouncements of any elected official (frequently looking for deeper personal or political motives—which, in fact, often lie beneath the surface), so they have come to believe that exceptional leaders, too, are little more than clever and successful politicians of the past. Significantly, whereas the 1934 edition of the *Encyclopedia of the Social Sciences* included a brief but incisive essay on statesmanship by a celebrated British scholar, a more recent edition omits all mention of statesmanship as a category of political thought.

In addition, discounting the idea of political wisdom reflects how little value is assigned to excellence in an egalitarian age.[15] As modern democracies increasingly disdain all social and economic distinctions, it becomes less fashionable to recognize that anyone excels at anything—a tendency that is especially pronounced where the political profession is concerned.

From this frame of mind comes the modern propensity to debunk the very idea of exemplary or wise leadership. To the debunkers, vague historical determinants or narrow self-interest, not free will, are the true motive forces in history, and it is naive to believe that some leaders really do care about the public good. This cynical view leads to a drastically reduced opinion of outstanding leaders in world history. It is as if "the old histories full of kings and generals whom our ancestors foolishly mistook for heroes are . . . to be replaced by a kind of hall of fame of clever operators."[16]

The most serious consequence of this increasing reluctance to recognize political achievement is that it makes political life less attractive to capable and conscientious individuals who might choose to distinguish themselves by serving public rather than private interests. By denying public officials the respect they are due, a democratic society can do itself considerable harm. A pervasive belief that corrupt and mediocre politicians are everywhere can become a self-fulfilling prophecy, causing only the corrupt or mediocre to seek public office.

DEMAGOGUES

Unlike Neville Chamberlain, a sincere but misguided leader of high moral principles, Adolf Hitler was an opportunistic leader and an example of the most dangerous species of politician—the demagogue. Originally, in ancient Greece, a demagogue was a leader who championed the cause of the common people. Today the term *demagogue* is applied to a leader who exploits popular prejudices, distorts the truth, and makes empty promises to gain political power. Generally, demagogues combine unbridled personal ambition, unscrupulous methods, and great popular appeal.

If true leaders represent the ideal, demagogues represent the perversion of both truth and leadership. Exceptional leaders genuinely care about achieving justice and the public good; demagogues only pretend to care about such things in order to gain a public position that they can exploit for their own advantage, at the expense of the very public interest they pretend to champion.

Demagogues come to power primarily in democratic societies, where leaders must gain popular approval to hold office. Unlike great democratic leaders, however, demagogues are rarely remembered after they leave power. Occasionally, they leave an indelible mark. When this happens, it is with the achievement of infamy rather than fame.

American political history is punctuated with the rise and fall of demagogues. Some had a purely local impact; others affected the entire nation. All are remembered chiefly with scorn.

Theodore Bilbo (1877–1947)   As governor and senator, Bilbo dominated Mississippi politics from the 1920s through the 1940s. He campaigned equally hard against blacks and his political opponents, linking them whenever possible. His campaign rhetoric was colorful and outrageous. In the heat of one political campaign, he denounced his opponent as a "cross between a hyena and a mongrel . . . begotten in a [racial slur deleted] graveyard at midnight, suckled by a sow, and educated by a fool."[17] Although Bilbo's white supremacy politics and down-home language endeared him to a great many Mississippians, not everyone was impressed. Even political allies viewed him as a self-serving political operator.

According to one writer, Bilbo was "pronounced by the state Senate in 1911 'as unfit to sit with honest upright men in a respectable legislative body,' and described more pungently by his admirers as 'a slick little bastard.'"[18] And in the eyes of the editor of the *Jackson Daily News*, Bilbo stood "for nothing that is high or constructive, . . . nothing save passion, prejudice and hatred, . . . nothing that is worthy."[19]

Huey Long (1893–1935)   Theodore Bilbo has mercifully escaped the attention of most American historians; Huey Long, a politician from the neighboring state of Louisiana, has not. Known to his Cajun constituents as the Kingfish, Long was far more ambitious than Bilbo. Of humble origins, he completed the three-year law program at Tulane University, passed a special examination from the Louisiana Supreme Court, and became a licensed attorney at the age of twenty-one. In his own words, he "came out of the courtroom running for office."[20] Three years later he was elected state railroad commissioner, and in 1928 he gained the Louisiana governorship.

Huey Long governed Louisiana with an iron hand during his four-year reign (1928–32) and his subsequent term as U.S. senator, which was cut short by his assassination in 1935. As governor, Long controlled every aspect of the state's political life. Surrounded by bodyguards and aided by a formidable political machine, he used state police and militia to intimidate voters, handed out patronage and political favors, created a state printing board to put unfriendly newspapers out of business, ordered a kidnapping on the eve of a crucial election vote to avoid personal political embarrassment, and generally acted more like a despotic ruler than a democratically elected governor. Under his autocratic rule,

Huey Long (1893–1935), Louisiana's controversial governor and, later, U.S. senator, exemplified demagoguery in his control of the state's powerful political machine. Under the guise of a populist, Long managed to gain power by offering hope to the disenfranchised.

© Bettmann / CORBIS

men could be—and were—arrested by unidentified men, the members of his secret police, held incommunicado, tried, and found guilty on trumped-up charges. A majority of the State Supreme Court became unabashedly his. . . . A thug, making a premeditated skull-crushing attack upon a Long opponent, could draw from his pocket in court a pre-signed pardon.[21]

Despite these excesses and a penchant for luxury, Long always took care to picture himself as "just plain folks." The true villains in American society, he said, were rich corporations such as Standard Oil, which consigned ordinary people to lives of poverty while enriching a few corporate officers.

To counteract this alleged thievery by big business, and to create a popular platform for the upcoming presidential race in 1936, Long developed an unworkable (but popular) Share the Wealth program, tailor-made to appeal to people suffering through the Great Depression. Long's proposal included restrictions on maximum wealth, mandated minimum and maximum incomes, so-called homestead grants for all families, free education through college, bonuses for veterans, and pensions for the aged, as well as the promise of radios, automobiles, and subsidized food through government purchases. However implausible and impractical this program seems, it should be remembered that the people to whom Huey Long was appealing were not inclined to quibble or question. They needed someone to believe in.

Like many other demagogues, Long gained power by promising hope to the hopeless. Demagogues generally vow to defeat the forces of evil that, according to them, are solely responsible for the people's plight. Of course, those forces— blacks in the case of Bilbo, corporations for Long—invariably do not exercise anything like the controlling influence attributed to them. Nonetheless, once accepted as the champion of the little people against enemies they themselves have conjured up, demagogues often have been able to manipulate the unsuspecting populace for their own illicit ends.

Joseph McCarthy (1908–1957)   During the 1950s, an obscure politician from Wisconsin named Joseph McCarthy identified a demon that greatly alarmed the American people and then claimed to find evidence of this malignant force in all areas of public life.

While serving as a Republican senator from Wisconsin, McCarthy attracted national attention by making the shocking "revelation" that the U.S. Department of State had been infiltrated by communists. For approximately four years, he leveled charges of treason against a wide array of public officials, college professors, and Hollywood stars. Using his position as chairman of the Senate Committee on Investigations, McCarthy badgered, intimidated, and defamed countless people in and out of government. As his accusations helped to create a national climate of fear, his power grew, and those who opposed him did so at their own risk.

In 1954, McCarthy accused the secretary of the army of concealing foreign espionage operations. That accusation, along with innuendos aimed at General George C. Marshall—next to President Dwight D. Eisenhower, perhaps the most respected public servant in America—marked a turning point. McCarthy had gone too far. Ironically, his unscrupulous methods were exposed in the Senate investigations that resulted from his own irresponsible accusations. The hearings received national radio and television coverage and made front-page headlines in every major newspaper in the country. In the end, McCarthy was cast into obscurity as rapidly as he had been catapulted into national prominence.

POLITICIANS

Citizens in democratic states frequently make disparaging remarks about politicians without realizing how much like the rest of us they really are. As a distinctive type of political leader, politicians are individuals whose main (but not only) concern is gaining or maintaining elected office, and who exercise political power for the purpose of representing their constituencies, doing what they believe to be necessary or right (or doing what they can get away with). Politicians are noteworthy because they are found only in democratic states. Authoritarian states have rulers and officials who engage in politics but are not politicians.

Most politicians, like most other jobholders, have neither great vision nor outstanding abilities. On a day-to-day basis, they do the best they can, given the limitations they operate under. Much of the time, they want to do the right thing, although they may have difficulty keeping moral or ethical issues in clear focus and even more difficulty taking political risks. Generally they are not corrupt, but they often *are* corruptible. They are no better—and no worse—than most people. In a word, they are *ordinary*.

A problem arises when citizens expect politicians to be extraordinary. In democracies, politicians have to juggle contradictory expectations. They are expected to be ordinary, identifying with the common citizen; at the same time, they are expected to display uncommon devotion to duty and country.

The would-be leader in a democratic society faces the perennial question of whether to act as a delegate, carrying out the voters' (presumed) wishes, or as a trustee, exercising independent judgment on behalf of his or her constituents. The political system itself requires elected representatives to be responsive if they wish to be reelected. But true leaders do not follow the pack, they *lead* it—and therein lies the politician's dilemma.

Legislators as Delegates

In a country the size of the United States (to say nothing of India), it is impossible for each individual to personally represent his or her own interests. The national legislature is the key to performing this vital function because it is typically the most representative branch of government. According to the ***delegate theory of representation,*** a legislature "is representative when it contains within itself the same elements, in the same proportion, as are found in the body politic at large. It is typical of us; we are all in it in microcosm."[22]

In this model of representative democracy, elected representatives are obliged to act as instructed delegates. The representative, according to this theory, is a receptacle of public opinion; in effect, the voters hire someone to serve as a kind of proxy in the legislature. This perspective easily accommodates focus groups and opinion polls to help legislators decide what stands to take on important issues. As a bonus, the most responsive legislators are also the most likely to be reelected (although in the United States virtually all incumbents have a huge advantage).

Underlying the delegate theory is a belief in the common sense and decency of the people. One prominent advocate of this theory, holding that there is a "relative equality of capacity and wisdom between representatives and constituents," argues that it would be "arbitrary and unjustifiable for representatives to ignore the opinions and wishes of the people" and that political issues often involve "irrational commitment or personal preference, choice rather than deliberation, the more necessary . . . that the representative consult with the people's preferences and pursue their choice."[23]

This approach also militates against corruption, according to its advocates. Legislators who are expected to act on the basis of constituents' opinions are under a constraint that makes illicit deals unlikely.

Legislators as Trustees

Detractors say the delegate theory of representation requires elected officials to be too passive—in effect, to act as followers rather than leaders. The foremost critic of the delegate theory was Edmund Burke (1729–1797), the famed eighteenth-century British writer and legislator.

Burke argued that legislators ought to retain a certain independence of thought and action. Specifically, according to Burke, the elected representative needed to isolate specific complaints about real problems from the grumbling of an irascible (and possibly irrational) electorate. He contended that the politician as legislator must listen to the complaints of constituents but not give all complaints equal weight: Competent legislators distinguish between complaints that arise from defects in human nature (and cannot be remedied) and those that "are symptoms of a particular distemperature" of the day.[24] Understood in this fashion, popular opinion becomes a valuable barometer. If legislators wish to get a reading on popular sentiment or whether controversy is brewing on a particular issue, they must first consult public opinion.

Given this relationship between public opinion and political representation, what role did Burke assign to the legislator? To put it bluntly, he believed that a natural aristocracy made up of the best and the brightest should govern, and that elected officials should act as trustees for their constituents. In other words, the legislators should act according to their understanding of the public good and not merely as a mouthpiece or puppet of the voters. As Burke declared in a famous speech to his own constituents, "Your representative owes you not his industry only, but his judgment; and he betrays, instead of serving you, if he sacrifices it to your opinion."[25]

Burke's so-called *trustee theory of representation* fits into his larger philosophy of government. Good government, he argued, must involve not only good will but also "virtue and wisdom." To be workable, in other words, representative government must be based on upright behavior and careful deliberation, with an eye toward discovering and carrying out the true public good. Burke characterized his own Parliament as "a *deliberative* assembly of *one* nation, with *one* interest, that of the whole—where not local purposes, not local prejudices, ought to guide, but the general good, resulting from the general reason of the whole."[26]

Burke believed that a wide gulf separated members of the legislature from ordinary constituents. He held that in a sound republic, representatives should be wiser and better informed than constituents and hence should be able, after careful deliberation, to solve most of the political problems that beset a nation. Finally, he argued that the welfare of the whole nation (the public or national interest) should take precedence over the welfare of any of its parts (local or special interests). For these reasons, Burke stressed the importance of the legislator as leader rather than follower.

Politicos

Some American political scientists have used the term *politico* to describe American legislators who successfully reconcile the functions of delegate and trustee. Specifically, politicos are political representatives who fight for approval of the bread-and-butter legislation favored by their constituents while taking independent stands on issues that do not directly engage the "pocketbook" interests of those constituents. For example, the fourth legislative district in Kansas has been called the general aviation center of America (housing, among others, the bulk of Boeing's military business); therefore, it is not surprising that its congressional representative must reflect constituents' interests by casting hawkish (conservative) votes on national security issues, while being accorded more latitude on other political matters.[27] Although politicos generally champion the special economic interests of their district or state, the positions they take can be issue-oriented. Thus, it is not surprising to see liberal senators from rural states sometimes oppose gun control legislation, a position that reflects the opinions of a majority of their most politically active constituents.

William Fulbright (1905–1995), while serving as senator from Arkansas, gave a speech at the University of Chicago shortly after the conclusion of World War II in which he articulated the politico's approach to the problem of democratic leadership:

> The average legislator early in his career discovers that there are certain interests, or prejudices, of his constituents which are dangerous to trifle with. Some of these prejudices may not be of fundamental importance to the welfare of the nation, in which case he is justified in humoring them, even though he may disapprove. The difficult case is where the prejudice concerns fundamental policy affecting the national welfare. A sound sense of values, the ability to discriminate between that which is of fundamental importance and that which is only superficial, is an indispensable qualification of a good legislator. As an example of what I mean, let us take the poll-tax issue and isolationism. Regardless of how persuasive my colleagues or the national press may be about the evils of the poll tax, I do not see its fundamental importance, and I shall follow the views of the people of my state. Although it may be symbolic of conditions

which many deplore, it is exceedingly doubtful that its abolition will cure any of our major problems. On the other hand, regardless of how strongly opposed my constituents may prove to be to the creation of, and participation in, an ever stronger United Nations organization, I could not follow such a policy in that field unless it becomes clearly hopeless.[28]

Fulbright's own career in the Senate (1945–75) would seem to provide an example of the politico in action. Often he voted against legislation, especially civil rights measures, that in all likelihood he personally favored. He realized that because his constituents' racial views, at that time, were sharply opposed to his own, he could not remain in office without deferring to the deep-seated prejudices of the Arkansas majority. Fulbright sometimes justified this approach on the ground that many civil rights issues were not of fundamental importance.

Fulbright's deference to his home state's majority opinion on the question of race relations gave him great latitude in the area of foreign policy, an area in which the Arkansas voters had little interest. In time, he became the chairman of the powerful Senate Foreign Relations Committee and was acknowledged widely as a leading spokesman for liberal causes in the realm of foreign policy—even though he represented a conservative state.

Appeasers

Politicians who are able to "get things done" are usually praised, provided they do not get the wrong things done. Appeasers form an interesting subset of ordinary politicians because of the wide chasm between the actions they intend and the results they achieve. What they believe to be the public interest and what is actually good for the nation turn out to be two very different things. Thus, if they win, the country loses.

Perhaps the best (or worst) example of an appeaser was Neville Chamberlain, prime minister of Great Britain from 1937 until 1940. In retrospect, it is clear that during this pre–World War II period, Germany was rapidly rearming. But Chamberlain earnestly believed in the futility and waste of military armaments and warfare, and he was equally convinced that negotiation and compromise could and should form the basis of all politics, including international politics. As late as October 1938, Chamberlain contended in the House of Commons that "fresh opportunities of approaching this subject of disarmament are opening up before us, and I believe that they are at least as hopeful today as they have been at any previous time" and asserted that

> to such tasks—the winning back of confidence, the gradual removal of hostility between nations until they feel that they can safely discard their weapons, one by one, . . . I would wish to devote what energy and time may be left to me before I hand over my office to younger men.[29]

Many of Britain's "younger men," however, were soon to die on the battlefield, thanks to Hitler's uncompromising militarism. Chamberlain's ever-so-civilized analysis of international politics that led to his attempt to appease a savage dictator was not without vision or sincerity; it was merely wrongheaded.

CITIZEN-LEADERS

Occasionally, an individual can decisively influence the course of political events without holding an official position in the government. An individual's unique dedication to a cause, personal magnetism, or even outright courage can garner an impressive political following. Such a person is called a citizen-leader. Here we look at four examples of such grassroots leadership.

Václav Havel   In the mid-1960s at the age of twenty-nine, Václav Havel (1936–) gained worldwide acclaim for his satiric, absurdist plays, including *The Garden Party* (1964) and *The Memorandum* (1965). In the summer of 1968, Havel and thirty other Czech cultural figures signed a statement calling for the revival of the outlawed Social Democratic party in Communist-controlled Czechoslovakia. In August of that same summer, the increasing but cautious trend toward liberalization within Czechoslovakia that had begun in 1963 was swiftly and successfully thwarted when the Soviet Union invaded the country to reassert hard-line Soviet control.

During the conflict, Havel played a key role in putting the Free Czech Radio on the airways and used this underground radio broadcast to direct daily commentary to Western intellectuals as a plea for assistance. Over the next two decades, Havel became Czechoslovakia's most famous playwright. His plays often contained biting satire aimed at the communists who ruled in Prague. But his writings were not the only reason for his increasing notoriety. He also became Czechoslovakia's foremost dissident and human rights champion. In 1977, Havel coauthored the Charter '77 manifesto, which denounced Czechoslovakia's communist rulers for failing to abide by Basket Three of the 1975 Helsinki Accords in which all signatories promised to respect civil and political rights. For such acts of political defiance, Havel was jailed repeatedly, serving sentences that often included hard labor. Despite these punishments, he was not silenced.

In December 1989, after Czechoslovakia's communist regime collapsed under the crushing weight of popular civilian discontent, Havel became president by consensus. That Havel had been in prison at the beginning of 1989 made his sudden ascent to power all the more remarkable. But then no other public figure in Czechoslovakia could come close to matching the moral authority Havel had accumulated during three decades of courageous citizen-leadership. Havel remained in office for over three years. Then, on the verge of Czechoslovakia's disintegration into two ethnic nation-states (the Czech Republic and Slovakia), he resigned.

But Havel would not long absent himself from public life. On January 26, 1993—little more than six months after his resignation—the Czech parliament elected Havel to a five-year term as president of the Czech Republic. Despite his prominent position, Havel did not always take an active role in governing his nation; yet he remained an important national figure. Although most Czechs distrusted and disavowed politicians, many respected Havel as the only living Czech leader who not only talked and wrote about "living in truth"—but also practiced what he preached.

Martin Luther King, Jr. An outstanding citizen-leader was the renowned civil rights champion Martin Luther King, Jr. (1929–1968). From the moment he became president of the newly formed Southern Christian Leadership Conference in 1957, King's national prominence grew. He led sit-ins, marches, demonstrations, and rallies throughout the South, all aimed at ending racial segregation and overcoming racial discrimination in jobs and housing. Practicing nonviolent civil disobedience, protesters under King's leadership openly broke the law (which sanctioned segregated lunch counters, required parade permits, forced African Americans to sit at the back of buses, and so on), and then accepted punishment for their action.

King intended to stir the conscience of the nation by reaching legislators and judges and, in the end, the American people. As he stated in his famous 1963 "Letter from Birmingham Jail" (King had gone to Birmingham, Alabama, to lead an economic boycott aimed at desegregating public facilities and was jailed for organizing an unlicensed parade):

> I submit that an individual who breaks a law that conscience tells him is unjust, and willingly accepts the penalty by staying in jail to arouse the conscience of the community over its injustice, is in reality expressing the very highest respect for law.[30]

King's hope was clear: "We must see the need of having nonviolent gadflies to create the kind of tension in society that will help men to rise from the dark depths of prejudice and racism to the majestic heights of understanding and brotherhood."[31]

The influence of King and other African American civil rights leaders including Roy Wilkins, Malcolm X, Whitney Young, the Reverend Jesse Jackson, and Vernon Jordan has been decisive. Although extremely controversial at the time, direct action proved crucial to the passage of the landmark 1964 Civil Rights Act, which banned discrimination in public accommodations and employment. Later, other civil rights legislation was passed, further ensuring equal treatment under the law for all citizens. In 1964, King was awarded the Nobel Peace Prize for his efforts. Four years later, at the age of thirty-nine, King was assassinated.

Rosa Parks Rosa Parks (1913–) stirred the conscience of a nation with a single act of courage. On December 1, 1955, she left work after spending a long day as a tailor's assistant at a Montgomery, Alabama, department store. Boarding a bus to go home, she found a seat. Soon, however, a white man who was standing demanded her seat. (Montgomery's customary practice required that all four blacks sitting in the same row with Rosa Parks would have to stand in order to allow one white man to sit, since no black person was allowed to sit parallel with a white person.)[32] Parks stayed put:

> I was thinking that the only way to let them know I felt I was being mistreated was to do just what I did—resist the order. . . . I had not thought about it and I had taken no previous resolution until it happened, and then I simply decided that I would not get up. I was tired, but I was usually tired at the end of the day, and I was not feeling well, but then there had been many days when I had not felt well. I had felt for a long time, that if I was ever told to get up so a white person could sit, that I would refuse to do so.[33]

The bus driver had Parks arrested.

Many historians date the origin of the American Civil Rights movement to the Montgomery bus boycott, conducted in the wake of Rosa Parks's arrest. Her single act of symbolic defiance is remembered today as an act of political valor that drew attention to racial injustice and led to a chain of events that eventually changed the nation forever.

Patty Wetterling   Patty Wetterling, a St. Joseph, Minnesota, mother of four, would have given all she owned not to have become a political activist. On October 11, 1989, a masked man abducted her eleven-year-old son Jacob. She would never see him again. At first, there was little she could do but search and grieve. In time, she established the Jacob Wetterling Foundation, one of whose goals was to underwrite lobbying efforts to pass state and national laws protecting children from abduction and sexual molestation. In 1991, she successfully lobbied in favor of a Minnesota law that required convicted sex offenders leaving prison to register a permanent residence with state authorities. In 1996, again partially due to her efforts, Minnesota's legislature approved a community notification program. It required state officials to evaluate the likelihood of convicted, soon-to-be released sex offenders committing other sex crimes, and neighbors were to be warned about those "most predatory offender[s]." Experience shows that sex offenders are difficult to rehabilitate and have high recidivism rates.

In 1994, Patty Wetterling helped persuade Congress to pass legislation (the Jacob Wetterling Act) that encourages states to enact laws requiring released sex offenders to register with local law enforcement agencies and enables those agencies to distribute information about sex offenders, including their names, addresses, and photographs.[34]

Many parents have praised the work of Patty Wetterling, but some civil libertarians see the new sex-offender laws as violations of the privacy and liberty rights of offenders who have already served their prison sentences.[35] Nonetheless, Patty Wetterling is a good example of a citizen-leader who, in the face of unspeakable evil and unbearable sorrow, entered the political arena and made a difference.

 # GATEWAYS TO THE WORLD: EXPLORING CYBERSPACE

For more information on political leaders, past and present, enter the name of the leader as the keyword in your search. For instance, a search using *Winston Churchill* as the keyword returned the following URL:

http://www.winstonchurchill.org/index.html

This site is maintained by the Churchill Center in Washington, D.C. It contains a vast array of materials relating to the former British prime minister, including speeches, famous quotes, photographs, and a links page.

Summary

Political leaders who occupy governmental positions can be classified as true leaders, demagogues, or ordinary politicians. Citizen-leaders hold no official office but can exert significant political influence.

True leaders, who are relatively rare, display an overriding concern for the public good, superior leadership skills, and keen practical wisdom in extraordinary situations in which the well-being (or the very existence) of a nation is at stake. Historically, they have been motivated at least in part by the lure of fame. Modern neglect of the concept of statecraft has led some observers to view it as a dying art.

Most prevalent in representative democracies are ordinary politicians. All elected officials must decide whether to exercise positive leadership or merely represent the views of their constituents. According to the delegate theory of democratic representation, politicians should act primarily as conduits for the expressed wishes of the electorate; the trustee theory, by contrast, stresses the importance of independent judgment in political office. Politicians who seek to combine these two concepts of representation are known as politicos. Some ordinary politicians can be classified as appeasers—often well-meaning but naive or incompetent public servants whose errors in judgment can lead to disaster. More sinister is the demagogue, who combines reckless personal ambition, unscrupulous methods, and charismatic appeal. Demagogues are most prevalent in democracies, and their fall is often as sudden and spectacular as is their rise to power.

Citizen-leaders combine dedication to a cause, personal ability or magnetism, and opposition to governmental policy (or established practice). They inspire others and attract a sympathetic following, frequently on a worldwide scale. They exert a moral force generated by the power of the cause they personify.

Key Terms

true leaders	statesman
demogogues	delegate theory of representation
ordinary politicians	trustee theory of representation
citizen-leaders	politico
statecraft	

Review Questions

1. How can political leaders be classified? Explain the differences between the various categories.

2. Why is the study of political leadership an important aspect of the overall study of politics?

3. Why are true leaders so rare?

4.   Describe two competing theories of representation. Which one makes the most sense to you and why?

5.   What is a demagogue? Name some demagogues. What motivates demagogues? Does democracy have any natural defenses against demagoguery? If so, what are they?

6.   What is the nature of exemplary leadership? Name four exemplary leaders and explain in detail what makes any one of them exemplary.

Recommended Reading

ADAIR, DOUGLASS. "Fame and the Founding Fathers." In *Fame and the Founding Fathers: Essays by Douglass Adair.* New York: Norton, 1974. Adair's essay on the relationship between fame and statecraft in the founding of the United States is a classic.

ALEXANDER, ROBERT J. *Rómulo Betancourt and the Transformation of Venezuela.* New Brunswick, N.J.: Transaction Books, 1982. An admiring biography of Venezuela's leading democratic statesman.

BURNS, JAMES MACGREGOR. *Leadership.* New York: HarperCollins, 1982. An exhaustive study of all facets of the leadership phenomenon.

FRISCH, MORTON, and RICHARD STEVENS, ed. *American Political Thought: The Philosophic Dimension of American Statesmanship.* 2nd ed. Itasca, Ill.: Peacock, 1983. A collection of essays on American statesmen that features a brief but outstanding introduction.

GARROW, DAVID J. *Bearing the Cross: Martin Luther King, Jr., and the Southern Christian Leadership Conference, 1955–1968.* New York: Random House, 1988. An in-depth examination of the life and accomplishments of America's greatest twentieth-century citizen-leader.

GILBERT, MARTIN. *Churchill. A Life.* New York: Henry Holt, 1991. A comprehensive one-volume biography written by his foremost biographer.

JAFFA, HARRY. *Crises of the House Divided: An Interpretation of the Issue.* Chicago: University of Chicago Press, 1982. Documents the political wisdom that characterized Abraham Lincoln's statecraft.

JORDAN, VERNON E. JR. (with Annette Gordon Reed). *Vernon Can Read! A Memoir.* New York: Public Affairs, 2001. Recounts the struggles of one of America's most prominent African-American leaders to climb the ladder of success and to promote the cause of racial equality in the process.

LONG, HUEY. *My First Days in the White House.* New York: Da Capo Press, 1972. A fanciful and amusing piece of propaganda written by one of America's foremost demagogues.

MEER, FATIMA. *Higher Than Hope: The Authorized Biography of Nelson Mandela.* New York: HarperCollins, 1991. A detailed account of the life of a former political revolutionary who has become one of the world's most distinguished leaders.

PITKIN, HANNAH, ed. *Representation.* New York: Atherton Press, 1969. A rich collection of essays with a straightforward and enlightening introduction by the editor.

WILDAVSKY, AARON. *The Nursing Father: Moses as a Political Leader.* Tuscaloosa: University of Alabama Press, 1984. A thoughtful analysis of political leadership in a biblical context.

Notes

1. Robert C. Tucker, *Politics as Leadership* (Columbia: University of Missouri Press, 1995), iii.
2. Walter Lippmann, *A Preface to Morals* (Boston: Beacon Press, 1960), 280. The quotations that follow are from 279–283.
3. See Harry Jaffa, "The Emancipation Proclamation," in *100 Years of Emancipation*, ed. Robert Goldwin (Skokie, Ill.: Rand McNally, 1964), 1–24.
4. Douglass Adair, "Fame and the Founding Fathers," in *Fame and the Founding Fathers: Essays by Douglass Adair* (New York: Norton, 1974), 10.
5. Ibid., 8.
6. Alexander Hamilton, John Jay, and James Madison, *The Federalist* (New York: Modern Library, n.d.), 470.
7. Robert J. Alexander, *Rómulo Betancourt and the Transformation of Venezuela* (New Brunswick, N.J.: Transaction Books, 1982), 435.
8. Aaron Wildavsky, *The Nursing Father: Moses as a Political Leader* (Tuscaloosa: University of Alabama Press, 1984).
9. Alexander, *Rómulo Betancourt*, 436.
10. Ibid.
11. John Edwin Fagg, *Latin America: A General History*, 2nd ed. (New York: Macmillan, 1969), 627.
12. Martin Gilbert, *Churchill* (Garden City, N.Y.: Doubleday, 1980), 100–126.
13. Ibid., 127.
14. U.S. Department of State, *Selected Documents*, April 1979.
15. Alexis de Tocqueville, *Democracy in America*, vol. 2 (New York: Schocken Books, 1961), 102–106.
16. Morton Frisch and Richard Stevens, "Introduction," in *American Political Thought: The Philosophic Dimension of American Statesmanship*, ed. Morton Frisch and Richard Stevens (Dubuque, Iowa: Kendall/Hunt, 1976), 5.
17. Quoted in Roman J. Zorn, "Theodore G. Bilbo: Shibboleths for Statesmanship," reprinted in *A Treasury of Southern Folklore: Stories, Ballads, Traditions, and Folkways of the People of the South*, ed. B. A. Brotkin (New York: Crown, 1949), 304.
18. James W. Silver, *Mississippi: The Closed Society* (Orlando, Fla.: Harcourt, 1964), 19.
19. Ibid.
20. Hodding Carter, "Huey Long: American Dictator," in *The Aspirin Age: 1919–1941*, ed. Isabel Leighton (New York: Simon & Schuster, 1949), 347.
21. Ibid., 361.
22. Joseph Tussman, as quoted in Marie Collins Swaley, "A Quantitative View," in *Representation*, ed. Hannah Pitkin (New York: Atherton Press, 1969), 83.
23. Hannah Pitkin, "The Concept of Representation," in *Representation*, ed. Pitkin, 21.
24. Quoted in Harvey Mansfield, Jr., *Statesmanship and Party Government: A Study of Burke and Bolingbroke* (Chicago: University of Chicago Press, 1965), 23.
25. Edmund Burke, "The English Constitutional System," in *Representation*, ed. Pitkin, 175.
26. Ibid.
27. In 1992, fourth district representative Dan Glickman compiled a moderate-to-liberal political record but was rated 100 percent when casting votes in favor of national security, according to the national security index of the American Security Council, a pronational defense organization that believes U.S. interests are maximized by developing and maintaining large-scale military defense systems. Glickman maintained

such a record from his initial election in 1976 until his defeat in the 1994 election by Republican Todd Tiahrt, a former Boeing company manager. Glickman subsequently was appointed secretary of agriculture. See Michael Barone and Grant Ujifusa, *Almanac of American Politics, 1994* (Washington, D.C.: National Journal, 1994), xv, 502–505.

28. Cited in Malcolm Jewell and Samuel Patterson, *The Legislative Process in the United States* (New York: Random House, 1966), 32.

29. Martin Gilbert, *Churchill: A Life* (New York: Henry Holt, 1996), 993.

30. Martin Luther King, Jr., "Letter from Birmingham City Jail," in *Civil Disobedience: Theory and Practice* (New York: Pegasus, 1969), 78–79.

31. Ibid., 75.

32. David J. Garrow, *Bearing the Cross: Martin Luther King, Jr., and the Southern Christian Leadership Conference, 1955–1968* (New York: Random House, 1988), 11.

33. Ibid., 12.

34. The amendment requiring states to provide information to the community about released sex offenders was named Megan's Law after another famous case. Megan Kanka was a seven-year-old New Jersey girl raped and murdered in 1994 by a neighbor who had a record of sexual assault against children. Megan's parents, like Patty Wetterling, led intense campaigns at the state and federal levels to enact sexual predator laws.

35. See, for instance, Caroline Louise Lewis, "The Jacob Wetterling Crimes Against Children and Sexually Violent Offender Registration Act: An Unconstitutional Deprivation of the Right to Privacy and Substantive Due Process," *Harvard Civil Rights—Civil Liberties Law Review* 31 (1996): 89–119. Despite such arguments, the courts have upheld these laws.

Chapter 12

APPROACHES TO THE PUBLIC GOOD

IDEOLOGIES AND ISMS

AT ONE POINT in Lewis Carroll's delightful *Alice's Adventures in Wonderland*, Alice becomes lost, only to encounter the Cheshire Cat, sitting on a tree branch. "Would you tell me, please, which way I ought to go from here?" asks Alice. "That depends a good deal on where you want to get to," replies the Cat. "I don't much care where," says Alice. "Then it doesn't matter which way you go," muses the Cat.

Like Alice lost in the forest, nations and their governments frequently find themselves unsure of where they want to go, not knowing which road to take. Political leadership can be woefully deficient or hopelessly divided. But intelligent understanding of programs and policies, as Alice's encounter with Cheshire Cat illustrates, can take place only as a means to fulfill definite goals. Nations, like individuals, cannot know what course to follow if they do not have an agreed upon destination.

POLITICAL ENDS AND MEANS

In politics, ends and means are inextricably intertwined. Debates over what particular new policy is desirable almost always assume that *something* must correspond to the **public good** or be in the public interest—that certain common goals will benefit the political community as a whole. Usually, in democratic politics, there are debates about means but not about ends. For example, politicians may disagree over whether a tax cut at a particular time will help to promote national prosperity (by encouraging saving and investment, balancing the national budget, reducing the rate of inflation, and so on), but arguments of this kind concern ways and means rather than purposes or ends. Although they may disagree about the best monetary and fiscal strategies, both sides would agree that the national government should promote economic growth and stability.

In some countries, the government's aims and activities have little to do with the public interest and everything to do with the personal lust for power.[1] In most democracies, the public good is generally associated with the certain core values such as security, prosperity, equality, liberty, and justice (see Chapter 13). These goals represent the political buoys by which the ship of state is kept on course. Arguments about whether the ship should tack this way or that, given the prevailing political currents and crosswinds, comprise the essence of most public policy debates. How closely the government comes to reaching its desired destinations is the ultimate test of the leadership's performance.

IDEOLOGIES AND THE PUBLIC INTEREST

People often have only vague ideas about public policy and how the government works or what it is doing at any given time.[2] But most people lean toward conservative or liberal views. When people stop merely "leaning" and adopt a rigid, closed system of political ideas, they are apt to embrace an *ideology*. An ideology is a kind of filter that "true believers" (adherents) use to interpret events, explain human behavior, and justify political action. Ideologies range from all-embracing theories of humanity and social organization (for example, Marxism) to loose collections of ideas that change over time (liberalism).

The use of "ideological" labels in political discourse is a semantic convenience that allows us to discuss various kinds of political orientations more easily and succinctly. An American conservative, for example, generally favors a strong national defense, limiting social welfare programs underwritten by the federal government, deregulation of business and industry, and similar programs. An American liberal, by contrast, tends to favor public assistance programs, reductions in military spending, and governmental regulation in such areas as the food and drug industry, occupational safety and health, housing, transportation, and energy.

Most Americans are neither doctrinaire liberals nor doctrinaire conservatives; in fact, very few Americans can be accurately described as ideologues. To be an ideologue, one must adhere strictly and tenaciously to an ideology or "party line." Individuals who are inclined to think for themselves or who are politically apathetic (the great majority of Americans) obviously do not fit this description.

In this chapter, ideologies are grouped under three headings: antigovernment ideologies, right-wing ideologies, and left-wing ideologies. The terms *left* and *right* have their origins in the European parliamentary practice of seating parties that favor social and political change to the left of the presiding officer and those opposing change (or favoring a return to a previous form of government) to the right. Of course, not every political viewpoint fits neatly into these two categories. This is especially true of extremist ideologies.

Antigovernment Ideologies

People who oppose any form of government, no matter how limited, embrace *anarchism.* The development of an anarchist ideology is often credited to the Russian revolutionary Mikhail Bakunin (1814–1876), who reveled in the "joy of destruction" and called for violent uprisings by society's beggars and criminals. Anarchism bears a close relationship to *nihilism,* which holds that the total destruction of all existing social and political institutions is a desirable end in itself. This extremely negative ideology has had relatively little impact outside of prerevolutionary Russia (and possibly Spain), although some contemporary terrorist groups appear to be anarchists or nihilists.

Libertarians are less hostile to the idea of formal government, although they believe that government must be kept to a bare minimum. (For this reason, they are sometimes called minimalists.) Proponents of *libertarianism* stress the preeminent importance of individual freedom. Libertarians generally oppose public policies that limit self-reliance and free choice—even those aimed at public safety or income security for the elderly. Libertarians insist that the invisible hand of the marketplace can regulate the interplay of social and economic forces better than the intrusive hand of the government, and the individual's right to privacy should encompass a very wide range of economic and moral choices. For example, libertarians defend the right of a citizen to print and distribute pornographic materials no matter how obscene or repugnant those materials might be to the majority

Controversial Nation of Islam leader Louis Farrakhan's implicit criticism of the U.S. government and its policies is reflected in his advocating causes of black self-sufficiency and separatism.

(including most libertarians). They generally oppose the draft on the ground that joining the armed forces ought to be a matter of personal choice.

Right-Wing Ideologies

At the opposite end of the political spectrum from anarchism and libertarianism are ideologies that stress the paramount importance of a central authority and political order. It may seem strange, but just a century ago, monarchy was a prevalent form of government throughout the world. Whether they are called kings or emperors, czars or sultans, sheikhs or shahs, monarchs have ruled in all ages and all places. Those who have held fast to the crown in the face of revolutionary challenges and popular demands for democratic reform are known as royalists or *monarchists.* Aristotle regarded monarchy—rule by a wise king—as the best form of government (although he recognized that wise kings, as opposed to tyrants, were very rare). It is also important to remember that several important countries are still ruled by monarchs—Jordan, Morocco, Saudi Arabia, and the oil-rich Persian Gulf states, to name a few.

Fascism   As the principal ideology of the extreme Right, however, monarchism was superseded in the twentieth century by *fascism,* an ideology that emphasizes the superiority of one race of people, as well as an unqualified obedience to authority. Fascism exerted a powerful influence in Europe and South America from the 1920s to the 1940s. Most commonly studied, of course, are the principal Axis powers (Germany, Italy, and Japan) in World War II. But there were other important instances of fascism as well—for example, in Spain, Hungary, and Argentina.

Despite its elitist character, fascism enjoyed genuine mass appeal, in part due to its ultranationalistic coloration. In addition to this heavy stress on the concept of nation (and, in Hitler's case, race), fascism had varied ideological roots including romanticism, xenophobia, populism, and even, oddly enough, a hierarchical, nonegalitarian, and particularistic form of socialism. (Nazi Germany, an example of a right-wing ideology put into practice, is discussed in detail in Chapter 5.)

One of the distinguishing features of many extreme right-wing ideologies is a blatant appeal to popular prejudices and hatred.[3] Such an appeal often strikes a responsive chord when large numbers of people, who are part of the racial or ethnic majority, have either not shared fully in the benefits of society or have individually and collectively suffered a severe financial setback. People in this situation, especially if they lack formal education and political discernment, may well be predisposed to believe a demagogue's explanation for their plight. Generally, scapegoats are blamed—a racial, ethnic, or religious minority group; an opposing political party; a foreign country; and the like.

On the Continent, a recession increased xenophobia and anti-immigrant feelings in the 1990s and led to demonstrations and acts of violence, especially in France and Germany (where the ultraright, pronationalist National Front and the National Democratic parties showed intermittent signs of strength). In the United States, the influence of the American Nazi party and the Ku Klux Klan (KKK) has lingered as hate groups continue to hold fast to a doctrine of white supremacy, which supplies the premise for a whole range of extremist policies dealing with immigration (foreigners must be kept out), civil rights (African Americans, Jews, and other minorities are genetically inferior and do not deserve the same constitutional protections as whites), and foreign policy (threats to white America must be met with deadly force). Both groups are organized along paramilitary lines, and both preach violence. Although the KKK has shrunken to perhaps fewer than 10,000 members, its long history of bigotry and violence toward African Americans (symbolized by the white sheets worn by its members and crosses set ablaze at rallies) makes it a group whose activities are closely monitored by the government.

The Religious Right The religious right emerged as an important nationwide political force in 1980. The election of a conservative Republican, Ronald Reagan, as president both coincided with and accelerated efforts to create a new right-wing political coalition in the United States. The coalition that emerged combined the modern political techniques of mass mailings, extensive political fund-raising, and the repeated use of the mass media (especially television) with a call for the restoration of traditional values, including an end to abortion, the reinstatement of prayer in the public schools, a campaign against pornography, the recognition of the family as the basis of American life, and a drive to oppose communism relent-lessly on every front.

This movement contained a large, core component of fundamentalist or evangelical Protestants, alternately called the New Religious Right or the New Christian Right, who saw politics as an outgrowth of core religious values. The New Christian Right was most obviously identified throughout the 1980s with the political views of television evangelist Jerry Falwell and his Moral Majority movement. Political observers disagreed both about the size of the New Right's political following and about whether it was in the mainstream of American politics. Critics labeled the New Right extremist and dangerous. More sympathetic observers, however, argued that there is no law against mixing politics and morality or politics and religion.

The New Right suffered a setback when evangelical minister Pat Robertson failed to win the Republican party's nomination for the presidency in 1988 and when pundit Pat Buchanan's campaign fizzled in 1992. Both Robertson and Buchanan had gained national recognition via cable television, with Robertson hosting the Christian television talk show *The 700 Club* and Buchanan appearing as the conservative voice on the public affairs program *Crossfire*. Although not everyone on the New Right, or even among Christian conservatives, supported them, both Robertson and Buchanan advocated core conservative values. The New Right and its Christian supporters continue to focus their efforts on gaining

© Bettmann / CORBIS

Christian Coalition head Randy Tate has become a conservative spokesperson for political issues.

influence within the Republican party. One in five Republican voters nationally can be classified as a Christian conservative, according to some estimates.

The Christian Coalition, another conservative group, has roots in the Pentecostal church. (Pat Robertson's Assemblies of God church is Pentecostal; members of Jerry Falwell's Moral Majority are mostly born-again, evangelical Christians). Boasting as many as 1 million members, the Christian Coalition produces and widely distributes a candidate scorecard, evaluating political candidates' positions on key issues. Its members focus on getting elected to local school boards in order to advocate for patriotism (as opposed to multiculturalism), religion, and a return to the basics in education, teaching abstinence in sex education classes (or doing away with sex education altogether), and restoring law and order within the schools.

The Christian Coalition has met with some success, but the organization's strategy of seeking elected office raises two interesting questions. First, are the efforts of the Christian Coalition best understood as a legitimate and laudable attempt by politically concerned citizens to involve themselves in public affairs or as a potentially worrisome blurring of the separation between church and state? Second, is the Christian Coalition an interest group or a political party?

Capitalism   The most powerful ideology in the Western world today is *capitalism.* The collapse of communism, with its explicit rejection of private property, the profit motive, and social inequality, was a triumphant moment for the proponents of *free enterprise* and the *free-market economy.* Indeed, the Cold War was in no small measure an ideological contest between the United States and the Soviet Union over this very issue.

Capitalism is the ideology of mainline conservatives in the United States and Western Europe. It is the philosophical basis for powerful organizations (and lobbies) as the United States Chamber of Commerce and the National Association of Manufacturers (NAM) and for powerful multinational corporations (MNCs) such as General Motors, Microsoft, and McDonald's.

What is capitalism? It is both an economic theory based on the principles found in Adam Smith's *Wealth of Nations* and an ideology that extols the virtues of individualism, hard work, independence, and personal initiative. As an economic theory it stresses the role of free-market forces—mainly supply and demand—in regulating economic activity, determining prices, values, and costs, and allocating scarce resources. It opposes government interference (in theory) and government regulation (in practice). It applauds the notion that, in the words of President Calvin Coolidge, "the business of America is business."

As an ideology, capitalism opposes "social welfare" and "government giveaways." Along with Calvinists,[4] conservatives tend to believe that wealth is a sign of success and a reward for virtue. Rich people deserve to be rich. Poverty is the fault of poor people themselves, who are lazy, indolent, and irresponsible. Ameliorating poverty is the job of charity and the church, not government. Conservatives also tend (or pretend) to believe in the "trickle down" theory: If the most enterprising members of society are permitted to succeed and to reinvest wealth rather than handing it all over to the tax collector the economy will grow, prosperity will trickle down to the lower levels, and everybody will be better off. Although conservatives are often reluctant to say these things publicly, many do think exactly this way (and say so, to each other).

Left-Wing Ideologies

Left-wing ideologies posit a view of human beings living together cooperatively, freed from demeaning and invidious social distinctions. In the realm of economics, these ideologies are rooted in the principle of *collectivism,* which holds that the public good is best served by common (as opposed to individual) ownership and administration of the political community's means of production and distribution. Collectivism is thus fundamentally opposed to the theory of *capitalism,* which contends that individual ownership of the means of production, in the form of private wealth (capital), offers the most efficient and equitable way of enriching the community as a whole. In modern times, the collectivist principle has been expressed most often in the form of *socialism,* which can be defined as "an ideology that rejects individualism, private ownership, and private profits in favor of a system based on economic collectivism, governmental, societal, or industrial-group ownership of the means of production and distribution of goods, and social responsibility."[5]

The French revolutionary François-Noël Babeuf (1760–1797), who advocated economic equality and common ownership of land, is the father of modern socialism. Babeuf's ideas were adapted and moderated by the so-called *utopian socialists,* including the Comte de Saint-Simon (1760–1825) and Charles Fourier (1772–1837), who envisioned an ideal (utopian) society based on collectivism, cooperation, and benevolence. Louis Blanc (1811–1882) advocated a considerably more down-to-earth form of socialism, including the establishment of worker-controlled councils and workshops; Blanc was active in worker uprisings in 1848. Out of this ferment evolved the theories and methods espoused by most left-wing ideologies of the twentieth century, from revolutionary communism to democratic socialism.

Revolutionary Communism   The extreme left-wing ideology of *revolutionary communism* or Marxism evolved principally from the writings of Karl Marx (1818–1883) and his associate, Friedrich Engels (1820–1895). Marx broke with the utopian socialists by asserting that the collectivist ideal could be attained only by open class conflict and that scientific "laws" of history preordained the outcome of that conflict. This emphasis on the inevitability of and the necessity for revolution by the *proletariat* (working class) distinguishes Marxism, or communism, from other forms of socialism.

Marx and Engels opened *The Communist Manifesto* (1848) with the bold assertion, "All history is the history of class struggle." This statement is based on two premises: (1) that economic, or material, forces are behind all human activities, and (2) that in history, change, and progress are produced by a constant clash of conflicting economic forces—or, to use the term borrowed from the German philosopher G. W. F. Hegel (1770–1831), by the *dialectic process.* All societies, Marx contended, evolve through the same historical stages, each of which represents a dominant economic pattern (the thesis) that contains the seeds of a new and conflicting pattern (the antithesis). Out of the inevitable clash between thesis and antithesis comes a synthesis, or new economic stage. What we now call the Industrial Revolution was, according to Marx, the capitalist stage of history, which succeeded the feudal stage when the *bourgeoisie* (urban artisans and merchants) wrested political and economic power from the feudal landlords. The laws of *dialectical materialism,* as Marx termed this view of history, made the rise of capitalism inevitable. Equally inevitable, according to those same laws, was conflict between capitalists and the proletariat, which would result in victory for the workers and the advent of a stable and classless society. (The utopian idea of the classless society is discussed in Chapter 2.)

Marxist theory holds that the main feature of modern industrial capitalism is the streamlining of society into two antagonistic classes—the capitalists, who own the means of production, and the proletariat, who have no choice but to work long hours for subsistence wages. The difference between those wages and the value of the products created through the workers' labor is *surplus value* (excessive profits), which the capitalists pocket. In this way, capitalists systematically exploit the workers and unwittingly lay the groundwork for a proletarian revolution.

This revolution, according to Marx and his adherents, will come about in the following way. Under the so-called *law of capitalist accumulation,* capitalists must expand at the expense of their competitors or be driven from the marketplace. As the stronger capitalists expand, they eliminate the weaker ones and capture an ever-increasing share of the market. Eventually, the most successful competitors in this dog-eat-dog contest force all the others out, thus ushering in the era of monopoly capitalism, which immediately precedes the downfall of the whole capitalist system. Why should capitalism be overthrown at this stage, when it appears that the monopoly capitalists have taken the reins of power? Because at the same time that the rich have been getting richer, the poor have been getting poorer. As human labor is replaced by machine labor, in an effort to gain a competitive edge, unemployment grows, purchasing power dwindles, and domestic markets shrink. This built-in tendency toward business recession and depression in turn gives rise to still more unemployment, even lower wages, and so forth. Countless human beings become "surplus labor"—jobless, penniless, and hopeless. This is known as the *law of pauperization* and it is inescapable. For orthodox Marxists, the "crisis of capitalism" and the resulting proletarian revolution are equally inevitable. Because capitalists will not relinquish their power, privilege, or property without a struggle, the overthrow of capitalism can occur only through violent revolution.

The belief that violent mass action is necessary to bring about radical change was central to the theories of Marx's follower V. I. Lenin (1870–1924), the founder of the Communist party of the Soviet Union and the foremost leader of the Russian Revolution of 1917. Marxist–Leninists, as they sometimes are called, argue that parliamentary democracy and "bourgeois legality" are mere superstructures designed to mask the underlying reality of capitalist exploitation. As a result, these revolutionary communists held no special brief for the kind of representative institutions prevalent in the United States and Western Europe.

With the fall of communism in the Soviet Union and Eastern Europe, Marxism has lost a great deal of its luster. Even so, the doctrine retains some appeal among the poor and downtrodden, primarily due to its crusading spirit and its promise of deliverance. In many ways, revolutionary Marxism resembles a militant fundamentalist religion, not unlike Islam in recent times and Christianity in the early Middle Ages. The British philosopher Bertrand Russell illustrated the parallels between Marxism and Christianity as follows:[6]

To understand Marx psychologically, one should use the following dictionary:

Yahweh (God)	= Dialectical Materialism
The Messiah	= Marx
The Elect	= The Proletariat
The Church	= The Communist Party
The Second Coming	= The Revolution
Hell	= Punishment of the Capitalists
The Millennium	= The Communist Commonwealth

According to Russell, the terms on the left give the emotional content of those on the right, and this analogy helps to explain Marxism's great emotional appeal.

Communism and Democracy   There has never been a strong Communist party in the United States, and relatively few American citizens would admit to having had any sympathy with communism. Yet in many other parts of the world, communist parties have, until recently, flourished. In the former Soviet Union, Eastern Europe, China, North Korea, Vietnam, Cuba, and several other Third World countries, communist parties have dominated under the banner of Marxism (in most cases, Marxism–Leninism).

Especially in the Third World, communists or Marxists spearheaded "national wars of liberation" aimed at the overthrow of existing governments after World War II. In many other countries, most notably in Western Europe, nonruling communist parties achieved democratic respectability. The Communist parties of France, Italy, and Spain, to cite but three examples, were legally recognized and popularly accepted participants in national elections and, occasionally, in coalition governments. For the most part, these parties played by the political rules and earned a considerable measure of public trust, although they never came close to winning the majority vote needed to gain control of the national government. In the 1970s, Communist party leaders in Italy and Spain led a movement called *Eurocommunism.* The Eurocommunists renounced a number of time-honored tenets of Marxism–Leninism, including advocacy of violent revolution, belief in the dictatorship of the proletariat, and dogmatic attachment to the principle of democratic centralism, which demands strict obedience to the party line and forbids dissent.

Although the influence of European communist parties has declined notably of late, it has not completely disappeared. Thus, after the French Communist party gained an impressive election victory in May 1997, three communists were appointed to the cabinet.

Democratic Socialism   In contrast to revolutionary communism, *democratic socialism,* the other main branch of socialist ideology, embraces collectivist ends (and hence rejects capitalism), but it is committed to democratic means. Unlike orthodox Marxists, democratic socialists believe in *gradualism*—reform rather than revolution.

In general, democratic socialists—also called "social democrats"—favor a greatly expanded role for government and a highly constricted role for the marketplace. Most socialist parties advocate the nationalization of key parts of the economy—transportation, communications, public utilities, banking and finance, insurance, and such basic industries as automobile manufacturing, iron and steel processing, mining, and energy. They also champion the modern-day *welfare state,* in which the government assumes broad responsibility for the health, education, and welfare of its citizens.

The goal of the welfare state is to alleviate poverty and inequality through large-scale income redistribution. Sometimes described as a cradle-to-grave system, the welfare state usually features free university education, free (or heavily subsidized) medical care, generous public assistance (family allowances), pension plans, and a variety of other free or subsidized services. To finance these programs and services, socialists advocate heavy taxation, including steeply progressive income taxes and stiff inheritance taxes designed to close the gap between rich and poor. Such policies are required by socialist ideology because it tends to equate social justice with economic equality.

After World War II, democratic socialism had a major impact in Western Europe (and a number of developing countries). Many European countries feature prominent social democratic parties. In Germany, for example, the major center left party is formally named the Social Democratic Party (SDP). Classic examples of welfare states could be found in Scandinavia and Great Britain. Notably, François Mitterrand, a socialist, was elected President of France in 1981, and in national elections held shortly thereafter, his party won enough legislative seats to form the first left-wing government in the history of the Fifth Republic (which dates from 1958). Still, with a few exceptions such as Denmark and Sweden, democratic socialism's political influence declined dramatically throughout Western Europe during the 1990s. A number of political parties that had championed socialist principles either declined in power or became friendlier to free markets and economic competition. Britain's Labour party, which won control of the government in 1997 under the leadership of moderate Tony Blair, is a prime example of the mellowing of Europe's social-democratic parties in recent years.

Democratic socialism as an organized political force has had little impact on postwar U.S. politics. In the 1930s, presidential candidate Norman Thomas ran on the Socialist party ticket and attracted attention and voter support. Both before and after World War I, the socialists polled over 900,000 votes in national elections. But the elections of 1912 and 1920 represented the high-water marks of socialism in the United States. Why has this been the case?

Americans tend to be individualistic and distrustful of "big government," and especially after World War II, they came to identify socialism with communism and to reject it on that basis. Nonetheless, many public programs that are now widely accepted and firmly entrenched closely resemble measures long advocated by democratic socialists the world over. Examples include Social Security, Medicare, family assistance, unemployment compensation, and federally subsidized housing. Welfare state measures, in other words, have fared much better in the United States than has the socialist ideology that spawned them.

Radical Egalitarianism   Radical egalitarianism is not a straightforward ideology in the sense that it owes its existence to the writings of a single individual or consists of one or two overarching and clearly defined principles; nor is it universally recognized. Nevertheless, radical egalitarianism represents a clearly identifiable approach to the public good. Radical egalitarians champion a world of complete equality. They hold that most conventional, everyday distinctions accepted by society (who succeeds, what is read and studied, and so on) have resulted primarily from bias or ethnocentrism. Radical egalitarians feel strongly that racial minorities, women, homosexuals, individuals with disabilities, and others outside the mainstream have suffered and continue to suffer from social discrimination, and now every effort must be made to ensure their advancement, success, and full equality. These groups have been neglected for too long (in favor of privileged white males); they must therefore be made both the object and the source of study, and works written about them and by them must be read as part of any college curriculum. Finally, the argument goes, these groups have not been examined adequately because of systemic discrimination and bias endemic in Western civilization; therefore, other societies and civilizations must be explored and perhaps emulated as alternatives.

The radical egalitarian analysis of American higher education, society, and civilization is highly controversial. Conservative critics object to the radical egalitarians' characterization of American society and Western civilization, bemoan their perceived lack of concern with excellence and achievement, and bristle when their critique is rejected as racist, sexist, homophobic, or otherwise biased. These critics suggest that radical egalitarians have created an emotionally charged climate where only "politically correct" thought is accorded respect. In the 1990s, the political correctness controversy raged on American college campuses, often as a kind of semantic shorthand for debate on the desirability of a world view governed by radical egalitarian assumptions.

ISMS AND AMERICAN POLITICS

American politics is essentially a tug-of-war between liberals and conservatives. Because these two labels often generate confusion, and because it is difficult to understand the central issues in American politics apart from the liberal–conservative distinction, we must analyze at length these two American approaches to the public good.

Labels In American Politics

Contemporary American liberalism and conservatism evolved from a 300-year-old *liberal tradition* in Western political thought. Most fundamentally, this tradition taught that the purpose of government was to safeguard individual rights. Today, *American liberalism* stresses social, political, and economic equality, all championed in the name of securing and expanding civil rights. By contrast, *American conservatism* favors policies designed to promote prosperity and equal opportunity, often coached in terms of safeguarding individual property and economic rights. Thus, both American liberals and conservatives champion individual rights; they simply disagree about which rights are most important.

Several factors make it difficult to define precisely what liberalism and conservatism mean in the context of contemporary U.S. politics. What are those factors?

To begin with, the role of ideology is strictly limited in the United States by a political culture in which everyday politics involves a struggle among opposing interests rather than a conflict over irreconcilable ideas or principles. Usually, the public stands taken by elected officials are shaped to reflect local economic interests, to coincide with the shifting social or economic moods of the national electorate, or to confront a particularly pressing problem. Therefore, although American politics has its share of doctrinaire liberals and conservatives, in practice American politicians tend to be more pragmatic than dogmatic.

Liberals or conservatives frequently find themselves on the same side of a controversial issue. For example, it is generally true that conservatives favor laws against pornography whereas liberals oppose such statutes. (Hence it is sometimes said, tongue in cheek, that liberals buy the books that conservatives want to ban, whereas conservatives form censorship committees and read the books as a group.) Nonetheless, certain so-called minimalist conservatives, or libertarians, oppose all restrictions on the sale, display, distribution, or ownership of any kind of reading material. And certain liberal—even radical—advocates of women's rights would join conservatives in banning such books, arguing that pornography exploits and degrades all females for the gratification of a few perverted (or profiteering) males.

Some issues that divide society into liberal and conservative camps in one era simply become irrelevant in another. Conservatives once defended the power and privilege of the aristocracy, but all formal titles of nobility were outlawed by the Constitution more than two centuries ago. In Europe, where hereditary titles were previously the key to wealth and power, they are now an anomalous throwback to the past, a quaint reminder of their former preeminence. Although conservatives, more often than liberals, still tend to represent the interests of the rich, no serious political figure in this country would dare suggest the resurrection of a formal aristocracy.

Common Themes

At one time, the terms *liberalism* and *conservatism* may have reflected coherent and clearly defined alternatives. In contemporary American political life, however, they are not distinct and completely formed ideologies, as are communism and fascism.

In the United States, both liberalism and conservatism have developed from, and represent variations on, a fundamental set of political principles.[7] This American creed owes much to the political writings of John Locke. As summed up in the Declaration of Independence, it holds that all human beings are created equal; that they are endowed with certain unalienable rights, including the rights of life, liberty, and the pursuit of happiness (Jefferson's expansion of Locke's "right to property"); and that government exists to protect those rights and acquires legitimacy by ruling according to the consent of the governed. The Declaration also states that when government becomes unmindful of the reasons for which it was created, the people have the right to alter or abolish it.

Note that the Declaration of Independence, in very general terms, specifies those ends of government to which we referred at the beginning of this chapter. *Liberty* is explicitly mentioned, as is the individual's right to life, or *security*. *Prosperity* is alluded to in the form of government's obligation to safeguard a person's right to pursue happiness (after all, the pursuit of happiness cannot exclude the pursuit of wealth in a commercial society). *Equality* is taken to be a fundamental human condition, and American citizens are guaranteed, among other things, equal liberty.

Finally, it is assumed that a government which does not adequately protect or respect the individual's right to life, liberty, and the pursuit of happiness is not worthy of its good name; such a government, the Declaration implies, violates the principle of *justice* and can be altered or abolished. In the U.S. Constitution, which has the avowed purpose to "establish Justice, insure domestic Tranquility, provide for the common defense, promote the general Welfare and secure the Blessings of Liberty," these basic ends of government are spelled out even more clearly.

Conservatives: The Primacy of Economic Rights

Conservatives in the United States generally stress the primacy of economics and economic rights. In so doing, they echo and expand on arguments first propounded by certain seventeenth- and eighteenth-century political philosophers and economists.

John Locke (1632–1704)   Although John Locke is recognized primarily as a political philosopher, he also contributed greatly to the idea of the *commercial republic,* an economic concept that forms the core of modern conservatism. Locke declared clearly and emphatically that individuals have a *right* to property—especially property they acquire through their own exertions—and that one of the primary purposes of government should be the protection of private property. He thus provided the political rationale for property rights, legal liabilities, and contractual obligations—the foundations of the commercial state. In addition, he gave the acquisitive instinct a newfound respectability in intellectual discourse.

Many earlier philosophers, from Aristotle to Thomas Aquinas (1224–1274), had cautioned against excessive concern for worldly possessions. Locke, in contrast, envisioned a society in which individuals would constantly endeavor to improve their lot, the spirit of enterprise and invention would flourish, and money would serve as the universal medium of exchange. Wealth could then be accumulated, reinvested, and expanded. Society would prosper—and a prosperous society, Locke reasoned, would be a happy one.

Baron de Montesquieu (1689–1755)   While Locke developed the general theory of the commercial republic, the French political philosopher Baron de Montesquieu, in his famous *Spirit of the Laws* (1748), identified a number of specific advantages associated with business and commerce. In Montesquieu's view, nations that trade extensively with other nations would be predisposed toward peace because war disrupts international commerce. He also asserted that commerce would help to produce more just political orders by opening up new avenues for individual self-advancement; in other words, through hard work and perseverance, even those born into poverty could become wealthy. In addition, an emphasis on commerce would inoculate a society against religious fanaticism, as a preoccupation with creature comforts and "keeping up with the Joneses" would replace the fanatical zeal that leads to religious strife. A final advantage of a commercial order would be its positive effect on individual morality. A commercial democracy, Montesquieu believed, would foster certain modest bourgeois virtues, including "frugality, economy, moderation, labor, prudence, tranquility, order, and rule."[8]

Adam Smith (1723–1790)   After Locke had laid the political foundations for the commercial state and Montesquieu had pointed out the advantages of such a state, the Scottish economist Adam Smith explained its operating principles. Smith was persuaded that both individual happiness and social harmony are closely tied to ways in which goods and services are produced. In his enormously influential *Inquiry into the Nature and Causes of the Wealth of Nations* (1776), he set out to delineate how a commercial society can function in an orderly and prosperous fashion without central government regulation or planning of economic affairs. More than any other work, this book provided the rationale for modern capitalism.

Like Locke before him, Smith was impressed with the central role of self-interest in human activity. In the economic marketplace, he argued, self-interest not only spurs individuals to work but also prompts them to select occupations that correspond to specific social needs:

> It is not from the benevolence of the butcher, the brewer, or the baker, that we expect our dinner, but from their regard to their own self-interest. We address ourselves, not to their humanity but to their self-love, and never talk to them of our own necessities but of their advantages.[9]

Smith famously theorized about the "invisible hand" of the marketplace, expressed in the *law of supply and demand.* This law, he argued, determines market value. Where supply is large and demand is small, the market value (or price) of the item in question will be driven down until only the most efficient producers remain. Conversely, where demand is great and supply is low, the market value of a given item will be driven up. Eventually, prices will decline as competition intensifies, again leaving only the most efficient producers in a position to retain or expand their share of the market. In this way, the market automatically seeks supply-and-demand equilibrium.

Smith believed that self-interest and market forces would combine to sustain economic competition, which would in turn keep prices from ranging very far from the actual cost of production (if they did, producers would be undercut by eager competitors). In this view, self-interest and market conditions make prices self-adjusting: high prices provide an incentive for increased competition and low prices lead to increased demand and hence increased production.

Finally, Smith's *free-enterprise theory* holds that individuals voluntarily enter precisely those professions and occupations that society considers most valuable because the monetary rewards often are irresistible even if the work itself is not particularly glamorous.[10] Taken as a whole, these concepts define what has come to be known as *laissez-faire* ("let the people do as they wish") *capitalism*—the idea that the marketplace, unfettered by central state planning, is the best regulator of the economy.

Modern Conservatism   Building on the writings of Locke, Montesquieu, and Smith, contemporary conservatives usually stress the right of people to pursue happiness as individuals (rather than members of a collective), emphasizing the right to hold, accumulate, and dispose of property. They also tend to defend the interests of business and corporate industry, arguing along the lines of Adam Smith that the private pursuit of wealth will ultimately lead to public prosperity. Finally, conservatives generally decry state intervention in the marketplace (such as social welfare programs that redistribute wealth) and bureaucratic "meddling" in business affairs (for example, federal regulations mandating minimum environmental standards).

Conservatives argue the quest for individual affluence brings with it certain collective benefits, including a shared belief in the work ethic, a love of order and stability, and a healthy self-restraint on the part of government. These collective "goods" are most likely to result from a political system that ensures the best possible conditions for the pursuit of personal gain. It may be that Montesquieu's "frugality, economy, moderation, labor, prudence, tranquility, order, and rule" are not the highest ideals, but to the conservative, they provide the best available insurance for a decent and stable political order.

Liberals: The Primacy of Civil Rights

Like conservatives, liberals stress that individuals are endowed with certain rights. But unlike conservatives, the rights liberals hold most dear are *civil rights*. Thus, they tend to be vigorous defenders of individual or groups who have been discriminated against, such as racial minorities, women, and the poor. Liberals generally espouse vigorous governmental action to promote equal rights. At the same time, they generally oppose most governmental restrictions on freedom of expression as well as efforts to "legislate morality" for the purpose of upholding community standards and traditions.

Behind this emphasis on personal liberties lies a fundamental belief in the virtue of individuality. Protection of and respect for the uniqueness and dignity of each person in the society should be the overriding goal of government, in this view. The case for individualism was eloquently stated in John Stuart Mill's *On Liberty* (1859):

> He who lets the world, or his own portion of it, choose his plan of life for him, has no need of any other faculty than the ape-like one of imitation. He who chooses his plan for himself, employs all his faculties. He must use observation to see, reasoning and judgement to foresee, activity to gather materials for decision, discrimination to decide, and when he has decided, firmness and self-control to hold to his deliberate decisions. And these qualities he requires and exercises exactly in proportion as the part of his conduct which he determines according to his own judgement and feelings is a large one. It is possible that he might be guided in some good path, and kept out of harm's way, without any of these things. But what will be his comparative worth as a human being? It really is of importance, not only what men do, but also what manner of men they are that do it. Among the works of man, which human life is rightly employed in perfecting and beautifying, the first in importance surely is man himself. . . . Human nature is not a machine to be built after a model, and set to do exactly the work prescribed for it, but a tree, which requires to grow and develop on all sides, according to the tendency of the inward forces which make it a living thing.[11]

Mill goes on to note that individuality is constantly threatened by the stifling conformity of mass opinion. Precisely for this reason, liberals argue, individuality requires protection against governments founded on majority rule. A democratic society, they point out, tends to confuse quantity and quality of opinion and to equate numerical superiority with political truth; in the process, dissenters are often frowned on or even persecuted.

In the eyes of Mill and his intellectual heirs, individualism is good for society and individuals alike, for it is from the creativity, dynamism, and inventiveness of individuals that social progress springs. Following this line of logic, liberals often argue that by granting citizens the full range of freedom to develop their talents and disseminate their ideas, government can set up a symbiotic relationship in which both the individual and society can prosper and grow.

Essential Differences

At the root of the differences between American liberals and conservatives lie contrasting opinions about human nature. Liberals believe in the essential goodness of human beings. Even though they do not deny that some individuals act in antisocial ways, they tend to view such miscreants as victims of their environment. Most present-day American liberals would say, for instance, that to reduce crime, society must alleviate the conditions of poverty, racism, and despair that breed antisocial behavior. In other words, human beings are equal in dignity and deserve to be treated as such both by their government and by their fellow citizens.

Conservatives take a dimmer view of human nature. They consider human beings to be inherently selfish and often unruly. Individuals seek to advance themselves ahead of others, but they differ in motivation, ability, moral character, and luck. Such differences, conservatives argue, are beyond the ability of any government to minimize. Consequently, they have fewer qualms than their liberal compatriots about disparities in wealth or privilege within society. In addition, they are generally less inclined to attribute antisocial behavior to environmental factors, contending instead that there will always be some "bad apples" in society.

Another difference between conservatives and liberals is that the latter view themselves as part of an evolving historical process through which the human condition has improved and will continue to improve. In other words, liberals take a progressive view of history, believing that the average person is better off now than a generation ago or a century or two ago. This belief leads to the conviction that future social arrangements, both at home and abroad, can be constructed to bring out the best in all human beings. Hence liberals tend to be forward-looking and optimistic about the long-term possibilities for making society and the world a better place.

Conservatives, by contrast, look to the past for guidance in meeting the challenges of the present. They dispute the notion that change can be equated with progress. To them, a political community is a fragile organism held together by shared beliefs and common values. Custom and convention, established institutions (such as the family, church, and government), and deeply ingrained social reflexes provide for conservatives the only sound basis for a stable social order. Like society itself, traditions should never be changed (or exchanged) too rapidly. Most conservatives, in sum, would subscribe wholeheartedly to Edmund Burke's admonition that when change is not needed, there is no need to change.

Conservatives, Liberals, and Public Policy

The conservative-versus-liberal orientations toward change, human nature, and society help to explain the current tension between the two groups, which one observer refers to as a "culture war."[12] Underlying the issues being debated (the purpose, composition, and importance of such social institutions as the family, education, the arts, law, and politics) is a moral disagreement. The conservative impulse toward tradition and orthodoxy culminates in the belief that right and wrong are universal values grounded in a transcendent philosophy or religion. By contrast, the liberal attachment to diversity and tolerance are reflected in the belief that moral and political decisions are intensely personal matters. For example, most liberals oppose prayer in schools, favor broad legal and social rights for gays and lesbians, and champion women's right to abortion, whereas many conservatives take the opposite stance on these issues. Conservatives typically argue that to ban prayer from schools, to recognize the rights of homosexuals, or to allow abortion is at some level morally wrong, whereas liberals typically argue that such practices, by denying individual choice, violate what is morally right.[13]

Liberals and conservatives also differ over issues of human nature and human rights. A devotion to property rights, along with a belief that prosperity is the

GATEWAYS TO THE WORLD: EXPLORING CYBERSPACE

The following is a list of the URLs for Web sites related to various ideologies. These sites are included purely for instructional purposes; the author does not necessarily endorse any of the ideas or ideologies to which specific sites are dedicated.

Anarchism

http://flag.blackened.net/daver/anarchism/anarchism.html

Nihilism

http://www.ws5.com/nihilism/; http://members.aol.com/nihilist01/

Libertarianism

http://www.libertarian.org/

Nazism and Fascism

**http://www.fordham.edu/halsall/mod/modsbook43.html;
http://remember.org/hist.root.what.html**

Religious Right

http://www.cc.org/

Socialism

http://www.gn.apc.org/socint/contents.html

Communism

http://www.marxists.org/

Democratic Socialism

http://www.dsausa.org/

essence of human happiness, generally leads conservatives to favor unregulated commerce and industry and to oppose governmental interference in the marketplace. For the same reasons, they tend to oppose social programs that involve large-scale redistribution of wealth, heavy or progressive taxation, governmentally mandated health insurance programs, and the like. These attitudes lead contemporary conservatives to favor "less government," and where government programs are necessary or unavoidable, they believe state and local governments are closer to the people and therefore trust them far more than the federal government. On another level, a somewhat harsh view of human nature predisposes conservatives to be tougher than liberals in dealing with perceived threats to personal safety and public order—thus, they typically favor stiffer sentences for criminals—and national security. They do not share the liberal concern with protecting provocative speech—especially when those involved are perceived as "radicals." Finally, in the realm of equality, conservatives generally believe that an excessive concern with economic equality can undermine the incentive system that, they argue, has made the United States successful and prosperous. For example, governmental attempts to secure economic equality through such devices as an affirmative action program are thought to stifle individual initiative and sever the link between personal merit and pecuniary reward.

Because liberals tend to picture the world as a benign place and human nature as inherently good, they are apt to see opportunities for cooperation, accommodation, and remedial action where conservatives see challenges, threats, and dangers requiring firmness and, when necessary, force. Thus, in foreign affairs, liberals tend to favor reduced defense spending, whereas conservatives tend to follow the old adage, "Fear God and keep your powder dry." In domestic affairs, liberals generally believe that society as a whole benefits from wholesale governmental intervention to provide disadvantaged or unfortunate persons with public housing, public works jobs, universal health insurance, and so on. No matter what the level of prosperity in the society at large, they argue, gross inequalities in the distribution of wealth must be readjusted by public policy, for if all humans are truly created equal, then no one should have to suffer the indignities of grinding poverty in a society where some live in luxury. Discrimination against any American can best be averted by strong affirmative action programs and by vigorous government enforcement. Moreover, believing that the perpetrators of crime are also victims (of economic and social injustice) and recognizing that the poor have the most difficult encounters with the criminal justice system, liberals demand maximum legal protection for the rights of the accused. Finally, for American liberals, individuality can best be protected by prohibiting government from interfering with any exercise of the constitutional rights of free speech, press, religion, assembly, association, and privacy.

Summary

All governments seek to attain certain social and economic goals in accordance with their view of the public good. How they implement these goals depends on the ideologies—the organized sets of beliefs about the public good—that they embrace.

Ideologies can be classified as antigovernment (anarchism, libertarianism), right-wing (monarchism, fascism), or left-wing (revolutionary communism, democratic socialism, radical egalitarianism) in orientation. U.S. politics is dominated by two other ideological tendencies: liberalism and conservatism. It is surprisingly difficult to differentiate clearly between these two viewpoints, principally because liberalism and conservatism in the United States share many fundamental values and assumptions. Conservatives stress economic rights; liberals emphasize civil rights. Liberals believe in the basic goodness of human nature; conservatives take a less charitable view of human nature. Liberals look to the future, believing that progress will ensure a better life for all; conservatives look to the past for guidance in dealing with the problems of the present. These differences are reflected in the divergent public policy aims espoused by the two ideological groups.

Key Terms

public good	bourgeoisie
ideology	dialectical materialism
anarchism	law of capitalist accumulation
nihilism	law of pauperization
libertarianism	Eurocommunism
monarchists	democratic socialism
fascism	gradualism
capitalism	welfare state
free enterprise	liberal tradition
free-market economy	American liberalism
collectivism	American conservatism
socialism	liberalism
utopian socialists	conservatism
revolutionary communism	law of supply and demand
proletariat	laissez-faire capitalism

Review Questions

1. Constitutional governments might define the public good in terms of attaining what goals?

2. Why might it be said that the performance of a government depends essentially on its ability to help realize the public good?

3. What is *ideology*? Is it a scientific term that is easily applied to a political analysis? Why or why not?

4. How does revolutionary communism compare with democratic socialism? On which political questions do the two movements agree? On which do they disagree?

5. How can we distinguish between a liberal and a conservative in the United States? What fundamental assumptions separate these two ideologies?

Recommended Reading

BERNSTEIN, EDWARD. *Evolutionary Socialism: A Criticism and Affirmation.* Translated by E. C. Harvey. New York: Schocken Books, 1961. A classic work espousing the cause of evolutionary socialism.

D'SOUZA, DINESH. *Illiberal Education: The Politics of Race and Sex on Campus.* New York: Random House, 1992. A controversial and influential attack on political correctness as practiced on American college campuses.

FRIEDMAN, MILTON. *Capitalism and Freedom.* Chicago: University of Chicago Press, 1994. A classic argument in favor of minimal governmental participation in the private sector.

GALBRAITH, JOHN KENNETH. *The New Industrial State.* 4th ed. Boston: Houghton Mifflin, 1985. A vigorous argument that concentrated economic power requires a powerful, active government.

HAYEK, FRIEDRICH. *The Road to Serfdom.* Chicago: University of Chicago Press, 1956. A classic attack on the welfare state.

HEYWOOD, ANDREW. *Political Ideologies: An Introduction.* New York: St. Martin's Press, 1992. A comprehensive survey of contemporary ideology.

HUNTER, JAMES DAVISON. *Before the Shooting Begins: The Search for Democracy in America's Culture War.* New York: Free Press, 1994. Hunter continues (see next entry) his examination of America's culture war, examining the basis of America's political beliefs, and contending that this deep split endangers the nation's democratic future.

———. *Culture Wars: The Struggle to Define America.* New York: Basic Books, 1991. An argument that America is fundamentally split politically according to different moral perspectives.

MACRIDIS, ROY. *Contemporary Political Ideologies, Movements and Regimes.* 6th ed. Reading, Mass.: Addison-Wesley, 1995. A summary of the characteristics and relative importance of the ideologies that have shaped our world.

MILL, JOHN STUART. *On Liberty.* New York: Viking Press, 1982. A profoundly important work whose discussion of individualism is vital to an understanding of the root assumptions of liberalism.

TUCKER, ROBERT, ed. *The Marx-Engels Reader.* 2nd ed. New York: Norton, 1978. Marx's writings, including the *Manifesto,* must be read if one is to understand modern revolutionary communism; this book contains a good selection of those writings.

Notes

1. Aristotle, *The Politics,* ed. and trans. Ernest Barker (New York: Oxford University Press, 1962), 1279a, 112.

2. This discussion builds on Andrew Heywood, *Political Ideologies: An Introduction* (New York: St. Martin's Press, 1992), 6–8. Heywood's (and our) discussion in turn builds on a definition offered in May Selinger, Politics and Ideology (London: Allen & Unwin, 1976).

3. The Anti-Defamation League of B'nai B'rith, *Hate Groups in America: A Record of Bigotry and Violence* (New York, n.d.), 11.

4. Calvinists are Protestants who follow the teachings of John Calvin (1509–1564); strict Calvinists believe in predestination, which holds that some people are chosen by God for salvation and others are eternally damned.

5. Jack C. Plano and Roy Olton, *The International Relations Dictionary* (Santa Barbara, Calif.: ABC, 1982), 81.

6. Bertrand Russell, *A History of Western Philosophy* (New York: Simon & Schuster, 1965), 364.

7. Martin Diamond, Winston Fisk, and Herbert Garfinkel, *The Democratic Republic: An Introduction to American Government* (Skokie, Ill.: Rand McNally, 1971), 4–5.

8. Baron de Montesquieu, *The Spirit of the Laws,* trans. Thomas Nugent (New York: Hafner Press, 1949), bk. 5, chap. 6, 46.

9. Adam Smith, *An Inquiry into the Nature and Causes of the Wealth of Nations* (New York: Modern Library, 1965), 14.

10. As is pointed out in Robert Heilbroner, *The Worldly Philosophers: The Lives, Times and Ideas of the Great Economic Thinkers* (New York: Modern Library, 1965), 14.

11. John Stuart Mill, *On Liberty* (Lake Bluff, Ill.: Regnery/Gateway, 1955), 85.

12. James Davison Hunter, *Culture Wars: The Struggle to Define America* (New York: Basic Books, 1991). Our discussion generally follows, but does not duplicate, Hunter's.

13. Ibid. As Hunter makes clear, this is not a disagreement between the religious and nonreligious; rather, often the dispute is waged by those within religions.

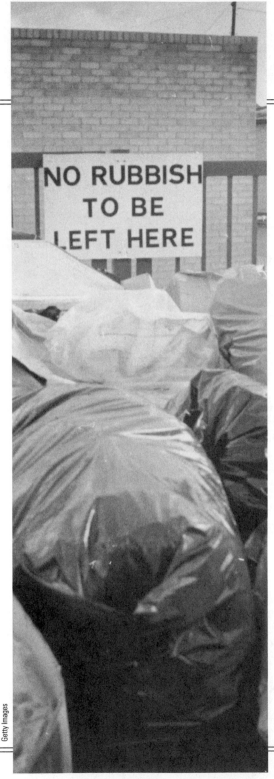

Getty Images

Chapter 13

Issues in Public Policy

Principles, Priorities, and Practices

CHAPTER 12 IDENTIFIED five core values: security, prosperity, equality, liberty, and justice. These values can easily be translated into policy aims, but deciding precisely how to translate them into actual policy is not easy. Debates over the changing issues of public policy are the very substance of politics in democratic countries.

Because a comprehensive, comparative study of public policy issues is beyond the scope of this text, we will focus mainly on the United States. Many of the policy questions and problems addressed in this chapter, however, arise in other democracies as well. Together we will explore alternative ways of dealing with some of these questions at different points along the way.

THE PURSUIT OF SECURITY

The first goal of virtually every independent state is to provide a reasonable amount of security for its citizens. With some notable exceptions, such as tyrannies that deliberately implant suspicion and fear among their citizens, governments tend to view individual and group security as important in its own right and as a prerequisite for the achievement of all other worthwhile ends. Among influential political philosophers, Thomas Hobbes (1588–1679) argued most strenuously that safety from harm constituted the chief justification for a government's existence. Hobbes was not alone in this contention, however: The venerable Aristotle may have stressed other, higher aims of politics, but he also understood clearly that the first goal of political life was the protection of life itself.[1]

Security from Foreign Enemies

National security became a commonplace expression in the post–World War II vocabulary of American politics. Protecting the United States from foreign and domestic enemies has been the highest national priority, as reflected in soaring defense spending and, in the 1980s, gaping budget deficits. But with the fading of the Cold War, the question arises: Has the world changed so fundamentally now as to drastically alter America's priority and greatly diminish the importance of military preparedness?

From 1945 until the late 1980s, the most important national security dispute within the United States focused on the Soviet threat. Those who saw the Soviet Union as powerful but peace-loving questioned high levels of arms expenditures and favored collaborative efforts (above all, strategic arms reductions) between the two superpowers. Other observers, who believed the Soviet Union to be a dangerous expansionist power bent on world domination, championed high defense budgets and favored concerted efforts to develop new high-tech weapons systems. This American national security debate was basically a disagreement about the motives of Soviet leaders and the character of the Soviet system.

With the collapse of the Soviet Union in the early 1990s, high levels of American defense spending became increasingly difficult to justify to American taxpayers. But skeptics pointed out that the world had not suddenly become a completely safe place even if many Americans *felt* safer. Economic and strategic threats to American interests were always possible (witness Iraq's invasion of Kuwait in 1990), and the persistence of regional or local conflicts, coupled with the proliferation of mass-destruction weapons (ballistic missiles, as well as nuclear, chemical, and biological weapons), meant that new dangers were appearing on the horizon.

Yet as the decade of the nineties continued, it appeared that the danger of a major war on the scale of World War II had receded. Liberals and conservatives agreed and, citing mounting budget deficits and changing political circumstances, advocated sizable force reductions and cuts or slowdowns in weapons development and acquisition programs. (However, they did not always agree on the rate and total size of these reductions.) Still, defense budgets reflected scaled-down military assumptions (see Figure 13-1). From the Cold War peak in 1986, Pentagon personnel (active, reserve, and civilian) declined by almost 20 percent. Active-duty military also saw a 20 percent reduction (from 4.4 million to 3.5 million).

Then came the terrorist attacks of September 11, 2001, and the mood of the country changed in a single morning. Having suffered a direct hit and with a gaping hole in its side, the Pentagon was suddenly at the forefront of the national policy arena once again. The Congress and the country were back in the Cold War groove ready to spend "whatever it takes" to make America safe for democracy, safe from terrorists within, and safe from enemies who harbor terrorists abroad.

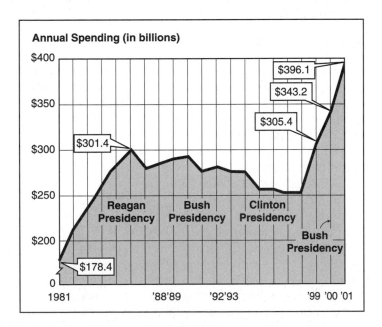

FIGURE 13-1   Military Spending on the Rise

In the 1990s, active-duty forces dipped below the post–World War II low in 1950. Military spending fell dramatically in the 1990s, but has risen again to Cold War levels in recent years.

SOURCE: Defense Department. Reprinted from the *Sioux Falls Argus Leader,* May 18, 1997, 11C.

Gone was the euphoria of the 1990s, gone was the illusion of invulnerability, gone was the sense that America was "special" and that catastrophes only happen to others.

Security from Enemies Within

September 11 placed a premium on the role of government in protecting the lives and property of individual citizens from enemies within—fellow citizens, spies, and unfriendly aliens. Today, this "new" national security issue is on the front burner; it receives even more attention than old international security issues (and provokes far more controversy). The debate has brought to light the difficulty of making a clear policy distinction between terrorism and crime. Clearly, terrorist acts—as all acts of violence against innocents—are criminal acts. But terrorism is motivated by political aims and often supported by "state sponsors" abroad (among others, Afghanistan, Iraq, Iran, and North Korea). Are terrorists, therefore, to be treated differently than "ordinary" felons? Do they deserve the same constitutional protections as, say, accused murderers and rapists? What if the accused also happen to be U.S. citizens? Terrorism is the focus of a later chapter, so we confine our discussion to violent crimes in this chapter, touching on terrorism only insofar as it is relevant to issues of crime and punishment.

There is little agreement as to what causes crime, what society ought to do about it, and whether all acts currently classified as crimes should continue to be punished (for example, possession or personal use of marijuana). Although it has declined of late, the long-term crime rate in the United States has risen dramatically over the past fifty years. Why?

According to some experts, crime is essentially a social phenomenon, a reflection of personal frustration or alienation caused by poverty and neglect, racial discrimination, and unequal economic opportunity. Why else, they ask, would the crime rate be highest in urban slums, where median incomes and living standards are the lowest? In this view, crime is a product of governmental neglect and social indifference.

Other experts point to different social phenomena to explain the increase in crime. They stress the dramatic decline of the traditional American family and note the increasing number of children at risk. Additionally, they emphasize the declining importance of community and neighborhoods and cite the resulting sense of isolation and individualism now predominant in American life. Where social bonds (and associated emotions such as shame) are weakened, they contend, so are constraints limiting socially undesirable or illegal behavior. Finally, these experts also blame popular culture spread by the mass media. Not only does contemporary American culture glorify violence (here encompassing everything from popular music to television advertisements), but it persistently endorses values more compatible with crime, such as immediate gratification and self-expression (as opposed to deferred gratification and self-restraint).[2]

Those who see poverty and income inequality as the root cause of crime champion government programs to help alleviate those conditions. By contrast, critics who emphasize the decline of family and culture believe that there is little

Defining Crime Down

AP / Wide World Photos

Daniel Patrick Moynihan

Why have Americans accepted such a high level of crime? One intriguing (and controversial) answer was suggested by New York Senator Daniel Patrick Moynihan, who is also a social scientist, in a much discussed article, "Defining Deviancy Down."[3] Faced with a high crime rate, Moynihan contends, Americans have denied its importance by redefining (i.e., defining down) what they considered to be normal. Years ago, a high crime rate was understood to be a severe social pathology; now, it has become accepted as a normal condition of society about which little can be done.

Moynihan supplies a striking example. On February 14, 1929, four gangsters gunned down seven rival gangsters in the infamous St. Valentine's Day Massacre. Moynihan observes that the nation was shocked, the event became a legend, the St. Valentine's Day Massacre merited *two* entries in the *World Book Encyclopedia*, and "the Massacre" influenced an amendment to the Constitution which ended Prohibition (a policy thought to have caused much gang violence).

Moynihan notes that with today's drug traffic, this form of violence has returned, but, by contrast, "at a level that induces denial." Americans today accept violence they once rejected as deviant and unacceptable behavior. Sadly, concludes Moynihan, "Los Angeles has the equivalent of a St. Valentine's Day Massacre every weekend."

government can actually do to reduce crime, except increase the probability of "swift and sure" punishment.

A different approach to reducing crime involves the decriminalization of certain so-called victimless crimes. The justification for such a position is simply practical—that it would reduce police, prosecutorial, and prison time and costs—but philosophical as well. Acts as different as prostitution and vagrancy share a common focus: Each is undertaken freely by an individual or among individuals, and no specific member of society is harmed.

The decriminalization debate has focused on drug legalization. Originally advocated on behalf of marijuana, the argument has been extended lately to include cocaine as well. Advocates of decriminalization argue that the undesirable social aspects of drug addiction occur primarily because many addicts rob and steal to support a habit made expensive by the government's declaring it to be illegal. Legalize drugs, and the price will drop significantly and the associated crime rate will decrease (as will the profits made by organized crime). Opponents of legalization dispute this claim. Although they agree that legalization may truly lessen the cost to society imposed by presently addicted individuals, legalization would also inevitably increase the number of addicts, thus harming society by creating an unproductive, self-destructive, and growing number of drug-addicted citizens. In the end, the main argument against legalized drug addiction proves to be the same as that made against legalizing victimless crimes—that society ultimately bears the final cost, whether it be in a drug-addicted citizenry or in neighborhoods frequented by prostitutes and vagrants, whose very presence often threatens the security and stability of these neighborhoods.

Decriminalization of drugs and prostitution is not likely to happen any time soon in the United States, but if more Americans were to visit the Netherlands and spend time in its capital, Amsterdam, they might question whether the Dutch model would not work in the United States. In Amsterdam, drugs and prostitution are allowed but only in restricted areas under no-nonsense police supervision and control. Prostitutes are required to have frequent medical checkups, and tough illegal drug trafficking laws are vigorously enforced. Today, Amsterdam is one of the most attractive, prosperous, and impressive cities in Western Europe.

Another crime-related public policy debate has focused on the issue of gun control. While many conservatives contended that restricting the sale and ownership of weapons would not reduce the violent crime rate, support for this view began to wane. Thus, in 1993, Congress passed the *Brady Bill* requiring a five-day waiting period prior to the purchase of a handgun, and in 1994, it placed restrictions on the sale of assault weapons.

The relationship between gun control and anti-terrorism in the post–9-11 climate raises an interesting question. It is possible that the American public's heightened concern with safety and security, coupled with the government's efforts to prevent future terrorist attacks, will lead to greater restrictions on the possession of handguns and other weapons; at the same time, there will almost certainly be those who argue that the citizen's supposed constitutional right to bear arms is more important than ever now that foreign enemies are targeting civilians.

Social Security

Many modern governments have also sought to provide for social security, often defined broadly to include poverty, hunger, illness, and old age, as well as natural disasters such as floods, hurricanes, fires, and other acts of God. What is government's proper role in helping individuals combat these perennial threats to life and health? Food stamps, farm subsidies, pensions, health and unemployment benefits, and student aid are all designed to provide citizens with financial assistance (security) when and where it is needed.

The scope of the federal government's obligations in these areas came under intense scrutiny in the 1990s. Critics of welfare argued that government "giveaway" programs encourage the very behavior they trying to combat (by encouraging people not to work). In 1996, welfare reform gave states more authority (and flexibility) in implementing welfare programs and limited welfare payments for those unwilling to work.

Among the most pressing budget problems is the solvency of the Social Security Trust Fund that provides retirement and health care benefits to senior citizens. Social Security makes monthly remittances to older Americans and Medicare covers seniors' doctor and hospital bills. Both have grown dramatically in recent decades. Because Americans are forced to pay into the Social Security pension fund until they retire (normally at age 65), these benefits are aptly called *entitlements* (government expenditures that Americans expect as a right, with Social Security and Medicare the two most expensive ones). Entitlements are politically sensitive because major interest groups (such as American Association of Retired Persons or AARP) and large numbers of voters (especially senior citizens) are prepared to punish politicians who want to cut these programs.

Both Medicare and Social Security suffer from a similar problem: Expenditures are rising far more quickly than projected revenues. Part of the problem is that Americans are living longer, making the program more expensive. Far more troubling (from a public policy standpoint) is the demographic trend line, specifically the large number of baby boomers (people born in the years immediately following World War II) approaching retirement who will draw on these government programs. For instance, when Medicare was established in 1965, there were 5.5 people paying money into the Medicare program for each recipient drawing money out. By 2040, the ratio will decrease to a very narrow 2.2 to 1.0 margin. Medicare has also been hit hard by the rapidly rising cost of health care. From 1980 to the mid-1990s, the cost of the Medicare program increased 11 percent annually, making it the fastest-growing federal program (Figure 13-2).

There is at least one other problem with the Social Security Trust Fund that politicians prefer not to talk about. For many years, the government has used trust fund monies to cover revenue shortfalls (budget deficits). When government fails to balance the public budget, it either has to borrow money from the private sector (primarily through the sale of savings bonds) or take it out of public "savings"— that is where the Social Security Trust Fund comes in.

Despite the perennial plundering of this fund, the federal government was in debt to the tune of $5.8 trillion in 2001. The interest payments on this debt amounted to $360 billion in 2001. By comparison, NASA's budget was $14 billion, while $32 billion went to education and $41 billion to roads. Thus, while demographic trends mentioned earlier pose a serious problem for public pension funds in many developed countries at present, government action and dubious (even deceitful) accounting practices have also contributed to the severity of the problem in the United States.

Meanwhile, expectations continue to rise. Americans who have paid into the system for years understandably expect (and demand) to get full benefits when they retire.

The high cost of social programs such as Medicare and Medicaid (which pays medical expenditures for poor Americans) reminds us that the costs of treating illness in a modern industrial society are considerable. Yet hazards caused by humans can also endanger the health and safety of the public. Thus, the government tests new medicines before they are placed on the market and sets minimum safety standards for public transportation. Particularly noteworthy are governmental efforts to protect the environment from human destructiveness. Manda-

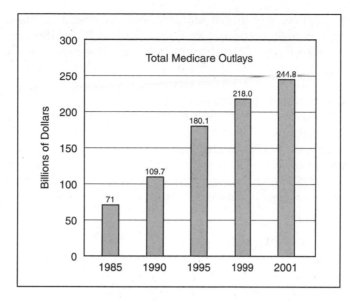

FIGURE 13-2   The Rising Cost of Medicare

More than 37 million Americans receive Medicare. It is the fastest-growing federal entitlement program, as well as the second most expensive, making up roughly 12 percent of the budget. Only Social Security costs more.

SOURCE: From Steve Langdon, "With Campaign Dust Settling, Medicare Chances Brighter," *Congressional Quarterly* (January 18, 1997): 179; Robert Pear, "Experts Say Cost of Medical Insurance Is Underestimated," *New York Times*, November 30, 2000, A1; Social Security Administration, "Status of the Social Security and Medicare Programs," www.ssa.gov/OACT/TRSUM/tsumary.html, accessed May 21, 2002.

tory clean air standards, environmental impact statements, increasingly stringent waste disposal requirements, and vigorous recycling efforts all aim at protecting the environment. Government conservation efforts also seek to protect endangered species of wildlife. Increasingly, environmental concerns, such as limiting acid rain and reducing river pollution, are not confined to national borders but involve international agreements (as they were in the North American Free Trade Agreement signed by the United States, Canada, and Mexico).

In recent years, there has been increasing public support for many environmental programs, although the Green Party has not made the inroads in national elections in the United States that it has in many other developed countries (for example, Germany and France). Critics sometimes complain, however, that the government's efforts hamper industrial development and economic growth and that the cost (in terms of needless delays and red tape) is too high.

Security from One's Own Actions

Occasionally, the government acts to protect individuals from doing themselves physical harm. For example, some states have adopted laws requiring motorcyclists to wear safety helmets or banning the sale of harmful drugs. Governmental intervention in personal affairs may also extend to questions of morality. The Eighteenth Amendment, which established Prohibition, was the most conspicuous example of national legislation aimed at preventing citizens from harming themselves morally as well as physically. Other examples include the various local, state, and federal laws banning the sale or distribution of pornography and those outlawing prostitution.

Defenders of moralistic legislation assert that no community can ignore the moral character of its citizens, especially when violating certain norms of behavior has adverse social consequences. Opponents of such statutes reply that governmental action of this type unduly restricts personal liberty. They also point out that people voluntarily participate in the prohibited actions and that each person ought to be able to determine his or her best interest.

THE PURSUIT OF PROSPERITY

Observers frequently characterize the United States as a commercial nation in which citizens are forever in search of financial security and the consumer is king. A century and a half ago, Alexis de Tocqueville noted that Americans were prey to constant agitation caused by their relentless pursuit of individual affluence. The condition has always been a salient characteristic of American society. In fact, the Founders envisaged a society of hardworking citizens dedicated to the entrepreneurial principles of self-reliance, upward mobility, and the profit motive.[4]

In establishing a commercial republic, the Founders consciously launched a political experiment that had been championed by philosophers and economists (including John Locke and Baron de Montesquieu) for over 100 years. In their view, a political order that encouraged the growth of commerce and trade would provide the best means of ensuring a robust national economy. Such a society, in which success was based on hard work and natural ability rather than accidents of birth, would enable citizens to achieve and acquire as much wealth as they desired or needed.

During the nineteenth century, the influence of Adam Smith's free-market philosophy, the rise of the business corporation, and the advance of technology transformed the commercial state into the capitalist state. By definition, *capitalism* means the private (and usually unregulated) ownership, manufacture, and distribution of goods and services. By the beginning of the twentieth century, however, the federal government had begun to enforce regulations designed to protect citizens from monopolies, abusive business practices, and other perceived economic injustices. This trend in public policy was strengthened enormously during the Great Depression of the 1930s, when, under the initiative of President Franklin Roosevelt, the government instituted a number of programs designed to buttress the economic security of ordinary citizens. In the 1960s and 1970s, Medicare, special training and jobs programs, and expanded welfare and food stamp benefits, supplemented unemployment compensation and Social Security.

By the 1980s, federal intervention in the economy had become so pronounced that many economists referred to a *mixed economy,* containing elements of both private enterprise and welfare-state socialism. In fact, however, the level of "intervention" was still far below that found in most Western democracies, but myopic politicians playing to a myopic public failed to note this fact.

Indeed, former president Ronald Reagan and, a decade later, Newt Gingrich and the Republicans in Congress suggested that government had gone way too far in its efforts to ensure individual economic prosperity and security. (Never mind the fact that federal budget deficits soared during the Reagan presidency.) During President Clinton's first term, conservatives in Congress were able to team up with special interests (the American Medical Association, pharmaceutical companies, and highly paid hospital administrators, among others) to defeat a proposal to create a national health care system that would protect every citizen. In the United States today, some 40 million Americans (including many children) have no health insurance and many cannot afford to pay for a single visit to a licensed physician much less to spend a night in a hospital.

Budget Deficits and the National Debt

Annual federal expenditures in the United States total an astounding $1.7 trillion. When the federal government spends more than it collects in a year, it produces a *budget deficit.* The accumulated deficits over the years become the *national debt.* Most economists agree that the trend and magnitude of the national debt have an important long-term effect on the economic health and security of the United States. At the same time, most economists also agree that the ratio of the debt to the gross national product (GNP)—about one-third (30 percent)—is in itself nothing to get terribly alarmed about. What *is* alarming in the eyes of some economists is the rate of growth in the debt.

Losing Interest: The National Debt   Budget deficits increased dramatically during the 1980s and 1990s. In 1981, when President Reagan assumed office, the national debt totaled less than $1 trillion. By 1988, at the end of President Reagan's term in office, it had surpassed $2.5 trillion; by 1997, it approached $6 trillion (which is where it stands today). This acceleration in the national debt had serious consequences. The government had to borrow ever more money to pay its bills, and needed to make enormous interest payments. By the late 1990s, more than fifteen cents of every federal tax dollar went to cover interest on the national debt (another way to think about this is that for every dollar Americans spend on government, they receive less than eighty-five cents in goods and services).

Between 1992 and 2000, both President Bill Clinton and the Republican-controlled Congress addressed the problems posed by the mushrooming national debt and budget deficits declined sharply in the late 1990s. Also, annual budget deficits as a percentage of gross domestic product (GDP) decreased significantly. Amidst a generally robust economy, Democrats and Republicans agreed in the spring of 1997 to a long-term budget plan that would balance the budget by 2001. Meanwhile, tax revenues increased faster than expected due to the strong economy, suggesting that a balanced budget and possibly even a budget surplus might result earlier than anticipated. Thus, a problem that had appeared virtually insoluble a few years before was at least temporarily placed on the back burner.

All that changed suddenly after September 11, when the Congress voted huge sums for cleanup and reconstruction efforts in New York City, bailing out hard-hit airlines (among others), and prosecuting the "war" against international terrorism at home and abroad. The budget surplus (if in fact there ever was one) quickly vanished, as did all talk "inside the beltway" of a balanced budget in 2002.

Meanwhile, Wall Street was also adversely affected by the attacks on the World Trade Center (only a few blocks away in Manhattan) as the stock market fell sharply. Whole sectors of the economy (the airlines and tourism, for example) were hurt, as well, and consumer confidence plummeted in the weeks following the calamity. Some enterprises teetered on the brink of bankruptcy and others laid off workers. The Federal Reserve lowered interest rates repeatedly (until they reached the lowest levels in four decades) in an effort to stave off a recession.

The Tax Burden: Too Light Or Just Right?   Americans tend to think taxes are too high and yet the United States has the lowest tax rates in the developed world. Most Western democracies, for example, allocate 40–50 percent of GDP to government; in Italy, Great Britain, Germany, and Canada the figure is about 45 percent, but in France it is over 50 percent. By contrast, in the United States, taxes account for barely more than 30 percent of GDP, and the income tax burden has been falling in recent years. In 1999, the average American family saw less than 9 percent of its income go to pay federal, state, and local taxes. One-third of all eligible taxpayers paid no income tax at all in 1999. A family of four with a median income of about $55,000 paid less than 8 percent, the lowest level since 1965, and even the top 1 percent (earning over $700,000 a year) paid only 22.2 percent.[5]

The reasons for these relatively low tax rates are political, cultural, and ideological. Americans have three mutually reinforcing aversions: an aversion to high taxes and "big government"; an aversion to "welfare," which—incredibly—translates into the absence of a national health insurance system (found in virtually every other postindustrial democracy); and an aversion to government ownership of enterprises (including public utilities, railroads, airlines, and port facilities).

President Franklin Delano Roosevelt once said that the federal tax code "might as well have been written in a foreign language." In fact, if it were written in a foreign *country*, it would almost certainly be far simpler and make more sense. The bewildering federal income tax rules—which are impossible to understand or interpret—are a taxpayer's nightmare and an accounting firm's dream come true. Attempts at "tax simplification" have failed. In 1986, the U.S. Congress passed a law directing the IRS to fix the system. A few years later, a "hypothetical" listing of family income and expenses was sent to fifty tax experts to determine this mythical family's tax liability. The result was fifty different "bottom lines" ranging from a tax bill of $12,500 to nearly $36,000![6]

The Byzantine U.S. tax system works remarkably well for the rich and the working middle-class alike. Due to relatively low income tax rates, the United States taxes its wealthiest citizens at a much lower rate than other industrial democracies. At the same time, because taxes on consumption (sales taxes) are also low, the middle class does not get "squeezed" nearly as much as most tax-payers *feel* like they do—grumbling about taxes is perhaps the oldest national pas-time. Remember the Boston Tea Party and the rallying cry of the American Revolution: "No taxation without representation"?

Consumption taxes generally do not hit the rich very hard at all because they spend a much smaller portion of their income on food, clothing, transportation, and other basic necessities. High turnover taxes hit the middle-class much harder for the same reason: they spend a far larger portion of their income on life's neces-sities. To put things into perspective, however, it helps to look at other countries. European countries, for example, use a so-called value added tax (VAT), a kind of turnover tax that is assessed at every stage in the manufacture and sale of any product—in this manner, the total tax "take" is built into the price of a finished product and passed along to the consumer. Rates vary widely among European countries, with the lowest rates set at 19 percent; the highest rates reach 25 per-cent. By contrast, sales taxes in the U.S. are rarely more than 6 percent and in Min-nesota, for example, groceries are exempt (eating in restaurants, however, is not).

In the United States, 58 percent of all federal revenues comes from personal and corporate income taxes, but the income tax burden on individuals is much heavier than on corporations. In fact, corporate income tax amounts to only about 10 percent of federal revenues today, a dramatic decline from the 1950s and 1960s, when it stood at about 25 percent. In the meantime, Social Security payroll taxes (34 percent of the total) are the fastest-growing source of federal revenue and accounted for the entire budget "surplus" in 2000–01 (and before).

Educational Malaise

Americans tend to measure the value of education primarily in terms of its practi-cal benefits—how much a high school diploma or college degree is worth in dol-lars and cents.[7] Students are urged to remain in high school and attend college because education leads to high-paying jobs.

Education also has social and economic implications for the nation as a whole. A skilled and technically trained work force is particularly important if the United States is to compete in global markets.

It is frequently asserted that there is a national crisis in American education. Signs of such a crisis have been reported for years. In some schools, guns, drugs, and gangs endanger students and teachers alike. Declining college entrance exam-ination scores, countless cross-cultural comparisons revealing that American stu-dents score worse on mathematical tests than comparable European and Asian students, high failure rates on elementary-level literacy tests given by large Amer-ican corporations all have been cited as examples of a failure of American primary and secondary education (see Figure 13-3). According to the National Assessment of Education (1990), "Large proportions, perhaps more than half, of our elemen-tary, middle-, and high school students are unable to demonstrate competency in challenging subject matter in English, mathematics, science, history, and geogra-phy," even though the public schools are well funded.[8] Moreover, U.S. businesses

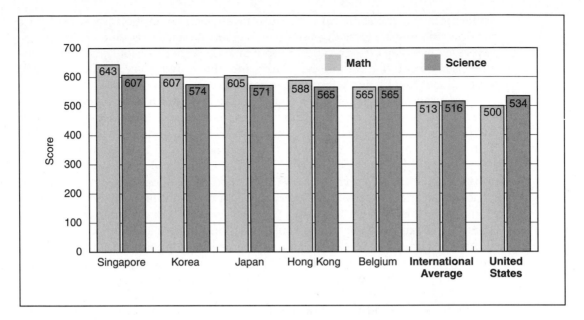

FIGURE 13-3   Comparing Students Worldwide

American students generally score somewhere in the middle in international comparisons. According to a recent study, eighth grade American students scored slightly below average in mathematics (ranking twenty-eighth when compared to students from forty-one nations) and just above average in science (seventeenth out of forty-one on that same list). *Note:* Margin of error is plus or minus ten points for each country.

SOURCE: IEA Third International Mathematics and Science Study (TIMSS, 1994–95).

spend $30 to $35 billion a year training students in skills that they should have learned in school. Grade inflation is widely recognized as a pervasive and corrosive force in education at all levels. Teachers pamper students more and more and expect less and less. Given these deteriorating standards, what is to be done?

Some educational reformers advocate national school testing that would identify strong and weak schools and act as a catalyst for improvement. Other proposals champion parent and student choice, arguing that encouraging competition within education would also encourage more thorough teaching and learning. Some conservators, including President George W. Bush, favor a voucher system, in which government transfer payments would partly offset the cost of attending private and parochial schools that meet state accreditation standards.[9] Voters defeated a voucher plan in California in a 1993 referendum. Still, support for voucher programs remains and gained new impetus after the Republicans won back the presidency in 2000. Because many reformers believe that private schools are doing a better job (especially Roman Catholic schools), they reason that stiff competition would force public schools to improve or wither away.

Meanwhile, educational experimentation flourishes. In Baltimore and Minneapolis, private for-profit corporations have managed public schools, and New York state has charter schools. All sorts of private schools have been founded across the country and the home schooling movement continues to grow.

Public school administrators and teachers have generally opposed fundamental reforms. They worry that a voucher system would turn the public schools into holding pens for the least desirable students. They have also expressed doubts about whether standardized tests can accurately measure educational achievement. Finally, they point out that many of the worst problems faced by the public schools reflect larger social problems—including crime, a breakdown of the family, drug use, and lack of interest in education—that public schools are powerless to solve. One thing nearly everyone agrees on, however, is that well-educated citizens are essential to economic success both individually and collectively.

Income Distribution

Prosperity depends not only on the amount of wealth in a society but also on its distribution. Income distribution raises both economic and moral questions. Consumers must make enough money to afford the goods and services the economy produces. If they do not, and if those goods and services cannot be exported, they cannot consume (buy things) and the economy will slide into recession. From a moral standpoint, glaring economic inequalities are difficult to justify in a society that has long professed to believe in "an honest day's work for an honest day's pay."

There is a large and growing disparity between the incomes of richest and poorest members of society. In 1994, for example, the top one-fifth of U.S. households earned more than 13.5 times the income of the bottom one-fifth (see Figure 13-4). Moreover, while the overall U.S. poverty rate in 2000 was 11.3 percent, broken down by race it was 9.4 percent for whites, 22.1 percent for blacks, 21.2 percent for Hispanic Americans, and 10.8 percent for Asian Americans.[10]

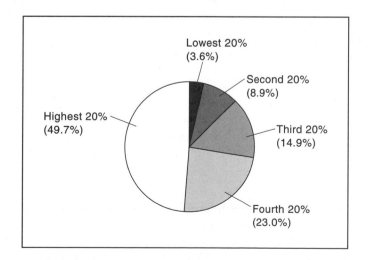

FIGURE 13-4   Household Income Inequality, 2000

SOURCE: U.S. Department of Commerce, Bureau of the Census, Current Population Survey, 2000 and 2001, accessed May 12, 2002 at *www.census.gov/hhes/www/img/incpov00/fig12.jpg*

Disturbing trends that first became obvious in the 1980s continued in the 1990s. As one observer points out, during the 1980s "the strong, the well-educated, the well-married, and the well-off *within* these groups made gains above the national average," but "a disproportionate number of women, young people, blacks and Hispanics were among the decade's casualties." The worst off were inner-city residents as well as a "growing underclass of high school dropouts, unwed mothers, female heads of households, unemployable young black males and homeless persons of all races," whose growing existence "provoke[d] . . . questions about the nation's future."[11]

Conservatives take a different view of economic inequality. Rather than focusing on the extreme differences in income, they emphasize that the United States has always had a large middle class and that it would be self-defeating to level society through legislative action (policies designed to redistribute income). Rather, policies that benefit those who work hard, take economic risks, invest wisely, and provide goods and services that people want are proven to work best.

Fiscal conservatives also point out that income distribution figures do not include government transfer payments (for example, unemployment compensation, food stamps, aid to families with dependent children, and so on) designed to assist the less fortunate in society. Such welfare programs, when carefully monitored and limited in scope, help the poor without depriving others of the incentives that are needed to motivate the vast majority of working-class citizens whose labors insure the nation's continued prosperity.

Neither liberals nor conservatives have all the answers. How, for example, does society help a high school dropout, who is also a sixteen-year-old single mother, not only survive but also to have a chance at success in life?

THE PURSUIT OF EQUALITY

Equality is a bedrock principle of American political life. The assertion in the Declaration of Independence that "all men are created equal" reflects the notion that "life, liberty, and the pursuit of happiness" are the birthright of all Americans, not just the privileged few. A century before the Declaration of Independence was written the English political philosopher John Locke argued that "life, liberty, and property" are natural rights to which all human beings are entitled. Thus, the idea of *equal rights*—as distinct from equal results—has deep roots in the Anglo-American political tradition.

Racial Discrimination

In matters of race and gender, however, American practice has not lived up to the principle of equal rights for all. Discrimination against African Americans has been an indisputable fact of political life in the United States. Until the 1860s, the institution of slavery made a mockery of American ideals. On the eve of the Civil War, in the infamous Dred Scott case, the Supreme Court ruled that no blacks whether slave or free were citizens; Chief Justice Roger Taney argued that blacks were "so inferior" that they had "no rights which the white man was bound to respect."

The outcome of the Civil War meant an end to slavery, but it did not ensure equality under the law. Nor did enactment of the Fourteenth Amendment, which, among other things, guaranteed that no person shall be denied "the equal protection of the laws." Ironically, it was the Supreme Court, the guardian of the Constitution, which largely nullified the intent of this amendment.

Two Landmark Cases   In the *Civil Rights Cases* (1883), the Court ruled that an act of Congress prohibiting racial discrimination in public accommodations (restaurants, amusement parks, and the like) was unconstitutional.[12] The equal protection clause of the Fourteenth Amendment, the justices held, was intended to prohibit only *state* discrimination, not private discrimination. Discriminatory acts committed by individuals having no official connection with state government, in other words, were beyond the range of the federal government and, therefore, of the federal courts. If, for example, a restaurant owner turned away black citizens, the owner would merely be exercising the rights of a private individual, and no congressional remedy would be constitutional.

Thirteen years later, in *Plessy v. Ferguson* (1896), the Court went even further.[13] In upholding the constitutionality of a state law mandating racially segregated railway carriages, the Court in *Plessy* devised the notorious *separate-but-equal doctrine.*

Homer Plessy (described by the Court as of "seven-eighths Caucasian and one-eighth African blood") had taken a seat in the white section of a train, only to be told that he was required to move to the "colored" section. A nearly unanimous Court rejected Plessy's claim that the segregation law violated his right to equal protection of the law, arguing that the law was neutral on its face; that is, it provided equal accommodations for persons of both races. The Court majority went so far as to suggest that if "the enforced separation of the two races stamps the colored race with a badge of inferiority," that "is not by reason of anything found in the act, but solely because the colored race chooses to put that construction upon it."

In both the *Civil Rights Cases* and *Plessy v. Ferguson*, only Justice John M. Harlan dissented. On each occasion, he argued that the Court's decision had the effect of defeating the egalitarian purpose behind the Fourteenth Amendment, which he declared had "removed the race line from our government systems." Because he believed that no government, at any level, possessed the constitutional power to pass laws based on racial distinctions, he viewed the Constitution as "color-blind." Harlan's dissenting opinion in *Plessy* would not become law, however, for another fifty-eight years.

Through the decisions handed down in the *Civil Rights Cases* and *Plessy v. Ferguson*, the Court not only sanctioned strict racial segregation in the South but also helped to legitimize a social system in which blacks were discriminated against, brutalized, and even murdered.

Racial Equality: Free At Last?   Legally protected or dictated racial segregation was the norm throughout the South (and in many parts of the North, as well) into the twentieth century. Beginning in the late 1940s, however, the Supreme Court began to reinterpret the old legal formulas with a view toward promoting racial equality. For example, in *Shelley v. Kraemer* (1948), it held that judicial enforcement of discriminatory private contracts was unconstitutional.[14] The Court ruled that legal enforcement of such agreements amounted to "state action" for the purpose of discrimination, which was prohibited by the Fourteenth Amendment. Also, although it declined to outlaw them outright, the Court began to insist that segregated state facilities be *truly* equal. Thus, in *Sweatt v. Painter* (1950), it held that the University of Texas law school had to admit blacks because the state could not provide a black law school of equal quality and reputation.[15]

In the famous case of *Brown v. Board of Education of Topeka* (1954), the Court finally overturned the separate-but-equal doctrine.[16] In that case, the justices declared that segregated schools were unconstitutional because "separate educational facilities are inherently unequal."

The *Brown* decision sparked a heated political debate over the meaning of "equality" in the United States. Despite an initial howl of protest, a national consensus gradually emerged. Ten years later, Congress passed the Civil Rights Act of 1964, the first of a series of federal laws aimed at realizing racial equality. It was a sign of the changing times that the 1964 act contained an equal-accommodations section very similar to the one ruled unconstitutional in the *Civil Rights Cases*.[17] By the late 1960s, after a decade of intense civil rights activities and the most serious

© Bettmann / CORBIS

In two landmark Supreme Court decisions, Civil Rights Cases *(1883) and* Plessy v. Ferguson *(1896), the strict racial segregation in the South was upheld by majority decision. Justice John M. Harlan's dissenting opinion in* Plessy, *that the Constitution is "color-blind," would not become law for almost fifty-eight years.*

civil disorders since the Civil War, the government was fully committed to the goal of ensuring equal rights under the law for all citizens. The public policy battle between advocates of racial equality and of white supremacy thus gave way to an increasingly complex and heated debate over the appropriate means to the goal of equality.

The Busing Controversy   The question of how far the government could and should go to promote equal rights was crystallized in the school busing controversy of the 1970s and 1980s, which grew out of an ambiguity in *Brown v. Board of Education*. In that case, as we have seen, the Court ruled that legal segregation in education was unconstitutional. In accepting the view that black children tended to learn more in integrated schools, however, the Court seemed to imply that merely ending legal or de jure segregation might not be sufficient. There still remained the problem of de facto segregation resulting from the socioeconomic effects of poverty—that is, from the concentration of much of the African American population in inner-city slums.

But how could segregated residential patterns be broken down for the purpose of integrating schools? One obvious possibility was to integrate school districts by transporting schoolchildren across district lines. Not only did busing offer the most straightforward way of integrating urban schools, but it also served to demonstrate in clear and unequivocal terms the nation's firm commitment to "equal opportunity." The onset of school busing—which in some instances was ordered by federal district courts and scrutinized by federal judges—put every locality in the nation on notice that henceforth racially homogeneous schools would not pass the constitutional test of "equal protection of the laws."

Critics attacked school busing on several grounds. Some of the opposition came from parents who harbored prejudice toward minorities, but much more came from parents who simply believed that neighborhood schools were best for all children no matter where they happened to reside. Others argued that the schools should not be turned into "social laboratories." School administrators feared that parental interest and participation would decrease as the physical distance between home and school increased.

Finally, unhappiness with busing coincided with a national "crisis of confidence" in the public schools.[18] Declining student test scores, drug and discipline problems, lax academic standards, and presentiments of future funding problems provided unmistakable signs that all was not well with the public schools.

Was busing a good idea? Yes and no. It did put pressure on local officials and school boards to improve facilities and conditions in inner-city schools. It also made it clear to skeptics that the federal government was serious about equality of educational opportunity. On the other hand, busing often had the effect of simply redistributing minorities from one part of the city to another. Some localities did attempt to bus children between the predominantly black inner city and the predominantly white suburbs, but the Supreme Court generally invalidated such plans unless it could be shown that the outlying school districts had practiced some form of governmentally imposed discrimination for which busing provided an appropriate remedy.[19]

Affirmative Action or Reverse Discrimination?

As controversial as the busing question proved to be, it was overshadowed in the late 1970s by a controversy over *affirmative action*. At issue here were governmental programs and regulations that accorded special preference to minorities in job hiring and promotion, admission to colleges and professional schools, and similar situations. The aim was to remedy the persistent effects of past and present discrimination against minorities. Like busing, these programs were established in the name of equality. But, many people asked, were such programs really fair? Were they even constitutional? Those who opposed affirmative action argued that this policy amounted to *reverse discrimination.*

If the Constitution permitted preferential treatment of minorities, did it also provide the majority with protection against reverse discrimination? This question was answered in part in 1978, when the Supreme Court handed down a ruling in a suit brought by Allan Bakke, a white student who had unsuccessfully sought admission to the medical school of the University of California at Davis.[20] Bakke contended that the medical school's special-admissions program (which set aside certain places for minority students, several of whom had significantly lower grade-point averages and standardized test scores than Bakke did) had unfairly undercut his chances of acceptance simply because of his race. In a close (and rather unclear) decision, the Court agreed with Bakke that rigid affirmative action quotas were unconstitutional and ordered that he be admitted to the medical school. It also indicated, however, that preference for minorities could be maintained under certain circumstances. The Supreme Court reaffirmed the *Bakke* decision in later rulings.[21]

However, the Supreme Court has also upheld several broadly based preferential hiring programs (drawing the line at plans that provided minorities with preferential protection against layoffs).[22] Similarly, it has upheld the use of affirmative action in the employment of women, taking the position that they may be preferred over better qualified men in order to improve gender balance in the workforce.[23]

On the other hand, the Court has more recently limited governmental preferences for minority-owned businesses, thus appearing to reverse (or at least dilute) earlier decisions.[24] It is not clear, therefore, exactly where affirmative action ends and reverse discrimination begins in the eyes of the Supreme Court. Two generalizations are possible. First, the Constitution gives Congress considerably more latitude than state and local governments to remedy the past effects of discrimination. Second, color-conscious affirmative action programs at the state and local levels are most likely to be upheld when there is clear evidence of specific (and not general social) discrimination against minorities.[25]

Affirmative action programs remain controversial and many have been contested in the courts. This point was illustrated most dramatically when, in November 1996, voters passed the California Civil Rights Initiative, prohibiting the state's government from discriminating or granting preferences on the basis of race, sex, color, ethnicity, or national origin. This voter effort to limit affirmative action programs was almost immediately contested in the courts, which acted to delay implementation for several months.

Advocates of affirmative action programs contend that preferences are justified (or indeed necessary) because minorities have suffered systematic discrimination for generations. Moreover, the argument continues, African Americans and other minorities have always been underrepresented in the professions. While blacks comprise approximately 12 percent of the population, they constitute less than 4 percent of the lawyers, judges, physicians, engineers, and college and university professors. Affirmative action is therefore required to remedy this situation, which arises from social circumstances rooted in historic injustice (especially slavery and racial segregation).

Opponents of affirmative action focus on the individuals harmed by such policies rather than on the group being helped. Any form of institutionalized discrimination, as seen from this perspective, unfairly punishes people for attributes that have nothing to do with merit. Fairness dictates that decisions about admissions, hiring, and the awarding of government contracts must be made according to relevant criteria applied in an equitable manner. Opponents of affirmative action also argue that society is punished when the most competent individuals are not allowed to succeed. According to this view, true justice does not demand a society in which each race is represented proportionally in each profession; it requires only equality of opportunity. Such equality demands, as Justice Harlan asserted, that the Constitution be color-blind.

Who Needs Protection?

Are there other groups besides African Americans who ought to be eligible for preferential treatment? Have Native Americans not also been discriminated against? What about Hispanics? Asian Americans have also suffered because of bias—but they are overrepresented in such fields as mathematics and computer science. Does this type of success negate any claim to preferential treatment?

The question of gender-based discrimination has raised even thornier issues. From the early 1970s through the 1980s, this debate centered on the ill-fated Equal Rights Amendment, which would have guaranteed that "equality of rights under the law should not be denied or abridged by the United States or by any State on account of sex." Do women need special protection as a historically disadvantaged "minority"? Are they entitled to preferential treatment to remedy the effects of past sex discrimination? If so, what are the policy implications? For instance, federal law requires only males to register for the military draft.[26] Does this law recognize only the natural physical differences between the sexes? Does it favor men by treating women as so physically and emotionally inferior (weak, slow, uncoordinated, fickle, prone to panic, unstable, and so forth) as to be incapable of serving in the military? Or does it favor women by exempting them from an unpleasant obligation? The same controversies have embroiled a number of other statutes, including statutory rape laws that make it illegal for males to have sexual relations with underage females but not for females to have sex with underage males.[27]

The poor and disadvantaged comprise yet another group often thought to deserve preferential treatment. What is poverty? Is it present only when people

The belief that they have been the object of discrimination, and have been denied equal rights, has informed many protest movements in the United States. Here Candice Gingrich, half sister of former House Speaker Newt Gingrich, addresses a rally which both advocated gay and lesbian rights and condemned violence directed against members of theses groups.

are teetering on the brink of starvation? Or is anybody who does not have a decent standard of living poor? What is a decent standard of living? Some experts classify as poor a certain percentage of the population at the lowest end of the income scale, but that says nothing about how people on the bottom actually live—in affluent Western societies, the lowest 20 percent live better than the vast majority of the people in poor Third World countries.

Opponents of social welfare programs maintain that poor people often live in squalor because they have bad habits and bad attitudes which they refuse to change; government can do little to alleviate the effects of personal failure. Others contend that poor people are often unfortunate victims of an indifferent society and a dog-eat-dog economic system; government has an obligation to use its powers to advance the cause of economic and social equality.

Finally, there is the issue of whether other groups—gays and lesbians, for example—have been the object of past discrimination and whether they are entitled to legally mandated protection from discrimination in the competition for jobs, schooling, and social benefits. In 1992, Colorado voters passed a measure prohibiting the state from enforcing specific legal protections or extending preference to gay citizens who believed they were disadvantaged or discriminated against. The referendum was overturned in 1996, when the Supreme Court held that the measure was discriminatory and therefore unconstitutional.[28] This case and others like it raise a larger question: What legal protections are due all Americans?

THE PURSUIT OF LIBERTY

As surely as equality is a primary goal of contemporary political life, so too is liberty. Slogans extolling the virtue of political freedom resound throughout the history of the American republic. "Give me liberty or give me death," declared Patrick Henry in a phrase that has been enshrined as a national motto.

The Value of Liberty

Political liberty in the Western world has long been understood as freedom from governmental restraint. Such freedom has commonly been seen as a valuable political asset for four principal reasons:

1. Life is robbed of its meaning if an individual cannot freely choose how to lead it. Because such freedom of choice is a distinctly human trait, liberty means the opportunity to act in a distinctly human way. Also, freedom is a prerequisite for human dignity. Because most adult citizens are capable of assuming moral responsibility for their own actions, the absence of freedom deprives individuals of the opportunity for self-realization and keeps them in a permanent state of arrested development. In other words, the absence of freedom reduces adults to the status of children.

2. Liberty is based on the assumption that individuals know best what they want and need to be happy. Fulfillment, according to this view, can be achieved only when individuals decide for themselves how best to spend their time and money.

3. Liberty is necessary for the meaningful exchange of ideas, as well as for social progress. Only in a free society can the full range of human ideas, inventions, and opinions be explored and exploited for the benefit of society. Freedom of expression is necessary to keep the government honest, as well.

4. The absence of liberty frequently results in abuses of power. Allowing the government to encroach on anyone's liberty threatens everyone's liberty. For example, we might all agree that a certain type of behavior is highly desirable—say, bathing regularly—and further that freedom in this particular instance is not necessarily a good thing (a constitutional right to practice poor hygiene?). Yet if the police can fine the person sitting next to me on the bus for not taking a shower what is to prevent the police from arresting me for not combing my hair or shaving?

Liberty and the First Amendment

In the United States, legal questions involving individual freedom often turn on the First Amendment, which provides that:

Congress shall make no law respecting an establishment of religion, or prohibiting the free exercise thereof; or abridging the freedom of speech, or the press; or the right of the people peaceably to assemble, and to petition the government for a redress of grievances.

Thus, the First Amendment protects four important aspects of citizen liberty: freedom of speech, freedom of the press, freedom of religion, and freedom of peaceable assembly. Because the language of the First Amendment is brief and general, the first three rights in particular have required an unusual amount of judicial interpretation.

Freedom of Speech   Most authorities agree that the overriding purpose behind the First Amendment was the protection of political speech. In a republic, open debate between political opponents is vital to the effective functioning of the political system. Most of the time, the *exercise* of free speech is not controversial, even though the speech itself might be.

However, freedom of speech can become a hotly contested issue when individuals who represent unpopular causes or who challenge the integrity or legitimacy of the political system try to exercise it. Extremists often arouse strong passions. Nazi speakers understandably arouse a particularly high level of revulsion among Jews, and Ku Klux Klan spokesmen have the same effect on African Americans. During the early days of the Vietnam War, youthful protesters were often depicted as unpatriotic and disloyal. Several years later, after the war had become unpopular, defenders of the U.S. role in Vietnam were booed and shouted down when they spoke on college campuses. The First Amendment, however, safeguards the right of all citizens to express political opinions, no matter how repugnant or unpopular, subject only to a few limitations (that the speech not be part and parcel of an illegal act, that it not foment riot, that it not constitute a direct personal provocation—so-called fighting words—and so on).

Of course, the protections offered by the freedom-of-speech clause are not confined to political speech alone. The Supreme Court has placed a very broad interpretation on *speech*, defining it as synonymous with *expression*. Artistic expression, symbolic statements (such as black armbands), and advertising are among the areas that, according to the Court, are protected by the First Amendment.

Once it is determined that an activity comprises symbolic free speech, its content or message makes no difference. Thus flag burning has been upheld as a protected form of symbolic free speech.[29] As with pure speech cases, the context of symbolic free speech is almost always constitutionally more important than its content. The Ku Klux Klan's burning of a cross in an isolated field may be an objectionable act, but it is nonetheless a constitutionally protected form of symbolic expression.[30] Burning a cross on someone's lawn is a different matter altogether.[31]

Freedom of the Press   The freedom of the press guarantees public access to news and information by protecting publishers from almost all forms of official censorship. In other words, newspapers and periodicals can publish what they wish, including criticisms and indictments of the government. The same holds true for the broadcast media. A diverse and unhampered press, the Founders believed, is crucial to self-government because in a democracy, every citizen is an important decisionmaker (in the voting booth) and because even popularly elected officials need someone (or something) to keep them honest.

The Supreme Court has consistently reaffirmed that under the Constitution, the press cannot be subject to *prior restraint.* This means that except in times of war or grave national emergency, the government does not have the power to prevent a newspaper or a periodical from publishing material of any sort—even papers classified as secret by the government or information that a trial judge may later rule as constituting prejudicial pretrial publicity.[32]

Freedom of Religion   By prohibiting the establishment of a state-sponsored religion, the First Amendment requires the government to be neutral in religious matters—neither to help nor to hinder any religion. This requirement complements the clause that guarantees citizens the free exercise of religion. Taken together, these two clauses ensure that citizens may practice any religion in any manner they like, within reasonable limits.

When religious practices pose a threat to society, however, government has the power to outlaw them. No court in the land, for instance, would uphold ritual murder on the ground that the free exercise of religion was guaranteed by the Constitution. Even certain religious practices that do not present any obvious danger to society, such as polygamy, are not constitutionally protected.[33] Nonetheless, the courts have allowed a reasonable latitude in the exercise of religion, upholding the right of conscientious objectors to refuse induction into the armed services, the right of Amish children to be exempted from public education requirements, and the right of Jehovah's Witness schoolchildren to refrain from saluting the flag (on the ground that such a practice would constitute, under their religion, worship of a graven image).

A more controversial matter has been school prayer. In a number of decisions, the Supreme Court has held that prayer, even if nondenominational, and Bible reading in public schools violate the establishment clause of the First Amendment.[34] In addition, clergy are not permitted to give nondenominational prayers at high school graduation exercises.[35] The Supreme Court has gone so far as to disallow a moment of silence in the public schools if a teacher suggests that it might be used for prayer.[36] Observing that public schools, teachers, and school boards are creatures of state government and that student enrollment in the public schools is mandated by state compulsory education laws, the justices have consistently ruled that school prayer unconstitutionally involves the state in the establishment of religion.

Some Court critics argue that these decisions should be reversed. School prayer, they contend, helps keep alive the religious traditions that made this country great and that alone can stem moral decadence among the country's youth. In rebuttal, defenders of the Court's decisions emphasize that daily prayer and Bible-reading sessions in the schools adversely affect the liberty of students who hold minority or no religious beliefs. The cause of religious freedom, they maintain, is best served by an absolute minimum of governmental interference in matters of faith.

The establishment clause has also been invoked in the public debate over governmental assistance to parents whose children attend private schools, particularly church-related or denominational schools. The argument has often been made that parents should have a maximum amount of choice in determining where their children go to school. All parents, as citizens, pay taxes to support the public schools, but sometimes they prefer to send their children to private or religiously sponsored schools for religious, social, or educational reasons. Because these parents must also pay private school tuition, policymakers question whether the government should aid parents who choose to send their children to such schools by granting them tax credits or some other financial assistance. As noted earlier, with this sort of financial relief in mind, various "voucher" plans have been drafted in Congress over the past few years.

The Right to Privacy

The First Amendment protects a number of freedoms. There are, however, other liberties not explicitly protected by that amendment (or by any other provision in the Bill of Rights).

Primary among such liberties is the so-called right to privacy, or right of choice, which generally means the right of adult citizens to decide personal issues free of governmental interference. Citing this right to privacy, the Supreme Court has ruled that women have a substantial, though not unlimited, right to choose an abortion. Initially, the Supreme Court took particular care to eliminate roadblocks

Since the 1973 Supreme Court's ruling in Roe v. Wade *affirming a woman's right to an abortion, pro-choice and antiabortion activists in the United States have demonstrated vocally and sometimes violently. The bombing of abortion clinics and shooting deaths of doctors and assistants working in these facilities have escalated the battle over abortion to frightening new levels of advocacy.*

Hazel Hankin / Stock, Boston

to the exercise of that right. More recently, however, the Court (with a more conservative bent) has become a less enthusiastic supporter of this right, ruling that the existence of a woman's right to an abortion does not require that public funds be spent to reimburse poorer women for the cost of abortions. Nor is the government required to pay public employees for performing or assisting in abortions.[37]

Objections to the Supreme Court's initial decision affirming a woman's right to an abortion have come largely from right-to-life groups, whose members believe that human life begins at conception and that abortion therefore amounts to legalized murder. A human embryo or fetus, they argue, possesses constitutional rights, including a right to life that in all but rare cases (such as when the mother's life would be threatened by pregnancy or childbirth) outweighs the mother's right to privacy. The right-to-life movement has publicized its position by protesting and sometimes blockading clinics that perform abortions. In 1994, however, legal limitations were imposed on such protests. First, Congress passed a law guaranteeing women unhampered access to abortion clinics; the law also restricted protesters from inhibiting a woman's ability to obtain an abortion. The same year, the Supreme Court held that antiabortion activists could be sued under the RICO (Racketeer Influenced and Corrupt Organization) law, if blockading abortion clinics inflicted economic harm on those performing abortions.[38] Still, as the Supreme Court noted in 1997 when it modified restrictions on abortion clinic protests, the free speech and expression rights of antiabortion demonstrators also require constitutional protections.[39]

Several Supreme Court justices have defended the pro-choice position by developing a new concept of privacy based on a right "to define one's own concept of existence, of meaning, of the universe, and of the mystery of human life."[40] This language has become increasingly important to those who contend there is a right to die, arguing that patients who are terminally ill or in unbearable pain should have the legal option of medically assisted suicide. However, in 1997, the Supreme Court unanimously refused to recognize a constitutional right to die.[41]

THE PURSUIT OF JUSTICE

In the following discussion, the term *justice* is narrowly defined as a particular end of government, achieved through the courts and the criminal justice system. A just society in this sense is one in which civil and criminal rules are applied fairly and the punishment fits the crime.

Crime and Punishment

No society can afford to let seriously antisocial or criminal behavior go unpunished. By punishing people who violate its rules, a society makes clear that such behavior will not be tolerated. The severity of the punishment demonstrates exactly how undesirable a particular behavior is. There are four rationales behind the punishment of antisocial behavior. First, the protection of society is advanced when *incarceration* is imposed upon criminals. Second, punishment of one criminal may dissuade other individuals from committing a similar crime (*deterrence*).

Third, punishment is an essential precondition for reeducating criminals, so that they can eventually resume normal and productive lives *(rehabilitation)*. Finally, punishment compensates the innocent victim of crime, who deserves the satisfaction of seeing the perpetrator punished *(retribution)*.

Justice as Fair Procedure

An old legal cliché holds that 90 percent of fairness in the law is fair procedure. Procedural safeguards are essential to prevent the innocent from being falsely accused and the accused from being falsely convicted. These safeguards, which comprise what is known as *due process of law,* are outlined in the Bill of Rights of the Constitution, particularly in the Fourth, Fifth, and Sixth Amendments. Under the Constitution, citizens have the legal right (1) not to be subjected to unreasonable searches and seizures by the government; (2) not to be tried twice for the same offense; (3) not to incriminate themselves; (4) to receive a speedy and public trial by an impartial jury; (5) to be informed of the nature of the charge made against them; (6) to be confronted by any witnesses against them; (7) to obtain witnesses in their favor; and (8) to have legal counsel.

Of course, each of these constitutional guarantees is subject to judicial interpretation. Taken as a group, however, they represent the heart of our system of justice. In the words of one observer:

> When a man is brought into court and is accused of having committed a grave offense against society, all the machinery of the state is set in motion to bring him to justice. The public prosecutor or the district attorney often has a veritable army at his disposal, all trained to ferret out information that may be relevant to the crime, all paid by the state to spend their working hours questioning witnesses, examining evidence, and building a case that will presumably lead to conviction of the accused. The latter, on the other hand, usually has very limited means at his disposal. More often than not, a defendant is fortunate if he has enough assets to pay the fees of an attorney. Few men can hire teams of private investigators who can devote their time, skills, and resources exclusively to the search for evidence and the building of a defense. No private citizen can match the modern state when the latter brings all its forces into play after he has been accused of having violated the law.[42]

Thus, procedural guarantees are essential to the protection of defendants from miscarriages of justice.

The Limits of Legal Protection

Despite these important safeguards, the criminal justice system does not always produce justice. The poor, for example, have always received a substantially lower level of legal aid. And historically, the greatest injustices in this country have stemmed from racial prejudice. For a long time, this was particularly true in the South, where the imposition and severity of punishment correlated more closely with race than with any other consideration. Black men who were convicted (often falsely) of raping white women were commonly sentenced to death or life in prison, whereas whites accused of similar crimes against black women were often not even brought to trial.

Whenever such blatant injustices have occurred, legal procedures have failed. But if shortcomings are sometimes easy to recognize, the best ways to correct defects in the system usually are not. Virtually every due-process guarantee has been the object of bitter controversy. For example, the Constitution clearly states that a defendant has the right to an attorney. This seems straightforward enough.

But what if the accused cannot afford to hire an attorney? Does the state have an obligation to provide an attorney for an indigent person accused of a felony? What about an indigent person accused of a misdemeanor? And what about appeals? Must the state provide legal counsel for a defendant who, after having been convicted of a crime, wishes to appeal the case? If so, must counsel be provided for every appeal the defendant wishes to make or for only the first appeal?[43]

The definition and application of procedural protections for the accused, then, often raise complex questions. Few people would disagree with the assertion that certain protections are necessary if justice is to be served. To the contrary, it has often been argued, quite plausibly, that the rights themselves must be *broadened* in application to afford meaningful protection for the accused. Obviously, however, there are limits to the scope of these legal safeguards. Were they to be applied as broadly as is theoretically possible, the monetary cost could become prohibitively high, or it could become next to impossible to convict anyone accused of anything, or the judicial process could become so sluggish that justice itself would be impeded or undermined. In the end, the proper scope of procedural safeguards must be determined by balancing the rights of the accused against the obligation of government to punish those who are truly guilty of violating the law.

In wartime, constitutional guarantees and due process are circumscribed in ways that would not be acceptable under any other circumstances. During the Civil War, for example, President Abraham Lincoln even suspended habeas corpus. At one point, the Chief Justice of the Supreme Court, Roger Tancy, was frozen in an eyeball-to-eyeball confrontation with the U.S. military over this very issue and had to back down when it became clear that the chief executive was on the side of the generals.

Fast-forward to the fall of 2001. After the shocking events of September 11, an outraged President George W. Bush buoyed by an astoundingly high (roughly 9 to 1) public approval rating asked Congress to pass sweeping new antiterror legislation (called the PATRIOT Act) that gave the Justice Department unprecedented powers of investigation and interrogation, search and seizure, arrest and detention, and, finally, surveillance (including telephone wiretaps and e-mail monitoring) provided that these activities were carried out for purposes of combating terrorism. The 175-page bill was rushed through the House of Representatives by the Republican majority in that body and passed with slight modifications in the Democratic Senate with only one opposing vote (Senator Russell Feingold of Wisconsin). The scope, haste, and "hype" associated with the PATRIOT Act illustrate clearly the tendency of public opinion to accept (even demand) restrictions on freedom in times of crisis and of legislators to hand over the "keys to the kingdom" to a popular commander in chief. It is worth noting, however, that most of Europe's parliamentary democracies place fewer obstacles in the path of the police and security forces in normal times than would be acceptable in the United States (see box on page 406).

Terrorism and Civil Liberties: The Tricky Balance

How Other Countries Do It

As Congress wonders how to balance security and liberty, it might be wise to take a look at other countries. Broadly speaking, other countries' security laws get tougher the farther you travel away from the Anglo-Saxon mold.

Britain's troubles in Northern Ireland have left its government with broad powers of arrest and detention, but these are balanced by a long tradition of civil liberties and a dislike for identity cards. Germany is tough on political extremists because of its Nazi past and a struggle with left-wing terrorism in the 1970s, but it is tolerant toward most groups claiming a religious basis, such as Islamic fundamentalists (not Scientologists, though). Germans have to carry identity cards, but they enjoy strict laws preventing government agencies from passing on personal data.

In France, Spain, and Italy, the tentacles of power reach wider. Failing to produce an identity card if you are checked in the street can result in a visit to the local police station, especially if you happen to look foreign. Even when tracking down common criminals, investigating magistrates, working with the police, have far-reaching powers to tap telephones, order searches, look

into bank accounts and put suspects behind bars without bringing charges—in France, for up to four years. French journalists working on stories about terrorism and corruption have been detained by the police. The Spanish secret service has monitored telephone calls by politicians, and even by the king.

In Japan, the balance tilts even further away from civil liberties. Japanese police have wide powers of arrest and of interrogation. Maybe that is why only 1 percent of defendants in criminal cases are acquitted. People have to register their addresses with the local authorities (which, until a few years ago, collected fingerprints from all foreign residents). The government's powers to seize assets were increased after the nerve-gas attack by the Aum Shinrikyo sect in 1995.

Like America's, most governments now want more powers. Britain's Human Rights Act is being reviewed. Germany is likely to scrap the special status enjoyed by religious groups and to relax its privacy laws. In Spain and France, search powers are likely to be expanded still further. Only the Japanese will see no real change: with domestic security already so tight, the government is working out how to let its army go abroad.

SOURCE: Adapted from *The Economist*, October 20, 2001, 31.

The Exclusionary Rule   No due-process issue has raised the question of fairness more sharply than the so-called *exclusionary rule*. Essentially, the exclusionary rule holds that when evidence has been illegally obtained, it cannot be entered in a court of law. The Supreme Court, in promulgating this rule, argued that the Fourth Amendment's prohibition against illegal searches and seizures would be meaningless if illegal police behavior were not discouraged by the certain knowledge that any evidence obtained in violation of the Constitution would be excluded from the courts.[44] In the view of the Court, then, the exclusionary rule provides an indispensable barrier to deliberate abuse of police powers.

Critics of this rule (including several Supreme Court justices) focus their arguments on the serious problems it causes police officers, whose searches and seizures must conform to very complex guidelines handed down by the courts.[45] Few searches and seizures, they point out, conform to textbook cases; most of the time, the police officer on the spot is compelled to make a spur-of-the-moment decision. Police officers, charged with protecting the public, often find themselves in dangerous situations; they do not have the luxury of slow deliberation in safe circumstances enjoyed by judges and juries.

At the heart of the dispute over the exclusionary rule lie several important differences of opinion. Advocates tend to view most law enforcement officers as overzealous, while critics see them as well-intentioned victims of convoluted and confusing laws. In addition, advocates of the rule see it as a valuable guarantee of justice, whereas opponents see it as an impediment to law enforcement. The Supreme Court has tried to strike a balance between these two poles by allowing the admission of illegally obtained evidence when the error was unintentional by the police and when they had demonstrated a good-faith effort to comply with the law.[46] This "harmless error" exception to the exclusionary rule attempts to balance the rights of the accused and the safety of the public.

Judicial Discretion   Until recently, the prevailing legal theory has been that wide discretion should be accorded to prosecutors (to prosecute, plea-bargain, or not prosecute), judges (to pronounce indeterminate sentences), and parole boards (to determine how much actual time a convicted criminal should serve). The rationale behind judicial and administrative discretion in this realm is that individuals accused or convicted of similar crimes differ significantly in background, motivation, and exposure to crime, as well as prospects for rehabilitation and other factors. With discretionary authority, magistrates and other officials can take such individual circumstances into account when determining charges or the severity of sentences. Discretion is considered even more important as the number of crimes rises and the number of prison cells remains almost static; in these circumstances, judges are sometimes reluctant to send any but the most hardened criminals to overcrowded and understaffed prisons.

This aspect of the judicial system has been attacked by many critics as arbitrary and open to all sorts of subtle abuses. They assert that prosecutors make decisions based on political considerations or individual whim, judges sentence according to pet theories of the law, and parole officers are easily fooled by clever convicts. These loopholes and uncertainties in the judicial system, it is alleged, severely dilute the deterrent effect of punishment. Even worse, critics charge, the convicted felon's punishment depends too much on circumstances that ought to be irrelevant in judicial matters, such as which judge happens to try which case. The force of these arguments has led a number of states to adopt such legal reforms as the reduction or elimination of indeterminate sentences.

Capital Punishment   The public debate over the propriety of capital punishment has been waged on at least two separate levels. In practical terms, experts differ radically over the question of whether capital punishment actually deters future murders. The evidence has been so fragmentary and the interpretations are so diverse that a definitive answer is unlikely. On another level, there is bitter controversy over whether capital punishment is morally defensible.

Interestingly, both sides emphasize the sanctity of human life. Defenders of capital punishment contend that justice demands the imposition of the death penalty precisely because justice places such a high value on human life—because society is morally obligated to condemn the murder of innocent persons in the harshest possible way.

GOALS IN CONFLICT

Most Americans do not maintain hard and fast convictions about politics, if only because determining how the public good is to be attained is no simple task. Certainly, the five aims of government examined in this chapter—security, prosperity, equality, liberty, and justice—are not easy to realize. As we have seen, controversial and complex issues arise within each category, and the best way of pursuing the various ends of public policy is rarely obvious.

Many times, the goals themselves conflict. For example, one important end of government is liberty. But during times of war, the government often restricts individual liberty by imposing curfews, limiting profits, restricting the job mobility of certain workers, prohibiting protests, establishing "relocation" camps, and so on in the name of national security. The antiterrorist law the Bush Administration pushed through Congress in the wake of the 9-11 attacks on the World Trade Center and the Pentagon was a stark reminder of the tension between liberty and security in times of crisis.[47] At times, judges limit freedom of the press to ensure justice for a defendant in a highly publicized trial. Governmental rules, formulated in the name of equality, may compel employers to pay minimum wages or meet tough safety standards, thus curtailing liberty or making prosperity harder to achieve. When a society embraces as many as *five* core values (liberty, equality, security, prosperity, and justice) it has to strive for the optimal balance among all five rather than the maximization of any one.

And how does one evaluate the performance of government in terms of these five public policy goals? Alexis de Tocqueville made the incisive observation, in *Democracy in America* (1831), that the more nearly equal people become, the more glaring even the slightest departure from equality appears to be. In other words, the closer a political system comes to fulfilling the goal of equality, the more it appears to fail when it has not fully reached that goal. Much the same can be said with respect to the other chief ends of government. And because competing interests and demands always prevent the full realization of any one goal, there is always the danger in a democracy that citizens and leaders alike will suffer from myopia or, in a crisis, get caught up in a war hysteria or patriotic outpouring. There is nothing wrong with patriotism provided it does not distort our perception of reality or undermine the balance between security and liberty as some critics feared it might in the fall of 2001.

Moderation—what the Greeks called the Golden Mean—is the key to political stability in democratic societies. Moderation inoculates citizens against unreasonable political expectations. It also guards against single-minded efforts to achieve one end of government at the expense of other essential ends. Discussions of public policy in a democracy can be inflamed by the zealotry and fanaticism of those who obsessively pursue singular and unattainable goals. Shrill cries may then drown out the quieter voices of those who understand that without patience and moderation, democracy will inevitably fail to strike the delicate balances that are the essence of good government.

GATEWAYS TO THE WORLD: EXPLORING CYBERSPACE

http://www.nationalsecurity.org/

Designed and supported by the Heritage Foundation, this site provides publications, discussions by policy experts, and links to other sites dealing with a variety of national security issues.

http://garnet.berkeley.edu:3333/budget/budget-1.html

This site is a project of the Center for Community Economic Research at the University of California–Berkeley. It provides a hands-on simulation for users to attempt to balance the budget by making fiscal policy decisions in a number of areas.

http://asa.ual.lib.umich.edu/chdos/rights/citizen.html

This is a citizen's guide to civil rights and civil liberties with links to Internet resources in each of these areas arranged by subtopic.

http://www.aad.english.ucsb.edu

This home page for the Affirmative Action and Diversity Project provides a variety of documents and links from both the pro and con positions.

http://www.policy.com

This site provides information on a variety of areas of public policy as well as links to think tanks, journals, government documents, and other sources relating to the policy area.

Summary

Public policy issues revolve around five universal goals of democratic government: security, prosperity, equality, liberty, and justice. Security is the most fundamental goal of government because other values cannot be pursued or preserved without it. In pursuing security, government attempts to protect citizens from foreign enemies, from fellow citizens, from natural enemies, and even, in some instances, from themselves.

In the United States, the goal of prosperity has historically been associated with a free-enterprise economy based on the idea of the commercial republic. In the twentieth century, however, the government has attempted to promote the economic well-being of individuals through social welfare and other programs. These programs have sparked heated debate over the proper role of government in economic matters, especially as the budget deficit has worsened. Problems in the educational system endanger American competitiveness in the international economy. The income distribution of Americans also made for a lively topic of national debate.

The question of equality in the United States has been closely identified with the effort to end racial discrimination. Two landmark Supreme Court cases in the post–Civil War period helped to perpetuate state laws and public attitudes upholding established patterns of racial inequality. In modern times, the case of

Brown v. Board of Education (1954) spearheaded the Civil Rights movement, which culminated in legislative, judicial, and administrative measures aimed at bringing about genuine racial equality. These civil rights gains were followed by new controversies over the issue of mandatory school busing to achieve racial integration and affirmative action guidelines designed to rectify past inequalities. Other major public policy issues related to equality have involved the rights of various ethnic groups, women, and the poor and disadvantaged.

The pursuit of liberty is a core value of American society. Among the personal liberties protected explicitly by the First Amendment are freedom of speech, freedom of the press, and freedom of religion. The right to privacy, or freedom of choice, is another significant aspect of personal liberty in the United States.

The pursuit of justice as a goal of government can be narrowly defined as the attempt to ensure equitable and efficient operation of the criminal justice system. The true test of justice, then, is whether the courts fairly and impartially apply the laws of the land. All societies punish antisocial or criminal behavior through criminal justice systems. In the United States, this system strives to uphold a commitment to due process, or fair procedure. Due-process safeguards, as enumerated in the Constitution and interpreted by the courts, pose several difficult problems in modern society. The controversial exclusionary rule attempts to balance the defendant's right to due process against society's right to be protected against criminals. Questions of judicial discretion and capital punishment also involve balancing defendants' and society's rights.

Conflicts among these five goals always prevent any one of them from being fully realized. In evaluating the relative importance of each goal in public policy issues, therefore, citizens must assume a moderate and rational point of view.

Key Terms

national security	affirmative action
Brady Bill	reverse discrimination
entitlements	prior restraint
mixed economy	retribution
budget deficit	due process of law
national debt	exclusionary rule

Review Questions

1. What are some political issues that involve security concerns?

2. What economic problems does the United States face today?

3. Contrast the ideal of equality and the practice of equality in U.S. history.

4. Why is liberty valuable? How is it protected in the United States?

5. What issues currently plague the American criminal justice system? Why are they important?

6. What is the relationship between the public good and moderation?

Recommended Reading

Because public policy questions are forever changing, exposure to current information and thoughtful opinion is vital. Appropriate reading would include highly respected newspapers (such as the *New York Times* and the *Washington Post*), weekly news magazines (such as *Time* and *Newsweek*), magazines of opinion (including the *Nation*, the *New Republic, Atlantic, Harper's, Commentary,* and *National Review*), and certain scholarly journals that specialize in public policy questions (such as *The Public Interest*). One collection that covers themes discussed in the last several chapters is Henry Aaron et al., eds., *Values and Public Policy* (Washington, D.C.: Brookings Institution, 1994).

Notes

1. Aristotle, *The Politics,* ed. and trans. Ernest Barker (New York: Oxford University Press, 1962), 1252b, 5.
2. Daniel Patrick Moynihan, "Defining Deviance Down," *American Scholar* 62 (Winter, 1993), 1.
3. James Q. Wilson, *Thinking About Crime* (New York: Basic Books, 1983), 234–240.
4. Martin Diamond, personal communication.
5. See Glenn Kessler, "The Lightened Federal Tax Load," *Washington Post National Weekly Edition,* April 3, 2000, 18.
6. "Don't Feel Alone If Tax Confusing: 50 Experts Differ over Family Return," *Lincoln Star* (AP report), February 18, 1989, 2.
7. As Tocqueville pointed out; see Alexis de Tocqueville, *Democracy in America,* ed. and trans. by J. P. Mayer (Garden City, N.Y.: Doubleday, 1966), 302, 459–468.
8. Although there are great disparities among schools. See Jonathan Kozol, *Savage Inequalities: Children in America's Schools* (New York: Crown, 1991).
9. Of course, such problems also raise a First Amendment establishment clause question.
10. "Poverty in the U.S.: 2000," U.S. Census Bureau, September 2001, 2.
11. Kevin Phillips, *The Politics of Rich and Poor* (New York: Random House, 1990), 202.
12. *Civil Rights Cases,* 109 U.S. 3 (1883).
13. *Plessy v. Ferguson,* 163 U.S. 537 (1896).
14. *Shelley v. Kraemer,* 334 U.S. 1 (1948).
15. *Sweatt v. Painter,* 339 U.S. 629 (1950).
16. *Brown v. Board of Education of Topeka,* 347 U.S. 483 (1954).
17. And it was upheld as a legitimate exercise of the government's commerce power; see *Heart of Atlanta Motel v. United States,* 379 U.S. 241 (1964), and *Katzenbach v. McClung,* 379 U.S. 294 (1964).
18. See Peter Schotten, "The Establishment Clause and Excessive Governmental— Religious Entanglement: The Constitutional Status of Aid to Non-Public and Secondary Schools," *Wake Forest Law Review* 15 (1979): 240–244.

19.   *Milliken v. Bradley,* 418 U.S. 717 (1974).

20.   *Regents of the University of California v. Bakke,* 438 U.S. 265 (1978).

21.   In fact, the Supreme Court may have gone beyond *Bakke,* by letting stand a federal court's decision that race cannot be a factor for purposes of (law school) admission. See *Texas v. Hopwood,* 116 S. Ct. 2581, cert denied (1996), 84 Fed. 3d 720 (1996).

22.   *Wygant v. Jackson Board of Education,* 476 U.S. 267 (1986).

23.   *Johnson v. Transportation Agency, Santa Clara County,* 480 U.S. 616 (1979).

24.   *Adarand Construction, Inc. v. Pena,* 515 U.S. 200 (1995).

25.   See, for instance, *United States v. Paradise,* 480 U.S. 149 (1987); *City of Richmond v. J.A. Croson Co.,* 488 U.S. 469 (1989); and *Metro Broadcasting, Inc. v. Federal Communications Commission,* 497 U.S. 547 (1990).

26.   *Rostker v. Goldberg,* 453 U.S. 57 (1981).

27.   *Michael M. v. Superior Court,* 450 U.S. 464 (1981).

28.   *Romer v. Evans,* 116 S. Ct. 1620 (1996).

29.   *Texas v. Johnson,* 491 U.S. 397 (1989).

30.   *Brandenberg v. Ohio,* 395 U.S. 444 (1969).

31.   This issue was resolved in *R.A.V. v. St. Paul,* 505 U.S. 112 (1992). A white eighteen-year-old male burned a cross on the lawn of the only black family living in a St. Paul, Minnesota, neighborhood. Although he might have been arrested for trespassing or disturbing the peace, he was charged under a local hate crime ordinance that made it illegal to place "on private or public property, a symbol, object, or graffiti, including but not limited to a burning cross or Nazi swastika, which one knows or has reasonable grounds to know arouses anger, alarm, or resentment in others on the basis of race, color, creed, religion, or gender." The Supreme Court decreed in 1992 that the ordinance, on its face, violated the First Amendment.

32.   See *New York Times, Co. v. United States,* 403 U.S. 713 (1971); and *Nebraska Press Association v. Stuart,* 427 U.S. 539 (1976).

33.   *Reynolds v. United States,* 98 U.S. 145 (1879).

34.   Most notably in *Abington School District v. Schempp,* 374 U.S. 203 (1963); and *Engle v. Vitale,* 370 U.S. 421 (1963).

35.   *Lee v. Wiesman,* 505 U.S. 577 (1992).

36.   *Wallace v. Jaffree,* 472 U.S. 38 (1985).

37.   The original case upholding a woman's right to an abortion is *Roe v. Wade,* 410 U.S. 113 (1973). Other important cases include *Harris v. McRae,* 448 U.S. 297 (1980); *Webster v. Reproductive Health Services,* 492 U.S. 490 (1989); and *Rust v. Sullivan,* 500 U.S. 173 (1991). Also see *Planned Parenthood of Southeast Pennsylvania v. Casey,* 505 U.S. 833 (1992).

38.   *Schenck v. Pro Choice Network of Western New York,* 117 S. Ct. 855 (1997).

39.   *N.O.W. v. Scheidler,* 510 U.S. 249 (1994).

40.   *Planned Parenthood of Southeast Pennsylvania v. Casey,* 505 U.S. at 851 (1992).

41.   *Washington v. Glucksberg,* 117 S. Ct. 82258 (1997).

42.   Burton Leiser, *Liberty, Justice, and Morals: Contemporary Value Conflicts* (New York: Macmillan, 1973), 192.

43.   The answer provided by the Supreme Court is that the state must provide effective assistance of counsel through the first appeal. See *Douglas v. California,* 372 U.S. 353 (1963), and *Ross v. Moffitt,* 417 U.S. 600 (1974).

44.   *Mapp v. Ohio,* 367 U.S. 643 (1961).

45.   See, for instance, Chief Justice Burger's dissent in *Bivens v. Six Unknown Agents of the Federal Bureau of Narcotics,* 403 U.S. 897 (1970).

46.   *United States v. Leon,* 468 U.S. 897 (1984).

47.   See, for example, "The Battle in Congress," *The Economist,* October 20, 2001, 31, 34.

© Bettmann / CORBIS

© Thomas A. Ferrara / Corbis Sygma

© Bettmann / CORBIS

POLITICS BY VIOLENT MEANS

© Bettmann / CORBIS

REVOLUTION

IN THE NAME OF JUSTICE

FEW WORDS ARE used as loosely as *revolution* and *revolutionary*. Television commercials abound with descriptions of "revolutionary" new shaving creams and household appliances or automobiles that will bring about a "revolution" in transportation. Societies and governments can also be revolutionary. But what exactly constitutes a revolution or a revolutionary government? Fundamentally, the adjective *revolutionary* denotes great change. Thus, a truly revolutionary shaving cream, appliance, or automobile would be a fundamentally new and better product than shaving creams, appliances, or automobiles of the past. The word *revolution* is frequently used in precisely this fashion: The so-called Industrial Revolution, for example, represented a fundamental change in the mode of production, one that altered the way national economies operated and societies were structured.

In a political context, a **revolution** is a phenomenon that brings about a fundamental change in an existing government and society. Usually, it is accompanied by violence and cultural upheaval. However, not just any political change constitutes a revolution. If a coup d'état brings to power one set of leaders, whose policies mirror those they replace and the country or society is affected little by that action, no revolution has occurred, and the resulting government cannot properly be called a revolutionary government.

THE PERSISTENCE OF REVOLUTION

Revolutions have occurred throughout human history, particularly during times of strong population expansion and rapid economic change.[1] Significant changes in governmental structure took place in many Greek city-states in the seventh and sixth centuries B.C.E., in Rome in the first century B.C.E., in the Islamic world in the eighth century A.D., and in Europe, particularly from 1500 to 1650 and from 1750 to 1850.

In the twentieth century, revolutions have occurred more frequently than ever before. In a sense, revolutions are part of a surge in national violence that has marked most of the century. In the 1930s, the renowned Harvard sociologist Pitirim Sorokin made an impressive study of "internal disturbances" in eleven political communities. In western Europe alone, he was able to identify no fewer than 1,622 such disturbances in the post–World War I era, of which fully 70 percent "involved violence and bloodshed on a considerable scale."[2] Moreover, he found that in every country studied, for every five years of relative peace there was one year of "significant social disturbance." Overall, Sorokin concluded that the twentieth century was the bloodiest and most turbulent period in history— and that judgment was made before World War II.

Subsequent events have borne out this judgment. For example, in the period from 1945 to 1970, fully 40 of the approximately 100 developing countries witnessed at least one military takeover. And between 1943 and 1962, attempts to overthrow an existing government occurred in virtually every country in Latin America, in two-thirds of the countries of Asia, and in half the African countries that had gained independence.[3] Between 1946 and 1959, the *New York Times* reported 1,200 separate instances of "internal war," including "civil wars, guerrilla wars, localized rioting, widely dispersed turmoil, organized and apparently unorganized terrorism, mutinies, and coups d'état."[4] Recent times have seen no decrease in revolutions, rebellions, and civil disturbances. If violence, organized and unorganized, has always been an integral part of political life, in the twentieth century it has become both better organized and more prevalent.

Not all revolutions are violent, however. In Eastern Europe, one country after another broke away from the Soviet Union in 1989 and most turned toward a market economy and parliamentary democracy. In all but a few instances—Romania, for example—these revolutions came about with a minimum of violence and bloodshed. In Czechoslovakia it even came to be called the Velvet Revolution because the changeover from communist dictatorship to constitutional government was so smooth. The newly independent Baltic republics of Estonia, Latvia, and Lithuania, are also notable examples of peaceful mass revolution. In each case, a process of political transformation was initiated without great upheaval, destruction of property, or loss of life.

MODERN REVOLUTIONS: TWO TRADITIONS

The idea of modern revolution—the belief "that a nation's people, by concerted political struggle, could fundamentally transform the political order that governed their lives and, with it, the social and economic structure of society"—can be traced to the late eighteenth century.[5] Although revolutions in general have a long history, dating back to the slave revolts of antiquity, modern revolutions possess a distinctive attribute: the idea of using the anger of the lower classes not merely to destroy the prevailing social order but also "to create a new and different one in which the traditional forms of oppression did not exist."[6] For this reason, it is often recognized that modern revolution is usually "characterized by a set of emotion-laden utopian ideas—an expectation that the society is marching toward a profound transformation of values and structures, as well as personal behavior."[7]

Modern revolution, and its attendant desire to establish a new, just social order, usually is traced to the *French Revolution* of 1789. But the *American Revolution,* begun in 1776, provides an alternative, albeit less appreciated, model of modern revolution. The American and French Revolutions, among the most important political events of the modern age, influenced the destiny of generations to come. Both revolutions championed profoundly important political changes that ultimately were animated by visions of a new kind of political order.

Yet, the two revolutions differed dramatically in many other respects. As one astute observer contends:

> It is certainly indisputable that the world, when it contemplates the events of 1776 and after, is inclined to see the American Revolution as a French Revolution that never quite came off, whereas the Founding Fathers thought they had cause to regard the French Revolution as an American Revolution that had failed. Indeed, differing estimates of these two revolutions are definitive of one's political philosophy in the

Begun with "the first blow for liberty," or the Battle of Lexington, the American War for Independence was the first successful anticolonial revolution.

modern world: there are two conflicting conceptions of politics, in relation to the human condition, which are symbolized by these two revolutions. There is no question that the French Revolution is, in some crucial sense, the more "modern" of the two. There is a question, however, as to whether this is a good or bad thing.[8]

The American Revolution

There is no doubt that the Founders considered the American War for Independence fought against King George III to be a legitimate revolution. In waging a war against England in the 1770s, the American colonists became the instigators of the modern world's first successful anticolonial revolution. The colonists' break with Great Britain in time became complete and irreparable. For that reason, it is tempting to say that the American *Revolutionary War* created a model for what have become known as wars of national liberation. However, the American Revolution differed decisively from almost all twentieth-century revolutionary upheavals.

Historical Significance   To understand the historical significance of the American Revolution, we must first examine the political opinions of its leaders. It is noteworthy that the American freedom fighters saw the Revolutionary War as a special and unique experience. "From the very beginning," according to one authority:

it was believed by those who participated in it—on the western side of the Atlantic—to be quite a remarkable event, not merely because it was their revolution, but because it seemed to them to introduce a new phase in the political evolution of mankind, and therefore to be touched with universal significance.[9]

In addition to contemporaneous political treatises, the Founders were well acquainted with world history and with the writings of the great political philosophers, including Montesquieu, Locke, Rousseau, Hume, and Voltaire.[10] Given this familiarity with classical political thought they were not inclined to overestimate the value of new or experimental approaches to politics.

The revolutionaries of 1776 believed that the divorce they demanded had universal meaning and the language of liberty contained in the Declaration of Independence was the timeless expression of that meaning. In other words, the Founders perceived an intimate relationship between the words ("truths") they promulgated and the deeds they performed.[11] Thus, to discover what was truly revolutionary about the American Revolution, it is necessary first to focus on what the American revolutionaries wrote about government and then to observe what they did about it.

Justification   The clearest exposition of the American revolutionary credo can be found in the Declaration of Independence. In addition to proclaiming separation from Great Britain, the Declaration enunciated the reasons for that separation.

The British government, it asserted, had grievously violated the principles of good government. Following John Locke's lead, Thomas Jefferson (the chief author) argued that those principles were twofold: that government must conform to the will of the majority (according to the Declaration's precise language, such a government must be based on "the consent of the governed") and must protect the inalienable rights of all individuals to "life, liberty, and the pursuit of happiness." These principles, in Jefferson's view, established the criteria by which the legitimacy of all governments in all times and places should be measured. A good (or legitimate) government, in other words, draws its authority from the consent of the governed and acts to ensure the inalienable rights of all its citizens.

By making human rights the philosophical basis of good government, the Declaration of Independence departed significantly from past precedent and contemporary practice. Formerly, governments had come into existence to guarantee order, to build empires, to punish impiety, or to enforce obedience. Now, for the first time in history, a political regime dedicated itself unequivocally to the principle of securing popular rights and liberties.

It followed from the Declaration's principles that governments that repeatedly jeopardized rather than protected those rights forfeited their claim to rule. Having stated this conclusion in the Declaration, the colonists continued to wage their war for independence.

Although initially they had desired only to be treated as equal British subjects, with the drafting of the Declaration of Independence they insisted on complete self-government. Nor would just any government do; they wished ultimately to create a government consistent with the self-evident truths they had pronounced in the Declaration. And these truths, they believed, were applicable far beyond the boundaries of the thirteen colonies. Jefferson found *universal* meaning in the enduring words of the document he had drafted:

> May it be to the world, what I believe it will be (to some parts sooner, to others later, but finally to all), the signal of arousing men to burst the chains under which monkish ignorance and superstition had persuaded them to bind themselves and to assume the blessings and security of self-government.[12]

Social and Political Changes   Jefferson's sentiments were expressed in language that ranks with the best revolutionary rhetoric of his or any other time—certainly, it stirred citizens to fight and die for the cause. Even so, it would be a mistake to view the American Revolution solely in the context of the fighting that ensued. While the historic battles raged, great social, economic, and religious changes took place. Restrictive inheritance laws such as primogeniture and entail were abolished; large British estates were confiscated and redistributed in smaller holdings; royal restrictions on land settlements were repealed; important steps to secure religious equality and separation of church and state were taken; and old families lost power, their places "taken by new leaders drawn from younger men, from the common people, and from the middle classes."[13]

Important political changes also occurred, as every colony wrote a new constitution. Drafted in the heat of war, these constitutions perpetuated preexisting systems of local self-government (especially in terms of the executive branch) while protecting individual liberties. The concepts and principles incorporated in these documents were then reflected in the Articles of Confederation and, eventually, in the U.S. Constitution. The importance of this preoccupation with the rule of law, or legality, and procedural correctness cannot be overemphasized.

What we might call the *constitutional process* culminated in the creation of popular government, or government by majority rule, at a time when the people of Europe were still largely subject to the autocratic rule of monarchs. Moreover, the colonists' steadfast concern for constitutionality was instrumental in defusing or preventing conspiracies and cabals that could have divided the new nation into many feuding political subdivisions.

A Moderate Revolution   In retrospect, the moderation with which the American Revolution was fought seems truly remarkable (so remarkable, in fact, that some political scientists do not classify it as a true revolution). The conflict was marked by a "rare economy of violence when compared to other revolutions."[14]

In comparison with later revolutionary conflicts (such as the French Revolution, the Russian Revolution, and the Spanish Civil War), civilian reprisals between insurrectionists and loyalists were mild. Also, the leaders of the American Revolution were never purged or murdered, as so many instigators of later revolutions would be. To the contrary, "[t]he military chief [Washington] became the first president of the Republic and retired at his own choice; the author of the Revolutionary Manifesto [Jefferson] was its first Secretary of State."[15]

What accounted for the unique orderliness of this revolution? Most important, the colonial leaders combined a Lockean attitude toward revolution with the pursuit of realistic, down-to-earth political goals. By "Lockean attitude," to which we will return later, we mean that, with few exceptions, the Founders regarded the revolution as a necessary evil. It was necessary because they knew of no other way to wrest independence from Great Britain, but it was an evil insofar as it caused suffering, bloodshed, and devastation. The American Revolution remains unique precisely because it was not led by fanatics and zealots who embraced an inflexible ideology or who thought that any means were appropriate to achieve their political ends. Rather, its leaders were contemplative individuals who continually questioned themselves (and one another) about the correctness of what they were doing. Although there was no lack of enthusiasm on the part of the revolutionary leadership, "this enthusiasm was tempered by doubt, introspection, anxiety, and scepticism."[16] In short, the American Revolution never took its own goodness for granted.

These tempered revolutionary values were placed in the service of sober and clear-eyed goals. Essentially, what the colonial leaders wanted from the revolution was separation from England and the formation of a system of government founded on consent and respect for the rights and liberties of the people. Significantly, these political visions fell within the realm of human possibility. The Revolutionary War itself was far from an impossible dream, as the eventual American victory amply demonstrated. And the intertwined concepts of self-government and the protection of citizens' rights had been evolving in the colonies at both the state and township levels in advance of the revolutionary conflict. Unlike later revolutionaries, the colonial leaders did not attempt to immediately institute something radically new and different. Understanding the dangers inherent in quixotic or utopian idealism, they knew that "the political pursuit of impossible dreams leads to terror and tyranny in the vain effort to actualize what cannot be."[17]

Far from being an event marked by such terror and tyranny, the American Revolution was, in the words of one authority, "a revolution of sober expectations."[18] Sobriety, moderation, and prudence were the watchwords of this revolution and the chief characteristics of the "well-ordered union" the Constitution would later ordain.

The French Revolution

The French Revolution was quite a different affair. For years, France had experienced growing political instability and popular dissatisfaction. Seeking to preserve the sharp class distinctions that marked French society, the aristocracy had repeatedly frustrated attempts at economic and political reform. Furthermore, the government had demonstrated a clear inability to cope with changing circumstances. Even a skilled and intelligent monarch, which Louis XVI (1774–92) certainly was not, would have found it difficult to overcome the liability of governmental institutions that were decentralized and hard to coordinate. In addition, by the late 1780s, the government was facing increasing difficulties in raising taxes to pay off the massive debt left from earlier wars. Then, just at the wrong time, from the point of view of those in power, economic reversals occurred. Although the economy had been growing, the fruits of that growth were terribly maldistributed. Particularly hard hit were the urban poor and the peasants, many of whom faced the probability of crushing material deprivation rather than the promise of continued economic development.

By 1789, eddies of discontent had swelled into a sea of dissension. Middle- and upper-class reformers demanded both political and social changes. In their most moderate form, these demands included restrictions on class privileges and reform of the system of taxation. Some leaders wanted more radical changes, including the creation of a political order governed by the principles of popular sovereignty.

All these demands were put forward at the May 1789 meeting of the *Estates-General,* a giant parliament elected by broad male suffrage and divided into three estates, or houses, representing the clergy, nobility, and commoners. After considerable debate (and a good deal of turmoil), a majority of the delegates, led by the numerically preponderant Third (commoner) Estate, formed a popular National Assembly. In addition to asserting the right to approve or reject all taxation, the members of this body demanded an end to aristocratic privileges.

These actions constituted a direct attack on the monarchy. Louis XVI responded with predictable ineptitude, applying just enough force to incense his opponents. When he marshaled his troops in an effort to bar the National Assembly from meeting, the delegates promptly repaired to a nearby indoor tennis court, where they resolved to meet continuously until they succeeded in drafting a constitution. Wavering somewhat, the king made concessions in the area of tax reform several

The storming of the Bastille on July 14, 1789, constituted a direct attack against the monarchy. Louis XVI conceded too little too late, and "liberty, equality, and fraternity" swept France.

days later but refused to abolish the privileges of the aristocracy. At the same time, he deployed troops in strategic positions. However, both these measures proved inadequate, and the threat of force proved inconsequential. Sporadic outbursts of violence, including the storming of the *Bastille*, followed swiftly, and as violent activity directed against the king's power became a prominent feature of French political life Louis XVI was forced to accede to demands for a constitution.

The New Constitution   In the two years it took to draft the French constitution of 1791, an egalitarian spirit swept the land. Aristocratic privileges were abolished, and church land was confiscated. A political document of fundamental importance, the *Declaration of the Rights of Man,* enshrined a slogan epitomizing the egalitarian spirit of the times: "liberty, equality, fraternity." The new constitution created a constitutional monarchy. No longer would Louis XVI rule autocratically according to divine right. Although the constitution placed the king at the head of the armed forces and charged him with responsibility for foreign affairs, it assigned most legislative powers to the National Constituent Assembly, which was given the power of the purse as well as the power to declare war. A new elective administration was also created, and voting laws were liberalized.

Thus, a stunning democratization of French political and social life was achieved in an amazingly brief period. The king's power, hitherto almost unlimited, had been undermined and radical social reforms were being implemented.

Political Instability   The constitutional monarchy set up by the 1791 constitution lasted less than one year, during which time the nation foundered without effective political leadership. Naturally, the king despised the new government that had been imposed on him. (At one point, Louis XVI even tried to flee the country to join opponents of the new government, but he was caught and returned to Paris.) The constitution barred former members of the Constituent Assembly from serving in the new legislature, which meant that inexperienced lawmakers held sway. Additional problems arose when the newly elected local administration failed to perform efficiently and when interests that had lost power under the new reforms, especially the Catholic Church and the aristocracy, began to oppose the new regime. A war with Austria and Prussia exacerbated existing difficulties, and the expected economic improvements were not forthcoming. Persistent rumors of the king's imminent return to absolute power swirled through Paris, inspiring a widespread fear of counterrevolution that undermined the political optimism brought on by the reforms.

The Rise of Radicalism   In the chaotic political and social environment of the early 1790s, events moved swiftly. Louis XVI was convicted of treason, deposed, and then beheaded in June 1793. A committee of political radicals intent on refashioning French society and unafraid to use violence thereupon took over the reins of government. The first priority of the new leader, Maximilien Robespierre (1758–1794), was to win the war against Austria and Prussia. This aim required military conscription and strict discipline on the battlefield, as well as national unity on the home front. In the ensuing atmosphere of external emergency, all political opposition was considered treasonous. This situation, though perhaps deplorable, was not unexpected—then as now political repression during times of war was a common phenomenon. But Robespierre was not satisfied simply to enforce national unity. In addition, he wished to create a regime of virtue—to rebuild French society from the ground up, so to speak, by remaking the French citizenry in the image of moral perfection. According to one authority:

> Robespierre wanted a France where there should be neither rich nor poor, where men should not gamble, or get drunk, or commit adultery, cheat, or rob, or kill—where, in short, there would be neither petty nor grand vices—a France ruled by upright and intelligent men elected by the universal suffrage of the people, men wholly without greed or love of office, and delightedly stepping down at yearly intervals to give place to their successors, a France at peace with herself and the world.[19]

However grandiose, Robespierre's utopian idealism was not meant merely as a statement of what *ought* to be; for him, it represented a manifesto to be carried out with ardor and thoroughness. Determined to create a "new citizen," Robespierre could not countenance the goal of individual freedom or the individual pursuit of happiness, as the American revolutionaries had. How could such latitude for individual choice exist in a world divided between absolute good and absolute evil? Robespierre was committed not to the creation of a free country but to the establishment of a "despotism of liberty." The institutionalization of virtue, however, comprised only one aspect of the idealism of the French Revolution. Compassion for the poor was another aspect. Emancipation from want, and even the promise of permanent abundance, became an important goal of Robespierre's revolution, which was waged in the name of the oppressed against the greed and avarice of the oppressors.[20] Only through such a policy, Robespierre believed, could the emergence of a virtuous and contented citizenry be ensured.

The New Agenda   To advance virtue and end poverty in the shortest possible time, Robespierre proposed a sweeping reformulation of French life. Governmental institutions, legal arrangements, social practices—everything was to be changed. Even a new calendar was proposed, as a symbol of the belief that a new era of history had dawned. The spirit of change was total, and heaven on earth was the ultimate goal. One observer has noted that the reigning spirit was that of "undiluted, enthusiastic, free floating messianism . . . satisfied with nothing less than a radical transformation of the human condition."[21]

The problem with messianism, however, is that only God (or God's messenger) can fulfill its glorious promises. Robespierre possessed no such divine qualifications. He and his compatriots soon discovered that it was one thing to proclaim a new order and quite another to *keep* order. Policy disputes emerged as disillusionment reacted with unlimited expectations in a volatile mix. Active opposition to the new rulers began to spread.

The Reign of Terror   Robespierre's response to the growth of opposition and the seemingly intractable difficulties involved in day-to-day government was to reinforce the regime of virtue with mass executions, which became known as the *Reign of Terror*. Executions by guillotine ordered by the Committee of Public Safety became commonplace, particularly in Paris. Originally aimed at the active opponents of the regime, governmental violence soon moved forward with a momentum of its own. It came to include people who shared Robespierre's vision but disagreed with his methods. Later, those who were merely suspected of dissenting became victims of the guillotine. Deep distrust enveloped those in power, as the survivors feared for their own safety. Eventually, this collective fear led to the overthrow and execution of Robespierre himself. During his yearlong rule, some 40,000 people had been summarily executed—an astonishing number in the eighteenth century.

Consequences of the Revolution   The results of the French Revolution are not easy to evaluate. Clearly, it did not achieve its desired ends. After Robespierre's fall, a corrupt and incompetent government known as the Directory assumed power. In 1799, that regime gave way to the dictatorship of Napoléon Bonaparte (1804–15), who managed to restore order and stability. Under Napoléon, France tried to conquer all of Europe in a series of ambitious wars that ultimately led to the country's defeat and Napoléon's downfall.

Thus, no popular government followed on the heels of the French Revolution. After Napoléon's deposition, in fact, the monarchy was reinstituted. Many worthwhile and long-lasting changes did come about, however. For instance, the monarchy installed in power in 1815 was significantly more limited in its powers than the pre-Revolutionary regime had been. Moreover, important social and political reforms stemming from the revolutionary era were retained, and the government was now more centralized and more efficient. Despite these changes, however, the restored monarchy stood in sharp contrast to the egalitarian vision of a new society that had inspired Robespierre and his followers.

The Two Revolutions Compared

If the American Revolution can be characterized as a revolution of sober goals, the French Revolution might be described as one of infinite expectations. In the beginning, the French revolutionaries believed that everything was possible for the pure of heart. The goals of the extremists were utopian, and to realize the extreme ends they sought, they were forced to use extreme means, including terror. Incredibly, America's best-known radical, Thomas Paine, found himself in a French prison during the revolution because his politics were not sufficiently extreme. In the thirteen colonies, most of the revolutionaries were political moderates. In France, moderates were executed or imprisoned.

The American Revolution, with its more modest aims, managed to produce the first great example of republican government in the modern age. France had no such luck. Yet the many revolutionary movements of the twentieth century were influenced far more by the French than the American example.[22]

It is understandable why the French Revolution—with its desire to eradicate poverty and its compassion for the oppressed—has fired the imagination of revolutionaries everywhere. But if concrete and lasting results are to be achieved, political ends must be realistic; otherwise, impossible dreams can turn into inescapable nightmares.

THE DESIRABILITY OF REVOLUTION: BURKE, PAINE, AND LOCKE

Is revolution more likely to improve the lot of the people or make things worse? More than 200 years ago, British conservative Edmund Burke and American revolutionary Thomas Paine carried on a memorable debate over this question. Much of the debate coincided with the early phase of the French Revolution. The pivotal issue was whether that revolution was really in the interest of the French people in whose name it was being waged and, more generally, whether revolutions were beneficial or detrimental to society.

Burke's Position

The French Revolution inspired Edmund Burke (1729–1797) to write perhaps the most famous critique of revolution ever written in the English language, *Reflections on the Revolution in France* (1790). Burke did not believe that the French Revolution resulted from deep-seated economic and social forces. To his mind, the real revolutionaries had been the philosophers who had expounded the subversive doctrine of rationalism and worshiped the god of science. By teaching that government existed to fulfill certain simple goals (for example, to secure individual rights), he argued, revolutionaries had created misleading impressions—most important, that radical change almost always brought great improvements. This way of thinking undercut what Burke believed to be two of the most important foundations of political society: religion and tradition.

Burke argued that dangerous political abstractions were at the heart of the French Revolution. By grossly oversimplifying politics and engendering unwarranted expectations at odds with French history and tradition, simplistic concepts such as "liberty, equality, fraternity" endangered the public order, on which all other political values and virtues ultimately rested. Good order, he noted, was the foundation of all good things.

The science of good government—how to run, maintain, or reform it—could not be mastered through philosophical speculations, Burke contended. He saw government as an "experimental science," whose practitioners needed the wisdom and insight born of experience. And experience, by its very nature, he argued, could not be acquired overnight; rather, it was accumulated, nurtured, cherished, and, above all, transmitted from generation to generation. Burke's view implied a veneration of the past as well as a respect for age and achievement. Society, to his mind, was an intricate tapestry of laboriously handcrafted institutions possessing an inner logic and perpetuated by the force of habit, custom, and convention.

This sober view of government, and of human capacities and limitations, led Burke to stress the importance of pragmatism and prudence in politics. Prudence, he said, was the "first of all virtues." As for pragmatism, he maintained that given the complexity of humanity and society, no simple, all-embracing political formula could work the kind of profound changes promised by the French theorists.

Finally, Burke criticized the extreme impatience of those who glorified revolution. Arguing in favor of gradual and deliberate reform, he warned that unless political change occurred slowly and circumspectly, the main mass of the population would end up in worse straits than ever: "Time is required to produce that union of minds which alone can produce all the good we aim at. Our patience will achieve more than our force."[23]

By promising more than any political order can ever deliver and raising unrealistic expectations for some immediate utopian breakthrough, revolution may both dazzle the masses by visions of a bountiful (but unattainable) future and blind them to the wisdom of the past. In short, though politics can be understood as the "art of the possible," in the distorted mirror of revolution it becomes the science of the impossible.

Paine's Rebuttal

Thomas Paine (1737–1809) attempted to refute the Burkean view of revolution in his *Rights of Man*, written in two parts in February 1792 and addressed specifically to Burke. In defining the legitimacy of popular revolution, Paine stressed the many injustices perpetrated by the British monarchy on the American colonists. For Paine, tyranny and monarchy were as one. Monarchies, he declared, thrive on ignorance and are wrong in principle:[24]

> All hereditary government is in its nature tyranny. An heritable crown, or an heritable throne, or by what other fanciful name such things may be called, have no other significant explanation than that mankind are heritable property. To inherit a government, is to inherit the people, as if they were flocks and herds.[25]

In another passage, he wrote:

> When we survey the wretched condition of man under the monarchical and hereditary systems of government, dragged from his home by one power, or driven by another, and impoverished by taxes more than by enemies, it becomes evident that those systems are bad, and that a general revolution in the principle and construction of government is necessary.[26]

In support of these generalizations, Paine cited numerous examples of royal injustice and corruption. The greatest injustice, he believed, was denial of the people's right to choose their own government. It seemed obvious to him that the people should in no way be bound by their ancestors' decisions. "Every age and generation must be free to act for itself, in all cases, as the ages and generations which preceded it. . . . The vanity and presumption of governing beyond the grave is the most ridiculous and insolent of all tyrannies."[27]

Paine saw revolution in France as emphatically just. In seeking to overthrow the monarchy, he contended, the French people were merely exercising a fundamental right (which grew out of their equal, natural right to liberty). Paine possessed an almost religious faith in the essential goodness and wisdom of the people. This faith pushed him to the conclusion that when the French Revolution is compared with that of other countries, it becomes apparent "that *principles* and not *persons,* were the meditated objects of destruction."[28]

Locke's Perspective

While Burke abhorred popular revolution, Paine glorified it.[29] Roughly a century earlier, John Locke (1632–1704) had taken something of a middle ground between these two extremes in his *Second Treatise on Government.* Locke began with the premise that to escape the inconveniences of anarchy in the state of nature, human beings consent to be governed. For Locke, then, consent formed the basis for both civil society and formal government, with the latter existing chiefly to protect the rights deemed essential to human life. He then raised this question: What happens if the government, contrary to its raison d'être, endangers the life, liberty, and property of its citizens? In such a case, he concluded, the government has exercised "force without right," and the people have the right to resist and defend themselves. In Locke's words:

> The end of Government is the good of Mankind, and which is *best for Mankind,* that the People should be always expos'd to the boundless will of Tyranny, or that the Rulers should be sometimes liable to be oppos'd, when they grow exorbitant in the use of their power, and imploy it for the destruction, and not the preservation of the Properties of their People?[30]

Locke did not glorify revolution. He admonished that popular rebellion should not be launched on a mere impulse. The people will accept individual errors and instances of misrule, he asserted, but they will not accept "a long train of Abuses, Prevarications and Artifices."[31] Locke even suggested that his doctrine of rebellion could serve as a deterrent to revolution: Awareness of the people's right to rebellion, he pointed out, would cause governments to think twice before engaging in repressive actions. Finally, he noted that cognizance of the *right* of the people to revolt against an oppressive government amounts to little more than the recognition that under sufficiently oppressive conditions, the people *will* revolt. Therefore, whether the government acknowledges such a right is immaterial:

> If the majority of the people are persuaded in their Consciences, that the Laws, and with them their Estates, Liberties, and Lives are in danger, and perhaps their Religion, too, how they will be hindered from resisting illegal force used against them, I cannot tell. This is an Inconvenience, I confess that attends all Governments.[32]

In proclaiming what has come to be known as the **right to revolution,** Locke seemingly did little more than endorse what he saw as a fact of political life. That point, however, does not diminish the importance of Locke's theory. His doctrine of rebellion was itself revolutionary in the late seventeenth century. Even in England, where a few decades earlier King Charles I had been beheaded, the question of whether dynastic rulers had a divine right to wield the scepter and command the sword was still being debated. In most other European nation-states, monarchs took the doctrine of divine right for granted. Not surprisingly, these kings did not trifle with anything so mundane as the will of the people, for they believed their authority stemmed from the will of God.

Locke's theory of revolution helped to sound the death knell for the doctrine of divine right. Revolution, Locke claimed, becomes necessary when government acts contrary to its reason for being. Does revolution ensure good government? Not necessarily—it may lead only to anarchy or more tyranny. Does revolution create the *possibility* of better government? Definitely. Often, Locke declared, only by revolting can the people replace tyranny and seize the opportunity to create a new and better government, one that will protect their rights to life, liberty, and property.

Thus, Locke made no utopian claims about the relationship between revolution and political revitalization. As he saw it, revolutions may stem from the desire for better government, but they cannot guarantee that happy result. New governments, he argued, are invariably new only in the sense that they supersede previous governments. Like Aristotle before him, Locke assumed the existence of a finite number of governmental forms. So revolutions could not be considered as quests for new forms of government, but quite literally as revolutions *(revolvings)* from one enduring form of government to another.[33]

Revolution, thus defined, hardly seemed a romantic endeavor. In Locke's view, it involved the exchange of one imperfect form of government for another, perhaps less imperfect form; it invariably encompassed great changes in the larger society; and it implied in almost every case the use of political force and violence. The tendency of revolutions toward upheaval meant that the process was to be feared, even if the goal was eminently desirable. Locke's sober view of rebellion has not been eclipsed; as one leading contemporary scholar has pointed out, "a period of terror and the emergence of coercive and aggressive regimes are the outcomes of revolutions."[34]

THE CAUSES OF REVOLUTION

Locke held that revolutions are necessary and proper when citizens simply cannot endure anymore. But what specifically is it they "cannot endure"? What causes citizens to discard ingrained political habits and support revolution?

The Traditional Explanation

To many observers, both history and common sense suggest that injustices perpetrated by government over a prolonged period foster the conditions in which the seeds of revolution can germinate. This traditional explanation of the cause of revolution originated with Aristotle, who observed in the fourth century B.C.E. that, although sedition may spring from small occasions, it ordinarily does not turn on small issues. The spark that ignites a revolution, in other words, should not be confused with the underlying causes of revolt. In most cases, Aristotle postulated, revolutions are caused by the administration of unequal justice. Under every political order competition for honors and wealth may give rise to the popular belief that one or both have not been fairly distributed. Revolution, then, may grow out of the tension created between the numerous poor (democrats), who want equality, and the wealthy few (oligarchs), who wish to preserve their power and riches.

Aristotle's concern with the perennial tension between rich and poor in political life established a theme in Western political thought that has gained importance with the passage of time. James Madison, for example, declared in *The Federalist* (No. 10) that the "most common and durable source of faction is the various and unequal distribution of property" and then set out to develop a theory of government under which this common source of political tension might be lessened.

A half century later, Karl Marx declared inequality in wealth to be the ultimate cause of all revolutions. According to Marx, revolution is synonymous with class warfare and invariably stems from pervasive injustice. As the economic distance between wealthy capitalists and impoverished workers increases, so does the possibility of revolution.

The Social Psychology of Revolution

What persuades the ordinary individual to disregard the strong social pressure for conformity and participate in a revolutionary movement? Marx held that desperation caused by poverty and social alienation is the chief psychological spur to revolutionary action, and his explanation has been widely accepted in modern times. A few years before Marx outlined this position in *The Communist Manifesto* (1848), however, Alexis de Tocqueville had offered an alternative view. In studying the French Revolution, Tocqueville observed, "it was precisely in those parts of France where there had been the most improvement that popular discontent ran the highest. There, economic and social improvement had taken place, and political pressure had lessened, but still there existed the greatest amount of unrest."[35]

Tocqueville concluded that economic improvement leads to revolution because once the people see that some improvement is possible, they inevitably yearn for more. No longer are they willing to put up with inconveniences and annoyances—only *real* improvement, *immediate* improvement, will satisfy them. Thus is the incentive for revolution born, he argued.

The positions of Marx and Tocqueville seem incompatible, but in 1962, James C. Davies wrote a celebrated article in which he suggested "both ideas have explanatory and possibly predictive value, if they are juxtaposed and put in the proper time sequence."[36] Davies came to this provocative conclusion after making a careful study of Dorr's Rebellion of 1842, the Russian Revolution of 1917, and the Egyptian Revolution of 1952. After discerning in these events a remarkably similar pattern of revolutionary development, he concluded that revolutions are most likely to erupt when conditions have been getting better for a prolonged period of time and then suddenly take a sharp turn for the worse. Elaborating on Davies's thesis, two authorities subsequently argued that the rates of earlier economic growth (and the speed of any economic decline) are especially significant factors in this regard. The higher the growth rate in per capita gross national product prior to a revolutionary upheaval and "the sharper the reversal immediately prior to the revolution," they declared, "the greater the duration and violence of the revolution."[37] In other words, revolutions stem not so much from terrible suffering as from crushing disappointment. Intense discontent, bred by the failure to acquire the goods and experience the conditions of life to which people believe they are rightfully entitled, induces them to revolt.[38]

Modern Theories of Revolution

To say that revolutions grow out of injustice, or perceived injustice, reflects a philosophical consideration of revolution. Such a view emphasizes the importance of injustice as a cause of action; that is, the *idea* that government has acted unfairly or unjustly is seen as a principal cause of revolution. But what *specific* political, economic, and social conditions can lead to revolutionary fervor? Modern-day social scientists try to explain the revolutionary process in more precise terms than did the older political philosophers, often relying on extensive case studies.[39]

Explaining Revolution   A threshold question confronting contemporary social scientists asks: What level of generalization can both account for the many different revolutions around the world and still provide a general understanding of revolution's core nature? Some observers emphasize that contempory revolutions (occurring between 1970 and 1990, in this instance) differ from both very early revolutions, which engulfed past monarchies and empires, and early twentieth century communist revolutions in Russia and China. Between 1970 and 1990, revolutions tended (1) to take place in small, urbanized nations (usually in the Third World); (2) to be animated by ideologies, opposition to Western colonial rule, and ethnic and religious claims; and (3) to be shaped (or constrained) by the Cold War generally and by superpower and international intervention specifically.[40] Although these distinctions reveal important facts about the revolutions of the 1970s to 1990s, they do not undermine the meaningful generalizations we can make about revolution.[41] Furthermore, since 1990, the world has changed dramatically as a result of the end of the Cold War. For instance, in states that had been part of the former Soviet Union, revolution has taken place in a far different political environment than it had a decade earlier. Anti-Russian sentiment has replaced anti-Western ideology, and the large power conflict between the United States and the former Soviet Union has evaporated. Despite such serious and ongoing political changes, the writings of contemporary social scientists yield important findings about the general nature of revolution.

According to political scientists Ted Gurr and Jack Gladstone, a revolution is best conceptualized as an interactive process that continues over time.[42] The machinery of government breaks down in stages as political crises ensue; both influential citizens and government leaders become alienated.

Governmental leaders are increasingly perceived as inept: unable to exercise effective authority; incapable of stabilizing the economy; powerless to ensure domestic order; weak and irresolute in the face of external threats. Thus, the established government comes to be perceived as illegitimate by nearly everyone (including the *elites*), and loses its right to rule.[43] Precisely for these reasons successful revolutionaries usually have the support of wealthy (possibly even aristocratic) patrons and are able to mobilize many discontented, as well. This explanation of revolution as an interactive process appears compatible with the traditional theory of revolution. It helps explain how injustice or the perception of injustice is at the root of revolution. Contemporary scholarship details how this process takes place. It examines the types of crises facing prerevolutionary states, the factors leading to a general loss of confidence in government, and the besieged governments' often hapless responses.

Prerevolutionary Problems   Prerevolutionary countries typically face perilous difficulties. Serious economic hardships can be particularly debilitating, for example, economic stagnation and decline, excessive debt, and the high costs associated with fighting internal wars. *Economic penetration*—the influence that one or more other nations have on the economic life of the prerevolutionary country—is also sometimes a factor. The influx of foreign capital into a less developed nation can induce the government to adopt new policies that endanger its immediate existence (for example, a nation may encourage the production of crops for export rather than local consumption to earn the foreign exchange necessary for industrialization and economic growth).

Demographic factors may exacerbate economic difficulties. Rapid population growth, such as exists in many Third World nations, can slow or reverse economic growth and promote economic inequality. Ethnic, racial, or religious tensions may increase national instability, especially when one particular group grows at a fast rate. Moreover, rapid urbanization can create a number of serious problems in working-class neighborhoods. For instance, when landless or land-poor peasants must move from their traditional rural homes to the unfamiliar surroundings of the city in search of jobs, such problems as social disruption, ill-planned urbanization, inadequate housing, poor sanitation, and deficiencies in medical and educational services often follow. In addition, crime usually increases, particularly when there is a high percentage of alienated young males.[44]

Governments unable to protect citizens from foreign nations are at risk for revolution. However, governments that lose wars are even more at risk. In these countries, which typically suffer severe economic setbacks, the failed war effort may lead to a climate conducive to radical change.[45] Finally, upheavals in neighboring states can spill over into and affect vulnerable governments in the vicinity.

Governmental Responses   Mounting economic, demographic, and political pressures in prerevolutionary nations often lead to citizen discontent (criticism, lawlessness, riots, and acts of terrorism), forcing governments to act. Sometimes, governments are impeded by powerful vested interests; for example, when the bureaucracy includes officials from the rich landholding class, landed interests are often able to block reforms designed to defuse a serious, and potentially revolutionary, domestic crisis.[46] At other times, governments' actions are inhibited by widespread internal corruption. Whatever the structural or behavioral problems faced by these governments, none can tolerate long-term criticism, lawlessness, or acts of terrorism. If a government's response is unjust or inept, or if it fails to act at all, it risks losing the confidence of its supporters and becomes highly prone to revolutionary demands.

Surprisingly, governments that do little or nothing are as much at risk of being overthrown as governments that act decisively, or even repressively. In a study of the French Revolution, Alexis de Tocqueville noted that French citizens took up arms against the monarchy precisely when it began softening. He concluded "generally speaking, the most perilous moment for a bad government is one when it seeks to mend its ways."[47] Tocqueville believed that underlying this paradox (as well as his contention that reform, not repression, is the great accomplice of revolution) is a psychological truth:

> Patiently endured so long as it seemed beyond redress, a grievance comes to appear intolerable once the possibility of removing it crosses men's minds.... For the mere fact that certain abuses have been remedied draws attention to the others and now appears more galling; people may suffer less, but their sensibility is exacerbated.[48]

In sum, tyrants cannot afford to institute reforms because to do so would be to admit past injustices and to activate "the rancor and cupidity of the populace."[49]

Modern studies provide some support for Tocqueville's observations. In a major analysis of the role of the armed forces in revolutionary episodes, one writer argues that revolution never succeeds when the armed forces remain loyal to the government in power and can be effectively employed.[50] When internal security measures are applied too late, too haphazardly, or as the last resort of a desperate government, there is a good chance that official acts of repression may only make matters worse. Apparently, governments that shrink from the systematic use of physical force in revolutionary situations run the greatest risk of being overthrown.

Successful Revolutions   For revolutions to occur there must be charismatic leaders willing to take the deadly risks associated with overthrowing an established (often repressive) regime.[51] At the same time, revolutionary leaders need the support of others in high positions and with technical skills. The right moment to win over the elites is when the government offends or threatens or undermines them in some way. Elite alienation poses the greatest danger to the prerevolutionary government when it occurs within the armed forces.[52] If the generals (and other senior military officers) withdraw support from (or turn against) the ruler(s), it is almost always fatal for the government in power.

Revolutionary change is frequently orchestrated from above. However, all revolutionary change depends on the new government's success in gaining or holding a mass following, which in turn often depends on the degree of citizen discontent prior to the revolutionary events. The causes of popular discontent can include "widespread dissatisfaction over economic conditions, especially among urban peoples; frustration about the lack of opportunities for real political participation, especially among young students and the middle classes; widespread anger about foreign interventions and official corruption; and rural hostility toward the predatory and repressive policies of urban-based regimes."[53] In short, it is the popular perception of injustice, whether true or false, that fuels the fires of all-out revolution in the modern era.

Finally, revolutions are not likely to take place unless most or all of the factors discussed earlier exist simultaneously. Thus, even a nation with nettlesome economic and social problems would probably not be prone to revolution unless it came also to display the other elements of prerevolution, such as the existence of revolutionary leaders, strong elite and citizen support for radical action, and a general loss of public confidence in the existing government's capacity to rule. It is the coincidence of these factors occurring together that makes revolutions happen.

The Dangers of Mass Movements   The Spanish philosopher José Ortega y Gasset (1883–1955) published his famous book *The Revolt of the Masses* in 1930, after the fascists had taken over in Italy, shortly before Hitler's accession to power in Germany, and just about the time that Stalin was consolidating his power in Soviet Russia.[54] He wrote with horror about "the accession of the masses to complete social power" and argued that "the masses, by definition, neither should nor can direct their own personal existence, and still less rule society in general [which] means that actually Europe is suffering from the greatest general crisis that can afflict peoples, nations, and civilizations."[55]

The twentieth century witnessed some of the bloodiest mass movements in history. All failed. The words of Ortega y Gasset are particularly poignant in the light of the calamitous results of modern revolutions:

> As they say in the United States: "to be different is to be indecent." The mass crushes beneath it everything that is different, everything that is excellent, individual, qualified and select. Anybody who is not like everybody, who does not think like everybody, runs the risk of being eliminated.[56]

And "being eliminated" is exactly what has happened to countless victims who have been sacrificed on the altar of revolutions run amok.

Summary

In political terms, a revolution involves significant changes in the form of a nation's government. Such changes have become increasingly common in many parts of the world during the modern era.

There are two basic revolutionary traditions, the American and the French. The American Revolution was more limited than the French Revolution and sought more moderate goals. The French revolutionary leaders, unlike their more pragmatic American counterparts, sought radical and complete change in the social, political, and moral fabric of their country.

The question of whether revolution is desirable has been fiercely debated since the late eighteenth century, when Edmund Burke stressed the many dangers associated with revolution and Thomas Paine emphasized its many benefits. Earlier, John Locke had taken a more moderate position in arguing that revolution is necessary and justified when it is directed against an oppressive government.

The precise causes of revolution are difficult to isolate. Aristotle argued that injustice is at the root of popular rebellion. But what convinces the ordinary citizen to participate in a revolution? Karl Marx contended that worsening economic and social conditions lead to participation in revolutions. Alexis de Tocqueville asserted that improving conditions are to blame, for they cause individual hopes to outrun social reality. A modern view is put forth by James C. Davies, who combines Marx's and Tocqueville's positions in arguing that revolutions are most likely to erupt when sharp economic or social reversals follow a period of rising expectations and moderate improvements. More recent studies on the causes of revolution emphasize that it is an ongoing process and reflects a crisis of legitimacy.

Facing difficult economic, political, or social problems, governments act ineptly or unjustly. They thereby lose the confidence of elites in society, and the masses are mobilized as revolutionary leaders plan the existing government's overthrow and the creation of a new political order. Mass-movement revolutions have ultimately all failed but in the process they have, ironically, victimized many innocent people.

Key Terms

revolution	Bastille
French Revolution	Declaration of the Rights of Man
American Revolution	Reign of Terror
Revolutionary War	right to revolution
Estates-General	economic penetration

Review Questions

1. In politics, what is the meaning of the word *revolution*? Have revolutions become more or less prevalent in the twentieth century in comparison with previous eras?

2. In what important respects were the American Revolution and the French Revolution similar? In what important respects did they differ?

3. In the debate over the desirability of revolution between Edmund Burke and Thomas Paine, what position did each take? What were Burke's chief arguments? How did Paine respond?

4. What was John Locke's view of revolution? Why did he assert the right of citizens to overthrow their government? In what sense does Locke occupy a middle ground between Paine and Burke?

5. According to Aristotle, what is the principal cause of revolution? How have modern social scientists sought to go beyond Aristotle's philosophical insights into revolution?

6. Has contemporary research shed any new light on the causes of revolution? If so, have any common elements arisen from recent theoretical research, or are the findings contradictory?

7. What theories have been advanced to explain how and why individuals become sufficiently disenchanted to join a revolutionary movement?

Recommended Reading

BRINTON, CRANE. *The Anatomy of Revolution.* Magnolia, Mass.: Peter Smith, 1990. A classic study of revolution that contains valuable historical insights into the causes and signs of revolution.

DAVIES, JAMES C. "Toward a Theory of Revolution." *American Sociological Review* (February 1962): 5–18. An influential essay that contends that sudden economic reversals, not oppression, cause revolutions.

GOLDSTONE, JACK A., ed. *Revolutions: Theoretical, Comparative, and Historical Studies.* 2nd ed. San Diego: Harcourt, 1993. A fine collection of readings, many of which examine specific revolutions.

———, TED GURR, and FARROYH MOSHIRI, eds. *Revolutions of the Late Twentieth Century.* Boulder, Colo.: Westview Press, 1991. An excellent summary of the literature, collection of case studies, and theoretical contribution to our understanding of revolution.

GREENE, THOMAS. *Comparative Revolutionary Movements.* 3rd ed. Englewood Cliffs, N.J.: Prentice-Hall, 1989. A wide-ranging discussion of revolution and the extent and limits of our knowledge of this phenomenon.

GURR, TED. *Why Men Rebel.* Princeton, N.J.: Princeton University Press, 1970. Gurr argues that citizens' perceptions of relative deprivation cause revolution.

ORTEGA Y GASSET, JOSÉ. *The Revolt of the Masses.* New York: Norton, 1993. (First published in 1930.)

SCHUTZ, BARRY, and ROBERT SLATER, eds. *Revolution and Political Change in the Third World.* Boulder, Colo.: Lynne Rienner, 1990. A good collection of case studies.

SKOCPOL, THEDA. *States and Social Revolutions: A Comparative Analysis of France, Russia, and China.* Cambridge, England: Cambridge University Press, 1979. A thorough examination of why revolutions occur, emphasizing the importance of community structure and international pressure.

Notes

1. Jack A. Goldstone, "Revolutions in World History," in *Revolutions: Theoretical, Comparative, and Historical Studies,* 2nd ed., ed. Jack A. Goldstone (San Diego: Harcourt, 1993), 320.

2. Quoted in Thomas Greene, *Comparative Revolutionary Movements* (Englewood Cliffs, N.J.: Prentice-Hall, 1989), 5.

3. Ibid., 5.

4. Ibid., 6.

5. Ted Robert Gurr and Jack Goldstone, "Comparisons and Policy Implications," in *Revolutions of the Late Twentieth Century,* ed. J. Goldstone, T. R. Gurr, and F. Moshiri (Boulder, Colo.: Westview Press, 1991), 324. Another way of distinguishing between modern and traditional revolutions is reflected in the linguistic distinction between *revolution* and *rebellion* (in other words, *revolution* is itself something of a revolutionary term). Yet this distinction is not uniformly made in the literature and therefore we have chosen not to employ it in this chapter.

6. Barrington Moore, Jr., *Reflections on the Causes of Human Misery and upon Certain Proposals to Eliminate Them* (Boston: Beacon Press, 1972), 170.

7. James Dougherty and Robert Pfaltzgraff, Jr., *Contending Theories of International Relations,* 3rd ed. (New York: Harper & Row, 1990), 321. The authors cite the scholarly writings of Hannah Arendt, among others.

8. Irving Kristol, "The American Revolution as a Successful Revolution," in *Readings in American Democracy,* ed. Paul Peterson (Dubuque, Iowa: Kendall Hunt, 1979), 52–53.

9. Cecilia Kenyon, "Republicanism and Radicalism in the American Revolution: An Old-fashioned Interpretation," in *The Reinterpretation of the American Revolution, 1763–1789,* ed. J. Greene (New York: Harper & Row, 1968), 291.

10. See, for instance, Bernard Bailyn, "Political Experience and Enlightenment in Eighteenth-Century America," in *The Reinterpretation of the American Revolution,* ed. Greene, 282–283.

11. Martin Diamond, "The Revolution of Sober Expectations," in *Readings in American Democracy,* ed. Peterson, 66.

12. Jefferson to Roger C. Weightman, June 24, 1826, in *The Political Writings of Thomas Jefferson: Representative Samples,* ed. Edward Dumbauld (Indianapolis: Bobbs-Merrill, 1965), 9.

13. Benjamin Wright, *Consensus and Continuity, 1776–1787* (New York: Norton, 1967), 3. Here Wright relies on the work of J. Franklin Jameson.

14. Ibid., 1.

15. Ibid.

16. Kristol, "The American Revolution," 53.

17. Diamond, "The Revolution of Sober Expectations," 73.

18. Ibid., 65.

19. Crane Brinton, *The Anatomy of Revolution* (New York: Random House, 1966), 122–123.

20. Hannah Arendt, *On Revolution* (New York: Penguin, 1976), 60.

21. Kristol, "The American Revolution," 6.

22. Ibid., 61.

23. Edmund Burke, *Reflections on the Revolution in France* (Indianapolis: Library of Liberal Arts, 1955), 197.

24. Thomas Paine, "The Rights of Man," in *Thomas Paine: Representative Selections,* ed. H. Clark (New York: Hill & Wang, 1967), 159.

25. Ibid., 184–185.

26. Ibid., 162.

27. Ibid., 61.

28. Ibid., 70.

29. Nonetheless, Burke became something of a supporter of the American cause in the Revolutionary War, urging his nation to recognize the legitimacy of the Americans' grievances.

30. John Locke, "An Essay Concerning the True Original Extent and End of Civil Government," in *Two Treatises on Government* (New York: New American Library, 1963), 466.

31. Ibid., 463.

32. Ibid., 452–453.

33. See Joseph Cropsey, *Political Philosophy and the Issues of Politics* (Chicago: University of Chicago Press, 1977), 157–162.

34. Jack Goldstone, "An Analytical Framework," in *Revolutions of the Late Twentieth Century,* ed. J. Goldstone, T. R. Gurr, and F. Moshiri (Boulder, Colo.: Westview Press, 1991), 50.

35. Alexis de Tocqueville, *The Old Regime and the French Revolution* (Garden City, N.Y.: Doubleday, 1955), 176.

36. James C. Davies, "Toward a Theory of Revolution," *American Sociological Review* (February 1962): 6.

37. Raymond Tanter and Manus Midlarsky, "A Theory of Revolution," *Journal of Conflict Resolution* 11 (1967): 272, table 6.

38. Ted Gurr, *Why Men Rebel* (Princeton, N.J.: Princeton University Press, 1970), 3–21.

39. As pointed out by Jack A. Goldstone in "Theories of Revolution: The Third Revolution," *World Politics* (April 1980): 425–453.

40. The last two sentences constitute the premise of J. Goldstone, T. R. Gurr, and F. Moshiri, eds., *Revolutions of the Late Twentieth Century* (Boulder, Colo.: Westview Press, 1991). These three characteristics are identified in Goldstone, "An Analytical Framework," 325.

41. As Goldstone admits, his study of revolutions since 1970 is consistent with his understanding of revolutions generally. See Goldstone, "An Analytical Framework," 37–38.

42. This discussion builds heavily on Gurr and Goldstone, "Comparisons and Policy Implications," 324–352.

43. Barry Schutz and Robert Slater, "A Framework for Analysis," in *Revolution and Political Change in the Third World,* ed. B. Schutz and R. Slater (Boulder, Colo.: Lynne Rienner, 1990), 7–9. Also see Gurr and Goldstone, "Comparisons and Policy Implications," 331.

44. Since the publication of his *Thinking about Crime* in 1975, James Q. Wilson's writings on crime in America have emphasized that socializing young males comprise the greatest challenge for a law-abiding society; there are now suggestions in the literature that this demographic fact also has implications for revolution. Compare Gurr and Goldstone, "Comparisons and Policy Implications," 335 (who emphasize age, not gender), and James Q. Wilson, *Thinking about Crime* (New York: Basic Books, 1975).

45. Walter Lacqueur, "Revolution," in *International Encyclopedia of the Social Sciences* (New York: Macmillan/Free Press, 1968), 501. See also Robert Hunter, *Revolution: Why? How? When?* (New York: Harper & Row, 1940), 126.

46. Theda Skocpol, *States and Social Revolutions: A Comparative Analysis of France, Russia, and China* (Cambridge: Cambridge University Press, 1979), 249.

47. Tocqueville, *The Old Regime,* 176.

48. Ibid.

49. Ibid., 187.

50. D. E. H. Russell, *Rebellion, Revolution and Armed Forces: A Comparative Study of Fifteen Countries with Special Emphasis on Cuba and South Africa* (Orlando, Fla.: Academic Press, 1974).

51. Charismatic leadership is a particularly important element in totalitarian revolution. See Chapter 3.

52. Gurr and Goldstone, "Comparisons and Policy Implications," 353–354.

53. Ibid., 334.

54. José Ortega y Gasset, *The Revolt of the Masses* (New York: Norton, 1993). First published in 1930.

55. This quote is taken from an excerpt published on the Internet at *The History Guide,* www.historyguide.org/europe/gasset.html, accessed May 13, 2002.

56. Ibid.

© Thomas A. Ferrara / Corbis Sygma

TERRORISM
WEAPON OF THE WEAK

IN FEBRUARY 1993, a yellow Ryder rental van containing a 1,200-pound bomb exploded in the parking garage of the World Trade Center in New York City. The blast instantly created a 200-foot crater in the basement of the world's second tallest building. Although over a thousand people were injured, remarkably only six people died. Shocked Americans observed in disbelief a devastating terrorist attack against the symbol of America's economic might and one of the most famous buildings in the world. Eight and a half years later, on September 11, 2001, lightning struck again when both World Trade Center towers were hit by hijacked commercial airliners loaded with highly volatile jet fuel. The towers burned for a short time and then imploded with an incredible force that rocked downtown Manhattan, killing thousands of people still trapped inside, creating a firestorm of debris, and sending a huge cloud of smoke, dust, and ash skyward that lingered over the city like an eerie, foul-smelling pall for days.

In 1993, many Americans had wondered: Was the attack on the World Trade Center an isolated act or a sign of things to come? In a short time, the answer was clear. Terrorist attacks in the United States, and acts of terrorism perpetrated against Americans, would become a grim fact of life—and death (see Table 15-1).

Ground Zero—a scene of total devastation where the World Trade Center towers stood so proudly before September 11, 2001.

TABLE 15-1

Terror Target: Americans

April 1983	Suicide bombing of the U.S. embassy building in Beirut, Lebanon, kills 63.
October 1983	Suicide truck bombing of Marine barracks in Beirut kills 229.
December 1988	Pan Am flight explodes over Lockerbie, Scotland, killing all 270 people aboard.
February 1993	Bomb in a van explodes beneath the World Trade Center in New York City, killing 7 and injuring 1,042.
June 1993	Federal investigators break up plot by Islamic radicals to bomb the United Nations and two Hudson River tunnels.
January 1995	Police in Manila, Philippines, arrest members of an Islamic terrorist group, testing bombs, allegedly to bomb several U.S. airliners in mid-flight over the Pacific. The accused leader of the plot, Ramzi Ahmed Yousef, is later arrested in Pakistan and is also charged with planning the World Trade Center bombing.
April 1995	A truck bomb destroys the federal building in Oklahoma City, Oklahoma, killing 168 and wounding over 600. Two Americans are charged (and later convicted).
November 1995	A car bomb explodes outside a U.S. Army training office in Riyadh, Saudi Arabia, killing 5 Americans and wounding 30 others.
April 1996	The FBI arrests Theodore J. Kaczynski, a Montana hermit, and accuses him of an 18-year series of bomb attacks carried out by the "Unabomber." (Kaczynski is ultimately convicted.)
June 1996	A truck bomb explodes outside an apartment complex in Dhahran, Saudi Arabia, killing 19 Americans and wounding 280.
July 1, 1996	Federal agents arrest 12 members of the "Viper Militia," a Phoenix, Arizona, group accused of plotting to blow up government buildings.
July 17, 1996	TWA flight 800 explodes and crashes shortly after takeoff from New York, killing all 230 passengers; the cause is still undetermined.
July 27, 1996	A pipe bomb explodes at a concert during the Summer Olympics in Atlanta, Georgia, killing one and wounding 111.
August 1998	The U.S. embassy buildings in Kenya and Tanzania are bombed, killing 224 people, mostly Kenyan passers-by in the capital of Nairobi.
October 2000	Speedboat-bomb attack on the USS *Cole* in Aden, Yemen, killing 17.
September 11, 2001	Four commercial jet airliners are hijacked from East Coast airports: two are crashed into the World Trade Center towers killing thousands, one is crashed into the Pentagon , and the fourth one crashes into a field in Pennsylvania.

SOURCE: *Wall Street Journal,* July 29, 1996, A14; *The Economist,* September 15, 2001, 18.

Despite these disturbing attacks on (and in) the United States, several other regions of the world have suffered far more from terrorism in recent decades. Terrorism has plagued many of the developing countries around the world, particularly in Asia and Africa (for example, in Algeria, where the government has struggled to survive recurrent attacks, and Israel, where suicide bombings are a constant threat to civilians). Persian Gulf states face similar problems. In fact, no Muslim government from North Africa to the Persian Gulf is free from the threat of terrorism.

Nor is any region safe from terrorism in today's world. Several South American countries (especially Peru, Colombia, and Mexico) have been plagued by terrorism for many years. The most advanced industrial nations of Western Europe are not immune, either. One striking example is Great Britain, where Irish Republican Army (IRA) ultranationalists have conducted a terrorist campaign against British control of Northern Ireland (also known as Ulster) since the late 1960s.

Given the prevalence of terrorism, no one can escape or ignore its effects. There are many little-noticed (and quickly forgotten) incidents that serve to illustrate this point. During the spring and summer of 1994, for example, German police discovered (and foiled) four attempts to sell nuclear materials that could have been used to construct an atomic bomb. In August 1994, 350 grams of atomic fuel were discovered on a Lufthansa flight from Moscow to Munich. Two days later, a German man was arrested for trying to sell a sample of pure plutonium to a police informant.[1] The smuggling of biological and chemical weapons for sale on the black market poses a danger, as well. In short, scenarios involving terrorists who conspire to use weapons of mass destruction (WMD)—from anthrax to a "dirty" radiation bomb— can no longer be confined to novels or movies. As Americans discovered after September 11, 2001, this sort of thing is now a terrifying and very real possibility.

WHAT IS TERRORISM?

Despite its prevalence, *terrorism* remains an elusive concept. Some definitions emphasize terrorism's use of violence in the service of politics. According to *Webster's New World Dictionary*, terrorism is "the use of force or threats to demoralize, intimidate, and subjugate, especially such use as the political weapon or policy." Another source defines terrorism as "the deliberate attack on innocent civilians for political purposes."[2] Terrorism has been defined in many ways but most all definitions take into account several factors, including violence, the desire for publicity, political motive, and intimidation aimed at civilian populations.[3] As we will see later in the chapter, our definition of terrorism implies both a strategy and tactics.

Terrorism comes in many forms.[4] For example, some experts attempt to designate terrorist activities according to whether they (1) are controlled or directed by a government, or (2) involve nationals from more than one country (see Table 15-2). Thus, *state terrorism* exists when a government perpetrates terrorist tactics on its own citizens, such as occurred in Hitler's Germany. In contrast, *international terrorism*, sometimes called *state-sponsored terrorism*, exists when a government harbors international terrorists (as the Taliban government in Afghanistan did in the case of Osama bin Laden and the al Qaeda organization), finances international terrorist operations, or otherwise supports international terrorism (that is, terrorism *outside* of its own borders). During the Cold War, the United States frequently accused the Soviet Union of underwriting (with money and arms) anti-American terrorist groups around the world. The Soviet Union responded that the

Terrorism: Five Definitions

Terrorism by nature is difficult to define. Acts of terrorism conjure emotional responses in the victims (those hurt by the violence and those affected by the fear) as well as in the practitioners. Even the U.S. government cannot agree on one definition. The adage, "One man's terrorist is another man's freedom fighter" is still alive and well. Following are several definitions of terrorism.

Terrorism is the use or threatened use of force designed to bring about political change. —Brian Jenkins

Terrorism constitutes the illegitimate use of force to achieve a political objective when innocent people are targeted. —Walter Laqueur

Terrorism is the premeditated, deliberate, systematic murder, mayhem, and threatening of the innocent to create fear and intimidation in order to gain a political or tactical advantage, usually to influence an audience. —James M. Poland

Terrorism is the unlawful use or threat of violence against persons or property to further political or social objectives. It is usually intended to intimidate or coerce a government, individuals or groups, or to modify their behavior or politics. —Vice President's Task Force, 1986

Terrorism is the unlawful use of force or violence against persons or property to intimidate or coerce a government, the civilian population, or any segment thereof, in furtherance of political or social objectives. —FBI Definition

SOURCE: Adapted from *www.terrorism.com*, accessed May 18, 2002.

U.S. government did the same when it was in the American interest to do so. Iran, Iraq, Libya, Sudan, Syria, North Korea, and Cuba have all been on the U.S. government's list of perpetrators of suspected state-sponsored terrorism for many years. Afghanistan was also on this list, of course, prior to the fall of the Taliban regime in late 2001.

TABLE 15-2

Classifying Terrorism

Type	Controlled or Directed by Government?	Involving Nationals from More than One State?
State terrorism	yes	no
International terrorism	yes	yes
Domestic terrorism	no	no
Transnational terrorism	no	yes

SOURCES: Adapted from Charles W. Kegley, Jr., ed., *International Terrorism: Characteristics, Causes, Controls* (New York: St. Martin's Press, 1990), 5; and Edward Mickolus, "Trends in International Terrorism," in *International Terrorism in the Contemporary World*, ed. Marius H. Livingston et al. (Westport, Conn.: Greenwood Press, 1978), 45.

Domestic terrorism is practiced within a single country by terrorists with no ties to any government. The aim of domestic terrorism is typically to strike fear and sow seeds of discord in a society and to discredit or overthrow existing political institutions. Unlike the United Kingdom, Spain, and several other Western countries, the United States had been largely exempt from such acts, until the Oklahoma City federal office building bombing in 1995, the summer 1996 bombing at the Olympics in Atlanta, and numerous bombings of abortion clinics. *Transnational terrorism* arises when terrorist groups that are not backed by any government and are operating in different countries cooperate with each other, or when one such group's terrorist actions cross national boundaries.

Today, the global nature of modern terrorism has blurred the distinction between the domestic and international forms of terrorism.[5] Looked at differently, all terrorism not actually carried out by governments can be viewed as *antistate terrorism,* which can in turn be divided into two types. Groups seeking to regain control over their homelands, such as Basques in Spain, Irish Catholics in Northern Ireland, Tamils in Sri Lanka, Sikhs in India, and Chechens in Russia have carried out *nationalist–separatist terrorism.* This type of terrorism usually is confined to a specific nation, although its practitioners may receive arms, money, and support from other radical groups, private donors abroad, or even from foreign governments. In contrast, groups seeking to destabilize society in the name of some abstract belief have engaged in *ideological terrorism.* The ideology may be based on a virulent brand of Marxism or Islam.[6] It may be fascist or anarchist in inspiration. Examples include the Red Army Faction in Germany, the Red Brigades in Italy, the Shining Path in Peru, the Islamic Jihad in Egypt, Osama bin Laden's al Qaeda (the Base), and, certain far-right militia groups in the United States. Often such groups also have international links.

Sometimes terrorism can be both nationalist–separatist and ideological. One example is HAMAS (Islamic Resistance Movement), which has violently opposed peace negotiations between Israel and the Palestine Liberation Organization (PLO) over the future of the Israeli-occupied West Bank and Gaza Strip. HAMAS is a nationalist–separatist movement that seeks the destruction of Israel and the establishment of a radical Islamic state. But it is also motivated by ideology, namely a brand of Islamic fundamentalism that stresses militancy and *jihad* (holy war). The lesson of HAMAS is clear: Defining terrorism is easier than classifying it and some terrorists belong in more than one category.

The Origins of Terrorism

There is clearly a link between terrorism and religious fundamentalism—Islamic extremism is an obvious case in point. However, many terrorists are not religious and few religious fundamentalists engage in acts of terrorism. Still, it is noteworthy that terrorism appears to have its roots in religion—specifically, its origins can be traced to three obscure religious sects (the names of which have entered into our vernacular).[7]

The *Thugs*, a Hindu sect finally destroyed in the nineteenth century, after having operated for many, many centuries in India, were highway ambushers who secretly killed thousands of other Hindus apparently out of some perverse sense of religious duty. An extremist Jewish group known as the *Zealots* killed outsiders and helped provoke rebellion against pagan Rome in 66–73 A.D. Beginning in the eleventh century, a Shi'ite Muslim sect, the *Assassins,* murdered outsiders in a campaign to "purify" Islam. Toward the end of the Middle Ages and later during the Reformation violent sects arose within Christianity as well.[8]

However, modern-day revolutionary terror is usually traced to more secular roots, often to the French Revolution or to the writings and deeds of nineteenth-century Russian anarchists.[9] Regarding the type of contemporary terrorism we see on the nightly news, some experts contend it sprouted from seeds planted in the late 1960s; a few even cite 1968 as the year of its inception. The confluence of turbulent and unsettling events in the late 1960s included racial strife in the United States, an escalating conflict in Vietnam, and the Arab–Israeli Six-Day War of 1967. The year 1968 brought these glimpses of things to come:

- Three Palestinian terrorists seized an Israeli El Al airliner and forced its crew to fly the plane to Algeria, one of the first of many acts of air piracy.

- The Baader-Meinhof gang announced its presence in West Germany by torching a Frankfurt department store.

- Yasir Arafat, an advocate of armed struggle against Israel, became the leader of the Palestine Liberation Organization.

- The assassination of Martin Luther King, Jr., precipitated an outbreak of domestic violence in the United States by such groups as the Black Panthers and the Weathermen.[10]

In addition, at least three longer-term historical forces helped to create a climate conducive to terrorism. First, direct military confrontations and conflicts became infinitely more dangerous in the nuclear age (what might start out as a conventional war, say between India and Pakistan, could escalate out of control). Therefore, nations whose interests coincided with certain terrorist objectives sometimes provided moral, financial, or military support to these groups. In this manner, terrorism became a kind of proxy for violence between nations. Second, European colonialism had drawn to a close, leaving many newly formed nations to work out a host of unresolved territorial, national, and religious disputes. The result was a variety of low-intensity wars, many punctuated by terrorist activity, within and between these nations. Third, a reverence for life and a concern for the individual, common to democratic societies, combined with dramatic up-close-and-personal worldwide television news coverage to make terrorist incidents major media events. Thus, the impact of such incidents—the publicity "payoff" from the terrorist's point of view—has been greatly magnified since the 1960s.

But it was in the 1970s that terrorism and *counterterrorism,* or opposing terrorism, became major growth industries. According to one estimate, the number of terrorist incidents multiplied tenfold between 1971 and 1985.[11] The level of terrorism remained high throughout the 1980s (see Figure 15-1). Precise figures vary widely, however, reflecting, among other things, differences in how

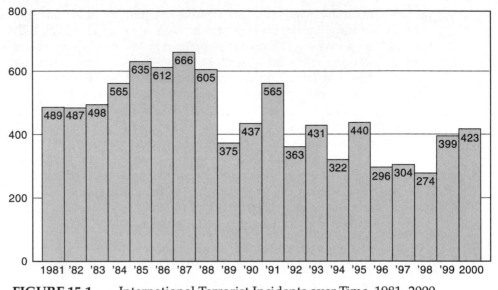

FIGURE 15-1   International Terrorist Incidents over Time, 1981–2000
SOURCE: U.S. Department of State, Office of the Coordinator of Counterterrorism, *Patterns of Global Terrorism,* online at www.state.gov/s/ct/rls/pgtrpt/2000/2452.htm, accessed May 14, 2002.

terrorism is defined. Risks International, for example, put the total number of terrorist incidents in 1985 at slightly over 3,000, while the U.S. government conservatively counted less than one-fourth that number.[12]

In any case, terrorism has risen sharply since the 1960s and remains a serious threat. In 2001, it became *the* major threat facing the United States. Prior to that time, terrorism plagued countries in Western Europe, Latin America, and Asia (see Figure 15-2) far more than the United States. (Surprisingly, terrorism was actually less common in the Middle East than in other regions of the world except North America in the late 1990s.)

The Logic of Terrorism

Why do terrorists act as they do? Often terrorist acts are designed to undermine support for and confidence in an existing government by creating a climate of fear and uncertainty. Terrorists use violence as a form of psychological warfare on behalf of an "overvalued idea" (see p. 457) or cause.

Terrorists are emphatically anti–status quo: they seek to bring about change or chaos, either as an end in itself or as a prelude to change. Terrorists find the present state of affairs intolerable and despair at ever seeing things change using peaceful methods of protest and political action. Terrorists often aim not so much to spark an immediate revolution as to provoke the government into acts of repression—to make the government look weak or inept, and thereby to prepare the way for a future revolution.

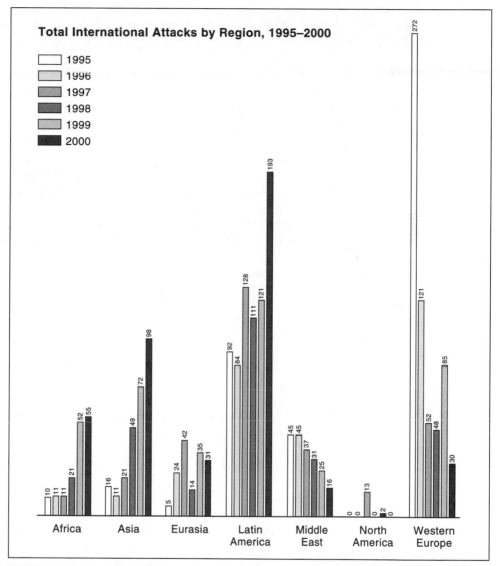

FIGURE 15-2   Total International Attacks by Region, 1995–2000
SOURCE: U.S. Department of State, Office of the Coordinator of Counterterrorism, *Patterns of Global Terrorism, 2000,* online at www.state.gov/s/ct/rls/pgtrpt/2000/2453.htm, accessed May 14, 2002.

Terrorism often does not strike where governments are most unjust but where they are the most vulnerable. Indeed, one expert on terrorism notes, "societies with the least political participation and the most injustice have been the most free from terrorism in our time."[13] Societies with the most participation and the least injustice are, by logical extension, potential targets of terrorist attack. The United

States and the United Kingdom are certainly not weak judged by military or economic standards, but terrorism has afflicted both.

Terrorist Tactics

Terrorism has often been described as the weapon of the weak against the strong. Typically individuals or tiny groups lacking in resources are the perpetrators of terrorist acts. The targets they favor are defenseless. Terrorism requires little money and can be funded by actions normally associated with common crime (such as armed robbery).

Terrorists' weapons of choice are often crude and cheap (for example, small arms and dynamite) but, as we now know, they can also be highly sophisticated (for example, passenger airplanes used as guided missiles or a particularly lethal form of anthrax). Terrorist tactics have become all too familiar. Planting bombs at crowded train terminals, kidnapping wealthy business executives, and blowing up airliners no longer seem extraordinary or even unusual.

Although terrorism usually is directed at innocents, it may also be directed at world leaders. Terrorist groups have been blamed for many assassinations, including Italy's former Prime Minister Aldo Moro (1978), Queen Elizabeth's cousin, Earl Mountbatten (1979), Egyptian president Anwar Sadat (1981), Indian prime minister Indira Gandhi (1984), and her son and former prime minister Rajiv Gandhi (1991). Terrorists have also attempted to assassinate Pope John Paul II (1981), former British Prime Minister Margaret Thatcher (1984), and her successor, John Major (1991). It is possible—though conjecture at this point—that the White House was one of the intended targets of the September 11 attacks. If so, the conspirators probably hoped to kill the American president.

The relationship between terrorist tactics and objectives is revealed in the Brazilian terrorist Carlos Marighella's chilling and incisive *Mini-Manual for Urban Guerrillas,* a forty-eight page do-it-yourself handbook for aspiring terrorists and revolutionaries. It spells out how to blow up bridges, raise money through kidnappings and bank robberies, and plan the "physical liquidation" of enemies. The book offers a range of practical advice: Learn to drive a car, pilot a plane, sail a boat; be a mechanic or radio technician; keep physically fit; learn photography and chemistry; acquire "a perfect knowledge of calligraphy"; study pharmacology, nursing, or medicine. It also stresses the need to "shoot first" and aim straight.

In general, terrorists champion violence above all other forms of political activity. Furthermore, revolutionaries such as Marighella glorify violence, not as a necessary evil but as a positive form of liberation and creativity.[14] According to Marighella, terrorism succeeds when strategies and tactics come together:

> The government has no alternative except to intensify repression. The police roundups, house searches, arrests of innocent people, make life in the city unbearable. [The government appears] unjust, incapable of solving problems. . . . The political situation is transformed into a military situation, in which the militarists appear more and more responsible for errors and violence. . . . Pacifists and right-wing opportunists . . . join hands and beg the hangmen for elections.[15]

Rejecting the "so-called political solution," the urban guerrilla must become more aggressive and violent, resorting without letup to sabotage, terrorism, expropriations, assaults, kidnappings and executions, heightening the disastrous situation in which the government must act.[16]

An urban guerrilla group called the Tupamaros terrorized Uruguay from 1963 to 1972, seeking to overthrow the government. The Tupamaros became the very embodiment of Marighella's revolutionary principles and have since served as an inspiration for terrorists and extremists throughout the world. Significantly, the Tupamaros threat in Uruguay ended only after most of the guerrillas were murdered in a brutal government crackdown. Today, Uruguay is a peaceful, democratic country.

Acts of Terrorism versus Acts of War

When al Qaeda operatives hijacked four commercial airliners on September 11, 2001, and successfully flew three of the planes into large buildings, two of them filled entirely with civilians, and a third with unarmed military and civilian personnel, they were carrying out a terrorist act *by definition* and an act of war *only by inference or interpretation*. When Japanese kamikaze pilots flew fighter planes into American warships anchored in Pearl Harbor on December 7, 1941, it was an act of war first and an act of terror only incidentally, if at all. The Japanese surprise attack was perfectly executed: in one blow it sank most of the battleships of the U.S. Pacific Fleet. In warfighting jargon, this attack was a classic example of the preemptive strike. However heinous and treacherous it appeared at the time (and still does) to Americans, it was extremely successful as a single strategic event. (Of course, in the perspective of the entire war, it takes on a very different aspect: It galvanized the American people like nothing else could have and gave President Franklin Roosevelt the green light to ask Congress for a declaration of war on Japan and Germany.)

These two events—the 9-11 attacks and Pearl Harbor—are often compared, but they clearly belong in different categories. Pearl Harbor was the result of a decision made by the government and military high command of an established state with which the U.S. had diplomatic relations at the time of the attack: It was without question an act of war. Moreover, the attack was directed exclusively against *military* targets—the Japanese pilots could have hit civilian targets in Hawaii but did not. Finally, the attacks were not designed to overthrow or destabilize the U.S. government or any other government, but rather to cripple U.S. naval power in the Pacific and thus forestall American interference with Japan's imperialist designs in Asia.

The 9-11 attacks contrast sharply on all three points. They were not undertaken by an established state (although Afghanistan harbored the al Qaeda network's top leaders and many of its fighters); they were directed mainly at civilians; and the attacks were clearly aimed at exposing the vulnerability of the United States, embarrassing the government, and undermining American economic might, while tarnishing the Pentagon's image both at home and abroad. Even more to the point, these attacks were designed to rally support for Osama bin Laden's extreme brand of Islamism and lead to the eventual toppling of "apostate" governments in the Arab world (including bin Laden's native Saudi Arabia).

Characteristics of Terrorist Groups

More than 600 terrorist groups exist worldwide.[17] They tend to be small and tight-knit, seldom numbering more than 100 members and usually less than several dozen. Many of the most notorious terrorists groups are found in the Middle East and are associated with Islamic fundamentalism—Abu Nidal organization, al Qaeda, Islamic Jihad, HAMAS, and Hizballah (Party of God) are five contemporary examples. Because such groups are often ethnically and politically homogeneous—sometimes close friends or even relatives of one another—terrorist cells are extremely difficult to penetrate or monitor, frequently confounding the best efforts of intelligence agencies to do so.

As the world learned after the release of the bin Laden videotape in mid-December 2001, al Qaeda operates on a "need-to-know" basis, closely guarding and compartmentalizing information within its own ranks, much like official intelligence services. This emphasis on counterintelligence is essential for the success and survival of terrorist groups and networks, especially under conditions of greatly heightened security in the United States, Europe, the Arab world, and elsewhere.

Even so, the life span of most terrorist groups is only about five to ten years. By the same token the leaders of terrorist groups usually do not hold power for more than a few years (although again there are exceptions, the most notorious being Abu Nidal, the shadowy figure behind the hijacking of the cruise ship *Achille Lauro* and bombings of the Rome and Vienna airports in the mid-1980s and Osama bin Laden, founder of al Qaeda and the prime mover behind the 9-11 hijack-bombings). Finally, terrorist groups seldom operate from a fixed location. Terrorists

© Corbis Sygma

Osama Bin Laden—the wealthy Saudi mastermind behind a series of terrorist attacks on U.S. targets that culminated in the destruction of the World Trade Center.

often have relatively little training, use unsophisticated equipment, and acquire the "tools of the trade"—some of which could be purchased at any hardware store—by theft. Of course, this description does not fit the perpetrators of the 9-11 attacks.

Terrorism in Algeria: A Contemporary Example

In Algeria, the line between Islamic fundamentalism and terrorism—or between revolution and civil war—was difficult to discern in the 1990s. Algeria most clearly exhibits tendencies seen in other Arab nations such as Egypt and Saudi Arabia, where terrorism has become a tactic of Islamic extremist groups seeking to overthrow established secular governments in the region.

Algeria gained its independence from France in 1962 after a long, violent revolutionary struggle. For some thirty years thereafter, pro-Marxist military strongmen ruled Algeria most of the time. Eventually, however, a core of Muslim fundamentalists became dangerously discontented. From this disquiet emerged the political organization Islamic Salvation Front (FIS). Later, when Algeria's first multiparty elections were held in 1991, the FIS gained a dazzling first-round victory. However, in 1992, the military simply canceled the second round of elections and installed a new president. This cynical act radicalized the FIS and prompted it to go underground. Even worse, it split the armed Islamist movement in Algeria and gave the most extreme *jidadist* elements—advocates of all-out terrorism—the upper hand. At the end of 1992, the Armed Islamic Group (GIA) emerged as a murderous alternative to the somewhat milder (less violent and uncompromising) FIS.

Algeria's terrorist nightmare began with GIA attacks primarily on the police, security forces, and government officials. Soon the terrorists began targeting other groups as well. In 1993 and 1994, there were dozens of attacks on opposition groups, foreigners, intellectuals, journalists, and other civilians. Between 1995 and 1998, only about 25 percent of the attacks were directed against security forces and government officials; the rest of the attacks—almost 75 percent—struck at civilians (see Table 15-3). Schools and school employees were also among the favorite targets of the attackers.

As the strategy changed (mainly targeting civilians), the insurgents' tactics also changed. In 1996, there were more bombings than assassinations, violent clashes with security forces, and organized armed attacks (see Table 15-4). Earlier bombings were aimed mainly at government buildings and police stations. After the mid-1990s the bombings increasingly targeted markets, cinemas, and restaurants, as well as schools.

According to one Middle East authority on the Algerian Islamist movement:

> Violence reached its ultimate level of cruelty in a series of massacres that began at the end of 1996. At least 67 massacres took place between November 1996 and July 1999, but most of these massacres took place in 1997 (42 massacres). . . . These massacres involved militants armed with guns, crude bombs, knives, and axes descending on villages at night to kill their inhabitants, often by hacking them to death and slitting their throats. Other atrocities involved fake security checkpoints set up by militants to identify specific targets—e.g. state employees and men with conscription papers.[18]

TABLE 15.3

The Targets of Algerian Islamist Activities from 1992 to 1998*

Year	Police and Security	Government Officials	Opposition Groups	Foreigners	Intellectuals and Journalists	Civilians	Total
1992	28	1	0	2	2	5	38
1993	43	26	1	10	7	1	88
1994	25	18	12	19	15	14	103
1995	31	17	11	10	27	37	133
1996	18	8	3	3	6	49	87
1997	19	5	3	0	0	98	125
1998	7	0	0	0	0	60	67
Total	171	75	30	44	57	264	641

*Measured in the number of separate attacks in each category, not in the total number of victims.
SOURCE: The data was collected from the Chronology section of *The Middle East Journal* and *Middle East International*. Only records that specify the date and place of an episode were included. Many reported incidents were not included in these numbers because they do not provide enough information to ensure their reliability. Although this procedure significantly underestimates the incidence of violence in Algeria, it does reliably reflect trends in violence.

The government countered with lethal force directed against the terrorists. Later, it also promised political reform. In November 1996, constitutional amendments espoused by the government were popularly ratified. The amendments appeared to move Algeria toward a limited democracy. However, they curtailed the radical Islamic groups, retained preponderate power in the executive branch, and banned all political parties based on religion, language, or religion (thus, during the June 1997 elections, the FIS and similar groups could not run candidates and could only urge citizens not to vote).

The FIS condemned the new constitution and continued to struggle against the regime until September 1997 when its armed wing, the Islamic Salvation Army (AIS), declared a cease-fire. But it was the vicious bands of zealots and thugs that comprised the GIA, not the AIS, which had carried out most of the bloody massacres. Not surprisingly, the hard-line "eradicators" in the government favored finding and killing the terrorists rather than trying to negotiate with them—this stance was understandable given the fact that the GIA had shown no proclivity toward compromise.

The election of a new president in 1999 broke the ice. The government released some political prisoners and pushed through the Law of Civil Reconciliation, extending amnesty to rebels who had not committed atrocities. The AIS, which benefited from a general amnesty due to its 1997 cease-fire, began disbanding its militia under state supervision at the end of 1999. Thousands of AIS rebels have taken advantage of the general amnesty granted by the regime, and at the beginning of 2000 even some GIA militias began declaring that they would abide by the cease-fire. Nevertheless massacres still take place in Algeria, although less frequently than in the bloody years between 1994 and 1998.

TABLE 15-4

The Methods of Algerian Islamists during the Insurgency from 1992 to 1998*

Year	Peaceful Demonstrations	Violent Clashes	Bombings and Sabotage	Assassinations and Armed Attacks	Total
1992	5	15	10	14	44
1993	0	19	4	62	85
1994	0	16	10	73	99
1995	0	8	43	68	119
1996	0	9	42	25	76
1997	0	10	34	63	107
1998	0	11	22	46	79
Total	5	88	165	351	609

*The data is arrived at in the same manner as in Table 15-1.

All the while, Algeria suffers from widespread economic and social problems. Despite Algeria's extensive oil and natural gas reserves, the people are overwhelmingly poor. Unemployment hovers at 25 percent. In 1997, more than half of its population was under twenty years of age (important because unemployment typically hits youth the hardest, which may, in part, explain why terrorists and revolutionaries are disproportionately young). Furthermore, unsettling ethnic divisions persist. Most notably, Berbers are a sizable minority who feel alienated and powerless, a feeling that was intensified when Algeria moved to make Arabic its sole official language, upsetting Berber speakers (as well as French speakers). These lingering problems continue to be largely ignored as the regime focuses on the continuing threat from militant Islamists in its midst who seek to turn Algeria into a theocratic state.

WHO (AND WHAT) IS A TERRORIST?

The horrors visited on Algeria by terrorists in the 1990s are hard for normal people living normal lives to comprehend. Who are the perpetrators of these terrorist acts? Where do they come from? How do terrorists differ from common criminals, guerrilla fighters, and revolutionaries? What causes certain individuals to turn to terrorism?

Classifying Terrorists: Criminals, Guerrillas, or Revolutionaries?

What gives terrorism its distinctive characteristics? Terrorism and fanaticism are closely associated. But how is fanaticism of this kind best understood? U.S. foreign policy treats terrorism as essentially a *political* phenomenon and classifies terrorists as subversives. This approach stresses the illegitimacy of all terrorism and advocates combating it with swift punishment and due vigilance. Critics of this approach (including some European countries and NATO allies) view terrorism as primarily a *social* problem. Although these governments are not averse to punishing terrorists (and have done so themselves in some cases), they tend to sympathize with the social classes or ethnic communities that terrorists claim to represent, and argue that terrorism will disappear only when the underlying causes of injustice, despair, and hopelessness are ameliorated.

The United States and Israel are on one side of this philosophical divide; Europe is on the other side. The Arab world is divided: Islamic fundamentalism is anathema to Egypt, Algeria, and Jordan, but embraced by Sudan. Saudi Arabia is ambivalent, both fearing Islamic fundamentalism and relishing its role as the birthplace of Islam and defender of the faith. Even where the governments suppress extreme Islamist groups, many people secretly sympathize with them. In Palestine, sympathy with groups like HAMAS and Hizbollah is widespread and hardly a secret. Many Arabs admit that throughout the Arab world, people express admiration for Osama bin Laden. Indeed, in some countries Osama reportedly has become the most popular name for baby boys.

In the West, however, there is general agreement that terrorists are criminals, though by no means ordinary, run-of-the-mill criminals. Killing and kidnapping, robbing banks, and hijacking airplanes are heinous crimes no matter who perpetrates them or why; they are terrorist acts when the motive is political. When serial murderers go on a killing spree, innocent people die and whole communities can be terrorized. But the aim of mass murderers is not to terrorize communities and certainly not to achieve political ends. They are mass murderers first and "terrorists" only incidentally. Occasionally, terrorists cooperate with criminals or criminals adopt terrorist tactics, but such circumstances are relatively rare and are usually confined to narcoterrorists—armed rebels in countries such as Colombia and Peru who are associated with powerful drug lords, both of whom seek to undermine legitimate political authority and defeat (or co-opt) the government's security forces.

If terrorists are not ordinary criminals, neither are they ordinary guerrillas or "freedom fighters," as they sometimes claim. Guerrillas often constitute the armed wing of a revolutionary movement or party—Mao's Red Army is perhaps the most famous example. Guerrilla forces engage the government's armed forces in battle. No one would claim that guerrilla forces never commit atrocities against civilians (or, for that matter, that the soldiers in uniform never do), but most insurgent violence is directed at governments and their security forces. By contrast, terrorists primarily target civilians and noncombatants, a strategy designed to sow the seeds of fear and doubt so people will not cooperate with the police and military and to show people that the government cannot protect them.

All terrorists are revolutionaries, though not ordinary revolutionaries. Certainly many revolutionaries in the twentieth century have at times resorted to terror—both before and after taking power. But ordinary revolutionaries concentrate primarily on overthrowing the government *in existing circumstances* rather than trying to precipitate a political and social crisis by artificial means (mass terror)—in other words, radically changing the circumstances. To that end, revolutionaries attempt to build a subversive party; infiltrate the government, the police, and the military; spread propaganda; agitate among trade unions; recruit and indoctrinate the young; and incite strikes, riots, and street demonstrations. Thus, terrorism in the hands of revolutionaries is a tactic, not a strategy; in the hands of terrorists, terror is both a tactic *and* a strategy. Terrorists often appear to share the view of Emile Henry, a Frenchman who, when charged with throwing a bomb in a café in 1894, replied, *"Il n'y a pas d'innocents"* ("No one is innocent").

Identifying Terrorists

One notion holds that urban poverty breeds terrorism, and therefore that any theory of modern terrorism must look at its social context, including urban decay, the breakdown of the family structure, youth unemployment, and the dehumanizing effects of surviving in a fast-paced, overcrowded, and often impersonal city, and, of course, Western intrusion—first colonization and now globalization. People unable to cope with or accept these stresses react in different ways. Some turn to crime; others to alcohol or drugs; and some drop out. A tiny fraction become associated with terrorism. Those who do become terrorists do not all come from urban backgrounds. They are not all poor. Although some terrorists grow up in the midst of urban poverty, others merely react against it. Osama bin Laden was born into a fabulously wealthy family in Saudi Arabia. In fact, many terrorists are well educated and come from relatively privileged backgrounds; they have merely observed severe injustice or have experienced it vicariously. Most terrorists are male, single, and young.[19]

TERRORISM AND SOCIETY

Many people in many places in this world have genuine, legitimate, deeply felt grievances. Perhaps if these grievances could be removed, terrorism would disappear.[20] Possibly so, yet there are many societies where individuals and groups have been treated unfairly but terrorism has not reared its ugly head. Why? Consider this: Totalitarian states do not have a problem with terrorism, and even nations with ruthless authoritarian governments seldom do.[21]

Societies most prone to terrorism are often those with weak states—that is, with unstable political structures (government, bureaucracy, security forces, party system, and so on) and fragmented political cultures. Weak states can take the form of unpopular and illegitimate authoritarian governments or permissive and quarrelsome democracies.[22] But if weak governments of all kinds correlate with incidents of terrorism, it is also worth noting that democracies are *by nature* vulnerable to terrorism and ill-suited to carry out sweeping counterterrorist programs (see Figure 15-3). Let us see why.

Youthful Recruits

The Shi'ite suicide bomber who drove her explosives-packed Peugeot into an Israeli Army convoy in southern Lebanon in 1985 was sixteen years old. The Jordanian who tried to assassinate a United Arab Emirates diplomat in Rome in 1984 was twenty-two. Of the *Achille Lauro*'s four hijackers, the oldest was twenty-three; the youngest, nineteen. Research puts the median age of terrorists at 22.5 years. In

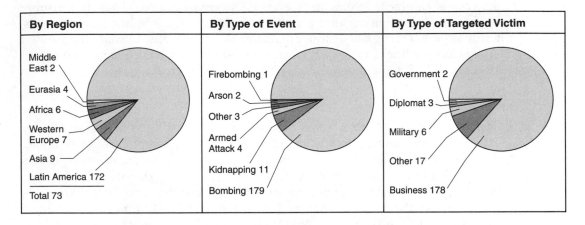

By Region	By Type of Event	By Type of Targeted Victim
Middle East 2	Firebombing 1	Government 2
Eurasia 4	Arson 2	Diplomat 3
Africa 6	Other 3	Military 6
Western Europe 7	Armed Attack 4	Other 17
Asia 9	Kidnapping 11	Business 178
Latin America 172	Bombing 179	
Total 73		

FIGURE 15-3   Anti-American Terrorist Attacks by Type, 2000

SOURCE: U.S. Department of State, Office of the Coordinator of Counterterrorism, *Patterns of Global Terrorism,* 2000. Online at *www.state.gov/s/ct/rls/pgtrpt/2000/2461.htm,* accessed May 14, 2002.

Northern Ireland, twelve- and fourteen-year-old terrorists have been arrested; fourteen- and fifteen-year-old children are recruited by Arab and Iranian groups, sometimes for particularly dangerous missions.[23] A German psychologist who interviewed captured members of the Red Army Faction noted elements of an "adolescent crisis" among terrorists, while an expert on the Provisional Irish Republican Army (PIRA) observed a "terrorist tradition" at work in some countries where "whole families pass on to their children that [terrorism] is the way you struggle for your rights."[24]

Eric Hoffer touches on the susceptibility of certain youths to fanatical causes in *The True Believer.* He places them in a group he calls "misfits," a category he further breaks down into temporary and permanent. Hoffer writes:

> Adolescent youth, unemployed college graduates, veterans, new immigrants and the like are of this category. They are dissatisfied and haunted by the fear that their best years will be wasted before they reach their goal.[25]

At the same time, although they tend to be "receptive to the preaching of a proselytizing movement," Hoffer argues that they "do not always make staunch converts."

The Psychology of Terrorism

According to one expert on the psychology of terrorism, "terrorists with a cause" are the most dangerous to democratic society.[26] Who are these rebels? What motivates them? Not surprisingly, many of the most common traits exhibited by members of terrorist groups are associated with adolescence, including:[27]

- *Oversimplification of issues.* Terrorists see complex issues in black-and-white terms; they have no interest in debate; they often live out a "fantasy war" imagining that the people overwhelmingly support their cause.

- *Frustration.* Terrorists feel that society has cheated them, that life is unfair, and that they deserve far more; they are unwilling to wait or work for something better and believe that the only way to get is to take.

- *Orientation toward risk taking.* Many terrorists seek situations involving adventure and are easily bored.

- *Self-righteousness.* Terrorists display belligerent assertiveness, dogmatism, and intolerance of opposing views.

- *Utopianism.* Terrorists harbor an unexamined belief that heaven on earth is just over the horizon—the only thing standing in the way is the corrupt and oppressive existing order.

- *Social isolation.* Terrorists, one expert notes, are often "people who are really lonely." For some, a terrorist cell may be the only "family" they have.

- *A need to be noticed.* Terrorists share a need to feel important, a desire to make a personal imprint by getting news coverage.

- *A taste for blood.* Interviews with captured terrorists, testimony by relatives and acquaintances, and eyewitness accounts by former hostages point to a final, startling characteristic: Some terrorists kill without an ounce of remorse.

Terrorists often oversimplify reality; thus, they may see victims as mere objects—a habit of mind observed among Nazi guards at extermination camps during the Holocaust.[28] In a similar vein, Paul R. McHugh, a distinguished psychiatrist at the Johns Hopkins School of Medicine, argues that terrorists, like other actors with a "ferocious passion," have an "overvalued idea" defined as "a thought shared with others in a society or culture but in the patient held with an intense emotional commitment capable of provoking dominant behaviors in its service."[29] One type of clinical disorder prompted by an overvalued idea is anorexia nervosa. According to Dr. McHugh, Adolph Hitler (anti-Semitism), Carrie Nation (temperance), and John Brown (abolitionism) are three historical figures with overvalued ideas. Two contemporary examples are the Unabomber and Jack Kevorkian (assisted suicide).

Those who suffer from personality disorders associated with overvalued ideas are commonly called fanatics. Once again, Hoffer's discussion of fanatics in *The True Believer* proves apropos. Fanaticism (excessive, blind devotion), whether political or religious, is almost always based on hatred, according to Hoffer. In this view, the fanatic places hatred in the service of a cause or a vision. Hatred is in turn a unifying force for like-minded fanatics, whereas love is divisive. Thus, hatred provides a reason for living, often appealing to individuals who are insecure, have little sense of self-worth, or lack meaning in their lives.

Hoffer's characterization of the fanatical state of mind merits attention:

> The fanatic is perpetually incomplete and insecure. He cannot generate self-assurance out of his individual resources—out of his rejected self—but finds it only by clinging passionately to whatever support he happens to embrace. This passionate attachment is the essence of his blind devotion and religiosity, and he sees in it the source of all virtue and strength. Though his single-minded dedication is a holding on for dear life, he easily sees himself as the supporter and defender of the cause to which he clings.

And he is ready to sacrifice his life to demonstrate to himself and others that such indeed is his role. He sacrifices his life to prove his worth.[30]

Nor are fanatics necessarily motivated by a good cause. They embrace a cause not primarily because it is just or holy but because they have a desperate need for something to hold on to. It is this need for passionate attachment that turns a cause into *the* cause. From there it can be a short step to *jihad* or a terrorist campaign.[31]

Although terrorism is not necessarily a reflection of social injustice, it often is. For example, in the case of Algeria, which Amnesty International called the most violent country in the Middle East at the end of the 1990s, terrorism was a response to the military's illegal cancellation of a national election in 1992. Still, when all is said and done, it is still a mystery how anyone can commit barbarous acts that violate the most elementary standards of morality out of idealism or religious fervor.

Terrorism and the Media

Terrorists seek publicity. As they see it, the more attention they can get, the better. Why? Because media coverage—above all, the dramatic images that flash across our television screens—draws worldwide attention to the act itself and the overvalued idea, the cause, embraced by those who perpetrated it. Not only is this coverage politically prized, it also is personally gratifying—it makes otherwise obscure and nondescript individuals feel important. Moreover, the prime-time exposure terrorists frequently get on CNN and other network news all over the world is free. And of course, the most daring, deadly, or otherwise sensational terrorist acts receive the most extensive media attention. Without any question, the two fatal blows struck against the World Trade Center are the most widely and repetitively televised terrorist acts in history.

In light of terrorists' need for publicity, many political analysts outside the profession of journalism blame the rapid rise of terrorism in part on the media— television, in particular. After all, bad news makes for better headlines and better copy than good news, and bad news that is also sensational and shocking garners the most attention and the highest Nielson ratings (which in turn translates into higher advertising revenues for the networks). In this sense, at least, terrorism is tailor-made for television.

In a market economy, simply reporting the news is not enough; the news industry must also sell the news. The share of the viewing audience—the news market—that chooses to watch television news determines how much companies will pay to advertise their products. Thus, the producers of news shows are loath to pass up a good story, even if it means playing into the hands of terrorists.

In defense of the media, is there any doubt that, say, an airplane hijacking involving hundreds of innocent people is newsworthy? The media do, after all, have a responsibility to keep people informed. And even if one network decided not to cover a particular terrorist incident or pay only slight attention to it, would the others ignore it too? In the final analysis, collusion and censorship are the only "solution"—but the cure, in this instance, would be worse than the disease. When democratic governments engage in constitutionally questionable activities in response to terrorist acts, the perpetrators of terrorism win a moral and political victory. Ironically, protests and demonstrations that might result from censorship, surveillance, wiretapping, and other internal security measures have the potential under favorable circumstances to destabilize a society—and imperil democratic institutions—far more than terrorism itself.

Media self-restraint is the only attractive solution. Realistically, the news industry is not likely to cut back significantly on its reporting of terrorism until public opinion turns against such reports. As consumers of news, we often get what we demand and, in that sense, deserve what we get.

COUNTERING TERRORISM

The question facing democratic societies is not how terrorism can be stopped but how terrorism can be slowed without curtailing basic freedoms. This issue has faced the United States and its European allies since the late 1960s. With the recent demise of the Soviet Union and rise of the Russian mafia—as well as the continuing threat from Iraq, the al Qaeda network, and others—the threat of nuclear terrorism has risen appreciably, underscoring the need of established governments everywhere to confront and defeat worldwide terrorism.[32]

Domestic Legislation

Authoritarian and totalitarian states are free to deal quickly and harshly with terrorists and accused terrorists. Democratic states, however, are committed to following the rule of law whenever and wherever possible. Over the last two decades, many democracies have enacted new laws or adapted old laws to deal more effectively with terrorists and terrorism.

One approach adopted by democratic states has been to pass new legislation. For instance, in the United States skyjacking was made a federal crime, as was committing an act of violence against any airline passenger within the United States or any *American* passenger outside the United States. In the wake of the first World Trade Center bombing and the Oklahoma City bombing, Congress passed the Antiterrorism and Effective Death Penalty Act in April 1996. This act provided federal law enforcement officials with more money and new tools to fight terrorism, tightened immigration, and loosened deportation procedures for aliens suspected of being terrorists.

But in 2001—on that fateful day in September—the second assault on the World Trade Center painfully revealed the utter inadequacy of all previous counterterrorist measures in the United States. President George W. Bush quickly set up a new cabinet-level Office of Homeland Security designed to coordinate the work of all federal departments and agencies engaged in any aspect of counterterrorism. The president also issued a controversial directive creating military tribunals for suspected terrorists, and reportedly:

> . . . was considering the possibility of trials on ships at sea or no United States installations, like the naval base at Guantánamo Bay, Cuba. The proceedings promise to be swift and largely secret . . . [and] the release of information might be limited to the

barest facts, like the defendant's name and sentence. Transcripts of the proceedings . . . could be kept from public view for years, perhaps decades.[33]

The major changes in the government's power over legal aliens in the United States are to be found in a new law pushed through Congress after the 9-11 attacks. The complete name of this law—necessary to produce the desired acronym—is the Uniting and Strengthening American by Providing Appropriate Tools Required to Intercept and Obstruct Terrorism Act of 2001, more commonly known as the USA Patriot Act. The act broadens the notion of who is to be considered a terrorist suspect and provides the attorney general with sweeping personal authority to detain Arabs and Muslims, as well as other foreigners; it permits the government to deny entry into the United States to any foreigner who publicly endorses terrorism or belongs to a terrorist group; it expands the definition of "terrorist activity" to include any foreigner who uses "dangerous devices" or raises money for a terrorist group, *wittingly or unwittingly;* finally, it allows the government to detain any foreigner the attorney general considers a menace.

Taken together the antiterrorist measures growing out of executive orders and the new law give the federal government peacetime powers of surveillance and infiltration unprecedented in modern times within the borders of the United States. Polls indicated that the vast majority of Americans considered these measures appropriate and did not think they jeopardized civil liberties. Still, there was a vocal minority on both the right and the left that dissented strongly, expressing alarm and dismay at what they viewed as the erosion of individual liberties and constitutional guarantees (especially Articles I, IV, V, and VI of the Bill of Rights).

Another approach has been to proscribe membership in terrorist organizations. In the United Kingdom, specific terrorist groups are outlawed, including the IRA and the Irish National Liberation Army, as is the solicitation of funds for these groups. Italy, France, the Netherlands, and Greece have passed laws banning terrorist groups and criminalizing membership in them. In addition, France, Britain, and Sweden have tightened visa requirements in an effort to curb acts of terrorism committed by foreign nationals, while Italy and Sweden have made it easier for police to tap telephones and open mail to detect letter bombs. However, when such measures are adopted by democracies, they inevitably raise civil liberties issues, as we have seen.

Cooperation among Nations

International efforts to combat terrorism undertaken by the United Nations have proven ineffective, as have the regional approaches undertaken by the Organization of American States (in 1971) and the Council of Europe (in 1977).[34] By contrast, some bilateral agreements among allies, or among adversaries with similar interests, have proven more effective in curtailing terrorism. For instance, the 1973 agreement between the United States and Cuba brought an end to a wave of skyjackings of American planes to Havana. Another example is the 1986 agreement between the United States and Great Britain to expand their extradition treaty by eliminating the political offense exemption for serious crimes of violence. After the 9-11 attacks, the United States was able to gain the support and active cooperation of many governments—including Pakistan and Russia—in support of its worldwide antiterrorist campaign. The NATO countries were particularly supportive, none more so than Great Britain, led by Prime Minister Tony Blair.

Intelligence sharing about terrorist activities among friends and allies has received a good deal of attention but has had only limited success in combating terrorism. Interpol is an international police agency headquartered in France, and there is also an organization that brings interior ministers and chiefs of police of certain cooperating nations together from time to time to exchange information and coordinate investigations of terrorism in Western Europe. These organizations have reportedly facilitated the capture of terrorists in some instances and occasionally prevented terrorist acts from occurring. In one particularly striking example of international cooperation, high-ranking FBI and CIA officials have cooperated with Russian internal security agencies to fight organized crime in Russia and ferret out its suspected links to both international terrorist groups and would-be smugglers of nuclear weapons materials.

International cooperation also can achieve short-term successes when it is targeted at particular terrorist problems and when strong leadership and coordination exist among the cooperating nations. This was illustrated both positively and negatively in April 1986, when President Ronald Reagan ordered the bombing of Libya, a nation widely believed to have supported international terrorism. Initially only the British supported the U.S. strike; the French, fearing terrorist reprisals, refused to allow U.S. warplanes based in the United Kingdom to fly over French territory.

But the punitive U.S. air strike against Libya was successful and signs of an emerging multinational consensus soon began to appear. On April 21, 1986, the European Community voted to impose economic sanctions against Libya, and in the summer of 1986, Libyans were expelled from Britain, West Germany, France, Italy, Spain, Denmark, Belgium, the Netherlands, and Luxembourg. Later, Libyans accused of blowing up a passenger plane (Pan Am Flight 103) over Lockerbie, Scotland, in December 1988 were caught and finally placed on trial in May 2000 before the World Court at the Hague in the Netherlands. Although the event was anticlimactic coming so long after the Lockerbie tragedy, it nonetheless demonstrated that intergovernmental cooperation can bring terrorists to justice.

Unilateral Counterterrorist Measures

Some counterterrorist strategies appear to be obvious, but appearances can be deceiving. For example, most every nation substantially strengthened airport security after bloody terrorist massacres at the Vienna and Rome airports in 1985, but the United States obviously did too little too late prior to the 9-11 attacks: In one morning four commercial airplanes were hijacked almost simultaneously from three different East Coast airports, and the hijack teams apparently managed to get on the planes with weapons (knives and box cutters).

Many authorities believe that retribution and deterrence are the only effective approach to dealing with terrorism. In this hawkish view, deterrence against terrorism requires, at a minimum, a steadfast refusal to negotiate concessions to terrorists, especially when hostages or unremitting attacks on civilian targets are involved (see "Peru's 'Shining Path' to Success against Terrorism"). To do otherwise is self-defeating and tantamount to rewarding evil, inviting future attacks of a similar nature.

Where counterterrorism has worked, a unifying thread has been the demonstrated will and ability of the government to take harsh and preemptive (proactive) military or paramilitary countermeasures against terrorists. The daring

Peru's "Shining Path" to Success against Terrorism

Sendero Luminoso—the "Shining Path"—came into existence in 1980 at the same time Peru became a democracy. Initially an agrarian-based terrorist organization that burned ballot boxes and hung dogs, the Shining Path later turned its attention to perpetrating widespread violence that sometimes verged on regional war, including public bombings, assassinations of local officials, and civilian murders. By 1992, this 5,000-strong organization had caused over 23,000 deaths and $20 billion worth of damage. Headed by Abimael Guzmán, a charismatic former philosophy instructor with middle-class origins, the Shining Path espouses a Maoist-like ideology. A hallmark of the group is its opposition to all other organizations—government and nongovernment, civilian, reform, and radical. Among its enemies: a smaller, less violent leftist terrorist organization, the Tupac Amaru Revolutionary Movement (MRTA), with whom it successfully battled for control over highly profitable drug operations during the late 1980s and early 1990s. The Tupac Amaru would fade from the political scene, only to reemerge in December 1996, when Tupac Amaru guerrillas seized the Japanese ambassador's residence during a diplomatic reception and held numerous high-level officials hostage, many for four months (they were freed when the residence was stormed and the guerrillas killed).

Guzmán and the Shining Path confronted a series of weak democratic governments in Peru throughout the 1980s. None was able to subdue hyperinflation, high unemployment, massive foreign debt, widespread poverty, drug overlords, and government corruption (not to mention terrorism). On April 5, 1992, however, events in Peru changed dramatically. Determined to embark on a tougher, more decisive course of action, President Alberto Fujimori assumed complete power; he suspended the constitution, dissolved the elected congress, and purged much of the judiciary. Fujimori was criticized worldwide for his military-backed coup. Yet within six months, Guzmán was in prison. Moreover, in 1993, the number of political killings dropped by 50 percent, and in 1994, that number continued to decline. Fujimori's economic policy also succeeded: Peru's 7 percent growth rate made it one of the most robust economies in Latin America, and its inflation rate declined significantly.

After Guzmán's capture, the Shining Path seemed to disintegrate as thousands of its members were imprisoned. It would later be rejuvenated, however. Although its membership was significantly reduced and its ideology more diffuse, the Shining Path continued under the ostensible command of Oscar Ramirez Durand (a long-time associate of Guzmán). Its trademark random acts of violence were resumed, but at substantially reduced levels; its heavy involvement in the illegal drug trade also continued.

And what about the future? Barring an extreme economic downturn in Peru, the Shining Path will most likely either remain a terrorist nuisance, or transform itself into a different kind of threat to society—one specializing in organized crime (a transformation already adopted by several terrorist groups in Colombia and Brazil).

July 1976 raid by Israeli commandos at Uganda's Entebbe Airport proved that terrorists are not invincible even after they have taken hostages and dug in, as did the successful commando assault on Tupac Amaru Revolutionary Movement (MRTA) guerrillas holding hostages in the Japanese Embassy in Lima, Peru, in December 1996. Success in hostage rescue operations necessitates highly skilled, quick-hitting commando units, such as Germany's GCG-9, which freed hostages from a Lufthansa airliner hijacked to Mogadishu, Somalia, in 1977; Britain's Special Air Services (SAS); and the U.S. Delta Force. Local police agencies are not equipped or trained to deal with terrorism:

> When you are operating with the SAS on the ground in an area like Armagh [in Northern Ireland], you very quickly realize that you are fighting a war, not taking part in a police operation. Night after night . . . IRA active-service units [infiltrate] from the safety of the South and [move] about freely in areas they made safe for themselves by murder, torture, kneecappings and other intimidation. They are using sophisticated weapons, [including] heavy machine-guns, rocket launchers, landmines and massive quantities of explosives. Through audio surveillance, you listen to the planning sessions at which the orders are given for acts of sabotage that will involve indiscriminate civilian casualties.
>
> Civilian police procedures cannot deal with this kind of threat. If you locate a team . . . in the process of organizing an attack on a shopping center with milk churns packed with high explosives and nails, you send a fighting patrol to attack it, you don't call the local bobby.[35]

However, the availability of special counterterrorist units such as the British SAS is not enough; governments also must be willing to use them. As one expert notes, the central objective of counterterrorist policy is "to establish an unmistakable pattern of failure and retribution."[36] Debacles, such as the 1980 U.S. attempt

Counterterrorism in Italy: A Historical Success Story

In the 1970s, Italy was the most terror-ridden country in the West. The extreme left-wing Red Brigades kidnapped and killed hundreds of judges, industrialists, and politicians—symbols of capitalism and the establishment. From 1969 to 1983, more than 14,000 acts of terrorist violence were recorded, 409 people were killed, and 1,366 were injured.

In 1978, the Red Brigades kidnapped Aldo Moro, a former prime minister and one of Italy's leading politicians. When the government refused to negotiate with Moro's abductors, he was murdered. In the end, however, it was the terrorists who lost. Shocked and outraged, the public demanded a tough counterterrorist program. Thereafter, the Red Brigades went into sharp decline.

How did Italy do it? First, the police infiltrated Red Brigades terror cells and subsequently arrested hundreds of members. Second, reduced prison sentences were offered to repentant terrorists who supplied information about the activities and whereabouts of other terrorists. Third, the police concentrated on a limited and manageable number of terrorist targets such as airports, harbors, and border crossings. Finally, new laws gave the police greater ability to tap phones and use other resources more effectively.

Deprived of sympathy for their causes, Italy's terrorists were isolated, and today they pose little threat to the country's stability.

GATEWAYS TO THE WORLD:
EXPLORING CYBERSPACE

http://nsi.org/terrorism.html

The National Security Institute sponsors and maintains this site, which includes facts about antiterrorism legislation, suggested precautions against terrorism, and facts and commentary on terrorism. This page also provides a number of links to government and nongovernment Web sites dealing with terrorism.

http://www.terrorism.net

In the words of the designers of this page, it "is an attempt to provide a single resource for people interested in the areas of Terrorism, Counter-Terrorism and International Crime." The page includes discussion groups, publications, travel advisories, and a links page.

---

to free hostages in Iran, and Egypt's 1985 attempt to recapture an Egyptian airliner hijacked to Malta, are bound to occur—sometimes with tragic consequences. But the long-term consequences of acting indecisively can be even more tragic.

Other steps that governments can take include controlling arms and explosives and, perhaps most important (though most difficult), developing better internal intelligence-gathering capabilities against terrorism. Only by getting information on terrorists' hideouts, movements, and plans can attacks be prevented; only by knowing in advance when and where terrorists plan to strike can targets be defended.

Obviously, the nature of democratic societies and the constitutional framework in which police and investigative agencies function present obstacles to any government faced with a terrorist threat. Citizens, quite properly, are unaccustomed to spying on friends, family members, neighbors and coworkers, and intelligence gathering is divided among several agencies, in part to prevent any one of them from gaining too much power. In the United States, for example, intelligence and counterintelligence are strictly separated; the CIA is responsible for foreign intelligence and is forbidden to engage in domestic spy operations against U.S. citizens or groups—counterintelligence is the function of the FBI. The need to bridge this bureaucratic abyss after 9-11 was the prime reason behind President Bush's decision to create the new Office of Homeland Security.

Private Measures

Finally, private citizens and firms have developed strategies to protect themselves.[37] Just as many governments were "hardening" their embassies and other overseas facilities in the 1980s and 1990s, private companies were spending billions of dollars annually on security services and hardware in the United States and elsewhere.[38] This figure rose sharply after September 11, 2001. Most citizens cannot afford to hire private security guards, however. But public awareness can make the terrorist's job a great deal more difficult. In Israel, for example, where terrorism is a constant threat and everyone is acutely aware of it, officials claim that 80 percent of bombs in public places are disarmed because suspicious objects are usually noticed and reported in time.[39] Most security experts in the United States agree that any future success in countering terrorism will depend heavily on greater vigilance on the part of ordinary citizens as well as on the government's part. Likewise, most commercial airline pilots agree that if hijacking stops it will be because passengers are prepared to subdue terrorists not because sky marshals happen to be on board.

CAN TERRORISM BE CONTAINED?

Contemporary terrorism poses a continuing problem and is not likely to go away anytime soon. The dangers appear to be growing: nuclear terrorism, as noted earlier, is no longer a wildly implausible possibility, nor is the threat of biological and chemical attacks.

It is clear that there is no single or totally effective solution to terrorism. Still, as we have seen, there are ways of limiting the opportunities available to terrorists and of deterring, punishing, or simply eradicating terrorism before it reaches epidemic proportions (as it did in Italy and Ecuador in the 1970s and early 1980s and in Algeria in the 1990s).

Despite specific successes, however, there remains a momentous problem: even one terrorist can be too many. Indeed, one well-trained terrorist with a small support system—a few friends, safe houses, and supplies—can inflict enormous damage. Terrorism can never be eradicated entirely in this imperfect world, but with patience, perseverance, courage, and vigilance it can be contained and liberty can be preserved (although perhaps not without periods of constriction)—that is one of the lessons of the recent past.

Summary

Terrorism, which can be understood as a political effort to oppose the status quo by inducing fear in the civilian population through the widespread and publicized use of violence, has become an everyday occurrence in the contemporary world. While it has ancient roots in religious conflict, contemporary terrorism can be traced to the 1960s.

Terrorists seek to create a climate of chaos and confusion in the belief political instability will hasten the downfall of the government. They form groups that are close-knit, homogeneous, small, and (often) short-lived. Terrorists can pose great challenges to countries facing political and economic problems; Muslim fundamentalism in Algeria provides such an example.

Although terrorists violate the law, they are not *criminals* in the everyday sense of the term. Nor are they guerrillas or ordinary revolutionaries. All terrorists are revolutionaries, but not all revolutionaries are terrorists. A terrorist is a kind of revolutionary who does not seek to obtain political power but whose primary objective is to protest and combat the perceived injustice of the existing political order through random acts of violence. Terrorists tend to be young, single males who share a variety of key psychological characteristics, including fanaticism and hatred.

Weak authoritarian governments and democracies are disproportionately threatened by terrorism. Democracy and terrorism are implacable enemies. Democracy depends for its existence on citizens' willingness to compromise and respect other people's opinions, whereas terrorists are zealots willing to undertake any action for the sake of their cause. Furthermore, democratic societies are by nature open and vulnerable to terrorist attacks. This vulnerability is both physical and psychological.

The problem democracies face in countering terrorism is complicated by the need to preserve individual freedoms while also protecting national security. Still, various singular and cooperative measures democracies have undertaken show promise of containing—though not eliminating—terrorism.

Key Terms

terrorism
state terrorism
international terrorism
domestic terrorism
transnational terrorism

antistate terrorism
nationalist–separatist terrorism
ideological terrorism
counterterrorism

Review Questions

1. How is terrorism different from common crime? From guerrilla warfare?

2. What tactics do terrorists typically employ, and how are their ends and means related?

3. What are the psychological roots of terrorism and the characteristics of the typical terrorist?

4. Why are democracies vulnerable to terrorism? Assess the terrorist threat to constitutional democracies.

5. What obstacles stand in the way of an effective counterterrorist policy?

6. What steps have constitutional democracies taken to protect themselves from terrorism? What more, if anything, can be done?

Recommended Reading

ASCENCIO, DIEGO, and NANCY ASCENCIO. *Our Man Is Inside.* New York: Little, Brown, 1983. A gripping account of a hostage situation in Bogotá, Colombia, in which fifteen ambassadors, including the U.S. ambassador to Colombia, were held captive by Marxist terrorists for sixty-one days.

CLARK, RICHARD C. *Technological Terrorism.* Old Greenwich, Conn.: Devin-Adair, 1980. Deals with the danger of fissionable or fusionable materials being diverted into the hands of terrorists; also examines chemical and biological weapons, Andromeda strains, and so on; makes policy suggestions.

CLUTTERBUCK, RICHARD. *Protest and the Urban Guerrilla.* New York: Abelard-Shuman, 1974. Examines the roots of protest and violence in Britain and Northern Ireland; surveys the rise of urban guerrilla movements worldwide; and ponders the implications of terrorism for the future of democratic societies.

COMBS, CINDY C. *Terrorism in the Twenty-First Century.* Upper Saddle River, N.J.: Prentice-Hall, 1997. A balanced, comprehensive text that covers virtually every aspect of terrorists, terrorism, and terrorist acts.

HACKER, FREDERICK J. *Crusaders, Criminals, Crazies: Terror and Terrorism in Our Time.* New York: Norton, 1977. A probing, essential study of the psychology of the terrorist.

JENKINS, BRIAN, ed. *Terrorism and Personal Protection.* Newton, Mass.: Butterworth, 1985. The best and most comprehensive book on the subject by an impressive collection of experts.

KEGLEY, CHARLES W., JR., ed. *International Terrorism: Characteristics, Causes, Controls.* New York: St. Martin's Press, 1990. A good collection of essays with well-crafted introductions by the editor to the book's three parts (characteristics, causes, controls).

KIDDER, RUSHWORTH M. "Unmasking Terrorism." *Christian Science Monitor,* May 13–21, 1986 (five-part series). Examines the origins and development of terrorism since the late 1960s, the problem of state-sponsored terrorism, the terrorist mentality, the manipulation of the media, and recent efforts to curb terrorism.

LAQUEUR, WALTER. *Terrorism.* New York: Little, Brown, 1979. A penetrating study of the origins, ideology, and sociology of terrorism by a leading scholar and writer; also examines various theories and surveys the modern history of terrorism.

LONG, DAVID E. *The Anatomy of Terrorism.* New York: Free Press, 1990. A balanced, thoughtful analysis of contemporary terrorism. A useful appendix lists and describes specific terrorist groups.

RIVERS, GAYLE. *The Specialist: Revelations of a Counterterrorist.* Lanham, Md.: Madison Books, 1985. Ostensibly a true story about the underworld of terrorism and counterterrorism, written under a pseudonym by a mercenary who specializes in carrying out antiterrorist operations under contract to Western (and other) governments; reads like a James Bond thriller.

WEINBERG, LEONARD, and PAUL DAVIS. *Introduction to Political Terrorism.* New York: McGraw-Hill, 1989. An excellent overview of terrorism.

WHITE, JONATHAN. *Terrorism: An Introduction.* Belmont, CA: Wadsworth, 2000. A readable basic text that touches all the bases and contains two chapters on terrorism in the United States. Includes a useful appendix entitled, "An Introductory Dictionary of Extremism."

Notes

1.   Cindy Coombs. *Terrorism in the Twenty-First Century* (Upper Saddle River, N.J.: Prentice-Hall, 1997), 1–2.

2.   "Nihilism and Terror," *New Republic,* September 29, 1986, 11.

3.   See also Martha Crenshaw, "The Causes of Terrorism," in *International Terrorism: Characteristics, Causes, Controls,* ed. Charles W. Kegley, Jr. (New York: St. Martin's Press, 1990), 113.

4. Two classification schemes are subsequently discussed. They are not exhaustive of those contained in the literature. The initial discussion here follows Kegley, who cites Edward Mickolus "Trends in International Terrorism," in *International Terrorism in the Contemporary World,* eds. Marius H. Livingston et al. (Westport, Conn.: Greenwood Press, 1978); see Charles W. Kegley, Jr., "Characteristics, Causes, and Controls of International Terrorism: An Introduction," in *International Terrorism,* ed. Kegley, 5.

5. Ibid.

6. The distinction between religion and ideology breaks down completely when adherents pursue patently political ends and use religion to justify the means. Islamic extremists, for example, frequently call for *jihad* (holy war) against Israel and the "Crusaders" (to use Osama bin Laden's epithet), but every Muslim knows that the Koran (Islam's holy scripture) strictly forbids the taking of innocent life and makes no exceptions. Terrorism certainly has no more of a place in Islam than it has in Christianity.

7. For a more complete discussion see David Rapoport, "Religion and Terror: Thugs, Assassins, and Zealots," in *International Terrorism,* ed. Kegley, 146–157. Also see Leonard Weinberg and Paul Davis, *Introduction to Political Terrorism* (New York: McGraw-Hill, 1989), 19–23.

8. Weinberg and Davis, *Political Terrorism,* 22.

9. Compare Rapoport, "Religion and Terror," 146, and ibid., 24–26.

10. Rushworth M. Kidder, "Unmasking Terrorism," *Christian Science Monitor,* May 13, 1986, 19. (Part of a five-part series.)

11. Ibid., 20.

12. Ibid. See also Figure 15-1 in this chapter.

13. Walter Laqueur, *Terrorism* (Boston: Little, Brown, 1977), 220.

14. Paul Johnson, "The Seven Deadly Sins of Terrorism," in *International Terrorism,* ed. Kegley, 65.

15. Carlos Marighella, *Mini-Manual for Urban Guerillas,* trans. by Gene Hanrahan (Chapel Hill, N.C.: Documentary Publications, 1984). (Originally published in Spanish in 1970.)

16. Claire Sterling, *The Terror Network: The Secret War of International Terrorism* (New York: Holt, 1981), 21–22.

17. Statistics from David E. Long, *The Anatomy of Terrorism* (New York: Free Press, 1990), 165.

18. Mohammad M. Hafez, *Middle East Journal* 4 (Fall 2000): 584–585.

19. Long, *The Anatomy of Terrorism,* 17.

20. Walter Laqueur, "The Futility of Terrorism," in *International Terrorism,* ed. Kegley, 69. Although Laqueur notes this view, he does not advocate it.

21. As has been often noted. See, for instance, Henry Dietz, "Revolutionary Organization in the Countryside: Peru," in *Revolution and Political Change in the Third World,* ed. Barry Schutz and Robert Slater (Boulder, Colo.: Lynne Rienner, 1990), 135.

22. Laqueur, "Futility of Terrorism," 70; and Walter Laqueur, "Reflections on the Eradication of Terrorism," in *International Terrorism,* ed. Kegley, 207.

23. Coombs, *Terrorism in the Twenty-First Century,* 68.

24. Rushworth M. Kidder, "Unmasking Terrorism," *Christian Science Monitor,* May 15, 1986, 18.

25. Eric Hoffer, *The True Believer* (New York: Harper & Row, 1951), 49.

26. See Frederick J. Hacker, *Crusaders, Criminals, Crazies: Terror and Terrorism in Our Time* (New York: Norton, 1977).

27. Kidder, "Unmasking Terrorism," May 15, 1986, 19.

28. Regarding the lack of remorse, see Long, *Anatomy of Terrorism*, 19.
29. Paul McHugh, *The Weekly Standard*, December 10, 2001.
30. Hoffer, *True Believer*, 80.
31. Ibid., 81.
32. Much of this discussion is based on Weinberg and Davis, *Political Terrorism*, chap. 8, 151–188. We acknowledge our debt to their scholarship.
33. Matthew Purdy, "Bush's New Rules to Fight Terror Transform the Legal Landscape," *New York Times* (online edition), December 16, 2001.
34. Weinberg and Davis, *Political Terrorism*, 168–170.
35. Gayle Rivers, *The Specialist: Revelations of a Counterterrorist* (New York: Charter Books, 1985), 40.
36. Richard Clutterbuck, *Protest and the Urban Guerrilla* (New York: Abelard-Shuman, 1974), 287.
37. See generally Brian Jenkins, ed., *Terrorism and Personal Protection* (Boston: Butterworth, 1985).
38. Kidder, "Unmasking Terrorism," May 21, 1986, 16.
39. Ibid., 17.

Chapter 16

WAR

POLITICS BY OTHER MEANS

The Causes of War
Human Nature • Society •
The Environment

Theories of War: A Critique
Beyond Politics • Beyond Economics •
The Danger of Oversimplification

Total War: Wars Everybody Fights

Accidental War: Wars Nobody Wants

Nuclear War: Wars Nobody Wins

Is War Ever Morally Justified?
The Just War Doctrine • Evaluating the
Just War Doctrine • The Nuremberg
War Crimes Trials

WAR IS THE central problem of international politics. In the famous words of the Prussian military theorist, Carl von Clausewitz (1780–1831), "War is a continuation of politics by other means." Governments are always conscious of the possibility that diplomacy (politics) will fail and that war with a neighboring state or perhaps between rival ethnic or religious groups *within* a state can break out at any time. Indeed, the most glaring defect of politics on all levels is its inability to prevent armed conflict in its myriad forms.

Most often when people think about war they have in mind *interstate wars*— that is, conflicts involving two or more nation-states. *Civil wars* are conflicts that occur within a single country; wars of this type have actually become more common than wars between sovereign states in the contemporary world. *Guerrilla warfare* is a low-tech form of fighting usually waged in rural areas by small, lightly armed mobile squads (often fed and sheltered by sympathetic villagers). Guerrillas typically carry out selective acts of violence primarily against the army, the police, and the government in an attempt to weaken or topple the ruler(s). *Low-intensity conflicts,* a fourth category, occur when one state finances, sponsors, or promotes the sporadic or prolonged use of violence in a rival country (by hiring mercenaries or underwriting guerrillas, for example).

In terms of lives lost, property damaged or destroyed, and money drained away, war is without any doubt the most destructive and wasteful of all human activities. Perhaps 35 million people, including 25 million civilians, perished as a result of warfare in the twentieth century alone (and this estimate was made in 1990, with ten years remaining in the century!).[1] General William Tecumseh Sherman knew firsthand the horror of war (as a military leader he had, in fact, been a feared practitioner of it). In a speech delivered fifteen years after the American Civil War, he declared: "There is many a boy who looks on war as all glory but boys, it is hell."

Unfortunately, not everyone sees war the way an older and wiser General Sherman did. Some of history's most illustrious (or infamous) personalities have reveled in the "glory" of war. Others, while not condoning bloodshed, have acknowledged war's perverse attractions. In the eighth century B.C.E., the Greek poet Homer noted that men grow tired of sleep, love, singing, and dancing sooner than they do of war. And in his poetry, he celebrated the self-sacrifice and courage that war demanded. The Greek philosopher Aristotle, writing some 500 years later, listed courage as the first, though not the foremost, human virtue. To Aristotle, courage in battle ennobled human beings because it represented the morally correct response to fear in the face of mortal danger, which in turn endangered the political community.

This emphasis on the benefits of war was not confined to the ancient Greeks, or even to ancient writers as a group. Perhaps no writer in modern times typified the tendency to rationalize war better than the German philosopher G. W. F. Hegel (1770–1831), who argued that "if states disagree and their particular wills cannot be harmonized, the matter can only be settled by war." There is nothing particularly shocking about this statement, although it does seem rather pessimistic. Hegel went on to argue, however, that war is actually salutary because "corruption in nations would be the product of prolonged, let alone 'perpetual' peace."

How Many Wars Are Fought a Year?

One might think it would be easy to determine how many wars are fought each year, but it is not necessarily so. Consider the year 1996. The Central Intelligence Agency counted twenty-eight armed conflicts throughout the world. During that same year, the Center for Defense Information listed twenty-seven active conflicts and ten unsettled conflicts that had become nonviolent. Meanwhile, the National Defense Council Foundation tallied a much higher sixty-four conflicts. How could this be?

There are several explanations. First, many public-policy research organizations (often called "think tanks") have a political orientation. The National Defense Council Foundation is a conservative association that supports defense expenditures. Thus, it is hardly surprising that it sees a much more dangerous world (and therefore calculates a greater number of armed conflicts) than does the liberal Center for Defense Information,

which sometimes criticizes allegedly high levels of national defense expenditures. Nor is it surprising that the National Defense Council Foundation defines world conflicts far more broadly than does the Center for Defense Information. The foundation counts not only the usual military conflicts but also domestic sources of violence, including significant violence resulting from drugs and organized crime.

But even if such differences did not exist, war counting would remain a difficult task. Defining wars by assigning a threshold of casualties is virtually impossible, because neither side in battle offers reliable information, while access by objective observers is usually limited or barred. Nor are wars or battles necessarily limited by national boundaries. For instance, the National Defense Council Foundation classified Bosnia and Serbia as separate conflicts while the CIA combined them into a single Balkan conflict.

During times of peace, Hegel reasoned, society becomes flabby, factious, and disunified. "As a result of war, nations are strengthened, but peoples involved in civil strife also acquire peace at home through making war abroad."[2]

Hegel contended that "world history is the world court." In other words, for Hegel the ultimate test of validity or worth is not some abstract moral standard, but success. And because the success in world politics is measured, above all, in terms of power and size, it follows that *might* and *right* are synonymous.

The German philosopher Friedrich Nietzsche (1844–1900) further radicalized this idea. Nietzsche disdained conventional morality in general and despised the Christian ethic of humility in particular (he regarded it as a weakness). What Nietzsche admired most both in individuals and nations was the aggressive exercise of power. He celebrated the will to power and praised the salutary effects of war on nations and civilizations.[3] This theme would be revived with a vengeance half a century later by a bellicose dictator, Adolf Hitler, and his equally bellicose ally, Benito Mussolini. Mussolini, like Hegel and Nietzsche, scoffed at pacifism. According to Mussolini, the father of Italian fascism, "war alone brings to their highest tension all human energies and puts the stamp of nobility upon the peoples who have the courage to meet it."[4]

In a perfect world there would be no war. But war is a constant in *this* world and always has been. The reality of war persists side by side with the hope that war might one day be eradicated. Throughout the ages, many political thinkers (not to mention utopian dreamers) have maintained that reason or God or history might sooner or later deliver the world from the agonies of war. But even among these optimists there has been little agreement about the root causes. Yet, if war is ever to be eradicated, it is first necessary to isolate its causes.

THE CAUSES OF WAR

Why war? There is no simple answer. Nor is the answer always the same for different wars. Indeed, it depends on so many variables, starting with the times.

Indeed, the causes of war differ from one era to another. For example, any detached observer living in Europe or the Middle East in the twelfth century A.D. would probably have attributed the frequency and ferocity of war at that time to religious zealotry. The Crusades, which began at the end of the eleventh century and continued for 200 years, were marked by the kind of unmerciful slaughter that, paradoxically, has often accompanied the conviction that "God is on our side."

Religion played a minor role in most of the major wars of the twentieth century (it did help fuel many regional and local wars, however). In no sense was religious fanaticism the cause of World War I, for instance. Many observers attribute the outbreak of that conflict to *nationalism* run amok, a phenomenon that was virtually unknown in the twelfth century. Others stress the *arms race* conducted by European nations, arguing that the momentum of military preparations carried Europe inexorably into war. Still others blame *imperialism:* The scramble for colonial territories in the latter half of the nineteenth century led to war, they contend, when there were no longer any "unclaimed" colonial lands left in Asia and Africa.

Likewise, religion did not play a major role in World War II. Ideology (national socialism in Germany, fascism in Italy, and communism in the Soviet Union) was a factor, but the main "ism" behind the aggressive policies of Germany, Italy, and Japan was *ultranationalism* or what the distinguished scholar of international politics Hans J. Morganthau called *nationalistic universalism.* The Korean War (1950–53) and the Vietnam War (1963–75) were fought for both geopolitical reasons or *reasons of state* and ideological reasons. It can be argued (and has been by some discerning historians) that this mixing of pragmatism and idealism was a factor in the unsatisfactory outcomes (from an American viewpoint) of both these wars.

On the surface, then, the causes of World War I and World War II differed radically from those of the Crusades. But whatever the proximate (or immediate) causes (religious zealotry, nationalism, and so on), every war represents another outbreak of the same old disease, even if the symptoms and severity of the malady have changed.

Philosophers and theologians, hoping to find the keys to peace by studying war, have for 2,000 years attempted to discover the root causes of war. After World War II, the most destructive war in history, political scientists tried using statistical and mathematical models to learn more about this problem. Quantitative research of this kind represents an effort to match the methodological rigor and precision of the natural sciences. In the words of John Vasquez, one of the foremost advocates of this approach:

> Philosophical analyses of the physical world, for example, even when conducted by such a brilliant thinker as Aristotle, did not produce a cumulative body of knowledge. A substantial advancement in our understanding came only with the development and application of the scientific method. Only through the use of controlled observation, the collection of evidence, careful inferences, and the belief that hypotheses must always be tested before being accepted was progress made. No matter which privileged theories are challenged, [this process] will be necessary before any real knowledge about war and peace is acquired.[5]

What has the scientific approach to the study of war achieved thus far? According to Vasquez, it has "helped refine thinking about war and raised serious questions about existing explanations of war."[6]

Other political scientists are not so sure.[7] For example, James Dougherty and Robert Pfalzgraff conclude that "[d]espite the proliferation of statistical studies of war (both inductive and deductive), none have been so definitive as to resolve the most significant problems . . . within a few decades, they are more likely to be relegated to footnotes than regarded as classics."[8] Greg Cashman takes a middle-of-the-road position in this debate:

> Although no single theory seems to have anywhere near universal validity, social scientific research has not been completely fruitless. Some theories have been identified as lacking a factual basis and have been relegated to the status of mythology. But several theories, having been validated by real-world events, have emerged as more useful and warrant our sincerest attention. . . . Thus, a winnowing-out process is occurring in the scholarship of war studies. Even though the investigations undertaken by social scientists during the last four decades have not culminated in the creation of a single, unified theory of war, they have certainly added greatly to our understanding of the causes of war.[9]

We begin our inquiry into the causes of war by looking at three alternative theories of war found in the writings of several of the West's most notable political thinkers. One interpretation emphasizes flaws in human nature. A second stresses defects in society (including government). A third sees inadequacies in the natural environment (scarcity of food, water, land, natural resources, and so on) as the key to understanding social and international conflict.[10] After examining in detail these three contending interpretations, we will look at the findings of several contemporary studies for corroboration or refutation.

Human Nature

Those who attribute war to flaws in human nature advance a variety of explanations for the all-to-human tendency to misbehave. Christianity has had a profound influence on Western political thought in this regard. Drawing on the Old Testament, early Christian thinkers viewed the human race as irreparably flawed by *original sin*—that is, by Adam and Eve's violation of God's law in the Garden of Eden. The story of the fall as recorded in the book of Genesis is about moral failing and human frailty in the face of temptation. It is in a very real sense a universal story with universal significance; world history in a nutshell.

According to Saint Augustine (354–430), the influential early Christian theologian, war is the price we pay for our corrupt nature. Many secular thinkers have displayed a similar pessimism, without citing original sin as the cause. The Greek philosopher Plato attributed wars at least partly to the feverish human passion for worldly possessions and creature comforts. The sixteenth-century Italian thinker Niccolò Machiavelli painted an equally depressing picture of the interaction between human nature and politics. In *The Prince,* Machiavelli asserted that political success and moral rectitude are often inversely related: Rulers tend to prosper in direct proportion to the dirty politics they practice for the sake of self-gratifying political ends.

If some have looked to religion and others to philosophy for an explanation of aggressive human tendencies, others have turned to psychology. Sigmund Freud (1856–1939), the founder of psychoanalysis, believed that human beings are born with a "death wish"—innate self-destructive tendencies—that they somehow manage to redirect into other activities most of the time. During times of conflict, Freud theorized, combatants direct these destructive tendencies against each other. Thus, wars serve a psychotherapeutic function: They offer an outlet for otherwise self-destructive impulses. Critics argue that this theory is too clever by half—in fact, the soldiers who do the fighting and killing are *not* the ones who decide to go to war and the decisionmakers (who are careful to stay out of harm's

In our age of mass destruction, only the symptoms and severity of the disease have changed. In August 1945 in Hiroshima, Japan, the dropping of the atomic bomb leveled whole sections of the city and signaled a new era of potential devastation.

way) are not the ones who fight wars. Most soldiers kill because they have a job to do and because they do not want to *be* killed, not because they are *by nature* violent, aggressive, or destructive.

Other psychologists have argued that aggression is an innate human drive constantly seeking an outlet, that aggression is a normal human response to frustration, or that human beings exhibit the same sort of "territorial imperative" which supposedly accounts for the aggressive behavior of many of the lower species of the animal kingdom. According to the territorial imperative theory, latent aggressions are deeply rooted in human nature, and threats to an individual's or group's territory (property, loved ones, and so on) are apt to trigger aggressive action.

Still other observers contend that the ultimate cause of war is not lodged in the human soul or psyche but rather in the human brain. People are neither depraved nor disturbed; rather, they are obtuse—not simply ignorant, but too stupid to understand the futility of war. In the words of a prominent pacifist writing between World Wars I and II:

> The obstacle in our path . . . is not in the moral sphere, but in the intellectual. . . . It is not because men are ill-disposed that they cannot be educated into a world social consciousness. It is because they—let us be honest and say "we"—are beings of conservative temper and limited intelligence.[11]

Thomas Hobbes (1588–1679) had a different, but hardly more flattering, explanation for war. He also saw human beings in the *state of nature* as brutes of limited intelligence. (He lived during the Puritan Revolution in England and was horrified at the prospect of a return to a kind of primordial anarchy, "a war of every man, against every man.") But Hobbes was, above all, a realist who sought to understand human nature as it is, not as it ought to be. The only way to know what people are *really* like, Hobbes believed, is to look at how they would behave outside of civil society as we know it—that is, in a state of nature. The conclusions he drew from this exercise are fascinating and continue to influence how we think about politics, war, and the possibility of peace even today.

Hobbes on War   According to Hobbes, in the state of nature human beings are governed by a keen instinct for self-preservation. They fear death above all and especially shrink from the prospect of sudden, violent death. This fear of death, however, does not result in meekness or passivity; on the contrary, aggression and violent behavior are the norm:

> So that in the nature of man, we find three principal causes of quarrell. First, Competition; Secondly, Diffidence; Thirdly, Glory. The first maketh man invade for Gain; the second, for Safety; and the third, for Reputation. The first cause [men to turn to] Violence to make themselves Masters of other mens persons, wives, children, and cattell; and the second, to defend them; the third, for trifles, at a word, a smile, a different opinion, and other signe of undervalue. . . .
>
>   Hereby it is manifest, that during a time men live without a common Power to keep them all in awe, they are in that condition which is called war; and such a war, as is of every man, against every man.[12]

Hence, the state of nature, for Hobbes, is a state of war.

Hobbes applied this same logic to international politics in his own time, which was a perpetual state of war. Just as individuals in the state of nature are governed by base motives and drives, he declared, leaders with similar motives and drives govern nations. And just as the state of nature lacks a government to protect people from each other, so the international system lacks a government to protect nations from each other.

Hobbes theorized that there are three kinds of disputes that correspond to the three defects in human nature: *aggressive wars,* caused by competitive instincts; *defensive wars,* caused by fears; and *agonistic wars,* caused by pride and vanity. Through this compact theory Hobbes sought to explain not only how human beings would act outside the civilizing influence of society and government (human beings constantly at each other's throats if not for the civilizing effect of government-imposed law and order) but also why nations sometimes go to war over issues that make no sense to outsiders.

The Hobbesian Legacy   Hans Morgenthau, like Hobbes, argued forcefully that human beings are deeply flawed. According to Morgenthau, "Human nature, in which the laws of politics have their roots, has not changed since the classical philosophies of China, India, and Greece endeavored to discover these laws," and "politics, like society in general, is governed by objective laws that have their roots in human nature."[13] The key to understanding the operation of these laws is the "concept of interest defined as power." Conceptualizing politics in this way means that human beings are motivated by self-interest, which predisposes human behavior toward an eternal "struggle for power." Morgenthau made this point particularly clear when he stated, "international politics, like all politics, is a struggle for power. Whatever the ultimate aims of international politics, power is always the immediate aim." Like Hobbes before him, Morgenthau rejected the mistaken ("idealist") view that "assumes the essential goodness and infinite malleability of human nature." Instead, he embraced the "realist" view "that the world, imperfect as it is from the rational point of view, is the result of forces inherent in human nature."[14]

According to Morgenthau, and the *realist school* of political theory his writings inspired, human nature and the drive for self-aggrandizement are a leading, if not *the* leading, cause of competition and conflict. Such an analysis hardly presents a flattering picture of humankind. But this view, however compelling, is not the only plausible explanation of why wars are fought.

Society

Not all political thinkers attribute the causes of war to the human psyche or human nature. Some blame modern society in general, organized into a state (an exclusive or "members only" political association), while still others contend that particular kinds of political states pose disproportionate dangers to peace. In this section, we examine the different approaches of political theorists and leaders who blame society or the state (the political framework of society) for war's destructiveness.

Rousseau: Property Is to Blame   "Man is born free, and everywhere he is in chains." With this attack on the modern nation-state, the French philosopher Jean-Jacques Rousseau (1712–1778) began the first chapter of his classic *Social Contract* (1762), in which he directly challenged Hobbes's assertion that human beings are naturally cunning and violent. Rousseau started from the premise that human beings are naturally "stupid but peaceful" creatures, quite capable of feeling pity for those who are suffering. (Note how this notion contrasts with the "stupid but violent" thesis encountered earlier.) Seen in this light, Hobbes simply erred in attributing innate characteristics such as ambition, fear, and pride to human beings in the state of nature. Rousseau was convinced that these are attributes of social man not natural man (here the term *man* is used in the classic sense to mean all humans irrespective of gender). Antisocial behaviors, paradoxically, have social causes; they are sure signs of human corruption. Society, not human nature, is to blame. Rousseau is quite explicit on this point: "It is clear that . . . to society, must be attributed the assassinations, poisonings, highway robberies, and even the punishments of these crimes."[15]

Indeed, Rousseau believed that society is the cause of all kinds of problems, including war. Specifically, he blamed the institution of private property—a preoccupation of all eighteenth-century European societies—for the miseries that have beset the human race since it abandoned its natural innocence for the false pleasures of civilization. Property divides human beings, he argued, by creating unnecessary inequalities in wealth, status, and power among citizens within particular nations and, eventually, among nations:

> The first person who, having fenced off a plot of ground, took it into his head to say *this is mine* and found people simple enough to believe him, was the true founder of civil society. What crimes, wars, murders, what miseries and horrors would the human race have been spared by someone who, uprooting the stakes or filling in the ditch, had shouted to his fellow-men: Beware of listening to this imposter, you are lost if you forget that the fruits belong to all and the earth to no one.[16]

Specifically, Rousseau postulated that just as the creation of private property led to the founding of the first political society, the original founding mandated the creation of additional nation-states. And because each of these nations remained in a state of nature vis-à-vis the others, there arose great tensions that eventually led to the "national wars, battles, murders, and reprisals, which make nature tremble and shock reason."[17] With the "division of the human race into different societies," Rousseau concluded:

> the most decent men learned to consider it one of their duties to murder their fellow men; at length men were seen to massacre each other by the thousands without knowing why; more murders were committed on a single day of fighting and more horrors in the capture of a single city than were committed in the state of nature during whole centuries over the entire race of the earth.[18]

Rousseau's view that private property is the root of all evil has exerted a profound influence on modern intellectual history. Even among political thinkers who reject Rousseau's specific diagnosis of the corruption of the nation-state, there has been widespread acceptance of his general theory that "man is good but men are bad." Several twentieth-century variations on this theme have appeared. As we shall see, each differs in substantial ways from the others, but all share the assumption that the fatal flaw leading to war resides in society rather than in human nature.

Nationalism Is to Blame   Many modern thinkers hold that war is inherent in the very existence of separate societies with sovereign governments. The main manifestation of these potent separatist tendencies is nationalism (sometimes referred to, in its most extreme forms, as jingoism or chauvinism). Nationalism commonly denotes the patriotic sentiments felt by the citizens of a given country toward their homeland. According to one authority:

> Each nation has its own rose-colored mirror. It is the particular quality of such mirrors to reflect images flatteringly: the harsh lines are removed but the character and beauty shine through! To each nation none is so fair as itself. . . . Each nation considers (to itself or proclaims aloud, depending upon its temperament and inclination) that it is "God's chosen people" and dwells in "God's country."[19]

Small wonder that nationalism has been called an idolatrous religion. Although it may foster unity and a spirit of self-sacrifice within a society, between societies it has led, directly or indirectly, to militarism, xenophobia, and mutual distrust.

Nationalism can be manipulated in support of a war policy, and warfare can in turn be used to intensify nationalism. The chemistry between nationalism and war is sufficiently volatile to have caused many *internationalists* (theorists favoring peace and cooperation among nations through the active participation of all governments in some sort of world organization) to single out nationalism as the main obstacle to achieving peace and harmony among the peoples of the world.

To the extent that nationalism is an artificial passion—one that is socially conditioned rather than inborn—political society is to blame for war. This type of reasoning has led some starry-eyed idealists to suggest a radically (critics would say "deceptively") simple formula for eliminating war: Do away with the nation-state and you do away with nationalism; do away with nationalism and you do away with war. Others have sought more practical remedies—fix the nation-state rather than try to abolish it.

Wilson and Kant: Tyranny Is to Blame   Many observers identify nationalism as the major cause of modern conflict, but others (not implausibly) blame despotism for the two calamitous world wars of the last century. It was President Woodrow Wilson who championed this notion and actually tried to build a new world order on its conceptual foundations. After World War I, Wilson sought to secure lasting peace through a treaty based on his *Fourteen Points*—principles that he hoped and believed would lead to a world without war. The cornerstone of this proposed new world order was the right of *national self-determination,* the right of people everywhere to choose the government they wished to live under. Wilson expected self-determination to lead to the creation of democracies, which he viewed as naturally more prone to peace than dictatorships.

But why should democracies be any more reluctant to go to war than dictatorships? The eighteenth-century German philosopher Immanuel Kant (1724–1804) first provided the explanation, one that appears to have deeply impressed Wilson. (So germane are Kant's writings to Wilson's ideas that one authority has suggested, "Woodrow Wilson's Fourteen Points were a faithful transcription of both the letter and spirit of Kant's *Perpetual Peace*."[20]) Kant postulated that to remain strong, nations must promote education, commerce, and civic freedom. Education, he theorized, would lead to popular enlightenment, and commerce would produce worldwide economic interdependence, each of which would advance the cause of peace. Most important, through expanded political freedom, individual citizens would become more competent in public affairs. And because liberty is most pronounced in republican regimes, such governments would be the most peace-loving *by nature*. The reason is simple: In republics—unlike monarchies or aristocracies—the citizens who decide whether to support a war are the same citizens who must then do the fighting. In Kant's own words:

> A republican constitution does offer the prospect of [peace-loving behavior], and the reason is as follows: If . . . the consent of the citizens is required in order to decide whether there should be war or not, nothing is more natural than that those who would have to decide to undergo all the deprivations of war will very much hesitate to start such an evil game. . . . By contrast, under a constitution where the subject is not a citizen and which is therefore not republican, it is the easiest thing in the world to start a war . . . as a kind of amusement on very insignificant grounds.[21]

© Bettmann / CORBIS

Honored in Britain at the end of World War I, American president Woodrow Wilson had hoped to make the world "safe for democracy." However, Wilson's theory of national self-determination was ultimately unsuccessful in halting wars between nations.

Kant envisioned an evolutionary process whereby steady, if imperceptible, progress would be made toward a peaceful world order as governments everywhere became increasingly responsive to popular majorities. Eventually, he felt, war would become little more than a historical curiosity.

Kant's linking of republicanism and peacefulness became Wilson's political credo. Both Kant and Wilson looked to the reconstruction of the nation-state as the key to a world without war. More specifically, both called for the global extension of democracy, education, and free trade to promote peace. Wilson, in particular, placed enormous faith in the morality and common sense of the ordinary person; he became convinced that the ideal of national self-determination would be the key to humanity's political salvation. He also believed that if the peoples of the world were given an opportunity to make a conscious choice among alternative forms of government, they would universally choose liberal democracy and peace. Finally, Wilson felt that if democratic institutions existed in all nations, the moral force of both domestic and world public opinion would serve as a powerful deterrent to armed aggression.

Lenin: Capitalism Is to Blame   Among those who did not agree that world peace hinged on the creation of more democracies and the elimination of dictatorships was an equally famous contemporary of Wilson's, V. I. Lenin (1870–1924), the leader of the Russian Revolution and the first ruler of the former Soviet Union. Lenin was as violently opposed to bourgeois democracy, as Wilson was enthusiastic about it. Although both extolled the virtues of national self-determination, they held very different interpretations of that concept. Wilson assumed that given the choice between democracy and some other system, any nation would choose democracy. In contrast, Lenin assumed that any nation given a choice between capitalism and communism should choose communism. For Wilson, the primacy of politics was self-evident; for Lenin, as a follower of Karl Marx, wars were waged solely in the interest of the monopoly capitalists.

In an influential tract titled *Imperialism: The Highest Stage of Capitalism,* Lenin advanced the Marxist thesis that Western imperialism—the late-nineteenth century scramble for colonial territories—was an unmistakable sign that capitalism was teetering on the brink of extinction. Imperialism, according to Lenin, was a logical outgrowth of the cutthroat competition characteristic of monopoly capitalism. Lenin theorized (correctly) that capitalists would always seek foreign markets where they can make profitable investments and sell (or dump) industrial surpluses. Thus, monopoly capitalists through their financial power and the political influence that accompanies it, push their societies into war for their own selfish purposes. In Lenin's own words:

> When the colonies of the European powers in Africa, for instance, comprised only one-tenth of that territory (as was the case in 1876), colonial policy was able to develop by methods other than those of monopoly-by the "free grabbing" of territories, so to speak. But when nine-tenths of Africa had been seized (approximately, by 1900), when the whole world had been divided up, there was inevitably ushered in a period of colonial monopoly and, consequently, a period of particularly intense struggle for the division and the redivision of the world.[22]

In sum, Lenin held that because war is good business for the capitalists of the world, capitalists make it their business to promote war.

Lenin's analysis of the causes of war seems far removed from the Wilsonian thesis that tyranny leads inevitably to international conflicts, and yet the two views coincide at one crucial point. Lenin and Wilson both believed that the nation-state—more precisely, a particular defect of a certain *type* of nation-state—produces wars. These two leaders were contemporaries and enemies. They were on opposite sides of the ideological fence, so to speak. But like Rousseau they both believed that if only some glaring defect in society—the type of government for Wilson, the type of economy for Lenin—could be eradicated, lasting world peace would ensue. Change is the key: Change the offending part of the nation-state, and human beings can live together in peace and harmony.

The Environment

Other theorists argue that war is often caused by scarcity and the insecurity associated with the fear of natural predators—cold, hunger, disease, snakes, storms, and so on. This view accords with the ideas of the philosopher John Locke (1632–1704).

The Lockean Perspective   In his *Second Treatise on Civil Government* (1690), Locke argued forcefully that wars reflect conditions inherent in nature rather than defects in human nature or society. Simply stated, his proposition is that environmental circumstances beyond human control frequently place human beings in do-or-die situations that make conflict inevitable. Like Hobbes before him, Locke was not blind to the imperfections in human beings. Locke's examination of the state of nature led him to agree with Hobbes that self-preservation is the most basic human instinct. At this point, however, the two thinkers diverged. In the words of one authority:

> Locke's state of nature is *not* as violent as Hobbes's. If, as it seems, force will commonly be used without right in Locke's state of nature, it is not because most men are vicious or savage and bloodthirsty; Locke does not, as Hobbes does, speak of every man as the potential murderer of every other man. The main threat to the preservation of life in the state of nature lies not in the murderous tendencies of men but rather . . . in the poverty and hardship of their natural condition.[23]

Locke believed that poverty and hardship are inevitable in the state of nature because he observed that great exertions are required to provide for our daily needs. Even then, we still have to protect our property, which is coveted by neighbors who have less than we do and by others who are hungry and poor. In this manner, Locke saw circumstances rooted in scarce resources (food, land, and so on), rather than internal character flaws, as the principal cause of human conflict.

Locke's views on human beings, society, and nature have a great bearing on the issues of war and peace. If the origins of war lie within human beings, as Hobbes believed, the eradication of war can come about only by changing the inner self. If the problem lies in society, as Rousseau and Lenin contended, the solution is to reconstitute society (or the state) to remove the particular defects thought to give rise to aggressive behavior. If the problem lies neither in humans nor in society but in nature, the solution must be to transform nature.

Interestingly, the transformation of nature was precisely how Locke proposed to end human conflict in domestic society. Civil government, he asserted, must create the conditions to encourage the process of economic development. Through economic development, a major cause of social tension—the natural "penury" of the human condition—would be greatly mitigated. At the same time, if the uncertainties of nature were replaced with the formal rules of organized society, the need for every human being to be constantly on guard against the depredations of others would be lessened greatly. Human beings would thus finally leave the state of nature, with all its anarchy and danger.

But in leaving one state of nature humanity ironically found itself inhabiting another—the often brutal world of international politics. Although Locke did not apply his theory of politics to the realm of international relations, his reasoning lends itself readily to such an application. Before the invention of government, human beings lived in domestic anarchy; likewise, in the absence of an effective world government, nations exist in international anarchy. In this sense, the relationships among nation-states differ little from relations among individuals before the formation of civil society. The international state of nature, no less than the original state of nature, is perpetually a *potential* state of war. Thus, each nation-state behaves according to the dictates of self-preservation in an environment of hostility and insecurity, just as each individual presumably did in the state of nature.

One of the most common and valued prizes of war is territory. And judging from all appearances, the desire for more land and resources—property, in the Lockean sense—is also one of the most common objectives of war. Recall that Lenin attributed the European scramble for colonial territories toward the end of the nineteenth century to the search for new markets, cheap labor, and raw materials—that is, property. Significantly, Lenin held that the propensity for capital accumulation (money and property) described by Locke was directly responsible for the phenomenon of imperialism, which Lenin predicted, would lead inevitably to war. Even if Lenin overstated the case against capitalism, one thing is certain: territoriality has always been associated with war (and always will be).

Locke wrote at a time when there was still plenty of land in the world that remained "unclaimed" (by Europeans) and uncultivated. He noted that even in the state of nature, human relations were probably fairly harmonious, so long as no one crowded anyone else. It stands to reason that as growing populations begin to place ever-greater pressures on easily available resources, however, the drawing of property lines becomes progressively more important. If, as Locke's analysis suggests, prehistoric people felt threatened by the pressures of finite resources, imagine how much greater those pressures have become in modern times.

Nature's Scarcity: Malthusian Nightmares   Many contemporary writers have elaborated on the theme of resource scarcity propounded by Locke and, later, by Thomas Malthus (1766–1834) in his famous *Essay on the Principle of Population* (1798). Richard Falk, for example, has identified "four dimensions of planetary danger," including the "war system," population pressures, resource scarcities, and "environmental overload."[24] These four dimensions of danger, according to Falk, are interrelated aspects of a single problem and hence must be treated as a group.

Falk's assumptions about the causes of international conflict are consistent with Locke's political understanding:

> . . . international society is, of course, an extreme example of a war system. Conflicts abound. Vital interests are constantly at stake. Inequalities of resources and power create incentives to acquire what a neighboring state possesses.[25]

Just as humans were constantly vulnerable to the depredations of others in the state of nature, so predatory neighbors continually threaten nation-states. Throughout history, then, violence has played a vital role in the conduct of foreign affairs because, Falk argues, conditions beyond the control of individual nation-states compel them to regard their own security as being directly proportionate to their neighbors' distress. Hence, even after the unprecedented destruction wrought by World Wars I and II "many efforts were made, often with success, to moderate the scope and barbarism of war, but no serious assault was mounted to remove the conditions that cause war."[26] What exactly are these conditions? Professor Falk

© Reuters NewMedia Inc. / CORBIS

Plagued by civil war and weakened by famine, an estimated two million people died in Somalia between 1991 and 1992.

argues that access to food and water supplies had a great bearing on the earliest wars. And these considerations, moreover, have not lost their relevance in the modern world:

> Given the present situation of mass undernourishment (more than two-thirds of the world population), it is worth taking account of the ancient link between war and control of food surplus, as well as the age-old human practice of protecting positions of political and economic privilege by military means.[27]

Even more basic than the issue of adequate food and water supplies, Falk points out, is the need to control the population explosion. In many ways, population pressure underlies the entire crisis of planetary organization. Under such conditions, it is understandable that no nation in the world, no matter how powerful, feels terribly secure in our times. The oil crisis of 1973 served as a dramatic reminder of the vulnerability of even the richest and most powerful countries. Not only oil but also many other raw materials, such as bauxite, copper, and tin, are maldistributed and in short supply. At the same time, the poorest countries continue to experience shortages in the most basic of all raw materials—food.

THEORIES OF WAR: A CRITIQUE

The three general views on the ultimate causes of war examined in this chapter are based on one of the most fundamental concepts in Western political philosophy—the triad of humanity, society, and nature. All three theories have some measure of validity. Together, they can help explain the origins of war in general. Individually or in combination, they help explain why particular wars are undertaken. Yet even when isolated, war's causes are complex and difficult to apply. For instance, while it is likely that a self-interested and perhaps violence-prone human nature is one factor that inclines nations' leaders to wage war, not all leaders are equally self-interested or violent. Moreover, not all leaders are equally constrained by their nations' political or legal restraints or by their opponents' military capabilities, nor do they all perceive danger or risk in the same way. Regarding nation-states, it appears that different characteristics may make them seem more or less warlike, but it is not clear which characteristics are associated with a tendency toward warfare. Finally, while a shortage of resources or food may incline some nations toward conflict, it may also lead to the opposite response: a greater desire for cooperation (and the help that can accompany it).

No single explanation can adequately explain the causes of war. Oversimplifying the problem only obstructs the search for answers. Idealism and pious pronouncements offer hope to a war-weary world, but that hope is misplaced.

Beyond Politics

Although it seems reasonable to assume that, all else being equal, nations exhibiting intense nationalism are more warlike than are politically apathetic nations, all else is seldom equal. Indeed, national-attribute explanations "have done a relatively poor job in explaining the incidence of war."[28]

But what about the Wilsonian view that democracies are naturally peaceful and tyranny is the primary cause of war in the modern world? Down through the ages, many political thinkers have stressed the relationship between dictatorial and belligerent or aggressive behavior. Aristotle, for instance, maintained that tyrants are "warmongers" who plunge their nations into war "with the object of keeping their subjects constantly occupied and continually in need of a leader."[29] Some modern political writers, such as Hannah Arendt, argue that totalitarian governments are *inherently* aggressive.[30] Two major conflicts (World War II and the Korean War) were initiated by totalitarian dictatorships in the twentieth century. Moreover, Stalin in the 1930s, Hitler in the 1940s, Mao in the early 1950s, and Pol Pot between 1975 and 1979 all waged war in the form of blood purges and mass murder at home. These episodes of extremely lethal state behavior strongly suggest that totalitarian rulers are prone to coercive force.

There are other reasons to associate dictatorships and organized violence. Dictators exercise absolute control over the armed forces, police, and instruments of propaganda. Often they have themselves been war heroes who rode to power on the wings of military victory—successful soldiers who take over governments are rarely squeamish about the use of force. For such rulers, war can provide a popular diversion from the tedium and rigors of everyday life; it can act as an outlet for pent-up domestic hostilities that might otherwise be directed at the dictator; it can help unify society and justify a crackdown on dissidents; or, finally, it can be used by the dictator to rejuvenate a stagnant economy or an uninspired citizenry.

But these observations, however suggestive, are not conclusive proof that despotism always or disproportionately causes wars. One problem is that such an analysis is not simple to apply, as an analysis of the Vietnam War illustrates. The Kennedy, Johnson, and Nixon administrations blamed that war on communist aggression. Critics of U.S. foreign policy, however, blamed much of the problem on misguided or provocative American actions in Southeast Asia. Thus, depending on the evidence one regards as most valid, the Vietnam War can be used to "prove" either that dictatorships are more prone to war than democracies or that democracies are no more immune to crusading militarism than dictatorships.

In general, representative democracies have not been notably successful at avoiding war. In this century, for example, India, the world's largest democracy, has waged several bloody wars against Pakistan, and the United States has remained anything but aloof from warfare, as the U.S.-led military action against Iraq in 1991 reminds us. Nor have democratic nations always been simply unwilling participants in war. The United States did not go out of its way to avoid fighting the Spanish-American War of 1898. And it is difficult to overlook U.S. intervention in the Mexican Revolution in 1914, when President Wilson (no less!) ordered American Marines to seize the Mexican port of Veracruz, and later sent a punitive expedition into Mexico against the forces of Pancho Villa.

In addition, quantitative analyses of interstate conflict do not support the conclusion that democratic nations are less warlike than either authoritarian or totalitarian states.[31] In fact, democracies engage in military action about as often as other types of government; some evidence suggests that democracies may start wars less frequently but join them more often.[32] In one respect, however, the Kantian-Wilsonian pro-democracy, antidictatorship theory of war does hold true: Democratic states rarely, if ever, fight each other (see Table 16-1).[33] There has not been a real war between democracies in over a century and a half.[34]

The recognition that democratic states fight other states but not each other is the *paradox of democratic peace.* One multifaceted explanation is that

> Expectations of war and threats of war between democracies are almost certainly reduced by the presence of a common political culture, by a mutual identity and sympathy, by stronger people-to-people and elite-to-elite bonds, by the ability of interest groups within these countries to form transnational coalitions, by more frequent communication, and by more positive mutual perceptions.[35]

The matter of *reciprocal* national perceptions may be particularly important. Consider that governmental power is more fragmented and limited in democracies, that democratic political leaders are inclined to emphasize compromise over confrontation, and that constitutional democracies generally respect the individual rights. All of these factors tend to promote the peaceful resolution of political disputes in democracies. The presumption that democracies are not a threat to each other is closely linked to a general *perception* of common values and interests, thus greatly reducing the likelihood frictions will precipitate the kind of a crisis that sometimes lead to war.

Thus, when democracies go to war, they fight nondemocratic states. This suggests that the degree of political difference (or distance) between governments, as well as economic and cultural differences, may be important.[36] Such findings support Woodrow Wilson's conclusion that dictatorial regimes are the natural enemies of democracies, as well as Lenin's view that capitalist and communist nations are incompatible. One study of Latin American politics notes that "the more similar two nations are in economic development, political orientation, Catholic culture, and density, the more aligned their voting in the UN" and the less conflict there will be between them. By the same token, "the more dissimilar two nations are in economic development and size and the greater their joint

TABLE 16-1

Wars, 1816–1991

Types of Wars	Number of Wars[a]
Democracies vs. democracies	0
Democracies vs. nondemocracies	155
Nondemocracies vs. nondemocracies	<u>198</u>
Total	353

[a]Defined as any military action in which at least 1,000 people are killed.
SOURCE: Haiku Institute of Peace Research, (October 20, 1991) Chapter 18, 473.

technological capability to span geographic distance is, the more overt conflict they have with each other."[37]

Beyond Economics

If politics provides only a partial and limited explanation for conflict, Lenin's theory that wars are caused by economic factors, particularly capitalism, explains even less. One problem with this proposition is that wars preceded both capitalism and imperialism, proving that capitalism is certainly not the only cause of war.[38] Furthermore, there is little in the historical evidence to support Lenin's economic theory that capitalist states (as opposed to socialist or communist states) are particularly warlike. Although some wars can be explained by national economic motives such as imperialism, most cannot.[39] In addition, the relationship between capitalism and imperialism is not altogether clear. Some capitalist states have practiced imperialism and waged war, while others have avoided both (e.g., Sweden and Switzerland). Lenin's economic theory has difficulty accounting for such differences, or why numerous socialist states have exhibited a propensity to armed aggression. As one observer notes:

> The last half century has witnessed the Soviet invasion of the Baltic countries (1939), Finland (1939), Hungary (1956), Czechoslovakia (1968), and Afghanistan (1979); China has attacked Tibet (1956), India (1962), and Vietnam (1979); Vietnam has attacked Cambodia (1975); the Soviets and the Chinese have fought over the Ogaden (1977). Of sixty-nine international conflicts of the 1945–1967 period, socialist systems participated in fifteen—roughly 25 percent. This is compared to the fact that only approximately 15 percent of all countries had socialist economies.[40]

All of this does not mean that economics is unrelated to war. For instance, the U.S.-led coalition in the Persian Gulf War was driven by economic motives: to protect the vast oil fields of Arabia and to keep the vital lifelines linking the Middle East with Europe, Asia, and North America from Saddam Hussein's control. But when economic motives exist for waging war, they are often merely one of a number of influences. There is surprisingly little evidence to support the thesis that one kind of economic system, or a country's particular stage of economic development, or economics in general, is decisive in motivating nations to fight wars. When academic studies point to economics as a contributing cause of war, they often rely *solely* on a statistical correlation between economics and war, which as every scientist knows does not prove causality.

Since World War II, wars have been fought within the territory of developing states. Does this fact mean that countries with less advanced economies are more warlike? Not necessarily, because it also appears that these wars have often been instigated or even fought by industrialized nations. Post–World War II examples of such conflicts include those fought in Suez, Algeria, the Congo, Vietnam, Afghanistan, the Falkland Islands, and Iraq. Although a strong correlation between economic development and the frequency of military conflicts cannot be made, there is some evidence suggesting that nations with more developed economies actually have greater warlike tendencies than countries with less developed economies.[41]

The Danger of Oversimplification

Simplistic theories of war abound. For instance, some quantitative theorists have described in fine detail recurring patterns that often lead to war-making military alliances, followed by military buildups, the making of threats, a series of crises, and so on.[42] Additionally, such studies have shown that certain actions undertaken by political leaders in an effort to reduce the possibility of war (for example, making alliances) may actually increase its likelihood.[43] However, none of these studies proves that acts such as making or joining military alliances or any of the other steps associated with the pattern leading to war actually cause war. Rather, each of these phenomena may result from another, underlying cause. Furthermore, the "typical" pattern is itself somewhat limited, as it represents only those conflicts fought between major states of approximately equal power.[44]

Most war theorists have long held that large states are more inclined to war than small states.[45] They also believe that powerful states are more inclined than weak states to fight wars. This possibility makes good intuitive sense, as it amounts to saying that nations confident of winning are most inclined to fight wars.[46] However, defining a state's power is difficult; political leaders may miscalculate, overestimating their own strength and underestimating the adversary's (the Vietnam War is a sterling example).[47] Nations experiencing internal violence are also more likely to be war-prone for several reasons: A war may help to unify the nation, or internal conflict may make it an easy target.[48] Nations headed by leaders who are risk takers are more likely to go to war, too.

Another relevant factor is the sharing of common borders, particularly when many borders are shared or when they are shared by long-standing rivals.[49] Environmental factors are important as well because nations with large and growing populations, limited access to necessary resources, and a high level of technology have an obvious incentive to pursue expansionist foreign policy, whereas low-population, high-technology countries fight fewer wars. When these latter countries do fight, they tend to be victims rather than aggressors.[50] In sum, a large, powerful nation with a rapidly expanding population and advanced technology that shares many borders with neighboring states (or one border with a traditional enemy, or both) and is governed by a risk-oriented leader, would be a prime candidate for aggressive war, especially if it happened to be facing civil strife or armed rebellion.

Many of the factors discussed so far in this chapter, from human nature to scarce resources, and many of the characteristics associated with war (population size, economic development, and border problems, for example) are difficult or impossible to change, especially in the short run. American humorist Will Rogers once suggested that world peace could be advanced if nations—like people—could move; but nations cannot move (although populations can—and do—migrate).

Furthermore, the false belief that conflict can be eradicated, or that it can be traced to one single factor, can actually increase the possibility of war. As European history from 1919 to 1939 illustrates, concentrating solely on rearranging the international system while ignoring the role of human nature may encourage the ruthless to resort to war by removing impediments in the path of self-interested and ambitious rulers.[51] Had American, French, and British leaders in the 1930s not underestimated the role of the Nazi ultranationalistic ideology or of Hitler's evil designs, World War II may have been averted or contained.

An understanding of the complex causes and factors associated with war, then, may help to affect modest improvement in the international system of conflict management by dispelling illusions about the prospects for peace. In such important matters, simple solutions can be worse than no solutions at all, as some of history's foremost political simplifiers have also been among the foremost contributors to war.

TOTAL WAR: WARS EVERYBODY FIGHTS

Total war is a thoroughly modern phenomenon. It is different from the *limited wars* of the distant past in several crucial respects. First, it is unlimited as to ends (aims and objectives). That is, in a total war one or more of the belligerent states seeks total victory over its adversary and will stop at nothing short of *unconditional surrender.* Second, total wars are virtually unlimited as to means. States engaged in total warfare use advanced technology to enhance the range, accuracy, and killing power of modern weapons. Third, total wars are unlimited as to participation: they involve whole societies in the war effort.

The Napoleonic Wars are prototype of total war and represent the first such war ever fought. Napoleon fought that war as an all-out drive for hegemony. He recognized no limits on ends or means. He sought total domination of Europe and he possessed all the means available to a modern, centralized state at that time. (Of course, there were no weapons of the mass destruction in Napoleon's time, except for conventional armies who could be used in this manner once the enemy was defeated; thus, Napoleon's forces burned much of Moscow, including the Kremlin, to the ground after Russia's defeat.) Most importantly, Napoleon introduced the idea of mass conscription, recruiting (drafting, that is) thousands of young men into the modern world's first people's army. Prior to this time, armies were made of professional soldiers and paid mercenaries. Napoleon also used nationalism, propaganda, and patriotic symbols to mobilize the whole society behind the war effort. All these innovations were harbingers of the future: the total wars fought in the first half of the twentieth century can be considered as a single event with an interlude between two incredibly violent spasms—the horrific culmination of processes set in motion more than a century earlier.

After World War II, the concept of total war took on an even more ominous meaning due to major advances in the science and technology of war-fighting capabilities. The advent of the nuclear age utterly transformed both the strategy and tactics of war, both the logic of military force and the battlefield. Like the new face of war itself, this transformation was total.

ACCIDENTAL WAR: WARS NOBODY WANTS

We like to think that our leaders always know what they are doing—especially when it comes to matters of war and peace. But accidents do happen. What if a Pakistani arms smuggler was passing through India with a package containing "weaponized" anthrax? And what if the anthrax deadly spores were released in the center of New Delhi, the capital of India, when the Kashmiri taxi driver ran a red light and collided with a truck at a busy intersection? And what if that happened during a crisis with Pakistan? Is it not possible that India would think Pakistan was launching an all out war? Pakistan had nothing to do with the incident, but India might decide to retaliate immediately and ask questions later (waiting would be extremely risky in such a situation). In this scenario, an all-out nuclear war could result from accident and misperception, rather than from any rational choice on either side.

War by misperception—war resulting from the misreading of the situation—is perhaps the most common kind of war nobody wants. *Accidental war* is another possibility. An incorrect translation, a message not delivered, a diplomatic signal missed or misinterpreted—accidents of this kind precipitated unintended wars well before the advent of space-age weapons systems. In a technological era dominated by nuclear weapons and ballistic missiles, the danger of war by accidental means has gone up dramatically, as have the stakes. *War by escalation* could begin as a limited (and presumably localized) conflict between two nations in which neither side originally intended to use its most destructive weapons. But as casualties mount, and battlefield reverses occur, one side (most likely the one that is losing) may be tempted to up the ante by introducing more powerful weapons, which the other side would have little choice but to match. If both sides possess nuclear weapons, the dynamics of such a situation could move the antagonists toward nuclear war. Thus, what had started out as a limited, conventional war could move step-by-step up the ladder of violence until the conflict turned into an all-out struggle to the death.

Catalytic war can also generate violence and destruction well beyond any nation's intention. Historically, such wars are most likely to reflect alliance arrangements. If one member of the alliance is attacked the other(s) spring to that country's defense, thus enlarging the war. Nowadays, a catalytic war might originate as a localized conflict between, say, two developing countries that happen to have powerful allies. Local wars have always had the potential to turn into regional wars or even global wars (as happened in both world wars).

Other nightmare scenarios are also possible. For example, a saboteur or a madman might manage somehow to pull the nuclear trigger. All such scenarios— whether they involve sabotage, misperception, accident, escalation, or a catalytic event—show how war can occur without any premeditation or intent to commit aggression.

NUCLEAR WAR: WARS NOBODY WINS

Weapons of mass destruction (WMD) have only been used once. The United States dropped two atomic bombs on the Japanese cities of Hiroshima and Nagasaki to end World War II. President Truman waited for Japan's High Command to surrender after the first bomb leveled Hiroshima. Three days later, he gave the order to drop the second bomb. This time it did the trick: Japan surrendered. It was the first and last time atomic weapons were used in war. The flip side of Japan's defeat was America's victory. But it would be a big mistake to try to repeat that winning strategy. The reason is very simple. When the U.S. president decided to "go nuclear" in 1945 there were only two atomic bombs in the world and they were both in the American arsenal. President Truman did not have to risk *massive retaliation* (a response in kind) from Japan or any other country. The United States had a (short-lived) *nuclear monopoly.*

The former Soviet Union quickly developed its nuclear-weapons program and by the end of the 1950s had an arsenal of mass-destruction armaments and was even building long-range rockets called *ICBMs* (intercontinental ballistic missiles). Moscow actually beat the United States into outer space by launching *Sputnik,* the first earth-orbiting satellite in 1957. During the 1960s, the United States lost not only its nuclear monopoly (if it was not already lost a decade earlier), but also its aura of invulnerability. The era of massive retaliation and *brinkmanship* (reliance on nuclear weapons to intimidate adversaries) was superseded by the era of *mutual assured destruction (MAD)* or *mutual deterrence*—a situation in which both superpowers have the ability to withstand a nuclear *first strike* and still be capable of delivering a *second strike* that would result in *unacceptable damage* to the aggressor.

Both superpowers spared no effort to get (or stay) ahead in the nuclear arms race. By the early 1970s, both sides had a tremendous *overkill* capability—both sides had enough weapons of mass destruction to destroy the other many times over. Even more alarming was the fact that both sides had built nuclear submarines designed to act as mobile platforms for launching nuclear-tipped missiles and both sides were putting multiple warheads—called *MIRVs* (multiple independently targeted reentry vehicles)—on both land-based and sea-based missiles (technically known as submarine-launched ballistic missiles, or *SLBMs*). But if both sides wanted to win the arms race, neither side wanted to lose a war with the other and knew there would be no winners if deterrence ever failed. In the Cuban Missile Crisis (1963), that almost happened. It was a close call—a wake-up call. The two sworn enemies quickly established the now famous *hot line*—a direct communications link between the White House and the Kremlin—to avert a future calamity, one that might just happen by accident.

IS WAR EVER MORALLY JUSTIFIED?

So far, we have been looking at war primarily from the standpoint of the perpetrators of aggression. But what about the victims? Few observers would dispute that nations have the right to resist armed aggression. When national survival is at stake, self-defense is morally justified. So despite Benjamin Franklin's assertion that "there was never a good war or a bad peace," some wars may be both necessary and proper, but which ones? Who is to say? And how can we know for sure?

The Just War Doctrine

The venerable doctrine of the *just war* holds that under certain circumstances, a war can be "good"—not in the sense of being pleasant or intrinsically desirable, but in the sense of serving the welfare of a nation and the cause of justice. This concept was advanced initially by early Christian theologians such as Saint Augustine and later refined by medieval philosophers. In the modern age, Hugo Grotius (1583–1645) and other natural law theorists have reformulated it.

Among those who favor the concept of the just war, there has been unanimous agreement that defensive wars are justified. If a nation is the victim of an unprovoked attack, it is justified in waging war against its assailant. Some theorists expand this doctrine to give third-party nations the right to interfere on behalf of hapless victims of military aggression. The 1991 Persian Gulf War, which was preceded by Iraq's invasion and occupation of Kuwait, is an obvious case in point.

Most modern theorists limit the just war doctrine to defensive wars, but earlier writers did not always recognize this distinction. Saint Augustine, for example, abhorred war in all its guises but found it necessary to justify even aggressive wars under some circumstances, as when a state "has failed either to make reparation for an injurious action committed by its citizens or to return what has been appropriated."[52] Another early Christian theologian, Saint Ambrose (340?–397), argued that

Campaign against the Taliban and al Qaeda in Afghanistan.

nations have a moral obligation, not simply a right, to wage aggressive war for the sake of higher principle. "Man has a moral duty," he wrote, "to employ force to resist active wickedness, for to refrain from hindering evil when possible is tantamount to promoting it."[53] Ambrose was aware of the need for limitations on this kind of war. Aggressive wars, he declared, should be fought only for a clearly just cause.

The just war doctrine finds expression in five distinct postulates. First, war must be the last resort available to a legitimate government; there must be no other effective political alternatives available. Second, the cause of the conflict must be just; a war should be fought only for the purpose of deterring or repelling aggression or righting a wrong. Third, the war cannot be futile; there must be some probability that the nation undertaking the conflict can succeed. Fourth, there must be proportionality of both ends and means; that is, the war's purpose must justify the cost of the war in money and lives, and the means employed in conducting the war must be appropriate to the reason the war is fought. Finally, a just war must be waged in a manner that minimizes injury and death to civilians. If all of these conditions are met, a war can be considered justified.

The doctrine of the just war is rooted in a notion of justice that transcends immediate national interests. In contrast to the simplistic nationalism represented by such slogans as "My country right or wrong," the just war concept suggests a standard for measuring moral responsibility that transcends narrow national interest. The early Christian theologians based their notions of justice on Christian theological doctrines and scriptural teachings. More modern versions of the just war doctrine are grounded in a natural-law philosophy holding that there are self-evident truths concerning human welfare—truths that are obvious to rational human beings everywhere and that, taken together, point toward the true meaning of the ideal of "justice for all."

Evaluating the Just War Doctrine

Of the various criticisms that have been leveled against the just war doctrine, we focus on three of the most substantial: that the doctrine represents moral relativism, that it embodies an ethnocentric bias, and that it is politically unrealistic.

Moral Relativism   Some critics contend that the concept of the just war is based on highly subjective, and hence unverifiable, value judgments. This is known as *moral relativism.* Because there is generally much room for disagreement about who was to blame for starting a particular war, it is argued, any attempt to assign moral responsibility is bound to reflect the opinions of the observer more than the often uncertain facts of the situation. The only way to avoid this type of moral relativism is to confine oneself to describing what happened before and during wars, sticking to accurate and verifiable facts.

Ethnocentric or Nationalistic Bias   Similarly, it is charged that Western just war theorists only reflect their own culture while tending to ignore justifications for war advanced by other cultures or ideologies—an accusation of *ethnocentric bias.* For instance, the traditional Islamic concept of a *jihad* ("struggle" or "holy war") against temptation, evil, apostasy, or "infidels" offers a moral rationale for aggressive war that has rarely been acknowledged by Western proponents of the just war doctrine.

Political Naiveté   Several opponents of the just war doctrine raise the practical objection that even if it were possible to arrive at a firm, unbiased, and universally accepted standard governing just and unjust wars, the resulting doctrine would be extremely difficult to apply fairly. Just as individuals are not good judges in their own cases, it is argued, so nations are not competent to pass judgment on controversies involving their own interests and well-being. Without an impartial referee, critics contend, the just war doctrine remains a sham advanced by aggressor nations to justify self-serving policies and military interventionism.

Defenders of the just war doctrine point out that moral judgments concerning the conduct of wars have long been thought both natural and necessary: natural in the sense that "for as long as men and women have talked about war, they have talked about it in terms of right and wrong,"[54] and necessary because without them, all wars would have to be considered equally objectionable (or praiseworthy).

Admittedly, it cannot be proven scientifically that aggressive wars are any worse than preemptive or preventive wars, but no such proof is required any more than we need proof to know that cold-blooded murder is more reprehensible than killing in self-defense—a distinction supported by both the criminal law and common sense.

It is often said that just war theories work to the advantage of the people who promote them. This objection contains a great deal of truth. By itself, the just war doctrine provides no universally accepted, enforceable standards for constraining the behavior of nation-states. In our world, heads of state often engage in moral talk and immoral behavior. The idea of the just war is worth keeping, therefore, if not as a means of controlling that behavior, then as a method of evaluating it.

The Nuremberg War Crimes Trials

Following World War II, in what is history's most famous attempt to apply moral standards to wartime conduct, the Nazi leaders were charged in Nuremberg, Germany, with several types of crimes. First, they were accused of *crimes against peace* because they had waged aggressive war in violation of international treaties and obligations. Second, they were charged with *war crimes,* which encompassed violations of the accepted rules of war such as brutality toward prisoners of war, wanton destruction of towns, and mistreatment of civilians in conquered lands. Third, they were accused of *crimes against humanity,* including the persecution and mass murder of huge numbers of noncombatants.

Although the Nazis had not succeeded in eliminating the Jewish people from the face of the earth, they had come very close. The decision to punish Nazi leaders for the wholesale slaughter of European Jewry was prompted by an under-

GATEWAYS TO THE WORLD: EXPLORING CYBERSPACE

To find out more about a particular armed conflict, use the title of the conflict as the search term. For instance, try *Bosnia* or *Vietnam War* as keywords.

standable desire for retribution. German actions could not be justified by the exigencies of war (which, of course, Hitler had started). Furthermore, the scope of the atrocities committed by the Nazi state was unprecedented in modern world history. Moral indifference was singularly inappropriate under these extraordinary circumstances.

The crimes against humanity concept provided firm support for the just war doctrine (and vice versa). The moral principle violated by the Nazis, that the needless suffering and death of innocent people is to be avoided, was so clear and its violation so flagrant that Nazi actions were, beyond the slightest doubt, morally indefensible. The morality or immorality of many unfortunate actions in times of war may be problematical. Not so with the Holocaust, which is an unambiguous instance of criminal activity as defined under the just war doctrine.

Although the trials held at Nuremberg were justifiable, the idea of war crimes trials raises serious concerns. It is no simple task to apply the crimes against peace, war crimes, and crimes against humanity labels to concrete and often unique situations. The death camps violated all standards of law, justice, and decency, but what about the Allied firebombing of Dresden? Or the brutalities against German civilians tolerated (if not encouraged) by the Soviet army? Or the utter devastation visited on Hiroshima and Nagasaki? Questions of morality in war are often ambiguous.

There are more recent examples of genocide and ethnic cleansing, including politically motivated mass murder in Bosnia, Rwanda, Sierra Leone and elsewhere in the 1990s. Whether terrorists ought to be tried for war crimes is a complex legal and moral question we will not try to answer here. Suffice it to say that President George W. Bush treated the 9-11 attacks on the United States as acts of war; they were acts that violated the most universally accepted moral and religious principle of all, namely that there is *never* a justification for the slaughter of innocent people. Whether any of the al Qaeda leaders or operatives will ever stand trial for war crimes depends on when, where, and how they are captured (provided, of course, at least some of them are taken alive) and on whether President Bush carries through on his declared intent to try them before military tribunals rather than allowing the International Court of Justice (ICJ) to decide their fate.

Summary

Avoiding war is not always an objective of state policy. Some leaders—for example, Italy's fascist dictator Mussolini—have actually glorified it.

Many attempts have been made to identify the causes of war. The resulting theories can be divided into three categories: Some see human nature as the cause; others blame society; and still others believe that Mother Nature (an unforgiving environment) is the key. Thomas Hobbes thought that war was a product of human perversity; Jean-Jacques Rousseau maintained that human beings are basically good but society corrupts them; John Locke attributed human aggression to scarcities in nature (that is, circumstances beyond human control). Scarcities in nature encompass a wide variety of forces and factors, including hunger and famine, disease, storms, droughts, and so on.

All single-factor theories fall short in explaining the causes of war. Wars stem from a variety of factors—social, political, economic, and psychological. A large, powerful nation that shares boundaries with several neighboring states, is ruled by a risk-oriented leader, has access to modern technology, is experiencing (or expecting) internal conflict, and has a rapidly expanding population, is likely to be predisposed toward war.

Under conditions of high tension, war may occur even if none of the principals wants it. Such unintended wars may erupt because of misperception, misunderstanding, accident, escalation, or a catalytic reaction. The possibility of unintended war illustrates the potential difficulty in assigning moral responsibility. Often when war occurs, it is not clear who or what actually caused it.

Using war as an instrument of state policy violates international law and morality, but not all wars are equally objectionable. The just war doctrine holds that self-defense and the defense of universal principles are legitimate reasons for going to war. This doctrine, however, is frequently criticized on the grounds of moral relativism, cultural ethnocentrism, and political realism.

The Nuremberg war trials assigned guilt for criminal acts performed while waging a war of aggression. International lawyers developed a new category of war crimes—crimes against humanity—at Nuremberg. Although the Nuremberg trials were justified, such proceedings contain inherent pitfalls and must be approached with extreme caution.

Key Terms

interstate wars	catalytic war
civil wars	massive retaliation
guerrilla warfare	nuclear monopoly
low-intensity conflict	ICBMs
nationalism	brinkmanship
arms race	mutual assured destruction (MAD)
imperialism	mutual deterrence
ultranationalism	first strike
nationalistic universalism	second strike
reasons of state	unacceptable damage
original sin	overkill
state of nature	MIRVs
internationalists	SLBMs
national self-determination	hot line
paradox of democratic peace	just war
limited wars	moral relativism
unconditional surrender	ethnocentric bias
war by misperception	crimes against peace
accidental war	war crimes
war by escalation	crimes against humanity

Review Questions

1. Into what general categories do most explanations of the ultimate causes of war fall?

2. According to Thomas Hobbes, what is the root cause of all wars? What arguments did Hobbes offer in defense of his thesis?

3. What did Rousseau believe to be the root cause of war? How did his views differ from Hobbes's? What arguments did Rousseau advance to support his thesis?

4. Among those who believe that society is the ultimate cause of war, differences of opinion exist about precisely what aspect of society is most responsible for the belligerency of nation-states. What are the four alternative theories presented in the text?

5. How did John Locke explain the phenomenon of war? How did his view differ from those of Hobbes and Rousseau? What arguments did he offer in support of his thesis?

6. Which explanation of the causes of war seems most plausible? Explain your answer.

7. Why is it difficult simply to condemn the guilty party or parties whenever war breaks out?

8. In a world where the technology of warfare is advancing by leaps and bounds, it becomes increasingly probable that a war will start even though nobody intends to start one. In what ways might this happen?

9. Are all wars equally objectionable from a moral standpoint? Explain.

10. Are the arguments, pro and con, concerning the validity of the just war doctrine equally balanced? Explain.

11. What prompted the Nuremberg crimes trials? What are crimes against humanity? How does the just war doctrine fit into the picture?

12. Should, or could, Nuremberg-type trials be conducted after every war?

Recommended Reading

ARON, RAYMOND. *The Century of Total War.* Lanham, Md.: University Press of America, 1985. One of this century's most influential thinkers examines the causes and conditions of war in our age.

————. *The Great Debate: Theories of Nuclear Strategy.* Translated by Ernst Pawel. Lanham, Md.: University Press of America, 1985. A lucid analysis of strategic alternatives available to the Western alliance. First published in the early 1960s, it is still worth reading.

BROWN, SEYOM. *The Causes and Prevention of War.* 2nd ed. New York: St. Martin's Press, 1994. A multidisciplinary overview of human aggression and violence by a widely recognized authority on the politics of war and peace; concludes with an integrated strategy for peace.

CARR, EDWARD HALLETT. *The Twenty Years' Crisis, 1919–1939.* 2nd ed. New York: St. Martin's Press, 1969. An excellent case study of the influences and forces that led to World War II, written in 1939.

CASHMAN, GREG. *What Causes War? An Introduction to Theories of International Conflict.* New York: Lexington, 1993. An excellent summary of contemporary studies of war's causes.

GOLDWIN, ROBERT, and TONY PEARCE, eds. *Readings in World Politics.* New York: Oxford University Press, 1970. An excellent collection of classic writings on war and other aspects of international politics. The Butterfield, Clausewitz, Einstein, and Mead articles are particularly insightful.

KAGEN, DONALD. *On the Origins of War and Peace.* New York: Doubleday, 1995. Kagan examines in depth a number of case studies (from the Peloponnesian Wars to the Cuban Missile Crisis) which demonstrate that war is a persistent problem growing out of nations' competition for power.

MORGENTHAU, HANS J., *Politics among Nations: The Struggle for Power and Peace,* 5th ed. (New York: McGraw-Hill, 1992). An incisive theoretical and historical look at the world stage, what goes on behind the scenes, and the motives of the main actors—states. A classic.

MORRISEY, WILL. *A Political Approach to Pacifism: Book 1; Book 2.* Lewiston, New York: E. Mellen, 1996. A comprehensive historical and philosophical critique of pacifism, including what the author perceives to be its inadequacies.

RICHARDSON, LEWIS. *Statistics of Deadly Quarrels.* Chicago: Boxwood, 1960. A frequently cited quantitative study of war.

RUSSETT, BRUCE. *Grasping the Democratic Peace.* Princeton, N.J.: Princeton University Press, 1995. The best available extended discussion of why democratic governments do not wage wars upon one another.

SEABURY, PAUL, and ANGELO M. CODEVILLA. *War: Ends and Means.* New York: Basic Books, 1990. A sober discussion of war as a permanent part of the human condition.

SINGER, J. DAVID, and MELVIN SMALL. *The Wages of War, 1816–1965: A Statistical Handbook.* Ann Arbor, Mich.: InterUniversity Consortium for Political and Social Research, 1974. An exhaustive attempt to identify the correlates of war.

STOESSINGER, JOHN. *Why Nations Go to War.* 8th ed. New York: Bedford/St. Martin's, 2001. An attempt to explain the causes of war.

VASQUEZ, JOHN, and MARIE HENEHAN, eds. *The Scientific Study of Peace and War: A Text Reader.* New York: Lexington, 1992. An excellent collection of quantitative studies. It contains a learning package that provides an excellent introduction to statistical methodology.

WALTZ, KENNETH N. *Man, the State, and War: A Theoretical Analysis.* New York: Columbia University Press, 1965. An extraordinarily lucid account of the origins of war, emphasizing the importance of human nature, the state, and the international political system.

WALZER, MICHAEL. *Just and Unjust Wars.* New York: Basic Books, 1992. A comprehensive effort to develop a just war theory and apply it to modern conflicts.

WRIGHT, QUINCY. *A Study of War.* Abridged ed. Chicago: University of Chicago Press, 1983. This is probably the most famous study of war in the English language.

Notes

1. Paul Seabury and Angelo M. Codevilla, *War: Ends and Means* (New York: Basic Books, 1990), 6.

2. G. W. F. Hegel, *Philosophy of Right,* trans. T. M. Knox, in *Great Books of the Western World,* vol. 46, ed. R. Hutchins (Chicago: Encyclopaedia Britannica, 1952), 149.

3. Friedrich Nietzsche, *Human, All Too Human,* trans. Marion Farber (Lincoln: University of Nebraska Press, 1984), 230–231, aphorism #477.

4. Benito Mussolini, "The Doctrine of Fascism," trans. M. Oakeshott, in *Great Political Thinkers,* ed. William Ebenstein (New York: Holt, 1965), 621.

5. John Vasquez, "Introduction: Studying War Scientifically," in *The Scientific Study of Peace and War: A Text Reader,* ed. John Vasquez and Marie Henehan (New York: Lexington, 1992), xix.

6. Ibid., xxii.

7. For an excellent introduction to the statistical methodology associated with quantitative war studies, see Stuart Bremer, et al. (adapted by Marie Henehan), "The Scientific Study of War: A Learning Package," in ibid., 373–437.

8. James Dougherty and Robert Pfaltzgraff, Jr., *Contending Theories of International Relations: A Comprehensive Study,* 3rd ed. (New York: HarperCollins, 1990), 356.

9. Greg Cashman, *What Causes War? An Introduction to Theories of International Conflict* (New York: Lexington, 1993), 279.

10. This discussion comprises a variation of the classification scheme presented by Kenneth N. Waltz, *Man, the State, and War: A Theoretical Analysis* (New York: Columbia University Press, 1965). We acknowledge our debt to his scholarship.

11. The quotation is from Sir Norman Angell's *Neutrality and Collective Security,* cited in Edward Hallett Carr, *The Twenty Years' Crisis, 1919–1939* (New York: Harper & Row, 1964), 39.

12. Thomas Hobbes, *The Leviathan* (London: Everyman's Library, 1965), 64.

13. Hans J. Morgenthau, *Politics among Nations: The Struggle for Power and Peace,* 5th ed. (New York: McGraw-Hill, 1992), 3–4.

14. Ibid., 29.

15. Jean-Jacques Rousseau, *First and Second Discourses,* trans. Roger and Judith Masters, ed. Roger Masters (New York: St. Martin's Press, 1964), 197. The quotation is from Rousseau's *Notes, Second Discourse.*

16. Ibid., 195–196.

17. Ibid., *Second Discourse,* 141–142.

18. Ibid., 161.

19. Frederick Hartmann, *The Relations of Nations* (New York: Macmillan, 1978), 32.

20. William Galston, *Kant and the Problem of History* (Chicago: University of Chicago Press, 1975), 26–27.

21. Immanuel Kant, "Eternal Peace," in *Immanuel Kant's Moral and Political Writings,* ed. Carl Friedrich (New York: Modern Library, 1949), 438.

22. V. I. Lenin, *Imperialism: The Highest Stage of Capitalism* (New York: International Publishers, 1939), 124.

23. Robert Goldwin, "John Locke," in *History of Political Philosophy,* ed. L. Strauss and J. Cropsey (Skokie, Ill.: Rand McNally, 1963), 442.

24. Richard Falk, *This Endangered Planet: Prospects and Proposals for Human Survival* (New York: Vintage Books, 1972), 106–107.

25. Ibid., 107.

26. Ibid., 113.

27. Ibid., 155.

28. Cashman, *What Causes War?,* 157.

29. Aristotle, *The Politics,* trans. and ed. Ernest Barker (New York: Oxford University Press, 1962), 1313b, 245.

30. Hannah Arendt, *Totalitarianism* (New York: Harcourt, 1951), 113–114.

31. William Dixon, "Democracy and the Peaceful Settlement of International Conflict," *American Political Science Review* 88 (March 1994): 14.

32. On democracies' proclivity to join wars more often than other forms of government, see Stuart Bremer, "Are Democracies Less Likely to Join Wars?" (paper presented at the annual meeting of the American Political Science Association, Chicago, September 3–6, 1992).

33. For an extended discussion, see Bruce Russett, *Grasping the Democratic Peace* (Princeton, N.J.: Princeton University Press, 1993).

34. As pointed out by Cashman, *What Causes War?,* 129.

35. Ibid.

36. Ibid., 137–139.

37. Rudolph Rummel, "Some Empirical Findings," *World Politics* 21 (1969): 238–239.

38. This discussion selectively follows Cashman, *What Causes War?,* 132–134.

39. Morgenthau, *Politics among Nations,* 51–57.

40. Ibid., 133.

41. Michael Haas, "Societal Approaches to the Study of War," in *The War System*, ed. Richard Falk and Samuel Kim (Boulder, Colo.: Westview, 1980), 355–356, 365.

42. See John Vasquez, "The Steps to War," in *The Scientific Study of Peace and War: A Text Reader*, ed. John Vasquez and Marie Henehan (New York: Lexington, 1992), 343–370.

43. Jack Levy, "Alliance Formation and War Behavior: An Analysis of the Great Powers, 1495–1975," in *The Scientific Study of Peace and War: A Text Reader*, ed. John Vasquez and Marie Henehan (New York: Lexington, 1992), 3–36.

44. Vasquez, "Steps to War," 370.

45. Cashman, *What Causes War?*, 137.

46. Ibid.

47. Dougherty and Pfaltzgraff, *Contending Theories*, 354–355.

48. Ibid., 145–152; however, as Cashman notes, the evidence is not unanimous.

49. The studies are summarized in ibid., 142–145. See also Paul Diehl, "Arms Races to War: Testing Some Empirical Linkages," *Sociological Quarterly* 26 (Fall 1985): 331–349; and his "Continuity and Military Escalation in Major Power Rivalries, 1816–1980," *Journal of Politics* 47 (November 1985): 1203–1211.

50. Nazli Chourci and Robert North, "Lateral Pressure in International Relations: Concept and Theory," in *Handbook of War Studies*, ed. Manus Midlarsky (Boston: Unwin Hyman, 1989), 310–311.

51. Waltz, *Man, the State, and War*, 233.

52. Quoted in Lee McDonald, *Western Political Theory: From Its Origins to the Present* (Orlando, Fla.: Harcourt, 1968), 127.

53. Cited in Dougherty and Pfaltzgraff, *Contending Theories of International Relations*, 151, n. 24.

54. Michael Walzer, *Just and Unjust Wars* (New York: Basic Books, 1968), 1.

PART V

POLITICS WITHOUT GOVERNMENT

Chapter 17

INTERNATIONAL RELATIONS

THE STRUGGLE FOR POWER

IN 416 B.C.E., Athens sent ships and troops against the island of Melos, a neutral colony of Sparta that had wanted no part of war.[1] Negotiating from a position of overwhelming strength, the Athenians insisted on unconditional surrender, bluntly telling the Melians, "You know as well as we do that right, as the world goes, is only in question between equals in power, while the strong do what they can and the weak suffer what they must." The Melians responded by asking, "And how, pray, could it turn out as good for us to serve as for you to rule?" "Because," the Athenians answered, "you would have the advantage of submitting before suffering the worst, and we should gain by not destroying you." Undaunted, the Melians persisted in trying to persuade the Athenians that the interest of all would be enhanced by peaceful relations between the two states. The Athenians would have no part of this logic. With ruthless disregard for questions of justice, they reasoned that if Melos were permitted to remain independent, the Melians and others would take it as a sign of Athenian weakness. "[By] extending our empire," the Athenians pointed out, "we should gain in security by your subjection; the fact that you are islanders and weaker than others rendering all the more important that you should not succeed in baffling the masters of the sea." Thus, the cold calculus of power politics doomed the Melian state.

Athenian intransigence was met by Melian resolve. Undaunted to the end, the Melians repeated that above all they desired neutrality; failing that, they vowed to put their trust in the gods and the Spartans. The Athenians proceeded to besiege the island, and the Melians counterattacked. The Spartans came but did not stay. Then disaster struck:

> Reinforcements afterwards arriving from Athens in consequence, under the command of Philocrates, son of Demeas, the siege was now pressed vigorously; and some treachery taking place inside, the Melians surrendered at discretion to the Athenians, who put to death all the grown men whom they took, and sold the women and children for slaves, and subsequently sent out five hundred colonists and inhabited the place themselves.

This story reads like a particularly gruesome episode in the life of Harry Potter, one in which the satanic Voldemort is back stronger than ever. Unlike Hogwarts, however, Melos was a real place, and the tragedy depicted in the story really happened. The context was the Peloponnesian War (431–404 B.C.E.) and we know the Melians' cruel fate because the Greek historian, Thucydides, wrote about it.

GET REAL!: MACHIAVELLI AND MORGANTHAU

The greatest political thinker of the Italian Renaissance, Niccolò Machiavelli (1469–1527), taught that the wise ruler must always play to win. In his own words, "how we live is so far removed from how we ought to live, that he who abandons what is done for what ought to be done, will rather learn to bring about his own ruin than his preservation."[2] The prudent ruler, he argued, recognizes what must be done to preserve and enlarge his dominions and does not allow moral qualms to cloud his judgment. For example, rulers should keep their promises (in his words, "keep faith") only when it suits their purposes to do so:

> A prudent ruler ought not to keep faith when by doing so it would be against his interest, and when the reasons which made him bind himself no longer exist. . . . If men were all good, this precept would not be a good one; but as they are bad, and would not observe their faith with you, so you are not bound to keep faith with them.[3]

The teachings of Machiavelli, together with the fate of the Melians, suggest that morality plays a less significant role in politics among nations than it does in politics within nations. As long as international politics continues to resemble the state of nature, tensions between nations will persist, talking all too often will fail, reason all too often will take a holiday, and the only question left to answer will be who lives and who dies. And when survival is at stake, necessity is often a remorseless tyrant.

Machiavelli's intellectual honesty and relentlessly realistic approach to politics is the basis for what is perhaps the most successful political philosophy in the modern world—successful in the sense that it has withstood the test of time, it continues to be extremely influential, and since Machiavelli's time the evidence for its validity has continually mounted. The theory that nations act on the basis of interests rather than ideals is known as *political realism.* In contemporary times, it is most closely identified with the writings of Hans Morgenthau (1904–1980). Following Machiavelli's rationale, political realists pay little heed to the way nations *ought* to act. Rather, they focus on how nations actually *do* act and why they act as they do. Survival is the basic goal of national policy, and the best way to ensure survival is to enhance the nation's power. In international politics, Morganthau argues, whatever the ultimate aim might be, the immediate aim is *always* power. Thus, interest is defined as power; indeed, for Morganthau, these two concepts merge into one—it is in the best interest of every nation to seek power first and pursue other objectives second, and then only insofar as these enhance national power, prestige, and the like.

Political realists stress that success in international politics, even when confrontation is absent, ultimately depends on power. According to Morgenthau, power is "man's control over the minds and actions of other men."[4] The most important aspect of power in international politics is military force. Accordingly, political realists tend to favor a tough-minded approach to national defense (more is generally better than less), nuclear arms control (to be pursued cautiously), and participation in international organizations (of limited utility and not the hope of the future).

Yet military force and political power are not synonymous. Other factors, including geopolitical, economic, and social concerns, contribute to a nation's power as well. Even the personal charisma or competence of a political leader or the effectiveness of a nation's political institutions give it an edge in a competitive and dangerous world. According to Morgenthau, neglect of intangible factors such as charisma "accounts in good measure for the neglect of prestige as an independent element in international politics."[5]

Optimizing and balancing a nation's vital interests requires political prudence. Thus Morgenthau wrote, "Realism considers prudence—the weighing of the consequences of political action—to be the supreme virtue in politics."[6] Properly interpreted and applied, such prudence will correctly guide the affairs of a nation. A foreign policy based on a realistic appraisal of the national interest will avoid not only the dangers of hazardous timidity but also "the blindness of crusading frenzy [that] destroys nations and civilizations—in the name of moral principle, ideal, or God himself."[7] As Morgenthau saw it, then, the concept of the national interest is an antidote for the excesses and follies of misguided moralists. Obviously, what constitutes the national interest varies from country to country and even from year to year, although some interests are permanent and others temporary, some primary and others secondary, some general and others specific.

To the political realist, the successful statesman is one who masters the art of balancing national interests and objectives against national capabilities (or power). Prudence demands that a statesman, like a budget-conscious shopper in the supermarket, distinguish between items that are necessary and those that are merely desirable. The essence of statecraft lies in bringing the expectations and desires of a nation into line with the capabilities of the state and correctly differentiating between vital and expendable interests. Political realism places a premium on flexibility, objectivity, and lack of sentimentality in the conduct of foreign policy. Thus, the political realist would say that in international politics there are no permanent allies, only permanent interests. Statesmen cannot afford to operate on any other basis, according to Morganthau, no matter how reprehensible or immoral this same behavior would be in interpersonal relations.

In the perilous world of international politics, morality has a different face—different, that is, from morality in our domestic lives, both personal and political. Because other nations act on the basis of perceived interests rather than lofty ideals, one's own nation must do likewise. All nations try to gain an advantage at the expense of other nations—this form of collective behavior is readily observable and it is universal. Therefore, Morgenthau asserted, political realism not only explains why nations act the way they do but, in the true spirit of science, can also predict how nations will act.

THE CLASSICAL EUROPEAN SYSTEM

Machiavelli and Morganthau were both products of tumultuous times in European history, albeit very different times. Machiavelli was influenced by the fierce rivalries, intrigue, and conflict that characterized relations among the Italian city-states of the fifteenth and sixteenth centuries. Machiavelli lived at a time when the modern nation-state system was in its infancy. The formal launching of the classical European system did not occur until more than a century after his death. Morganthau was born in Germany shortly before World War I. One of the casualties of that war was the European system, which was characterized by a conscious effort to maintain *equilibrium* (or balance) among the participating states. This collective balancing act was interest-based but it depended on a common definition of "interest" (as we are about to see), an enlightened definition that emphasized self-preservation of each through a system that depended on the survival of all. Europe's famed *balance-of-power system* operated for almost three

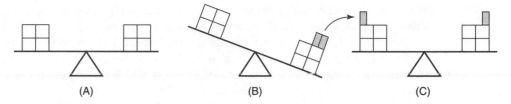

FIGURE 17-1   Adjusting the Balance of Power

Equilibrium (A) is upset by adding a new participant (B); it is restored (C) by the transfer of one state from one alliance to another.

SOURCE: Edward V. Gulick, *Europe's Classical Balance of Power* (New York: Norton, 1967).

centuries (see Figure 17-1). It began with the signing of the Treaty of Westphalia in 1648 and ended with the outbreak of World War I. With the short-lived exception of Napoleon's France, no state was able to establish hegemony on the Continent during this 266-year period—a remarkable achievement for any era.

Systemic Prerequisites

The international system functioned effectively because one nation, known as the *keeper of the balance,* repeatedly threw its political and military weight behind the weaker alliance during times of crisis and conflict. Great Britain acted in this capacity, and was ideally suited to it because of the nation's geographic detachment and military (especially naval) prowess. An island power in close proximity to the Continent, Britain could cast a relatively dispassionate eye on international disputes and rivalries across the English Channel. A major British concern, historically, was which power controlled the Lowlands (modern-day Belgium and Holland) just across the Channel, which at its narrowest point is a mere twenty-two miles wide. In a larger sense, Britain was an impregnable fortress as long as no single power succeeded in conquering the Continent. Finally, Britain's unchallenged naval supremacy and economic vitality made it a powerful ally or a formidable foe, while its lack of a large standing army removed any threat of British domination on the Continent.

Another important factor undergirding the traditional European system was a basic moral consensus—a common outlook held by nations all sharing a single civilization. Historians Edward Gibbon and Arnold Toynbee, as well as the philosophers Emerich de Vattel and Jean-Jacques Rousseau, have stressed the paramount importance of the cultural and religious traditions that pervaded European society and transcended national boundaries during the heyday of the balance-of-power system.[8]

Under these extraordinary conditions, "international politics became indeed an aristocratic pastime, a sport for princes, all recognizing the same rules of the game and playing for the same limited stakes."[9] Limiting the stakes meant that even when war broke out, the belligerents did not seek to annihilate each other. For the most part, Europe's rulers, imbued with the rationalistic outlook of the eighteenth-century Enlightenment, adopted a pragmatic approach to governing and viewed any kind of fanaticism as absurd and dangerous. Not only the stakes but also economic and military capabilities were limited: Few countries could afford to squander the national wealth on high-risk adventures, and military action was constrained by the absence of modern technology.

Another fortuitous aspect of this pan-European culture was the absence of ideology. Realignments occurred as circumstances changed, adding to the smooth functioning of the system. Structural rigidity would have impeded the balancing process and made an all-out war more likely.

The Demise of the European Consensus

What happened to upset the relatively stable international order that had prevailed for over 250 years in Europe? First, Napoleon's nearly successful attempt in the early nineteenth century to conquer Europe—creating the first mass-conscription, popular army in modern history—heralded the rise of modern nationalism (see Chapter 16). Although France's bid for hegemony ultimately failed, it was a harbinger of things to come and demonstrated the power of a nation united by a common cause. The cause itself was rooted in the explosive idea of human equality enshrined in both the American and French Revolutions of the late eighteenth century. Between the Napoleonic wars and World War I, ideas such as national self-determination and universal rights changed fundamental assumptions about politics and, in so doing, undermined the old aristocratic order.

In the nineteenth century, the Industrial Revolution also ushered in economic and technological changes that transformed the art of warfare. For example, Prussia used railroads to move troops in victorious military campaigns against Austria (1866) and France (1870). New instruments of war were not far off either—military applications of the internal combustion engine, for example, included self-propelled field artillery and, by World War I, combat aircraft.

A final factor that helped to undermine the European system was the rigidity of military alliances. Toward the end of the nineteenth century, coalitions were becoming fixed and hardened while nations were steadily accumulating military power. Unprecedented peacetime outlays for military research and development, the creation of relatively large, standing armies, and a spiraling arms race reflected and reinforced the increasing division of Europe into two opposing alliances. This development set the stage for World War I, which signaled the beginning of the end of the classical balance-of-power system. It would take another world war to finish the job.

THE CONTEMPORARY GLOBAL SYSTEM

World War II produced a new configuration, one that continues to shape world politics to the present day. Replacing the European system was a *global* one dominated by two preeminent powers. In this new *bipolar system,* both sides diverted huge resources toward development of total war capabilities, and each regarded the other as its ideological nemesis. The Cold War between the United States and the Soviet Union after 1945 lasted nearly half a century and ended only with the disintegration of Soviet power in 1991. It is appropriate, therefore, to discuss the structural characteristics of world politics during the heyday of this Soviet–American rivalry before turning our attention to the contemporary global system.

The End of Eurocentrism

One of the most pronounced changes in international politics after World War II was the reduced influence of European nations, which had since the seventeenth century been the fulcrum of the international balance of power. Actually, Europe's decline was foreshadowed by the increasing prominence of two non-European powers, the United States and Japan, evident already in the late nineteenth century. But it was not until World War II had physically shattered Europe that the traditional great powers, Great Britain, France, and Germany, became second-rank states. Britain was forced to abandon a worldwide empire; France was preoccupied with the reconstruction of its economy, society, and government after the Nazi occupation; Germany was defeated, occupied, and partitioned into zones from which two new states—the Federal Republic of Germany (West Germany) and the German Democratic Republic (East Germany)—would emerge. The Soviet Union, which had suffered the heaviest war losses of all, rose miraculously from the ashes more powerful than ever.

The colonial empires of Britain, France, Belgium, and the Netherlands disintegrated rapidly after World War II. From these former colonial territories emerged scores of new nations, which turned to the two industrial power blocs for economic and military aid. The Third World thus became one arena where the bipolar power struggle was played out. The hallmark of this struggle was the Cold War.

The Advent of Bipolarity

Although the transition from a European to a global international system had begun before World War II, the war greatly accelerated the process—in part by removing the European states as primary actors on the world stage. In place of the former great powers, of which there were seven at the outbreak of the war, were two *superpowers*—the United States and the Soviet Union. The United States formed a kind of protectorate over the western half of war-torn Europe, and the Soviet Union created a "satellite" empire in the eastern half.

The United States, which was the first to develop and use the atomic bomb, enjoyed a short-lived nuclear monopoly after World War II. The Soviet Union, to the surprise and dismay of Western observers, successfully tested an atomic device in 1949—serving notice that it, too, had the right stuff to become a full-fledged superpower.

In terms of military might, global reach, and economic resources in the 1950s, the United States and the Soviet Union dwarfed all other nations. However, the ideological chasm dividing them precluded collaboration of any kind.

The Primacy of Ideology

The two superpowers on opposite sides of the globe dominated the international scene, making them natural rivals. And because one was capitalist and democratic and the other communist and dictatorial, the rivalry turned especially dangerous and acrimonious. At the conclusion of World War II, Allied mistrust of Joseph Stalin, the Soviet dictator, was greatly heightened by his nation's permanent occupation of eastern Europe, which the Red Army had liberated from the Germans, and by Stalin's attempt to force the Western powers to abandon West Berlin. No less alarming to the United States and its allies was the Soviet atomic bomb test in 1949.

The Soviets, meanwhile, interpreted U.S. foreign policy actions, including the cutoff of lend-lease aid, the refusal to grant large loans, and the launching of the *Marshall Plan* as proof that "American imperialism" was plotting the destruction of the "world socialist system." Stalin's chief ideologue, Andrei Zhdanov, declared at a Communist party conference in 1947 that the world had been divided into two camps. This two-camp doctrine had its counterpart in the Western notion of a "world Communist conspiracy," which posited that a secret Soviet blueprint aimed to subvert all democratic societies. Although these beliefs may seem exaggerated in retrospect, extreme rhetoric on both sides—fueled by the clash of ideologies—lent credibility to such an interpretation.

American-led efforts at containment were epitomized in Western Europe by the creation of a powerful military alliance, the *North Atlantic Treaty Organization (NATO)*. The Soviet Union countered with a military pact of its own, the Warsaw Treaty Organization (commonly known as the *Warsaw Pact*), linking Moscow and Eastern Europe. The aura of confrontation that permeated the two alliance systems left little room for compromise or conciliation. At its inception, then, the Cold War was waged by two extraordinarily powerful nations whose aims, interests, and values seemed incompatible. At the very least, each sought to block the ambitions of the other; at worst, each sought to bring about the other's collapse. In this respect, the postwar system contrasted sharply with the traditional European system it had replaced: The ends of war and diplomacy were no longer limited to such finite objectives as the acquisition of territorial tidbits or the assertion of royal entitlements.

The Danger of Nuclear War

When the European balance of power held sway, nations observed certain rules that limited war aims. Limitations on available means of warfare also checked the ambitions of adventurous nations. Two technological breakthroughs in the twentieth century, however, greatly expanded the destructive potential of military weaponry. First came the development of airborne bombers and, later, missile delivery systems whose capabilities would have staggered the imagination a century earlier. Second, advances in nuclear physics led to the invention of fission (atomic) and fusion (hydrogen) bombs capable of leveling entire cities. From these scientific and technological advances grew the formidable U.S. and Soviet arsenals of increasingly accurate land- and sea-based missiles, armed with multiple nuclear warheads. The two nations commanded a vast overkill capacity: Each side deployed enough nuclear weapons to destroy the other many times over. Under such circumstances, all-out war would have amounted to mutual suicide. This realization, as we shall see, played a major role in promoting a new international security scheme intended to ensure human survival in a world threatened with almost instantaneous destruction.

Mutual Deterrence

At the heart of the post–World War II balance-of-power system was deterrence. The unprecedented mass destructiveness of nuclear weapons elevated the concept of deterrence—that is, preventing conflict—over the notion that national defense required nations such as the United States and the Soviet Union to respond without restraint to an aggressor nation's attack. Deterrence began not as an abstract idea but as a historical necessity. The United States lost its nuclear monopoly shortly after World War II but continued to enjoy a measure of nuclear superiority until the mid-1970s. In 1957, however, the Soviet Union put the first artificial satellite *(Sputnik)* into orbit. The Soviet space shot demonstrated to the world that the USSR had the technology to build long-range rockets—that is, to launch offensive weapons from Soviet soil, aimed directly at U.S. targets.

By the late 1960s, the era of invulnerability was over for the United States: The Soviets had built a land-based missile force against which there was no adequate defense. Now both sides stared into the nuclear abyss. *Deterrence* became the new watchword in a great debate over military strategy and an integral part of the post–World War II balance of power. According to deterrence theory, nations acquire nuclear weapons not with the intention of using them but to deter other nations' use. In this sense, public expenditure for such weapons is markedly different from money appropriated for such projects as schools, libraries, and parks. If these facilities were *not* used, it would represent a serious domestic policy failure. By contrast, if nuclear weapons ever *were* used, it would constitute a far more serious foreign policy failure—one that could jeopardize the very survival of humanity.

Thus, deterrence is fundamentally psychological. As such, it incorporates some of the elements of a high-stakes poker game. Like poker, deterrence involves a contest of wills based on a certain reality. Because survival hangs in the balance, players must minimize risks. Bluffing is part of the process. Therefore, if Country A successfully uses military power to keep Country B from pursuing its desired foreign policy objective, Country B's prestige is damaged and Country A gains a psychological edge. Nuclear deterrence depends not only on the realities of power but also on the perceptions each side has of the other's will, intentions, and resolve in the face of grave danger.

A number of assumptions underlie nuclear deterrence theory. First, deterrence holds that nations have communicated to potential adversaries a clear will to use weapons of mass destruction if attacked. Second, despite the resulting mutual distrust, decisionmakers on both sides are rational, and therefore neither side will launch a nuclear strike unless it can protect itself from a counterattack. Third, each side possesses a second strike nuclear capability, meaning that enough of the attacked nation's nuclear capabilities would survive a surprise attack (first strike) to make possible a retaliatory blow—or second strike—adequate to inflict unacceptable damage on the attacker.

To ensure the survivability of its nuclear forces, the United States built three separate but interrelated nuclear weapon delivery systems after World War II. This so-called *triad* consisted of land-based intercontinental ballistic missiles (ICBMs), submarine-launched ballistic missiles (SLBMs), and manned bombers (known as the Strategic Air Command, or SAC), some of which were always aloft. The Soviet Union also had a three-pronged deterrence system that depended heavily on land-based missiles and warheads, which it possessed in larger numbers than the United States. The United States' sea-based deterrent was more powerful than the Soviet Union's, however.

Deterrence and the arms race went hand in hand for decades after World War II. Influencing the direction and pace of the arms race were a number of factors. First, each nation had specific goals and priorities that placed varying limits on expenditures for armaments. Second, each superpower had been swayed by its perception of what the other was doing. Thus, an accelerated Soviet weapons buildup in the 1970s prompted the United States to launch a major rearmament program. One corollary of this effort was that a stable balance was not possible when one nation, particularly a nation with an expansionistic foreign policy, possessed a clear advantage in number and strength of nuclear weapons. Finally, technology exerted its own pernicious influence. On the one hand, because technological knowledge cannot be unlearned, both nations were wary of disarmament proposals; on the other, the possibility that another nation might achieve a technological breakthrough provided an incentive to continue high levels of weapons research and development.

Nuclear deterrence worked for several decades, but it was fraught with tension and danger. Although both superpowers consistently reassured the world that they intended to use their nuclear weapons only for defensive purposes, the nuclear arsenals themselves often exacerbated the fear and mistrust that fueled the arms race in the first place.

U.S. FOREIGN POLICY PAST AND PRESENT

Distinguishing clearly between ends and means is critical in the analysis of international politics, and in the formulation of foreign policy. By foreign policy ends, we mean the overarching goals that animate and motivate nations. By foreign policy means, we refer to the strategies or policies that nations adopt to pursue their goals. Goals or objectives are by nature long-range, deeply rooted, and slow to change. Strategies or policies, in turn, can be pragmatic or tactical, and largely dictated by the goals that nations set. Strategies can vary from time to time and can be global or regional. Like every nation, the United States has had to decide between two basic orientations (or strategies). Perhaps more than any other country in the world, the United States changed its foreign goals—and its definition of the *national interest*—in the middle of the twentieth century.

What Is the National Interest?

Two important and recurring types of goal orientation are seen in international politics: a defensive *status quo strategy* versus an offensive *expansionist strategy*. Most nations say they are engaging in the first (a status quo strategy) even when they are pursuing the second (an expansionist strategy). To some extent, this hypocrisy is deliberate ("the tribute that vice pays to virtue") and to some extent it is perhaps simple self-delusion—after all, it is human nature to rationalize our behavior when we cannot justify it.

To the casual observer, it may at times appear as though there is no difference between the behavior of defensive status quo states and aggressive expansionist states, but the motives and goals of the two are quite different. Nations seeking to expand want to change existing power relationships, often at the direct expense of nations wishing to freeze existing relationships. As a rule, expansionist states are dissatisfied with the status quo (the existing configuration of power and prestige in the world). For this reason, they are moved to provoke wars, initiate arms races, promote revolutions abroad, and seek generally to destabilize the international system (which they tend to reject as fundamentally illegitimate and unjust). Such actions generally create a strong moral pressure against these nations, although each case must be evaluated individually.

Although the distinction between aggressive and defensive states is clear in theory, it is extremely blurred in practice. Thus, if no rival nation is engaging in an arms buildup, status quo states are content to stay at existing levels of military readiness. But if a dissatisfied rival state is adding new weapons to its already existing arsenal, then it stands to reason that even the most satisfied status quo state(s) will be compelled to imitate this behavior—out of very different motives, however. In the one instance, the motive is expansion, in the other self-preservation.

Some states balk at the dangers inherent in such a system and attempt to opt out of international power politics altogether. These states pursue a strategy of **_neutrality_** or a strategy of **_nonalignment_**. Neutrality means not taking a stand one way and simply sitting on the sidelines, whereas nonalignment means not choosing sides in general but not necessarily remaining neutral on all issues and in all situations.

Status quo strategies are essentially conservative. Nations adopting such strategies aim to uphold the existing balance of power; they cherish stability, peaceful intercourse among nations, and above all, legitimacy. Status quo states generally seek to use instruments such as international law, multilateral arrangements, and global authorities (for example, the League of Nations and the United Nations) to legitimize the existing distribution of power and prestige in the world. Frequently, they refuse to recognize revolutionary governments on the grounds that such

Manifest Destiny

The United States has always pretended to pursue a status quo policy, even when it was in fact expanding. The story of how the United States grew from thirteen states (the original colonies) huddled along the Atlantic seaboard into a vast empire stretching across an entire continent from ocean to ocean is known to every schoolchild in America but teachers rarely present it as a story about American imperialism or expansionism—unless, perhaps, the children and the teacher are Native Americans. Spaniards and Mexicans would have reason to quarrel over this point, as well, as people living in Texas, Arizona, California, or Florida (among other states) ought to know. Even Russians might object (they ventured into Alaska before the United States existed). Expansionists in the U.S. Congress called it "Manifest Destiny" but, as Shakespeare said, a rose by any other name is still a rose.

governments seized power unlawfully or pose a threat to the stability of the regional or global balance, or that to reward violence and lawlessness with international acceptance undermines respect for law and order everywhere. American foreign policy after World War II provides the most vivid illustrations this policy—indeed, the United States refused to recognize the existence of the Chinese government for more than two decades after the Communist takeover on the mainland in 1949.

However, few states consistently follow status quo strategies on all fronts. Sometimes the political posture of a particular nation shifts between, say, expansionism and pursuit of the status quo. The diplomatic history of the United States illustrates this tendency. Although at various times it has practiced a policy of both continental and extracontinental expansion (see "Manifest Destiny" box on previous page), the United States has for much of its history followed a strategy of maintaining the regional and international status quo. Two examples of this policy are the Monroe Doctrine and the post–World War II effort to contain a perceived Soviet aggression. Both are examined in the next section.

Pursuing the National Interest

There is an important distinction between a nation's long-term goals and its short-term policies. The gap between goals and policies raises three key points. First, regardless of whether a nation pursues a status quo or an expansionist strategy, it may simultaneously carry out different policies to deal with different problems. For example, a nation may seek to preserve the status quo by signing a peace treaty with one nation to launch an expansionistic attack on another: Nazi Germany, which pursued an expansionist policy, signed a nonaggression treaty with the Soviet Union in August 1939 for strategic advantage in conquering eastern Europe.

Or a nation may choose a strategy of expansionism when it believes that striking first and occupying a potential enemy's territory are necessary to its own survival. These examples emphasize the second point: that power strategies are flexible; they change with circumstances and can be applied and altered whenever the nation's ruling leadership deems it appropriate. The United States has frequently invaded or intervened militarily in Latin American countries—the declared intent has always been to defend the status quo or to free the oppressed from tyranny (although, not surprisingly, many Latin Americans see things very differently).

The Monroe Doctrine: Enshrining the Status Quo   President James Monroe promulgated the *Monroe Doctrine* in his annual message to Congress on December 2, 1823. In this address, he pledged that the United States would respect strictly the existing political configurations in the Western Hemisphere. "With the existing colonies or dependencies of any European power we have not interfered and shall not interfere," Monroe observed. But as for

> the governments who have declared their Independence, and maintain it . . . we could not view any interposition for the purpose of oppressing them, or controlling in any other manner their destiny, by any European power, in any other light than as the manifestation of an unfriendly disposition towards the United States.[10]

With this declaration, the United States served notice that henceforth Washington would resist any attempt by an outside power to upset the hemispheric balance of power. In effect, the Monroe Doctrine asserted the right of the United States of America to maintain a preeminent position in roughly one-half the world—the half believed to be vital to its national security.

History, Conflict, and Foreign Policy: The Case of the Middle East

To illustrate the complex and ambiguous nature of foreign policy goals in international relations, we need look no further than to the prolonged conflict between Israel and the Arab world.

After World War II, Jewish nationalists, or Zionists, waged a successful war against the British and the Arabs for a homeland in Palestine. In defense of this action, they cited historical, Biblical, and legal authority and argued that in the aftermath of the Holocaust, Jews could live in security only in a Jewish homeland. The war they fought, however, was not without its innocent victims. Palestinian Arab refugees who had fled in droves rather than live in a Jewish state regarded the Israelis as imperialists. Arab nationalists everywhere took up the cause, declaring a holy war against Zionism and vowing to destroy the newborn state of Israel. Not surprisingly, Arab nations in the region refused to recognize Israel's right to exist as a sovereign state.

Subsequently, radical Palestinian groups directed acts of terrorism against the Israeli population with the complicity of several Arab governments, notably Egypt. In 1956, Egypt seized the Suez Canal from Great Britain and France, who then actively backed Israel in the ensuing war with Egypt over which nation would control access to the canal. This episode only strengthened the Arab belief that Zionism and Western imperialism were conspiring to dominate the Muslim nations of the Middle East.

After more than a decade of smoldering hostilities, another war erupted. In 1967, reacting to bellicose Egyptian threats and to intelligence reports suggesting that Egypt was on the verge of an attack, Israel launched a preemptive military operation that resulted in the so-called Six-Day War. After less than a week of fighting, the Israelis had routed their enemies and occupied large tracts of Arab territory, including the Sinai Peninsula and Gaza Strip in Egypt, the Golan Heights in Syria, and the West Bank of the Jordan

River in Jordan. The hitherto partitioned city of Jerusalem fell under complete Israeli control. Humiliated by this abject defeat, Egypt and Syria prepared for yet another round of fighting. In 1973, they attempted to revise the post-1967 status quo by attacking Israeli-held territories. The Israelis were again equal to the challenge, but this time they suffered a setback in the early going. With the United States acting as a mediator, the Egyptians eventually regained the Sinai desert by agreeing to a peace treaty with Israel in 1979 (the Camp David accords), but the other Arab nations charged Egypt with selling out to Zionism and "imperialism."

Conflict between Israelis and Palestinians intensified in the 1980s as Israel invaded Lebanon in 1982 to counteract cross-border attacks by the PLO and other militant Palestinian groups. Later, Palestinians launched the first *intifada* (uprising) against Israeli occupation in the West Bank and Gaza Strip. The 1990s brought a short-lived lull in the fighting and an abortive agreement on the first steps toward creation of a Palestinian state. The peaceful coexistence of Palestinian-Arabs and Israelis broke down in 2000 when the PLO rejected an Israeli plan for a final settlement that, although considerably more generous than any previous Israeli offer, did not go far enough to satisfy PLO leader, Yasir Arafat. The second *intifada*, even more violent than the first, ensued. Interestingly, each side constantly sought to justify its position on the ground that it was merely maintaining its power. Arab critics claimed the moral high ground, asserting that they were simply defending the Palestinians' right to self-determination; the Israelis cited the Holocaust and Israel's right to exist as a sovereign nation.

Similar ambiguities crop up all the time in international politics. Fortunately, competing claims do not preclude judgments about nations' foreign policy goals; they merely make such judgments more difficult to reach.

Containment: Expanding the Status Quo   Another important example of American status quo policy, *containment,* originated in the late 1940s and remained in force until 1991 when the Soviet Union first faltered and then disintegrated. World War II had drastically altered the European (and thus global) balance of power and, in the aftermath of the war, the United States was thrust for the first time into the role of paramount world leader—a role challenged by a formidable adversary. Under the redoubtable leadership of Joseph Stalin, the Soviet Union appeared to present a grave new threat to the security of the United States. At the time, it seemed as if Alexis de Tocqueville's century-old prophecy that the United States and Russia had each been "marked out by the will of Heaven to sway the destinies of half the globe"[11] was about to be fulfilled.

American policymakers eventually decided to deal with the perceived Soviet threat through a policy of containment, the main outlines of which were delineated in a celebrated article published in the prestigious journal *Foreign Affairs* in July 1947. The anonymous author, "Mr. X," turned out to be George F. Kennan, the then-influential director of the State Department's Policy Planning Staff and later an ambassador to the USSR. "It is clear," Kennan wrote:

> that the main element of any United States policy toward the Soviet Union must be that of a long-term, patient but firm and vigilant containment of Russian expansive tendencies. . . . Soviet pressure against the free institutions of the Western world is something that can be contained by the adroit and vigilant application of counter-force at a series of constantly shifting geographical and political points.[12]

Kennan went on to predict that if a policy of containment were applied consistently for a decade or so, the Soviet challenge would diminish significantly. He also suggested (prophetically, it can now be said) that if containment proved successful, the totalitarian Soviet state would ultimately fall victim to severe internal pressures.

This "new" doctrine of containment was actually nothing more than the age-old status quo policy applied to Europe. Its apparent novelty stemmed mainly from the specific adaptation of status quo initiatives to the unique set of circumstances that prevailed after World War II.

The first major test of containment came in 1947, when it appeared that Greece was about to fall victim to a communist insurgency. After Great Britain, which had historically played the role of guarantor of the status quo in the eastern Mediterranean, declared that it could no longer afford to underwrite the legitimate government of Greece, the United States stepped in. In an urgent message to Congress requesting authority to provide foreign aid to the embattled governments of Greece and Turkey, President Harry Truman enunciated the containment principle that came to be known as the *Truman Doctrine:* "I believe that it must be the policy of the United States to support free peoples who are resisting attempted subjugation by armed minorities or by outside pressures."[13] When Congress approved the president's request, containment became the official policy of the U.S. government.

After a communist government gained power in Czechoslovakia in February 1948, the United States countered with the European Recovery Program, commonly known as the Marshall Plan, a $16.5 billion program aimed at the reconstruction of the war-torn economies of Western Europe. This program was designed to promote the recovery of Western Europe not only economically but also spiritually and politically as well. At the time, it was feared that communism might come in "through the back door"—meaning that the powerful Communist parties of France and Italy might be able to capitalize on the demoralization of the general populace and, with the covert backing of Moscow, seize power in Paris and Rome as they had done in Prague. Thus, the Marshall Plan formed an integral part of the overall U.S. effort to preserve the status quo after World War II.

In 1949, the United States broke a tradition that dated back to its founding by sponsoring a peacetime military alliance, NATO, comprising nearly all the Western European countries plus Canada and the United States. NATO represented the logical extension of containment from the economic realm to the military realm.

The fall of Mainland China to the Communists in 1949 provoked another great wave of anxiety throughout the United States. When, in 1950, fighting broke out in Korea between the communist regime in the north and the noncommunist one in the south, the United States decided to apply containment as vigorously on the Asian perimeter as it had on the European. Although technically fought under the flag of the United Nations, the Korean War was actually waged in the main by the United States in pursuit of its own national interest, the preservation of the postwar status quo, this time in Asia.

During the 1960s, what had started out as a policy designed to prevent the spread of communism, first in Europe and then in Asia, turned into a firefighting strategy of anticommunist interventionism in the Third World. Military equipment, economic aid, diplomatic support, and the American nuclear umbrella were all extended to specific nations deemed to be under threat of communist subversion or insurgency. Military intervention was considered an appropriate response under certain circumstances. This strategy of military containment reached its high-water mark when hundreds of thousands of U.S. troops were sent to South Vietnam, between 1964 and 1972, to help that nation in its battle against communist guerrillas and North Vietnamese forces. After the Vietnam War, the United States placed much less reliance on large-scale military intervention to maintain the international status quo, although the main thrust of U.S. foreign policy did not change.

By the early 1990s, the U.S. policy of containment had lost its raison d'être. The Soviet Union's decision to grant autonomy to its former eastern European satellite nations, its backing of the U.S.-led coalition against Iraq in 1991, and its disintegration later that year made it obvious that the American policy of containment had served its purpose. The breakup of the Soviet Union at the end of 1991 provided the last measure of convincing evidence that the Soviet threat could no longer be treated as the cornerstone of American foreign policy, thus making the American policy of containment obsolete.

THE GREAT DEBATE: REALISM VERSUS IDEALISM

There is a tendency to associate political realism with an aggressive pursuit of nation interests—not necessarily expansionist, but interventionist. Political realists are seldom advocates of restraint in crisis situations. For example, in the crisis presented by the 9-11 terrorist attacks on the United States, the conservative, Republican administration of President George W. Bush called for an aggressive pursuit of the perpetrators as well as punitive measures against any state(s) that harbored international terrorists. The methods the United States used were violent—bombing and inserting Special Operations combat teams in order to (1) overthrow the Taliban government, and (2) kill or capture Osama bin Laden and his al Qaeda terrorist network.

Clearly, violent methods do not always denote a strategy of expansionism. The United States was not trying to colonize Afghanistan. Oddly enough, defenders of the status quo (especially conservatives) routinely associate violence with aggression and aggression with expansionism. However, defenders of the status quo (again, especially conservatives) tend to use violence or even sponsor insurgencies as part of a strategy aimed at defeating revolutionary movements. The champions of a *counterinsurgency strategy* claim to be idealistic but the rest of the world, with few exceptions, see armed intervention by any outside power as imperialistic. For example, the Reagan administration (1980–88) aided a variety of anticommunist insurgents around the world in the 1980s, including groups in Central America (the Contras in Nicaragua), in Asia (the *Mujaheddin* rebels in Afghanistan), and in Africa (UNITA guerrillas in Angola). The fact that President Reagan called the guerrilla forces he liked "freedom fighters" did not fool anybody (except perhaps in the United States). These examples demonstrate the importance (and difficulty) of moral objectivity in foreign policy analysis. A strategy aimed at changing the existing distribution of power and wealth is not necessarily a sign of imperialism or idealism; more likely it is evidence that realism has swayed policymakers, rightly or wrongly, to take a certain course of action.

To understand what expansionism is, one must also understand what it is not. For example, not every state with a territorial claim against another state or a desire for change in the global distribution of power and wealth is aggressive or expansionist. A border dispute does not in itself constitute evidence that either contending country has an appetite for empire. Neither does the demand by many developing countries for a "new international economic order" (meaning a redistribution of global wealth). Challenging the status quo in this way is hardly proof of aggression both because the objectives are limited and reasonable and because the methods are primarily political and diplomatic (pressure or persuasion) rather than military or economic (intimidation and coercion).

During the Cold War, political realism provided an invaluable perspective from which to view international relations. Power expansion or power maintenance strategies and combative regional strategies were adopted and scrutinized as the United States and the Soviet Union pursued survival and ascendancy and as other nations often reacted. During this time, the realist notion of the struggle for power among self-interested nations provided a complete explanation of nation-state behavior for many (but hardly all) political scientists. However, with the disintegration of the Soviet Union and the passing of the Cold War, debates about the applicability of political realism and national self-interest have become more heated.

Blowback

The concept of *blowback* is at the center of a storm over American foreign policy that as been raging in academic circles (but has gone largely unnoticed by the general public) since the end of the Cold War. Chalmers Johnson, an expert on Asia, who wrote a best-selling book of the same name, popularized this term.[14] Analysts at the Central Intelligence Agency (CIA) actually invented the term *blowback* for internal use. Later students of international relations adopted it. According to Johnson:

> It refers to the unintended consequences of policies that were kept secret from the American people. What the daily press reports as the malign acts of "terrorists" or "drug lords" or "rogue states" or "illegal arms merchants" often turn out to be blowback from earlier operations.[15]

As examples, Johnson cites the 1988 bombing of Pan Am flight 103 over Lockerbie, Scotland, which, he asserts, "was retaliation for a 1986 Reagan administration aerial raid on Libya that killed President Muammar Qadaffi's stepdaughter."[16] He also suggests that drug trafficking in the U.S. is in part the result of past U.S. support for dictators and anticommunist insurgents in Latin America and that terrorist attacks against U.S. targets are blowback, citing a 1997 report to the Pentagon's chief of acquisitions and technology: "Historical data shows a strong correlation between U.S. involvement in international situations and an increase in terrorist attacks against the United States."[17]

The picture Johnson paints is nothing short of alarming:

> The most direct and obvious form of blowback often occurs when the victims fight back after a secret American bombing, or a U.S.-sponsored campaign of state terrorism, or a CIA-engineered overthrow of a foreign political leader. All around the world today, it is possible to see the groundwork being laid for future forms of blowback.[18]

This dark admonition, written in 1999, looked prophetic in days after terrorists leveled the World Trade Center and blew a large hole in the side of the Pentagon using hijacked passenger airplanes as weapons. In this same passage, Johnson wrote about the 1990–91 Persian Gulf War and its aftermath and specifically about the suffering caused by the U.S.-imposed economic blockade on Iraq, charging "it helped contribute to the deaths of an estimated half million Iraqi civilians due to disease, malnutrition, and inadequate medical care." Osama bin Laden and the al Qaeda high command "justified" the 9-11 attacks on the grounds that (1) the U.S. has defiled the sacred soil of Saudi Arabia by stationing military forces in the country; (2) the U.S. has supported Israel's repression of Palestinians' rights, and (3) the U.S. has waged economic war against Iraqi civilians.

President Bill Clinton blamed bin Laden for the terrorist attacks on two U.S. embassies in 1998 in Nairobi (the capital of Kenya), and Dar es Salaam (the capital of Tanzania). He retaliated by bombing a pharmaceutical plant in Khartoum (the capital of Sudan) and an al Qaeda training camp in Afghanistan. Neither of these air strikes accomplished its intended purpose, but the attack against Sudan was particularly embarrassing to the United States when it turned out that the pharmaceutical plant was not manufacturing chemical weapons of mass destruction as the United States had alleged. However:

Government spokesmen continue to justify these attacks as "deterring" terrorism, even if the targets proved to be irrelevant to any damage done to facilities of the United States. In this way, future blowback possibilities are seeded into the world. The same spokesmen ignore the fact that the alleged mastermind of the embassy bombings, bin Laden, is a former protégé of the United States. When America was organizing Afghan rebels against the USSR in the 1980s, he played an important role in driving the Soviet Union from Afghanistan and only turned against the United States in 1991 because he regarded the stationing of American troops in his native Saudi Arabia during and after the Persian Gulf War as a violation of his religious beliefs.[19]

Again, Johnson's analysis and indictment are particularly compelling in the light of the tragic 9-11 events. Johnson cites many examples of incidents likely, in his estimation, to produce future blowback in our relations with Japan (Okinawa), South Korea (the 1980 Kwangju massacre), China, Indonesia, and others. Although Johnson's critique is incisive in places, and there is no doubt a good deal of truth in the book, his views are controversial and by no means shared by other academic or government experts. Indeed, in the wake of 9-11 many Americans tended to be suspicious of *any* criticism of U.S. foreign policy, viewing it as unpatriotic. And there were plenty of college professors who jumped on the bandwagon, too.

In Search of a New Foreign Policy

Amid this controversy, some international theorists contend that not much has changed in the post–Cold War era. They continue to apply a traditional interpretation of the national interest to world politics. However, changed circumstances (namely the demise of the Soviet Union) now direct the United States to adopt a largely isolationist, or internally focused, foreign policy. According to these post–Cold War realists, the United States can no longer afford to police the world, nor does its security and prosperity any longer require it. Instead, the United States "must anchor its security and prosperity in a less-than-utopian set of objectives [and] think in terms not of the whole world's well-being but . . . of purely national interest."[20]

Accepting the anarchic system of competing nation-states as a given, *neo-isolationists* advise against trying to change the world. Instead, they say, the United States should minimize its involvement in foreign conflicts. International discord is an inherent part of the international system, whose members display glaring differences in size, natural resources, economic development, historical experiences, and so forth.

Adopting such an inward-looking interpretation of the national interest might rule out international economic initiatives not directly benefiting the United States. It would call into question the U.S. role in existing alliances (especially NATO) and international organizations (for example, the United Nations) and other multinational institutions (such as the World Bank and the World Trade Organization). Finally, it could leave the world without a rudder (effective leadership, that is).

Political scientists Max Singer and Aaron Wildavsky take a different approach to understanding international politics in the post–Cold War era. They argue that despite talk of a "new world order," most contemporary critics fail to grasp the real world emerging in the post–Cold War period.[21] Unlike visionaries, who posit the existence of one political world, and Cold War realists, who identify three political worlds, Singer and Wildavsky argue that two such worlds exist, one comprising prosperous democratic states and the other impoverished nondemocratic states. Furthermore, prosperous democracies, which account for about 15 percent of the world's population, are called "zones of peace," whereas underdeveloped dictatorships are labeled "zones of conflict." The two worlds or zones are viewed as separate and separable. Singer and Wildavsky contend that power struggles and wars in the zones of conflict will continue to be the norm. In addition, peaceful competition, in the form of trade and investment, and economic cooperation will replace (as it already has) war in the zones of peace.

The policy implications of this analysis are far-reaching. For example, if two such separate and separable zones do exist, it would be possible for states in the zones of peace to remain aloof from the violence and bloodshed occurring in the zones of conflict. It would follow, then, that military intervention in regional conflicts would have to be undertaken with extreme caution. According to Singer and Wildavsky:

> [O]ur overall goal should be the advance of stable democracy so that zones of peace will be extended as soon as possible. We propose that the United States should pursue this goal in five ways: by making a clear distinction in our policy between democracies and nondemocracies; by minimizing trade barriers; by providing economic aid and advice; by providing an example and a market; and by working with other democracies to preserve peace and improve the international order, even if military intervention is required. But we should not have a policy of forcing democracy on authoritarian countries.[22]

Such an analysis exudes optimism in that it views the power of example "and the openness of our markets" as the most effective ways to influence the behavior of authoritarian regimes. Thus, although it takes a traditional realist view of politics among authoritarian states, it views politics among democratic nations very differently.

Idealism as Self-Interest: The Power of Morality

Political realism, with its emphasis on power, self-interest, and national interests, has proven remarkably influential. Yet, well before the Cold War ended, political realism's indifference to matters of morality had been extensively criticized. As we observed earlier, political realism has little use for the idea of morality; instead, it favors facts, interests, and power. Finding this rejection of morality disturbing, some political scientists support an alternative understanding of international relations called *idealism,* which considers values, ideals, and moral principles as the keys to describing, comprehending, and even changing the behavior of nation-states. A concern for ideals not only helps explain why nations act, but also furnishes guidelines for how nations ought to act. Often, idealists hold that nations, like human beings, desire peace and prosperity, but when political leaders are misled by irrational forces—for instance, by a misguided ideology or fervent nationalism—wars and international tensions result. In order to reduce world tensions, to restore rationality, and, ultimately, to help ensure peace, idealists emphasize the importance of international law and global organizations such as the United Nations.

Idealists often regard realists as cynics; realists counter that idealists are naive. Who is right? Perhaps, in a sense, they both are. Even the arch-realist, Hans Morganthau, did not deny that morality plays *some* role in international relations. Without taking account of morality it is impossible for realists or anyone else to account for certain actions of nation-states. Singer and Wildavsky note the pervasive influence of realism in the heyday of the Soviet–American rivalry: "Practically everyone believed that if a nation was [much] more powerful than its neighbors, it would use its power to control or conquer them."[23] But, of course, that never happened, not during the Cold War or after it, when the United States was widely hailed as the world's only superpower. Thus, national self-restraint can be explained by the influence of moral principle as well as by the complex interplay of power politics.

Some national leaders clearly give moral principle more weight than others in the formulation and conduct of foreign policy. In the United States, for example, President Woodrow Wilson emphasized national self-determination and collective security and President Jimmy Carter actively promoted global human rights—both presidents were committed to certain moral principles. Nations do sometimes act altruistically, for example by offering asylum to refugees who flee political persecution, economic disaster, or civil war. Between the two world wars, British leaders sought to alleviate harsh conditions imposed on Germany by the Treaty of Versailles, a stand hailed as "a noble idea, rooted in Christianity, courage, and common sense."[24]

The U.S. military action in Somalia from 1992 to 1994 was undertaken for the purpose of alleviating mass starvation. That intervention, which cost American lives and offered no political or economic advantage to the United States, cannot be explained by self-interest alone (if at all).[25] Indeed, it accomplished little or nothing other than to alienate Islamic extremists (including Osama bin Laden) who saw it as yet another example of American military intervention in the internal affairs of a Muslim society.

In most cases, a given nation's foreign policy contains elements of both ideals (moral principle) and self-interest. For instance, the Marshall Plan was magnanimous by any reasonable measure. Indeed, even Winston Churchill, who measured his words carefully and avoided hyperbole like the plague, called it the "most unsordid act in history."[26] But the Marshall Plan was also consistent with the United States' post–World War II status quo strategic policy of reestablishing a stable Western European community able to resist armed aggression from without and organized subversion from within. Similarly, Germany sent massive amounts of aid to Russia in the winter of 1991–92 in part for humanitarian reasons and in part out of fear that a failed Russia would destabilize Western Europe and unleash a horde of refugees in Germany's direction.

It is true that nations are most compassionate when they have something at

GATEWAYS TO THE WORLD: EXPLORING CYBERSPACE

http://www.ciia.org/links.htm;
http://www.psr.keele.ac.k/orgs.htm

These sites provide links to a variety of international relations sources.

http://politicalscience.wadsworth.com/russett71

This site is an extension of Bruce Russett and Harvey Starr's international relations textbook, *World Politics: The Menu for Choice,* from Worth Publishers/W. H. Freeman. It provides a number of links to areas of interest for students of international relations. The links are grouped by the topical, chapter layout of the text.

stake, but many nations understand that good deeds can also be good foreign policy and upholding high ideals can help to advance a nation's interests. Generosity is often rewarded with goodwill and the goodwill has an exchange value in international politics (as in all politics).

Nations have occasionally sacrificed concrete national interests for the sake of moral principle. Denmark during World War II illustrates this point. Although an occupied country, Denmark was granted a large degree of political autonomy by the Nazi government. In an effort to protect its Jewish citizens and other refugees, the Danish government and people openly defied German edicts aimed at isolating Jews from the general population and thereby put themselves at risk. Through acts of uncommon moral courage, the Danes were responsible for creating "an extraordinary obstacle which arose in the path of the German destruction machine: an uncooperative Danish administration and a local population unanimous in its resolve to save its Jews."[27] Both the consequences of Denmark's actions, and the actions themselves, were quite rare. Yet "little Denmark, too weak to seek self-preservation through power, limit[ed] its foreign policy largely to humanitarian causes, and . . . in the end survived Hitler's conquest."[28]

Recognizing that both morality and power can play a role in international relations, it is argued that an expanded understanding of national interest should include both factors. Moreover, the worldwide advancement of such moral principles as liberty, democracy, and human rights has been described as constituting an important national interest of democratic states. This idea is rooted in the assumption that a foreign policy indifferent to moral principle cannot be defended morally, as well as in the utilitarian supposition that a world composed of democratic nations, which respect freedom and human rights, would also be a safer world (as noted in Chapter 16, democracies do not go to war against each other). A democratic state's national interests often contain elements of both idealism and realism. This points to an important truth: Power without justice is mere expediency, while morality without power constitutes only good intentions.[29]

New World, Old Habits

The key assumption behind the idea of national self-interest in political realism theory is that sovereign states first look inward to define the interests that guide a nation's conduct in the world beyond its borders. Some contemporary critics, however, charge that this self-centered understanding of the national interest is outmoded. They argue that there is a "need for a new diplomacy and for new institutions and regulatory regimes to cope with the world's growing environmental interdependence" because "our accepted definition of the limits of national sovereignty as coinciding with national borders is obsolete."[30]

Today's profound environmental challenges (global warming, acid rain, air pollution, and disappearing rain forests), as well as the rapid depletion of nonrenewable natural resources, overpopulation, and world poverty, are global in scope and therefore require global solutions. "Think locally, act globally" is the motto of this school of thought. Its credo is that nations have a moral obligation not to pursue narrow self-interests to the detriment of seeking and finding solutions pressing global problems. In the interests of survival, the old world order needs to give way to a new world order in which global interests replace national interests. Thus, in an increasingly interdependent world, the best way for any given nation to ensure its prosperity and security is to look outward rather than inward, to open its doors to international cooperation, and to shed any nationalistic tendencies (such as excessive patriotism, protectionism, and isolationism) in favor of a new global consciousness.

This approach requires a drastic change in the way human beings think and behave. It also requires a much broader, and arguably more enlightened, definition of self-interest than anything put into practice in international politics in the past. To some, the new world order and global community sound like soft-boiled idealism. But adherents reject this charge, arguing that the policies and prescriptions they advocate are firmly rooted in human self-interest, and that global security and perhaps even self-preservation hinge on a radical rethinking of world politics. In today's world, they contend, yesterday's realism is not only obsolete but also dangerous.

What do you think? After all, it is the members of today's younger generation who will decide the fate of tomorrow's world.

New Patterns, Old Problems

The dissolution of the Soviet Union marked the end of the post–World War II balance of power. Countries have consequently had to redefine relationships with one another. As a result, it is sometimes asserted that a new world order is emerging. Understanding the dynamics of this brave new world is essential to any coherent view of contemporary international politics.

International politics currently does *not* exhibit a clear balance-of-power configuration whereby participants with incompatible aims, conflicting interests, and roughly equal power interact in predictable ways to maintain stability and peace as it did in Europe between 1648 and 1914. The emerging international order is marked by contradictory trends—for example, the movement toward (European) integration, which transcends traditional state boundaries, and the simultaneous rise of religious and ethnic particularism *within* existing nations, which has caused the breakup of three multinational states in Europe: the Soviet Union, Yugoslavia, and Czechoslovakia. The present state of international relations is most likely temporary and transitional and will in time yield to some more permanent arrangements.[31]

After the Cold War, What?

We live in an unbalanced world. The crumbling of the Soviet empire and the demonstration of U.S. military prowess in the war against Iraq in the early 1990s made clear that the United States prevailed as the world's sole remaining super-power. This conclusion was reinforced by the striking contrast between the stable U.S. economy and the disarray of the former Soviet economy, by the juxtaposition of domestic stability in the United States and the upheaval in various parts of the former Soviet Union, and by the vitality of the Western alliance system even after the Warsaw Pact ceased to exist.

Although there is no universally recognized definition of *superpower*, most analysts agree that a superpower must meet a three-part test. First, it must have a full range of power capabilities, including not only military muscle but also economic, political, diplomatic, and even moral clout. Second, it must have global reach, defined as the capacity to project power to all parts of the world. Third, it must be willing to assert its leadership role in the international arena. By this test, only the United States qualifies as a superpower. Japan and Germany are primarily economic powers. Britain and France have substantial diplomatic power and considerable military capability but are not regarded as great economic powers. The Russian Republic possesses formidable strategic nuclear capabilities and some diplomatic clout but is currently preoccupied with its own internal economic problems. China, a regional power, lacks global capabilities and an advanced industrial economy.

One immediate consequence of a unipolar world is a reduction in global tension (which was not, however, matched by a reduction in regional tensions in all cases). The nuclear stalemate that defined the Cold War is no longer a driving force in world politics. An eclipse of the ideological conflict (capitalism and democracy versus socialism and communism) that defined the post–World War II world has accompanied this reduction in friction. This "de-ideologization" does not mean that the world today is free of divergent interests and values. It only means that the way Americans have thought about the world for over four decades is suddenly subject to revision. Realism is still as necessary to national survival as ever, but exactly what constitutes a realistic foreign policy in the changed (and ever-changing) circumstances of today's world is far from obvious.

Another consequence of a unipolar world is that there are few *external* restraints on the world's sole surviving superpower, the United States. Although no nation is entirely free to do as it wishes (especially in a world where many nations have nuclear weapons), many of the restraints on the United States today are self-imposed. These can be economic (what can it afford to do?), political (how much foreign involvement will the electorate support?), or even moral (what kinds of actions ought a democratic nation committed to the protection of human rights undertake?).

A Global Economy

With the reduction of political conflicts among the world's most powerful nations, international economics assumes increasing importance. The buzzword in the capitals of the world is *globalization.* This is only natural, for the more that problems of war and peace recede, the more nations and leaders can turn to the next order of business, the pursuit of prosperity. There is no doubt that the world economies today are far more interdependent than at any other time in human history, but what does this mean? The short answer is that economic interdependence promises greater levels of both international cooperation and international competition.

This transformation of the world economy is driven by large multinational corporations and by the new information technology, each of which transcends national boundaries. Additionally, some problems simply necessitate international cooperation, including regional and worldwide environmental problems, limited forms of arms control, international debt repayment and relief concerns, and the coordination of economic policies during times of crisis. A particularly important worldwide economic question was addressed in late 1997 and early 1998 when many Asian nations experienced a sudden, sharp economic downturn.

Responding to the fear of a global economic meltdown, a large-scale rescue package was formulated that directly benefited a number of nations, including South Korea and Indonesia. The effort was headed by the *International Monetary Fund (IMF)*—an organization composed of the governments of many nations, designed to promote worldwide economic stability. The IMF coordinated large scale economic loans and, as a precondition for making the loans, it insisted that the nations it helped agree to important economic reforms.

Yet in the face of such cooperative efforts, economic competition among nations is also on the rise. Often governments attempt to benefit their citizens by subsidizing domestic industries or agriculture, by invoking tariffs on imports, or by erecting other trade barriers. Such protectionist practices inhibit free trade and can lead to international tensions, even among allies. A good example of such stress can be seen in the ongoing (and not always pleasant) trade negotiations between the United States and Japan. Occasionally, American and Japanese relations have been strained over the issue of the Japanese government's policy of protectionism. On the other side of the globe, trade talks between the United States and its European allies in 1993 and 1994 became acrimonious over the issue of governmental subsidization of agriculture. These examples serve as a reminder that competition as well as cooperation continues to exist in the increasingly important world of international economics and trade.

The Rise of Regionalism

Increasingly, the world's wealthiest nations are forming geographic economic blocs. Often, these blocs transcend the narrowest economic interests of individual nation-states and promise great financial rewards. Cooperation among Western European nations is especially noteworthy, especially in the realm of economics and trade. Thus, the European Union envisions becoming a single economy with a single currency and genuinely free trade within its borders (see Figure 17-2).

The European Union (EU) envisions a barrier-free market of more than 340 million people and more than $5 trillion in economic clout. Here are the members and how wealth and population are distributed:

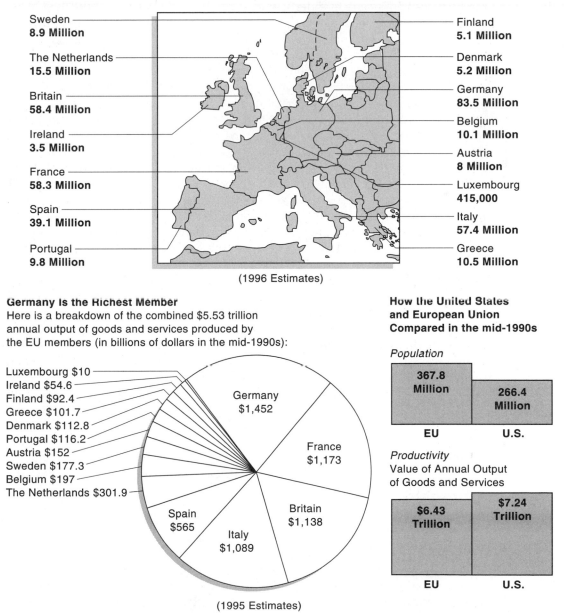

Sweden
8.9 Million

The Netherlands
15.5 Million

Britain
58.4 Million

Ireland
3.5 Million

France
58.3 Million

Spain
39.1 Million

Portugal
9.8 Million

Finland
5.1 Million

Denmark
5.2 Million

Germany
83.5 Million

Belgium
10.1 Million

Austria
8 Million

Luxembourg
415,000

Italy
57.4 Million

Greece
10.5 Million

(1996 Estimates)

Germany Is the Richest Member
Here is a breakdown of the combined $5.53 trillion annual output of goods and services produced by the EU members (in billions of dollars in the mid-1990s):

Luxembourg $10
Ireland $54.6
Finland $92.4
Greece $101.7
Denmark $112.8
Portugal $116.2
Austria $152
Sweden $177.3
Belgium $197
The Netherlands $301.9

Germany
$1,452

France
$1,173

Britain
$1,138

Italy
$1,089

Spain
$565

(1995 Estimates)

How the United States and European Union Compared in the mid-1990s

Population

367.8 Million	266.4 Million
EU	U.S.

Productivity
Value of Annual Output of Goods and Services

$6.43 Trillion	$7.24 Trillion
EU	U.S.

FIGURE 17-2 Forging an Economic Power: The European Union in the Mid-1990s
All GDP estimates here are based on purchasing power parity conversions.
SOURCE: *The World Factbook, 1996* copyright © 1996 by Claitor's Publishing. Reprinted with permission; CIA publications, 1996.

This economic collaboration among European nations has been evolutionary and grew out of years of prior economic (Common Market) and military (NATO) cooperation. Most impressively, this cooperative relationship has overcome centuries of rivalry and mistrust between France and Germany. Long-term plans for the European Union are grander yet; in December 1994, leaders of the twelve EU countries adopted a plan to expand by early in the twenty-first century to include over twenty members, including the former communist countries of Bulgaria, the Czech Republic, Hungary, Poland, Romania, and Slovakia. Meanwhile, earlier in 1994, the United States, Mexico, and Canada negotiated a far-reaching trade agreement (NAFTA); later that year, plans were made to expand the NAFTA agreement to Chile. In December 1994, an agreement among representatives of thirty-four nations in the Western Hemisphere pledged to negotiate a vast free-trade zone (the agreement was officially named the Free Area of the Americas) that would stretch from Canada to the tip of Argentina. Such an economic plan envisioned a market of 850 million consumers buying $13 trillion worth of goods and services. Finally, Japan has strengthened economic ties with other Pacific Basin nations, and it seems "that in the 1990s, Japan and the NICs of Asia [South Korea, Singapore, Hong Kong, and Taiwan] might form a powerful new economic bloc linked by trade, investment, and aid relationships."[32] This potential regional bloc is by far the most ill defined of these three alliances, and an emerging economic powerhouse, China, complicates its realization.

What will emerge from this new tripartite concentration of economic power? Of course, within these economic blocs there will be extended cooperation. Cooperation also means interdependence for better or worse, as the United States discovered in early 1995 when Mexico's peso devaluation threatened the stability of American financial markets. Nonetheless, based on these cooperative efforts, some visionaries go so far as to predict a scenario of future political integration that will transcend the boundaries of the nation-state.

An even more difficult question asks how these three geoeconomic blocs will coexist. Competition among them is inevitable, but there is also vast potential for economic cooperation. Finally, it is likely that nations in all three blocs will benefit greatly from membership in regional trade associations, very likely increasing the economic distance between themselves and the world's many developing nations. If so, regional groups may become big obstacles rather than stepping-stones to the emergence of a truly global economy.

The Curse of Ethnic Violence

While close regional economic cooperation may point to the emergence of political organizations beyond the self-sufficient nation-state, ethnic strife in some parts of the world threatens the nation-state's very existence. Although this topic is discussed in Chapter 8, a number of key points need to be made regarding its relevance in the emerging international order.

Worldwide, ethnic conflict has increased markedly during the past two decades. Disputes among different ethnic, religious, and racial groups within nation-states and between such groups and governments point to an important fact: Intense ethnic rivalries are not confined to any one world region but exist virtually everywhere.

Examples of ethnic animosity are almost unlimited. A few of the most prominent discontented ethnic groups include the Sikhs and Muslims in India, the Volga Tatars in the Russian Republic, the South Ossetians in Georgia, the French-speaking Quebecois in Canada, the Kurds in Iraq and Turkey, the Tamils in Sri Lanka, and the Timorese in Indonesia. Moreover, intense ethnic feeling among rival peoples within a country is almost always associated with political strife and violence. Ethnic tensions have led to riots, civil wars, acts of terrorism, and occasionally the disintegration of countries.

One particularly disturbing problem associated with ethnic strife involves refugees and other displaced peoples. In the summer of 1994, for instance, after a genocidal civil war in Rwanda led to the slaughter of 200,000 to 500,000 people, approximately 3 million refugees (or 40 percent of the country's population) attempted to cross the border into Zaire (now called The Democratic Republic of The Congo). Overwhelmed international relief agencies and the Zaire government faced problems of mass starvation and epidemic disease that defied human comprehension. The war in Bosnia also created millions of refugees, orphans, and asylum-seekers by the mid-1990s.

Though the divisive effects of ethnic tension usually are more mundane, even seemingly routine governmental duties such as census taking, which the U.S. Constitution requires the government to undertake every ten years, can be fraught with danger in other parts of the world. In Iraq, Lebanon, Kenya, and Pakistan, among other countries, ethnic disputes have delayed, prevented, or contested census taking because "the apportionment of legislative seats, revenue, and other public goods among various ethnic groups depends on what census results show."[33] Routine census taking has even led to warfare:

> In Assam, a state in northeast India, census results showing small changes in the proportion of Bengalis to Assamese in the 1970s paved the way for a violent reaction to an increase in Bengali names on electoral rolls later in the decade. Thousands died as a result. The census can become a life-or-death matter in an ethnically divided society.[34]

Finally, it is important to recognize that ethnic conflicts frequently are more complex than they seem. In a number of nations, such as many of the newly independent states of the former Soviet Union, there are peoples of various ethnic groups, all of whom make claims or desire independence from each other. Even in Canada many in French-speaking Quebec, which contains a quarter of Canada's 27 million people, have advocated independence to preserve their language and culture. Some 800,000 Indians within Quebec make that argument on the basis of their 10,000-year history, and representatives of Quebec's 7,000 Eskimos (or Inuit, as they prefer to be called) have said they would seek their own separate nation within Quebec, should Quebec gain its independence. Such claims emphasize that increasing ethnic feeling—culminating in disputes over politics, economics, language, discrimination, and culture—can be a divisive force in the world today, often fragmenting the political community into its most elementary parts.

The New Doomsday Scenario:
Averting a Silent Spring

In the United States and throughout the world, most environmental issues remained unrecognized until the 1960s. Since then, however, interest in environmental protection has expanded greatly, as have the number of environmental pressure groups and their ability to influence governments worldwide regarding global environmental protection. These so-called *green parties*, which advocate greater attention to environmental problems, exist in virtually every major industrialized country except the United States. Nonetheless, in this country environmentally related interest groups have blossomed. Such well-known and -financed groups as the Sierra Club, the Audubon Society, Save the Whales, and the National Wildlife Federation exert considerable political clout. Furthermore, research and policy institutes monitor the state of the environment and advocate ecology-conscious public policies.

It is hardly surprising that recent decades have witnessed a growing international awareness of environmental issues. Acid rain; global warming; the need to conserve water resources, forests, and fisheries; and the continued heavy use of the earth's nonrenewable natural resources such as oil, gas, and minerals have all recently provided incentives to governments to cooperate in fashioning international environmental agreements. Although thus far these agreements have been limited in scope, they are expected to become more numerous and even more important in the future.

The Old Doomsday Scenario:
Preventing Nuclear Proliferation

Because of the unprecedented scale of death and destruction they can inflict, atomic, biological, and chemical weapons—sometimes called ABC weapons—are in a class by themselves. (Atomic weapons are also known as nuclear weapons—the words *atomic* and *nuclear* are used interchangeably here.) In addition to causing an immense loss of life, damage to infrastructure, and widespread environmental devastation, the use of these weapons could conceivably result in genetic mutations with lasting consequences for future generations. Indeed, their effects are difficult to predict or control. The states that possess these weapons want to prevent other states from acquiring them. Iraq and North Korea are two countries that have sought to acquire weapons of mass destruction, a development vigorously opposed by the United States and its allies.

Although arms limitation treaties covering ABC weapons exist (see Chapter 18), many states refuse to sign or be constrained by them. Not surprisingly, national instability and regional conflicts are made more dangerous by the spread of mass-destruction weapons systems. Flash points, including Iraq in the Middle East and North Korea in Northeast Asia, threaten to undermine world stability. As Table 17-1 indicates, the number of nuclear "haves" is still quite small, but the number of nuclear powers has grown from only five in the 1960s to nine at present.

TABLE 17-1

Proliferation of Nuclear Weapons

Has Nuclear Weapons	Probably Has Nuclear Weapons	Has Pledged Not to Build Nuclear Weapons	Has Given Up Nuclear Weapons	Is Believed to Be Interested in Obtaining Nuclear Weapons
China	Israel	Algeria	Belarus	Iran
France		Argentina	Kazakhstan	Iraq
Great Britian		Brazil	Ukraine	Libya
India		Germany		North Korea
Pakistan		Japan		Syria
Russia		South Africa		
United States				

No less troubling is the fact that some developing countries that possess valuable natural resources—for example, oil-rich Libya, Iran, and Iraq—are believed to desire weapons of mass destruction. Nonetheless, these facts only hint at the true dimensions and dangers of the nuclear proliferation problem. Nowadays, the technology needed to build nuclear weapons is widely understood, and the necessary materials (for example, enriched uranium) are relatively easy to obtain. According to one estimate, by the year 2000 as many as forty nations may possess the means to manufacture nuclear weapons.[35] Given the military, political, and symbolic importance of such weapons, it is unrealistic to expect any slackening in the efforts of some nuclear "have-nots" (especially those with aggressive aims) to obtain them.

The greater the number of state or nonstate actors (for example, terrorists) with nuclear, biological, or chemical weapons, the greater the possibility that these weapons might be used intentionally or unintentionally. The danger of proliferation can take countless forms. For example, a kind of instant proliferation occurred when the Soviet Union disintegrated, leaving several former Soviet republics in possession of inherited nuclear arsenals. In response to heavy diplomatic pressure from the West, these formidable weapons, including large warheads and long-range missiles in the Ukraine and Kazakhstan, have now apparently all been relinquished to Russia.

One nightmare scenario became a reality in the fall of 2001—the anthrax attacks that followed in the wake of the 9-11 hijack-bombings in the United States were only one form of mass destruction weapons feared to have fallen in the hands of international terrorists. An even greater fear was the possibility that terrorist cells would launch attacks using crude atomic weapons to contaminate urban areas with radiation or obtain weaponized germs even more dangerous than anthrax (such as smallpox or pneumonic plague).

The IT Revolution

In the emerging, new international order, some trends point to a limited but noteworthy transcending of the nation-state (for example, the emergence of a global economy and the rise of cooperative transnational organizations such as the European Union), while others point to the nation-state's disintegration (as a result of pronounced ethnic violence, for instance). A curious fact of contemporary political life is that each of these seemingly contradictory trends is occurring simultaneously.

How does the information technology revolution fit into this complex pattern? Without a doubt, a true information revolution is taking place. The carrying capacity of the global communications network (computers, telephone, and television) has grown exponentially more powerful in the last two decades. According to Moore's Law (named for Gordon Moore, the cofounder of Intel), computing power per dollar doubles every eighteen months. A $2,000 laptop computer today is far more powerful than a $10 million mainframe computer was in the mid-1970s. Furthermore, in the 1970s, there were only about 50,000 computers in the world; today the number has skyrocketed to around 140 million. And whereas a transatlantic telephone cable could carry only 138 conversations simultaneously in 1960, a fiber-optic cable now can carry 1.5 million conversations at a time. The Internet (and World Wide Web) has an estimated 50 million users worldwide and the number continues to rise rapidly.

The most obvious political effect of the information revolution is to weaken individual governments' hold over citizens. Citizens worldwide now have access to independent sources of information. Everything from criticism of government, to pornography, to a criminal–terrorist "build your own nuclear bomb" Web page, can be accessed from any country, usually despite the efforts of government. The information revolution even threatens to undermine traditional cultures and civilizations that do not share Western values.

There are undoubtedly, important political consequences of the information revolution, some of which now can be only dimly perceived. For instance, it has been commonly assumed that technology enhances the ruthless grip of tyrannical rulers (recall George Orwell's description of "telescreens" and other technology used by totalitarian rulers in his classic novel *Nineteen Eighty-Four*). But the opposite may be more nearly true: The information revolution likely promotes worldwide freedom by making it more difficult for nondemocratic government to control their citizens. Furthermore, if technology helps promote free government, and if (as was shown in Chapter 16) democracies refrain from fighting wars with other democracies, could it be that an unintended consequence of the worldwide technology revolution will be the fostering of a more peaceful world?

Apocalyptic Visions: Culture Wars and Anarchy?

Even if the emerging international order can usher in a more peaceful era, it will not ensure peace. A cursory glance at human history is sufficient to remind us that conflict has existed throughout the ages. Thus, in today's post–Cold War era, observers question not whether future conflict will come about but whether (and how) it will differ from that of the past. Political scientist Samuel Huntington offers one of the most intriguing and disturbing visions of future conflict. He argues that the old clash of Cold War ideologies will be replaced by a "clash of civilizations":

[T]he fundamental source of conflict in this new world will not be primarily ideological or primarily economic. The great divisions among humankind and the dominating source of conflict will be cultural. Nation-states will remain the most powerful actors in world affairs, but the principal conflicts of global politics will occur between nations and groups of different civilizations. The clash of civilizations will dominate global politics. The fault lines between civilizations will be the battle lines of the future.[36]

Huntington defines a *civilization* as "the highest cultural grouping of people and the broadest level of cultural identity people have short of that which distinguishes humans from other species."[37] In addition, a civilization, large or small, and encompassing many nations or only one nation, is defined by two sets of characteristics. The first set includes objective factors, such as language, history, customs, institutions, and most importantly, religion.[38] Ideas compose the second important set of characteristics. Thus, while the ideas of individualism, liberalism, constitutionalism, human rights, equality, liberty, the rule of law, democracy, free markets, and the separation of church and state are significant aspects of Western culture, Huntington notes that they often "have little resonance in Islamic, Confucian, Japanese, Hindu, Buddhist, or Orthodox cultures."[39] Huntington suggests that future conflicts will increasingly be tied to strong cultural identification and people's willingness to fight and die in defense of traditions and values threatened by Americanization, Westernization, and globalization—which in the mind of many people in developing countries are indistinguishable from one another.

As noted earlier in the chapter, ethnic tension and conflict constitute a defining characteristic of the post–Cold War world. Huntington has examined the nature and geography of contemporary ethnic conflicts, including, for example, the tension between the Christianity-based civilization of Western Europe and the Islam-based civilization of the Arab Middle East and North Africa. Here, ethnic tensions have taken violent forms, including military interventions launched or led by Western nations (for example, the 1991 Persian Gulf War) and anti-Western acts of terrorism by radicals in Islamic Arab states (especially Iran, Iraq, Libya, Egypt, and Syria). Other clashes of cultures and civilizations exist in the Balkans (most notably, Bosnia), where Orthodox Christians and Muslims brutalize each other, as well as on the periphery of the old Russian (later Soviet) Empire. In Russia, Orthodox–Muslim conflicts in recent years have set Ossetians against Ingush and Armenians against Azeris in the Caucasus. Similarly, in Central Asia, Orthodox Russians live in tension with indigenous Muslim peoples, including Kazakhs, Uzbeks, Turks, Kyrghiz, and Afghans.

In Huntington's view, this clash of civilizations includes not only conflicts between regions of the world but also culturally rooted conflict in areas where two or more civilizations coexist. For instance, in Asia distinct Chinese and Japanese civilizations rival one another, as do Chinese and Tibetan (Buddhist), Chinese and Indian (Hindu), and Chinese and Muslim (Central and South Asia) societies. On the Indian subcontinent, a Hindu majority in India fights with its own large Muslim minority as well as with neighboring Pakistan.

In Europe, the cultural divide (or so-called Velvet Curtain) between Western nations—whose shared experiences include Roman Catholicism, the Renaissance, the Reformation, the Enlightenment, and the Industrial Revolution—and Eastern nations—which are mostly Slavic and Orthodox and remain largely untouched by the religious and intellectual developments of the West—has contributed to ongoing tensions long after the Iron Curtain disappeared. Finally, the Western Hemisphere is home to two distinct cultural heritages. North America (the United States and Canada) is predominantly anglophone and heavily influenced by British and north European culture, including Protestantism, whereas Mexico and Central and South America are predominantly Spanish-speaking and almost exclusively Roman Catholic and are rooted in a mix of Iberian culture and indigenous civilizations (for example, Incan, Mayan, and Aztec, among others).

Huntington stresses that the *kin-country syndrome*—whereby the peoples and leaders of various countries are culturally tied to one another—now manifests itself in international relations. In the 1991 Persian Gulf War, for example, both Arab elites and general populations outside of Iraq rallied against the West. Yet Arab support for another Arab-Islamic country, even one ruled by a ruthless dictator such as Saddam Hussein, is only one example of the kin-country phenomenon. Others include Turkish support of Azerbaijan (Muslim) against its longtime rival, Armenia (Orthodox); and the West's condemnation of Orthodox Serbs', but not Roman Catholic Croats', brutality against Bosnian Muslims. To many Muslim observers in the Arab world and southern Asia, the contrast between the West's forceful action against the Iraqi invasion of Kuwait (a former British protectorate) and its relatively weak response to Serbian aggression against Bosnian Muslims also suggests a kin-country bias.

Furthermore, Huntington identifies "torn countries," which contain populations embodying different civilizations and cultures, as prime candidates for disintegration. Actual and projected examples include the former Soviet Union, Yugoslavia, and Mexico. Conflict within torn countries can easily escalate into war involving states or groups from rival civilizations.

The most ominous element in Huntington's clash of civilizations theory is the possibility of global conflict between Western and non-Western civilizations (in Huntington's words, "the West against the rest"). Developing political ties between certain Arab states and China foreshadow a possible Islamic–Confucian alliance. Remarkably, the emergence of Osama bin Laden's al Qaeda movement under the banner of a virulently anti-Western, anti–Judeo-Christian, Islamist ideology supports Huntington's general thesis, even though he (Huntington) did not predict the precise form the first (but probably not the last) clash of civilizations in the new century would take. The fact that bin Laden formally declared a *jihad* against "Crusaders" (an obvious allusion to the medieval campaign European Christendom against Muslim "infidels") and made it "the duty of Muslims everywhere to kill Americans"[40] underscores the profound sense in which the American-led struggle against international terrorism is more than a confrontation between a rogue nonstate actor and the world's most powerful nation-state. Exactly *what* it means, however, is yet to be determined. Will the Arab states denounce not only bin Laden but terrorism in general? Will the United States find a way to accommodate Arab interests (and Palestinian aspirations) without scuttling its special relationship with Israel?

Huntington's thesis was widely discussed and highly controversial when it first appeared. Like most ideas in the fast-paced contemporary world, it soon faded into the void of yesterday's news and was forgotten—until September 11,

2001, that is. The shock and horror of that day and the images associated with it caused Americans to engage in collective soul-searching and to search for answers to the question: Why do they hate us so much? That search led back to recent books and articles about where the world is going in the new millennium. It led back to writings of scholars (especially Samuel Huntington and Chalmers Johnson), and a journalist named Robert Kaplan, who in 1994—the year after the *first* World Trade Center bombing—published a profoundly disturbing article entitled "The Coming Anarchy" in the *Atlantic Monthly* magazine.[41]

Kaplan argues that "The breaking apart and remaking of the atlas is only now beginning." The nation-state as we know it is obsolete and destined to be replaced not by larger regional groupings or a world-state (as some idealists foolishly predicted after World War II), in Kaplan's view, but by a formless force field of political whirlpools energized by huge and highly unstable urban concentrations—the teeming, chaotic, crime-infested cities (or "city-states") of the future. The picture Kaplan paints is bleak in the extreme:

> Imagine cartography in three dimensions, as if in hologram. In this hologram would be the overlapping sediments of group and other identities atop the merely two-dimensional color markings of city-states and the remaining nations, themselves confused in places by shadowy tentacles, hovering overhead, indicating the power of drug cartels, mafias, and private security agencies. Instead of borders, there would be moving "centers" of power, as in the Middle Ages. Many of these layers would be in motion. Replacing fixed and abrupt lines on a flat space would be a shifting pattern of buffer entities, like the Kurdish and Azeri buffer entities between Turkey and Iran, the Turkic Uighur buffer entity between Central Asia and Inner China (itself distinct from coastal China), and the Latino buffer entity replacing a precise U.S.-Mexican border. To this protean cartographic hologram one must add other factors, such as migrations of populations, explosions of birth rates, vectors of disease. Henceforward the map of the world will never be static. This future map—in a sense, the Last Map—will be an ever-mutating representation of chaos.[42]

West Africa presents a glimpse of this grim future in which borders virtually disappear, society becomes a boiling cauldron of ethnic conflict, police and political authority fade out of the picture, criminals, thugs, and corrupt officials (most likely in close collusion) take control of commerce, violence is random and rampant (perpetrated in large part by predatory gangs of armed youths scanning the landscape for anyone who might be a source of drug money), and disease stalks the countryside like a killer of last resort determined to hunt down the survivors (see "Anarchy in Africa" on the following page).

Whether future conflicts will occur as a consequence of disintegrating nation-state structures or become a global clash of civilizations is uncertain. However, there is little doubt that war clouds will continue to darken the playing field of politics on all levels—local, regional, and international. Nor is there any doubt that local conflicts will threaten the existence of some nations and the stability of many governments or that instability will spill over into neighboring countries. Success in containing conflict and minimizing war will depend in part on the effectiveness of the international institutions created after World War II for those purposes. These institutions, including, especially, the United Nations, are our focus in the final chapter of the book.

Anarchy in Africa

Tyranny is nothing new in Sierra Leone or in the rest of West Africa. But it is now part and parcel of an increasing lawlessness that is far more significant than any coup, rebel incursion, or episodic experiment in democracy. Crime was what my friend—a top-ranking African official whose life would be threatened were I to identify him more precisely—really wanted to talk about. Crime is what makes West Africa a natural point of departure for my report on what the political character of our planet is likely to be in the twenty-first century. The cities of West Africa at night are some of the unsafest places in the world. Streets are unlit; the police often lack gasoline for their vehicles; armed burglars, carjackers, and muggers proliferate. "The government in Sierra Leone has no writ after dark," says a foreign resident, shrugging. When I was in the capital, Freetown, last September, eight men armed with AK-47s broke into the house of an American man. They tied him up and stole everything of value. Forget Miami: direct flights between the United States and the Murtala Muhammed Airport, in neighboring Nigeria's largest city, Lagos, have been suspended by order of the U.S. Secretary of Transportation because of ineffective security at the terminal and its environs. A State Department report cited the airport for "extortion by law-enforcement and immigration officials." This is one of the few times that the U.S. government has embargoed a foreign airport for reasons that are linked purely to crime. In Abidjan, effectively the capital of the Cote d'Ivoire, or Ivory Coast, restaurants have stick- and gun-wielding guards who walk you the fifteen feet or so between your car and the entrance, giving you an eerie taste of what American cities might be like in the future. An Italian ambassador was killed by gunfire when robbers invaded an Abidjan restaurant. The family of the Nigerian ambassador was tied up and robbed at gunpoint in the ambassador's residence. After university students in the Ivory Coast caught bandits who had been plaguing their dorms, they executed them by hanging tires around their necks and setting the tires on fire. In one instance Ivorian policemen stood by and watched the "necklacings," afraid to intervene. Each time I went to the Abidjan bus terminal, groups of young men with restless scanning eyes surrounded my taxi, putting their hands all over the windows, demanding "tips" for carrying my luggage even though I had only a rucksack. In cities in six West African countries I saw similar young men everywhere—hordes of them. They were like loose molecules in a very unstable social fluid, a fluid that was clearly on the verge of igniting. "You see," my friend the Minister told me, "in the villages of Africa it is perfectly natural to feed at any table and lodge in any hut. But in the cities this communal existence no longer holds. You must pay for lodging and be invited for food. When young men find out that their relations cannot put them up they become lost. They join other immigrants and slip gradually into the criminal process."

"In the poor quarters of Arab North Africa," he continued, "there is much less crime, because Islam provides a social anchor: of education and indoctrination. Here in West Africa we have a lot of superficial Islam and superficial Christianity. Western religion is undermined by animist beliefs not suitable to a moral society, because they are based on irrational spirit power. Here spirits are used to wreak vengeance by one person against another, or one group against another." Many of the atrocities in the Liberian civil war have been tied to belief in *juju* spirits, and the BBC has reported, in its magazine *Focus on Africa*, that in the civil fighting in adjacent Sierra Leone, rebels were said to have "a young woman with them who would go to the front naked, always walking backwards and looking in the mirror to see where she was going. This made her invisible so that she could cross to the army's positions and there bury charms . . . to improve the rebels' chances of success."

Excerpted from Robert D. Kaplan, *The Coming Anarchy*. New York: Vintage Books, 2001, 4–6.

Summary

The workings of international politics differ significantly from those of national or domestic politics due to the absence of an overriding sovereign government. The fate of the Melians illustrates the preeminent role of military might in the international arena. The struggle for power is inherent in the nature of the international system. Every sovereign state strives to advance the national interests in competition with every other sovereign entity or challenger of the status quo. The concept of the national interest is ambiguous, however; it encompasses anything that a nation's leaders perceive as promoting the long-term security and prosperity of the state.

Students of international politics need to distinguish between foreign policy ends and means. Nations choose a variety of ends, but these are almost always overshadowed by one ultimate aim—the nation's pursuit of power. Some nations are satisfied with existing power relationships, seeking merely to maintain the status quo; others are dissatisfied and challenge the status quo. All states who seek to compete on the international scene are constantly engaged in behavior designed to enhance national power. A few nations, however, avoid choosing between power maintenance and power enhancement; they tend to reject power politics altogether.

The Monroe Doctrine was designed to perpetuate the regional status quo in the Western Hemisphere, and the containment of the perceived Soviet threat was a global status quo strategy adopted by the United States after World War II. In the post Cold War era, some political scientists employ political realism theory in arguing that the United States should pursue an isolationist foreign policy. Others suggest that key structural features of the international political system provide an important vehicle for understanding contemporary international relations and for determining U.S. foreign policy. Although in the past political realism has provided an understanding of international relations, today it is criticized for its rejection of moral principles and its focus on national interests despite pressing global problems.

The traditional balance-of-power system that formally came into being in Europe in 1648 was limited in size and scope. One advantage of the Eurocentric system was that all members shared certain common values and beliefs. Also, Great Britain acted as the keeper of the balance. The European system worked because means and ends were limited, alliances were flexible, and there was a singular absence of crusading zeal. Changes in these conditions during the nineteenth century presaged the collapse of the balance-of-power system.

After World War II, a bipolar system emerged in place of the old multipolar European system. Broader in geographic scope than its predecessor, this bipolar system featured a bitter rivalry between two superpowers, the United States and the Soviet Union. Deep ideological differences and the overriding danger of a nuclear holocaust characterized their rivalry. By the late 1960s, a strategic stalemate based on mutual deterrence made war between these two titans equally irrational for both.

With the disintegration of the Soviet Union and the end of the Cold War, a new international order is emerging. Significantly, this is not a balance-of-power system but is marked by contradictory tendencies. Moreover, there is reason to believe that it will be a temporary and transitional system.

The emerging international order is unipolar, headed by the United States. Cooperation and competition over economic issues increasingly dominate it. Furthermore, economic power is becoming concentrated in three regions centered in Western Europe, the United States, and Japan. Rising ethnic conflict throughout the world is a source of concern and a divisive force in the nations where it exists. Global environmental issues are increasingly receiving attention as a result of better international cooperation. However, the proliferation of dangerous weapons systems among developing nations continues to threaten world stability. Finally, although the source of future conflict is uncertain, one authority argues that it may arise from cultural differences and perhaps become a clash of civilizations.

Key Terms

political realism	expansionist strategy
equilibrium	neutrality
balance-of-power system	nonalignment
keeper of the balance	Monroe Doctrine
bipolar system	containment
Marshall Plan	Truman Doctrine
North Atlantic Treaty	neo-isolationists
Organization (NATO)	idealism
Warsaw Pact	globalization
triad	International Monetary Fund (IMF)
national interest	kin-country syndrome
status quo strategy	

Review Questions

1. What does Thucydides' account of the confrontation between the Melians and the Athenians reveal about the nature of international politics?

2. What does a Machiavellian approach to politics entail? What sort of worldview does this approach embrace?

3. What is the meaning of the term *national interest*? How do political realists use this term?

4. What two basic foreign policy strategies are available to sovereign states?

5. What is meant by a balance of power? How did the traditional European balance-of-power system work? What were its chief characteristics? Why did it function more or less successfully for some 260 years?

6. What brought about the decline and fall of the classical European balance-of-power system?

7. How did the post–World War II international system differ from its predecessors?

8. Is there a present-day balance of power?

9. What constitutes today's greatest threat to world peace?

Recommended Reading

BRZEZINSKI, ZBIGNIEW. *Global Turmoil on the Eve of the Twenty-First Century.* New York: Simon & Schuster, 1993. A penetrating examination of the influences and factors affecting nations and peoples in the contemporary international system.

CARR, EDWARD HALLETT. *The Twenty Years' Crisis, 1919–1939.* New York: Harper & Row, 1981. An excellent discussion of the relationship between power and morality in international politics, written in 1939. The author shows how the principles of international politics would have contributed to the tragedy of World War II.

DOUGHERTY, JAMES E., and ROBERT L. PFALTZGRAFF, JR. *Contending Theories of International Relations: A Comprehensive Study.* 4th ed. Reading, Mass.: Addison-Wesley, 1997. An intelligent and comprehensive explanation of all aspects of the discipline.

HARTMANN, FREDERICK H. *The Relations of Nations.* 6th ed. Englewood Cliffs, N.J.: Prentice-Hall, 1983. A basic textbook with insightful discussions of key concepts. Comprehensive in coverage.

HUNTINGTON, SAMUEL P. *The Clash of Civilizations and the Remaking of World Order.* New York: Simon & Schuster, 1996. An elaboration of the author's provocative thesis concerning the shape of future conflict, which first appeared in the journal, *Foreign Affairs,* summer 1993.

JOHNSON, CHALMERS. *Blowback: The Costs and Consequences of American Empire.* New York, Holt (Owl), 2000. A best-seller by widely acclaimed Asian expert who is highly critical of the interventionist impulse that has driven American foreign policy since World War II.

KENNAN, GEORGE F. *American Diplomacy, 1900–1950.* Chicago: University of Chicago Press, 1985. An elegantly written interpretive history of American foreign policy during the first half of the twentieth century.

KAPLAN, ROBERT D. *The Coming Anarchy: Shattering the Dreams of the Post Cold War.* New York, Vintage, 2000. A best-selling collection of articles by one of America's most incisive and pessimistic writers.

KEGLEY, CHARLES W., JR., and EUGENE R. WITTKOPF. *World Politics: Trend and Transformation.* 8th ed. New York: Bedford/St. Martin's, 2001. An introductory textbook that emphasizes interdependence in a changing global system.

KOTKIN, JOEL. *Tribes: How Race, Religion, and Identity Determine Success in the New Global Economy.* New York: Random House, 1994. The unhappy economic and political fallout of clashing multicultural peoples is detailed in this work.

MACHIAVELLI, NICCOLÒ. *The Prince.* New Haven: Yale University Press, 1997. This book has been required reading for students and practitioners of diplomacy for several centuries.

MCCLELLAND, CHARLES A. *Theory and the International System.* New York: Macmillan, 1966. A theoretical examination of the applicability of systems analysis and behavioral methods to political science.

MORGENTHAU, HANS J. *Politics among Nations: The Struggle for Power and Peace.* New York: McGraw-Hill, 1992. A classic English-language international politics text written by a leading theorist of political realism.

MOYNIHAN, DANIEL PATRICK. *Pandemonium: Ethnicity in International Politics.* New York: Oxford University Press, 1993. A sobering look at the new world order torn apart by ethnic conflict.

ROSECRANCE, RICHARD N. *Action and Reaction in World Politics: International Systems in Perspective.* Westport, Conn.: Greenwood Press, 1977. An imaginative attempt to put the history of Western international politics into a systems perspective.

RUBINSTEIN, ALVIN Z., ed. *America's National Interest in a Post–Cold War World.* New York: McGraw-Hill, 1993. A collection of readings that examine the U.S. role in the contemporary international political system.

SINGER, MAX, and AARON WILDAVSKY. *The Real World Order: Zones of Peace/Zones of Turmoil.* Chatham, N.J.: Chatham House, 1996. A provocative interpretation of international relations in the contemporary world.

SPANIER, JOHN. *Games Nations Play.* 9th ed. Washington, D.C.: C.Q. Press, 1995. A well-written and popular text that has withstood the test of time.

THOMPSON, KENNETH. *Morality and Foreign Policy.* Baton Rouge: Louisiana State University Press, 1980. An illuminating discussion of the relationship among political power, moral considerations, and the national interest in formulating and carrying out foreign policy.

VIOTTI, PAUL, and MARK KAUPPI. *International Relations Theory: Realism, Pluralism, Globalism.* 2nd ed. Englewood Cliffs, N.J.: Prentice-Hall, 1992. A useful, advanced text that includes readings and valuable bibliographical information.

WALTZ, KENNETH N. *Theory of International Politics.* New York: McGraw-Hill, 1979. This influential book set forth a theory of international relations emphasizing power relationships among states that became known as neorealism.

WOLFERS, ARNOLD. *Discord and Collaboration: Essays on International Politics.* Baltimore: Johns Hopkins University Press, 1965. A superb compilation of scholarly essays dealing with key concepts and issues in international relations.

ZEIGLER, DAVID W. *War, Peace, and International Politics.* 7th ed. Reading, Mass.: Addison-Wesley, 1997. A good basic text focusing on war as the age-old problem of international politics.

Notes

1. The quotations in this discussion are from Thucydides, "The Melian Conference," in *Readings in World Politics,* 2nd ed., ed. Robert Goldwin and Tony Pearce (New York: Oxford University Press, 1970), 472–478.

2. Niccolò Machiavelli, *The Prince,* in *The Prince and the Discourses* (New York: Modern Library, 1952), 56.

3. Ibid., 64.

4. Hans J. Morgenthau, *Politics among Nations: The Struggle for Power and Peace,* 5th ed. (New York: McGraw-Hill, 1992), 11.

5. Ibid., 22–23.

6. Ibid., 11.

7. Ibid.

8. Ibid., 221–223.

9. Ibid., 27.

10. Quoted in Alexander de Conde, *A History of American Foreign Policy: Growth to World Power,* vol. 1, 3rd ed. (New York: Scribner's, 1978), 130.

11.   Alexis de Tocqueville, *Democracy in America*, vol. 1 (New York: Schocken Books, 1961), 522.

12.   George F. Kennan, "Sources of Soviet Conduct," in *Caging the Bear: Containment and the Cold War*, ed. Charles Gati (Indianapolis: Bobbs-Merrill, 1974), 18.

13.   *Congressional Record*, 80 Cong., 1st sess. (March 1947), 1981.

14.   See Chalmers Johnson, *Blowback: The Costs and Consequences of American Empire* (New York: Holt, 2000.)

15.   Ibid., 8.

16.   Ibid.

17.   Ibid., 9.

18.   Ibid.

19.   Ibid., 11.

20.   See, for example, Alan Tonelson, "What Is the National Interest?" in *America's National Interest in a Post–Cold War World*, ed. Alvin Z. Rubinstein (New York: McGraw-Hill, 1994), 56. Also see Barbara Conry, *U.S. "Global Leadership": A Euphemism for World Policeman, Policy Analysis* No. 267 (CATO Institute, February 8, 1997).

21.   Max Singer and Aaron Wildavsky, *The Real World Order: Zones of Peace/Zones of Turmoil* (Chatham, N.J.: Chatham House, 1996), 5–6.

22.   Ibid., 199.

23.   Ibid., 5.

24.   Martin Gilbert, *The Roots of Appeasement* (New York: New American Library, 1966), xi.

25.   Although a few commentators suggested that President Clinton's policy helped to solidify political alliances with key African American leaders in Congress, this was not likely his main purpose. An interesting example of altruism took place in 1920–21, when a terrible famine occurred in the Soviet Union. Despite the Soviet government's avowed support of anticapitalist revolutions in the West, a relief organization (known as the Hoover Commission) was created by the U.S. government. Millions of dollars in food supplies were sent, and many lives were saved in the severely stricken Volga region. At the time, an official Soviet journal observed that "of all the capitalist countries, only America showed us major and real help." Quoted in Adam Ulam, *Expansion and Coexistence: Soviet Foreign Policy, 1917–1973*, 2nd ed. (New York: Praeger, 1974), 148. Also see John Lewis Gaddis, *Russia, the Soviet Union, and the United States: An Interpretive History* (New York: Wiley, 1978), 99–101.

26.   Quoted in Marvin Jones, *The Fifteen Weeks* (New York: Harbinger, 1955), 256.

27.   Raul Hilberg, *The Destruction of the European Jews* (New York: Harper & Row, 1961), 358–359.

28.   Arnold Wolfers, *Discord and Collaboration: Essays on International Politics* (Baltimore: Johns Hopkins University Press, 1965), 93.

29.   The argument that the realism-idealism distinction is better understood as the difference between principle and prudence is Nathan Tarcov's; see his "Principle and Prudence in Foreign Policy: The Founders' Perspective," *The Public Interest* 76 (Summer 1984): 45–60.

30.   Jessica Tuchman Mathews, "The Environment and International Security," in *World Security: Challenges for a New Century*, 2nd ed., ed. Michael Klare and Daniel Thomas (New York: St. Martin's Press, 1994), 286.

31.   Particularly helpful is Charles Krauthammer, "The Lonely Superpower," *New Republic*, July 29, 1991, 23–27. Our discussion follows Krauthammer in several important respects.

32.   Joan Edelman Spero, *The Politics of International Economic Relations*, 4th ed. (New York: St. Martin's Press, 1990), 229.

33. Donald Horowitz, "Ethnic and National Conflict," in *World Security Challenges for a New Century*, ed. Klare and Thomas, 175.

34. Ibid., 176.

35. Charles Kegley, Jr., and Eugene Wittkopf, *World Politics: Trend and Transformation*, 6th ed. (New York: St. Martin's Press, 1997), 395–396.

36. Samuel Huntington, "The Clash of Civilizations?" *Foreign Affairs* 72 (Summer 1993): 22–43; and Samuel Huntington, "If Not Civilizations, What? Paradigms of the Post-Cold War Era," *Foreign Affairs* 72 (December 1993): 24–39; Huntington has since published his view on this subject in a book entitled *The Clash of Civilizations and the Remaking of World Order* (New York: Simon & Schuster, 1996).

37. Huntington, "Clash of Civilizations," 24.

38. Ibid., 25, 26.

39. Ibid., 40.

40. Judith Miller, "A Child of Privilege Who Champions Terror," *New York Times*, September 14, 2001, online edition.

41. Robert D. Kaplan, *The Coming Anarchy* (New York: Vintage Books, 2001). This best-selling book is actually a collection of previously published articles.

42. Ibid., 50–51.

© Jason Szenes / Corbis Sygma

Chapter 18

INTERNATIONAL ORGANIZATION(S)

THE STRUGGLE FOR ORDER

Nonstate Actors on the World Stage
Multinational Corporations • INGOs and IGOs

The United Nations
Historical Background: The League of Nations • The Founding of the United Nations • The United Nations during the Cold War • The United Nations after the Cold War • Problems Underlying Comprehensive International Organizations

International Law
Usefulness • Compliance and Enforcement • International Law in the Modern Era • The Limitations of International Law • International Law Evaluated

The Continuing Quest for Peace

IF YOU WANT peace, prepare for war. This dictum has been the mantra of political realists since time immemorial. Indeed, history points to the conclusion that conflict is a part of the human condition and war can, at best, be prevented or deterred by a policy of vigilance and military readiness. But this view has always had its challengers. In a world where

> the price of gasoline at American service stations is now determined by people meeting in foreign capitals . . . the availability of color televisions to the American consumer is governed not simply by internal market forces but also by agreements between Washington, on the one hand, and Tokyo, Taipei, and Seoul, on the other . . . decisions reached in the Kremlin influence the level at which Americans are taxed and how the revenues generated will be spent . . . supplies determine welfare everywhere—indeed, where everything appears to be connected to everything else—[in this kind of world] new ways of thinking and new conceptual modes are needed.[1]

Today, national economies are increasingly submerged in the world economy, a possibility which certain visionaries foresaw and welcomed long before it had become a reality. These so-called *functionalists* argued that effective international organizations would promote worldwide cooperation and that cooperation would in turn create shared economic interests, promote international understanding, and decrease world tensions and hostilities. This school of thought—called *functionalism*—attracted considerable interest in the academic community after World War II. Its proponents believed that the practical advantages of peace, commerce, and cooperation transcending borders would eventually lead to the abandonment of narrow, national self-interest.

Yesterday's functionalism is today's *interdependence*—the new buzzword for the intricate web of close ties among nations that some say is transforming the very foundations of the international order. In particular, the steady growth and development of the world economy has given rise to supranational structures to ensure proper regulation and to remove artificial impediments (such as tariffs and trade quotas).

Growing regional trade ties and movement toward regional economic integration are evident in the decision of the European Union to create a unified economy in 1992. The emergence of supranational structures such as the Central American Common Market in the Caribbean, Mercosur in the southern cone of South America, the Asian Pacific Economic Cooperation Forum, and the South Asian Association for Regional Cooperation (SAARC) reflects a keen interest in regional integration outside of Europe as well. Increased cooperation and the substitution of economic competition for military conflict among nations will, in this view, be the final result. Eventually, rational self-interest will prompt all nations to recognize that unimpeded trade and investment across oceans, borders, and other frontiers is a boon to all nations.

But has the rise of such economic pacts aimed primarily at promoting prosperity also advanced the cause of world peace? And has the creation of global and regional organizations, including several universal international organizations (such as the United Nations), or the implementation and application of international law, truly promoted such cooperation? To answer these questions, we must first examine the various types of supranational structures in the world today.

NONSTATE ACTORS ON THE WORLD STAGE

International cooperation has been aided by entities other than nation-states. These entities are known generically as *nonstate actors*. Multinational corporations, nongovernmental organizations (NGOs), and international nongovernmental organizations are three major types of legitimate nonstate actors that have played important roles in world politics.

Multinational Corporations

Businesses "with foreign subsidiaries which extend the production and marketing of the firm beyond the boundaries of any one country" are commonly known as *multinational corporations (MNCs).* Indeed, "The contemporary multinational corporation is best viewed as a global network of subsidiaries."[2] General Motors, Microsoft, Exxon, Coca-Cola, McDonald's, and Intel are examples of powerful U.S.-based MNCs. The rise of the multinational corporation since the end of World War II—encompassing both businesses based in the United States and those in other nations as well—has been astounding. By the mid-1990s, it was estimated that MNCs employed 73 million people, representing nearly 10 percent of the world's paid nonfarm jobs and close to 20 percent of individuals employed in industrialized countries. MNCs directly or indirectly employed at least 150 million people and accounted for 20 percent of all paid, nonfarm jobs.[3] In addition, the world's 350 largest MNCs accounted for almost 40 percent of merchandise trade in the 1990s, while the sales of a number of the largest and wealthiest MNCs today exceed the gross domestic product of many nations.[4] Worldwide, MNCs aggregate sales amount to many trillions of dollars every year.[5] No wonder some see the new world order as fundamentally different from its predecessor:

> These are not the times for narrow balance-of-power considerations. As even an unchallenged superpower like the United States has seen, efforts to block the flow of trade and investment to nations such as Iran and Cuba are not just increasingly ineffective, but costly. Multinational corporations—once made vulnerable to the expropriation of property or blockage of funds, and forbidden to trade with hostile countries and to buy and sell freely the latest high technology and scarce commodities—are now more likely to guide foreign policy than follow it.[6]

A combination of improved technology and changing economic circumstances has contributed to the rapid growth of MNCs. Modern computers and communications and transportation technology have created the possibility for corporate expansion, integration, and personal mobility. The growth of the global economy has also aided this process (since 1950, world trade has increased more than tenfold), which has snowballed as increasing numbers of corporations have expanded overseas to obtain comparative advantages in terms of markets or lowered labor costs.[7]

The major banks of North America, Western Europe, and (until recently) Japan have been a collective source of funds for the worldwide expansion of MNCs. These giant banks are themselves multinational, maintaining branches and offices throughout the world, with trillions of dollars of assets. Over half of the largest multinational banks were Japanese in the early 1990s (prior to the downturn of the Japanese economy and the near collapse of Japan's financial system); most of the others were (are) located in the United States and Western Europe. Along with the World Bank and the International Monetary Fund, both specialized agencies of the United Nations, multinational banks play a crucial role in encouraging investment and economic development.

Commercial banks also have attempted to stabilize the world's financial system during unsettled times. In the winter of 1973–74, when the price of oil increased fourfold, and again in 1979–80, when oil prices more than doubled, great disparities in national wealth were created overnight, especially among developing countries. In these turbulent times, the international banking system provided stability by lending money invested by oil-rich nations to countries that were short on cash or could not afford to import necessary foodstuffs because of the high cost of oil.

Multinational corporations are here to stay. Some economists applaud them, arguing that they enhance worldwide competition, improve economic efficiency, and promote technology. Yet the rise of the multinational corporation has generated alarm in many quarters. Critics contend that MNCs too often pursue profits without regard to the damage they do to host countries in the process and that they have engaged in illicit interference in the internal affairs of host countries (for example, in Chile in the early 1970s). And, in this view, because they operate outside the legal control of any one national government, they represent a serious challenge to the sovereignty and independence of the traditional territorial state and to the integrity of the international system.

> Whatever the validity of these specific criticisms, there is little doubt that MNCs are collectively and individually a potent force in contemporary world politics. In the words of one well-known political scientist: Multinational firms that coordinate production on a global scale and distribute their output throughout the world are one of the most striking recent manifestations of global interdependence. As such they put into question the value of models of world politics that proceed from the assumptions of national self-sufficiency and of the exceptional character of cross-boundary relationships. . . . According to one view, they are the international counterpart of the nineteenth-century industrial revolution; according to another, they may be the skeleton of the world economy of the future.[8]

INGOs and IGOs

There are two basic types of international organizations. Organizations made up of private individuals and groups affiliate are called *international nongovernmental organizations (INGOs)* whereas international organizations in which the membership consists of governments are known as *international governmental organizations (IGOs)*. Both INGOs and IGOs comprise a rich variety of associations (see Tables 18-1 and 18-2). In this chapter, we focus on IGOs because they more directly influence world politics and the quest for international peace.

TABLE 18–1

Some Representative International Nongovernmental Organizations (INGOs)

Afro-Asian Peoples' Solidarity Organization	International Federation of Air Line Pilots Associations
Amnesty International	International Handball Federation
Arab Lawyers Union	International Olympic Committee
European Broadcasting Union	International Political Science Association
European Federation of the Plywood Industry	International Union Against the Venereal Diseases and the Treponematoses
Federation of Asian Women's Associations	
International Air Transport Association	International Union of Local Authorities
International Alliance of Women	Latin American Shipowners Association
International Chamber of Commerce	Nordic Association of Advertising Agencies
International Committee of the Red Cross	Rotary International
International Confederation of Accordionists	Salvation Army
International Confederation of Arab Trade Unions	Save the Children
International Confederation of Free Trade Unions	World Council of Churches
International Council Against Bullfighting	World Federation of Jewish Journalists
International Council of Scientific Unions	World Federation of Master Tailors
International Criminal Police Organization	World Federation of United Nations Associations

SOURCE: *Yearbook of International Organizations 2001*, 38th ed. vol. 3. Munich: K. G. Saur Verlag, 2001–2002. Reprinted with permission.

The first noteworthy IGO in the modern era was the Holy Alliance, formed in 1815 by Russia, Austria, and Prussia to suppress the revolutionary democratic movement in Europe. But IGOs truly came into prominence between the two world wars (1919–39). At that time there was a proliferation of international organizations associated with the newly formed League of Nations, which was the first truly universal (worldwide) IGO in history. By 1940, more than 80 IGOs and nearly 500 INGOs were in existence; following World War II, the number of both organizations increased substantially (see Figure 18-1).

Typically, IGOs have restricted membership based on territorial functional considerations and exist to advance a single goal.[9] But there are exceptions. For instance, the World Health Organization, while serving the single purpose of fighting illness, is open to universal membership. On the other hand, the Organization of African Unity restricts its membership regionally, but promotes a variety of cooperative goals that cut across economic, political, and social lines. The United Nations (UN) is the world's preeminent international organization, for reasons that are explained later in this chapter.

The vast array of supranational, transnational, and international structures in the world today has created what one writer calls "networks of interdependence."[10] We examine two particularly important types of IGOs, economic pacts (specifically the European Union) and military alliances (specifically the North

TABLE 18–2

Some Representative International Governmental Organizations (IGOs)

African Development Bank	International Labor Organization
African Groundnut Council	International Olive Oil Council
Arab Postal Union	International Red Locust Control Organization for Central and Southern Africa
Asian Development Bank	
Asian Pacific Economic Council	International Telecommunications Satellite Organization
Association of Southeast Asian Nations	International Whaling Commission
Central American Common Market	Latin American Free Trade Association
Conference on Security and Cooperation in Europe	North Atlantic Treaty Organization
Council for Mutual Economic Assistance	Organization of African Unity
European Economic Community	Organization of American States
European Space Agency	Organization of Petroleum Exporting Countries
Food and Agriculture Organization	Union of Banana Exporting Countries
Gulf Cooperation Council	UN Educational, Scientific, and Cultural Organization
Inter-American Tropical Tuna Commission	
International Bank for Reconstruction and Development (World Bank)	United Nations
	Universal Postal Union
International Civil Aviation Organization	World Health Organization
International Coffee Organization	

SOURCE: *Yearbook of International Organizations 2001*, 38th ed. vol. 3. Munich: K. G. Saur Verlag, 2001–2002. Reprinted with permission.

Atlantic Treaty Organization, which is currently undergoing a process of change induced by the end of the Cold War).

Economic Pacts   Trade treaties account for many of the most significant international agreements of the post–World War II period. The great majority of such compacts were bilateral (involving only two countries). There are at least five distinct forms of multilateral economic pacts, including:

- *Preferential trade arrangements.* In these pacts, several states agree to grant each other exclusive trade preferences, including tariff reductions. One prominent example: the **British Commonwealth,** made up of Great Britain and many of its former colonies.

- *Nondiscriminatory trade organizations.* These pacts are forged in order to promote closer trade relations on a global or regional scale. The **World Trade Organization (WTO)**—formerly the General Agreement on Trade and Tariffs (GATT)—is the most important contemporary example; another is the European Free Trade Association (EFTA), whose size and influence has dwindled with the emergence of the European Union (see the box on page 552).

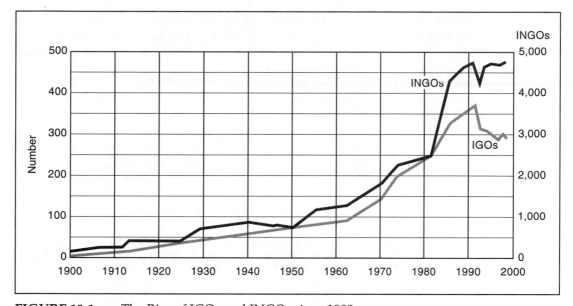

FIGURE 18-1   The Rise of IGOs and INGOs since 1900
SOURCE: Adapted from Kegley and Wittkopf, *World Politics: Trend and Transformation,* 6th ed., New York: St. Martin's Press, 1997, p, 146.

- *Free trade areas.* These arrangements go beyond preferential systems by completely eliminating trade barriers among members. Member governments surrender their sovereign right to determine trade policy with other member states while retaining total freedom to set their own national trade policies with nonmember states. A well-known example is the *North American Free Trade Agreement (NAFTA),* successfully negotiated among the United States, Canada, and Mexico in 1993 and scheduled to expand to Central and South America in future years.

- *Customs unions.* One step above free-trade areas on the ladder of economic integration, these economic pacts are based on free trade among the members and a common external tariff for all trade with nonmembers. One example is the Mercosur trade agreement, comprising four full members (Argentina, Paraguay, Brazil, and Uruguay) and two associated members (Chile and Bolivia), encourages free trade among its members while imposing a common external tariff of 14 percent on capital goods.

- *Economic unions.* These agreements establish a significant level of economic integration among nations and a partial surrender of sovereignty as well. The most impressive example of this type of supranational organization is the evolving *European Union (EU).* The EU is described more completely in the box on page 552).

Military Alliances   Although rarely described as IGOs, military alliances are, in fact, the first major form of intergovernmental organization to grow out of the modern state system. Since the emergence of this system of the seventeenth century, such alliances have been a prominent feature of international politics. The purpose of military alliances is simply to deter or fight enemies, both potential and immediate. Not surprisingly, alliances beget alliances. Thus, military alliances have often been part of arms races, which usually preceded major wars. This observation led a number of political scientists and world leaders to conclude that alliances were a form of international organizations which, paradoxically, were at odds with world peace and order. President Woodrow Wilson, for example, believed that military alliances were one of the main causes of World War I; as we will see, he tried to forge a new international organization based on the principle of "open covenants, openly arrived at" (the League of Nations). Such an organization, he believed, would erase the need for military alliances (which for

The Europe Union: History in the Making

The EU was previously known as the European Community (or Common Market). Its origins can be traced to 1952, when Belgium, France, West Germany, Italy, Luxembourg, and the Netherlands founded the European Coal and Steel Community (ECSC). In 1957, these six countries signed the two Treaties of Rome, which laid the legal foundations for creation of the European Economic Community (EEC) and the European Atomic Energy Community (Euratom) the following year. The institutions of the ECSC, EEC, and Euratom were merged into a single entity in 1967. Subsequently, nine additional member states have been admitted: Denmark, Ireland, and the United Kingdom in 1973; Greece in 1981; Portugal and Spain in 1986, and Austria, Finland, and Sweden in 1995. The list of countries being considered for admission at present features many former communist states in eastern Europe, including Bulgaria, the Czech Republic, Estonia, Hungary, Latvia, Lithuania, Poland, Slovakia, and Slovenia.

The Single European Act of 1987 provided for the creation of a *Single European Market* and codified agreement on majority voting in the Council (a political decision-making body consisting of the foreign ministers of the member states). The Single European Market provides the conceptual framework for the EU's present movement toward a total unification of all the national economies, including the establishment of a European Monetary Union (EMU)—the euro since

1999. These measures were already contemplated by the Maastricht Treaty, which transformed the EEC into the European Union.

Today, the EU provides for the free flow of goods and services, labor and capital, technology, and tourists within its vastly expanded borders. In addition, it sets common external tariffs and adjusts taxes and subsidies that affect trade within the community. Among its other avowed aims are establishing common foreign as well as fiscal and monetary policies among member states and promoting greater economic specialization and internal cooperative ventures.

Furthermore, it is noteworthy that the European Union has created political institutions that fulfill many of the functions of a supranational government. These institutions include the Council of Ministers, the Commission, the European Parliament, and the Court of Justice. The Council of Ministers and the Commission function as a dual executive, with the former directly representing the views of the member governments and the latter speaking for the interests of the EU as a whole. Important decisions must have the unanimous approval of the Council. The European Parliament is a deliberative body that advises and oversees but does not legislate. Since 1979, its members have been elected by a direct universal suffrage. The Court of Justice interprets and applies EU treaties and adjudicates disputes between member states and the EU bodies.

many centuries had been arranged behind the scenes and at times were maintained in secret).

But alliances did not disappear. After World War II, the United States sought to counter the perceived Soviet threat to Western Europe by creating the North Atlantic Treaty Organization (NATO). For the United States, it was the first peacetime military pact since George Washington, in his famous "Farewell Address," warned a young American nation against involvement in "entangling alliances." The Soviet Union countered by creating the Warsaw Treaty Organization (also known as the Warsaw Pact) in 1955.

The Warsaw Pact was disbanded when the communist regimes in Eastern Europe toppled in 1989 (only two years before the Soviet Union disintegrated). Thus, NATO had fulfilled its original mission. But rather than disband, something remarkable happened: It redefined its reason for being. Led by the United States, NATO became a new kind of alliance. No longer focused on defeating an enemy, NATO now sought to play a new role as peacekeeper in Europe. The first test of NATO's newly defined mission was an effort to limit the diameter and duration of the conflict in Bosnia by sending troops and conducting air strikes. NATO is again in the process of expanding. Ten of the original twelve members of NATO were located in Western Europe (and the United States and Canada were the other two members). By 1997, there were sixteen members; three former Warsaw Pact countries—Poland, Hungary, and the Czech Republic—joined as full members in 1999 to bring the total to 19. In 2002, NATO and Russia negotiated a potentially historic partnership agreement as well. NATO's expansion has been bolstered by two perceptions: that NATO's reason for being has changed from military to political, and that excluding eastern European countries from membership perpetuated the old East-West division of the continent long after the Cold War ended.

NATO's new role as Europe's "sheriff" is controversial. Some of NATO's critics even question whether its continued existence is justified now that the Cold War is over. Additionally, Russian nationalists have warned that admission of Moscow's former allies in Eastern Europe comprised an aggressive policy aimed at isolating the Russian Federation from Europe, and redividing Europe to Russia's disadvantage. Extreme Russian nationalists were especially strident on this issue. In the United States, critics of NATO's expansion contended that it would unnecessarily draw a new line of division in Europe (leaving important countries such as Estonia, Latvia, Lithuania, and the Ukraine on the other side and that it would poison relations between the United States and Russia, threatening European stability in the process.

Despite these controversies, NATO appears to be here to stay. Russia's adroit and popular president, Vladimir Putin, has taken various steps to institutionalize a rapprochement with the West—to this end, he has not tried to block NATO expansion, wisely choosing instead to extract Western concessions for his acquiescence in this ongoing process. Yet questions remain. Would it thrive in its new capacity as a new, peacekeeping alliance? What would be its ultimate size? And, most importantly, would it help or hinder peace and order in Europe?

THE UNITED NATIONS

The United Nations is the most ambitious attempt in history to construct a universal international organization capable of providing a framework for world peace and the military clout to enforce the world rule of law. But the establishment of the United Nations after World War II was not the first such attempt.

Historical Background: The League of Nations

To understand the United Nations, we must place it in historical context. Beginning in the nineteenth century, several international peacekeeping federations were founded, usually in the aftermath of increasingly destructive wars. The Holy Alliance, formed in 1815, in the wake of the Napoleonic wars, represented an attempt by Europe's major powers to control international events by means of meetings and conferences. A more elaborate organization was the *League of Nations,* set up in 1919, following World War I.

When the Covenant of the League of Nations was sealed in 1919, it was hailed by Wilsonians as the advent of a new age in world history. The actual machinery of the League of Nations included the Assembly, the Council, and the Permanent Secretariat. The Assembly was a deliberative body made up of representatives from each member state. Each representative in the Assembly cast one vote, and all votes carried equal weight. Motions on the floor of the Assembly required unanimous approval for passage, meaning that virtually every member state, no matter how tiny, enjoyed veto power over nearly every decision. The much smaller Council was made up of four permanent and four nonpermanent members. The role of the Council was to investigate and report on threats to the peace and to make proposals or recommend appropriate action to the Assembly. The two bodies were coordinated and supervised by the Permanent Secretariat, the administrative arm of the League.

The ambitious aims of the League of Nations included, above all, the maintenance of international peace through the promise of swift and certain retribution against aggressor nations—peace and punishment were two sides of the same coin. War (like crime) would not pay because an attack on any one member would be an attack on all. In this respect, the League became the institutional embodiment of President Woodrow Wilson's desire to replace the traditional balance of power with "a single overwhelming, powerful group of nations who shall be trustees of the peace of the world."[11] The key was to create a system of *collective security* so formidable no individual state—no single challenger of the status quo—would stand a chance against it. The combined military forces of all law-abiding nations were to be set against any state that violated international peace. In the view of the League's founders, the very existence of such a potential force would make it unnecessary to actualize it, because potential aggressors would be deterred—that is, they would not dare test it.

Despite President Wilson's inspired advocacy, the United States initially stayed on the sidelines (because the Republicans in the Senate led by Henry Cabot Lodge opposed passage of the treaty). That move foreshadowed the League's future misfortunes and its eventual demise. By the early 1930s, conflicting national interests and bitter rivalries had resurfaced with a vengeance.

In retrospect, the League was doomed to failure. First, it was supposedly a world organization but it lacked universal acceptance (both the United States and the upstart Soviet Union were conspicuously absent, though for very different reasons). Second, it was procedurally flawed: The requirement for unanimity prior to any military or police action guaranteed virtually paralysis in the face of a future crisis because every state large and small had a veto. Third, the collective security measures in the Charter were triggered by acts of aggression but the Charter failed to define *aggression*. Nor would the League's members ever agree on a definition either in the abstract or later in crisis situations when, for example, Hitler's Germany remilitarized the Rhineland, Italy invaded Ethiopia, Germany threatened (and ultimately invaded) Poland and Czechoslovakia, or Japan embarked on a career of conquest in Asia.

Finally, the success of the League depended, above all, on the United States. World War I had transformed the balance of power from one based in Western Europe to one that was truly global. It had also moved the United States front and center on the world stage. In the span of a few years, it had smashed the myth of a Eurocentric world. Henceforth the balance of power system would encompass all the nations and regions of the world, and the great powers would either be extinct (the Austro-Hungarian Empire and Czarist Russia) or eclipsed by the United States, the Soviet Union, Japan, and (eventually) China—all located outside of the territorial core of Europe.

The Founding of the United Nations

The vast destruction, shocking death toll, and terrifying new weapons of World War II sparked renewed efforts to ensure world peace through the establishment of a powerful international organization. The founders of the United Nations recognized that if the new organization was to have any chance of succeeding, it would have to represent an organizational improvement over the League of Nations. As already noted, the League's structure had at least two fatal flaws. First, its members were all treated as equals, irrespective of the realities of national power. In the Assembly, every member state had one vote, and every negative vote constituted a veto. And even in the Council, where the great powers were permanent members, the nonpermanent members exercised veto power. Consequently, the lesser powers had too much clout and the major powers too little. The other great weakness of the League was its incompleteness. The scope of the League's peace aims may have been worldwide, but its membership was limited. The absence of several great powers—particularly the United States—meant that the League's mandate was universal in theory but circumscribed in practice.

The founders of the United Nations in 1945 were intent on rectifying the defects in the League's collective security system. A major effort was made to ensure that no potential member state would be excluded from the new organization (see Figure 18-2). The General Assembly was designed as a deliberative body in which all UN members would have an equal voice and an equal vote. More important, the UN Charter created a Security Council entrusted with "primary responsibility for the maintenance of international peace and security." The charter specified that this body was to be made up of five permanent members (the United States, the Soviet Union [recently replaced by the Russian Republic], the United Kingdom, France, and China) and ten nonpermanent members. In contrast to the League, the so-called Big Five alone were given the right to veto certain specified important matters, such as the selection of the secretary-general, as well as proposed peacekeeping measures. In this manner, the UN Charter sought to correct the anomaly of legal equality in the midst of political inequality. In the United Nations, member states would have responsibilities commensurate with each one's capabilities.

Precisely how these responsibilities were conceptualized was spelled out in Chapter 7 of the UN Charter, titled "Action with Respect to Threats to the Peace, Breaches of the Peace, and Acts of Aggression." Article 39 specifies, "the Security Council shall determine the existence of any threat to the peace, breach of the peace, or act of aggression and shall make recommendations, or decide what measure shall be taken in accordance with Articles 40 and 42, to maintain or restore international peace and security." Subsequent articles spell out how the Security Council is expected to discharge its obligations. Article 41 deals with economic sanctions, including "complete or partial interruption of economic relations and of rail, sea, air, postal, telegraphic, radio, and other means of communication, and the severance of diplomatic relations." Article 42 contemplates situations in which economic sanctions may be inadequate; in such cases, the Security Council "may take action by air, sea, or land forces as may be necessary to maintain or restore international peace and security. Such action may include demonstrations, blockades, and other operations by air, sea, or land forces of Members of the United Nations." Other articles in Chapter 7 deal with organizing the military components of a full-fledged collective security system, including the establishment of the Military Staff Committee (Article 47).

The machinery of international peacekeeping outlined by these articles far surpassed the comparable machinery of the League of Nations. Moreover, the United Nations was intended to go well beyond merely maintaining peace and security, as the establishment of its so-called specialized agencies revealed. Through these agencies, the United Nations plays an important role in worldwide disaster relief, resettlement of refugees, technical assistance in the areas of food and agriculture, health concerns, and many other areas. In addition, the world body actively promotes a higher world standard of living through such agencies as the Economic and Social Council (ECOSOC) and the United Nations International Children's Emergency Fund (UNICEF). Finally, financial and developmental assistance has been extended to economically troubled states through the World Bank, the International Monetary Fund (IMF), and the United Nations Conference on Trade and Development (UNCTAD). The plethora of specialized agencies makes it clear that the United Nations was committed from the outset to promoting world welfare as well as preventing world war.

However, the UN Charter was clearly not designed as a blueprint for a world government. Article 2, paragraph 7, of the Charter makes it clear that matters

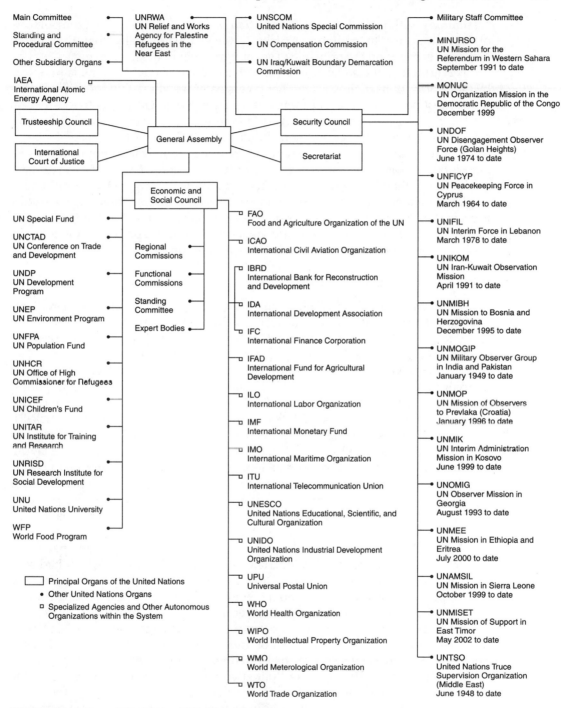

FIGURE 18-2   The United Nations System

The United Nations, the world's most important IGO, has spawned many affiliated, smaller IGOs.

SOURCES: Adapted from *The World Factbook 1996,* Central Intelligence Agency, 1997, and "Current Peacekeeping Operations," UN Department of Public Information, 1997.

"essentially within the *domestic jurisdiction* of any state" are beyond the purview of UN authority. In addition, Article 2 states unequivocally that the United Nations "is based on the principle of sovereign equality of all its members."

Nevertheless, the equality of all members of the United Nations is undercut by other provisions of the Charter that give greater weight within the organization to the most powerful or most prominent member states. The most obvious reason for these provisions was the need to guarantee the participation of the major states. But there was another, more subtle reason: Some of the United Nations' original supporters did view the new international organization not merely as an association of sovereign states but also as the forerunner of a world government. And if that possibility were ever to become a reality, the larger states would have to play a greater role than the smaller, less powerful states. Thus, the contradictions in the Charter mirror the mix of realism and idealism present at the creation of the United Nations; for "one-world" idealists they also represented the compromises of the past necessary to pave the way for the future.

The United Nations during the Cold War

Unfortunately, the United Nations could not escape some of the same problems that had destroyed the League of Nations. Individual nations were simply not ready to commit themselves to the extent that the organization's proper functioning required. Nor were they willing to surrender their sovereignty.

On the one hand, the charter at several points obligates member states to act in accordance with the rule of law and empowers the Security Council to punish them when they do not. On the other hand, it provides a number of loopholes and escape clauses for states that wish to evade or ignore their obligations. Article 51, for example, states that "nothing in the present Charter shall impair the inherent right of individual or collective self-defense." As long as "self-defense" is a lawful justification to resort to force, and as long as individual states are free to define self-defense broadly enough to cover virtually any action they deem to be in their national interest, such a provision invites aggression. The dilemma is obvious: Without escape clauses such as Article 51, the UN Charter would not have been acceptable; with them, it may not be enforceable.

Another problem plaguing the world body until recently was the persistent state of tension between the United States and the Soviet Union, which had seriously hampered the workings of the United Nations during the Cold War. Because each superpower at one time or another enjoyed a majority in the General Assembly, deadlock rather than decisive action became the hallmark of most UN deliberations. The consensus necessary to promote peace through collective security in the Security Council was also absent on most occasions—if the Soviet Union did not veto a controversial measure, the United States often did.

Despite these difficulties, the limited conflict-management functions of the United Nations were not always unsuccessful. At various times since its founding, it has contributed to peace by sending special mediators, truce supervision teams, or quasi-military forces to various parts of the world, including Cyprus, the Middle East, and the Congo. These efforts, though typically limited in scope and success, proved valuable.

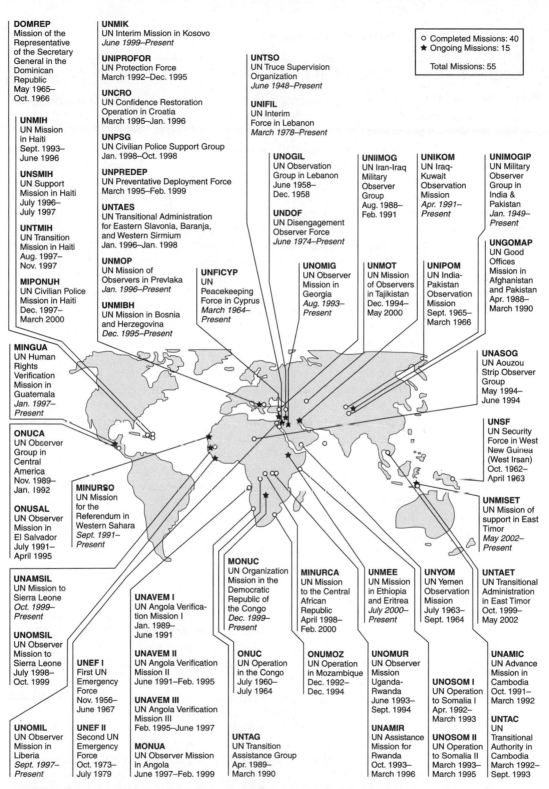

DOMREP
Mission of the Representative of the Secretary General in the Dominican Republic
May 1965–Oct. 1966

UNMIH
UN Mission in Haiti
Sept. 1993–June 1996

UNSMIH
UN Support Mission in Haiti
July 1996–July 1997

UNTMIH
UN Transition Mission in Haiti
Aug. 1997–Nov. 1997

MIPONUH
UN Civilian Police Mission in Haiti
Dec. 1997–March 2000

UNMIK
UN Interim Mission in Kosovo
June 1999–Present

UNIPROFOR
UN Protection Force
March 1992–Dec. 1995

UNCRO
UN Confidence Restoration Operation in Croatia
March 1995–Jan. 1996

UNPSG
UN Civilian Police Support Group
Jan. 1998–Oct. 1998

UNPREDEP
UN Preventative Deployment Force
March 1995–Feb. 1999

UNTAES
UN Transitional Administration for Eastern Slavonia, Baranja, and Western Sirmium
Jan. 1996–Jan. 1998

UNMOP
UN Mission of Observers in Prevlaka
Jan. 1996–Present

UNMIBH
UN Mission in Bosnia and Herzegovina
Dec. 1995–Present

UNTSO
UN Truce Supervision Organization
June 1948–Present

UNIFIL
UN Interim Force in Lebanon
March 1978–Present

UNOGIL
UN Observation Group in Lebanon
June 1958–Dec. 1958

UNDOF
UN Disengagement Observer Force
June 1974–Present

UNFICYP
UN Peacekeeping Force in Cyprus
March 1964–Present

UNOMIG
UN Observer Mission in Georgia
Aug. 1993–Present

UNIIMOG
UN Iran-Iraq Military Observer Group
Aug. 1988–Feb. 1991

UNMOT
UN Mission of Observers in Tajikistan
Dec. 1994–May 2000

UNIKOM
UN Iraq-Kuwait Observation Mission
Apr. 1991–Present

UNIPOM
UN India-Pakistan Observation Mission
Sept. 1965–March 1966

UNIMOGIP
UN Military Observer Group in India & Pakistan
Jan. 1949–Present

UNGOMAP
UN Good Offices Mission in Afghanistan and Pakistan
Apr. 1988–March 1990

○ Completed Missions: 40
★ Ongoing Missions: 15

Total Missions: 55

MINGUA
UN Human Rights Verification Mission in Guatemala
Jan. 1997–Present

ONUCA
UN Observer Group in Central America
Nov. 1989–Jan. 1992

ONUSAL
UN Observer Mission in El Salvador
July 1991–April 1995

MINURSO
UN Mission for the Referendum in Western Sahara
Sept. 1991–Present

UNASOG
UN Aouzou Strip Observer Group
May 1994–June 1994

UNSF
UN Security Force in West New Guinea (West Irsan)
Oct. 1962–April 1963

UNMISET
UN Mission of support in East Timor
May 2002–Present

UNAMSIL
UN Mission to Sierra Leone
Oct. 1999–Present

UNOMSIL
UN Observer Mission to Sierra Leone
July 1998–Oct. 1999

UNOMIL
UN Observer Mission in Liberia
Sept. 1997–Present

UNEF I
First UN Emergency Force
Nov. 1956–June 1967

UNEF II
Second UN Emergency Force
Oct. 1973–July 1979

UNAVEM I
UN Angola Verification Mission I
Jan. 1989–June 1991

UNAVEM II
UN Angola Verification Mission II
June 1991–Feb. 1995

UNAVEM III
UN Angola Verification Mission III
Feb. 1995–June 1997

MONUA
UN Observer Mission in Angola
June 1997–Feb. 1999

MONUC
UN Organization Mission in the Democratic Republic of the Congo
Dec. 1999–Present

ONUC
UN Operation in the Congo
July 1960–July 1964

UNTAG
UN Transition Assistance Group
Apr. 1989–March 1990

MINURCA
UN Mission to the Central African Republic
April 1998–Feb. 2000

ONUMOZ
UN Operation in Mozambique
Dec. 1992–Dec. 1994

UNMEE
UN Mission in Ethiopia and Eritrea
July 2000–Present

UNOMUR
UN Observer Mission Uganda-Rwanda
June 1993–Sept. 1994

UNAMIR
UN Assistance Mission for Rwanda
Oct. 1993–March 1996

UNYOM
UN Yemen Observation Mission
July 1963–Sept. 1964

UNOSOM I
UN Operation to Somalia I
Apr. 1992–March 1993

UNOSOM II
UN Operation to Somalia II
March 1993–March 1995

UNTAET
UN Transitional Administration in East Timor
Oct. 1999–May 2002

UNAMIC
UN Advance Mission in Cambodia
Oct. 1991–March 1992

UNTAC
UN Transitional Authority in Cambodia
March 1992–Sept. 1993

FIGURE 18-3   UN Peacekeeping Operations Past and Present

SOURCE: United Nations, "Peacekeeping," www.un.org/peace, accessed May 22, 2002. Used with permission of the United Nations.

The United Nations after the Cold War

The mid- to late 1980s saw an unprecedented period of cooperation among the five permanent members of the Security Council, particularly between the United States and the Soviet Union. The catalyst was the Soviet Union's new conciliatory foreign policy initiated by Mikhail Gorbachev. After the collapse of the Soviet system in 1991, the United States exercised relatively uncontested influence in the United Nations. For the first time in its history, the United Nations was characterized by a unity of purpose rather than by sharp conflict between its two most powerful members. This era of increased cooperation produced two significant results. First, the United Nations embraced a particularly vigorous approach to international peacekeeping, sometimes bordering on peacemaking (see Figure 18-3).[12] Second, it sanctioned collective military action against Iraq after that nation invaded Kuwait.

Peacekeeping on the Rise   The presence of UN peacekeeping forces stationed all over the world at the start of the new millennium testified to the enhanced role of the United Nations in the post–Cold War international order. No fewer than 47,000 peacekeepers from eighty-eight countries were serving in fifteen UN operations. More peacekeeping projects have been launched since the end of the Cold War (1989–91) than during the entire Cold War era (roughly four decades). In all, a total of fifty-four peacekeeping operations were launched between 1948 and 2001.

Recent UN peacekeeping efforts have encompassed a wide array of missions, some of which were unprecedented for the organization. These efforts, in turn, varied greatly in scale. A mere fifty observers facilitated the Soviet Union's withdrawal from Afghanistan in 1988. By contrast, in 1989 personnel from 109 nations joined in an effort to secure peace and independence for Namibia, where UN peacekeepers were charged with creating the conditions for elections and securing the repeal of discriminatory and restrictive legislation, the release of prisoners, and the return of exiles.

Starting in 1991, almost 400 UN peacekeepers undertook a novel role in El Salvador: At the end of its civil war, they were to monitor and verify human rights violations and make recommendations for their own eventual elimination. Also, beginning in October 1991, UN peacekeepers in Cambodia were charged with implementing a peace agreement among four formerly warring factions. The agreement included the demobilization of the various armies, the repatriation of 350,000 refugees, and the assurance of elections. According to one expert, this task gave the United Nations "effective responsibility for administering the country during an 18-month transition period."[13] Some 40,000 peacekeepers, sent in 1993 to the former Yugoslavia, supported the negotiations leading to the U.S.-brokered peace settlement in November 1995. The presence of this force, combined with NATO military support and UN-sponsored sanctions, pressured Serbian dictator, Slobodan Milosevic, to negotiate in good faith. Later, after Milosevic was ousted following his defeat in national elections (and a popular groundswell when he tried to cancel the results), the United Nations was instrumental in bringing the brutal former president and other accused war criminals in Yugoslavia to justice.

Reuters / Petr Josek / Archive Photos

United Nations soldiers have sometimes played a crucial role in maintaining peace around the world. Here, in the face of sniper fire, a UN soldier escorts a Croatian woman to safety.

UN peacekeeping actions since the Cold War are more frequent and ambitious than ever before in the UN's history. Recently, the United Nations launched peacekeeping operations in Kosovo (Yugoslavia), Sierra Leone (West Africa), East Timor (formerly part of Indonesia), the Congo (central Africa), and the Horn of Africa (Ethiopia and Eritrea) in a single year (June 1999–July 2000). But these ventures are not risk-free and they come with no guarantee of success. For example, UN troops were sent to Somalia in 1992 to facilitate the safe distribution of food to starving people, but they were attacked by rebels who viewed the UN as a cat's paw for the West (the United States, in particular). UN peacekeepers generally try to avoid the use of deadly force but that is not always possible, given the tinderbox environments in which they are so often asked to operate. UN personnel involved in peacekeeping operations have suffered many casualties over the years, including over 1,600 fatalities since 1948. Peacekeeping in Lebanon (244 fatalities) and Cyprus (170 fatalities) has been particularly hazardous in times past. In both cases, there has never been closure (that is, a peace settlement acceptable to all warring parties) and so the UN presence has become a permanent fixture. Of the ten peacekeeping operations launched in the 1990s, most incurred fewer than fifteen fatalities; however, forty-six members of the United Nations Mission in Sierra Leone (UNAMSIL) were killed in Sierra Leone.

Nor can UN peacekeepers always implement political changes necessary to ensure future calamities—for example, widespread starvation—will be averted. In Cambodia, peace did not long survive the withdrawal of UN forces: In June 1997 an antidemocratic coup abruptly defeated the UN's ambitious efforts to promote

The United Nations and American Public Opinion

The United Nations continues to suffer from public mistrust, as well as widespread misunderstandings about what it really is and does. The image problem, ironically, has always had a particularly strong presence in the United States, the country in which the United Nations is located and which played the largest role in its creation. Much of the public mistrust of the United Nations is based on a misunderstanding. To view the United Nations as a world government in the making is to buy into an old myth.

The United Nations has evolved from a world organization originally charged with preventing war into one with a far less ambitious aim of promoting peace by acting in various conflict-abatement roles (for example, cease-fire monitoring, peace observation, and the interposition of quasi-military forces). It is also a convenient forum for member states to engage in ongoing dialogue while focusing attention on major global issues. Then, too, the UN contributes indirectly to peace maintenance by making economic and technical assistance available to the poorest of the poor nations.

Nor is it true that the United States is a mere captive of the United Nations. Indeed, some UN member states, including the United States, have at times refused to pay all or part of their dues when they have been displeased about something (in March 1998, the United States owed $1.3 billion in back dues). In all, the United Nations was owed a total of $2.5 billion in back dues—almost twice as much as the annual budget for the UN's main functions.

Although a portion of American public opinion believes the United States has shouldered a disproportionate burden, it is noteworthy that of the nearly 1,300 UN peacekeepers who have died in action since 1945, only 3 percent were Americans. Another little-recognized fact is the UN's sizable economic contribution to the U.S. economy. The total UN boost to the economy of the New York City area alone was $3.2 billion a year in the late 1990s, according to former Mayor Rudolph Giuliani; the UN presence in New York City has generated 30,600 jobs, yielding $1.2 billion in annual earnings.

democracy in that nation. In the former Yugoslavia, UN peacekeepers' initial attempts to promote a cease-fire were overwhelmed by the fury of the fighting and became effective only after NATO air strikes and ground support were brought to bear. In the end, the Serbian army was defeated and President Milosevic was forced to negotiate. One of the lessons of the wars in Bosnia and Kosovo is that UN peacekeeping efforts are unlikely to succeed in stopping regional conflicts without the military backing of major individual member states and regional military alliances (such as NATO). In fact, the experience in Yugoslavia and elsewhere makes a strong case for creation of new regional military groupings capable of acting as the law-enforcement apparatus of the United Nations.

Meanwhile, as already noted, some UN peacekeeping operations have become permanent fixtures without leading to a final settlement (Kashmir, Cyprus, and Lebanon are three prime examples). These institutionalized peacekeeping missions are a perennial drain on the UN budget, which is always stretched to the breaking point. In the mid-1990s, UN peacekeeping projects cost $3.2 billion a year, with about one-third of that amount remaining unpaid. Projected costs from July 2001 to June 2002 were $3–3.5 billion. In all, the total estimated cost of peacekeeping operations from 1948 to 2001 came to about $23 billion.

But it is necessary to put these figures into perspective, which critics of the United Nations seldom if ever do. By comparison, the U.S. defense budget for 2001 alone was $300 billion. The Pentagon's shopping list for the near future includes $48 billion for new helicopters, $67 billion for a new fighter (the F-22 Raptor), and $223 billion for a new Joint Strike Force JSF). Given these numbers, the amount spent on all the peacekeeping operations in history is infinitesimal. It is hard to imagine a better bargain for the world's taxpayers even if the success rate of peacekeeping operations continues to be measured in small fractions.

Collective Military Action   In August 1990, when Iraq invaded Kuwait, the United Nations (led by the United States) responded militarily. The collective military action recalled Woodrow Wilson's failed dream of collective security, wherein the League of Nations would exercise military force for the sake of maintaining peace and morality in the world. The UN response to Iraq also pointed back to a previous attempt at collective military action: In June 1950, when North Korea invaded South Korea, the United Nations (again led by the United States) responded with military force. But even that instance of collective security was problematical. The Soviet Union did not participate and in fact objected strenuously to the use of the United Nations as a legal pretext for what Moscow viewed as an American military intervention in defense of a client state, South Korea. Although the UN flag was raised, the so-called Korean conflict was in truth a war fought by the United States against North Korea and, later, the People's Republic of China. The supreme commander, General Douglas MacArthur, was responsible to the president of the United States, not the secretary-general of the United Nations.

It would be another four decades before the United Nations was again used in building an international coalition against an aggressor. The Cold War precluded any such effort—both superpowers used the veto to block enforcement actions proposed by the other.

In 1990–91, when the United States (backed by the British) launched Operation Desert Storm against Iraq, the Security Council became a forum for the major powers to meet and consult on how to respond to Iraqi aggression. It was the first major test of the United Nations in the post–Cold War era. The United States gained the Security Council's support for resolutions condemning Iraq, establishing tough economic sanctions, and ultimately approving the use of force to expel the Iraqi army from Kuwait. After the Gulf War's end, United Nations inspectors were allowed access to sites in Iraq suspected of hiding biological, chemical, or nuclear weapons. Iraq later would dispute the terms of these inspections, leading the United States to threaten bombing raids (an action at least temporarily avoided by the successful diplomatic efforts of UN Secretary-General Kofi Annan).

What the United Nations did *not* do before and during the Gulf War is equally important, however. The war against Iraq was predominantly an American effort. The United Nations did not provide any forces of its own. The secretary-general had no control over how the coalition forces were deployed or employed. There was no UN general staff, nor did the United Nations coordinate the military or diplomatic operations undertaken by coalition members (principally the United States and Great Britain). And the United Nations did not provide any funding. The war was financed in large part by contributions from America's richest allies, including Japan, Germany, Kuwait, and Saudi Arabia. So it is an exaggeration to call the war against Iraq a UN enforcement action. It would also be an exaggeration to call it an exercise in collective security. To be precise, it was a broad-based coalition forged by the United States with the imprimatur of the United Nations.

Problems Underlying Comprehensive International Organizations

Despite its successes, the United Nations has not lived up to all the expectations of its founders. Although its architects sought to solve the procedural problems associated with the League of Nations—such as the unanimity rule that prevented the League's Assembly from acting—the United Nations has had its share of similar problems. Procedural problems are often rooted in deep-seated political differences.

The Problem of Universality   All nations of significant size or consequence must be persuaded to join a comprehensive international organization and remain part of it, otherwise it is just a matter of time before a crisis somewhere reveals the inadequacy of the edifice and brings it crashing to the ground. As a minimum condition for success, all major powers must be members, as the experience of the League of Nations clearly demonstrated. The history of the United Nations also illustrates the importance of including all potential member states—especially those with the capacity to disrupt world peace. The absurdity of refusing to seat the People's Republic of China, which the United States excluded from the United Nations for two decades, is an obvious case in point. Today the United Nations is truly universal. In 2000, no fewer than 189 countries, including some so tiny that they are no more than a dot on the world map, claim full UN membership.

The Problem of Inequality   Small nations typically demand formal equality with large nations in international organizations—anything less would be an affront and might be seen as an invitation to outside intervention in the internal affairs of a sovereign state. By the same token, powerful nations insist that their superior strength be reflected in special procedural arrangements, such as the veto power of the permanent members of the UN Security Council. Anything less, they argue, would represent a diminution of their real importance in the world. Moreover, as the relative strengths of member states fluctuate, the original formula governing such matters needs to be revised. Some nations formerly considered great powers have to be demoted to make room for newcomers whose stars are rising. This is more than merely a "technical" problem. No international organization can remain viable unless it resolves the problem of inequality while remaining flexible enough to change with changing circumstances.

The Problem of Competence   Comprehensive international organizations are often powerless to do any more than the least cooperative members are willing to countenance even where individual states do not have veto power. For example, if developing countries band together they can block action in the General Assembly and probably get a permanent member of the Security Council to veto measures in that body as well. (Or theoretically they can defeat measures by majority vote in the Security Council.) As a result, international organizations tend to lack the competence to deal with a wide range of problems normally thought to fall within the realm of governmental action. The best they can do, as a rule, is deal with specific cases arising in general areas of common concern (for example, peacekeeping).

The Problem of Unity   In the past, the most successful international organizations have been alliances based on confronting a common enemy. The Holy Alliance, inspired by the fear of a resurgent France, is a case in point. The present-day Arab League is another: Without the unifying effect of facing a common enemy (Israel), the Arab states undoubtedly would have engaged in far more internecine squabbling over the past fifty years. Similarly, without the perceived threat of communist expansion in the late 1940s and early 1950s, the North Atlantic Treaty Organization would never have been founded. Finally, the high point of UN unity came in 1990–91, when most nations of the world joined the United States in opposing a common enemy, Iraq. When the original threat fades, however, the bonds of alliance tend to disintegrate. Disunity, or the absence of any real sense of community in the international arena, is a major obstacle to all forms of international organization, from the simplest to the most complex and comprehensive.

The Problem of Sovereignty   The problem of sovereignty—the supreme power a state exercises within its territorial boundaries—underlies all four problems previously mentioned. In the final analysis, sovereignty is indivisible: Either a nation has the last word in its own affairs or it does not. A nation can no more be partially sovereign, the nineteenth-century U.S. political leader John C. Calhoun once noted, than a woman can be partially pregnant. Thus, the creation of an effective world government would be possible only if existing governments could be persuaded to surrender sovereignty to a higher authority—a prospect most nation-states (and many scholars) consider too risky in a world dominated by fear, prejudice, and mistrust.

INTERNATIONAL LAW

Peace and harmony can only be advanced within the context of the present nation-state system. In this context, international law can buttress international organizations to promote a safer and more secure world.

For roughly 350 years, the international system has been regularized (if not exactly regulated) by an evolving body of *international law* defining the rights and obligations of states in relation to one another. The "rules of the game" have been freely adopted by sovereign governments and have been generally assumed of treaties. Other widely recognized sources of international law include custom and convention; general legal principles based on justice, equity, and morality; and the judicial decisions and teachings of eminent legal authorities.

The most famous codification of international law remains Hugo Grotius's *On the Law of War and Peace,* published in 1625, just twenty-three years before the formal establishment of the nation-state system in the Treaty of Westphalia. It was no accident that the rise of the modern international system coincided with the emergence of a set of rules governing the mutual relations of nations. Since the Treaty of Westphalia, international law has become a vital part of everyday world politics.

Usefulness

Consider for a moment the vast range of practical questions that could not be answered with any assurance apart from the rules and conventions of international law. How would territorial boundaries on land and sea be determined? If a river formed the boundary between two states, for instance, who would decide (1) whether the boundary should be drawn along the riverbed, along the river banks, or down the exact center of the river; (2) whether the river should be open to navigation for one state, both states, or neither state; or (3) whether upstream states have the right to build dams, reservoirs, and hydroelectric power plants on rivers that wend their way into the territory of the downstream states? What if the river changes course? Questions of this kind would crop up in many other areas of international relations. What would guarantee the safety of diplomatic representatives accredited to this or that foreign government? How would traffic on the high seas be regulated? Who would decide whether neutral states should have the right to carry on normal commercial relations with belligerents in times of war? These are only a few of the vital issues that would be extremely difficult to resolve in the absence of a preexisting body of international law.

Compliance and Enforcement

Surprisingly, international law has generally been observed and respected by the states it is designed to constrain. One authority notes:

> During the four hundred years of its existence international law has in most instances been scrupulously observed. When one of its rules was violated, it was, however, not always enforced and, when action to enforce it was actually taken, it was not always effective. Yet to deny that international law exists at all as a system of binding legal rules flies in the face of all evidence.[14]

The enforcement of international law has always posed unique difficulties. Under almost all national governments, the punishment for a crime committed by an individual is carried out by arrest, trial, and possible imprisonment. But obviously, no world government rules in the international sphere (certainly not the United Nations), and just as obviously, governments cannot be arrested, placed on trial, or thrown in prison. Nonetheless, they can be punished. The functional equivalent of government in the realm of international politics is the balance of power. In other words, states perceived as "lawbreakers" can be subjected to diplomatic censure or economic embargo or blockade by other governments. In extreme cases, they can even be overrun, despoiled, and occupied.

Clearly, there is little truth in the assertion that international law has no muscle behind it and nation-states are never constrained to obey its dictates. Rather, the real difference between international and national law has to do with constancy: Whereas ordinary citizens generally expect to be punished if they break the law, governments can more often break the law and get away with it. Even so, political pressures to conform to the requirements of international law are real and meaningful. A recent example was the reluctant decision of the Serbian government to turn ex-President Milosevic over to the UN War Crimes Tribunal.

Fear of political repercussions is not the only reason that most of the time most governments play by the rules. As we saw earlier, every country has much to gain from the existence of a uniform body of international rules and regulations. Without such rules, international trade, travel, and tourism would be greatly impeded, and international financial transactions, foreign investments, technological transfers, and postal and telecommunications links would hardly be possible. And without the elaborate and widely respected rules of diplomatic immunity, few governments would send diplomatic representatives to foreign capitals. Under the circumstances, it is doubtful whether any government can afford to treat international law cavalierly for long. Faced with the discouraging prospects of diplomatic isolation, economic disruption, and military retaliation, governments have usually violated treaties, conventions, and common rules of good conduct only under the most extraordinary, extreme, or extenuating circumstances.

Even so, power is the coin of all politics and law without the police to enforce it is a farce. In the international arena, the participants play the role of the police either individually or collectively. Thus, the balance of power is "an indispensable condition of the very existence of International Law."[15]

International Law in the Modern Era

Prior to World War II, the Geneva and Hague Conventions constituted the most important body of international law and set forth the rules of war. Since 1945, international law has advanced in several important areas, most notably in arms control. Looking forward, it is likely that international law will be increasingly concerned with environmental issues. Each of these important examples of contemporary international law will be examined in the following sections.

The Geneva and Hague Conventions   Until the mid-nineteenth century, the rules of warfare were governed by custom. In 1856, several of the great powers endorsed the first of a series of multilateral international conventions—the Declaration of Paris, which limited war at sea by outlawing privateering and specifying that a naval blockade had to be effective to be legally binding. More important was the *Geneva Convention* of 1864 (revised in 1906), which laid down rules for the humane treatment of the wounded on the battlefield. Of still greater importance was the *Hague Convention* of 1899, which codified for the first time many of the accepted practices of land warfare. A second Hague convention, in 1907, revised

TABLE 18-3

Major Bilateral Arms Control Agreements between the United States and the Former Soviet Union/Russia

Date	Agreement	Principal Objectives
1963	Hot Line Agreement	Establishes a direct radio and telegraph communication system between the governments to be used in times of crisis
1971	Hot Line Modernization Agreement	Puts a hot line satellite communication system into operation
1971	Nuclear Accidents Agreement	Creates a process for notification of accidental or unauthorized detonation of a nuclear weapon; creates safeguards to prevent accidents
1972	Antiballistic Missile (ABM) Treaty (SALT 1)	Restricts the deployment of antiballistic missile defense systems to one area and prohibits the development of a space-based ABM system
1972	SALT I Interim Agreement on Offensive Strategic Arms	Freezes the superpowers' total number of ballistic missile launchers for a five-year period
1972	Protocol to the Interim Agreement	Clarifies and strengthens prior limits on strategic arms
1972	High Seas Agreement	Creates procedures to prevent crisis-provoking incidents on the oceans
1973	Agreement on the Prevention of Nuclear War	Requires superpowers to consult if a threat of nuclear war emerges
1974	Threshold Test Ban Treaty with Protocol	Restricts the underground testing of nuclear weapons above a yield of 150 kilotons
1974	Protocol to the ABM Treaty	Reduces permitted ABMs to one site
1976	Treaty on the Limitation of Underground Explosions for Peaceful Purposes	Broadens the ban on underground nuclear testing stipulated in the 1974 Threshold Test Ban Treaty; requires on-site observers of tests with yields exceeding 150 kilotons
1977	Convention on the Prohibition of Military or Any Other Hostile Use of Environmental Modification Techniques	Bans weapons that threaten to modify the planetary ecology
1979	Salt II Treaty (never ratified)	Places ceilings on the number of strategic delivery vehicles, MIRVed missiles, long-range bombers, cruise missiles, ICBMs, and other weapons; restrains testing

the 1899 codes with regard to the rights and duties of belligerents and of neutral states and persons; it also prescribed rules concerning the use of new weapons such as dumdum bullets, poison gas, and gas-filled balloons for bombing.

Arms Control Treaties   No issue seemed more important or aroused more passion than the bilateral arms control agreements negotiated between the United States and the former Soviet Union during the Cold War (see Table 18-3). Although these agreements were both numerous and controversial, they affected nuclear deterrence only at the margin—altering neither country's fundamental dependence on nuclear deference to maintain peace.

Date	Agreement	Principal Objectives
1987	Nuclear Risk Reduction Centers Agreement	Creates facilities in each national capital to manage a nuclear crisis
1987	Intermediate-range Nuclear Force (INF) Treaty	Eliminates U.S. and USSR ground-level intermediate- and shorter-range nuclear weapons in Europe and permits on-site inspection to verify compliance
1990	Chemical Weapons Destruction Agreement	Ends production of chemical weapons; commits cutting inventories of chemical weapons in half by the end of 1999 and to five thousand metric tons by the end of 2002
1990	Nuclear Testing Talks	New protocol improves verification procedures of prior treaties
1991	START (Strategic Arms Reduction Treaty)	Reduces arsenals of strategic nuclear weapons by about 30 percent
1992	START I Protocol	Holds Russia, Belarus, Ukraine, and Kazakhstan to strategic weapons reductions agreed to in START by the former USSR
1992	Open Skies Agreement	Permits unarmed surveillance aircraft to fly over the United States, Russia, and their allies
1992	Cooperative Threat Reduction Agreement	Provides a variety of equipment and support to assist Russia in the safe destruction of strategic delivery systems, the transportation of nuclear warheads, the physical protection of nuclear-weapon storage sites, warhead accounting, and chemical and biological weapon destruction and facility dismantlement
1993	START II	Cuts the deployed U.S. and Russian strategic nuclear warheads on each side to between 3,000 and 3,500 by the year 2003; bans multiple-warhead land-based missiles
1995	HEU Agreement	Reduces risk of diversion or theft of nuclear-weapons-grade highly enriched uranium (HEU) recovered from dismantled nuclear warheads through government purchase and use as civilian reactor fuel
1997	Fissile Material Cut-Off Treaty (FMCT)	Bans production of fissile material for nuclear weapons or other nuclear explosive devices
1997	Core Conversion Agreement	Obligates the United States to facilitate the conversion of Russia's three remaining plutonium production reactors to no longer produce weapons-grade plutonium; originally intended to be complete by the end of 2000, this project will now likely be implemented by 2002
1997	START III	Pledges the agreement that was renewed at the September 1998 Moscow Summit for the United States and Russia to deploy no more than 2,000 to 2,500 strategic nuclear warheads each on CBMs, SLBMs, and heavy bombers by December 31, 2007, pending ratification of the START II Treaty

SOURCE: Charles W. Kegley, Jr. & Eugene Wittkopf, *World Politics: Trend and Transformation,* 8th ed., Bedford/St. Martin's (2001), 580–581.

The demise of the Soviet Union, a perceived improvement in relations between the United States and Russia, and the existence of nuclear weapons in the newly created nations of Belarus, Ukraine, and Kazakhstan, all spurred the United States and Russia to reach much more consequential arms limitation agreements. Most notably, the 1993 *START II (Strategic Arms Reduction Treaty II)* agreements cut nuclear warheads by 60 percent over already reduced levels from two years earlier. Furthermore, START II banned multiple warheads on land-based missiles while reducing submarine-launched multiple warheads. Underlying START II was each nation's hope that this agreement, "could reduce the chances of a war of annihilation by banning the nuclear weapons that both powers would be most likely to use in a preemptive strike."[16]

Over the past forty years, a number of important arms control measures enacted have been multinational, agreed to by many or most of the world's nations. Some of the most noteworthy agreements include:

- The 1959 *Antarctic Treaty* prohibited all military activity on the Antarctic continent and accorded each signatory the right of aerial surveillance. It also prohibited dumping of nuclear wastes and encouraged cooperation in scientific investigations.

- The 1967 *Outer Space Treaty* banned nuclear weapons from outer space, prohibited military bases and maneuvers on the moon and other planets, and barred claims of national sovereignty in outer space.

- The 1968 *Nonproliferation Treaty* restricted signatories from transferring or receiving nuclear weapons or materials. While most of the world's nations have signed this agreement, several of the signatories have not consistently obeyed their provisions, and a number of other key nations, including Iran, Iraq, Libya, Pakistan, and India have not signed it.

- The 1971 *Seabed Treaty* banned nuclear weapons from the bottom of the world's oceans outside each state's twelve-mile territorial limit.

- The 1972 *Biological Weapons Convention* pledged the destruction of biological stockpiles while outlawing the production and storage of such weapons.

- The 1993 *Chemical Weapons Convention* intends to eliminate chemical weapons within ten years. The U.S. Senate ratified this treaty in April 1997.

There are limits to what such pacts can be expected to accomplish. Governments usually do not sign agreements that require them to act contrary to how they would act in the absence of such agreements. For example, the United States claimed to have had no intention of developing chemical weapons (nor did it rely on those weapons for its national security) at the time it ratified the Chemical Weapons Convention. Where a proposed agreement on international rules of conduct has required the negotiating parties to relinquish something important to them, international law has not fared so well.

International Law and the Environment The existing body of international law dealing with the environment is likely to grow considerably in the future. Precisely for that reason, some experts believe that past arms-limitations treaties will provide a precedent for a new era of transnational environmental agreements.

With few exceptions, such as the Montreal Protocol, which bans substances dangerous to the ozone layer (see box on p. 571), the number and scope of most other international environmental agreements have been limited. Like armaments, environmental concerns have traditionally fallen under the rubric of national sovereignty. However, resource depletion, the preservation of endangered species, and human-induced changes in the biosphere are issues that, like the possibility of nuclear war, affect all countries.

The global warming treaty (considered by world leaders at Kyoto, Japan, in December 1997) is a good example of the difficulty of fashioning comprehensive international environmental law. Many scientists—including geophysicists and

International Law and the Environment: The Montreal Protocol

The Montreal Protocol, formally known as the Montreal Protocol on Substances that Deplete the Ozone Layer, has been hailed as the most significant environmental pact in history and a model agreement for ushering in a new era of international law. Prompted by worldwide concern about the erosion of the ozone layer, which shields the planet from cancer-causing ultraviolet radiation, twenty-three nations in 1986 endorsed a plan to reduce chlorofluorocarbons (known as CFCs and widely used in automobile air conditioners) 50 percent by 1999. At a meeting in London in 1990, the agreement was modified, banning all CFCs by the year 2000. Two years later, representatives from more than eighty nations agreed in Copenhagen to move up the ban of CFCs to 1996 and to outlaw several other harmful substances as well. In 1992, the United States unilaterally announced its compliance with the provisions of the modified Montreal Protocol.

The unprecedented scope of the amended Montreal Protocol pleased many who feared for the environment and stressed the need for international cooperation. Still, implementing the agreement was fraught with difficulties. International funding to help developing nations purchase ozone-friendly technologies was very slow in coming. Criticism of the treaty's provisions came from opposite directions. Some saw the treaty as unnecessary; others believed it did too little or that loopholes would allow for exemptions from the bans.

Still, there was some early evidence that this important international compact may be working. A Dutch study published in 1997 compared what would have happened under three scenarios—one with no restrictions on ozone-destroying chemicals, another with the 1987 Montreal Protocol, and a third with the more stringent Copenhagen agreement. The results were impressive. "If you compare it to what would have happened otherwise, then you see a tremendous . . . kind of success story," noted one of the researchers (the results of the study are illustrated below).[17]

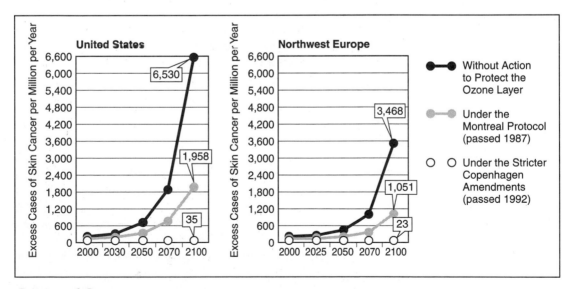

Ozone and Cancer

A 1992 international agreement to cut down on ozone-depleting chemicals should prevent millions of skin cancers. Scientists' projections of the skin cancer rate: Excess cases of skin cancer per million per year.

SOURCE: Associated Press/World Wide Photos; Amy Kranz.

meteorologists—predict a major warming in the earth's temperature over the next century. The worldwide effects of global warming could be calamitous, adversely affecting the world's climate, destroying agricultural land, and causing a rising sea level that will threaten many coastal cities.

A major cause of global warming is carbon dioxide, created when coal, oil, and other fossil fuels are burned in internal combustion engines, but there is political opposition in the United States to any treaty that would discourage, penalize, stigmatize, or limit energy use. Labor unions such as the AFL-CIO worry about lost jobs. Numerous business executives from major manufacturing industries complain about the imposition of additional government regulations. Skeptics question the computer models and doubt whether global warming will actually take place, or argue that it can be easily or effectively controlled.

Meanwhile, there are vast differences internationally. European nations favor pro-environmental standards that could not pass the U.S. Congress. A small number of Caribbean and South Pacific nations, seeing themselves most at risk from global warming (for example, even a two-foot rise in sea level would endanger their coastal businesses and poison their drinking water), champion even more stringent standards than those advocated by their European counterparts. Meanwhile, numerous developing nations, including China, India, and Brazil, have exempted themselves from any agreement. And oil-producing nations, such as Saudi Arabia, see any future treaty as economically harmful and continue to oppose it outright.

One of the first major foreign policy decisions that President George W. Bush announced upon moving into the Oval Office was that he would not sign the Kyoto Treaty. This decision was widely criticized abroad and met with wildly divergent reactions at home. The uncertain future of the global warming treaty points to another respect in which international environmental treaties are like arms limitations treaties: They take many years to negotiate, many more to implement, and are forever at the mercy of politicians and politics.

The Limitations of International Law

Treaties intended to outlaw war (such as the unsuccessful Kellogg-Briand Pact of 1928, eventually ratified by sixty-four nations) and agreements designed to promote peace and international understanding (such as the UN Charter) rarely withstand the test of time or the pressures of national ambition. Even modest "friendship" pacts solemnly signed by neighboring nations have been breached over the centuries.

The contemporary international system lacks three practical prerequisites necessary to establishing the world rule of law. First, there is currently no single source of international legislative authority beyond the General Assembly of the United Nations, whose powers are negligible. Second, no international executive office possesses the power to initiate or enforce international law. (Symbolically, the secretary-general of the United Nations could lay claim to this duty; but here again, the office commands no real power.) Third, there is no way to force sovereign governments to submit disputes to the World Court for adjudication or accept the verdict even when they do.

Enforcement must be left to individual nation-states, which too often enforce decisions unreliably or not at all. As long as international law lacks the predictability and coherence that give the rule of law its unique value, it will remain more of a convenience for governments than a constraint on them.

The World Court   The lack of international law enforcement capabilities is reflected most clearly in the workings of the *World Court.* The World Court itself is still a somewhat obscure institution which meets in The Hague (Holland's old capital). Properly known as the International Court of Justice (ICJ) and one of the six principal organs established by the UN Charter, the Court is a fully constituted judicial body, complete with judges, procedural rules, and the solemn trappings of a dignified tribunal. But, most important, it lacks a clearly defined jurisdiction.

The World Court is one of the few courts in the Western world that does not have a permanent backlog of cases; in fact, until recently, it sometimes had no cases at all. This paucity of work stemmed not from an absence of international disputes but from the Court's poorly defined jurisdiction, which depends on the will of the parties involved. For the Court to gain jurisdiction over an international dispute, the nations involved must confer jurisdiction on it in accordance with Article 36 of the Statute of the International Court of Justice. Article 36 specifically stipulates:

> Parties to the present Statute *may* at any time declare that they recognize as compulsory . . . *in relation to any other State accepting the same obligation,* the jurisdiction of the Court in all legal disputes concerning: (1) the interpretation of a treaty; (2) any question of international law; (3) the existence of any fact which, if established, would constitute a breach of an international obligation. [Emphasis added]

In other words, governments are legally obligated to abide by a decision of the Court only when they have given their prior consent to the Court's adjudication of a case. They may make a declaration of intent to accept the Court's jurisdiction in advance, as Article 36 invites them to do, or they may simply choose to submit certain cases on an ad hoc basis.

In the first twenty years of the World Court's existence, forty-two governments declared their intent to accept the *compulsory jurisdiction* of the Court. Although this seemed like a large step in the direction of a law-based world order, in international affairs, as in life in general, things are not always as they appear. The American "acceptance" of Article 36 is a case in point. Given its material affluence and attachment to due process of law, the United States might have been expected to push hard for a stable and orderly world founded on a respect for international law. Yet the U.S. declaration made on August 14, 1946, by which the United States ostensibly accepted the compulsory jurisdiction of the International Court of Justice, was actually a model of diplomatic sleight of hand. It states, in part:

> This declaration shall not apply to: a. disputes the solution of which the parties shall entrust to other tribunals by virtue of agreements already in existence or which may be concluded in the future; or b. disputes with regard to matters which are essentially within the domestic jurisdiction of the United States of America as determined by the United States of America; or c. disputes arising under a multinational treaty, unless

(1) all parties to the treaty affected by the decision are also parties to the case before the Court, or (2) the United States of America especially agrees to jurisdiction.

Together, these qualifications meant that the U.S. government agreed to compulsory jurisdiction only on the condition that such agreement did not compel it to accept the Court's jurisdiction. But the United States' qualified acceptance of compulsory jurisdiction was not unique. No government in the contemporary world has agreed unconditionally to commit itself to abide by the rulings of a world court.

The United States and the World Court   One might argue that if the United States or some other country took the lead in establishing a meaningful relationship with the World Court, perhaps other nations would follow suit. What would prevent the United States and, say, Great Britain from setting a positive example by promising to submit all future disputes between themselves to the compulsory jurisdiction of the World Court? At least on the surface, nothing would preclude this kind of contractual agreement between the two countries. But even if it were possible, why would it be necessary? For over a century, the United States and Great Britain have had very few disputes requiring protracted negotiations. And any disputes they might have in the foreseeable future are likely to be minor ones—close allies seldom face differences that require adjudication. Obviously, the efficacy of compulsory jurisdiction cannot be gauged accurately when two governments are on such amicable terms, and any differences that cannot be ironed out through normal diplomacy are *voluntarily* turned over to the jurisdiction of an international tribunal anyway.

The World Court's utility was tested in the 1980s, in the confrontation between Nicaragua's former Marxist (Sandinista) regime and the Reagan administration. In early 1985, Nicaragua filed suit against the United States in the World Court, charging Washington with aggression for mining the harbor at Corinto and supporting the Contra rebels. The State Department promptly announced that the U.S. government would boycott the proceedings and suspend bilateral talks with the Nicaraguan government. President Reagan justified these actions on the grounds that Nicaragua was using the Court for political and propaganda purposes.

In June 1986, the World Court ruled decisively against the United States in the case. At Nicaragua's initiative, the Security Council voted on whether to support the World Court's decision. The vote went against the United States 11 to 1. (It would have been approved overwhelmingly, with the United Kingdom, France, and Thailand abstaining, except for the U.S. veto.) Unfortunately, as this controversial case illustrates, the problem with compulsory jurisdiction, as with international law in general, is that it is least effective where it is most necessary.

In February 1998, the World Court again ruled against the United States in a high profile case. This time it was a dispute that stemmed from the terrorist bombing of Pan Am flight 103 over Lockerbie, Scotland, in 1988, in which 259 people died (plus 11 more on the ground). The United States and Great Britain led a successful fight for UN sanctions against Libya when the Libyan government refused to extradite two Libyan nationals suspected of perpetrating this terrorist act. The sanctions were imposed in 1992 and remained in effect. The Libyan government

© Owen Franken / CORBIS

The end of ideological rivalry between the two nuclear superpowers appeared to be a significant step toward a safer, saner world. It gave new opportunities for building world order, but provided no guarantee of perceptual peace.

then took the dispute to the World Court for relief, but the United States argued that the Court lacked jurisdiction. It was this procedural question that the judges finally decided in 1998.

But in this case, political and legal maneuvering went hand in hand. The United States had been pressuring Libya to turn over the suspects in the Lockerbie bombing for trial in the Netherlands under Scottish law rather than under international law. In this case, the ICJ would not be involved, but the trial would benefit from the aura of international legality associated with the country where the World Court sits. At the end of 1998, Libya agreed to the U.S. proposal and in April 1999 handed the suspects over to the United Nations. The highly publicized trial was held in 2000 and in January 2001 one of the two Libyans (a former Libyan intelligence agent) accused of the Lockerbie mass murders was found guilty by a panel of Scottish judges and sentenced to at least twenty years in prison. The other one was acquitted and allowed to return to Libya.

This verdict did not close the case nor did the United States agree to support an end to UN sanctions against Libya in its aftermath, but it did provide some degree of closure in a horrific case of international terrorism. In so doing, it set the stage for a rapprochement between Libya and the West (particularly the United States). And only eight months later, after the 9-11 terrorist attacks in the United States, it took on a whole new meaning, establishing a possible precedent for future trials in similar cases.

GATEWAYS TO THE WORLD: EXPLORING CYBERSPACE

For more information about a particular nonstate actor, use the name of the entity as your search term. For instance, to find out more about the role of the IMF in development, you should enter *International Monetary Fund* as your keyword. This search would lead you to sites such as <http://www.imf.org>, which is the home page for the IMF.

http://www.un.org

Official home page of the United Nations. It includes a wealth of resources for research, including a search engine.

http://www.un.org/law

This section of the UN Web site is devoted exclusively to international law. Among other features, this site includes the Law of the Sea, treaties online, and coverage of the International Criminal Tribunal for the former Yugoslavia (ICTY).

http://www.icj.cij.org

Official home page of the International Court of Justice (ICJ).

International Law Evaluated

Sovereign states generally place vital national interests ahead of a blind devotion to international law. Of course, nations differ on this matter—some break the precepts of international law infrequently; others may not care about such rules and obey them only as a matter of expedience. In either case, however, the fact that nations *can* refuse to be bound by it means that international law will be uniformly followed only when it is in the national interest of all governments to do so. In other words, respect for international law ultimately depends on national self-interest.

Are principles of justice, therefore, unimportant in international politics? Not exactly: They are of great value in understanding and evaluating the actions of governments and rulers. At times, governments can be punished (for example, through sanctions, as Iraq, Iran, Libya, North Korea, and many maverick states have discovered). Rogue rulers can also be punished as the eagerly awaited trial of former Yugoslav President Slobodan Milosevic before the International Court of Justice (World Court) in 2002 illustrates.

The first principle of international political life is national self-preservation. International law is useful when it serves the interests of national governments—especially powerful ones. At such times, the machinery of international justice (mainly the World Court) is likely to spring into action—indeed, more likely to get into the act now than during the Cold War. However, the major powers still prefer to seek traditional political and military solutions (where they have greater control over the outcomes), rather than judicial remedies (where they relinquish control to judges whose allegiances are unknown and unknowable). But the time is perhaps ripe for the role of international law and the prestige of the World Court to grow.

THE CONTINUING QUEST FOR PEACE

In 2001, the United Nations and Secretary-General Kofi Annan were awarded the Nobel Peace Prize for working toward a better-organized and more peaceful world. It was a sign of the times and a tribute to the achievements of the most successful comprehensive international organization in world history. To be able to describe the United Nations in these glowing terms without fear of contradiction says as much about the world (and world history) as it does about the UN. In truth, the UN's achievements have been modest, though not inconsequential.

Although balance-of-power politics and nuclear deterrence forged a relatively stable system of order after 1945, the end of the Cold War has given rise not only to new opportunities for order building but also to new dangers and sources of instability. Whether the proliferation of new international organizations—and the maturation of old ones—will counterbalance the ever-present forces of disorder remains uncertain.

International law and international organizations are not likely to replace diplomacy and war (or the threat of war) as the means by which nation-states resolve most disputes. Nor is respect for international law or the sanctity of treaties likely to increase enough so that countervailing force is no longer our chief means of preventing or limiting war.

International organizations can help with the Herculean task of conflict management but they will never resolve all conflicts everywhere. A more orderly world would, by definition, be one less predisposed toward war. Perhaps it would be a better world in every way. Even so, to propose that because war is the absence of order, the presence of order would automatically mean the absence of war is a logical fallacy of dangerous proportions.

In fact, there is no quick fix. No single act or event, no matter how momentous, can usher in a world without war. Ending the ideological rivalry between the world's most powerful states is a significant step toward a safer and saner world, but it is, regrettably, no guarantee of perpetual peace.

So the search continues. Even though peace remains elusive, the need to avoid wars—especially major wars involving weapons of mass destruction—is so compelling that people everywhere have a common interest in learning to manage conflict. But is conflict management good enough? Should we not strive to end conflict altogether? It has been said that politics is the art of the possible, or the best possible. Unfortunately, putting an end to conflict is not possible. However, in today's world learning to cope with conflict more successfully is necessary.

Summary

To what extent have international organizations and international law contributed to a more peaceful world? The removal of national barriers to trade, travel, and transfers of all kinds is reflected by the great increase in nonstate actors in the modern world, including multinational corporations, international governmental organizations, and international nongovernmental organizations. Multinational economic pacts and military alliances have also enhanced regional or worldwide interdependence.

This impressive network of international organizations and international pacts has not been free of national rivalries, however. And comprehensive international organizations have proved to be no more successful in bringing long-lasting peace and stability to the international arena. In the twentieth century, the League of Nations was torn apart by conflicting national interests. During the Cold War, the United Nations encountered many obstacles, although it enjoyed some limited success as a peacekeeping institution. Peacekeeping activity has expanded in the post–Cold War era. During this time, the United Nations sponsored collective military action against Iraq.

International law facilitates and regulates relations among sovereign and independent states whose interactions might otherwise be chaotic. Like the United Nations, international law in general has had a checkered history. Modern-day examples of international law include the Geneva and Hague Conventions, which set rules for warfare, and the multilateral arms limitation treaties. International environmental agreements are becoming an increasingly important part of international law. The limitations of international law are starkly apparent in the difficulties encountered by the World Court. The limitations of the United Nations and international law derive from their inability to prevail over the divisive influence of national interests.

Key Terms

functionalists (functionalism)
interdependence
nonstate actors
multinational corporations (MNCs)
international nongovernmental
    organizations (INGOs)
international governmental
    organizations (IGOs)
British Commonwealth
World Trade Organization (WTO)
North American Free Trade Agreement
    (NAFTA)
European Union (EU)
League of Nations
collective security

domestic jurisdiction
international law
Geneva Convention
Hague Convention
Strategic Arms Reduction Treaty II
    (START II)
Antarctic Treaty
Outer Space Treaty
Nonproliferation Treaty
Seabed Treaty
Biological Weapons Convention
Chemical Weapons Convention
World Court
compulsory jurisdiction

Review Questions

1. Identify nonstate actors in international politics. What impact have they had on the international system?

2. What prompted the founding of the United Nations? How does it differ from the League of Nations?

3. What does the UN Security Council do and how does it make decisions?

4. Where were UN peacekeeping operations most prevalent prior to the 1990s? How has the international context of peacekeeping changed since the end of the Cold War? Identify the setting for three or four of the most ambitious peacekeeping missions in recent years.

5. Does international law serve a useful purpose in contemporary international relations? Comment.

6. What are the limitations of international law?

7. How effectively has the World Court functioned?

8. What would have to be done to enhance the role of international law in world politics?

9. Do trends in world politics appear to favor a larger future role for the International Court of Justice or a smaller one?

Recommended Reading

AKEHURST, MICHAEL. *A Modern Introduction to International Law.* 6th ed. New York: Routledge, 1987. A good introductory text on international law.

BENNETT, A. LEROY. *International Organizations: Principles and Issues.* 6th ed. Englewood Cliffs, N.J.: Prentice-Hall, 1994. A good introductory text on international organizations.

BRIERLY, J. L. *The Law of Nations.* 6th ed. New York: Oxford University Press, 1978. A classic text.

CLAUDE, INIS L., JR. *Swords into Plowshares: The Problems and Progress of International Organizations.* 6th ed. New York: McGraw-Hill, 1994. A classic introduction focusing on the theoretical and practical problems of the League of Nations and the United Nations. The author presents an incisive analysis of the difficulties international organizations have encountered in trying to carry out their peacekeeping efforts.

D'AMATO, ANTHONY, ed. *International Law Anthology.* Cincinnati, Ohio: Anderson, 1994. An excellent compilation of documents and writings covering all aspects of international law.

HENKIN, LOUIS. *How Nations Behave: Law and Foreign Policy.* 2nd ed. New York: Columbia University Press, 1979. An incisive analysis that uses case studies and concrete examples to show how international law is interwoven into foreign policy process.

HINSLEY, F. H. *Power and the Pursuit of Peace: Theory and Practice in the History of Relations between States.* Cambridge, England: Cambridge University Press, 1967. A scholarly historical study of proposals and schemes for the international management of conflict from the Middle Ages to the modern age.

JACOBSON, HAROLD K. *Networks of Interdependence: International Organizations and the Global Political System.* 2nd ed. New York: McGraw-Hill, 1984. A highly detailed study of public and private international organizations.

KEOHANE, ROBERT O., and JOSEPH S. NYE. *Power and Interdependence: World Politics in Transition.* 2nd ed. Glenview, Ill.: Scott, Foresman, 1989. A groundbreaking work that challenges the realist theory of international relations and attempts to construct an alternative theory based on the concept of interdependence.

KLARE, MICHAEL, and DANIEL THOMAS, eds. *World Security: Challenges for a New Century.* 2nd ed. New York: St. Martin's Press, 1994. An important collection of readings, with selections on organizational efforts to improve international cooperation.

RIGGS, ROBERT, and JACK PLANO. *The United Nations, International Organizations, and World Politics.* 2nd ed. Belmont, Calif.: Wadsworth, 1994. A complete description of the history, structures, successes, and failures of the United Nations.

STOESSINGER, JOHN G. *The United Nations and the Superpowers: China, Russia, and America.* 4th ed. New York: McGraw-Hill, 1977. A useful, well-written volume that focuses on the performance and interaction of the United States and the former Soviet Union at the United Nations.

VON GLAHN, GERHARD. *Law among Nations.* 6th ed. 1992. A comprehensive guide to international law.

Notes

1. Charles W. Kegley, Jr., and Eugene Wittkopf, *American Foreign Policy: Pattern and Process,* 2nd ed. (New York: St. Martin's Press, 1987), 149–150.

2. The first quote is in Joan Edelman Spero, *The Politics of Economic Relations,* 4th ed. (New York: St. Martin's Press, 1991), 104; the second is in Bruce Kogut, *Foreign Policy* (Spring 1998): 7; online at www.findarticles.com/cf_dls/m1181/n110/20492572/.

3. As stated in the United Nations' *World Investment Report.* For a summary, see Francis Williams, "Global Business: A Fact of Life—UNCTAD's World Investment Report Assesses Role of Multinationals," *Financial Times,* August 31, 1994, 4.

4. Lester Brown, et al., *Vital Signs: The Trends That Are Shaping Our Future* (New York: Norton, 1993), 74.

5. Charles W. Kegley, Jr., and Eugene Wittkopf, *World Politics: Trend and Transformation,* 6th ed. (New York: St. Martin's Press, 1997), 129.

6. Kogut, *Foreign Policy,* 1; online reprint at findarticles.com.

7. Joan Edelman Spero, *The Politics of Economic Relations,* 112–113.

8. George Modelski, ed., *Transnational Corporations and World Order* (New York: Freeman, 1979), 3.

9. Kegley and Wittkopf classify IGOs by the breadth of their membership and the number of their goals. Here we follow their lead. See Kegley and Wittkopf, *World Politics,* 144–148.

10. Harold K. Jacobson, *Networks of Interdependence: International Organizations and the Global Political System* (New York: Knopf, 1979).

11.   Cited in Inis L. Claude, Jr., *Power and International Relations* (New York: Random House, 1962), 97.

12.   Margaret Karns, "Maintaining International Peace and Security: UN Peacekeeping and Peacemaking," in *World Security: Challenges for a New Century*, 2nd ed., eds. Michael Klare and Daniel Thomas (New York: St. Martin's Press, 1994), 199. Our discussion of the United Nations' role since the Cold War follows Karns's, and we are indebted to her scholarship.

13.   Karns, *Maintaining International Peace*, 206.

14.   Hans J. Morgenthau, *Politics among Nations: The Struggle for Power and Peace*, 5th ed. (New York, Knopf, 1978), 281.

15.   Lassa Francis Oppenheim, *International Law: A Treatise*, vol. 1, 2nd ed. (London: Longman, 1912), 93.

16.   Kegley, Jr., and Wittkopf, *World Politics*, 472.

17.   The quotation is from an Associated Press wire story; the article to which it refers is Henry Slapper, Guus J. M. Velders, John S. Daniel, Frank R. de Gruijl, and Jan C. van der Leun, "Estimates of Ozone Depletion and Skin Cancer Incidence to Examine the Vienna Convention Achievements," *Nature* 384 (November 1996): 256–258.

GLOSSARY

accidental war In the modern age, the unintentional launching of a nuclear attack because of a mistake or miscalculation.

administrative decentralization The transfer of governmental powers from a central seat of power to local bureaucracies.

affirmative action Giving preferential treatment to a socially or economically disadvantaged group in compensation for opportunities denied by past discrimination.

alienation The feeling on the part of ordinary citizens that normal political participation is of no consequence or that they are barred from effective participation.

American conservatism A perspective in the United States that emphasizes prosperity, security, and tradition above other values. (See also *American liberalism*.)

American liberalism A perspective in the United States that emphasizes individualism, equality, and civil rights above other values. (See also *American conservatism*.)

American Revolution (1775–83) Also called the War of Independence and Revolutionary War, this epoch-making event led to end of British rule over the thirteen American colonies and the formation of the United States of America in 1787–89; usually dated from the Declaration of Independence in 1776.

anarchism A system that opposes in principle the existence of any form of government, often through violence and lawlessness.

Antarctic Treaty An international agreement that prohibits all military activity on the Antarctic continent and allows for inspection of all nations' facilities there. It also nullifies all territorial claims to Antarctic land and pledges the signatories to peaceful cooperation in exploration and research.

antistate terrorism Terrorism directed against the government or institutions that comprise the state.

appellate court A court that reviews cases on appeal from district courts.

arms race reciprocal military buildups between rival states; a process that tends to accelerate research, technology, and development in weapon systems and, according to some experts, is a potential cause of war.

ascriptive society A society wherein an individual's status and position are ascribed by society on the basis of religion, gender, age, or some other attribute.

Asian flu A term used to describe the widespread financial turmoil in Asian stock markets, financial institutions, and economies in 1997.

authoritarianism Term applied to states in which all legitimate power rests in one person (dictatorship) or a small group of persons (oligarchy), individual rights are subordinate to the wishes of the state, and all means necessary are used to maintain political power.

authority Command of the obedience of society's members by a government.

autocracy Unchecked political power exercised by a single ruler.

balance of power system The key concept in a classic theory of international relations positing that nations of approximately equal strength will seek to maintain the status quo by preventing any one nation from gaining superiority over the others. In a balance-of-power system, participating nations form alliances and fight limited wars, with one nation acting as a "keeper of the balance," alternately supporting rival blocs to prevent a power imbalance.

Balfour Declaration Named for the British foreign secretary who in 1947 declared that the United Kingdom favored "the establishment in Palestine of a national home for the Jewish people" and pledged to "facilitate the achievement of this object, it being clearly understood that nothing shall be done which

582

may prejudice the civil and religious rights of the existing non-Jewish communities in Palestine or the rights and political status enjoyed by Jews in any other country.

barrister In Great Britain, an attorney who can plead cases in court and be appointed to the bench.

Bastille At the time of the French Revolution (1789), the Bastille was the infamous royal prison in Paris; the mass storming of the Bastille on July 14, 1789, and the freeing of the prisoners constituted a direct attack against the monarchy and symbolized the end of an era in French history; the revolutionaries then used the guillotine against none other than the reigning Bourbon dynasty, King Louis XVI and his extravagant wife, Queen Marie Antoinette.

Basic Law The West German constitution, adopted in 1949.

behavioral engineering The carefully programmed use of rewards and punishments to instill desired patterns of behavior in an individual or an animal.

behavioralists Theorists whose study of politics emphasizes fact-based evaluations of action.

behavioral psychology A school of psychological thought that holds that the way people (and animals) act is determined by the stimuli they receive from the environment and from other persons and that human or animal behavior can be manipulated by carefully structuring the environment to provide positive stimuli for desired behavior and negative stimuli for unwanted behavior.

bicameralism Division of the legislature into two houses.

bill of attainder A legislative decree that declares a person guilty and prescribes punishment without any judicial process.

Biological Weapons Convention A 1972 international arms control treaty that pledged the destruction of biological weapons stockpiles and outlawed the production and storage of such weapons.

bipolar system The breakdown of the traditional European balance-of-power system into two rival factions headed by the United States and the former Soviet Union, each with overwhelming economic and military superi-ority and each unalterably opposed to the politics and ideology of the other.

bourgeoisie In Marxist ideology, the capitalist class.

Brady Bill Named after former President Ronald Reagan's first press secretary, James Brady, this bill (which became law in 1994) requires a five-day waiting period for the purchase of a handgun; intended to give local law enforcement time to ascertain that the purchaser is not a convicted felon. (Brady was shot and severely wounded during a 1981 assassination attempt on President Reagan.)

brinkmanship In diplomacy, the deliberate use of military threats to create a crisis atmosphere; the calculated effort to take a tense bilateral relationship to the brink of war in order to achieve a political objective (for example, deterring a common enemy from carrying out an act of aggression against an ally).

British Commonwealth A prominent example of a preferential trade arrangement, in which several states agree to grant each other exclusive trade preferences; includes Great Britain and many of its former colonies.

British Raj British colonial rule on the Asian sub-continent from the eighteenth century to 1947 when India and Pakistan became independent.

budget deficit When the federal government spends more than it collects in revenue in a year. Over time, these deficits aggregate into the national debt and have significant long-term implications for the economic health and well-being of a country. (See also *national debt*.)

Bundesrat The upper house in the German federal system; its members, who are appointed directly by the *Länder* (states), exercise mostly informal influence in the legislative process.

Bundestag The lower house in the German federal system; most legislative activity occurs in this house.

Camp David Accords A 1979 agreement by which Israel gave the Sinai back to Egypt in return for Egypt's recognition of Israel's right to exist; the two former enemies established full diplomatic relations and pledged to remain at peace with one another.

capitalism A market-based economic system based on the private enterprise and driven by the profit motive, as contrasted with the centrally planned economic system pioneered by the former Soviet Union; the opposite of communism.

catalytic war A conflict that begins as a localized and limited encounter but grows into a general war after other parties are drawn into the conflict through the activation of military alliances.

cells Small, tightly knit organizational units at the grassroots level of V. I. Lenin's Bolshevik party.

Central Committee The group that directed the Soviet Communist party between party congresses. Its members were chosen by the party leadership.

charismatic leader A political leader who gains legitimacy largely through the adoration of the populace. Such adoration may spring from past heroic feats (real or imagined) or from personal oratorical skills and political writings.

checks and balances Constitutional tools that enable branches of government to resist any illegitimate expansion of power by other branches.

Chemical Weapons Convention A 1993 international arms control treaty to eliminate chemical weapons within ten years. It calls for the destruction of chemical weapons stockpiles and the monitoring of companies making compounds that can be used to produce nerve agents, to end production of chemical weapons.

citizen-leaders Individuals who influence government decisively even though they hold no official position.

citizenship The right and the obligation to participate constructively in the ongoing enterprise of self-government.

civic education The process of inculcating in potential citizens the fundamental values and beliefs of the established order.

civil disobedience Violation of the law in a nonviolent and open manner to call attention to a legal, political, or social injustice.

civil war A war between geographical sections or political factions within a nation.

coalition government In a multiparty parliamentary system, the political situation in which no single party has a majority and the largest party allies itself loosely with other, smaller parties to control a majority of the legislative seats.

cohabitation In France, the uneasy toleration of a divided executive.

Cold War The high level of tension between the United States and the former Soviet Union, in which diplomatic maneuvering, hostile propaganda, economic sanctions, and military buildups were used as weapons in a struggle for dominance.

collective ministerial responsibility In the British system, the principle that holds cabinet members jointly responsible for all the actions and decisions of the government; ministers (equivalent to department "secretaries" in the U.S. government) do not disagree publicly or openly with official policy or with the prime minister on any policy matter, although they may (and no doubt do) debate issues and express dissenting opinions privately.

collective security In international relations, the aim of an agreement among several nations to establish a single powerful bloc that will be turned on any nation that commits an act of aggression; because no single nation could ever overpower the collective force, aggression would be futile.

collectivism The belief that the public good is best served by common (as opposed to individual) ownership of a political community's means of production and distribution.

collectivization The takeover of all lands and other means of production by the state.

colonialism The policy of seeking to dominate the economic or political affairs of underdeveloped areas or weaker countries. Also called imperialism.

common law In Great Britain, laws derived from consistent precedents found in judges' rulings and decisions, as opposed to those enacted by Parliament. In the United States, the part of the common law that was in force at the time of the Revolution and not nullified by the Constitution or any subsequent statute.

Commonwealth of Independent States (CIS) A loose federation of newly sovereign nations created after the collapse of the Soviet Union. It consisted of almost all the republics that previously had comprised the USSR.

community Any association of individuals who share a common identity based on geography, ethical values, religious beliefs, or ethnic origins.

compulsory jurisdiction A legal obligation to abide by the decision of a court; in the first twenty years of the World Court's existence, forty-two governments declared their intent to accept its compulsory jurisdiction.

concurrent powers Joint federal and state control.

conservatism A political philosophy that emphasizes prosperity, security, and tradition above other values. (See also *liberalism*.)

constitution Delineation of the basic organization and operation of government.

constitutional democracy A system of limited government, based on majority rule, in which political power is scattered among many factions and interest groups, and governmental actions and institutions must conform to rules defined by a constitution.

constitutionalism See *rule of law*.

containment The global status quo policy followed by the United States after World War II; the term stems from the U.S. policy of containing attempts by the Soviet Union to extend its sphere of control to other states as it had done in eastern Europe. NATO, the Marshall Plan, and the Korean and Vietnam Wars grew out of this policy.

conventional participation Engaging in the most common and least demanding of political activities, including voting, following political issues in the media, and attending political rallies.

counterterrorism Methods used to combat terrorism.

country As a political term, it refers loosely to a sovereign state and is roughly equivalent to *nation* or *nation-state;* the word "country" is often used as a term of endearment—for example, in the phrase "my country 'tis of thee, sweet land of liberty . . ." in the patriotic song every American child learns in elementary school; *country* has an emotional dimension not present in the word *state*.

coup d'état The attempted seizure of governmental power by an alternate power group (often the military) that seeks to gain control of vital government institutions without any fundamental alteration in the form of government or society.

crimes against humanity A category of crime, first introduced at the Nuremberg trials of Nazi war criminals, covering the wanton, brutal extermination of millions of innocent civilians.

crimes against peace A Nuremberg war crimes trials category, covering the violation of international peace by waging an unjustified, aggressive war.

Dayton Accords A peace agreement signed in Paris, France, in 1995 aimed at ending the war in Bosnia; the settlement gave 49 percent of Bosnia to the Serbs and 51 percent to the Muslims and Croats, kept Sarajevo as the capital, and created a central government with a collective presidency and parliament.

Declaration of the Rights of Man Enacted by French National Assembly in August 1789, this brief manifesto was intended as the preamble to a liberal-democratic constitution to be written later; it affirmed the sovereign authority of the nation but limited that authority by recognizing the right to individual life, property, and security.

delegate theory of representation A theory that elected officials should reflect the views of their constituencies.

demagogues Those who use their leadership skills to gain public office through appeals to popular fears and prejudices, then abuse that power for personal gain.

Democracy Wall A wall located in the heart of Beijing on which public criticism of the regime was permitted to be displayed in 1978.

democratic correlates Those conditions or circumstances thought to relate positively to the creation and maintenance of democracy within a nation.

democratic socialism A form of government based on popular elections, public ownership and control of the main sectors of the economy, and broad welfare programs in health and education to benefit citizens.

demokratizatsiia Mikhail Gorbachev's policy of encouraging democratic reforms within the former Soviet Union, including increased electoral competition within the Communist party.

dependency theory Holds that the developing nations remain poor and dependent on the rich nations long after colonialism has officially ended because the industrialized states (the West) use every means available (political, economic, military, and cultural) to prevent competition from less developed countries (LDCs) where labor is cheap and abundant and to perpetuate a world economic system which keeps the price of raw materials and farm commodities low.

developing nations Nations without provisions for transition of political power and assurance of public services and individual safety.

devolution In the context of U.S. federalism, the policy of giving states and localities more power to make laws, policies, and decisions without interference from Washington, D.C.

dial groups Public opinion groups in which individuals are given a dial on which to register their instant approval or disapproval.

dialectical materialism Karl Marx's theory of historical progression, according to which economic classes struggle with one another, producing an evolving series of economic systems that will lead, ultimately, to a classless society.

dictatorship of the proletariat In Marxist theory, the political stage immediately following the workers' revolution, during which the Communist party controls the state and defends it against a capitalist resurgence or counterrevolution; the dictatorship of the proletariat leads into pure communism and the classless society.

direct democracy A form of government in which political decisions are made directly by citizens rather than by their representatives.

disciplined parties In a parliamentary system, the tendency of legislators to vote consistently as a bloc with fellow party members in support of the party's platform.

district court The court in which most federal cases originate.

divided executive Situation in French government when the president and the prime minister differ in political party or outlook.

domestic jurisdiction Matters that are essentially within the purview of a sovereign state.

domestic terrorism A form of terrorism practiced within a country by people with no ties to any government.

Dr. Bonham's case English court case (1610) in which jurist Edward Coke propounded the principle that legislative acts contrary to the rule of law are null and void.

dual executive In a parliamentary system, the division of the functions of head of state and chief executive officer between two persons; the prime minister serves as chief executive, and some other elected (or royal) figure serves as ceremonial head of state.

due process of law A guarantee of fair legal procedure; it is found in the Fifth and Fourteenth Amendments of the U.S. Constitution.

Duma Officially called the State Duma, it is the lower house of the Federal Assembly, Russia's national legislature, reestablished in the 1993 constitution, after having been abolished in 1917. It comprises 450 members, half of whom are elected from nationwide party lists, with the other half elected from single-member constituencies.

dystopia A society whose creators set out to build the perfect political order only to discover that they cannot remain in power except through coercion and by maintaining a ruthless monopoly over the means of communication.

economic penetration The influence that one or more other nations exert on the economic life of a prerevolutionary nation.

entitlements Government expenditures that provide benefits that are deeply ingrained in the fabric of American life and that Americans expect as a matter of right because they have made mandatory tax contributions to government-run retirement and health insurance funds.

Estates-General The legislature of France before 1789, in which each of the three estates (clergy, nobility, and commoners) was represented.

ethnic cleansing The practice of clearing all Muslims out of towns and villages in Bosnia by violent means.

ethnocentric bias The inability of nations to be reasonably objective when judging their own acts because of ideology or nationalism.

eugenics The science of controlling the hereditary traits in a species, usually by selective mating, in an attempt to improve the species.

Eurocommunism In western Europe, a modification of traditional Soviet communist theory that renounced violent revolution and dictatorship in favor of control of the existing governmental structure through elections.

European Union (EU) The economic association of European nations; formerly known as the Common Market or European Economic Community.

exclusionary rule In judicial proceedings, the rule that evidence obtained in violation of constitutional guidelines cannot be used in court against the accused.

expansionism A strategy by which a nation seeks to enlarge its territory or influence.

ex post facto law A law that retroactively criminalizes acts that were legal at the time they were committed.

fascism A totalitarian political system that is headed by a popular charismatic leader and in which a single political party and carefully controlled violence form the bases of complete social and political control. Fascism differs from communism in that the economic structure, although controlled by the state, is privately owned.

Federal Assembly This is Russia's national legislature, a bicameral parliament, established under the 1993 constitution, comprising a lower chamber (State Duma) and an upper chamber (Federation Council).

Federation Council The upper house of the Federal Assembly, Russia's national legislature, established under the 1993 constitution, with 178 members, composed of two deputies (representatives) from each of the eighty-nine territorial units.

federalism A system of limited government based on the division of authority between the central government and smaller regional governments.

first past the post An electoral system used in the United Kingdom and the United States in which legislative candidates run in single-member districts and the winner is decided by plurality vote; this system favors broad-based, entrenched political parties and tends toward a two-party configuration; critics contend that it is undemocratic because it places a huge hurdle in the path of small or new parties and forces voters to decide between voting for a major-party candidate near the center of the political spectrum or wasting their votes on a third-party candidate who cannot possibly win.

first stage of communism In Marxist theory, the period immediately following the overthrow of capitalism during which the proletariat establishes a worker dictatorship to prevent counterrevolution and seeks to create a socialist economic system.

first strike A surprise or preemptive attack using nuclear weapons.

First World The industrialized democracies.

focus groups Small numbers of people who, led by a communications expert, react to and discuss particular agenda items.

free enterprise Another term for private enterprise unencumbered by heavy state regulation or restrictions; the opposite of state-controlled enterprise or state ownership of businesses and industries.

free-market economy A decentralized economy in which prices, wages, and interest rates, as well as the mix of goods and services produced, are determined by the forces of supply and demand rather than by the state.

French Revolution (1789) Brought down the Bourbon monarchy in France in the name of *"liberté, egalité, and fraternité"* (liberty, equality, and fraternity), introduced the contagion of liberalism in a Europe still ruled by conservative, aristocratic, and royalist institutions, and ushered in the rule of Napoléon Bonaparte; prelude to the First Republic in France and to the Napoleonic Wars.

functionalism/functionalists In political thought, the theory that the gradual transfer of economic and social functions to international cooperative agencies (for example, specialized UN agencies such as UNESCO) will eventually lead to a transfer of actual authority and integration of political activities on the international level.

fusion of powers In a parliamentary system, the concentration of all governmental authority in the legislature.

gender gap A term used to refer to differences in voting between men and women in the United States. This disparity is most obvious in political issues and elections that raise the issue of appropriateness of governmental force.

Geneva Convention A body of international law dealing with the treatment of the wounded, prisoners of war, and civilians in a war zone.

Gestapo In Nazi Germany, the secret state police—Hitler's instrument for spreading mass terror among Jews and political opponents.

glasnost Literally "openness," this term refers to Mikhail Gorbachev's curtailment of censorship and encouragement of political discussion and dissent within the former Soviet Union.

glasnost-first model A theory of development which argues that liberalizing political reforms should precede economic reforms.

Gleichschaltung Hitler's technique of using Nazi-controlled associations, clubs, and organizations to coordinate his revolutionary activities.

globalization The process by which values, attitudes, preferences, and products associated with the most technologically advanced democracies are being spread around the globe via mass media and trade.

government The persons and institutions that make and enforce rules or laws for the larger community.

gradualism The belief that major changes in society should take place slowly, through reform, rather than suddenly, through revolution.

Great Leap Forward Mao Zedong's attempt, in the late 1950s and early 1960s, to transform and modernize China's economic structure through mass mobilization of the entire population into self-sufficient communes in which everything was done in groups.

Great Proletarian Cultural Revolution A chaotic period beginning in 1966, when the youth of China (the Red Guards), at Mao Zedong's direction, attacked all bureaucratic and military officials on the pretext that a reemergence of capitalist and materialist tendencies was taking place. The offending officials were sent to forced labor camps to be "reeducated."

green revolution A dramatic rise in agricultural output, resulting from modern irrigation systems and synthetic fertilizers, characteristic of modern India, Mexico, Taiwan, and the Philippines.

guerrilla warfare The tactics used by loosely organized military forces grouped into small, mobile squads that carry out acts of terrorism and sabotage, then melt back into the civilian population.

gulag archipelago Metaphorical name for the network of slave labor camps established in the former Soviet Union by Joseph Stalin and maintained by his secret police, to which nonconformists and politically undesirable persons were sent.

Habeas Corpus Act An act, passed by the English Parliament in 1679, that strengthened the rights of English citizens to the protection of law.

Hague Convention A widely accepted set of rules governing conduct in land wars, the use of new weapons, and the rights and duties of both neutral and warring parties.

Hare plan In parliamentary democracies, an electoral procedure whereby candidates compete for a set number of seats, and those who receive a certain quota of votes are elected. Voters vote only once and indicate both a first and a second choice.

hot line The secure direct line of communication between Washington and Moscow created in 1963 at the height of the Cold War to prevent an accidental nuclear Armageddon.

human nature The characteristics that human beings have in common and that influence how they react to their surroundings and fellow humans.

Hundred Flowers campaign A brief period in China (1956) when Mao Zedong directed that freedom of expression and individualism be allowed. It was quashed when violent criticism of the regime erupted.

ICBMs Intercontinental ballistic missiles.

idealism A political philosophy that considers values, ideals, and moral principles as the key to comprehending, and possibly changing, the behavior of nation-states.

ideological terrorism A form of terrorism, usually Marxist in outlook, aimed at overthrowing a government.

ideology Any set of fixed, predictable ideas held by politicians and citizens on how to serve the public good.

illegal participation Political activity that is against the laws of the state.

imperialism A policy of territorial expansion (empire-building) often by means of military conquest; derived from the word *empire*.

individualism According to Alexis de Tocqueville, the direction of one's feelings toward oneself and one's immediate situation; a self-centered detachment from the broader concerns of society as a whole. According to John Stuart Mill, the qualities of human character that separate humans from animals and give them uniqueness and dignity.

initiative A vote by which citizens directly repeal an action of the legislature.

interdependence In political thought, the theory that no nation can afford to isolate itself completely from the political, economic, and cultural activities of other nations and that as a result, a growing body of international organizations whose interests transcend national concerns has arisen.

International Monetary Fund (IMF) An international organization established by the United Nations, composed of the governments of many nations, designed to promote worldwide monetary cooperation, international trade, and economic stability. It also helps equalize balance of payments by allowing member countries to borrow from its fund.

interest group An association of individuals that attempts to influence policy and legislation in a confined area of special interest, often through lobbying, campaign contributions, and bloc voting.

international governmental organizations (IGOs) International organizations of which governments are members.

internationalists Theorists favoring peace and cooperation among nations through the active participation of all governments in some sort of world organization.

international law The body of customs, treaties, and generally accepted rules that regulate the rights and obligations of nations when dealing with one another.

international nongovernmental organizations (INGOs) International organizations made up of private individuals and groups.

International Revolutionary party The dominant political party in Mexico from 1929 to the present; the PRI had never lost an election until 2000, when Vincente Fox of the National Action party won the presidency.

international terrorism A form of terrorism involving one country against the government of another; sometimes called state-sponsored terrorism.

intifada An Arabic word meaning "uprising"; the name given to the prolonged Palestinian uprising against Israeli occupation in the West Bank and Gaza in 1987–93 and again in 2001–02; the second intifada has been particularly violent involving the frequent use of suicide bombers by extremist Palestinian groups and a brutal crackdown by Israel in the occupied territories.

interstate wars Conflicts between sovereign states.

Iron Law of Oligarchy The elitist theory that because of the administrative necessities involved in managing any large organization, access to and control of information and communication become concentrated in a few bureaucrats, who then wield true power in the organization.

islands of separateness Family, church, or other social organizations through which internal resistance to the prevailing totalitarian regime can persist.

judicial review The power of a court to declare acts by the government unconstitutional and hence void.

junta A ruling oligarchy, especially one made up of military officers.

justice Fairness; the distribution of rewards and burdens in society in accordance with what is deserved.

just war A war fought in self-defense or because it is the only way a nation can do what is right.

Kashmir A disputed territory between India and Pakistan; most of Kashmir is controlled by India which has a Hindu majority but Kashmir's population is predominantly Muslim, the religion of Pakistan; India and Pakistan have fought three major wars over Kashmir since independence in 1947 and tensions mounted again in 2000–01; India possesses nuclear weapons and Pakistan may also have a limited number of atomic bombs in its military arsenal.

keeper of the balance The nation in a balance-of-power system that functions as an arbiter in disputes, taking sides to preserve the political equilibrium.

kin-country syndrome Phenomenon wherein countries whose peoples and leaders are culturally tied to one another take similar positions.

Knesset The unicameral Israeli parliament.

kulaks A class of well-to-do landowners in Russian society that was purged by Joseph Stalin because it resisted his drive to establish huge collective farms under state control.

Kuomintang The Chinese Nationalist party, led by Chiang Kai-shek, defeated by Mao Zedong in 1949.

laissez-faire capitalism Capitalism that operates under the idea that the marketplace, unfettered by central state planning, is the best regulator of the economic life of a society.

law of capitalist accumulation According to Karl Marx, the invariable rule that stronger capitalists, motivated solely by greed, will gradually eliminate weaker competitors and gain increasing control of the market.

law of pauperization In Karl Marx's view, the rule that capitalism has a built-in tendency toward recession and unemployment, and thus workers inevitably become surplus labor.

law of supply and demand This principle, which forms the basis of capitalist or market-based economics, holds that the best regulator of the economy is the "invisible hand" of the market place; the supposedly rational results of free and unfettered economic activity; patterns of production, distribution, investment, and consumption that result from rational decisions of free individuals (producers, consumers, entrepreneurs, and workers) all pursuing their own selfish interests.

legitimacy The exercise of political power in a community in a way that is voluntarily accepted by the members of that community.

legitimate authority The legal and moral right of a government to rule over a specific population and control a specific territory; the term *legitimacy* usually implies a widely recognized claim of governmental authority and voluntary acceptance on the part of the population(s) directly affected.

liberal arts education Education that stresses the development of critical thinking skills through the study of literature, philosophy, history, and science.

liberal tradition In Western political thought, a 300-year-old tradition which takes the position that the purpose of government is to champion and protect individual rights. However, there is continuing disagreement between the followers of American liberalism and American conservatism about which individual rights are most important.

liberalism A political philosophy that emphasizes individualism, equality, and civil rights above other values. (See also *conservatism*.)

liberalization In the former Soviet Union, the relaxation of repressive internal policies. Periods of liberalization and repression alternated throughout Soviet history.

libertarianism A system based on the belief that government is a necessary evil that should interfere with individual freedom and privacy as little as possible; also known as minimalism.

limited government The concept that government cannot undertake an action, no matter how many people desire it, that conflicts with an overriding principle (such as justice) embodied in the constitution.

limited wars The opposite of all-out wars, particularly all-out nuclear warfare.

list system Method of proportional representation by which candidates are ranked on the ballot by their party and are chosen according to rank.

lobbyists People who attempt to influence governmental policy in favor of some special interest.

Lok Sabha The lower house of India's Federal Parliament; the directly elected House of the People; in India as in the United Kingdom and other parliamentary systems, governments are formed by the majority party (or a coalition of parties) in the lower house following national elections.

low-information rationality The idea that voters can make sensible choices (for example, casting a ballot wisely) even though they lack knowledge and sophistication about public policy, candidates, current events.

low-intensity conflict Occurs when one state finances, sponsors, or promotes the sporadic and prolonged use of violence in a rival country.

loyal opposition The belief, which originated in England, that the out-of-power party has a responsibility to formulate alternative policies and programs; such a party is sometimes called the loyal opposition.

Magna Carta A list of political concessions granted in 1215 by King John to his barons that became the basis for the rule of law in England.

majority rule The principle that any candidate or program that receives at least half of all votes plus one prevails.

Marshall Plan A post–World War II program of massive economic assistance to western Europe, inspired by the fear that those war-devastated countries were ripe for communist-backed revolutions.

Marxists Followers of the political philosophy of Karl Marx (1818–1883), who theorized that the future belonged to the industrial underclass ("proletariat") and that a "classless society" would eventually replace one based on social distinctions (classes) tied to property ownership; during the Cold War (1947–91), the term was often mistakenly applied to everyone who embraced the ideology or sympathized with the policies of the Soviet Union or the People's Republic of China against the West.

Massive retaliation Military-strategic doctrine based on a plausible standing threat of nuclear reprisal employed by the United States in the 1950s during the short-lived era of the American nuclear monopoly; according to this doctrine, if the Soviet Union attacked U.S. allies with conventional military forces the United States would retaliate with nuclear weapons.

mass line Mao Zedong's belief that any problem could be solved by instilling individuals with ideological fervor, thereby inspiring and mobilizing the masses to action.

mass media The vehicles of mass communication, such as television, radio, film, books, magazines, and newspapers.

mass-mobilization regimes Totalitarian states at their most active stage of encouraging citizen participation in rallies and political meetings.

mass movement Any large group of followers dedicated to a leader and/or ideology and prepared to make any sacrifice demanded of them for the sake of the movement.

Meiji Restoration The end of Japan's feudal era, in 1868, when a small group of powerful individuals crowned a symbolic emperor, embarked on an economic modernization program, and established a modern governmental bureaucracy.

MIRVs Multiple, independently targettable, reentry vehicles; this is the name given to intercontinental missiles containing many nuclear warheads that can be individually programmed to split off from the nose cone of the rocket upon reentry into the earth's atmosphere and hit different specific targets with a high degree of accuracy.

mixed economy An economic system that combines both publicly and privately owned enterprises.

mixed regime A nation in which the various branches of government represent social classes.

Moghuls Muslim invaders who created a dynastic empire on the Asian sub-continent; the greatest Moghul rulers were Babur (1483–1530), Akbar (1556–1605), Shah Jahan (1628–1658), and Aurangzeb (1658–1707); Shah Jahan was the architect of the Taj Mahal.

monarchists Adherents to a system based on the belief that political power should be concentrated in one person (for example, a king) who rules by decree.

Monroe Doctrine A status quo international policy laid down by U.S. president James Monroe, who pledged the United States to resist any attempts by outside powers to alter the balance of power in the American hemisphere.

moral relativism The idea that all moral judgments are inherently subjective and therefore not valid for anybody but oneself; the belief that no single opinion on morality is any better than another.

mosaic society A society characterized by a large degree of sociocultural diversity (often found in African and Latin American nations) that can pose significant barriers to the nation's development.

Motor-voter law A statute that allows residents of a given locality to register to vote at convenient places such as welfare offices and drivers' license bureaus; the idea behind laws of this kind is to remove technical obstacles to voting and thus promote better turnouts in elections.

multinational corporation (MNC) A company that conducts substantial business in several nations.

multinational states Sovereign states which contain two or more (sometimes many more) major ethnolinguistic groups (or nations) in the territories they control; notable examples include India, Nigeria, Russia, China, as well as the former Yugoslavia.

mutual assured destruction (MAD) A nuclear stalemate in which both sides in an adversarial relationship know that if either one initiates a war the other will retain enough retaliatory ("second strike") capability to administer unacceptable damage even after absorbing the full impact of a nuclear surprise attack; during the Cold War, a stable strategic relationship between the two superpowers.

mutual deterrence The theory that aggressive wars can be prevented if potential victims maintain a military force sufficient to inflict unacceptable punishment on any possible aggressor.

North American Free Trade Agreement (NAFTA) Signed in 1994 by the United States, Mexico, and Canada, NAFTA established a compact to allow free trade or trade with reduced tariffs among the three nations.

nation Often interchangeable with *state* or *country* in common usage, this term actually denotes a specific people with a distinct language and culture or a major ethnic group— for example, the French, Dutch, Chinese, and Japanese people all constitute a nation as well as a state, hence the term *nation-state*; not all

nations are fortunate enough to have a state of their own, however—modern examples include the Kurds (Turkey, Iraq, and Iran), Palestinians (West Bank and Gaza, Lebanon, Jordan), Pashtuns (Afghanistan), Uighurs and Tibetans (China).

National Action party The main opposition party in Mexico; the PAN's candidate, Vincente Fox, was elected president in 2000.

National Assembly Focal point of France's bicameral legislative branch that must approve all laws.

national debt The accumulation over time of annual budget deficits, that is, when the federal government spends more than it collects in revenue each year. It forces the government to borrow money to pay its bills and results in substantial payments of interest on those loans, which diverts important federal tax dollars from the government's annual coffers.

national interest The aims of policies that help a nation to maintain or increase its power and prestige.

national security Protection of a country from external and internal enemies.

national self-determination The right of a nation to choose its own government.

nationalist–separatist terrorism A form of terrorism carried out by groups seeking their own homeland, with activities confined to a specific nation.

nation building The process by which inhabitants of a given territory—irrespective of ethnic, religious, or linguistic differences—come to identify with symbols and institutions of their nation-state.

nation-state A geographically defined community administered by a government.

NATO (North Atlantic Treaty Organization) A military alliance (founded in 1949) consisting of the United States, Great Britain, Canada, Germany, France, Italy, Greece, Turkey, Portugal, Norway, Belgium, Denmark, the Netherlands, Iceland, and Luxembourg. Previously, its principal aim was to prevent Soviet aggression in Europe.

neo-isolationists Label sometimes given to foreign policy critics who argue that the United States has too many commitments overseas and would be better off concentrating on domestic issues.

neutrality The policy of giving the very highest priority to staying out of war by adopting a non-threatening posture toward neighboring states, maintaining a strictly defensive military capability, and refusing to take sides in conflicts; Finland, Sweden, and Switzerland are among the countries that have pursued a policy of neutrality most successfully.

new federalism During the Nixon administration, the federal government provided unrestricted (or minimally restricted) funds to states and localities under this program; later, under President Ronald Reagan it was reincarnated as a policy aimed at cutting federal funds going to the states.

new industrial countries Countries with flourishing economies, thriving export industries, and a burgeoning middle class; examples include South Korea, Taiwan, Singapore, and Thailand.

new science of politics The eighteenth-century concept that political institutions could be arranged to produce competent government while preventing tyranny from developing out of an overconcentration of power.

nihilism A philosophy that holds that the total destruction of all existing social and political institutions is a desirable end in itself.

no-confidence vote In parliamentary governments, a legislative vote that the sitting government must win to remain in power.

nomenklatura The former Soviet Communist party's system of controlling all important administrative appointments, thereby ensuring the support and loyalty of those who managed day-to-day affairs.

nonalignment A policy specific to the Cold War in which many developing countries—formerly known as Third World countries—preferred not to ally themselves with either the United States and its allies (the West) or the Soviet Union and its allies (the East); nonalignment differs from neutrality in that it does not commit a state to non-aggression or non-involvement in local conflicts and, unlike neutrality, it did not become an important concept in international relations until after World War II.

Nonproliferation Treaty (NPT) An international agreement, drafted in 1968, not to aid nonnuclear nations in acquiring nuclear weapons; it was not signed by France, China, and other nations actively seeking to build these weapons.

nonstate actors Entities other than nation-states, including multinational corporations, nongovernmental organizations (NGOs) and international nongovernmental organizations, that play a role in international politics.

nonviolent resistance A passive form of confrontation and protest; also called civil disobedience at times.

nuclear monopoly When only one side in an adversarial relationship possesses a credible nuclear capability; the United States enjoyed a nuclear monopoly for roughly a decade after World War II.

oligarchy A form of authoritarian government in which a small group of powerful individuals wields absolute power.

ordinary politicians Individuals who concentrate on getting reelected.

Outer Space Treaty An international agreement, signed by the United States and the former Soviet Union, that banned the introduction of military weapons into outer space, prohibited the extension of national sovereignty in space, and encouraged cooperation and sharing of information about space research.

overkill Having a much larger nuclear arsenal than is (or would be) needed to wipe out an adversary completely.

Palestine The territory south of Lebanon and Syria and west of Jordan known in Biblical times as Judea and Samaria; today most of this territory forms the nation-state of Israel established in 1947 with the help of the United States and Great Britain.

Palestinian Arabs The Arab inhabitants of the former territory of Palestine most of which is now the state of Israel; Palestinian Arabs, like most other Arabs, are Muslims; millions of Palestinians were displaced after World War II when Jewish immigrants, mostly from Europe, realized a longstanding Zionist dream to recreate a Jewish homeland in the historical place where Judaism was born; the creation of Israel was accomplished by armed struggle rather than negotiation, setting the stage for what has become a permanent state of war between Palestinian Arabs (many of whom still live in refugee camps) and the state of Israel.

paradox of democratic peace Democratic states are often militarily powerful, fight other states, engage in armed intervention, and sometimes commit acts of aggression, but they do not fight each other.

parliamentary sovereignty In the United Kingdom, the unwritten constitutional principle that makes the British parliament the supreme law-making body; laws passed by Parliament are not subject to judicial review and cannot be rejected by the Crown.

parliamentary system A system of democratic government in which authority is concentrated in the legislative branch, which selects a prime minister and cabinet officers who serve as long as they have majority support in the parliament.

participation Active involvement in politics, running the gamut from voting to mass protests and even armed rebellion or terrorism.

partiinost The spirit of sacrifice, enthusiasm, and unquestioning devotion required of Communist party members.

Party Congress The highest Soviet political body, which met every five years. It supposedly represented the party membership but actually served to legitimize the policies of the ruling elite.

patron–client relations A form of political participation, most often found in developing countries, in which, within a hierarchical system, influential persons obtain benefits in return for votes, payoffs, or political power bases.

peer group A group of people similar in age and characteristics.

perestroika Term given to Mikhail Gorbachev's various attempts to restructure the Soviet economy while not completely sacrificing its socialist character.

perestroika-first model A theory of national development that emphasized that liberalizing, market-oriented reforms should be undertaken before political reforms were attempted.

Petition of Right An act, passed by the English Parliament in 1628, that established due process of law and strictly limited the monarch's powers of taxation.

philosopher-kings Wise philosophers who govern Plato's ideal city in *The Republic*.

plebiscite A vote by an entire community on some specific issue of public policy.

pluralists Theorists who believe that in any large democracy, the political system is decentralized and institutionally fragmented and therefore that control of the power structure is possible only by single-issue coalitions in confined areas of special interest.

police powers Powers of states to maintain the internal peace and order, provide for education, and generally safeguard the people's health, safety, and welfare.

Politburo A small clique that formed the supreme decision-making body in the former Soviet Union. Its members often belonged to the Secretariat and were ministers of key governmental departments.

political action committees (PACs) Groups organized to raise campaign funds in support of or in opposition to specific candidates.

political apathy Lack of interest in political participation.

political development A government's ability to exert power effectively, to provide for public order and services, and to withstand eventual changes in leadership.

political efficacy The ability to participate meaningfully in political activities, usually because of one's education, social background, and sense of self-esteem.

political party Any group of individuals who agree on some or all aspects of public policy and organize to place their members in control of the national government.

political penetration Promotion of economic development through road and bridge construction and telephone line installation to create a more integrated national economy.

political realism The philosophy that power is the key variable in all political relationships and should be used pragmatically and prudently to advance the national interest; policies are judged good or bad on the basis of their effect on national interests, not on their level of morality.

political socialization The process by which

members of a community are taught the basic values of their society and prepared for the duties of citizenship.

politico A legislator who follows the will of constituents on issues that are most important to them and exercises personal judgment in areas that are less important to constituents or fundamentally important to the national welfare.

politics The process by which a community selects rulers and empowers them to make decisions, takes action to attain common goals, and reconciles conflicts within the community.

power The capacity to influence or control the behavior of persons and institutions, whether by persuasion or coercion.

prefects In France, the heads of major governmental agencies.

presidential system A democratic form of government in which the chief executive is chosen by separate election, serves a fixed term, and has powers carefully separated from those of the other branches of government.

prior restraint The legal doctrine that the government does not have the power to restrain the media from publication except in cases of dire national emergency.

private interest groups Groups organized to advance the self-interest of their members.

proletariat In Marxist theory, the working class.

propaganda The use of mass media to create whatever impression is desired among the general population and to influence thoughts and activities toward desired ends.

proportional representation Any political structure under which seats in the legislature are allocated to each party based on the percentage of the popular vote each receives.

public good The shared beliefs of a political community as to what goals government ought to attain (for example, to achieve the fullest possible measure of security, prosperity, equality, liberty, or justice for all citizens).

public interest groups Groups that promote causes they believe will benefit society as a whole.

public opinion A view held by citizens that influences the decisions and policies of government officials.

public opinion polling Canvassing citizens for their views.

purge The elimination of all rivals to power through mass arrests, imprisonment, exile, and murder, often directed at former associates and their followers who have (or are imagined to have) enough influence to be a threat to the ruling elite.

question hour In the United Kingdom, the times set aside Monday through Thursday every week for Her Majesty's Loyal Opposition (the party out of power) to criticize, and scrutinize the actions and decisions of the Government (the party in power); twice each week the Prime Minister must answer hostile questions fired at him or her by the Opposition, as well.

Rajya Sabha The upper house of India's Federal Parliament; the indirectly elected Council of States.

random sampling A polling method that involves canvassing people at random from the population. (See also *stratified sampling*.)

recall Direct voting to remove an elected official from office.

rectification In Maoist China, the elimination of all purported capitalist traits, such as materialism and individualism.

referendum A vote through which citizens may directly repeal an action taken by the legislature.

Reign of Terror In the French Revolution, the mass executions, ordered by Maximilien Robespierre and his Committee of Public Safety, of all persons whose political outlook differed from their utopian ideal.

representative democracy Citizen participation whereby polling leads to the election of representatives.

republic A form of government in which sovereignty resides in the people of that country, rather than with the rulers. The vast majority of republics today are democratic or representative republics, meaning that the sovereign power is exercised by elected representatives who are responsible to the citizenry.

retribution The punishment of criminals on the ground that they have done wrong and deserve to suffer.

reverse discrimination When affirmative action aimed at giving historically disadvantaged groups greater access to jobs, housing, and educational opportunities becomes an obstacle to members of the majority, it is sometimes given this label; an unintended consequence of giving preference to minorities and gender discrimination.

revolution A fundamental change in the political and social institutions of a society, often accompanied by violence, cultural upheaval, and civil war.

revolution of rising expectations A revolution achieved through development that Third World nations experience as they emulate First and Second World successes.

revolutionary communism The ideology that the capitalist system must be smashed by a violent uprising by the working class and replaced with public ownership and a government-controlled economic system.

Revolutionary War The American War of Independence (1775–83); see *American Revolution*.

right to revolution John Locke's theory that when governmental actions undermine the essential rights of life, liberty, and property, citizens have a right to revolt and replace the government with one that will rule correctly.

rule of law The concept that the power and discretion of government and its officials ought to be restrained by a supreme set of neutral rules that prevent arbitrary and unfair action by government. Also called constitutionalism.

salami tactics The methods used by V. I. Lenin to divide his opponents into small groups that could be turned against one another and easily overwhelmed.

Seabed Treaty An international agreement that forbids the establishment of nuclear weapons on the ocean floor beyond the twelve-mile territorial limit.

second stage of communism In Marxist theory, a utopian classless society in which individual fulfillment and social cooperation and harmony are achieved and from which war has been entirely eliminated.

second strike Retaliation in kind against a nuclear attack(er); this "second-strike capability" paradoxically minimizes the likelihood that a nuclear confrontation will lead to an actual nuclear exchange.

Second World The communist states.

sedition The fomenting of revolution.

separation of powers The organization of government into distinct areas of legislative, executive, and judicial functions, each responsible to different constituencies and possessing its own powers and responsibilities.

simple majority The largest bloc of voters in an election.

SLBMs Submarine-launched ballistic missiles.

socialism An ideology favoring collective and government ownership over individual or private ownership.

soft money Campaign contributions to national party committees that do not have to be reported to the Federal Election Commission so long as the funds are not used to benefit a particular candidate; the national committees funnel the funds to state parties which generally operate under less stringent reporting requirements; critics are that soft money is a massive loophole in the existing system of campaign finance regulation and that it amounts to a form of legalized corruption.

solicitor In Great Britain, an attorney who can prepare court cases and draw up contracts and other legal documents but cannot plead cases or become a judge.

sovereignty A government's capacity to assert supreme power successfully in a political state.

Star Chamber Historically, a British court whose jurisdiction was extended to allow the king arbitrarily to punish anyone who disobeyed a royal decree.

state In its sovereign form, an independent political-administrative unit that successfully claims the allegiance of a given population, exercises a monopoly on the legitimate use of coercive force, and controls the territory inhabited by its citizens or subjects; in its other common form, a state is the major political-administrative subdivision of a federal system and as such is not sovereign but rather depends on the central authority (sometimes called the national government) for resource allocations (tax transfers and grants), defense (military protection and emergency relief), and regulation of economic relations with other federal subdivisions (nonsovereign states) and external entities (sovereign states).

state building The creation of political institutions capable of exercising authority and allocating resources effectively within a nation.

statecraft The wise management of the affairs of state.

stateless nations Peoples (or nations) that are scattered over the territory of several states or dispersed widely and who have no autonomous, independent or sovereign governing body of their own; examples of stateless nations include Kurds, Palestinians, and Tibetans. (See *nation*.)

state of nature The condition of human beings before the creation of a social code of behavior and collective techniques to control normal human impulses.

statesman A politician in a position of authority who possesses exceptional political skills, practical wisdom, and concern for the public good and whose leadership has a significant positive effect on society.

state terrorism Usually violent methods used by a government's own security forces to intimidate and coerce its own people.

status quo strategy A national policy of maintaining the existing balance of power through collective security agreements, diplomacy, and negotiation, as well as through "legitimizing instruments" such as international law and international organizations.

Strategic Arms Reduction Treaty II (START II) A treaty negotiated between the United States and the former Soviet Union that limited strategic nuclear weapons.

strategic polling A type of polling used to determine what positions candidates ought to take or what political advertisements will project positive candidate images.

stratified sampling A manner of polling in which participants are chosen on the basis of age, income, socioeconomic background, and the like, so that the sample mirrors the larger population; the opposite of *random selection*.

straw polls Unscientific surveys; simple, inexpensive polls open to all sorts of manipulation and misuse.

subversion The attempt to undermine a government, often using outside assistance.

Supreme Court The federal court of last resort, settling cases that raise particularly trouble-some questions of legal interpretation or constitutional principle.

terms of trade In international economics, the valuation (or price) of the products (commodities, manufactures, services) countries buy on the world market relative to the valuation of the products they sell; the structure of prices for different kinds of goods and services in international trade—for example, if manufactures are generally high-priced relative to minerals and agricultural products, then the terms of trade are unfavorable for countries that produce only farm commodities or raw materials.

terrorism Political activity that relies on violence or the threat of violence to achieve its ends.

theocracy A government based on religion and dominated by the clergy.

Third World Collectively, the developing nations of Asia, Africa, and Latin America, most of which were once European colonies; Third World nations tend to be poor and densely populated.

Tiananmen Square massacre In 1989, unarmed civilian workers and students marched in Tiananmen Square in Beijing to demand democratic freedom and government reforms. Army troops responded with force, killing 1,500 demonstrators and wounding another 10,000.

totalitarianism A political system in which every facet of the society, the economy, and the government is tightly controlled by the ruling elite. Secret police terrorism and a radical ideology implemented through mass mobilization and propaganda are hallmarks of the totalitarian state's methods and goals.

tracking polls Repeated sampling of voters to assess shifts in attitudes or behavior over time.

traditionalists Theorists whose study of politics is based on examining fundamental and enduring questions.

traditional societies Such societies are rooted in the past, resistant to change, and often very poor and agrarian, with high birthrates and widespread illiteracy.

transnational terrorism Exists when terrorist groups in different countries cooperate or when a group's terrorist actions cross national boundaries.

true believer A person who is totally committed to the revolutionary movement and fanatical in his or her devotion to, and self-sacrifice for, the cause.

true leaders Individuals who, through the exercise of uncommon political wisdom and skills, lead their countries through times of national stress.

Truman Doctrine President Harry Truman's pledge of U.S. support for any free people threatened with revolution by an internal armed minority or an outside aggression.

trustee theory of representation The theory that elected officials should be leaders, making informed choices in the interest of their constituencies.

tutelage The system of central bureaucratic supervision of all local decisions found in a unitary system of government (for example, France).

tyranny of the majority The political situation in which a dominant group uses its control of the government to abuse the rights of minority groups.

ultranationalism Extreme nationalism often associated with fascism; a militant right-wing orientation typically characterized by militarism, racial bigotry, and xenophobia.

unacceptable damage In warfare, a level of destruction that would make the temptation to commit aggression unattractive to a would-be perpetrator; in nuclear-strategic doctrine, the objective of a second-strike capability necessary to deter a preemptive or preventive nuclear attack (a first strike).

unconditional surrender Giving an all-but-vanquished enemy a stark choice between surrendering immediately (placing itself entirely at the mercy of the victor) and being utterly destroyed.

unconventional participation Political activity that is legal but considered inappropriate by a majority of citizens.

unitary system A system in which the government may choose to delegate affairs to local government.

utopia Any visionary system embodying perfect political and social order.

utopian socialists Individuals who believed that public ownership of property could be effectively accomplished and could solve most important political problems.

war by misperception Armed conflict that results when two nations fail to perceive each other's true intentions accurately.

war crimes Crimes committed during warfare that constitute gross violations of the generally accepted rules of war.

war by escalation In an armed conflict, the movement from fighting on a relatively local and limited scale to all-out warfare, usually initiated when the underdog of the moment chooses to increase its military forces, rather than lose, until both sides have committed their total capabilities.

Warsaw Pact A military alliance between the former Soviet Union and its satellite states, created in 1955, that established a unified military command and allowed the Soviet army to maintain large garrisons within the satellite states, ostensibly to defend them from outside attack.

Weimar Republic The constitutional democracy founded in Germany at the end of World War I by a constitutional convention convened in 1919 at the city of Weimar; associated with a period of political and economic turmoil, it ended when Hitler came to power in 1933.

welfare state A state whose government is concerned with providing for the social welfare of its citizens and does so usually with specific public policies, such as health insurance, minimum wages, and housing subsidies.

winner-take-all system Electoral system in which the candidate receiving the most votes wins.

World Court Also known as the International Court of Justice, the principal judicial organ of the United Nations; the Court hears any case brought before it by parties who voluntarily accept its jurisdiction.

World Trade Organization (WTO) A nondiscriminatory trade organization organized to promote closer trade relations on a global or regional scale; formerly the General Agreement on Trade and Tariffs (GATT).

Zionism The movement whose genesis was in the reestablishment, and now the support of, the Jewish national state of Israel.

CREDITS

INDEX

Page numbers followed by f indicate figures; t, tables.